CENSUS OF INDIA 1891

Census of India 1871-1951, 9 Sets In 384 Bindings (9788121258876) Rs. 700000

Census of India 1891, 28 Vols. In 49 Bindings (978-81-212-7129-5) Rs. 125000

1. General Report (9788121269834) Rs. 1450
2. General Tables For British Provinces And Feudatory States (9788121269810) Rs. 2710 (Vol. I)
3. General Tables For British Provinces And Feudatory States (9788121269797) Rs. 950 (Vol. II)
4. Assam - Report (9788121269773) Rs. 2390 (Vol. I, V.1)
5. Assam - Tables (9788121269759) Rs. 2210 (Vol. II, V.2)
6. Assam - Provincial Tables (9788121269735) Rs. 1310 (Vol. II, V.3)
7. The Lower Provinces of Bengal and their Feudatories - The Report (9788121269711) Rs. 1660 (Vol. III)
8. The Lower Provinces of Bengal and their feudatories - The Administrative Tables (9788121269698) Rs. 4200 (Vol. IV)
9. The Lower Provinces of Bengal and their feudatories - The Caste Tables (9788121269674) Rs. 2600 (Vol. V, Pt. 1)
10. Lower Provinces of Bengal - The Provincial Tables (9788121269650) Rs. 1980 (Vol. V, Pt. 2)
11. Berar or the Hyderabad Assigned Districts (9788121269636) Rs. 3360 (Vol. VI)
12. Bombay and Its Feudatories - Report (9788121269612) Rs. 4010 (Vol. VII, Pt. 1)
13. Bombay And Its Feudatories - Imperial Tables (9788121269599) Rs. 790 (Vol. VIII, Pt. 2)
14. Imperial Series - Burma Report (9788121269575) Rs. 2320 (Vol. IX-V.1)
15. Imperial Tables - Burma Report (9788121269551) Rs. 3360 (Vol. X-V.2)
16. Provincial Tables Burma Report (9788121269537) Rs. 3510 (Vol. X-V.3)
17. Provincial Tables Burma Report (9788121269513) Rs. 3630 (Vol. X-V.4)
18. The Central Provinces And Feudatories - The Report (9788121269490) Rs. 2290 (Vol. XI, Pt. 1)
19. The Central Provinces And Feudatories - Imperial tables and supplementary returns (9788121268936) Rs. 2010 (Vol. XII)
20. Madras The Report On The Census (9788121269476) Rs. 2870 (Vol. XIII)
21. Madras - Tables I to XVII-C, British Territory (9788121269452) Rs. 3490 (Vol. XIV)
22. Madras - Tables A TO E, British Territory. Tables for feudatory States and A Caste Index (9788121269438) Rs. 2820 (Vol. XV)
23. The North Western Provinces and Outh - Report and Provincial Tables (9788121268912) Rs. 3100 (Vol. XVI, Pt. 1)
24. The North - Western Provinces and Oudh- Imperial Tables (9788121269414) Rs. 2000 (Vol. XVII, Pt. 2)
25. The North - Western Provinces and Oudh- Imperial Caste Tables (9788121269391) Rs. 3020 (Vol. XVIII, Pt. 3)
26. Punjab and Its Feudatories - The Report on the Census (9788121269377) Rs. 2710 (Vol. XIX, Pt. 1)
27. Punjab and Its Feudatories - Imperial Tables and Supplementary Returns for the British Territory (9788121269353) Rs. 1370 (Vol. XX, Pt. 2)
28. Punjab and Its Feudatories - Imperial Tables and Supplementary Returns for the Native States, Together With A Caste Index (9788121269339) Rs. 4910 (Vol. XXI, Pt. 3)
29. Report on The Census of The Districts of Ajmere-Merwara (9788121269056) Rs. 720 (Vol. XXII)
30. His Highness The Nizam's Dominions - Report (9788121269315) Rs. 2240 (Vol. XXIII, Pt. 1)
31. His Highness The Nizam's Dominions - Report (9788121269292) Rs. 2410 (Vol. XXIII, Pt. 2)
32. His Highness The Nizam's Dominions - Imperial And Supplementry Tables and Caste Index (9788121269278) Rs. 3390 (Vol. XXIII, Pt. 3)
33. Baroda - Report (9788121269254) Rs. 3810 (Vol. XXIV, Pt. 1)
34. Baroda - Tables (9788121269230) Rs. 2620 (Vol. XXIV, Pt. 2)
35. Mysore - Report (9788121269216) Rs. 2590 (Vol. XXV, Pt. 1)
36. Mysore - Imperial Tables (9788121269193) Rs. 1600 (Vol. XXV, Pt. 2)
37. Mysore - Tables (9788121269179) Rs. 5320 (Vol. XXV, Pt. 3)
38. Mysore - Supplementary Tables (9788121269155) Rs. 3590 (Vol. XXV, Pt. 4)
39. Mysore- Supplement to the Mysore census report of 1891 being a list of villages in the Mysore province and : comparing the population as per Censuses of 1891, 1881 & 1871 (9788121279024) Rs. 5350 (Vol. XXV, Pt. 5)
40. Rajputana - The Report, Imperial Tables And Supplementary Returns (9788121269131) Rs. 2330 (Vol. XXVI, Pt. 1)
41. Rajputna - The Provincial Tables and Remarks (9788121269117) Rs. 550 (Vol. XXVI, Pt. 2)
42. Central India (9788121269094) Rs. 2000 (Vol. XXVII)
43. Kashmir State - The Report on the census and Imperial and supplementary Tables (9788121269070) Rs. 2290 (Vol. XXVIII)
44. The Census of Calcutta (9788121269032) Rs. 890
45. Report on the census of Cochin (9788121269018) Rs. 790 (Pt. 1)
46. Report on the census of Cochin - The Final Census Tables with Appendices (9788121268998) Rs. 910 (Pt. 2)
47. Report on the Census of Coorg (9788121268974) Rs. 730
48. Report on the census of Travancore -Report (9788121274029) Rs. 4220 (Vol. I)
49. Report on the census of Travancore -Appendix (9788121268950) Rs. 5300 (Vol. II)

Owing to the antiquity and rarity of this book, certain pages are regrettably absent, and readability is compromised due to the blurring of the original text. If you possess any insights regarding the availability of these missing sections, kindly inform us. Your assistance is crucial in ensuring the completion of this significant work for the benefit of future generations.

CENSUS OF INDIA, 1891

BOOK-42: VOLUME XXVII

CENTRAL INDIA

R. H. GUNION

GYAN

Published by

Gyan Publishing House
5, Ansari Road
Daryaganj, New Delhi-110002
Phone: 011-47034999, 9811692060
E-mail: books@gyanbooks.com

Distribution Network
gyanbooks.com
India, USA, Canada, UK, Australia

ISBN: 978-81-212-7129-5 (Set) 28 Vols. In 49 Bindings
978-81-212-6909-4 (PB) Book-42, Vol. XXVII

First Published, 1893

2nd Impression 2024

Printed at: Gyan Press, Delhi.

CENSUS OF INDIA 1891

CENSUS OF INDIA, 1891.
VOLUME XXVII.

CENTRAL INDIA.

BY

R. H. GUNION,

PRINCIPAL OF THE RESIDENCY COLLEGE, INDORE,
AND *EX-OFFICIO* ASSISTANT TO THE AGENT TO THE GOVERNOR GENERAL IN CENTRAL INDIA.

CALCUTTA:
OFFICE OF THE SUPERINTENDENT OF GOVERNMENT PRINTING, INDIA.
1893.

No. 1277 of 1893.

FROM

R. H. GUNION, Esq.,

Superintendent of Census Operations in Central India,

TO

THE FIRST ASSISTANT TO THE AGENT TO THE GOVERNOR-GENERAL IN CENTRAL INDIA.

Dated Indore Residency, the 18th April 1893.

SIR,

I have the honour to forward herewith my report on the late Census of Central India, which I was appointed to superintend by Foreign Department letter No. 2577 I., dated the 5th August 1890.

2. The Indore Census office was in existence from that date till October 1892. At first it was the medium of the Census Commissioner's instructions being communicated to the Durbars through the various Agency offices and directly to the Durbars of Indore and Dewas. When the work of enumeration was over, the office was constituted as an abstracting office for the Indore Agency, and continued at the same time to superintend the work of the other abstracting offices according to the instructions received from time to time from the Census Commissioner regarding the abstraction and tabulation of the Census Returns. When the Tabulation Registers were completed and sent in to Indore from the Agency centres, the office became a compilation office for the whole of Central India.

3. Mr. Munchershah Bazonji Ragi, Assistant Record-keeper in the office of the Agent to the Governor-General in Central India (and now Tutor to His Highness the Raja of Dewas, Junior Branch), was selected for special duty in connection with the Census, and his services have been at my disposal during the time that the Census operations lasted. I am doing Mr. Munchershah no more than justice when I say that I could not have had a more energetic and capable assistant.

4. The report comprises—

(*a*) An account of Central India and its political and dynastic divisions, followed by remarks on the returns of the Census, compared, where comparison was possible, with those of the Census of 1881.

(*b*) A concise history of the Census operations in Central India from their inception in March 1890 till the completion of this report.

(*c*) The Tables, Imperial and Supplementary.

5. I beg to thank the Political Agents in Central India, on whom the Census threw a great deal of additional work, for their prompt attention to the instructions of the Census Commissioner, and for their forbearance and courtesy to myself personally.

I have the honour to be,

SIR,

Your most obedient Servant,

R. H. GUNION,

Superintendent of Census Operations in Central India.

INDEX.

CHAPTER I.

SECTION.	PAGE	PARA.
I.—General description of Central India	1	1—5
II.—Political Agencies and States in Central India	2	6—8
III.—Density of Population	9	9—17
IV.—Towns and Villages: Urban and Rural population	12	18—29
V.—Movement of the population	16	30—33
VI.—Religion	19	34—38
VII.—Population by Age Periods	19	39—45
VIII.—Caste	22	46—69
IX.—Occupation	25	70—97
X.—Special Tables referring to Cantonment and Railway population	28	98—99

CHAPTER II.

SECTION.	PAGE	PARA.
I.—Preliminary arrangements	29	1—9
II.—Form of Village Registers, Indents for Enumeration Books for Native States, Cantonments and Railways	32	10—31
III.—Arrangements made by Durbars for carrying out the enumeration in the various States	40	32—82
IV.—Compilation of returns based on the Enumerator's Abstract	48	83—87
V.—Abstraction and Tabulation	50	88—101
VI.—Compilation of Tabulated Returns	63	102—106
VII.—Cost of the Central India Census	71	107—114

APPENDIX I.

	PAGE
Results of Sir John Malcolm's partial Census of Malwa compared with those of the 1891 Census	75

APPENDIX II.

Statement showing the distribution over the different Agencies of the Territory of Gwalior and Indore. 76

TABLES—IMPERIAL AND SUPPLEMENTARY.

TABLE.		PAGE
I.—Area, houses and population		1
II.—Variation in the enumerated population since last Census		3
III.—Towns and villages classified by population		5
IV.—Towns according to population compared with the preceding Census		7
V.—Towns arranged territorially, with population by religion		11
VI.—Religions		15
VII.—Ages by Religions (Parts A to I)		17
VIII.—Total population, by Age, and Civil Condition of persons enumerated on the British India Schedule		35
VIIIA.—Civil Condition by Religion and Age of persons enumerated on British India Schedule (Parts A to I)		37
IX.—Education, by Religion and Age, of persons enumerated on British India Schedule (Parts A to I)		55
X.—Parent-tongue of persons enumerated on British India Schedule		73
XI.—Birth-place		77
XII.—Persons of Unsound Mind, by Age, enumerated on the British India Schedule		83
XIIA.—Persons of Unsound Mind, by Caste, Tribe or Race, enumerated on the British India Schedule		87
XIII.—Deaf Mutes, by Age, enumerated on the British India Schedule		89
XIIIA.—Deaf Mutes, by Caste, Tribe or Race enumerated on the British India Schedule		91
XIV.—Blind, by Age, enumerated on the British India Schedule		93
XIVA.—Blind, by Caste, Tribe or Race, enumerated on the British India Schedule		95
XV.—Lepers, by Age, enumerated on the British India Schedule		99
XVA.—Lepers, by Caste, Tribe or Race, enumerated on the British India Schedule		101
XVI.—Castes, Tribes and Races, by Nationality or traditional occupation		103
XVII.—Occupations, by Age—Part A.—(Provincial Summary)		164
XVII.—Occupations—Part B—(Provincial Distribution)		233
A.—Christians, by Sect and Race—Part I	These tables apply only to persons enumerated on the British India Schedule.	279
A.—Races—Part II		283
B.—Christians, by Race and Age		287
C.—Literate by Language known—(Provincial Summary)		289
Supplementary Statement of Area and Population		293
Supplementary Table shewing the population of Central India (Native States and British occupations) by Religions		297
Table shewing the percentage of the total population belonging to the Principal Religions		305

REPORT

ON THE

CENSUS OF CENTRAL INDIA, 1891.

CHAPTER I.

SECTION I.—GENERAL DESCRIPTION OF CENTRAL INDIA.

Geographical description of Central India.

Central India, the aggregate of States under the political care of the Agent to the Governor General in Central India, may be roughly described as a great triangle, the base of which is the course of the Narbada from Mathwar, adjoining Rewa Kantha, to about 60 miles east of Hoshangabad, continued in an imaginary line to about 60 miles east of the town of Rewa; and the apex is the most northerly point in the course of the Chambal, about 30 miles south of Agra. The triangle is by no means a perfect one: Rajputana stretches into it on the north-west, the North-Western Provinces on the north-east, and the Central Provinces on the south-east; while the Indore territory in Nimar extends over the Narbada into Kandesh and British Nimar; and there is a break of continuity near Jhansi, between the States of Urchha and Datia.

2. Central India has otherwise been described as two irregular and detached tracts of territory, converging near Jhansi, and stretching in an arc east and west across the middle of the continent.

Geographical confusion of States and Agencies.

3. This immense territory, covering 78,219 square miles, contains 79 States, Thakurats, etc., more or less independent. The larger of these are broken up into isolated parts, Gwalior and Indore, for instance, having territory in almost all the agencies into which Central India is politically divided; and this geographical confusion is aggravated by the fact that parts of Tonk and Jhalawar, States under the Rajputana Agency, lie in Central India, while parts of Gwalior and Indore lie in Rajputana.

Sir John Malcolm's census, and the census of 1881.

4. A census of certain selected areas in Malwa was taken by Sir John Malcolm about 1820. This partial census will be noticed hereafter, and an attempt will be made to compare its results with those of the census of 1891. But the census of 1881 was the first systematic attempt to enumerate the population of Central India. Many difficulties were experienced in that census, for some of which inefficient administration was responsible. This was largely due to the absence of geographical homogeneity in the areas to be dealt with; to the country being split up into so many States, large and small; and to the intermixture already referred to of States and Agencies. There were other difficulties as well: great trouble was met with in the enumeration of the Bhils in the south-west corner of the Agency and of the Kols, Gonds, etc., in its eastern portion. In the latter the wildness and difficulty of the country, the want of means of internal communication, and the apathetic indifference of the Durbars to the advantages to be derived from an accurate record of population, combined to make the enumeration difficult, and its results more or less untrustworthy.

5. The report on the census operations of 1881 says :—

"Sufficient has been said to make it clear that no accurate deductions can be drawn from, or statistics erected upon, the figures which the statements contain. It is, in short, not safe to regard them otherwise than as a rough estimate of the people, and the facts connected with their existence. Possibly, when the time occurs for taking another census, the introduction of improved communications, with a concomitant increased prosperity of the country, may have induced more advanced ideas of administration, and an ability to discern the numerous fiscal advantages to be gleaned from a correct record of all details affecting the population. Meanwhile, what we now have is not altogether useless; many facts have been collected which are either of interest or importance, and the figures will serve as a foundation, though only an imperfect one, on which to rear a more carefully constructed fabric hereafter; whilst for the Province as a whole, it is not unreasonable to suppose that inaccuracies, exaggerations, and diminutions may have, throughout the many States, in some measure corrected themselves, and brought out for the whole a more accurate total than the manner in, and the circumstances under, which the census was taken would justify our crediting."

It is to be acknowledged that the hope expressed by the writer of that report, that the census of 1891 would be a much better one than that of 1881, have been in general fully realised. All the States have co-operated in the census as they would not have done had their rulers not been awake to the advantages to be derived from it; and it is worthy of particular note that Rewa, which in 1881 was characterised as "the most backward State in India," made in 1891 all its own census arrangements, both for enumeration and the subsequent tabulation of returns, and carried them out with a degree of accuracy and despatch which would have done credit to many districts in British India.

SECTION II.—POLITICAL AGENCIES AND STATES IN CENTRAL INDIA.

6. The following are the agencies, or political charges, into which Central India is divided:

(1)—The Indore Agency, the districts immediately under the Agent to the Governor General, whose First Assistant holds, with regard to those districts, the position of a Political Agent.

The Indore Agency.

The Indore Agency comprises the City of Indore, seven Parganas of the Indore State (Mhow, Samwer, Khudel, Harsola, Hatod, and Banganga); the town of Dewas, and a considerable amount of adjoining Dewas territory; the Gwalior Parganas of Neori and Bhaurasa; the Thakurat of Bagli; and three other guaranteed Thakurats.

The towns* and villages in the Indore Agency are as under :—

State.	Towns.	Number of Villages.
Indore	Indore City Gautampura.	387
Dewas (Senior)	Dewas	112
Dewas (Junior)		122
Bagli	......	55
Gwalior Parganas of Neori and Bhaurasa	......	103
	Mhow Cantonment. Indore Residency.	

* Of over 5,000 inhabitants.

As regards the State of Indore, the greater part of its territory lies in other Agencies. Adjoining the City of Indore is the British Residency, a limited area assigned by treaty for the head-quarters of the Agent to the Governor General; and about 14 miles to the south-west is the cantonment of Mhow. As regards the State of Dewas, a great part of its territory, as will be seen presently, is distributed over the Western Malwa, Bhopal, and Bhopawar Agencies.

The two Gwalior Parganas, Neori and Bhaurasa, are parts of the Malwa Prant of that State, and are under a Mukhtiarkar (equivalent in rank to a Suba), whose head-quarters are at Neori.

Gwalior Agency.

(2)—The Gwalior Agency, or the political charge of the Resident at Gwalior, is the most homogeneous of all the Agencies in Central India, containing, as it does, no territory not belonging to Gwalior, except the petty State of Kaniadhana; the small guaranteed holdings of Seopur-Baroda, Kathon and Pahargarh; and a few villages belonging to the Maharaj of Khotoli in Kotah. The Gwalior territory in this Agency forms one of the three Prants (Gwalior, Malwa and Esagarh) into which the Maharaja Sindiah's dominions are divided. It is this Prant alone which is directly under the Resident, the others being divided between the Indore, Bhopal, Western Malwa, Bhopawar, and Guna Agencies.

The river Chambal separates the Gwalior Prant on the north-east and north-west from the British districts of Agra and Etawa, and from the Rajputana States of Dholpur, Karauli and Jaipur.

Below is a list of the districts in the Gwalior Prant, with the Parganas belonging to each :—

Districts.	Parganas.	Districts.	Parganas.
Towargarh	Gormi. Porsa. Aino. Ambah. Gohad.	Sabalgarh	Sabalgarh. Seopur. Dodhar. Bijeypur.
Gird Gwalior	Gird. Antri. Pachor. Nurabad.	Narwar	Narwar. Mangroni. Bhiterwar. Aron. Sipri. Kolaras. Pahari.
Bhind	Bhind. Mau. Ater. Omari. Mehagawa.	Bhander	Bhander. Indarkhi. Daboh. Karera. Pichor.
Sikarwari	Bagchini. Maugarh. Jigni. Jora.		

Note.—The Parganas of Esagarh and Chanderi were for census purposes taken as parts of the Gwalior Agency.

In the district of Gird Gwalior lie the City of Lashkar, the fortress of Gwalior, and the abandoned Cantonment of Morar. Adjoining these is the British Residency.

The chiefship of Kaniadhana was transferred to the Gwalior from the Bundelkhand Agency in 1888.

The towns and villages in the Gwalior Agency are as under :—

State.	Towns.	Number of Villages.	Remarks.
Gwalior . . .	Lashkar . . Bhind. Karaia. Sabalgarh. Gohad. Baroda. Morar. Seopur. Narwar. Bhander. Chanderi.	4,027	The number of villages includes 96 villages of Guaranteed Thakurats.
Kaniadhana . .	...	47	

(3)—The Bhopal Agency comprises the State of Bhopal; the States of Narsinghgarh, Rajgarh, Khilchipur, Maksudangarh, Kurwai, Basoda, Muhamadgarh, and Pathari; the Pindara Jagirs; six guaranteed Thakurats of Gwalior, and two of Indore; the Gwalior districts of Bhilsa, Ganj-Basoda, and Sujalpur of the Esagarh Prant, and Sonekach of the Malwa Prant; the Indore districts of Zirapur, Machalpur, Gagroni and Nimawar; Sironj belonging to Tonk; Sarangpur belonging to Dewas; and Larawat belonging jointly to Dewas and Dhar.

Bhopal Agency.

The Bhopal Parganas are :—

Gairatganj, Chhipaner, Piklon, Siddikganj, Mahalpur, Garhi, Jaithari Debipura, Jawar, Islamnagar, Bari, Barely, Deori, Chandpura, Silwani, Bhairaunda, Daurahia, Bhuri, Dewanganj, Bilkisganj, Shahganj, Tal Sehore, Ichhawar, Ashta, Nazirabad, Raisen, Mardanpur, Udepura. Tehsil Huzur, Sewas, and Bersia.

The Narsinghgarh Parganas are :—

Narsinghgarh, Chhapahera, Pachor, and Khujner.

The Rajgarh Parganas are :—

Rajgarh, Kothda, Karanwaj, Kalipith, Nawalganj, Talen, and Biaora.

The Khilchipur Parganas are :—

Khilchipur, Bhojpur, Kherkhedi, Wamangaon, and Piplia.

The Kurwai Parganas are :—

Kurwai, Suthalia, Layra, Soharwasa, Battisi, and Mahabalpur.

The Gwalior Guaranteed Thakurats are :—

Agra Barkhera, Tappa, Dhabla Dhir, Kankarkhera, Kamalpur, Dhabla Ghosi, Dariakheri, Baodia, and Alnia.

The Indore Guaranteed Thakurats are :—

Patharia and Kherirajpur.

The Gwalior Parganas are :—

Sujalpur, Malhargarh, Sonekach, Bhilsa, and Basoda.

The Indore Parganas are :—

Zirapur, Machalpur, Tingachpur, Talen, Harangaon, Gagron, Kantaphod Satwas, Rajore, and Nimawar.

Bhopal, the most important State in the Bhopal Agency, has no outlying territory in other Agencies. Sehore, 23 miles south-west of the City of Bhopal, is the head-quarters of the Agency and a Cantonment.

The towns and villages in the Bhopal Agency are as under :—

State.	Towns.	Number of Villages.
Bhopal	Bhopal . . . . . Ashta. Bersia. Sehore. Ichhawar. Sehore Cantonment.	3,167
Gwalior	Bhilsa . . . . . Sujalpur. Mangaoli.	1,540⅓*
Narsinghgarh	Narsinghgarh . .	419
Rajgarh	Biaora	631
Tonk	Sironj	390
Khilchipur	......	223
Maksudangarh	......	77
Kurwai	......	92
Basoda	......	22
Muhamadgarh	......	17
Pathari	......	19
Pindara Jagirs	......	5
Gwalior Guaranteed Thakurats . .	......	15
Indore	......	566⅓*
Indore Guaranteed Thakurats . . .	......	2
Dewas (S. and J. Branches) . . .	......	73
Dhar	......	4⅓*
Suthalia	......	20
Agra Barkhera	......	34

Bundelkhand Agency.

(4)—The Bundelkhand Agency, which extends over 10,227 square miles, comprises thirty States, large and small, as under :—

Urchha.	Alipura.	Bihat.
Panna.	Gaurihar.	Pahra.
Datia.	Tori Fatehpur.	Jigni.
Chhatarpur.	Paldev.	Taraon.
Charkhari.	Jasso.	Rebai.
Bijawar.	Lugasi.	Belhari.
Ajaigarh.	Sarila.	Eijna.
Samthar.	Garauli.	Dhurwai.
Baoni.	Bhaisonda.	Kamta Rajaula.
Baraundha.	Beri.	Banka Pahari

* The small district of Sundarsi (one village) belongs jointly to Gwalior, Indore and Dhar.

The Pargana of Alampur, belonging to Indore, is included in the Bundelkhand Agency. The Cantonment of Nowgong is the head-quarters of the Agency.

The following list gives the names of the Parganas of the larger States :—

The Urchha Parganas are :—

Urchha, Terhi, Palhera, Jatwara, Teharowli, Baldeogarh, Pirthipur, and Paharsinghpur.

The Panna Parganas are :—

Panna, Samaria, Dharampur, Aktohan, Ghorra, Shahnagar, Pawai, Singhpur, Birsinghpur, and Bakswaha.

The Datia Parganas are :—

Datia, Indragarh, Seonda, Nadigaon, and Baroni.

The Chhatarpur Parganas are :—

Chhatarpur, Rajnagar, Mau, Deora, and Lauri.

The Charkhari Parganas are :—

Maharajnagar, Rampur, Bawan Chaurasi, Isanagar, and Satwara.

The Bijawar Parganas are :—

Rajauli, Satai, Shahgarh, Gulganj, Bamoura, and Karahia.

The Ajaigarh Parganas are :—

Ajaigarh, Zargati, Bangla, Barwara, Mahaiwa, and Pathar.

The Samthar Parganas are :—

Samthar, Lohargarh, Maharajgarh, Amargarh, and Sami.

The towns and villages in the Bundelkhand Agency are as under :—

State.	Towns.	Number of Villages.
Urchha	Tikamgarh	658
Panna	Panna	858
Datia	Datia	454
	Seonda.	
	Nadigaon.	
Charkhari	Maharajnagar	270
Chhatarpur	Chhatarpur	315
Samthar	Samthar	90
Bijawar	Bijawar	299
Ajaigarh	......	361
Other petty States	......	370
	Nowgong Cantonment.	

(5)—The Baghelkhand Agency, which covers about 11,323 square miles, includes Rewa and the small States of Nagode, Sohawal, Maihar, and Kothi.

Baghelkhand Agency.

The Rewa Parganas are :—

Rewa Tahsil, Ramnagar, Verdi, Tiothar, Madhogarh, Mauganj, and Manpur.

The towns and villages in the Baghelkhand Agency are as under :—

State.	Towns.	Number of Villages.
Rewa	Rewa Satna.	5,431
Maihar	Maihar	183
Nagode	Unchhera	334
Sohawal	...	173
Kothi	....	67

Western Malwa Agency.

(6)—The Western Malwa Agency. This Agency includes the States of Jaora, Ratlam, Sailana, and Sitamau; the guaranteed holdings of Piplauda, Panth-Piplauda, Bhatkheri, Lalgarh, Kalakhera, Narwar, Sarwan, Uparwara, Khojankhera, Shajasta, Tal, Bilode, and Sedri; 20 Parganas of Gwalior (Malwa Prant); 21 Parganas of Indore; the Alote Pargana of Dewas (Senior Branch); and the Ringnode and Garguchha Parganas of Dewas (Junior Branch).

The Gwalior Parganas are :—

Agar, Susner, Nalkhera, Barode, Shahjapur, Tonk, Mandsaur, Nahargarh, Bhaugarh, Afzalpur, Sukhera, Nimach, Jawad, Singoli, Gangapur, Ujjain, Barnagar, Khachhrod, Unail and Panbehar.

The Indore Parganas are—

Mehidpur, Kaitha, Jarda, Tarana, Jagoli, Karanjmakron, Rampura, Garote, Sunail, Kotri, Raipur, Manasa, Chandwasa, Kharaoda, Satkheda, Naraingarh, Antri, Kanjardah, Nandwas, and Depalpur.

The Western Malwa Agency contains the two cantonments of Nimach and Agar, the latter of which is also the head-quarters of the Political Agent.

The towns and villages in the Western Malwa Agency are as under :—

State.	Towns.	Number of Villages.
Gwalior	Ujjain Mandsaur. Nimach. Shahjapur. Barnagar. Khachhrod. Jawad. Agar. Nimach Cantonment.	2,454
Ratlam	Ratlam	218
Jaora	Jaora Tal-Mandawal	327
Indore	Rampura Mehidpur. Bhanpura. Tarana. Manasa. Sunail.	1,231
Sitamau	Sitamau	91

State.	Towns.	Number of Villages.
Sailana	Sailana	76
Tonk	Pirawa	121
Piplauda	...	24
Panth-Piplauda	...	10
Dewas (Senior)	...	75
Dewas (Junior)	...	61

Bhopawar Agency.

(7)—The Bhopawar Agency. This Agency contains the States of Dhar, Jhabua, Barwani and Ali Rajpur; the chief-ships of Jobat, Kathiwara, Mathwar and Ratanmal; the guaranteed Thakurats of Dotria, Kachhi-Baroda, Bakhtgarh, and Multhan; the guaranteed Bhumiats of Rajgarh, Garhi, Kalibaori, Bharudpura, Kothedis, Chiktiabad, Chhota Barkhera, Bara Barkhera, Jamnia, and Nimkhera; the Gwalior district of Amjhera (Malwa Prant); the Nimar districts of Indore; and the British Pargana of Manpur.

The Dhar Parganas are—

Dhar, Bari Khasgi, Badnawar, Nalcha, Mandu, Dharampuri, Kuks i, Thikr Sultanabad, and Nimanpura.

The Barwani Parganas are—

Barwani, Rajpur, Anjode, Jalgona, Patti, and Silawad.

The Jhabua Parganas are—

Jhabua, Rajola, Bori, Kanas, Ranapur, Kundanpur, Pitor, Rambhapur, Harinagar, Parmalia, Thandla, Khawasa, Karwad, Sarangi, Hanumangarh, Mehidawa, Raipuria, Lakhnaoda, Umarkotah, Kalianpura, and Bhagore.

The Ali Rajpur Parganas are—

Ratha, Takarwara, Walpur, Sondwa, Chhaktala, Phulmal, Chandpur, Amkhat, Barzar, Bhabora, Ziran, Nanpur, and Khatali.

The Gwalior territory comprises the Parganas of Amjhera, Tanda—Balwari Bagh, Bakanair, Dikthan, and Sagor.

The Indore part of Nimar contains the parganas of —

Maheshwar, Kesarwar, Pipalgond, Dargaon, Karhai, Mardana, Amleta Barwai, Katkut, Khargone, Sanawad, Muhamadpur, Khadgaon, Bhikamgaon, Silondri, Una, Barode, Balakwada, Palia Dawli, Nagalwadi, Brahmangaon, Chikalda, Lawani, Dahi, Hasilpur, Betma, and Pitlawad.

The towns and villages in the Bhopawar Agency are as under :—

State.	Towns.	Number of Villages.
Indore	Maheswar Khargone.	1,269
Dhar	Dhar Kuksi.	526
Barwani	Barwani	343
Jhabua		736

State.	Towns.	Number of Villages.
Ali Rajpur	......	326
Jobat	......	61
Kathiwara	......	46
Mathwar	......	35
Ratanmal	......	13
Guaranteed Thakurats	......	88
" Bhumiats	......	190
Gwalior	......	459
Dewas	......	31
Manpur (British Pargana)	......	32

8. The Guna Agency contains the petty States of Dharnaoda, Khiaoda, Bhadaura, Sirsi, Umri, Raghogarh, Parone, and Gurrah; the Gwalior Parganas of Myana, Pachhar, Arone, Ranod, Bajrangarh, Chachoda and Kumbraj; and Chhabra belonging to Tonk.

Guna Agency.

The towns and villages in the Guna Agency are as under:—

State.	Towns.	Number of Villages.
Tonk	Chhabra	187
Dharnaoda	......	30
Khiaoda	......	6
Bhadaura	......	12
Sirsi	......	35
Umri	......	27
Raghogarh	......	104
Parone	......	39
Gurrah	......	57
Gwalior	......	1,040

SECTION III.—DENSITY OF POPULATION.

7. In the Central India Census Report of 1881, Final Form I (General Statement of Area and Population) was the only table in which areas had any place. In that Form the States were not arranged as they were in the other tables; and in some cases the areas of more than one State were lumped together. As regards the areas given in the table referred to, the writer of the 1881 report says:—

Areas.

"Unfortunately the separate areas of some important States, one indeed the largest in Central India, cannot be ascertained; and it is impracticable therefore to frame any even approximate detailed statistics concerning the density of the population. We are dependent for our figures connected with areas on the Topographical Survey Department; and the classification adopted, notably for Gwalior and the twelve States which head the list of Statement I., *i.e.*, for a total area of 29,066·08 square miles,—a classification which is neither geographically nor politically correct; as well as that for many other States improperly grouped together, renders any calculation, founded on the exact area of each, quite impracticable. For the total of Central India the population is given at 9,261,907 souls, which, distributed over an area of 75,229·64 square miles, gives a density of 123·12 persons per square mile, which may be accepted as approximately correct."

8. For this census the Surveyor-General was requested to furnish the area of each State separately, and, in the case of States having territory in more than one Agency, the area of those States in each Agency; and to give, apart from those areas, the land occupied by Railways, Cantonments and Agency headquarters. But he could not furnish the areas of States by Agencies; the boundaries of the latter not being shown in the Topographical Standard Sheets. The consequence is that Table I of the present report has no area, except that of Central India as a whole. And even that area cannot be accepted as strictly accurate, having necessarily been made up from figures got from various sources. The only detailed areas available are those given in the Supplementary Statement of Area and Population on page 293. To furnish the State figures for that statement occupied much of the time of the Surveyor-General's office for five months. As the boundaries of only one or two of the Cantonments and Agency head-quarters were defined in the Surveyor-General's maps, all such areas are in the Supplementary Statement, included in the area of the States in which they lie. The areas also of land occupied by the various Railways is included in the State areas. In the 1891 census Agencies, and not States, as in 1881, are reckoned as districts for census purposes. The former is no doubt the more symmetrical mode of arranging the census returns; but what is gain in one way is loss in another, through it having been found impossible to procure Agency Areas.

---

9. As regards their total population, the Agencies into which Central India is divided fall into the following order:—

Total population of Central India.

Agency	Population
Bhopal	2,006,859
Gwalior	1,757,509
Baghelkhand	1,737,606
Western Malwa	1,619,368
Bundelkhand	1,508,053
Bhopawar	978,652
Indore	372,792
Guna	337,973
Total population of Central India	10,318,812

10. From the circumstances just mentioned, in order to get any information as to the density of population, how it varies district by district, how far it has changed since 1881, and in what direction the change has been, recourse must be had to the Supplementary Statement on page 293. Even that is not altogether what it professes to be: the area given for Gwalior, for instance, includes that of several petty States, which, though subsidiary to it, are not integral parts of its territory.

Density per square mile.

11. The area of Central India as a whole is 78,219·2 square miles. This figure includes Railways, Cantonments and Agency head-quarters, and the British Pargana of Manpur. The population of Central India, according to the present census, including the population of the Tonk districts in Malwa, and excluding that of the Indore and Gwalior districts in Meywar, is 10,318,812, or 131·92 per square mile.

Density by 1881 census.

12. In 1881 the area of Central India was returned as 75,229·64 square miles, and the total population as 9,261,907. But that return is admittedly incorrect. For one thing, it does not include the area of the Tonk districts (878 square miles), nor does the population as then returned include the population of those districts. In order, therefore, to compare the density of the population in 1881 and 1891 we must take the area as now given (which is at any rate approximately correct), minus the Tonk area, and subtract the 1891 population of the Tonk districts from the total 1891 population of Central India Such a calculation gives 119·76 per square mile as the density of the population in Central India in 1881, as against 131·08 in 1891.* Roughly speaking, there is an increase since 1881 of eleven persons per square mile.

13. It is worth noting here that Sir John Malcolm in 1820 found the population of those parts of Malwa which he subjected to a census to be 98 to a square mile, "which," he says, "may safely be taken as a scale for the present reduced population of Central India."†

Density of population by States compared with 1881.

14. Taking the chief States of Central India, the density of their population in 1881 and 1891 is as under:—

State.	Area.	Population.		Increase or Decrease.	Average Number of Persons per square mile.	
		1881.	1891.		1881.	1891.
Gwalior	25,846·3	3,071,524‡	3,482,351‡	+ 410,827	118·83	134·73
Indore	9,715·9	1,054,237	1,099,990	+ 45,753	108·51	113·22
Bhopal	6,996·9	954,901	952,486	— 2,415	136·49	136·14
Rewa	12,676·6	1,305,124	1,508,943	+ 203,819	102·96	119·03
Urchha	2,079·8	311,514	333,020	+ 21,506	149·77	160·12
Datia	912·5	182,598	186,440	+ 3,842	200·10	204·31
Panna	2,492·0	227,306	239,333	+ 12,027	91·21	96·04
Dhar	1,775·0	149,244	169,474	+ 20,230	84·08	95·47
Rutlam	729·5	87,314	89,160	+ 1,846	119·69	122·22
Jaora (including Piplauda).	691·5	120,077	130,442	+ 10,365	173·64	188·63
Dewas	882·5	142,162	152,073	+ 9,911	161·09	172·32
Rajgarh	957·2	117,533	119,489	+ 1,956	122·78	124·83
Narsinghgarh	669·6	112,427	116,280	+ 3,853	167·90	173·65

Gwalior.

15. The area of Gwalior appears to have been considerably over-estimated in 1881. As now stated, it includes several independent petty States in the Guna Agency, and several Guaranteed Thakurats in the Gwalior, Indore and Bhopal Agencies. The areas of those holdings cannot be separately stated; but taking their combined

* The density of those Tonk districts is above the average, being 206·12.

† Malcolm's *Central India*, Vol. II, p. 184.

‡ To make the comparison accurate for the Gwalior population, the figures for Cantonments within Gwalior territory are subtracted from the 1891 total, as they do not appear in 1881 as part of Gwalior, and the figures for Khaniadhana and Sitaman are deducted from the 1881 total, both these places being treated apart from Gwalior in 1891.

population, and applying the average density of the whole area given for Gwalior (134·73), the area of the Gwalior State by itself cannot be more than 24,700 square miles.

Rewa.

16. Rewa has made the greatest increase (seventeen) in the number of persons per square mile. This is rather striking, considering the barrenness of the greater part of the territory of Rewa. Indore with her miles and miles of fertile soil has increased only five per square mile. Gwalior stands next to Rewa with an increase of sixteen. But it must be borne in mind that in 1881 the census of Gwalior was taken very imperfectly, both the enumeration and the subsequent operations (done by State officials) having been very carelessly carried out.

Bhopal, etc.

17. The decrease in the population of Bhopal is remarkable, and there is nothing to explain it. Still more remarkable is the smallness of the increase (only three per square mile) in the population of Ratlam, considering the number of immigrants that work on the Godhra-Ratlam Railway must have brought into the State, and the large increase (fifteen per square mile) in the population of the adjoining state of Jaora. The increase in the number of villages (to be presently mentioned) in Ratlam makes the anomaly still more glaring. The nomadic habits of the Bhils can scarcely account for so great a disparity.

SECTION IV.—TOWNS AND VILLAGES: URBAN AND RURAL POPULATION.

18. The following table shows the towns and villages in Central India:—

State.	Number of Towns.				Number of Villages.			
	1881.	1891.	Increase.	Decrease.	1881.	1891.	Increase.	Decrease.
Gwalior . . .	20	23	3	...	9,780	9,551	...	229
Indore . . .	4	12	8	...	3,725	3,511	...	214
Bhopal . . .	5	6	1	...	3,006	3,167	151	...
Rewa . . .	3	2	...	1	5,078	5,432	354	...
Urchha . . .	1	1	...	...	652	658	6	...
Datia . . .	3	3	...	...	451	454	3	...
Panna . . .	1	1	...	...	867	858	...	9
Dhar	2	2	...	...	502	530	28	...
Ratlam . . .	1	1	...	...	162	218	56	...
Jaora	1	2	1	...	315	327	12	...
Dewas . . .	2	1	...	1	455	474	19	...
Rajgarh . . .	1	1	...	...	637	631	...	6
Narsinghgarh . .	1	1	...	...	416	419	3	...
Other States, etc. .	8	13	5	...	5,419	6,185	766	...
TOTAL .	53	69	16	...	31,465	32,415	950	...

Note.—The 1891 totals in this statement include 3 towns and 698 villages belonging to Tonk which the 1881 totals do not include.

Towns.

19. Several places that were reckoned as towns in 1881 are not so reckoned in 1891. Jhansi has become British territory. Four Gwalior towns besides Jhansi have disappeared, *viz.*, Burdu, Bhilgarh, Gungapur, and Kularas. Rajgarh was reckoned as a town of the State of that name in 1881, evidently by mistake for Biaora, which is the name of the capital of Rajgarh. Sarangpur* also (Dewas), Barigura (Rewa), Raswas (Bhopal) and Seora (Datia) are no longer reckoned as towns.

20. On the other hand, in this census 25 places are returned as towns, which were not so taken in 1881, *viz.* :—

Eight of Gwalior: Jawad, Karaia, Narwar, Mangauli, Sabalgarh, Bhander Gohad, and Chanderi.

Eight of Indore: Rampura, Maheshwar, Khargone, Bhanpura, Tarana, Manasa, Sunail and Gautampura.

Two of Bhopal: Bersia and Ichhawar.

One of Rajgarh: Biaora, which appeared wrongly as Rajgarh in the 1881 Report.

One of Nagode: Unchehra.

One of Jaora: Tal-Mandawal.

One of Sailana: Sailana.

There are also three towns in the Tonk districts in Central India, *viz.*, Sironj, Chhabra and Pirawa, which were not included in Central India in the 1881 census.

Villages.

21. The total number of villages in Central India is 32,415. In 1881 it was returned as 31,465. But in 1881 the Tonk territory in the Bhopal, Western Malwa and Guna Agencies, containing 698 villages, was not included. Allowing for those villages, and for the exclusion in 1881 of the Rewa and Nagode Villages in Allahabad and Jabalpur,† and setting the increase (24) in the number of places reckoned as towns against the decrease (8), there are 181 more villages in 1891 than there were in 1881.

22. There is a marked decrease in the number of villages in Gwalior and Indore; a slight decrease in Panna and Rajgarh; and an inexplicably large increase in Rewa and Ratlam. The decrease in the number of villages in Gwalior, taken along with the great increase (sixteen per square mile) in the population of the State, can be explained by the fact that the average number of persons in a village, as will be seen from a subsequent statement, has largely increased in Gwalior; and this is probably due to the prevalence of dacoity in some parts of the State. The large increase in the number of villages in Ratlam is the more striking, as the population of that State has increased only three per square mile

Average population of villages.

23. The total population of Central India is in this census returned as :—

Urban	964,538
Rural	9,354,274

In 1881 the figures were—

Urban	799,687
Rural	8,462,220

Leaving the urban population out of consideration for the present, we have an increase in the total rural population of 892,054. Deducting 156,354 for the rural population of the Tonk districts not included in 1881, we find the real increase to be 735,700.

* Sarangpur was in 1889 divided between the Senior and Junior Branches of the Dewas State; and neither of the parts now counts for a town.

† See page 71.

24. This 9,354,274, the amount of the rural population, is spread over 32,415 villages. Thus the average population of villages is 288 as against 269 in 1881. The following statement gives the figures for the larger States of the Agency :—

State.	Number of Villages.		Rural Population.		Population per Village.	
	1881.	1891.	1881.	1891.	1881.	1891.
Gwalior . . .	9,780	9,551	2,718,560	3,054 541	277·9	319·8
Indore . . .	3,725	3,511	969,928	950,690	260·3	270·7
Bhopal . . .	3,006	3,167	883,329	860,305	293 8	271·6
Rewa	5,078	5,432	1,271,098	1,478,546	250·3	272·1
Urchha . . .	652	658	293,170	315,410	449·6	479·3
Datia . . .	451	454	140,789	147,387	312·1	324·6
Panna . . .	867	858	212,630	224,628	245·2	261·8
Dhar . . .	502	530	127,808	144,698	254·6	273·0
Ratlam . . .	162	218	56,248	59,338	347·2	272·1
Jaora . . .	315	327	88,532	90,685	281·0	277·3
Dewas . . .	455	474	116,698	137,005	256·4	289·0
Rajgarh . . .	637	631	110,652	113,013	173·7	179·1
Narsinghgarh . .	416	419	101,027	107,719	242·8	257·0

25. The most remarkable fact in this statement is that in Gwalior the average number of persons in a village has risen from 277 to 319. The number of villages in Gwalior, as we have already seen, has decreased. The rural population in Gwalior has increased since last census in a higher ratio than the urban, and to a greater extent than in other States.

The abandonment of villages in consequence of dacoity is, as above stated, the probable reason of the decrease in the number of villages and of the increase in the average population of villages.

Number of persons to a house.

26. The following statement gives the number of persons to a house in the larger States :—

State.	Number of houses.	Population.	Number of persons to a house.
Gwalior	600,894	3,378,774	5·62
Indore	224,204	1,099,990	4·90
Bhopal	189,693	952,486	5·02
Rewa	278,153	1,508,943	5·42
Urchha	62,725	333,020	5·26
Datia	31,057	186,440	6 00
Panna	49,044	239,333	4·88
Dhar	33,573	169,474	5·04
Ratlam	20,670	89,160	4 31
Jaora	23,866	117,650	4·93
Dewas	28,778	152,073	5·28
Rajgarh	23,055	119,489	5·18
Narsinghgarh	20,602	116,280	5·64

The Supplementary Statement of Area and Population on page 293 does not distinguish occupied houses in urban from those in rural areas state by state, as Table I distinguishes them Agency by Agency.

Number of persons to a house in urban and rural areas.

27. As regards the number of persons to a house in urban and rural areas respectively, Sir John Malcolm wrote of his census:—"The number of persons to each house was found to differ considerably in different districts. In the City of Indore it was a fraction more than five, while in many villages near that capital the number did not exceed four. Perhaps five may be taken as the average."* It is a remarkable fact that in the census of 1891, the Indore Agency (which of course includes the City of Indore, and several of the districts which were included in Sir John Malcolm's census) is the only one in Central India which has a larger population per house in urban than in rural areas. The figures for the different agencies are as under—

Agency.	In Urban areas.	In Rural areas.
Indore	5·17	4·87
Gwalior	4·59	6·53
Bhopal	4·62	5·08
Bundelkhand	4·83	5·23
Baghelkhand	4·57	5·36
Western Malwa	4·77	4·96
Bhopawar	4·65	4·85
Guna	3·95	5·41

The high figure for Gwalior rural areas is noticeable in connexion with what has been said above regarding the increase in the population and the decrease in the number of villages.

Urban and rural population in 1881 and 1891.

28. The total urban population returned in 1891 is 964,538 as against 799,687 in 1881, an increase of 164,651. The total rural population returned in 1891 is 9,354,274 as against 8,462,220 in 1881, being an increase of 892,054. As has already been said, nine places taken as towns in 1881 were not so taken in 1891, and twenty-five places have been taken as towns in 1891 which were not so taken in 1881; so there are sixteen more towns in 1891 than there were in 1881. The aggregate population of the towns which have disappeared was, in 1881, 90,956, while the aggregate population of the, so to speak, new towns is 166,468 in 1891. As the definition of a town for census purposes was practically the same in 1891 as it was in 1881 (the stipulations as to Municipality, Markets, and Chaukidari Act not being applicable in Central India) those figures give some idea of the migration of the population from town to country and from country to town. For the whole Agency, the urban population has increased about 17 per cent., while the rural population

* Malcolm's *Central India*, Vol. II, page 184.

has increased only 9½ per cent. The subjoined statement gives the figures for the larger States—

State.	Total Population.		Increase or Decrease.	Urban Population.		Increase or Decrease.	Rural Population.		Increase or Decrease.
	1881.	1891.		1881.	1891.		1881.	1891.	
Gwalior	3,024,979	3,378,774	+353,795	306,419	324,233	+ 17,814	2,718,560	3,054,541	+367,308
Indore	1,054,237	1,099,990	+ 45,753	84,309	149,300	+ 64,991	969,928	950,690	— 13,843
Bhopal	954,901	952,486	— 2,415	71,572	92,181	+ 20,609	883,329	860,305	— 23,024
Rewa	1,305,124	1,508,943	+203,819	34,026	30,397	— 3,629	1,271,098	1,478,546	+207,448
Urchha	311,514	333,020	+ 21,506	18,344	17,610	— 734	293,170	315,410	+ 22,240
Datia	182,598	186,440	+ 3,842	41,809	39,053	— 2,756	140,789	147,387	+ 6,598
Panna	227,306	239,333	+ 12,027	14,676	14,705	+ 29	212,630	224,628	+ 11,998
Dhar	149,244	169,474	+ 20,230	21,436	24,776	+ 3,340	127,808	144,698	+ 16,891
Ratlam	87,314	89,160	+ 1,846	31,066	29,822	— 1,244	56,248	59,338	+ 3,090
Jaora	108,434	117,650	+ 9,216	19,902	26,964	+ 7,062	88,532	90,686	+ 2,154
Dewas	142,162	152,073	+ 9,911	25,464	15,068	— 10,396*	116,698	137,005	+ 20,307
Rajgarh	117,533	119,489	+ 1,956	6,881	6,476	— 405	110,652	113,013	+ 2,361
Narsinghgarh	112,427	116,280	+ 3,853	11,400	8,561	— 2,839	101,027	107,719	+ 6,692

Increase of population by sexes since 1881.

29. The total population according to the Census of 1891 is 10,318,812. Of these 5,395,536 are Males and 4,923,276 Females. In 1881 the figures were:—Total 9,261,907; Males 4,882,823 and Females 4,379,084. So there is a recorded increase of 1,056,905 in the total population; an increase in the males of 512,713, and in the females of 544,192. But it must be remembered that the 1891 figures include the population of the Tonk districts in Central India, which was not included in the figures of 1881. The population of those districts is now returned as 181,135 (Males 96,345 and Females 84,790). So the actual total increase is only 875,770 or 8·63 per cent; the actual increase in the male population is 416,363 or 7·85 per cent., and that in the female population is 459,402 or 9·49 per cent.

Section V.—MOVEMENT OF THE POPULATION.

Immigration.

30. Increase of population is of course due partly to natural causes and partly to immigration. To estimate the amount due to immigration we take Table XI along with Table II. We find the total number of persons born and censused in Central India according to the 1891 Census to be: Total 9,564,632, Males 5,034,533, Females 4,530,099, or 92·69; 93·30; 92·01 per cent., respectively. The immigrants are only about 6 per cent., divided as under:—

	Total.	Males.	Females.
From the Central Provinces	117,878	52,895	64,983
From Rajputana	240,317	118,841	121,476
From North-West Provinces	260,678	115,440	155,238
From elsewhere	135,307	83,827	51,480
Total immigration recorded in 1891 Census	754,180	361,003	393,177

* This is only an apparent decrease: see footnote on page 13.

Immigration by the 1881 Census.

31. The immigration recorded in the 1881 Census was as under :—

	Total.	Males.	Females.
From the Central Provinces . .	78,258	36,188	42,071
From Rajputana	137,744	71,278	66,466
From the North-West Provinces .	202,565	95,022	107,543
From elsewhere	65,276	39,348	25,928
Total immigration recorded in 1881 Census	483,843	241,836	242,007

32. Entering now into more detail, the following statement gives the proportion of immigrants for the different Agencies* of Central India :—

Immigration by Agencies.

Agency.	Born in Central India.	Born out of Central India.
Indore	84·30	15·70
Gwalior	94·84	5·16
Bhopal	93·29	6·71
Bundelkhand	90·98	9·02
Baghelkhand	95·24	4·76
Western Malwa	92·00	8·00
Bhopawar	90·44	9·56
Guna	92·48	7·48

33. As regards migration from one State in Central India to another, the intermixture of State and Agency boundaries makes it impossible to give figures of any approach to accuracy. For instance, Indore has territory in every Agency in Central India except Gwalior, Baghelkhand and Guna ; and a man returned as born in Indore may have been born in any one of the Agencies except those mentioned ; and such a man being returned among the population of the Indore Agency may, or may not, be resident in the Indore territory in that Agency. However, the movement from one State to another is very slight in Central India, as may be seen from the following statement regarding those States which have territory in one Agency only :—

Immigration by States.

State.	Total population.	Returned as born in the State.	Returned as inhabiting the Agency in which the State lies.		Returned as born in the State and inhabiting another Agency.
			Number.	Percentage.	Percentage.
Rewah	1,508,943	1,452,567	1,446,509	99·58	·42
Bhopal	952,486	873,178	866,052	99·18	·82
Urchha	333,020	321,497	316,084	98·54	1·46

For reasons already stated no comparison with 1881 is possible. See page 10.

State.	Total population.	Returned as born in the State.	Returned as inhabiting the Agency in which the State lies.		Returned as born in the State and inhabiting another Agency.
			Number.	Percentage.	Percentage.
Panna	239,333	222,075	209,836	94·91	5·09
Datia	186,440	182,580	160,525	87·92	12·08
Chhatarpur	174,148	171,892	169,821	98 79	1·21
Charkhari	143,108	117,471	117,158	99·73	·27
Bijawar	123,414	127,577	127,127	99·65	·35
Jhabua	119,787	135,952	134,612	99·08	·92
Rajgarh	119,489	104,684	102,437	97·85	2·15
Jaora	117,652	109,074	107,381	98·44	1·56
Narsinghgarh	116,280	101,471	98,061	96·63	3·37
Ajaigarh	93,048	82,708	79,819	96·05	3·95
Ratlam	89,160	86,623	79,688	91 99	8·01
Nagode	84,097	77,989	73 544	94·29	5·71
Barwani	80,266	31,754	31,745	99·97	·03
Maihar	77,546	65,627	63,911	97·92	2·08
Ali Rajpur	70,091	84,317	84,308	99·98	·02
Sohawal	43,853	37,675	35,385	93·92	6·08
Samthar	40,541	33,573	30,168	89·85	10·15
Khilchipur	36,302	33,463	32,885	98·27	1·73
Sitamau	33,307	28,180	28,018	99·42	·58
Sailana	31,512	28,001	25,442	90·86	9·14
Kothi	22,656	19,424	18,552	95·51	4·49
Kurwai	21,787	15,851	15,845	99·96	·04
Baraundha	18,596	15,580	14,415	92·52	7·48
Baoni	18,441	12,387	12,387	100·00	...
Raghogarh	18,132	14,922	14,793	99·13	·87
Alipura	15,280	11,276	11,275	99·99	·01
Jobat	15,047	14,019	14,019	100·00	...
Kaniadhana	14,871	12,195	12,054	98·92	1·08
Bagli	14,675	9,128	9,126	99·97	·03
Maksudangarh	14,422	10,605	9,923	93·56	6·44
Gurrah	10,854	7,548	7,483	99·13	·87
Gaurihar	10,148	7,457	7,457	100·00	...

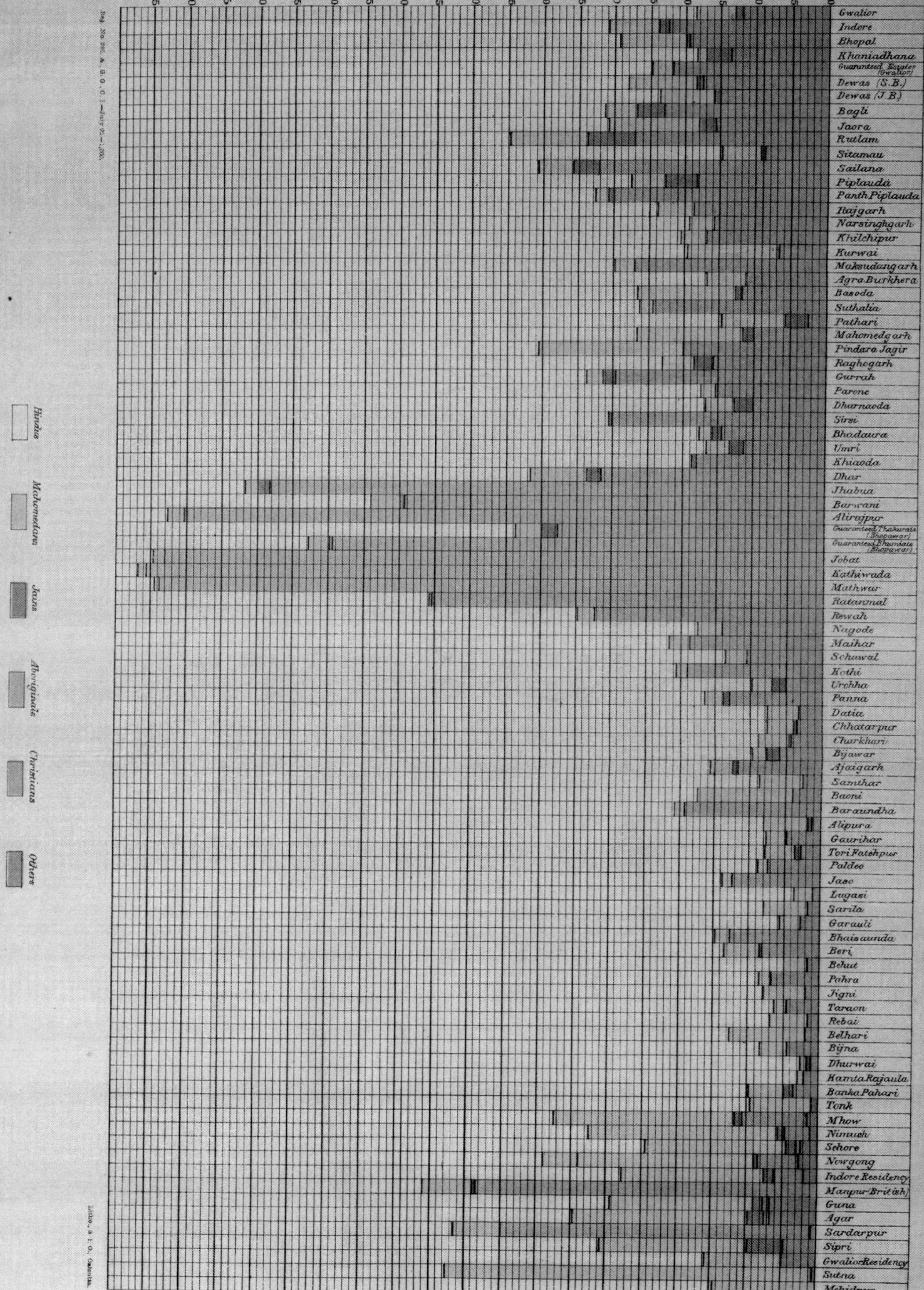

Hindus
Mahomedans
Jains
Aboriginals
Christians
Others
Gwalior
Indore
Bhopal
Khaniadhana
Guaranteed Estates (Gwalior)
Dewas (S.B.)
Dewas (J.B.)
Bagli
Jaora
Rutlam
Sitamau
Sailana
Piplauda
Panth Piplauda
Rajgarh
Narsinghgarh
Khilchipur
Kurwai
Maksudangarh
Agra Burkhera
Basoda
Suthalia
Pathari
Mahomedgarh
Pindara Jagir
Raghogarh
Gurrah
Parone
Dharnaoda
Sirsi
Bhadaura
Umri
Khiaoda
Dhar
Jhabua
Barwani
Alirajpur
Guaranteed Thakurats (Bhopawar)
Guaranteed Bhumiats (Bhopawar)
Jobat
Kathiwada
Mathwar
Ratanmal
Rewah
Nagode
Maihar
Sohawal
Kothi
Urchha
Panna
Datia
Chhatarpur
Charkhari
Bijawar
Ajaigarh
Samthar
Baoni
Baraundha
Alipura
Gaurihar
Tori Fatehpur
Paldeo
Jaso
Lugasi
Sarila
Garauli
Bhaisaunda
Beri
Behut
Pahra
Jigni
Taraon
Rebai
Belhari
Bijna
Dhurwai
Kamta Rajaula
Banka Pahari
Tonk
Mhow
Nimuch
Sehore
Nowgong
Indore Residency
Manpur-British
Guna
Agar
Sardarpur
Sipri
Gwalior Residency
Sutna
Mehidpur

SECTION VI.—RELIGION.

Population by religion.

34. The next point is religion, which is treated in Imperial Table VI and the Supplementary Statement of the Population of States by Religion on page 293. Of the total population of Central India, 7,735,246 are Hindus, 568,640 Musalmans, 89,984 Jains, 1,916,209 Aboriginals, 5,999 Christians, 837 Parsis, 1,825 Sikhs, and 72 Jews. The census of 1881 gave 7,800,396 Hindus, 510,718 Musalmans, 49,824 Jains, 891,424 Aboriginals, 7,065 Christians, 916 Parsis, 38 Jews.

35. The percentage of Hindus, Musalmans, Aboriginals and Jains in 1881 and 1891 respectively is shown below:—

	Hindus.	Musalmans.	Jains.	Aboriginals.
1881	84·22	5·51	·53	9·62
1891	74·96	5·51	·87	18·57

36. The marked decrease in the number of Hindus is no doubt due to many Aboriginals having been wrongly taken as Hindus in the census of 1881. The decrease in the number of Christians and Parsis is to be attributed to the abandonment of the Cantonment of Morar.

37. The following statement gives the percentage of Hindus, Musalmans, Aboriginals, Jains, Christians and others for each Agency:—

Agency.	Hindu.	Musalman.	Aboriginal.	Jain.	Christian.	Others.
Indore	76·04	12·29	8·92	1·51	·94	·02
Gwalior . . .	88·06	4·41	6·92	·57	·02	...
Bhopal	75·29	8·04	16·80	·53	·01	·02
Bundelkhand . .	89·17	3·62	6·29	·83	·04	·02
Baghelkhand . .	67·39	2·51	30·04	·02	·01	...
Western Malwa .	71·79	7·80	18·26	2·06	·05	·03
Bhopawar . .	44·52	4·77	49·48	1·24	...	...
Guna	82·48	3·74	12·24	1·42	...	·10
TOTAL .	74·96	5·51	18·57	·87	·05	·02

38. The Table on page 305, illustrated by the diagram on the opposite page, gives the percentage for States, and for the places in British occupation (Cantonments, Agency Head-Quarters and the Pargana of Manpur).

SECTION VII.—POPULATION BY AGE PERIODS.

Age of the total population by sexes.

39. We now come to deal with the ages of the population. In Imperial Table VII, seventeen

periods have been taken. The statement below shows the total number of persons, male and female, returned as coming under each age period :—

Age period.	TOTAL.	Males.	Females.
Under 1 year	294,188	148,599	145,589
1	156,064	76,725	79,289
2	260,260	126,476	133,784
3	318,639	151,142	167,497
4	316,752	158,123	158,629
5 to 9	1,497,365	782,080	715,285
10 to 14	1,103,466	641,130	462,336
15 to 19	784,898	430,680	354,218
20 to 24	870,602	431,257	439,345
25 to 29	947,316	481,576	465,740
30 to 34	1,032,901	543,758	489,143
35 to 39	1,621,937	335,734	286,203
40 to 44	775,259	411,970	363,289
45 to 49	309,606	173,162	136,444
50 to 54	457,459	233,392	224,067
55 to 59	117,450	62,133	55,317
60 and over	454,696	207,599	247,097

40. Some of these figures are very striking and even startling. The number of children returned as one year old is little more than half the number of those returned as under one year. Assuming that the ages were correctly stated to the enumerators, this would indicate a most alarming rate of infant mortality, which is not borne out by any known facts. At the same time it seems strange that a man, however ignorant, should not know whether his child was born more or less than a year ago. Again, the number of children returned as one year old is only a little more than half the number returned as two years old.

Age by Religion.

41. The statement below gives the percentage of Hindus, Musalmans, Aboriginals and Jains coming under each age period.—

Age period.	Hindus.		Musalmans.		Aboriginals.		Jains.	
	Males.	Females.	Males.	Females.	Males.	Females.	Males.	Females.
Under 1 year	2·71	2·87	2·75	3·06	2·92	2·24	2·49	2·78
1	1·41	1·59	1·26	1·46	1·50	1·73	1·29	1·29
2	2·28	2·06	2·12	2·64	2·69	3·16	1·93	2·16
3	2·72	3·29	2·37	2·99	3·43	3·97	1·94	2·33
4	2·85	3·12	2·42	1·78	3·27	3·77	1·94	2·33

Age period.	Musalmans.		Hindus.		Aboriginals.		Jains.	
	Males.	Females.	Males.	Females.	Males.	Females.	Males.	Females.
5 to 9	14·26	14·29	12·30	13·20	16·36	15·98	10·60	11·56
10 to 14	11·93	9·30	10·73	9·09	12·11	9·83	10·55	9·06
15 to 19	8·11	7·28	7·80	7·32	7·45	6·75	8·63	8·32
20 to 24	8·06	8·94	8·51	9·75	7·31	8·56	9·30	9·52
25 to 29	8·97	9·49	9·50	9·71	8·41	9·20	9·49	9·17
30 to 34	10·07	9·94	10·73	10·25	9·88	9·81	10·05	9·69
35 to 39	6·26	5·86	6·42	5·36	5·95	5·69	7·07	6·30
40 to 44	7·62	7·48	8·41	7·83	7·43	6·67	7·95	8·59
45 to 49	3·27	2·85	3·33	2·52	2·82	2·48	4·63	3·44
50 to 54	4·33	4·67	5·17	5·04	3·97	3·86	5·44	3·68
55 to 59	1·19	1·16	1·25	1·10	·91	·92	1·96	1·58
60 and over	3·85	5·16	4·85	5·07	3·48	4·18	4·53	5·86

Comparison with 1881.

42. In the 1881 Census five periods of age were adopted for Central India, *viz.* :—infants, 1 to 3 years; children, 4 to 15 years; youths, 16 to 30 years; adults, 31 to 50 years; old, above 51 years. As regards this classification the writer of the 1881 report says :—

"It is a matter of extreme difficulty to invent any classification which, while being intelligible to uneducated natives, shall also effect a correct registration of ages. The periods adopted were probably as good as any other under the circumstances, but they led, it is believed to abnormal registration under the terms *children* (larká larki) and *youth* (jawán). Most natives who are not either old or crippled prefer to be recorded as *jawán*, whilst a native boy may have reached the age at which he, in our society, would be considered a man, and still be called a "larká" by his parents. Thus we find that out of the whole population of Central India 6,102,298 have been recorded under these two denominations, *viz.* : 3,591,139 as youths, 2,511,159 as children. The number of infants (from 1 to 3 years) is recorded at 869,890, or only 9 per cent. ; the 2nd, 3rd, 4th, and 5th periods of age work out to 27, 40, 15 and 9 per cent. respectively. Infant males and females are almost exactly equal. Male children are 29 and females 25 per cent. Male youths and female youths number 39 and 38 per cent. respectively. Male adults 15, female adults 16, old males 8, old females 12 per cent."

43. The following statement attempts to compare the results of the 1891 Census as regards the age of infants with those of 1881 by combining the two classifications :—

Religion.	1 to 3 years.			
	1881.		1891.	
	Males.	Females.	Males.	Females.
Hindus and Aboriginals	9·07	9·82	7·42	8·45
Musalmans	8·28	9·34	8·51	10·17
Jains	7·97	9·28	7·67	8·57

44. These figures are not very satisfactory. Comparison as to other age periods has been tried, but with even more hopeless results, it being impossible to adapt the classification of 1891 to that of 1881.

45. It is noticeable that in children under 4 years females are considerably more numerous than males. Between the ages of 5 and 29, and 30 and 59, males largely predominate; while females over 60 are far more numerous than males. These statements apply to Hindus, Musalmans, Jains and Aboriginals both in this Census and in that of 1881. Among Hindus male infants under one year are more numerous than female. This was found to be the case both in 1881 and 1891.

SECTION VIII.—CASTE.

Castes, tribes, etc., in connexion with traditional occupation.

46. The subject of caste or tribe, in connexion with traditional occupation, is treated in Imperial Table XVI, the grouping being according to the scheme furnished by the Census Commissioner for India. This Table was a very difficult and costly one to compile, and it is questionable whether the result will be thought to be worth the trouble and expense. As regards the names of castes, the list may be accepted as complete; but whether they are correctly arranged in groups is another matter. A large number of castes, regarding the occupations of which nothing was known, have been thrown into group 45 (Miscellaneous and Disreputable Livers): miscellaneous they were; but doubtless they did not all deserve to be branded as disreputable.

Group 1.

47. Group 1 (Military and Dominant) contains 1,115,191 persons, or 10·80 per cent. of the total population of Central India. Of these, 601,972 are described as Rajput, 204,501 as Gujar, 84,231 as Chhattri, 56,529 as Jat, 35,608 as Maratha, 37,757 as Deswal (Musalman and Aboriginal), 24,241 as Rawat, 15,657 as Mirdha (Aboriginal), 14,724 as Thakur, and 14,399 as Raghubansi. The number of true Rajputs is, of course, much understated, many Rajputs having described themselves as Rathor, Rawat, etc. In the Baghelkhand Agency all the Rajputs seem to have been returned as Chhattris.

Group 2.

48. Group 2 (Minor Agricultural) contains 2,246,451 persons or 21·77 of the population. In this group the numerically strongest castes are the following:—

Caste	Number	Caste	Number
Kachhi	472,124	Dhakar	47,260
Ahir	373,591	Tamboli	24,398
Balai	346,546	Kalota	20,703
Lodha	252,658	Mankar	19,766
Kurmi	164,117	Ajna	18,692
Koli	123,455	Dhanuk	14,516
Mali	91,365	Loda	13,971
Dangi	58,691	Sondlia	10,097
Kunbi	57,884	Gaoli	10,042

49. The Kachhi caste is particularly numerous in the Gwalior and Bundelkhand Agencies; in the Indore Agency Kachhis number only 2,284. Of the Ahir caste 111,005 are found in the Bundelkhand Agency. The Balai caste is mostly in the Bhopal and Western Malwa Agencies. The Kurmi caste belongs almost exclusively to the Bundelkhand and Baghelkand Agencies, while the Kunbi caste (probably the same as Kurmi) is found in Indore, Bhopal and Bhopawar. Gwalior has no Kunbis and very few Kurmis. The Dhakars are almost all in Western Malwa.

50. Group 4 (Forest and Hill Tribes) contains 1,409,868 persons, or 13·66 of the population. The most numerous castes in this group are:—

Group 4

Bhil	354,177	Seheriya	70,004
Gond	254,449	Kotwar	28,335
Kol	217,274	Mewati	21,393
Bhilala	159,366	Korku	21,131
Mina	118,518	Bharud	11,444
Kirar	113,831		

51. There are 244,347 Bhils in the Bhopawar Agency, and 79,077 in Western Malwa; they are found in the other Agencies also, but in Bundelkhand and Baghelkhand their number is very small. The Gonds are almost all in the Baghelkhand and Bhopal Agencies; there are a few in Bundelkhand. Of Kols there are 210,045 in Baghelkhand, and very few anywhere else. The Bhilalas were not separately enumerated in 1881; in 1891 they were. They are nearly all in Bhopawar. Minas are found in all the agencies, Kirars and Seheriyas belong almost exclusively to the Gwalior, Bhopal and Guna Agencies. More than half of the Kotwars are in the Guna Agency. Mewatis are found everywhere except in Bundelkhand and Baghelkhand. The Korkus are nearly all in Bhopal. There are no Bharuds except in Bhopawar.

Group 5.

52. Group 5 (Priests) contains 947,741 persons or 9·18 per cent. of the population; 945,475 are Brahmans.

Group 6.

53. Group 6 (Devotees) contains 142,917 persons, or 1·38 per cent. of the population. Bairagis number 58,986, Gosains 35,950, Gelots 20,879, Fakirs 12,759, and Jogis 10,274.

Group 14.

54. Group 14 (Traders) contains 369,947 persons, or 3·61 per cent. of the population. 260,784 are Banias, and 14,930 Bohras. The number of Banias is understated, many of that caste being returned as Saraogi, Baiswar, Dasora, Hasora, etc. Of the Bohras 10,897 are in Western Malwa. There are 4,133 Mahajans and all of them in the Indore Agency have been returned as males; probably the females have gone with the Banias.

Group 18.

55. Group 18 (Barbers) contains 182,472 persons, or 1·76 per cent. of the population. The only castes under this group are Bari, Nai and Sirnai. The last named is found in the Western Malwa Agency alone, and numbers only 628 persons. A few Nais are Musalmans.

Group 19.

56. Group 19 (Blacksmiths) contains 107,076 persons, or 1·03 per cent. of the population; 599 Lohars are described as Musalmans: the others are all Hindus. The castes of Jotia and Kamar also appear among the blacksmiths, but their numbers are infinitesimal.

Group 20.

57. Group 20 (Carpenters and Turners) contains 228,108 persons, or 2·21 per cent. of the total population. The Kathi caste numbers 85,430, the Sutar 83,987, the Barhai 43,789; Jaugars appear only in Baghelkhand, and are all returned as females, while the Barhais in that Agency are all males.

Group 23.

58. Group 23 (Weavers, Calenderers and Dyers) contains 186,714 persons or 1·80 per cent. of the population. The mos numerous caste in this group is that of the Koris, who, however, are almost all in Bundelkhand and Baghelkhand. The Panika caste is found only in Baghelkhand, and is very numerous there. The Sali

caste numbers 13,691, almost all in Bhopawar. The Chhipa caste exists everywhere in considerable numbers except in Baghelkhand.

Group 26.

59. Group 26 (Shepherds and Wool Weavers) contains 182,089 persons, or 1·77 per cent. of the population, 171,332 are of the Gadaria caste. This caste is found in every Agency. The Gari caste, numbering 3,226, belongs to the Indore Agency exclusively. The Gadri caste is found only in the Guna Agency; and of 803 persons belonging to it only 17 are returned as males.

Group 27.

60. Group 27 (Oil-pressers) contains 211,285 persons, or 2·04 of the population. They are all of the Teli caste.

Group 28.

61. Group 28 (Potters) contains 166,698 persons, or 1·61 of the population. They are all of the Kumhar caste.

Group 35.

62. Group 35 (Fishermen, Boatmen, Palki-bearers, Cooks, etc.) contains 228,437 persons, or 2·21 per cent. of the population. The Kahar caste numbers 81,321. It is found in all the agencies; but there are very few in Indore, Bundelkhand and Guna. The Dhimar caste numbers 69,429, almost all in Bundelkhand. Kamkers (Musalman), 231 in number, are found only in Western Malwa, and are all females. Kirs (Hindu), on the other hand, are all males in Guna.

Group 38.

63. Group 38 (Leather workers) contains 958,121 persons, or 9·28 per cent. of the population. In this group Chamars alone number 888,018, and are found in every Agency. The Bhami caste numbers 13,444, but there are none of this caste in the Gwalior, Bundelkhand or Guna Agencies. The Mangi caste numbers 48,474, all in Baghelkhand.

Group 38A.

64. Group 38A (Low Castes not included in Group 38) contains 16,775 persons. This group has not worked out in a satisfactory manner, some of the abstracting offices having evidently included Dhers, Mahars and Mangs among the Chamars. The figures of the Indore Agency are remarkable for the small proportion of females.

Group 44.

65. Group 44 (Hunters, Fowlers, etc.) contains 187,714 persons, or 1·81 per cent. of the population. The Moghya caste numbers 110,784, mostly in Western Malwa. The Bagri caste, numbering 57,406, also belongs chiefly to Western Malwa. The Pardhi caste numbers 6,291, mostly in Bhopal.

Group 45.

66. Group 45 (Miscellaneous and Disreputable Livers) contains 163,900 persons, or 1·58 per cent. of the population. The anomalous composition of this group has already been remarked upon. Besides those properly belonging to it, as Khangars, Baoris, Sondias, etc., it includes a large number of castes for which a proper place could not be found elsewhere. In this group there is a caste called Savaya; in Guna 1,279 females are returned as belonging to it, and no males. Of the castes known to be disreputable, the Khangar caste numbers 38,121, most of them in Bundelkhand. The Sondhia caste numbers 8,044, almost all in Western Malwa. The "others" in Indore are remarkable for the absence of males.

Group 48.

67. Group 48 (Tribal Communities of Foreign Asiatic Origin or reputed Descent) contains 455,102 persons, or 4·41 of the population. In point of fact, this group includes a large proportion of the Musalmans, who, in Central India are 5·51 of the total

population. Among those included are 170,020 Pathans, 234,789 Sheikhs, 34,877 Sayyids, and 10,124 Moghals. These four tribes are well distributed over the Agencies. Arabs number 134, of whom 100 are in Bhopal, and the remainder in Western Malwa. Sunni is a strange tribe for 28 Musalmans in Indore to fancy they belong to, and equally strange is Shiah for 1838 in Bhopawar. Vilaitis so called number only 740, most of them in Western Malwa. Sidis number 474, divided between Indore and Western Malwa. Parsis number only 837, almost all in Indore and Western Malwa.

Group 50.

68. Group 50 (Non-Asiatic Races) contains 4,154 persons. The only noticeable point in this group is the French descent of 128 Christians in Bhopal, who represent the "Bourboun" family which entered the service of the Bhopal State in the time of Vizier Mahomed. They have decreased in number since 1881, having been returned then as amounting to 155.

Groups 51 and 52.

69. Group 51 (Eurasians) contains 1,535 persons. It is doubtful whether the names under this group denote any real distinction of race. In popular opinion Eurasians are the same as East Indians; and the Portuguese that are met with in Central India are scarcely to be differentiated from the Goanese. Group 52 (Christian Converts) contains only 310 persons. Possibly some who ought to have appeared among the Christian converts have been included among the Madrasis of Group 51.

SECTION IX.—OCCUPATION.

General untrustworthiness of occupation returns.

70. Tables XVII A and XVII B deal with Occupations, the former being a Provincial Summary by ages, and the latter showing the distribution of occupations over the different Agencies. These returns were even more troublesome and costly to compile than the Caste Table, and the information conveyed in them is at least as imperfect in points of detail. Something will be said hereafter, in connexion with the subject of tabulation, about the untrustworthiness of many of the entries in the occupation column of the enumeration book; and of course the abstractors could not make the registers more accurate than the data with which they were furnished.

71. It will be noticed that the totals of the two tables do not tally. This is due to the fact that the abstraction of the returns for the Tonk districts in Central India was done in the Rajputana Census Office; and as that office elected not to abstract occupations by ages, only the totals of occupations for those districts were sent to the Indore Census Office for compilation. Those totals are included in Table XVII B, but they could find no place in Table XVII A.

Scheme of classification of occupations.

72. The classification of occupations in these tables follows as closely as possible the scheme suggested by the Census Commissioner for India. Of this scheme the main classes are—

A.—Government.
B.—Pasture and Agriculture.
C.—Personal Services.
D.—Preparation and Supply of material Substances.
E.—Commerce and the Transport of Persons, Goods and Messages, and the Storage of goods.
F.—Professions, learned, artistic and minor.
G.—Indefinite Occupations, and Means of Subsistence independent of Occupation.

73. Subordinate to these seven classes are twenty-three orders, as under;—

A. I.—Administration.
II.—Defence.
III.—Feudatory State Service.

B. IV.—Live-stock breeding, etc.
V.—Agriculture.

C. VI.—Personal, household and sanitary services.

D. VII.—Food and drink.
VIII.—Light, firing and forage.
IX.—Buildings.
X.—Vehicles.
XI.—Supplementary requirements.
XII.—Textile fabrics and dress.
XIII.—Metals and precious stones.
XIV.—Glass, pottery and stone-ware.
XV.—Wood, cane and leaves.
XVI.—Drugs, gums, etc.
XVII.—Leather.

E. XVIII.—Commerce.
XIX.—Transport and storage.

F. XX.—Learned and artistic Professions.
XXI.—Sports and amusements.

G. XXII.—Indefinite occupations.
XXIII.—Independent of work.

74. These orders are divided into seventy-seven sub-orders, and in these sub-orders are included nearly five hundred separate occupations.

Class A.

75. The orders into which class A (Government) is divided are—

I.—Administration	76,025
II.—Defence	17,154
III.—Feudatory State Service	349,353

"Administration" contains 76,025 persons. But only 2,257 of those belong to the service of the Imperial Government, the total of the order being swollen by 73,678 persons in "Village Service," who would have been taken under "Feudatory State Service" had any place there been provided for them.

76. With regard to this class, it will also be noticed that it is only British troops which come under "Defence," those of Native States being included in "Feudatory State Service."

77. The two tables show a remarkable discrepancy under the head "Political Service," the one which includes the Tonk districts showing 116 persons belonging to that service, while the one which excludes those districts shows only 54.

78. The total number returned under "Feudatory State Service" is 349,358, of whom 115,581 come under "Army." No attempt has been made to distinguish officers from privates, the figures being in some cases utterly incongruous.

79. Adding the "Village Service" mentioned above to the total of "Feudatory State Service," we get the figure of 423,031, or 4·09 per cent. of the total population as depending on native state service for subsistence.

80. Class B (Pasture and Agriculture) contains 5,062,917 persons, or 49·06 per cent. of the population. These come under the two orders of—

Class B.

IV.—Live-stock breeding, etc.	97,177
V.—Agriculture	4,965,740

81. The only two occupations under "Live-stock" that are numerous are—

Cattle-breeders and dealers	22,093
Herdsmen	49,560

82. As regards "Agriculture," the Census Commissioner's scheme made distinctions between tenants and occupants, and also between cultivating and non-cultivating tenants. The Enumeration Book used in Central India scarcely admitted of those distinctions being made; and when the Agency returns came to be compiled, it was found that several of the Agencies had not returned a single tenant, either cultivating or non-cultivating, and had taken all the persons coming under the sub-order "Interest in Land" as Land *occupants*. Similarly the sub-order "Agricultural Labourers" is blank for several of the Agencies,

Those who till the land have not been distinguished as occupants, tenants, or hired labourers, the name Kheti being used for all three indifferently. Enough has been said to show that though the total is, no doubt, fairly accurate, no reliance can be placed on the details of the agricultural population.

Class C.

83. Class C (Personal and Household and Sanitary Services) contains 526,200 persons, or 5·09 per cent. of the population. Order VI, of the same title, is the only one under this class; and it includes personal and domestic servants of every kind, and also all employed in connexion with sanitation as scavengers, sweepers, etc.

Class D.

84. Class D (Preparation and Supply of Material Substances) contains 1,382,492 persons, or 13·45 per cent. of the population. These come under the under-mentioned orders:—

VII.—Food and Drink	238,227
VIII.—Light, Firing and Forage	108,259
IX.—Buildings	75,170
X.—Vehicles	509
XI.—Supplementary requirements	34,819
XII.—Textile Fabrics and Dress	330,857
XIII.—Metals and Precious Stones	131,341
XIV.—Glass, Pottery and Stoneware	65,140
XV.—Wood, Cane and Leaves	154,318
XVI.—Drugs, Gums, Dyes, etc.	15,729
XVII.—Leather, Horns, Bones and Grease	228,123

85. There are some very remarkable and inexplicable returns in this class. In Baghelkhand there are 10,985 grain-dealers, all females, 516 cocoanut-sellers, all males, and 12,862 firewood and grass gatherers, all males. Similarly, in Guna there are 1,375 country spirit distillers, only 17 of whom are females; and in Western Malwa there are 656 betel-leaf sellers, of whom only 9 are females. In Indore there are 1,502 female brick-makers, and only one male. A still more remarkable case is that of the building contractors, of whom there are in all 213 males, distributed over the Indore, Bhopal, Bundelkhand and Baghelkhand Agencies, and no females anywhere.

86. Under "Textile Fabrics" are shown a very large number of people (236,260) engaged in the preparation of cotton, about half of whom are weavers.

87. Under "Leather, etc.," appear 228,123 persons (Tanners, Shoemakers, Leather-dyers, Hide-dealers, etc). As the Chamars number 888,018 in the caste return, either comparatively few of them adhere to their traditional occupation, or else the name is used to cover many who do not properly belong to the caste.

Class E.

88. Class E (Commerce, Transport and Storage) contains 308,242 persons, or 3·04 per cent. of the population. These come under the two orders of—

XVIII.—Commerce	273,433
XIX.—Transport and Storage	34,809

89. As regards "Commerce" a very large number of persons come under the two designations of "Merchants unspecified" and "Shop-keepers otherwise unspecified." There are of the former 51,482, and of the latter 136,101. These two represent the common entries of "Baipar" and "Dukandari" in the Enumeration Books.

90. As regards "Transport and Storage" there has probably been considerable confusion between the "Carts and Carriages" of this order, and the "Vehicles" coming under order X of Class D: the latter are obviously fewer than they ought to be.

91. "Pack bullock Owners and Drivers" number 9,860, while the caste return gives 58,904 Banjaras. This is a striking instance of a caste being forced by the march of progress to desert its traditional occupation.

Class F. 92. Class F (Professions—learned, artistic and minor) is divided as under:—

XX.—Learned and Artistic Professions.
XXI.—Sports and Amusements.

93. Under order XX, the ministry of religion accounts for 69,059, including such as priests, religious mendicants, temple servants, etc., 140 persons have been returned as Hail-averters and 61 as Amuletiers.

Teachers and schoolmasters number 2,026, which seems a very small allowance, the males above 15 years of age, who may be supposed to be engaged in the work of teaching, being only 856, while the number of boys of school-going age in Central India is nearly a million and a half.

Medical practitioners of all kinds number only 4,804.

Under "Pictorial Art" come 2,299 Painters; but it is scarcely credible that there are so many in Central India following painting as a fine art. *Rangsaz*, rather than *Musawwar*, would probably be found to be their real profession.

94. The total number of persons who come under "Sports and Amusements" is 6,930.

Class G. 95. Class G (Indefinite Occupations and Means of Subsistence independent of Occupation) contains the following orders:—

XXII.—Indefinite	2,197,989
XXIII.—Independent of work	276,709

96. The order "Indefinite" is swollen by 2,190,099 persons returned as subsisting by "general labour"—the *mazduri* of the enumeration books. These amount to 21·22 per cent. of the population. "Miners unspecified" are 1,128, all in Baghelkhand, and no doubt represent the persons employed in the Umaria collieries.

97. Among the "Independent of work" 269,187 are returned as "Mendicants (not religious)."

"Prisoners" are only 1,548, which of course is much below what it ought to be. It is evident that the inmates of jails have not in most cases been entered as such, but as of the occupation which they followed, or chose to say that they followed, when they were free. This appears particularly in the Bundelkhand Agency, for which no prisoners have been returned, and from the Bhopal Agency, where 238 are returned, but all females.

SECTION X.—SPECIAL TABLES REFERRING TO CANTONMENT AND RAILWAY POPULATION.

98. The under-mentioned tables have reference only to Cantonment and Railway population, enumerated on the British India Schedule. The figures are those received from the Ajmir Census Office, in which the Abstraction and Tabulation of these Schedules was carried out.

Table VIII.—Population by age and civil condition.

Table VIIIA to Table VIII I.—Civil Condition by Age for the different Religions—Hindu, Musalman, Jain, Aboriginal, Christian, Parsi, Sikh, Jew.

Table IXA to IX I.—Education by Religion and Age.

Table X.—Parent Tongue.

Tables XII to XVA.—Infirmities (unsound mind, deaf-mutes, blind, lepers) by Age and Caste or Tribe.

99. The numbers prefixed to the caste groups in the infirmity tables are those of the Census Commissioner's classification of castes.

CHAPTER II.

SECTION I.—PRELIMINARY ARRANGEMENTS.

Census Commissioner's first instructions.

1. The Census operations in Central India began in April 1890 with the receipt of two Notes from Mr. Baines, Census Commissioner for India, extracts from which, bearing on the preliminaries of the Census in the Feudatory States, are here given :—

"The Political Agents should start and superintend the preliminary operations in the smaller States, and should aid the Durbar in the larger, keeping a watch, as far as possible, on the progress of the work, so as to prevent the delay that occurred in several States in the last Census. The question of the Census of guaranteed estates was raised in 1880-81, and was settled in favour of the guarantee-holders, so that it need not recur on this occasion. The Political Agents will arrange for the Census, and the results will be incorporated with those of the State within which the estate is situated. Detached portions of States in one Agency lying within the limits of another should be dealt with territorially, and be tabulated accordingly at the head-quarters of the latter, the results being afterwards communicated to the Durbar of the parent State. A note might be made below the general statement of area and population to show the aggregate extent of each State thus split up, or the results might be excluded from the total of the tabulating Agency and incorporated with those of the main State or its Agency.

"With regard to the operations themselves, the first step is to secure the preparation n each State of a register showing the name of each village with those of its outlying hamlets or other detached quarters. For towns, this should show the suburbs, mohallas, wards, streets or other sub-divisions. The number of houses or persons in each, as returned in 1881, should, if available, be also stated in the register. From this the circles should be marked off, an extract in full detail for each circle being prepared, with blank columns for the blocks and names and offices of the enumerators to be appointed. The demarcation of the blocks from this register should be made on consideration of the area that an enumerator can cover during the period allowed for the Census. If three villages are compact and two lie close together, the aggregate population not exceeding, for instance, 600 persons, one enumerator, provided with two or three separate books of schedules can easily take the whole in the course of a day. Some care, however, is needed to prevent portions only of several villages being included in one block. As far as possible the registration of the villages should be conducted with regard to territorial situation, though, no doubt, in many cases the interspersal of villages of other States will render this course out of the question. The standard block of 60 houses prescribed for British territory will probably be inapplicable in Central India, where a considerable area will not be enumerated at one and the same time. It will be for the Political Agents, however, to decide beforehand how many schedules should be bound into each enumeration book. On the last occasion that number was 100. This entails considerable trouble in checking the abstraction, so that it seems advisable to allot two or even three books of 40 schedules each in cases where either all the blocks are in a single village, or each block comprises more than one separate village. If this course be adopted, however, a column will have to be added to the circle register to show the number of books for which each enumerator is responsible. Care must be taken, too, in registering villages, that landing-places, camping-grounds, detached but inhabited temples, sarais, etc., are not omitted from the list.

"The preparation of the register should be begun before the rains, so that the blocks may be defined and an enumerator nominated for each by the beginning of October. The numbering of the houses, and the concurrent registration in the block-list, by which the enumerator is to be guided round his block, should then be started, and be completed by the end of December. The main points to be noted in connection with this task are (*a*) that the order in which the serial numbers run should be that in which they can most conveniently be visited ; (*b*) that the numbering should be serial for a village when not consisting of more than one supervisor's circle, or about 600 houses, not for a block, or for a circle, except as above specified ; (*c*) that the supervisors should see that the general definition of a house, especially in towns, is understood and applied as uniformly as circumstances permit. This definition is the dwelling-place of one or more families having a separate independent entrance from the public way (whether road, street, or lane, etc.) Special cases, such as enclosed quarters of towns, the quarters of low-caste menials outside the walls of the village, lodging-houses with galleries and outside staircases, the central house of a village, which not unfrequently forms a sort of fort full of the independent dwelling-places of relatives of the headman, all these require to be numbered under special instructions, as the definition fails to include them.

"Between October and January, the supervisors should be instructed in their duties, more particularly with reference to the schedule entries and the check upon the enumerators during the preliminary record. The best means of doing this is to organise a class of men sent up from each State for the purpose, who should be personally conducted round a block or a few houses by either the Political Agent himself, or some one specially trained by him in census details, so that a few spare schedules may be filled up by or in the hearing of the class of supervisors, who should be encouraged to bring forward any doubts or difficulties they may have chanced upon. Or, again, the instructing officer may depute one of these nominees to enumerate any person who may be in attendance in court or office on business, and correct and explain the record thus made. At all events, the men should be taught their work on some regular system, so that they in turn can teach the enumerators.

"The month of January should be taken up with the first round of the enumerator, on which he has to enter in his book the full details about all the ordinary residents in his block, by house-to-house visits. This round will be spread over from 15 to 20 days, and should be concluded by the 1st February. In towns, where the movement of the population is more frequent, it will be sufficient to begin on the 1st February, and finish on the 15th idem. During and after this record, the main work of the census in the direction of test and correction has to be performed, and this can only be properly done by house-to-house visitation. The mere inspection of a bundle of books brought by the enumerators or supervisors to a camp or office is necessarily only good for the correction of errors in the record, and leaves untouched the far more serious errors that may have occurred in the enumeration. Without expecting the same amount of check and inspection required in British territory, there is no reason why a considerable control should not be exercised in many parts of Central India by officials on tour, or when other opportunities occur. The preliminary record will not be made in cases where the enumeration is spread over some time, and not merely revised on a fixed date.

"The census itself will take place on the night of Thursday, the 26th February, and in Central India the towns and parts of the more thickly-populated country can probably be enumerated between nightfall and midnight on that date. In the rest of the tract, except certain hill and forest areas, it will apparently not be advisable to attempt more than a day-census, or revision of the preliminary record on the 26th and 27th. In the parts of the country inhabited by wild tribes, and very difficult of access, it is not practicable to take a synchronous census at all, so the enumeration will have to be effected by the aid of the tribal headman, beginning on a date to be fixed in consultation with the Agent to the Governor-General, according to circumstances, but ending with the 26th or 27th February.

"Copies of all circulars of a general nature issued by the Census Commissioner will be forwarded to the Agent to the Governor-General from time to time for information, so that the procedure in British territory may be learnt by those concerned with the operations in Feudatory States. It might be of advantage also to hold a meeting at Indore soon after the preliminaries have been started to discuss difficulties and arrange procedure. Probably the beginning of July would be a suitable time for such a consultation, and in addition to the Political Agents, delegates from the States, either the official specially entrusted with the local Census arrangements, or some one in general authority under the Durbar, might attend. The Census Commissioner hopes to be at Indore himself on this occasion, but if he is unable to be present, will obtain the sanction of a Local Government to the deputation of their Census Superintendent to attend the meeting and give his advice.

"In conclusion, it may be pointed out that with the record of 1881 as a basis for operations and the long period available on this occasion for preparation, the Census of 1891 should be taken not only with more ease, but also with considerable improvement in accuracy and despatch."

Census Conference at Indore.

2. Mr. Baines, Census Commissioner for India, made a flying visit to Indore early in March and went over the records of the 1881 Census to see what changes and modifica-

tions were desirable. He then arranged for a Census Conference to be held a few months later at Indore. Accordingly, he again visited Indore in July, and was met by almost all the Political Agents and by several officials who had been deputed by Native States for work in connection with the Census. At this Conference it was finally decided, after elaborate discussion, what the form of the Enumeration Book for Native States should be; and various other points of Census administration, such as the enumeration of wild tribes, etc., were considered.

Instructions to Political Agents. States asked to co-operate.

3. The Political Agents were informed that it was the intention of the Government of India to take a Census of the whole of India on the 26th February 1891, in which the Agent to the Governor-General had no doubt that the Durbars and Chiefs of Central India would give cordial aid and co-operation, as they had done in 1881. Intimation to that effect was to be at once made to the Durbars and guaranteed Thakurs under each Agency.

4. Full instructions, based on the Census Commissioner's notes, were issued to the Political Agents; and the functions of the different officials, to be appointed by the States to conduct the operations, were clearly defined. Those officials were—(1) an Enumerator for each block, (2) a Supervisor for each circle (of seven to ten blocks), and (3) a Superintendent for each town or Pargana.

Census of outlying districts.

5. Some difficulty arose as to the enumeration of the parts of Centra India States that lie in Rajputana, and *vice versa*. It was decided that the enumeration of the Chaumehla District of Jhalawar and of the Sironj, Pirawa, and Chhabra Districts of Tonk, should be conducted under the orders of the Rajputana political authorities by the Jhalawar and Tonk Durbars respectively; and similarly that the enumeration of the parts of Gwalior and Indore in Meywar should be conducted by the Gwalior and Indore Durbars under the orders of the Political Agent in Western Malwa.

6. Certain villages belonging te the district of Allahabad lie within the Baghelkhand Agency. The enumeration of those villages was arranged for by the Allahabad authorities. Again, several villages of the Rewa State lie within the district of Allahabad, and several villages of the Nagode State lie within the district of Jabalpur. The enumeration of those villages was arranged for by the Rewa and Nagode Durbars, respectively, under the orders of the Political Agent in Baghelkhand.

Detached portions of States within Central India.

7. As regards the enumeration of parts of States lying in different Political Agencies in Central India, the instructions issued from the Indore Census Office were in accordance with the principle laid down by the Census Commissioner (see page 29). A difficulty was raised by the Political Agent in Bhopal, who advocated what he considered a simpler system, *viz.*, that the enumeration of the detached portions of Gwalior, Indore, Dewas, and Dhar lying within the Bhopal Agency should be conducted by the Durbars of those States. It was decided that the general rule should be followed in all cases.

Question as to guaranteed Thakurats.

8. Several States represented that their rights would be infringed if the enumeration of the Thakurats under them were taken by the Thakurs themselves under the supervision of the Political Agent; but it was explained that the operations of the Census had no political significance, and that no rights could be created, destroyed, strengthened or weakened by anything done in connexion therewith. In the case of any difficulty arising regarding Thakurs, whose guarantee had been brought to notice since the Census of 1881, Political Agents were instructed to make a reference to the Agent to the Governor-General.

9. As has been already stated, the Census Commissioner did not contemplate a synchronous enumeration for hill tribes. But in Gwalior it was found possible to enumerate those tribes in the same way as the rest of the population. In Baghelkhand the hill tribes were enumerated by day on the 26th and 27th of February. In the Bhopawar Agency, in which Bhils form the majority of the population, some trouble arose from a Brahman of Jhabua having started a theory that the object of the Census was to procure some men and children to bury alive in the foundations of a new bridge. Some Bhils were reported to have left the country in terror; but the Jhabua Durbar promptly had the Brahman arrested and punished, and the excitement soon subsided.

Enumeration of hill tribes, etc.

SECTION II.—FORM OF VILLAGE REGISTERS, INDENTS FOR ENUMERATION BOOKS FOR NATIVE STATES, CANTONMENTS AND RAILWAYS.

10. No special forms for house and village registers were prescribed by the Census Commissioner. The following were recommended for use in Central India, and were uniformly adopted :—

Form of village registers and house lists.

Block List.

Village.	Sub-division (Hamlet, etc.)	Houses.			Remarks.
		Serial No.	Description—dwelling, shop, temple, etc.	Name of chief occupant.	
1	2	3	4	5	6

Village List.

STATE PARGANA CIRCLE

Village.			No. or letter of Block.	Houses.			Remarks.
Serial No.	Name.	Name of Hamlet, Quarter, etc.		Serial No.	Description (dwelling houses, temple, shop, etc.).	Name of chief occupant.	
1	2	3	4	5	6	7	8

Circle List.

STATE PARGANA {CIRCLE {SUPERVISOR

Villages.				Blocks.		
Serial No.	Name.	Names of Hamlets, etc.	Number of Houses.	Number or letter of Block.	Name and Office, etc., of Enumerator.	Remarks.
1	2	3	4	5	6	7

Sub-divisional Register.

STATE PARGANA CENSUS SUPERINTENDENT

Villages.				Circles.		
Serial No.	Name.	Number of Hamlets, etc.	Number of Houses.	Number or letter of Circle.	Name and Office, etc., of Supervisor.	Remarks.
1	2	3	4	5	6	7

An identical copy of the block list formed, as will be seen hereafter, a part of each enumeration book.

Form of the Enumeration Book for Native States.

11. At an early stage it was decided that the enumeration of Native States should be of a much simpler character than that of British districts, and should be made on a schedule of eight columns only, the British India fourteen-column schedule being used for the enumeration of Cantonments and Agency Head-quarters, of the Railway population, and of European residents in Native States. Careful consideration was given to the schedule, and the following form was finally adopted. It is here given both in English and in transliterated Hindi.

House No.

Serial Number.	Name.	Male or Female.	Age.	Religion.	Caste.	Birth-State or Province.	Occupation or means of subsistence.
1	2	3	4	5	6	7	8

Nambar Makan.

Nambar Shumar.	Namme valadi-at.	Mard ya Aurat.	Umr.	Mazhab ya Dharm.	Zat ya Kaum.	Jahan paidayish hui kisi riyasat ya kisi ahata amaldari Sarkar Angreze men.	Pesha ya aur tarik guzareka.
1	2	3	4	5	6	7	8

12. It was decided that 110 schedules should be bound in each book, each schedule being ruled for ten names, and that no variation from this rule should be permitted.

13. Each book was complete with Instructions to Enumerators ; a Specimen Schedule filled up so as to show the enumerators how to deal with the entries they were likely to have to record ; an Enumerator's Abstract, the use of which will appear hereafter ; and a Block List, as already mentioned.

14. The following is a translation of the Instructions to Enumerators.

INSTRUCTIONS TO ENUMERATORS.

A.—The First Round.

You will visit each house in your block to which has been given a number corresponding with the block list and enter in the blank schedules the name and particulars prescribed below for every person, young and old, males and females, residing in or taking meals from that house. You should use a fresh page for each house, and when there are more than ten persons in a house, continue the entries on the next page, which should be numbered, with the addition of the word " continued " in brackets after the number. Do not begin the entries for a fresh house in the middle of a page. If any ordinary resident in the house be absent for a few days, you should still enter that person as present. If there are any visitors in the house who are only stopping a day or two, as for a marriage, etc., do not enter them, unless they are going to stop till the 26th February. Write very clearly in the character you know best. Enter first the head of the family in each house, whether male or female, then the rest of the members of the family, then the servants residing on the premises, and lastly, visitors who are likely to stop some time in the house.

B.—The Second Round.

On the evening of the 26th and the morning of the 27th of February you will again visit your block, as before, and read over to the head of each family the entries made on your first visit, and ask him if any person has left the house, or any one has come who was not there before, or if any infant has been born. You will then enter those not entered before, and strike out the whole of the entries for those who have died or have left. But if any person has only left the house for a few hours to watch in the fields, etc., and is still taking meals from the house, you will consider him as present, and not strike his name out. After visiting all the houses, go to the dharamsalas, serais, and landing or encamping places, and count all the travellers, pilgrims, etc., you find there. When you are sure that every part of your block has been thoroughly visited, you should go to your Supervisor, and prepare the Abstract.

C.—*Rules for filling in the Schedule.*

Column 1.—(Serial number). Do not enter this number on your first visit, but fill it in on your second round.

Column 2.—(Name). If a child had not been named, enter the word "child." Enter all persons by name, but if there is any objection to giving the name of any female, enter the word "Female" in this column.

Column 3.—(Sex). Enter whether each person is *male or female*, even though you have already written "female" in column 2.

Column 4.—(Age). Enter the number of years each person has completed—and in the case of infants of less than one year old, write the word "infant" in this column. If the age cannot be stated exactly, guess what it is from the appearance of the person, or by inquiries from relatives. You must not, however, ask to see any female who is not voluntarily presented before you.

Column 5.—(Religion). Enter whether Hindu, Mussalman, Jain, Christian, Parsi, Bhil, etc.,

Column 6.—(Caste). Enter the caste of Hindus, as Brahman, Rajput, Bania, etc; the tribes of Mussalmans, as Saiad, Shaikh, Borah, Pathan, Arab, etc.; and of forest tribes as Bhil, Gond, etc.; and the races of Christians, as European, Eurasian, Native Christiain.

Column 7.—(Birth-State or Province). Enter the State, or if born in British Territory, the Province of birth, but not the zillah, parganah, village or town.

Column 8.—(Occupation, etc.). Enter the occupation of all who do work, and in the case of young children and women who do no work for wages, etc., enter the occupation of the person who supports them, prefixing the word "dependent" as agriculture, State military service, State writers, private service, trade (as shop-keeper, money-lender, etc.), priests, artisans (as carpenter, gold-smith weaver, potter, etc.), labourer, and mendicancy. You are not to leave this column blank even for infants, as these are supported by their parents, whose occupation is to be entered against the name of the infant, as above prescribed.

Note.—Do not write the word "ditto" in any column, and make a full entry as above prescribed in every column for every person, whether infant, or grown up.

15. The following is the English version of the Specimen Schedule:—

House No. *Specimen Schedule.*

Serial Number.	Name.	Male or female.	Age.	Religion.	Caste.	Birth-State or Province.	Occupation or means of subsistence.
1	2	3	4	5	6	7	8
1	Mansingh-Jaisingh	Male	39	Hindu	Rajput	Jodhpur	Zamindar.
2	Rupsingh-Mansingh	Male	8	Hindu	Rajput	Jodhpur	Zamindar.
3	Harisingh-Fatehsingh	Male	62	Hindu	Rajput	Panjab	Military service.
4	Shivshanker-Balram	Male	27	Hindu	Brahman	Ajmir	Priest.
5	Subhan Rao Malhar	Male	45	Hindu	Maratha	Indore	Domestic service.
6	Bale Khan-Shir Khan	Male	43	Mussalman	Pathan	Kabul	Private service (peon).
7	Amirchand-Tarachand	Male	32	Hindu	Oswal	Jaipur	Money-lender.
8	—Female	Female	35	Hindu	Rajputni	Udaipur	(Dependent) Zamindar.
9	—Female	Female	21	Hindu	Brahman	Oudh	Domestic service.
10	Jivkor	Female	38	Hindu	Ahir	Rewah	Domestic service.

16. The Enumerator's abstract was in the following form :—

Abstract.

(Not to be filled up till after the Census.)

STATE.	Circle Block No.
Zillah or Pargana Village	Name of Enumerator

Number of occupied houses.	NUMBER OF PERSONS.		
	Males.	Females.	Total.
1	2	3	4

Added by — Enumerator of Block No.

Re-added by — ,, ,, No.

Tested by — ,, ,, No.

Certified to be correct.

(Signed)

Date of certificate. The of 1891. *Supervisor.*

17. The Block List was in the following form :—

Block List.

Village.	Sub-division (Hamlet, etc.).	HOUSES.			REMARKS.
		Serial Number.	Description—dwelling, shop, temple, etc.	Name of chief occupant.	
1	2	3	4	5	6

18. Each book had a brown cartridge cover, with the following printed on it :—

ENUMERATION BOOK.

STATE *Zillah or Pargana*	CHARGE *Superintendent*	BLOCK No. *Enumerator*
TOWN OR VILLAGE	CIRCLE *Supervisor*	

No. of Blank schedules issued to Enumerator in this book.

Issued to Supervisor on the of 189	Issued to the Enumerator on the of 189
Returned by Supervisor on the of 1891.	Received from the Enumerator on the of 1891.
(Signed) *Charge Superintendent.*	(Signed) *Supervisor.*

19. It was arranged that both Urdu and Nagari versions of the book should be printed. The Nagari version was an exact transliteration of the Urdu.

Form of Enumeration Book used for Cantonments, Railways, etc.

20. In Cantonments and Agency Head-quarters the Census Commissioner decided that the fourteen-columned schedule of British India should be used for the enumeration of both the civil and the military population. These schedules were bound 104 in a book; but loose* (or household) schedules were also provided, and were freely used, especially at Mhow.

21. In the Cantonments in which British troops are stationed (Mhow, Nimach, and Nowgong) there is the civil authority of the Cantonment Magistrate co-existing with the military authority. In those Cantonments the enumeration within military limits was taken by the military authorities, while the enumeration outside strictly military limits was taken by the Cantonment Magistrates under instructions from the Political Agents. The Census Commissioner was at first inclined to think that Mhow was a special case, and that it would probably be necessary to have all the census arrangements for Mhow controlled by the General Officer Commanding; but it was afterwards decided to treat Mhow in the same way as the other Cantonments.

22. Agar, Guna, Sehore, and Sardarpur are Cantonments for Local Corps, and are all Agency head-quarters also. At Agar and Guna the military and civil authority is the same, the officer in command being Political Agent also. As such he took the census of the whole population, both military and civil. At Sehore the officer commanding the Bhopal Battalion took the census of the military lines, and the Political Agent took the census of the civil population. The same course was followed at Sardarpur. For Mahidpur, which used to be a cantonment, it was thought advisable that the arrangements for its enumeration should be made by the Political Agent in Western Malwa.

* Loose household schedules (of fourteen columns) were also provided for the enumeration of European residing in Native States.

23. The Agency Head-quarters which are not also Cantonments are Indore Residency, Gwalior Residency, and Sutna (Baghelkhand). In these the enumeration was of course conducted by the Political authorities. No special arrangements were considered necessary for the small detachments of troops stationed in them, except that the company of British infantry and the wing of Native infantry stationed at Indore were enumerated by the officer commanding the station under instructions from the General Officer commanding the Mhow Division.

Railways.

24. For the enumeration of Railway population also the fourteen-column schedule was used. All the arrangements were made by the Railway authorities, the only thing done by the Indore Census office being to prepare, and send to the managers of the different railways, mileage statements, showing the length of line in each Agency. The total mileage of railways in Central India is 823·50 miles, distributed as in the following table:—

Railway	Agency	Miles
Rajputana-Malwa Railway	Indore Agency	73·16
	Western Malwa Agency	151·65
Indian Midland Railway	Bhopal Agency	123·00
	Bundelkhand Agency	65·46
	Gwalior Agency	66·35
East Indian Railway	Bundelkhand Agency	68·38
	Baghelkhand Agency	87·00
Bengal-Nagpur Railway	Baghelkhand Agency	188·50
	TOTAL MILEAGE	823·50

Indent for Enumeration Books for Native States.

25. No record having been kept of the population of villages according to the Census of 1881, the preparation of the indent of books required for the enumeration of Native States was a very difficult and tedious task. It is to be hoped that it will be found possible to preserve, in manuscript at least, if they cannot be printed, the village registers of the 1891 Census. The preliminary arrangements for the next census will be much simplified thereby.

26. All the enumeration books for the Native States of Central India were printed at the Government Press, Calcutta.

27. The instructions of the Census Commissioner were that an indent for the books required, prepared on information received from the Political Agents, should be forwarded not later than August 1890. The Political Agents were instructed to base their calculations on the number of houses to be covered by the Census operations, if sufficient information was available; if not, their indents were to be made out as accurately as possible on such information as could be collected at an early date, on the basis, not of the population as estimated by the previous census, but of existing and ascertainable facts, bearing in mind that each enumeration book was to serve for the dwellers in not more than 100 houses.

28. It was arranged that both Urdu and Nagari books should be provided, the Nagari version, as already explained, being a literal transcription of the Urdu.

29. The indents of all the Agencies reached Indore in time to enable the Indore Census Office to forward the indent for the whole of Central India on the 18th of August, and to make timely provision for correcting the few miscalculations that were unavoidable.

Indent for the eight-columned Enumeration Books, of 110 pages each, required for the Native States in the Central India Agency.

Agency.	Number of Books. Hindi.	Urdu.
Gwalior Residency	7,310	...
Bhopal Agency	4,675	1,100
Bundelkhand Agency	4,712	275
Baghelkhand Agency	7,700	...
Western Malwa Agency	7,301	660
Bhopawar Agency	4,750	...
Guna Agency	1,655	15
Indore Agency	1,990	...
TOTAL	40,093	2,050

Indent for Enumeration Books for Cantonments, etc.

30. It having been arranged that the abstraction and tabulation of the books used in the census of Cantonments and Agency Head-quarters, and of European residents in Native States, should be done at Ajmir, it was ordered that the indents for those books should be forwarded by the military authorities, and (for the civil population) by the Political Agents, direct to the Provincial Superintendent of Census at Ajmir.

Indent for Enumeration Books and Household Schedules required for Cantonments and Agency Head-quarters in Central India.

Cantonment, etc.	Number of Hindi Books.	Number of Urdu Books.	Number of English Books.	Schedules.
Mhow Cantonment (Civil population)	...	...	100	550
Ditto (Military do.)	...	...	72	237
Nimach Cantonment (Civil do.)	...	83	...	77
Ditto (Military do.)	26	...	22	...
Nowgong Cantonment (Civil do.)	...	33	...	6
Ditto (Military do.)	...	...	19	55
Bundelkhand Agency Head-quarters	...	4	...	11
Indore Residency (Civil population)	10	30	...	75
Ditto (Military ditto)	7	...	2	10
Agar Cantonment	8	20	...	16
Mahidpur Cantonment	...	3	...	...
Guna ditto	22	...	8	11
Sardarpur ditto	11	...	...	10
Sutna ditto	...	5	3	...
Sipri ditto	16	...	2	3
Gwalior Residency Head-Quarters	8	...	...	3
Sehore Cantonment	...	55	...	22
Native States, for Europeans residing in Tour Offices of the Political Agents, etc.	...	...	50	1,000
TOTAL	108	241	270	2,086

31. The Indore Census office had nothing to do with the indents of books for the enumeration of the Railway population in Central India. Those indents were prepared by the authorities of the different railways, and forwarded by them to the Provincial Superintendents of Census to whom respectively it fell to take the census of those parts of the different lines that lie in British India. Thus, the indents for the Indian Midland and East Indian Railways were sent to Allahabad; that for the Bengal-Nagpur Railway to Nagpur; and that for the Rajputana-Malwa Railway to Ajmir.

Indent for Enumeration Books for Railways.

SECTION III.—ARRANGEMENTS MADE BY DURBARS FOR CARRYING OUT THE ENUMERATION IN THE VARIOUS STATES.

32. So far the report has dealt almost wholly with the Census Commissioner's instructions for the census of Central India, and their communication through the Indore Census office, to the Political Agents. It will be advisable at this stage to say something of the way in which those instructions were carried out, so far as may be gathered from reports received from the Political Agents, and from the Durbar Census officers appointed in the larger States. As the Indore Agency Census office was in direct communication with the Indore and Dewas census officials, a good deal of information exists for those States; and a very exhaustive and interesting report on Census operations in Gwalior was furnished to the Resident by the Chief Census officer of the Gwalior State.

Indore.

33. Mr. Krishnarao Gopal was appointed Chief Census officer for the Indore State. On his transfer to the interior he was succeeded by Messrs. K. S. Date and Fateh Singh as joint Census officers.

Agency employed in enumeration.

34. The work of enumeration in the Indore State was mainly carried out by official (unpaid) agency. Amins and Wahiwatdars were made Charge Superintendents; and Thanadars, Kotwals, and superior clerks were made Supervisors. A very few paid enumerators were employed: as a rule, Patwaris, Kanungos, Mandlois, and the clerks of Jagirdars and Ijaradars were made to act in that capacity. Not reckoning the amount paid in travelling allowances to State servants, the enumeration is understood to have cost the Indore Durbar R4,000.

Preparation of village lists.

35. The first thing done was to prepare a list of the villages in each pargana, and to divide those villages, and also the mohallas of towns, into blocks consisting of not more than 100 houses each. Then village registers were prepared on a Hindi version of the form given on page 32. The registers, with full marginal instructions for filling them in, were printed by the Durbar. Specimens of these registers were brought to the Indore Census office for inspection. Then the houses were numbered, care being taken that no house was omitted.

Definition of a house.

36. In Indore, as elsewhere, some difficulty arose regarding the definition of a house. That adopted by the Agra Conference ("the dwelling-place of one or more families with their resident servants having one principal entrance from the common way") could not be universally applied. For instance, there exist in Indore walled enclosures with only one entrance from the common way, but with several separate dwelling-places inside, the one behind the other, those behind being reached by the verandah of the front one. It was a question whether one number should be affixed to the entrance from the common way, or all the houses within the enclosure should be numbered. The latter course was adopted, as giving the actual number of houses more correctly. Other questions as to what should

and should not be taken as houses were considered on their merits, special instructions being issued to meet special cases.

37. Blocks made by the district authorities to consist of more than 100 houses were remodelled. No block was allowed to contain parts of two separate villages. The whole of the Indore territory under the Indore Agency was divided into 68 circles and 672 blocks.

38. As soon as possible, specimens of the Native State enumeration book as approved by the Census Commissioner, were supplied to the Census officers of the Indore State, that they might instruct the Charge Superintendents in the proper method of filling in the entries, who in their turn might impart this knowledge to the Supervisors, of whom there was to be one for every ten or twelve enumerators. To make sure that they thoroughly understood what they had to do, Charge Superintendents were required to send specimens of filled-in schedules to the Indore State Census officers for inspection.

39. The joint Census officers made a tour in the districts under the Indore Agency to see that the local arrangements were being properly carried out.

Preliminary record made on manuscript books.

40. A great part of the work of the preliminary enumeration was done before the 10th of February on manuscript books, specially prepared, to lessen the chance of the printed books being soiled or torn. The entries in the manuscript books were supposed to be copied into the printed books after the former had been inspected by the Charge Superintendents; but it is doubtful if this inspection was made, though strict injunctions were issued that it should be: if the inspection had been made, it is scarcely possible that so many omissions should have been found when the books came to be abstracted.

Dewas.

41. The Census officers of the Dewas State (Senior and Junior) received instructions direct from the Indore Agency Office, in the same way as the Indore officers did. Practically the same arrangements as those described above were carried out. A wrong system of numbering houses was in some cases adopted. Where several families occupied what would, by the Census Commissioner's definition, be one house, a *house* number was given to each *family*. This mistake was found out too late to be rectified, and must to some extent vitiate the return of occupied houses. The Dewas territory under the Indore Agency was divided into 64 circles and 293 blocks.

Guaranteed Thakurats in the Indore Agency.

42. The Thakur of Bagli took the census of all his villages, guaranteed and non-guaranteed, under instructions from the Indore Agency office. The Thakurat was divided into 9 circles and 40 blocks. No paid agency was employed in Bagli. The four villages which the Thakur of Pathari holds under Dewas (Junior Branch) are guaranteed, while the eight which he holds under Dewas (Senior Branch) are non-guaranteed. The Dewas Durbar (Senior Branch) wished to take the census of the latter, as had been done in 1881; but the Agent to the Governor General ruled that the Thakur of Pathari should take the census of all his villages. Similarly, the Thakur of Uni was allowed to take his own census, in spite of objections raised by Dewas (Junior Branch). So also was the Thakur of Karodia, who holds under Indore.

43. The Neori and Bhaurasa Parganas of Gwalior were divided, the former into 19 circles and 63 blocks, and the latter into 13 circles and 37 blocks.

Gwalior.

44. As was remarked above, a very full account exists of the census arrangements in the Gwalior State, and particularly in those parts of the State that are immediately under the Resident, in the very able report made by Mr. Raghunath Rao Dinkar, the Chief Census officer appointed by the Council of Regency. The following

Gwalior—*contd.*

sketch of census arrangements in Gwalior is in the main an abstract of Mr. Raghunath Rao's report.

45. Gwalior territory as a whole consists of three Prants:—Gwalior, Malwa, and Esagarh. These are sub-divided into districts or zillas, and the zillas into parganas. The Suba is the chief officer in a district, and the Tahsildar in a pargana. The Malwa Prant is under a Sar-Suba.

46. The original intention was that Mr. Raghunath Rao should direct the Census operations in the whole of the Gwalior State. But this arrangement was afterwards modified for reasons of convenience; and a special Census officer was appointed for Malwa; while the Subas of Esagarh and Bajrangarh were directed to make their own census arrangements under the instructions of the Political Agent at Bhopal and the Political Assistant at Guna respectively. The pargana of Esagarh* (with Chanderi), though under the Bhopal Agency, was, on account of its distance from Bhopal, taken along with the Gwalior Prant.

47. For census purposes the pargana was taken as the territorial unit, and divided according to the chaukis of head constables, these police divisions being better defined than the Kanungos' circles of the Revenue Department. A list of the villages under each chauki was drawn up by the officer in charge of the chauki, acting under the orders of the Tahsildar. To help and check the work of the Tahsildars, a Superintendent was appointed for each district.

48. Some irregular arrangements had been made, under the orders of the Political Agent in Bhopal, before the transfer above referred to was effected. In particular, the number of houses to be included in a block had been fixed at 36, while the enumeration books were intended for 100 houses. This of course seriously affected the indent for books; but it was thought too late to interfere with the arrangement already made, and it was allowed to stand.

Preparation of village lists.

49. The records of the 1881 Census, preserved in the Khatut-daftar, were not complete or accurate enough to furnish, even approximately, the number of houses to be censused in 1891; a fresh list of villages was necessary. Patwaris were made to send statements for their villages to the head constable of their chauki. These statements gave the name of each separate collection of houses (Thok or Tola) in the village, and the number of houses in each; and stated the description of the village, *i.e.*, whether it was khalsa, maafi or jagir. The puras belonging to a village were also entered.

50. From these Patwaris' statements each head constable prepared a list of the villages included in his chauki; and for the accuracy of all the entries in this list the head constable was held responsible. From these head constables' lists, the list for the pargana was prepared by the Tahsildar. In this list only the name and description of the villages, and the number of houses in each, were given. One copy was sent to the Suba of the district, and another to the central Census Office at Gwalior, the latter having to reach its destination before the 5th of September. Each Tahsildar had to attach to his list a copy of the Topographical Survey Map for his pargana, on which he had marked the census area under each head constable, had entered in their proper place all villages not given in the map, and had drawn a red circle round villages that had been deserted, or had fallen under foreign jurisdiction.

51. The Tahsildars' lists when received were compared with the Dehzhada in the Mal-Daftar, and finally a correct list of villages in Gwalior Prant and Esagarh Pargana was secured. They were found to amount to 5,632, or, deducting 942 deserted villages, 4,690.

* Esagarh is the name of a Prant as well as of a pargana.

Gwalior—*contd.*

52. In anticipation of arrangements afterwards to be made for the actual enumeration, Subas were informed that the following would be the names employed to designate the census areas and the officers in charge of them :—

Names of census areas and officials.

Block (Giroh Makanat)	Enumerator (Shumar Kunande)
Circle (Halka)	Supervisor (Janch Kunande)
Charge	Charge Superintendent
District	Zilla Superintendent.

53. In illustration and amplification of the definition of a house, as given by the Census Commissioner for India, instructions to the following effect were issued by the Gwalior Census office :—

Definition of *house*.

A compound with one opening to the public road, containing several dwelling places inhabited by the members of one family and their servants, was to be regarded as one house; but if such a compound contained separate dwelling places inhabited by families of different castes, each dwelling place was to be considered a separate house. A house of two or more storeys was to be taken as one house, although the inmates bore no relation to one another. Sarais, Mosques and Dharmsalas were to be taken as separate houses. Bungalows with outhouses, if in the same compound, were to be taken as one house; but if the outhouses were outside the compound, and had independent communication with the road, they were to be taken as separate houses from the bungalow. The several tenements of barracks and police lines were to be regarded as so many separate houses. Shops independently situated, and not forming parts of a dwelling house, were to be taken as houses by themselves.

54. The demarcation of blocks in the villages was done by each head constable for the villages of his chauki, in consultation with the Patwaris. In towns it was done by the Sub-Inspectors of Thanas under the supervision of the Tahsildar. The recognised sub-divisions of villages and towns were as far as possible kept intact. Care was taken to make each block compact and distinct from its neighbours. The circles, each of 10 blocks, or as near that number as was convenient, were arranged so as to form symmetrical wholes, a circular form being aimed at as far as possible. Strict orders were issued against including parts of a village in different circles.

Demarcation of blocks.

55. The blocks having been demarcated, every Patwari was required to draw up a list of the blocks in his village in the following form :—

Number of Circle.	Serial number of Blocks.	Description of Blocks	Name of Enumerater.	Office.
1	2	3	4	5

Gwalior—*contd.*

56. From these lists each head constable had to draw up a list of blocks for the area of his chauki in the following form :—

Serial number of Village.	Name of Village.	Nature of Village.	Number of Circle.	Serial number of Blocks.	Description of Blocks.	Name of Enumerator.	Office.	Name of Supervisor.	Office.
1	2	3	4	5	6	7	8	9	10

A similar list of blocks was drawn up for towns.

57. From these head constables' lists, each Tahsildar had to make up a list of blocks for his pargana, and forward it to his Suba and to the Chief Census office at Gwalior. The pargana lists all reached Gwalior in the month of October.

Numbering of houses.

58. The work of numbering houses was done in villages by the Patwaris, and in towns by the Sub-Inspectors of Police, assisted by the Patwaris of the towns and the Thana Moharrirs. Head constables had to visit all the villages in their chaukis twice, once to see the work begun, and again to see that it had been properly finished. The numbering was consecutive for the whole of a village and the puras attached to it, and, in towns, for the whole of a mohalla, or other town division. In Lashkar city the work of numbering the houses was supervised by the Thanadars, and by the Kotwals in Morar, Gwalior, and the quarter known as Maharaja Sindiah's Brigade.

59. After the numbering was completed, lists of blocks were prepared by Tahsildars (from lists furnished by the Patwaris) and forwarded to the Gwalior Census office. These lists were in the following form :—

Serial number.	Name of village, with description of block, where the number of houses exceeds one hundred.	Number of houses in each block.
1	2	3

Lists of the blocks into which towns were divided were made on a similar form.

60. It would have been easier to have had the houses numbered first of all; and the reason why that was not done was that the Gwalior Census Officer wished to make it imperative on the most careless Patwari to go three time round every house in his village—first for the preparation of the village list, second, for making rough circle and block lists, and third, for actually numbering the houses.

61. The Tahsildars' lists were revised in the Gwalior Census office, and blocks and circles not in accordance with the instructions were remodelled. As finally demarcated, there were, in Gwalior Prant and Esagarh Pargana 4,978 blocks and 585 circles.

62. It would seem that in 1881 the census was taken in Gwalior without any numbering of houses; for it is stated that this being done *for the first time*

in 1890 gave rise to fear among the ignorant villagers that a new and unheard of tax was about to be imposed. *Gwalior—contd.*

Agency employed in preliminary arrangements and in actual enumeration.

63. For preparing village lists, demarcating blocks and circles, and numbering houses, the state officials did all that was required. As we have seen, these were, in the descending scale, Tahsildar, Sub-Inspector or head constable, and Patwari. But for the actual work of enumeration, preliminary and final, special agency was considered necessary. The Revenue Department, it appears, does not provide a Patwari for every village: sometimes one Patwari has to manage a group of even large villages. The zemindars in the districts are generally illiterate; and the respectable and fairly educated residents in the villages were found in most cases to be so hostile to the operations of the census that no useful aid could be expected from them. For these reasons the Council of Regency was induced to sanction a large amount of paid agency.

64. But the difficulty did not end with this. When the Tahsildars were told that they were authorised to entertain such and such a number of paid enumerators, they replied that a sufficient number of competent men could not be got for money. Ultimately the responsibility of finding a sufficient number of fit men was thrown on the Subas of districts. About half the total number of enumerators were paid. In Lashkar and Morar no unpaid agency whatever was employed.

65. Each enumerator was provided with a card of appointment.

Arrangements for lands held in jagir.

66. The census arrangements above detailed were held to cover lands held in jagir; and the Inamdars were not, as a rule, asked to concern themselves with them. The three great Jagirdars, however, Jadho Saheb, Sitole Saheb, and Angre Saheb, were asked to arrange for the census each of his own jagir, and they gladly undertook to do so. Their arrangements, however, were carefully supervised by the Tahsildars in whose jurisdiction the jagirs severally lie. The Rajas of Pahargarh and Seopur-Baroda, and the Thakurs of Khatoli and Bhansauli objected to the Durbar authorities making census arrangements on their lands, and claimed a right to send their census returns direct to the Resident. Their objections and claims were valid according to the ruling of the Agent to the Governor General for the census of guaranteed estates,* that ruling being in accordance with the general practice in the Census of 1881; and the abovementioned Chiefs were allowed to make their own census arrangements for their holdings.

67. It was decided to procure the enumeration books from the Government of India in preference to printing them at the Durbar Press. Loose schedules, locally printed, were provided for the enumeration of travellers, boatmen, and wandering tribes. All the books and schedules were in Hindi, and no other language than Hindi was to be used in filling them up.

Railway premises and travellers by rail.

68. The census of railway premises and travellers by rail was, of course, arranged for by the Railway authorities, but that of outlying gate-lodges, etc., was left to the local census officials. Thirty-five enumeration books, of 12 schedules each, were procured and distributed to the enumerators of the villages within the boundaries of which the gate-lodges lay. These books were ordered to be sent, when filled in, to the Resident, for transmission to the Railway authorities.

Cantonments.

69. The rules for the census of cantonments and troops on the march were modelled on those prescribed for British India. Loose schedules seem to have been largely used in the military Census.

---

* Page 31.

Gwalior—*contd.*

70. There is not much river traffic in the Gwalior Prant; but it was thought advisable to take precautions to secure the inclusion in the census of persons in boats or at landing ghats on the census night. A policeman was stationed at every ghat on the night of the census to enumerate the people encamped on it, or sleeping in boats moored near. This was done on loose schedules, which were afterwards stitched to the books of the villages adjoining.

River travellers.

71. The police were entrusted with the census also of the houseless population. The station officers were furnished beforehand with as many loose schedules as they thought would be required for the camps within their jurisdiction. Precautions were taken to keep the camps stationary for some days before the census. The schedules were afterwards stitched to the village books.

Houseless population.

72. Adequate arrangements were made for the census of other travellers Officials on tour took the census of all persons attached to their camps. The population of such camps was included in that of the villages within the bounds of which they were pitched on the night of the census. People attending fairs or marriage festivals were enumerated by the police on loose schedules. Head constables were required beforehand to procure, and furnish to Subas, all the information they could regarding fairs and important marriages that would be likely to bring many people together on the night of the 26th of February. The schedules were attached to the books of the villages at which the gatherings were held.

Fairs, wedding parties, etc.

73. For the census of the Lashkar jail, arrangements were made by the Suba of Gird Gwalior, within whose jurisdiction it lies. For the district jails no special arrangements were considered necessary: they were taken as parts of ordinary blocks. Hospitals were treated in the same way. No preliminary enumeration was made in jails and hospitals.

Jails.

74. Having regard to the inefficiency of many of the Patwaris, and also of the paid men employed as enumerators when Patawaris were not available, it was considered necessary to begin the preliminary record a full month before the actual census. On the 15th of December, State servants were selected by the Subas from the different departments to act as Supervisors, and on the 28th such paid enumerators as were required were appointed. Each supervisor, on his appointment, received from his Charge Superintendent the enumeration books for his circle, and also a copy of the circle and block lists.

Preliminary record.

75. The method of filling in the entries having been fully explained to them, the enumerators were made to enumerate the inhabitants of ten houses on a manuscript copy of the schedule. Their entries were submitted to the Supervisors for inspection. The block lists were then copied by the enumerators into the pages provided for the purpose in the enumeration books, and the enumerators started on their first round, to make the preliminary record. For this manuscript books were used, the entries in which were not copied into the actual census books till they had been scrutinised by the Supervisors. For houses found unoccupied on the first round enumerators were directed to write "empty" on the top of the schedule, and leave the page blank.

76. In no part of Gwalior Prant and Esagarh Pargana was it considered necessary to arrange for a day census even of wild tribes.

Wild tribes.

77. The final enumeration on the night of the 26th of February was fixed to begin, in the districts, at sunset. In Lashkar, Morar, and Gwalior 9-30 P.M. was fixed, in order that persons arriving by the mail train from Agra might have time to reach their homes.

78. Lashkar city, being for police purposes separate from the Gird Gwalior district, in which it lies, was taken as a census division by itself, and the census officer's head clerk was intrusted with all the arrangements for the nine thanas into which it is divided. Enumerators were engaged for a month on R8, and durbar officials were made to act as Charge Superintendents and Supervisors. Gwalior—*contd.*

79. To guard against difficulties that might arise from the ignorant prejudices of the people, the following notification was published by the Durbar.

Notification.

"In any of the following cases, namely:—

(*a*) If any Census officer without sufficient cause refuses or neglects to act as such or makes any false return;

(*b*) If any person refuses to answer any question asked of him by a Census officer;

(*c*) If any person occupying any house, enclosure or other place refuses to allow access to any Census officer;

(*d*) If any person removes, obliterates, alters or injures before the 31st day of March 1891 any numbers which have been affixed to houses;

he shall be punished with fine which may extend to fifty rupees."*

80. It was estimated that the census of the Gwalior Prant would cost R29,583-6-9, divided as follows:—

Number.	Heads of Charges.	Estimated Cost.		
1	Census officer's allowance	2,700	0	0
2	Office Establishment	2,933	9	9
3	Pay of Superintendents for 7 districts	2,730	0	0
4	Pay of Enumerators	19,432	0	0
5	Maps in Hindi	240	0	0
6	Sign-boards in Lashkar city	400	0	0
7	Painting numbers on houses	272	12	6
8	Stationery	645	1	0
9	Miscellaneous	229	15	6
	TOTAL	29,583	6	9

*As the census arrangements above detailed do not in all respects conform to the instructions of the Census Commissioner for India, it is thought advisable to give here a note that was made on Mr. Raghunath Rao Dinkar's report, and sent to the Resident on the 15th January of 1891.

Note on Mr. Raghunath Rao Dinkar's report.

"The report generally is very satisfactory."

"It is matter of regret that so many paid enumerators are required in the districts and even in Lashkar city. The latter are to be paid R8 per mensem. The total sum to be paid in wages to enumerators is to be R19,432."

"It is not said whether the books supplied for the census of outlying gate-lodges on the railway are of the fourteen-columned kind, as they ought to be. They were not furnished through this office; so it is to be presumed that they are railway books. Special care will have to be taken that the enumerators know the difference between them and the Native State books."

"Objection might be taken to the prescribed use of loose schedules for the enumeration of troops on the march, of boatmen, etc., landing at ghâts on the night of the 26th February, of the houseless population, and of persons attending fairs and marriage parties. The use of loose schedules (except for European residents) was not contemplated in Central India. One would think that there would be information available to enable troops marching, and the attendants at fairs and important marriage parties, to be enumerated in the ordinary books. The same may be said of the so-called houseless population, who should be enumerated where they are whether they have houses or not. Ghâts should have been blocked with the adjoining villages."

"It is ordered that no preliminary record is to be taken in jails and hospitals. A preliminary record may not be necessary for jails, but it would be safer to have one for hospitals."

"It is satisfactory to see that a day census of Bhils is not considered necessary."

"The punitive clauses seem needlessly harsh, especially clauses *b* and *c*. It would have been better to adopt provisions similar to those of the British Census Act. That Act makes a reasonable reservation about women's names when there is an objection to giving them. Nor can it be necessary that a Census officer should have *access* to a house."

Other States.

81. To give in detail the census arrangements made by the other important States in Central India would be in effect, a repetition of what has been said above regarding Indore and Gwalior. So far as information is available, it appears that effective arrangements were made in all of them under the direction of the Political Agents concerned.

82. As regards Rewa, no trouble was anticipated in taking the census of the wild tribes inhabiting its more remote districts; but, in accordance with the instructions of the Census Commissioner for India, those tribes were enumerated by day on the 26th and 27th of February.

SECTION IV.—COMPILATION OF RETURNS BASED ON THE ENUMERATOR'S ABSTRACT.

83. After the actual enumeration on the 26th of February, and before the enumeration books were sent in to the Agency Head-quarters, the page in the enumeration book called the enumerator's abstract had to be utilised for the compilation of a rough return of occupied houses, and of the numbers of the population, urban and rural, by sex. This return was meant, in the words of the Census Commissioner, "not only to serve as a guide in abstraction, but for use in official returns for the year ending with the 31st of March 1891."

84. That urban and rural areas might be clearly distinguished for the purposes both of this return and of the subsequnet tabulation of the census figures, Political Agents were required to furnish beforehand lists of places which should for census purposes be considered as towns.

Instructions for the compilation of enumerator's abstracts.

85. Regarding the compilation of returns based on the enumerator's abstract the following circular was issued to Political Agents.

"It is presumed that everywhere Census officers have been or will be soon appointed according to the Census Commissioner's instructions. These officers are Enumerators, Supervisors, and Charge Superintendents. The function of each in the preparation of the abstract is as follows:—

1stly.—The Enumerator under the immediate eye of his Supervisor is to add up the number of (*a*) occupied houses, (*b*) males, (*c*) females in his block. The form adopted for Central India will not admit of visitors being shown as distinct from residents. Then the supervisor is to pass the book over to another enumerator for re-addition, and if the figures thus totalled tally with each other, the abstract form on the reverse of the specimen schedule in the book is to be filled in and signed by both the enumerators, and certified to be correct by the Supervisor.

2ndly.—When this has been done the Supervisor should proceed to enter the results in the *Circle Abstract,* which will be supplied to him in a form somewhat modified from that sketched in paragraph 3 in Note L, of date the 18th July 1890 from the Census Commissioner, India, and which he is to sign.

3rdly.—The Supervisor is to take his *Circle Abstract* to the Charge Superintendent who will be Chief Census officer in a pargana, town, or zilla, etc., who is to post the circle totals in to a *Summary* for his sub-division in the form shown in the annexed separate paper and pass it on after being satisfied of its correctness, to the Political Agent through the proper channel.

4thly.—The last thing to be done is for you, as Political Agent, to prepare an Agency Summary according to the form suggested in paragraph 5 of the note, including the totals for Cantonments and Railways, and to wire the results to the Census Commissioner for India, Simla, and to this office in the following concise form: "Houses——; Males——; Females——; Total——" You will be separately addressed regarding the despatch to you of the summaries of Cantonments and Railways.'

"You are further required to prepare a statement in the following form :—
(*Agency*).

Name of Town, Cantonment, etc., and total of rural areas.	Occupied Houses.	PERSONS.			REMARKS.
		Males.	Females.	Total	
A. Town A . . .					
Cantonment A . . .					
Town B, etc., . . .					
TOTAL *Towns* .					
B. Total *Rural areas* .					
Grand Total .					

and transmit it by post to this office as well as to that of the Census Commissioner for India, Simla. To prepare this statement it will be necessary for you to decide, in consultation with the State officials, on the principles laid down as under, what places are to be regarded as towns for census purposes :

(*a*) The population should be not less than 5,000, residing in houses more or less contiguous, not in scattered collections, as hamlets, etc.

(*b*) The place, though containing the above population, should not be merely a large village, but should have some distinctly urban character, as that of a market town.

"A list of towns in your agency should, before the census, be submitted for record to the Census Commissioner for India, Simla, and also to this office.

"It has been arranged to have extra copies of the Enumerator's Abstract, printed on separate slips of paper, in case those in the books become torn or dirtied, and these will reach you direct from the Press. They should be distributed to the Native States in your agency in proportion to the number of books indented by each.

"It has also been considered necessary to have the forms printed for the Circle Abstract, and Sub-divisional Summary in Hindi and Urdu and the Agency Summary in English. I am therefore to request that you will report at an early date the number of these forms which will be required in your agency. There should be no difficulty in arriving at the required number as the Circles and Sub-divisions are or should be marked out already."

CIRCLE ABSTRACT.

State——————*Pargana, Town, Zilla, etc.,*——————*Circle*——————

Village or ward of a town.	Block No.	No. of occupied houses.	TOTAL POPULATION.		
			Males.	Females.	Total.
1	2	3	4	5	6
Circle Total . . .					

Submitted to the Head Officer of Pargana (or Town, Zilla, etc.,) on the ——————*of*——————*1891.*

(Sd.)

Supervisor.

SUMMARY.

STATE.	PARGANA, TOWN, ZILLA, etc.,				
Circle.	Occupied houses.	Population.			REMARKS.
		Males.	Females.	Total.	
1	2	3	4	5	6
Pargana, etc., Total					

Tested and submitted through——————*to the Political Agent*
——————*on the*——————*1891.*

(Sd.)

Head of the Pargana, etc.

NOTE.—The *Agency Summary* will be in exactly the same form as the *Summary*, the first column being reserved for Parganas, etc.

86. The civil and military authorities in cantonments were similarly addressed as to the preparation of circle summaries and a sub-divisional summary for each cantonment, which latter was directed to be forwarded to the Political Agent concerned. A similar summary, also to be sent to the Political Agents was ordered to be prepared by the Railway authorities for the parts of their lines lying within the limits of each Agency.

87. The Agency summaries were in all cases to reach the Census Commissioner by the 8th of March, the totals being telegraphed to him not later than the 5th. The State returns were prepared with as much accuracy, and forwarded with as much punctuality as could reasonably be expected.

SECTION V.—ABSTRACTION AND TABULATION.

Tabulation registers.

88. For the tabulation of the Census Returns of Central India the following five registers were adopted :—

TABULATION REGISTER No. I.

RELIGIONS.

All Religions. *State*——————*Pargana*——————

Serial No.	Villages.	Block No.	MALES.								FEMALES.							
			Hindus.	Mahomedans.	Jains.	Aboriginals.	Parsis.	Christians.	Jews, etc.	Total males.	Hindus.	Mahomedans.	Jains.	Aboriginals.	Parsis.	Christians.	Jews, etc.	Total Females.

Size 2′ 3″ by 7½″

In this Register Jains and Aboriginals were shewn separately from Hindus as in the Abstraction sheet, and Aboriginals included Bhils, Gonds, etc.

TABULATION REGISTER No. II.

AGES BY RELIGION.

Religion. *State* __________ *Pargana* __________

Serial No.	Villages.	Block No.	MALES.																		FEMALES.																	
			Infant.	1	2	3	4	5—9	10—14	15—19	20—24	25—29	30—34	35—39	40—44	45—49	50—54	55—59	60 & over.	Total males.	Infant.	1	2	3	4	5—9	10—14	15—19	20—24	25—29	30—34	35—39	40—44	45—49	50—54	55—50	60 & over.	Total females.

Size 2′ 3″ by 7½″

Each religion had a register for itself. There was one for Hindus, one for Jains, one for Aboriginals, one for Musulmans, and so on.

TABULATION REGISTER No. III.

CASTES.

State __________ *Pargana* __________

Serial No.	Villages.	Block No.																								Total.

Size 2′ 3″ by 7½″

Castes were arranged according to religions, all castes of Hindus first, then the Aboriginal tribes, then Jains, then tribes of Musulmans, etc.

TABULTION REGISTER No. IV.

BIRTHPLACE.

State __________ *Pargana* __________

Serial No.	Villages.	Block No.																			Total.

Size 2′ 3″ by 7½″

States in Central India were to be entered first, then States out of Central India, and lastly British districts or provinces.

TABULATION REGISTER No. V. A.

Occupation by Age.

*State*________________ *Pargana*________________

Serial No.	Villages.	Block No.	Males.																	
																		Total Males.		
			0—4	5-14	15 & over.	0—4	5—14	15 & over.	0—4	5—14	15 & over.	0—4	5—14	15 & over.	0—4	5—14	15 & over.	0—4	5—14	15 & over.

Size 2' 3″ by 7½″.

Note.—There was a separate Register, No. V. B., for females.

Abstraction Sheets.

89 Four working sheets were required for abstracting the returns of the Enumeration Books. They were as follows :—

Abstraction Sheet No. I.

(From columns 3, 4 and 5 of the Enumeration Book.)

Agency__________ Charge__________ Signatures of { Abstractor__________
State__________ Circle__________ Totaller__________
Village__________ Block__________

Book No.______ Date of abstraction__________

Age.	Males.							Age.	Females.						
	Hindus.	Musalmans.	etc.				Total Males.		Hindus.	Musalmans.	etc.				Total Females.
Infant.								Infant.							
1 . .								1 . .							
2 . .								2 . .							
3 . .								3 . .							
4 . .								4 . .							
5—9 .								5—9 .							
10—14 .								10—14 .							
15—19 .								15—19 .							
20—24 .								20—24 .							
25—29 .								25—29 .							
30—34 .								30—34 .							
35—39 .								35—39 .							
40—44 .								40—44 .							
45—49 .								45—49 .							
50—54 .								50—54 .							
55—59 .								55—59 .							
60 and over								60 and over							
Total .								Total .							

Abstraction Sheet No. 2.

(From columns 3, 5 and 6 of the Enumeration Book.)

Agency________ Charge________ Block________

State________ Circle________ Book No.________

Village ________

Signatures of { Abstractor________ / Totaller________ } Date of abstraction____

Religions.	Castes.	Males.		Females.	
			Total.		Total.
TOTAL .					

Abstraction Sheet No. 3.

(From columns 3 and 7 of Enumeration Book.)

Agency________ Charge________

State________ Circle________ Signatures of { Abstractor________ / Totaller________ }

Village________ Block________

Book No.______ Date of abstraction______

Birthplace.	Males.		Females.	
		Total.		Total.
TOTAL .				

Abstraction Sheet No. 4.

(From columns 3 and 8 of the Enumeration Book.)

Agency________ Charge________

State________ Circle________ Signatures of { Abstractor________ / Totaller________ }

Village________ Block________

Book No.______ Date of abstraction______

Occupations.	Males.				Females.			
	0—4	5—14	15 and over.	Total.	0—4	5—14	15 and over.	Total.
TOTAL .								

Supply of forms for abstraction and tabulation.

90. An important preliminary to the work of abstraction and tabulation was the supply to the Agency offices of a sufficient number of the necessary working sheets and registers. The indent for enumeration books, which was based on the supposed number of blocks that had been demarcated, could not safely be followed. A block might include more than one village; and a large village might contain several blocks; whereas tabulation had to deal with *villages*, taking no account of the blocks into which they were divided for the purposes of enumeration.

91. Regarding the provision of working sheets and registers, the Political Agents were, in November 1890, addressed in the following terms:—

"It will be observed that a record is required of the number of villages and of the population of each. It is pointed out that if the abstraction were carried out by blocks, it would be impossible to obtain such a record in the abstraction sheets, as some of the blocks probably include more than one village. It is desirable, then, that the abstraction should be conducted in such a way that each village will be abstracted on its separate sheets, and your indent will be based therefore not on the number of blocks in any given pargana or area, but on the number of blocks relating to villages or towns, as a whole, *plus* the number of small villages therein included.

"The indents for tabulation registers should be based on the calculation given in the Census Commissioner's instructions, that is to say, on the number of working sheets, one register being sufficient to include the tabulated results of 20 working sheets (ten items on each page, twenty in all). A further number of registers will be required for town, pargana, and State registers, as well as for wastage: for these purposes 20 per cent. should be added to the calculation above specified."

"I annex a specimen form for exhibiting the indents in question, together with the figures on which they are based. The information now asked for should be submitted in the form in question at your early convenience."

POLITICAL AGENCY—BHOPAL.

I.—Bhopal State.

A.—TOWNS.

Name of Town.	Number of enumeration books required.	Number of sets of 4 abstraction working sheets required.		Number of sets of 6 tabulation registers required.		REMARKS.
		Hindi.	Urdu.	Hindi.	Urdu.	
Bhopal	70	...	115	...	7	
Ashta	55	...	84	...	6	
Islamnagar	21	...	33	...	3	

B.—PARGANAS.

Name of Pargana.	Number of enumeration books required.	Number of villages.	Number of sets of 4 abstraction working sheets required.		Number of sets of 6 tabulation registers required.		REMARKS.
			Hindi.	Urdu.	Hindi	Urdu.	
Bhopal	191	211	...	318	...	20	
Ashta	104	116	...	174	...	11	
Islamnagar	99	90	...	150	...	10	

Form B should not include the requirements of towns already shown under Form A.

Indent for registers, etc.

92. The Central India Agency indent for working sheets and tabulation registers was as under :—

	Agency.	Abstraction Sheets.							
		Sheet I. *Religion and Age.*		Sheet II. *Castes.*		Sheet III. *Birthplace.*		Sheet IV. *Occupation.*	
		Hindi.	Urdu.	Hindi.	Urdu.	Hindi.	Urdu.	Hindi.	Urdu.
1	Indore	6,000	500	12,000	1,000	6,000	500	12,000	1,000
2	Gwalior	11,600	...	23,200	...	11,600	...	23,200	...
3	Bhopal	13,700	4,300	27,400	8,600	13,700	4,300	27,400	8,600
4	Bundelkhand	12,000	500	24,000	1,000	12,000	500	24,000	1,000
5	Baghelkhand	15,000	...	30,000	...	15,000	...	30,000	...
6	Western Malwa	12,000	1,100	24,000	2,200	12,000	1,100	24,000	2,200
7	Bhopawar	7,000	...	14,000	...	7,000	...	14,000	...
8	Guna	2,000	30	4,000	60	2,000	30	4,000	60

	Agency.	Tabulation Registers.											
		No. 1. Religions.		No. 2. Ages by Religion.		No. 3. Castes.		No. 4. Birthplace.		No. 5A. Occupations by age: Males.		No. 5B. Occupations by age: Females.	
		Hindi.	Urdu.	Hindi.	Urdu.	Hindi.	Urdu.	Hindi.	Urdu.	Hindi.	Urdu.	Hindi.	Urdu.
1	Indore	500	100	4,000	800	4,000	800	2,000	400	2,000	400	2,00	400
2	Gwalior	625	...	5,000	...	5,000	...	2,500	...	2,500	..	2,500	...
3	Bhopal	700	300	5,600	2,400	5,600	2,400	2,800	1,200	2,800	1,200	2,800	1,200
4	Bundelkhand	...	700	...	5,600	...	5,600	...	2,800	...	2,800	...	2,800
5	Baghelkhand	800	...	6,400	...	6,400	...	3,200	...	3,200	...	3,200	...
6	Western Malwa	700	...	5,600	...	5,600	...	2,800	...	2,800	...	2,800	...
7	Bhopawar	400	...	3,200	...	3,200	...	1,600	...	1,600	...	1,600	...
8	Guna	150	10	1,200	80	1,200	80	600	40	600	40	600	40

Working of Abstraction Offices,

93. The working of the abstraction and tabulation offices will appear from the following circulars addressed to Political Agents.

Circular of 13th February 1891.

"1. The Census work subsequent to enumeration cannot now be fully explained, as the final forms to be adopted for the Native States in Central India have not yet been determined upon. But it is hoped that this note will prove useful for the work of abstraction and tabulation whatever final forms are afterwards prescribed. What additions or alterations appear necessary will be intimated from time to time.

" 2. The different operations in the working of the Census are :—

(1) Enumeration.
(2) Compilation of Enumerators' abstracts.
(3) Abstraction.
(4) Tabulation.
(5) Compilation.

"3. With regard to enumeration (which is to begin when lamps are lighted on the night of the 26th February 1891, and to be finished before the following morning), full instructions have already been issued, and, if those instructions are duly carried out, no difficulty ought to arise.

" 4. The compilation of Enumerators' abstracts should begin on the following day. This work ought not to take more than four days, even in States like Gwalior and Indore. In all cases it ought to have been finished in time for the books to reach the Agency head quarters in the first week of March. With regard to this also full instructions have been issued to all Political Agents, who, it is hoped, have taken care to have them communicated and explained to all Census officers in their respective charges.

" 5. As a preliminary to abstraction, the books should, as soon as they arrive at the Agency Head Quarters, be arranged according to charges, circles and blocks by the supervising establishment, who should have been entertained in February to make all necessary preparations for the reception of the books. The Agency Superintendent of Census, who will be responsible for the safe custody of the books, will pass a receipt to the Durbar officials for every parcel of books received. It is presumed that instructions have been issued to the officials in charge of the Census in each State to keep the books of each Pargana separate and arranged by blocks and circles.

" 6. The record-keepers, who are appointed before the Census, are presumed to have been provided with racks and all necessary furniture before the books arrive. The records keeper's duties are : to arrange the books, as soon as he gets them, according to Parganas and States, to label the shelves, and to open a register of the book thus arranged. When the books are given out for abstraction he has to take out the enumerator's abstracts from the books and deposit them under lock and key. He is to arrange the abstraction sheets in a cupboard or box, and be careful not to issue more of them at a time than are absolutely required. He is to keep strict account of the issue and receipt of books in the following form :—

ROOM No.

Date of Issue.	Books issued.			Population of each village.			Worker.		Signature of Room Inspector.	Date of Return.
	Pargana or State.	Block No.	Names of villages.	Males.	Females.	Total.	Abstraction or Reabstraction.	Name.		

" He issues and receives the books through the medium of the Room Inspectors, whose signature he is to take on his register. He is to lose no time in distributing the books to the Abstractors every morning.

" 7. The Room Inspector's duties are : to receive the books from the Record-keeper every morning for the Abstractors under his charge (passing a receipt for them to the Record-keeper) ; to pass the sheets to the Totallers as they are ready ; to return the books and sheets to the Record-keeper, when finished ; and to collect the unfinished books every evening and deposit them, duly labelled, with the name of the men to whom they belong, with the record-keeper, who will put them into a separate box provided for the purpose. He further is to see that the Abstractors do not scribble on the books and do not communicate with one another. He is to open a register and enter the books against the names of the Abstractors under his charge, as he gives them out, and on receiving them back duly finished he is to note against each book the number of entries made by each Abstractor ; this will show the average outturn of work, and the comparative efficiency of the Abstractors, whose pay should sink and rise accordingly.

"8. For Abstraction, four working sheets have been adopted :

No. 1 for Age and Religions.
No. 2 for Castes.
No. 3 for Birth-places.
No. 4 for Occupations.

For the working of these sheets there are two systems, which may be called the "Reading aloud system" and the "Independent working system."

On the first system a set of five men works simultaneously on one book, one man reading aloud and the other four making entries, each on one of the four sheets. The reader reads a line (to give an instance) :—

Male—10 years—Hindu—Rajput—Indore, dependent on weaver.

The 1st writer makes a mark thus :—" / " on the male side of his sheet under Hindu against 10-14.

The 2nd writer enters "Hindu" under Religion and "Rajput" under caste and makes a similar mark against Rajput in the male column.

The 3rd writer writes "Indore" under Birth-place and makes a mark against Indore in his male column.

The 4th writer writes "weaver" under Occupation and "dependent" on the line below and makes a similar mark against "Dependent" in the male column.

For easy reckoning when four entries have been made together, the fifth should be marked by a line drawn across all four thus ////

There is less chance of mistakes if the reader takes all the males in a book first and afterwards all the females.

The reader makes a tick with his pencil against each name as he reads it.

On the independent working system the entries are marked in the same way as is described above, but on this system a book is not completely abstracted by one set of five men simultaneously ; each sheet is filled up from the book separately by men who, if possible, work in four separate rooms according to the sheet on which they work. The men in each room work independently of each other, except in the case of Sheet I, for which it is thought better to have two men working (one reading and the other making the entries). So whatever be the number of clerks available there will always be twice as many engaged on Sheet No. 1 as on any of the others.

"9. Both systems have been tried here. The reading aloud system was the one that was worked in Central India in the 1881 Census, and it has many things to recommend it, especially when the working staff is small. The independent working system, though it is perhaps quicker than the other, undoubtedly requires more supervision and verification ; but as Mr. Baines, in his Circular No. 154 of 29th September 1890, recommends this system, it may be adopted in all the Census offices in Central India.

"10. To test the correctness of the figures it is necessary that 50 to 20 per cent of the books should be re-abstracted, and for this work the most efficient Abstractors should be selected.

"11. When books of several Parganas of a State have been abstracted (and a proportional number of them re-abstracted) a set of 4 men should be set apart for tabulation.

"12. There are five Tabulation Registers :—

No. 1 for Religions.
No. 2 for Ages by Religions.
No. 3 for Castes.
No. 4 for Birth-places.
No. 5 for Occupations.

Register Nos. 1 and 2 can be filled in directly from Abstraction Sheet No. 1. These two registers can be filled in by one Tabulator.

Register No. 4, which can be filled in from Abstraction Sheet No. 3, might be done by another Tabulator.

Register No. 3, which can be filled in from Abstraction Sheet No. 2, and Register No. 5, which can be filled in from Abstraction Sheet No. 4, should have two men working together, one man to dictate and the other to make entries."

"13. The tabulated returns should not be totalled by the Tabulators, but two men should be especially set apart for this purpose."

"14. It will be more convenient if for every 20 villages or blocks the complete set of Tabulation Registers is made up into one book. A complete book for 20 villages or blocks will contain as follows:—

1 Copy of Register No. 1.
16 Copies of Register No. 2 (each religion will be tabulated on a separate register, so 8 forms will be required for males and 8 for females).
8 Copies of Register No. 3 (the Caste Return of Hindus will be very long, so 8 copies of this register, 4 for males and 4 for females, had better be taken).
4 Copies of Register No. 4 (2 for males and 2 for females).
8 Copies of Register No. 5 (4 for males and 4 for females).'

37

"15. Thus a book of Tabulation Registers for 20 villages or blocks will contain in all 37 Registers. Care should be taken that the headings on each register are clearly written; and the totals of each village or town should be shown in red ink."

Circular of 5th March 1891.

"The Census Commissioner's remarks on this office note on abstraction and tabulation are as follows:—

1. It should now be taken as decided that Final Imperial Tables Nos. I, II, III, IV, V, VI, VII, XI, XVI, and XVII, as given in pages 83-89 of Census Proceedings, Part I (Enumeration), should be adopted for Central India. In consequence of the adoption of Final Table XVII in which information regarding occupation *by age* is required,—

(*a*) it will be necessary to divide the Male and Female columns in Abstraction Sheet No. 4 into 3 age periods, thus:—

Occupation.	Males.				Females.			
	0-4.	5-14.	15 and above.	Total.	0-4.	5-14.	15 and above.	Total.

(*b*) "dependents" on an occupation will not, as stated in paragraph 8 of the previous note, be taken apart from workers."

"2. The *independent working* system is to be adopted, as the Census Commissioner thinks that the *reading aloud* system is unsafe (*a*) because it admits of judging totals and consequently re-abstraction is necessary, (*b*) it introduces two extra elements of error— wrong dictation and wrong hearing."

"3. In the concluding portion of paragraph 8 it was suggested that Abstraction Sheet I should have two men working on it (one reading and the other making the entries), but after further experiment, undertaken on Census Commissioner's suggestion, it is thought advisable to have only one man for sheet No. 1."

"4. With reference to paragraph 10 of the note it is proposed that no special set of men should be appointed for re-abstraction, but that every abstractor should have his turn at that work. Thus there will be less chance of collusion; and it will be easy to arrange a system whereby all Abstractors not only lose marks by making mistakes, but also have a chance of earning marks by finding out the mistakes made by others."

"5. On Tabulation Registers a further note will be issued later on, as the Census Commissioner's suggestion on this office note require a further reference."

Circular of 20th March 1891.

"It is considered advisable to call the attention of the Census officers to the necessity of taking the enumerator's abstracts out of the books before the latter are given out for abstraction, and also of seeing that the abstracts are locked up, so that they cannot be used as guides by Abstractors or Totallers.

"It will be well also to make a rule that no one should have access to the Abstractors while they are at work, and that no, Abstractor should leave his desk till he has finished a book on which he has begun, and has returned it with his sheet to the Room Inspector. Further, care must be taken that the Abstractors do not total up for themselves the male and female entries in the book on which they are at work, because if they are once in possession of the actual totals they will be tempted to add or rub out a few ticks in their abstraction sheets so as to make the results tally.

"The following is recommended as the best method of keeping Census Records.

"As soon as all the books for one State are received by the Record-keeper, he will give them a serial number for each State in bold red-ink figures, and arrange them in the racks according to States, in order of serial numbers. He will issue the books with the blank abstraction sheets to the Room Inspector every morning in the order of the serial numbers, keeping a record of the same. The form given in the first note, paragraph 6, should be modified so as to give a column for the red-ink numbers. The Room Inspector, before issuing the books and abstraction sheets to his Abstractors, will write, with red ink in bold figures at the top of each abstraction sheet, the red ink number of the book with which that sheet is given out. The Room Inspector will bring every evening all the completed books and sheets to the Record-keeper, who will pass a receipt. The Record-keeper will arrange all sheets I in one folio, all sheets II in another, and so on according to the red-ink numbers.

"When about 100 books have been fully abstracted, the Superintendent should compare the totals of all the four sheets belonging to one book with one another, and if the totals of any of them are found not to tally, the book to which they belong should be given out for re-abstraction. The re-abstraction will show which of the Abstractors has gone wrong. But even when the totals on the sheets tally, it will be well to have a considerable number of books re-abstracted. This will lead to detection if any of the Abstractors do what is mentioned above, *viz.*, add or rub out ticks to accommodate their figures to a total already ascertained.

"The religion of Jains is to be shewn separately from that of Hindus, so is that of Aboriginals (Bhil, Gond, Moghya, Mang, Maher, Mina, Kol, Deswali, etc.)

"In Abstraction Sheet I, Jains and Aboriginals must, therefore, be abstracted by themselves. In this sheet, Bhils, Gonds, etc., will all be grouped under the heading Aboriginals.

"In Abstraction Sheet II, Jains must be entered as such both in the religion and caste columns and Aboriginals must be shewn in detail, *i.e.*, to say in the religion column the words "Aboriginal religion" should be entered and Bhil, Gond, etc., in the caste column.

"It was suggested in the first note, paragraph 14, that for every 20 villages a book of 37 registers of all kinds should be prepared. But the Census Commissioner has overruled this, and has decided that for each Pargana in a large State, and for a whole State, if it does not contain more than 150 to 200 blocks, all the registers of one kind should be bound separately, *i.e.*, all Registers I into one book, all Registers II into another, and so on. Thus for each Pargana or small State of 150 to 200 blocks there will be 5 books of Tabulation Registers, the book of Register I consisting (according to the number of blocks included) of 15 to 20 pages, that of Register II of 120 to 160 pages, that of Register III of 120 to 160 pages, that of Register IV of 60 to 80 pages, that of Register VA of 60 to 80 pages, and that of Register V B of 60 to 80 pages."

"The Census Commissioner has directed a tour to be made round all the Abstraction Offices in the Central India Agency. It is hoped that this will be done within a few weeks. In the meantime any doubts and difficulties that arise should be referred to the Indore Census Office."

94. By the middle of March all the Agency Abstraction offices were ready with their contingents of clerks, and work might have been begun at once, had the necessary forms been received in time from the Press at Calcutta. In most of the offices the few weeks of forced inactivity were utilised in practising the clerks in the proper method of doing their work, on manuscript forms, the instructors being those of their number, or of the supervising staff, who had had the advantage of a preliminary training in the Indore Office.

Delay in receipt of abstraction sheets, etc.

95. To secure as much uniformity as possible in the work generally and particularly in dealing with doubtful entries in the enumeration books, all the Agency Offices, except Guna, which is very much out of the way, were visited at least once by the Superintendent of Census Operations in Central India.

96. In Native States the cost of abstraction was understood to be borne by the Durbars, the Census grant providing only menial servants, the cost of accommodation, where such was incurred, and the supervising establishment, (Office Superintendent, Record-keepers, Room Inspectors and Totallers). But the State of Rewa asked to be allowed to pay for the whole establishment of its abstracting office, which, as has already been remarked, was distinct from the Baghelkhand Agency Abstracting Office at Sutna, and was personally looked after by Pandit Het Ram, C.I.E., the late Dewan.

Separate abstracting office for Rewa State.

97. The work of abstraction was a good deal retarded at first by several difficulties that had to be faced in all the offices alike. These were mainly due to errors and imperfections in the work of the enumerators. Entries such as "bacha," in column 3, as well as in column 2, were common. Sometimes persons were entered as Sikhs or Jains in column 6, and as Hindus in column 5. Aboriginals also were a source of difficulty in column 5. To obviate the difficulty as much as possible in the case of the latter, a list of all the aboriginal tribes known to exist in Central India was prepared in the Indore Office, and circulated, in Hindi and Urdu, to the Agency Offices. In countless cases names of towns were given in the Birth-place column, and from those it was often, of course, impossible to conjecture the Province or State of birth. To help the adjusting of such entries, an elaborate list of the chief towns in every district of British India was prepared and circulated. Other difficulties in the Birth-place column were such entries as "Ingrezi Ilaka," which was found on inquiry to mean the Central Provinces, and "Madhya Hindustan." Again persons described in column 6 as "sutars" or "lohars" by caste were frequently entered "mazduri" in column 8. In the latter column such entries as "bepar" or "naukari" were very common.

Difficulties in abstraction arising from imperfect entries in the Enumeration Books.

98. Notwithstanding these and other difficulties, there is every reason to believe that the work of abstraction, as well as of the subsequent operation of tabulation, was efficiently carried out all over Central India. An unfortunate blunder was made in the Bundelkhand Office, which made it necessary for Abstraction Sheet No. 4 to be done over again for a large number of books, the Superintendent of the Office having neglected the instructions issued in March 1891* as to the abstraction of occupations by age.

99. On the limits of permissible error in abstraction, the following circular, based on the instructions of the Census Commissioner, was issued on 1st May 1891:

"Attention has frequently been drawn to discrepancies in the abstraction sheets. The general direction in such cases is, in accordance with the Census Commissioner's instructions, that the books be abstracted over and over again till the sheets tally.

* See page 58.

"Some specimens of the test slips used in the Indore Abstracting Office for the comparison of the abstraction sheets accompany this note, and their adoption in all the agencies is recommended.

"But it is useless to expect that the abstraction can be more accurate than the materials on which it works; and taking into consideration the incorrect and careless entries in many of the enumeration books, and the difficulty arising therefrom in their abstraction, and seeing that the time also, by which the work should be finished, is very limited, it is thought advisable to relax the general direction and to make some attempt to fix certain limits within which the head of each office should be allowed to correct by adjustment the errors disclosed by those test slips.

"It is difficult to lay down more than general principles in a matter of this sort; but on the whole it may be said that it may be necessary to let pass no error in the total of each sex. In other details the error generally lies in an excess in the largest of several unequal partitions of the sheet. It is probable that the ages will be more correct in Sheet I than in those sheets which contain more comprehensive periods; and religion in the same way will be more correct in Sheet II than in Sheet I. In the case of religions, as a rule, a book will contain but a few items of a religion different from that of the majority, so that an error is speedily rectified by examination of the book itself for that one section of the community. When a sheet is passed as correct for occupations, but the ages do not correspond with those in Sheet I, it is safer to make the adjustment in the occupation sheet. Generally speaking, Sheet I, which has always been insisted upon as being the most important form of the four, should be altered as little as possible. The religion and occupation sheets should therefore be selected for such adjustment as is thought necessary.

"One rule must be observed throughout, and that is that no transfer of more than one entry per hundred in a sheet can be allowed, and this only on the understanding that the strictest scrutiny by means of the test slips has previously been made."

Test Slip. Sheets Nos. I & II.

Red Ink No.	Sheet No.	Hindus.	Mahomedans.	Jains.	Aboriginals.	Parsis.	Christians.		
	I								
	II								
	I								
	II								
	I								
	II								
	I								
	II								
	I								
	II								
	I								
	II								
	I								
	II								
	I								
	II								
	I								
	II								

Test Slip. Sheets Nos. I & IV.

Red Ink No.	Sheet No.	0—4		5—14		15 & above.	
	I						
	IV						
	I						
	IV						
	I						
	IV						
	I						
	IV						
	I						
	IV						
	I						
	IV						
	I						
	IV						
	I						
	IV						

100. Regarding the completion of the Registers and the form in which they were to be transmitted to Indore, the following instructions were issued in July 1891:—

"It is hoped that that the tabulation work in your agency is now in progress, and will be finished by the middle of August at the latest.

"I am to send herewith a copy of the list of States as arranged for compilation at Indore, and to say that your Tabulation Registers should be prepared in the order of that list. When ready for despatch to Indore the Registers should be packed in separate bundles by States and Parganas, a label being affixed to each bundle giving full details of its contents.

"With the Tabulation Registers you are requested to send a list of the number of occupied houses in each Pargana of the States in your agency.

"It is further requested that all possible care be taken in the preparation of the Tabulation Registers. Any doubts or difficulties that occur in filling up the Registers should be at once referred to the Indore office. The headings in the Registers should be written in 'Balbodh,' wherever practicable, and as distinctly as possible. The totals of each page should be brought forward till a Pargana, or, in the case of small States, a State is completely tabulated; the totals that are entered at the bottom of each page are to be brought forward to the top of the next page till the whole Pargana, or, in, the case of small States, the whole State is finished; but the totals entered in the last column of each page are to be brought forward and entered in the column of the next page immediately after the block number column till every ten blocks or villages are completely tabulated. It may be noted with reference to Register No. 1 (All Religions), that a column should be provided at the end of this register to show the total population of both the sexes in each village. Column I in all the registers is meant for the serial numbering of villages only."

101. Nothing can be said here regarding the abstraction and tabulation of the fourteen-column schedules on which, as has been seen, residents in cantonments and all Europeans were enumerated. Those schedules were abstracted at Ajmir, and the tabulated results sent to the Indore office for compilation.

SECTION VI.—COMPILATION OF TABULATED RETURNS.

102. The tabulated registers began to arrive at the Indore office in the month of July 1891, and the work of compilation was at once started. The staff employed was a selection of the most efficient members of the supervising staff of the Indore Agency Abstraction Office.

103. The various compilation sheets were in the form given below:—

Agency COMPILATION SHEET A.—PRELIMINARY TOTALS. Page

State.	Area in square miles.	Occupied houses.		Population.						Variation per cent.				Persons per square mile.	
				Total.		Males.		Females.		Occupied houses.	Population.				
		1891.	1881.	1891.	1881.	1891.	1881.	1891.	1881.		Total.	Males	Females	1891.	1881.

COMPILATION SHEET I.

Agency *For Table I.—Area, Houses, and Population.* Page

State.	Area in square miles.	Number of		Occupied Houses.			Population.								
							Both Sexes.			Males.			Females.		
		Towns.	Villages	Total.	In Towns.	In Villages.	Total.	Urban.	Rural.	Total.	Urban.	Rural.	Total.	Urban.	Rural.

COMPILATION SHEET II.

Agency *For Table II.—Variation in Population.* Page

State.	Both Sexes.			Males.			Females.		
	1891.	1881.	Difference	1891.	1881.	Difference	1891.	1881.	Difference.

COMPILATION SHEET III.

Agency *For Table III.—Towns and Villages classified by Population.* Page

State or Pargana.	Total Number of Town and Villages.	Total Population.	1—199		200—499		500—999		1,000—1,999		2,000—2,999		3,000—4,999		5,000—9,999		10,000—14,999		15,000—19,999		20,000—49,999		50,000 and over.	
			Number.	Population.	Number.	Population.	Number.	Population.	Number.	Population.	Number.	Population.	Number.	Population.	Number.	Population.	Number.	Population.	Number.	Population.	Number.	Population.	Number.	Population.

COMPILATION SHEET IV.

Agency *For Table IV.—Towns by Population.* Page

Town.	State.	Municipality, Suburbs or Cantonment.	Both Sexes.			Males.			Females.		
			1891.	1881.	Difference.	1891.	1881.	Difference.	1891.	1881.	Difference.

COMPILATION SHEET V.

Agency *For Table V.—Population of Towns by Districts and by Religion.* Page

State.	Town.	All Religions.																								Others.		
		Total.	Males.	Females.	Total.	Males.	Females.	Total.	Males.	Females.	Total.	Males.	Females.	Total.	Males.	Females.	Total.	Males.	Females.	Total.	Males.	Females.	Total.	Males.	Females.	Total.	Males.	Females.

COMPILATION SHEET VI.

Agency — *For Table VI.—Religion.* — Page / Males

STATE OR PARGANA.	Sex Total.											

COMPILATION SHEET VII.—Part Religion Page

Agency — *For Table VII.—Age, Religion.* — Males

STATE OR PARGANA.	Sex total.	Infant.	1	2	3	4	5—9	10—14	15—19	20—24	25—29	30—34	35—39	40—44	45—49	50—54	55—59	60 & over.

COMPILATION SHEET X.

Agency — *For Table XI.—Birthplace.* — Males

Enter the birthplaces in the following order :—(*a*) Districts and States within the Province ; (*b*) Districts and States contiguous to the Province ; (*c*) Other Provinces or States in India ; (*d*) Asiatic Countries beyond India ; (*e*) Countries beyond Asia.

STATE OR PARGANA.	Sex total.																

COMPILATION SHEET XIII.

Page

Agency

For Table XVI.—Castes, etc.

Males

STATE OR PARGANA.	SEX TOTAL.																				

COMPILATION SHEET XIV.

Page

Agency

For Table XVII.—Occupations.

Males

STATE OR PARGANA.	TOTAL.	0–4	5–14	15–	TOTAL.	0–4	5–14	15–	TOTAL.	0–4	5–14	15–	TOTAL.	0–4	5–14	15–	TOTAL.	0–4	5–14	15–

104. Instructions had been received from the Census Commissioner that as the work went on, concise statements should be made to him of the results arrived at by Agencies for inclusion in his own tables. For these concise statements slips in the following form were used :—

Slip 1.—For Table I.

PROVINCE , CENTRAL INDIA.

*Agency*____________

Heading.		Detail.	Total.
Area in square miles			
	Towns		
	Villages		
Occupied houses	Towns		
	Villages		
Total population	Towns		
	Villages		
Males	Towns		
	Villages		
Females	Towns		
	Villages		

Certified on the of 1891.

Slip 2.—For Table II.

PROVINCE , CENTRAL INDIA.

*Agency*____________

Heading.		Population.	Variation + or —.
Total population	1891		
	1881		
Males	1891		
	1881		
Females	1891		
	1881		

Certified on the of 1891.

Slip 1 (a).—For Table V.

PROVINCE , CENTRAL INDIA.

*Agency*____________

States.	Towns.	All Religions.			Hindus.		Musalmans.							
		Total.	Males.	Females.	Males.	Females.	Males.	Females.	Males.	Females.	Males.	Females.	Males.	Females.

Slip 3.—For Table III.

PROVINCE , CENTRAL INDIA.

*Agency*__________

Heading.		Number.	Population.
Total Towns and Villages.			
1	1— 199		
2	200— 499		
3	500— 999		
4	1,000— 1,999		
5	2,000— 2,999		
6	3,000— 4,999		
7	5,000— 9,999		
8	10,000—14,999		
9	15,000—19,999		
10	20,000—49,999		
11	50,000 & over.		

Certified on the of 1891.

Slip 4.—For Table VI.

PROVINCE , CENTRAL INDIA.

Agency..........

Religion.	Total.	Males.	Females.
All Religions.			
1. Hindu.			
2. Musalman.			
3. Jain.			
4. Aboriginal.			
5. Christian.			
6. Parsi.			
7. Buddhist.			
8. Sikh.			
9. Jew.			
10. Brahmo.			
11.			
12.			
13.			
14.			

Certified on the of 1891.

Slip 5.—For Table VII.

PROVINCE , CENTRAL INDIA.

*Agency*__________

Age-period.	Hindus.		Musalmans.		Jains.		Aboriginals.		Christians.		Parsis.						Total.		
	Males.	Females.	Males.	Females.	Males.	Females.	Males.	Females.	Males.	Females.	Males.	Females.	Males.	Females.	Males.	Females.	Males.	Females.	Total.
0																			
1																			
2																			
3																			
4																			
Total (0—4).																			
5—9																			
10—14																			
15—19																			
20—24																			
25—29																			
30—34																			
35—39																			
40—44																			
45—49																			
50—54																			
55—59																			
60 & over.																			
Total																			

Slip 5.—For Tables VII and VIII.

PROVINCE , CENTRAL INDIA.

*Agency*________ *Religion*________

Age-periods.	Males.				Females.			
	Single.	Married.	Widowed.	Total.	Single.	Married.	Widowed.	Total.
0								
1								
2								
3								
4								
Total (0—4)								
5—9								
10—14								
15—19								
20—24								
25—29								
30—34								
35—39								
40—44								
45—49								
50—54								
55—59								
60 & over.								
Total								

Slip 6.—For Table IX.

PROVINCE , CENTRAL INDIA.

*Agency*________ *Religion*________

Instruction.		Males.	Females.
All ages	Learning		
	Literate		
	Illiterate		
	Total		
0—14	Learning		
	Literate		
	Illiterate		
	Total		
15—24	Learning		
	Literate		
	Illiterate		
	Total		
25 & over	Learning		
	Literate		
	Illiterate		
	Total		

Certified on the of 1891.

Slip 7.—For Table XI.

PROVINCE , CENTRAL INDIA.

*Agency*________

Birthplace.	Total.	Males.	Females.	Birthplace.	Total.	Males.	Females.

Slip 8 for Tables XII to XV.

PROVINCE CENTRAL INDIA.

*Agency*________________

Age-periods.	Males.				Females.			
	Insane.	Deaf-mute.	Blind.	Leper.	Insane.	Deaf-mute.	Blind.	Leper.
0—4								
5—9								
10—14								
15—19								
20—24								
25—29								
30—34								
35—39								
40—44								
45—49								
50—54								
55—59								
60 & over.								
Total .								

Slip 9 for Tables XII A to XV A.

PROVINCE CENTRAL INDIA.

*Agency*________________

INFIRMITY.

Caste, etc.	Religion.	Males.	Females.
Total			

Certified on the of 1891.

105. In the submission of the slips difficulty and delay several times arose with regard to the Baghelkhand Agency in consequence of there being a few outlying villages of the States of Rewa and Nagode in the Allahabad and Jabalpur Districts, for which information had to be awaited from the Census Offices of the North-West Provinces and the Central Provinces respectively. It would save much trouble in the next census if the territorial system were strictly applied not only in the enumeration, but also in the subsequent operations of the census. In 1891 the enumeration and tabulation of the villages in question were carried out in British India; but the results were compiled with the population of the States to which the villages belong, and excluded from the totals of the two Provinces.

106. All the sheets, except those for Caste and Occupation, were compiled by the middle of May 1892. The greater part of the staff was then dispensed with, and the attention of the office concentrated on Tables XVI, XVII, and XVII A. These were very long and tedious to compile, and it is very questionable whether the result is worth the time and trouble that it took to attain it. The Caste and Occupation columns were those which had been most unsatisfactorily filled up in the Enumeration Books; and they were also those on which the abstractors had had to exercise most ingenuity in guessing what the entries meant. Many anomalies in the Agency tables are the consequence—anomalies which the Indore Office could do nothing to rectify at the time of compilation, and can now do very little to explain. But it may be said with some confidence that the best use was made that could be made of the materials available. When the Census Commissioner left for England in May 1892, the work was sufficiently advanced for a manuscript copy of Table XVI to be given to him. Tables XVI and XVII A were finished in October 1892, by which time nearly all the preceding tables had been printed.

SECTION VII.—COST OF THE CENTRAL INDIA CENSUS.

107. The cost to the Imperial Government of the 1891 Census in Central India is estimated at R42,987-4-4. The details are given below.

108. The cost of enumeration, apart from that of the office establishment at Indore (then very small) and of the Enumeration Books and their carriage from Calcutta to the Agency centres, was borne entirely by the States.

109. The total cost of the Enumeration Books and Schedules used in the Central India Agency (including those used for Railway and Cantonment population, and for European residents in Native States) was R7,782-15-11. From these enumeration charges there should be deducted the cost of the books supplied to the Gwalior State, R3,667-6-9, which the Durbar volunteered to pay for, and also a contribution of R200 made by the State of Bhopal.

110. The total cost of compiling the returns, so far as it was borne by the Census grant, was R33,253-9-2. This sum does not cover the cost of tabulating the fourteen-column schedules at Ajmir.

111. The charge on account of printing this report cannot yet be accurately stated. It is estimated at R5,635.

112. The following statement shews the cost to the Imperial Government of the 1891 Census in Central India :—

Headings.			Amount.	Amount.
Enumeration—			R a. p.	R a. p.
Establishment			818 0 0	
Contingencies			132 11 3	
Enumeration Books for Native States and Cantoı ments			7.782 15 11	
Total cost on account of Enumeration			...	8,733 11 2
Abstraction, Tabulation and Compilatıox—				
		R a. p.		
Establishment	1890-91	796 5 6		
	1891-92	17,472 10 11		
	1892-93	1,637 0 4	19,906 0 9	
Travelling Allowance	1890-91	37 15 6		
	1891-92	1,971 1 0	2,009 0 6	
Printing of forms at Government Press, India.	1890-91	2,068 3 5		
	1891-92	2,139 1 7	4,207 5 0	
Contingencies	1890-91	4.350 6 0		
	1891-92	2,738 11 10		
	1892-93	42 1 1	7,131 2 11	
Total cost on account of Abstraction, Tabulation, and Compilation			...	33.253 9 2
Honorarium to the Superintendent of Census Operations in Central India			...	1,000 0 0
TOTAL			...	42,987 4 4
Estimated cost of printing 1,000 copies of the Report			...	5.635 0 0
GRAND TOTAL			...	48,622 4 4

113. The item of R818 under heading *Enumeration* Establishment requires some explanation. The amount is the salary of the clerk in the Office of the Agent to the Governor General, who was deputed for duty in connection with the Census.

114. As regards the items of expenditure incurred in connection with tabulation, etc., in the year 1890-91, it should be explained that, although the actual tabulation of returns did not begin till April 1891, a good deal of preliminary expense was unavoidable. The supervising establishment of the Agency Office had to be entertained as early as Feburary 1891 ; furniture had to be supplied; and the travelling expenses of clerks sent to Indore for instruction, and distributed afterwards over the different Agency offices, had to be paid.

R. H. GUNION.

APPENDICES.

APPENDIX I.

Results of Sir John Malcolm's partial Census of Malwa compared with those of the 1891 Census.

Agency.	State.	Pargana, etc.	Number of Towns and Villages.		Number of Houses.		Population.	
			1820.	1891.	1820.	1891.	1820.	1891.
Indore	Indore	Indore City	...	...	4,235	15,746	63.560	82,984
		Indore Pargana	185	79	13,089	4,401	41,461	19,838
		Samwer	108	94	5,599	5,244	22,864	22,457
Do.	Dewas	Dewas Pargana (including Town)	232	236	7,157	13,674	30,588	72,213
Bhopal	Indore	Machalpur	56	78	2,270	3,667	12,161	20,767
		Zirapur	64	88	2,662	3,180	12,073	19,426
		Sundarsi	11	9	1,383	722	5,416	3,761
		Nimawar	24	83	1,083	5,763	4,497	27,609
		Rajore	24	109	2,384	5,932	9,538	29,653
		Kantaphod	30	47	2,187	2,713	8,700	12,348
		Harangaon	16	39	514	1,763	1,957	9,209
Do.	Dewas	Sarangpur	54	73	3,048	5,886	11,430	29,800
Western Malwa	Indore	Raipur	21	25	1,437	1,535	6,483	8,118
		Depalpur	139	132	8,524	8,189	34,310	40,220
		Sunail	26	29	2,065	2,224	8,471	11,004
		Kaitha	22	22	1,461	1,707	6,618	8,402
		Nandwas	23	31	430	1,239	1,938	5,840
		Bhanpura	49	83	3,273	7,705	13,406	34,141
		Tarana	141	153	6,577	8,682	26,171	41,909
		Rampura	364	111	18,251	7,035	73,489	30,057
		Mahidpur	14	133	3,876	7,896	11,486	38,306
Do.	Dewas	Alote	68	75	2,316	4,397	8,685	24,828
		Gurguchha	19	27	927	1,154	3,476	6,912
		Ringnode	31	34	1,489	2,526	5,583	12,426
Do.	Jaora	Jaora Pargana	...	80	4,886	8,914	20,210	44,012
		Tal	42	} 96	2,786	} 6,717	12,308	} 30,178
		Mandawal	35		1,481		9,116	
		Sunjeed	47	55	1,796	2,146	7,151	12,308
		Baroda	22	27	1,657	1,759	6,048	8,995
		Malhargarh	49	59	...	3,258	12,125	16,750
Bhopawar	Indore	Hasilpur	17	27	688	1,505	2,538	7,182
		Betwa	42	45	2,031	2,586	7,617	11,730
		Katkut	12	23	151	461	486	1,889
		Khargon	56	60	4,273	6,028	19,092	27,931
		Muhamadpur	27	45	1,230	3,293	5,320	17,264
		Mardana	11	16	411	1,081	1,548	6,152
		Amleta	8	11	175	358	759	2,087
		Una	13	83	421	3,909	1,710	20,278
		Bhikamgaon	15	108	426	3,569	1,649	17,599
		Nagalwadi	6	99	268	2,347	965	12,216
		Brahmangaon	12	30	146	1,542	527	7,685
		Khadgaon	8	53	167	1,850	565	9,411
Do.	Dhar	Dhar Pargana	151	141	7,573	8,625	30,795	40,509
		Badnawar	150	56	7,735	4,637	31,119	23,651
		Nalcha	10	39	557	1,762	2,173	9,095
		Dharampuri	45	112	1,223	5,147	4,586	28,589
		Kuksi	31	68	2,015	4,967	7,748	25,011
		Sultanabad	20	55	506	2,569	1,897	12,769

APPENDIX II.

Statement shewing the distribution over the different Agencies of the territory of Gwalior and Indore.

Gwalior State.

Agency.	Parganas.
Gwalior	Gormi.
	Porsa.
	Aino.
	Ambha.
	Gohad.
	Gird.
	Ountri.
	Pachaur.
	Nurabad.
	Bhind.
	Mau.
	Ater.
	Amari
	Mehagawa.
	Bagchini.
	Mangarh.
	Jigni.
	Jora.
	Sabalgad.
	Sivapur.
	Dodhar.
	Bijeypur.
	Narwar.
	Mangroni.
	Bhiterwar.
	Aron.
	Sipri.
	Kolarus.
	Pahari.
	Bhander.
	Indurkhi.
	Daboh.
	Karera.
	Pichor.
Indore	Neori.
	Bhaurasa.
Bhopal	Sundarsi.
	Sujalpur.
Bhopal	Malhargarh.
	Sonekach.
	Bhilsa.
	Basoda.
Western Malwa	Agar.
	Susner.
	Nalkhera.
	Barode.
	Shajapur.
	Tonk.
	Mandsaur.
	Nahargarh.
	Bhangarh.
	Afzalpur.
	Sukhera.
	Nimach.
	Jawad.
	Singoli.
	Gangapur.
	Ujjain.
	Barnagar.
	Khachrod.
	Unail.
	Panbehar.
Bhopawar	Amjhera.
	Tanda Balwari.
	Bagh.
	Bakanair.
	Dikthan.
	Sagor.
Guna	Myana.
	Pachhar.
	Arone.
	Ranod.
	Bajrangarh.
	Chachoda.
	Kumbraj.

APPENDIX II—*continued.*

INDORE STATE.

Agency.	Parganas.	Agency.	Parganas.
Indore	Mhow.	Western Malwa	Kharaoda.
	Samwer.		Sathkheda.
	Khudel.		Naraingarh.
	Harsola.		Antri.
	Hatod.		Kanjarda.
	Banganga.		Nandwas.
Bhopal	Zirapur.		Depalpur.
	Machalpur.	Bhopawar .	Maheswar.
	Tingachpur.		Kesarwar.
	Talen.		Pipalgond.
	Sundarsi.		Dhargaon.
	Harangaon.		Karhai.
	Gagron.		Mardana.
	Kantaphod.		Amleta.
	Satwas.		Barwai.
	Rajore.		Katkut.
	Nimawar.		Khargone.
Bundelkhand .	Alumpur.		Sanawad.
Western Malwa .	Mahidpur.		Muhamadgarh.
	Kaitha.		Khadgon.
	Jarda.		Bhikamgaon.
	Tarana.		Silondri.
	Jagoli.		Una.
	Karanj Makron.		Barode.
	Rampura.		Balakwada.
	Bhanpura.		Padlia Dhawli.
	Garote.		Nagalwadi.
	Sunail.		Brahmangaon.
	Kotri.		Chikalda.
	Raipur.		Lawani.
	Manasa.		Dahi.
	Chandwasa.		Hasilpur.
			Betma.
			Pitlawad.

G. I. C. P. O.—No. 5 C. C. I.—27-11-93—1,000.

TABLE I.

Area, Houses and Population.

TABLE I.—Area, Houses and Population.

AGENCIES.	Area in square miles.	NUMBER OF		OCCUPIED HOUSES.			POPULATION.								
							TOTAL.			MALES.			FEMALES.		
		Towns.	Villages.	Total.	Towns.	Villages.	Total.	Towns.	Villages.	Total.	Towns.	Villages.	Total.	Towns.	Villages.
1	2	3	4	5	6	7	8	9	10	11	12	13	14	15	16
Indore . .		5	779	74,786	28,306	46,480	372,792	146,385	226,407	201,944	82,682	119,262	170,848	63,703	107,145
Gwalior . .		11	4,076	281,137	41,032	240,105	1,757,509	188,520	1,568,989	948,805	101,582	847,223	808,704	86,938	721,766
Bhopal . .		12	7,317	397,901	33,178	364,723	2,006,859	153,328	1,853,531	1,052,777	81,434	971,343	954,082	71,894	882,188
Bundelkhand .		10	3,675	289,973	25,629	264,344	1,508,053	123,876	1,384,177	784,006	65,645	719,261	723,147	58,231	664,916
Baghelkhand .	78,169·2	4	6,188	325,176	10,543	314,633	1,737,606	48,211	1,689,395	872,222	25,920	846,302	865,384	22,291	843,093
Western Malwa .		21	4,688	327,824	51,855	275,969	1,619,368	247,585	1,371,783	851,033	128,419	723,514	767,435	119,166	648,269
Bhopawar . .		5	4,155	202,074	10,578	191,496	978,652	49,207	929,445	502,832	24,877	477,955	475,820	24,330	451,490
Guna . .		1	1,537	62,900	1,878	61,022	337,973	7,426	330,547	180,117	3,730	176,387	157,856	3,696	154,160
Total ..	78,169·2	69	32,415	1,961,771	202,999	1,758,772	10,818,812	964,538	9,854,274	5,395,536	514,289	4,881,247	4,923,276	450,249	4,473,027

TABLE II.

Variation in the enumerated population since last Census.

NOTE.—In 1881 the compilation was by States and not, as in this Census, by Agencies. Many of the Central India States have territory in more than one Agency; and, as all the registers of the 1881 Census have been destroyed, there are no figures available for comparison except in the case of the Baghelkhand Agency, none of the States under which have any outlying territory in other Agencies.

TABLE II.—Variation in the enumerated population since last Census.

AGENCIES.	Total.			Males.			Females.		
	1891.	1881.	Variation.	1891.	1881.	Variation.	1891.	1881.	Variation.
1	2	3	4	5	6	7	8	9	10
Indore	372,792	......	......	201,944	......	......	170,848	......	......
Gwalior	1,757,509	......	......	948,805	......	......	808,704	......	......
Bhopal	2,006,859	......	......	1,052,777	......	......	954,082	......	......
Bundelkhand	1,508,053	......	......	784,906	......	......	723,147	......	......
Baghelkhand	1,737,606	1,512,595	225,011	872,222	757,681	114,541	865,384	754,914	110,470
Western Malwa	1,619,368	......	......	851,933	......	......	767,435	......	......
Bhopawar	978,652	......	......	502,832	......	......	475,820	......	......
Guna	337,973	......	......	180,117	......	......	157,856	......	......
Total .	10,318,812	......	......	5,395,536	......	......	4,923,276	......	......

TABLE III.

Towns and Villages classified by Population.

TABLE III.—Towns and Villages classified by Population.

AGENCIES.	Total number of Towns and Villages.	Total Population.	1—199		200—499		500—999		1,000—1,999		2,000—2,999		3,000—4,999		5,000—9,999		10,000—14,999		15,000—19,999		20,000—49,999		50,000 & over.		Unclassed Population.
			Number.	Population.	Number.	Population.	Number.	Population.	Number.	Population.	Number.	Population.	Number.	Population.	Number.	Population.	Number.	Population.	Number.	Population.	Number.	Population.	Number.	Population.	
1	2	3	4	5	6	7	8	9	10	11	12	13	14	15	16	17	18	19	20	21	22	23	24	25	26
INDORE	784	372,792	413	42,238	266	81,929	65	43,134	24	31,572	10	24,237	1	3,297	2	14,394	...	...	1	15,068	1	31,773	1	82,984	2,166
GWALIOR	4,087	1,757,509	1,764	177,984	1,387	446,319	607	417,871	252	340,364	46	110,798	20	75,653	9	59,419	...	...	...	...	1	24,518	1	104,083	500
BHOPAL	7,329	2,006,859	4,207	428,784	2,378	735,617	541	363,307	152	207,114	21	51,090	18	67,619	9	59,377	2	22,861	...	...	...	...	1	70,338	752
BUNDELKHAND	3,685	1,508,053	1,735	163,184	1,087	352,864	561	386,869	228	308,435	47	113,029	17	59,796	4	26,895	4	51,632	1	17,610	1	27,566	...	...	173
BAGHELKHAND	6,192	1,737,606	3,260	310,155	2,083	656,049	654	435,897	165	218,707	20	47,206	6	21,381	3	18,670	...	...	...	...	1	23,626	...	...	5,915
WESTERN MALWA	4,709	1,619,368	2,428	250,774	1,595	496,133	483	320,361	142	189,951	26	61,396	14	53,168	13	84,631	3	33,239	1	15,291	4	112,142	...	...	2,282
BHOPAWAR	4,160	978,652	2,729	252,806	1,071	323,235	257	168,021	64	85,281	17	40,790	17	59,312	4	30,777	...	...	1	18,430	...	...	...	..	...
GUNA	1,538	337,973	1,010	87,234	391	118,203	114	76,114	14	18,422	2	5,442	6	25,132	1	7,426	...	...	...	...	...	...	...	...	...
Total	32,484	10,318,812	17,546	1,713,159	10,258	3,210,849	3,282	2,211,574	1,041	1,399,846	189	453,988	99	365,358	45	301,589	9	107,732	4	66,399	8	219,625	8	257,405	11,788

TABLE IV.

Towns according to population compared with the preceding Census.

TABLE IV.—Towns according to population compared with the preceding Census.

Towns.	Agency.	Total Population.			Males.			Females.		
		1891.	1881.	Variation.	1891.	1881.	Variation.	1891.	1881.	Variation.
1	2	3	4	5	6	7	8	9	10	11
1. Lashkar	Gwalior	104,083	88,066	+ 16,017	54,553	46,720	+ 7,833	49,530	41,346	+ 8,184
2. Indore (City)	Indore	82,984	75,401	+ 7,583	46,328	41,484	+ 4,844	36,656	33,917	+ 2,739
3. Bhopal	Bhopal	70,338	55,402	+ 14,936	36,891	28,466	+ 8,425	33,447	26,936	+ 6,511
4. Ujjain	Western Malwa	34,691	32,932	+ 1,759	18,292	16,970	+ 1,322	16,399	15,962	+ 437
5. Mhow (Cantonment)	Indore	31,773	27,227	+ 4,546	18,300	15,536	+ 2,764	13,473	11,691	+ 1,782
6. Rutlam	Western Malwa	29,822	31,066	− 1,244	15,322	16,544	− 1,222	14,500	14,522	− 22
7. Datia	Bundelkhand	27,566	28,346	− 780	14,213	14,574	− 361	13,353	13,772	− 419
8. Mandsaur	Western Malwa	25,785	22,596	+ 3,189	13,164	11,856	+ 1,308	12,621	10,740	+ 1,881
9. Morar	Gwalior	24,518	24,022	+ 496	15,375	15,418	− 43	9,143	8,604	+ 539
10. Rewa	Baghelkhand	23,626	22,016	+ 1,610	12,155	11,010	+ 1,145	11,471	11,006	+ 465
11. Jaora	Western Malwa	21,844	19,902	+ 1,942	11,010	10,336	+ 674	10,834	9,566	+ 1,268
12. Dhar	Bhopawar	18,430	15,224	+ 3,206	9,701	7,885	+ 1,816	8,729	7,339	+ 1,390
13. Tikamgarh	Bundelkhand	17,610	18,344	− 734	9,200	9,439	− 239	8,410	8,905	− 495
14. Nimach (Cantonment)	Western Malwa	15,291	13,069	+ 2,222	8,763	7,576	+ 1,187	6,528	5,493	+ 1,035
15. Dewas	Indore	15,068	11,921	+ 3,147	8,051	6,216	+ 1,835	7,017	5,705	+ 1,312
16. Panna	Bundelkhand	14,705	14,676	+ 29	7,766	8,194	− 428	6,939	6,482	+ 457
17. Maharajnagar	Ditto	13,068	13,196	− 128	6,668	6,934	− 266	6,400	6,262	+ 138
18. Chhatarpur	Ditto	12,957	13,474	− 517	6,604	7,028	− 424	6,353	6,446	− 93
19. Rampura	Western Malwa	11,935	...	...	6,133	...	...	5,802	...	...
20. Sironj	Ditto	11,737	...	...	6,676	...	...	5,061	...	...
21. Sehore (Cantonment)	Bhopal	11,124	10,389	+ 735	6,084	5,666	+ 418	5,040	4,723	+ 317
22. Shajapur	Western Malwa	11,043	9,247	+ 1,796	5,592	5,036	+ 556	5,451	4,211	+ 1,240
23. Nowgong (Cantonment)	Bundelkhand	10,902	7,492	+ 3,410	6,946	4,249	+ 2,697	3,956	3,243	+ 713
24. Barnagar	Western Malwa	10,261	7,908	+ 2,353	5,334	4,159	+ 1,184	4,927	3,758	+ 1,169
25. Bhilsa	Bhopal	9,670	7,070	+ 2,600	5,284	3,695	+ 1,589	4,386	3,375	+ 1,011
26. Indore (Residency)	Indore	9,345	7,690	+ 1,655	6,099	4,750	+ 1,349	3,246	2,940	+ 306
27. Maheshwar	Bhopawar	9,230	...	...	4,670	...	...	4,560	...	...
28. Bhind	Gwalior	9,188	7,412	+ 1,776	5,576	3,889	+ 1,687	3,612	3,523	+ 89
29. Khargon	Bhopawar	9,147	...	...	4,388	...	...	4,759	...	...
30. Khachrod	Western Malwa	9,034	9,489	− 455	4,504	4,922	− 418	4,530	4,567	− 37
31. Jawad	Ditto	8,920	...	...	4,555	...	...	4,365	...	...
32. Narsinghgarh	Bhopal	8,561	11,400	− 2,839	4,548	6,207	− 1,659	4,013	5,193	− 1,180
33. Mehidpur	Western Malwa	8,263	8,908	− 645	4,017	4,281	− 264	4,246	4,627	− 381
34. Samthar	Bundelkhand	7,865	7,891	− 26	4,192	4,289	− 97	3,673	3,602	+ 71
35. Agar (Cantonment)	Western Malwa	7,692	6,193	+ 1,499	4,137	3,281	+ 856	3,555	2,912	+ 643
36. Shopur	Gwalior	7,600	8,402	− 803	3,894	4,238	− 344	3,706	4,165	− 459
37. Bijawar	Bundelkhand	7,543	7,192	+ 351	4,114	3,711	+ 403	3,429	3,481	− 52
38. Chhabra	Guna	7,426	...	...	3,730	...	...	3,696	...	...
39. Karaia	Gwalior	7,132	...	...	3,655	...	...	3,477	...	...
40. Baroda	Ditto	6,780	6,787	− 7	3,380	3,364	+ 16	3,400	3,423	− 23

Table IV.—Towns according to population—Central India.

TOWNS.	AGENCY.	TOTAL POPULATION. 1891.	TOTAL POPULATION. 1881.	TOTAL POPULATION. Variation.	MALES. 1891.	MALES. 1881.	MALES. Variation.	FEMALES. 1891.	FEMALES. 1881.	FEMALES. Variation.
1	2	3	4	5	6	7	8	9	10	11
41. SUTNA	Baghelkhand	6,771	5,385	+ 1,386	3,802	3,053	+ 749	2,969	2,332	+ 637
42. SUJALPUR	Bhopal	6,669	7,136	− 467	3,351	3,695	− 344	3,318	3,441	− 123
43. BHANPURA	Western Malwa	6,626	...	...	3,290	...	...	3,336	...	...
44. BIAORA	Bhopal	6,476	...	...	3,339	...	...	3,137	...	...
45. MAIHAR	Baghelkhand	6,457	6,487	− 30	3,179	3,197	− 18	3,278	3,290	− 12
46. SEONDA	Bundelkhand	6,409	7,988	− 1,579	3,244	4,200	− 956	3,165	3,788	− 623
47. KUKSI	Bhopawar	6,346	6,212	+ 134	3,188	3,129	+ 59	3,158	3,083	+ 75
48. NIMACH	Western Malwa	6,309	5,161	+ 1,148	3,337	2,699	+ 638	2,972	2,462	+ 510
49. ASHTA	Bhopal	6,280	5,793	+ 487	3,215	3,083	+ 132	3,065	2,710	+ 355
50. NARWAR	Gwalior	6,190	...	...	3,174	...	...	3,016	...	...
51. MANGAULI	Bhopal	6,158	...	...	3,436	...	...	2,722	...	...
52. SABALGARH	Gwalior	6,111	...	...	3,213	...	...	2,898	...	...
53. BARWANI	Bhopawar	6,054	5,581	+ 473	2,930	2,767	+ 163	3,124	2,814	+ 310
54. BHANDER	Gwalior	5,967	...	...	3,065	...	...	2,902	...	...
55. SITAMAU	Western Malwa	5,861	5,764	+ 97	3,017	2,963	+ 54	2,844	2,801	+ 43
56. TARANA	Do.	5,840	...	...	2,973	...	...	2,867	...	...
57. PIRAWA	Do.	5,627	...	...	2,819	...	...	2,808	...	...
58. UNCHEHRA	Baghelkhand	5,442	...	...	2,714	...	...	2,728	...	...
59. BERSIA	Bhopal	5,437	...	...	2,832	...	...	2,605	...	...
60. GOHAD	Gwalior	5,378	...	...	2,778	...	...	2,600	...	...
61. MANASA	Western Malwa	5,130	...	...	2,601	...	...	2,529	...	...
62. TAL MANDAWAL	Do.	5,120	...	...	2,752	...	...	2,368	...	...
63. SAILANA	Do.	5,113	...	...	2,626	...	...	2,487	...	...
64. SEHORE	Bhopal	5,108	5,206	− 98	2,563	2,646	− 83	2,545	2,560	− 15
65. SUNEL	Western Malwa	5,096	...	...	2,578	...	...	2,518	...	...
66. NADIGAON	Bundelkhand	5,078	5,475	− 397	2,570	2,821	− 251	2,508	2,654	− 146
67. CHANDERI	Gwalior	5,073	...	...	2,553	...	...	2,520	...	...
68. GAUTAMPURA	Indore	5,049	...	...	2,523	...	...	2,526	...	...
69. ICHHAWAR	Bhopal	5,018	...	...	2,653	...	...	2,365	...	...
Total		952,750	...	...	506,179	...	...	446,571	...	...
Railways in Central India		11,788	...	...	8,110	...	...	3,678	...	...
GRAND TOTAL OF URBAN POPULATION		964,538	...	...	514,289	...	...	450,249	...	...

TABLE V.

Towns arranged territorially, with population by religion.

TABLE V.—Towns arranged territorial

Agency.	State.	Towns.	Total Population. Total.	Total Population. Males.	Total Population. Females.	Hindu. Total.	Hindu. Males.	Hindu. Females.	Musalman. Total.	Musalman. Males.	Musalman. Females.
1	2	3	4	5	6	7	8	9	10	11	12
Indore.	Indore	Indore City	82,984	46,328	36,656	60,240	34,069	26,171	18,106	9,824	8,282
		Mhow Cantonment	31,773	18,300	13,473	19,910	11,131	8,779	8,233	4,481	3,752
		Indore Residency	9,345	6,099	3,246	6,793	4,460	2,333	1,875	1,191	684
		Gautampura	5,049	2,523	2,526	2,988	1,468	1,520	1,168	596	572
	Dewas	Dewas	15,068	8,051	7,017	10,294	5,543	4,751	3,685	1,974	1,711
Gwalior.	Gwalior	Lashkar	104,083	54,553	49,530	76,867	40,752	36,115	23,038	11,695	11,343
		Morar	24,518	15,375	9,143	17,682	11,129	6,553	6,416	4,013	2,403
		Bhind	9,188	5,576	3,612	7,072	4,242	2,830	1,520	1,002	518
		Seopur	7,600	3,894	3,706	5,068	2,660	2,408	1,593	946	1,047
		Karaia	7,132	3,655	3,477	6,456	3,309	3,147	140	78	62
		Narwar	6,190	3,174	3,016	4,670	2,416	2,254	1,207	586	621
		Sabalgarh	6,111	3,213	2,898	5,057	2,650	2,407	987	521	466
		Bhander	5,967	3,065	2,902	5,035	2,622	2,413	846	395	451
		Gohad	5,378	2,778	2,600	4,596	2,371	2,225	635	327	308
		Chanderi	5,073	2,553	2,520	3,423	1,706	1,717	1,267	666	601
		Baroda	6,780	3,380	3,400	5,236	2,598	2,638	484	244	240
Bhopal.	Bhopal	Bhopal	70,338	36,891	33,447	32,487	17,267	15,220	35,788	18,492	17,296
		Sehore Cantonment	11,124	6,084	5,040	8,362	4,495	3,867	2,294	1,261	1,033
		Ashta	6,280	3,215	3,065	3,991	2,058	1,933	1,861	953	908
		Bersia	5,437	2,832	2,605	4,283	2,196	2,087	1,075	590	485
		Sehore Town	5,108	2,563	2,545	2,875	1,439	1,436	2,077	1,048	1,029
		Ichhawar	5,018	2,653	2,365	3,543	1,879	1,664	1,170	631	539
	Gwalior	Bhilsa	9,670	5,284	4,386	7,489	4,064	3,425	1,727	976	751
		Sujalpur	6,669	3,351	3,318	4,017	2,031	1,986	1,931	953	978
		Mangauli	6,158	3,436	2,722	4,389	2,460	1,929	1,131	621	510
	Narsinghgarh	Narsinghgarh	8,561	4,548	4,013	7,151	3,814	3,337	1,148	584	564
	Rajgarh	Biaora	6,476	3,339	3,137	4,969	2,553	2,416	1,134	581	553
	Tonk (Rajputana)	Sironj	11,737	6,676	5,061	7,709	4,288	3,421	3,912	2,330	1,582
Bundelkhand.	Datia	Datia	27,566	14,213	13,353	21,924	11,387	10,537	4,799	2,354	2,445
		Seonda	6,409	3,244	3,165	5,540	2,807	2,733	693	341	352
		Nadigaon	5,078	2,570	2,508	4,659	2,344	2,315	368	204	164
	Orchha	Tikamgarh	17,610	9,200	8,410	12,363	6,574	5,789	3,665	1,843	1,822
	Panna	Panna	14,705	7,766	6,939	11,741	6,204	5,537	2,180	1,133	1,047
	Charkhari	Maharajnagar	13,068	6,668	6,400	9,594	4,975	4,619	3,237	1,575	1,662
	Chhatarpur	Chhatarpur	12,957	6,604	6,353	10,348	5,329	5,019	2,095	1,039	1,056
		Nowgong Cantonment	10,902	6,946	3,956	6,653	4,097	2,556	3,269	1,999	1,270
	Samthar	Samthar	7,865	4,192	3,673	6,780	3,628	3,152	933	482	451
	Bijawar	Bijawar	7,543	4,114	3,429	5,661	3,119	2,542	1,279	689	590
Baghelkhand.	Rewa	Rewa	23,626	12,155	11,471	18,320	9,566	8,754	4,917	2,336	2,581
		Sutna	6,771	3,802	2,969	5,282	3,031	2,251	1,147	614	533
	Maihar	Maihar	6,457	3,179	3,278	4,811	2,361	2,450	1,236	602	634
	Nagode	Unchehra	5,442	2,714	2,728	4,317	2,140	2,177	939	480	459
Western Malwa.	Gwalior	Ujjain	34,691	18,292	16,399	23,329	12,370	10,959	9,476	4,897	4,579
		Mandsaur	25,785	13,164	12,621	16, 16	8,243	7,873	7,425	3,713	3,712
		Nimach Cantonment	15,291	8,763	6,528	10,337	5,935	4,402	4,126	2,258	1,868
		Shajapur	11,043	5,592	5,451	7,383	3,720	3,663	2,820	1,414	1,406
		Barnagar	10,261	5,334	4,927	6,319	3,250	3,069	2,451	1,291	1,160
		Khachrod	9,034	4,504	4,530	5,141	2,573	2,568	1,942	929	1,013
		Jawad	8,920	4,555	4,365	5,208	2,634	2,574	1,860	948	912
		Agar	7,692	4,137	3,555	4,944	2,702	2,242	1,915	997	918
		Nimach	6,309	3,337	2,972	3,830	2,027	1,803	1,306	701	605
	Rutlam	Rutlam	29,822	15,322	14,500	16,775	8,520	8,255	7,405	3,787	3,618
	Jaora	Jaora	21,844	11,010	10,834	9,350	4,725	4,625	9,896	4,943	4,953
		Tal Mandawal	5,120	2,752	2,368	3,348	1,733	1,615	1,239	734	505
	Indore	Rampura	11,935	6,133	5,802	7,460	3,891	3,569	3,356	1,613	1,743
		Mehidpur	8,263	4,017	4,246	4,715	2,359	2,356	2,704	1,259	1,445
		Bhanpura	6,626	3,290	3,336	4,759	2,369	2,390	1,436	707	729
		Tarana	5,840	2,973	2,867	4,661	2,379	2,282	973	489	484
		Manasa	5,130	2,601	2,529	3,993	2,028	1,965	570	287	283
		Sunel	5,096	2,578	2,518	2,765	1,432	1,333	1,012	471	541
	Sitamau	Sitamau	5,861	3,017	2,844	4,710	2 412	2,298	977	526	451
	Sailana	Sailana	5,113	2,626	2,487	3,764	1,927	1,837	624	316	308
	Tonk (Rajputana).	Pirawa	5,627	2,819	2,808	2,998	1,533	1,465	1,752	862	890
Bhopawar.	Indore	Maheshwar	9,230	4,670	4,560	7,144	3,647	3,497	1,324	639	685
		Khargon	9,147	4,388	4,759	6,579	3,170	3,409	2,359	1,132	1,267
	Dhar	Dhar	18,430	9,701	8,729	13,948	7,338	6,610	3,393	1,737	1,656
		Kuksi	6,346	3,188	3,158	3,563	1,798	1,765	1,368	661	707
	Barwani	Barwani	6,054	2,930	3,124	3,669	1,794	1,875	1,318	593	725
Guna.	Tonk (Rajputana).	Chhabra	7,426	3,730	3,696	5,704	2,910	2,794	1,493	691	802
	Railways in Central India		11,788	8,110	3,678	8,811	6,194	2,617	2,147	1,418	729
		Total	964,588	514,289	450,249	661,968	354,845	307,128	236,812	123,263	113,049

vith population by religion.

Jain.			Aboriginal.			Christian.			Parsi.			Sikh.			Jew.		
Total.	Males.	Females.	Total.	Males.	Females.	Total.	Males.	Females.	Total.	Males.	Females.	Total.	Males.	Females.	Total.	Males.	Females.
13	14	15	16	17	18	19	20	21	22	23	24	25	26	27	28	29	30
2,528	1,385	1,143	1,813	874	939	49	26	23	...	...	...	248	150	98	...	...	...
192	97	95	...	...	...	2,915	2,300	615	419	214	205	51	45	6	53	32	21
148	96	52	...	...	...	366	266	100	154	80	74	8	5	3	1	1	...
199	98	101	694	361	333	...	...	...	...	...	...	...	...	...	...	...	...
399	152	147	786	382	404	...	...	...	...	...	...	4	...	4	...	...	...
1,923	997	926	2,153	1,065	1,088	99	41	58	...	...	...	3	3	...	...	...	...
102	52	50	256	145	111	61	35	26	1	1	...	...	...	...	...	...	...
444	239	205	149	92	57	3	1	2	...	...	...	...	...	...	...	...	...
306	160	146	233	128	105	...	...	...	...	...	...	...	...	...	...	...	...
298	150	148	238	118	120	...	...	...	...	...	...	...	...	...	...	...	...
...	...	...	312	171	141	1	1	...	...	...	...	...	...	...	...	...	...
4	4	...	59	35	24	4	3	1	...	...	...	...	...	...	...	...	...
...	...	...	86	48	38	...	...	...	...	...	...	...	...	...	...	...	...
70	38	32	77	42	35	...	...	...	...	...	...	...	...	...	...	...	...
134	59	75	249	122	127	...	...	...	...	...	...	...	...	...	...	...	...
27	17	10	1,028	518	510	4	2	2	...	...	...	1	1	...	...	...	...
803	409	394	856	523	333	188	91	97	23	10	13	193	99	94	...	...	...
139	83	56	...	...	...	69	36	33	11	5	6	249	204	45	...	...	...
398	184	214	25	17	8	5	3	2	...	...	...	...	...	...	...	...	...
28	13	15	51	33	18	...	...	...	...	...	...	...	...	...	...	...	...
102	46	56	54	30	24	...	...	...	...	...	...	...	...	...	...	...	...
153	69	84	146	73	73	6	1	5	...	...	...	...	...	...	...	...	...
272	147	125	182	97	85	...	...	...	...	...	...	...	...	...	...	...	...
433	219	214	288	148	140	...	...	...	...	...	...	...	...	...	...	...	...
394	191	203	244	164	80	...	...	...	...	...	...	...	...	...	...	...	...
...	...	...	255	147	108	...	...	...	...	...	...	7	3	4	...	...	...
84	47	37	289	158	131	...	...	...	...	...	...	...	...	...	...	...	...
116	58	58	...	...	...	...	...	...	...	...	...	...	...	...	...	...	...
10	6	4	832	465	367	1	1	...	...	...	...	...	...	...	...	...	...
10	7	3	166	89	77	...	...	...	...	...	...	...	...	...	...	...	...
...	...	...	51	22	29	...	...	...	...	...	...	...	...	...	...	...	...
930	451	479	649	330	319	3	2	1	...	...	...	...	...	...	...	...	...
158	76	82	572	312	260	12	8	4	...	...	...	42	33	9	...	...	...
...	...	...	237	118	119	...	...	...	...	...	...	...	...	...	...	...	...
286	136	150	228	100	128	...	...	...	...	...	...	...	...	...	...	...	...
49	28	21	...	...	...	...	...	...	...	...	...	...	...	...	...	...	...
12	12	...	140	70	70	...	...	...	...	...	...	...	...	...	...	...	...
35	19	16	568	287	281	648	557	91	2	2	...	281	263	18	...	...	...
52	29	23	296	194	102	3	2	1	...	...	...	38	28	10	...	...	...
112	63	49	229	93	136	...	...	...	...	...	...	1	1	...	...	...	...
68	42	26	342	174	168	...	...	...	...	...	...	...	...	...	...	...	...
...	...	...	186	94	92	...	...	...	...	...	...	...	...	...	...	...	...
924	517	407	918	481	437	32	20	12	7	5	2	5	2	3	...	...	...
1,637	888	749	592	313	279	6	4	2	9	3	6	...	...	...	...	...	...
157	81	76	...	...	...	534	418	116	119	59	60	2	2	...	16	10	6
499	254	245	340	203	137	1	1	...	...	...	...	...	...	...	...	...	...
951	497	454	539	295	244	...	...	...	1	1	...	...	...	...	...	...	...
634	324	310	1,317	678	639	...	...	...	...	...	...	...	...	...	...	...	...
853	462	391	993	507	486	6	4	2	...	...	...	...	...	...	...	...	...
609	307	302	222	129	93	...	...	...	2	2	...	...	...	...	...	...	...
577	295	282	587	310	277	9	4	5	...	...	...	...	...	...	...	...	...
4,341	2,284	2,057	1,227	693	534	61	31	30	9	4	5	4	3	1	...	...	...
1,405	765	640	1,167	561	606	7	5	2	19	11	8	...	...	...	...	...	...
387	209	178	145	75	70	1	1	...	...	...	...	...	...	...	...	...	...
750	407	343	369	222	147	...	...	...	...	...	...	...	...	...	...	...	...
612	286	326	232	113	119	...	...	...	...	...	...	...	...	...	...	...	...
177	85	92	252	127	125	...	...	...	...	...	...	2	2	...	...	...	...
45	24	21	161	81	80	...	...	...	...	...	...	...	...	...	...	...	...
231	108	123	331	173	158	5	5	...	...	...	...	...	...	...	...	...	...
219	111	108	1,100	564	536	...	...	...	...	...	...	...	...	...	...	...	...
82	36	46	92	43	49	...	...	...	...	...	...	...	...	...	...	...	...
355	179	176	369	203	166	...	...	...	1	1	...	...	...	...	...	...	...
877	424	453	...	...	...	...	...	...	...	...	...	...	...	...	...	...	...
264	141	123	496	241	255	1	1	...	1	1	...	...	...	...	...	...	...
15	9	6	154	77	77	...	...	...	...	...	...	...	...	...	...	...	...
615	319	296	460	301	159	1	1	...	9	4	5	4	1	3	...	...	...
415	221	194	1,000	508	492	...	...	...	...	...	...	...	...	...	...	...	...
89	42	47	972	497	475	2	1	1	...	...	...	4	3	1	...	...	...
229	129	100	...	...	...	...	...	...	...	...	...	...	...	...	...	...	...
72	58	14	191	114	77	547	316	231	17	8	9	1	1	...	2	1	1
29,339	15,841	18,998	29,245	15,348	13,897	5,650	4,188	1,462	804	411	398	1,148	849	299	72	44	28

TABLE VI.

Religions.

TABLE VI.—Religions.

AGENCIES.	TOTAL POPULATION.			HINDU.			MUSALMAN.			JAIN.		
	Total.	Males.	Females.	Total.	Males.	Females.	Total.	Males.	Females.	Total.	Males.	Females.
1	2	3	4	5	6	7	8	9	10	11	12	13
Indore . .	372,792	201,944	170,848	283,493	153,266	130,227	45,828	25,019	20,809	5,659	3,090	2,569
Gwalior . .	1,757,509	948,805	808,704	1,547,683	836,805	710,878	77,673	42,252	35,421	10,056	5,340	4,716
Bhopal . .	2,006,859	1,052,777	954,082	1,511,116	793,942	717,174	161,354	85,635	75,719	10,828	5,570	5,258
Bundelkhand .	1,508,053	784,906	723,147	1,344,823	701,202	643,621	54,722	28,533	26,189	12,530	6,369	6,161
Baghelkhand .	1,737,606	872,222	865,384	1,171,088	590,068	581,020	43,723	22,377	21,346	474	250	224
Western Malwa	1,619,368	851,933	767,435	1,162,563	611,128	551,435	126,311	66,226	60,085	33,408	17,685	15,723
Bhopawar . .	978,652	502,832	475,820	435,705	223,508	212,197	46,388	24,199	22,189	12,222	6,333	5,889
Guna . . .	337,973	180,117	157,856	278,775	148,412	130,363	12,641	6,874	5,767	4,807	2,603	2,204
Total .	10,318,812	5,395,536	4,923,276	7,735,246	4,058,331	3,676,915	568,640	301,115	267,525	89,984	47,240	42,744

AGENCIES.	ABORIGINAL.			CHRISTIAN.			PARSI.			SIKH.			JEW.		
	Total.	Males.	Females.	Total.	Males.	Females.	Total.	Males.	Females.	Total.	Males.	Females.	Total.	Males.	Females.
	14	15	16	17	18	19	20	21	22	23	24	25	26	27	28
Indore . .	33,241	17,337	16,004	3,513	2,696	817	583	298	285	321	205	116	54	33	21
Gwalior . .	121,699	64,150	57,549	392	252	140	2	2	...	4	4	...	...	...	...
Bhopal . .	322,766	167,150	155,616	304	156	148	36	16	20	455	308	147	...	...	...
Bundelkhand .	94,974	47,926	47,048	677	576	101	2	2	...	325	298	27	...	...	...
Baghelkhand .	522,033	259,355	262,678	227	128	99	...	...	...	61	44	17	...	...	...
Western Malwa	295,730	155,937	139,793	844	611	233	191	104	87	303	231	72	18	11	7
Bhopawar . .	484,282	248,755	235,527	24	18	6	23	15	8	8	4	4	...	...	...
Guna . . .	41,384	21,949	19,435	18	15	3	...	...	...	348	264	84	...	...	...
Total .	1,916,209	982,559	933,650	5,599	4,452	1,547	837	437	400	1,825	1,358	467	72	44	28

TABLE VII.

Ages by Religions.—Part (A).

ALL RELIGIONS.

TABLE VII.—Ages by Religions.—Part (A). ALL RELIGIONS.

AGENCY.	TOTAL POPULATION.			AGE PERIODS.															
	Total.	Males.	Females.	Under 1 year.		1 year.		2 years.		3 years.		4 years.		Total 0—4.		5—9.		10—14.	
				Males.	Females.	Males.	Females.	Males.	Females.	Males.	Females.	Males.	Females.	Males.	Females.	Males.	Females.	Males.	Females.
1	2	3	4	5	6	7	8	9	10	11	12	13	14	15	16	17	18	19	20
Indore	372,792	201,944	170,848	5,504	5,713	2,847	3,027	4,248	4,485	4,430	4,969	4,532	4,607	21,561	22,801	22,213	21,276	19,368	14,392
Gwalior	1,757,509	948,805	808,704	26,354	22,890	12,530	11,632	20,414	19,735	25,084	25,216	28,305	25,672	112,687	105,145	134,230	113,744	110,999	70,247
Bhopal	2,006,859	1,052,777	954,082	28,806	29,344	14,170	14,595	25,942	27,161	28,744	32,152	30,697	30,894	128,359	134,146	144,951	134,635	119,886	85,775
Bundelkhand	1,508,053	784,906	723,147	19,504	18,128	11,312	11,777	17,605	18,886	23,176	25,610	23,476	24,075	95,073	98,476	121,759	110,608	99,059	71,094
Baghelkhand	1,737,606	872,222	865,384	24,900	24,530	14,117	15,311	22,781	25,774	29,725	34,744	28,708	30,679	120,231	13,138	146,637	138,812	121,929	93,175
Western Malwa	1,619,368	851,933	767,435	21,903	22,313	12,254	12,915	18,782	19,281	20,345	22,441	22,076	21,919	95,360	98,869	112,796	102,894	92,353	66,981
Bhopawar	978,652	502,832	475,820	17,592	18,586	6,813	7,379	12,663	14,132	14,354	16,530	14,757	15,361	66,179	71,988	72,394	69,428	57,137	47,158
Guna	337,973	180,117	157,856	4,036	4,085	2,682	2,653	4,041	4,330	5,284	5,835	5,572	5,422	21,615	22,325	27,100	23,888	20,399	13,514
Total	10,318,812	5,395,536	4,923,276	148,599	145,589	76,725	79,289	126,476	133,784	151,142	167,497	158,123	158,629	661,065	684,788	782,080	715,285	641,180	462,336

AGENCY.	AGE PERIODS.																			
	15—19.		20—24.		25—29.		30—34.		35—39.		40—44.		45—49.		50—54.		55—59.		60 and over.	
	Males.	Females.	Males.	Females.	Males.	Females.	Males.	Females.	Males.	Females.	Males.	Females.	Males.	Females.	Males.	Females.	Males.	Females.	Males.	Females.
	21	22	23	24	25	26	27	28	29	30	31	32	33	34	35	36	37	38	39	40
Indore	15,329	13,960	18,700	18,148	21,661	17,557	23,816	17,830	13,396	8,398	17,521	13,566	6,281	3,743	10,574	8,468	2,009	1,415	9,515	9,294
Gwalior	81,511	62,490	79,555	74,243	87,744	81,390	94,866	82,022	56,523	44,939	72,335	61,661	29,416	21,517	40,427	38,139	11,683	9,625	36,829	43,542
Bhopal	79,459	67,355	84,827	91,037	100,892	99,042	108,060	94,602	68,648	55,591	83,801	67,179	33,554	24,541	45,914	42,646	11,720	10,304	42,706	47,229
Bundelkhand	65,447	49,817	57,174	55,762	64,556	63,416	74,821	69,728	45,603	44,251	59,778	55,060	28,108	23,887	33,902	33,066	10,561	10,137	29,065	37,845
Baghelkhand	63,485	49,925	56,313	59,253	68,043	71,841	79,576	84,445	49,881	52,288	61,946	63,552	27,423	26,321	35,011	37,651	10,089	11,005	31,658	46,078
Western Malwa	71,606	61,436	79,549	80,576	74,238	69,486	90,535	78,682	59,215	47,093	65,884	59,073	27,789	20,669	38,926	37,779	9,162	7,335	34,520	36,562
Bhopawar	39,019	37,266	41,324	46,502	46,873	46,483	53,978	46,723	30,431	23,712	37,627	32,511	14,585	11,135	21,358	19,863	4,751	3,629	17,176	19,422
Guna	14,824	11,969	13,815	13,824	17,569	16,529	18,106	15,111	12,037	9,931	13,078	10,687	6,006	4,631	7,280	6,455	2,158	1,867	6,130	7,125
Total	480,680	354,218	481,257	439,345	481,576	465,744	543,758	489,143	335,724	286,203	411,970	363,289	173,162	136,444	233,392	224,067	62,133	55,317	207,599	247,097

TABLE VII.

Ages by Religions.—Part (B).

HINDU.

TABLE VII.—Ages by Religions.—Part (B). HINDU.

AGENCY.	TOTAL HINDUS.			AGE PERIODS.															
	Total.	Males.	Females.	UNDER 1 YEAR.		1 YEAR.		2 YEARS.		3 YEARS.		4 YEARS.		TOTAL 0—4.		5—9.		10—14.	
				Males.	Females.	Males.	Females.	Males.	Females.	Males.	Females.	Males.	Females.	Males.	Females.	Males.	Females.	Males.	Females.
1	2	3	4	5	6	7	8	9	10	11	12	13	14	15	16	17	18	19	20
INDORE	283,493	153,266	130,227	4,218	4,436	2,199	2,337	3,171	3,355	3,286	3,736	3,399	3,431	16,273	17,295	16,868	16,167	14,764	10,849
GWALIOR	1,547,683	836,805	710,878	23,390	20,014	11,234	10,338	17,859	17,049	21,910	21,872	24,750	22,170	99,143	91,443	118,366	99,552	98,572	61,458
BHOPAL	1,511,116	793,942	717,174	21,724	21,821	10,843	11,171	19,564	20,461	22,009	24,535	23,380	23,485	97,520	101,473	110,443	102,149	90,989	64,101
BUNDELKHAND	1,344,823	701,202	643,621	17,336	16,021	10,187	10,413	15,707	16,660	20,648	22,710	20,862	21,144	84,740	86,948	108,561	97,875	88,676	63,113
BAGHELKHAND	1,171,088	590,068	581,020	16,533	15,690	9,108	9,707	14,516	15,924	18,989	21,494	17,948	18,811	77,094	81,626	94,711	89,021	83,207	63,414
WESTERN MALWA	1,162,563	611,128	551,435	15,799	16,132	8,773	9,310	13,342	13,609	14,307	15,721	15,674	15,677	67,895	70,449	80,058	73,455	66,251	47,801
BHOPAWAR	435,705	223,508	212,197	7,922	8,338	2,865	3,111	5,085	5,589	5,314	6,296	5,477	5,718	26,663	29,052	27,528	27,476	25,116	20,121
GUNA	278,775	148,412	130,363	3,338	3,397	2,229	2,204	3,318	3,523	4,308	4,769	4,545	4,398	17,738	18,291	22,297	19,763	16,949	11,150
Total	7,735,246	4,058,331	3,676,915	110,260	105,849	57,438	58,591	92,562	96,170	110,771	121,133	116,085	114,834	487,066	496,577	573,832	525,458	484,524	342,007

AGENCY.	AGE PERIODS.																			
	15—19.		20—24.		25—29.		30—34.		35—39.		40—44.		45—49.		50—54.		55—59.		60 AND OVER.	
	Males.	Females.	Males.	Females.	Males.	Females.	Males.	Females.	Males.	Females.	Males.	Females.	Males.	Females.	Males.	Females.	Males.	Females.	Males.	Females.
	21	22	23	24	25	26	27	28	29	30	31	32	33	34	35	36	37	38	39	40
INDORE	11,735	10,692	13,657	13,775	16,302	13,343	18,323	13,643	10,308	6,488	13,544	10,457	4,878	2,881	7,970	6,506	1,517	1,076	7,127	7,055
GWALIOR	72,646	55,403	70,512	65,290	77,342	71,819	83,311	71,903	49,935	39,805	63,198	54,269	25,923	19,177	35,230	33,641	10,325	8,552	32,302	38,566
BHOPAL	60,505	51,506	64,070	68,267	76,014	74,724	81,008	70,673	51,810	41,665	62,115	49,983	25,209	18,521	33,939	31,615	8,862	7,693	31,458	34,804
BUNDELKHAND	58,793	44,657	51,125	49,780	57,756	56,559	66,747	61,935	40,878	39,503	53,236	48,933	25,173	21,438	30,178	29,756	9,542	9,142	25,797	33,982
BAGHELKHAND	44,848	34,575	40,356	40,870	48,038	49,290	54,217	56,986	34,368	35,055	41,111	44,212	19,478	18,706	24,123	27,203	7,370	7,742	21,147	32,320
WESTERN MALWA	51,392	44,147	57,369	58,204	53,525	49,688	65,381	56,719	42,748	34,019	47,478	42,522	19,996	14,921	27,863	27,492	6,459	5,387	24,713	26,631
BHOPAWAR	17,136	16,819	19,022	21,340	20,902	20,556	25,078	21,430	14,280	11,128	18,124	16,062	7,355	5,339	10,784	10,327	2,499	1,883	9,021	10,664
GUNA	12,389	10,004	11,359	11,320	14,490	13,667	14,864	12,425	9,897	8,171	10,725	8,880	4,976	3,876	5,988	5,426	1,787	1,541	4,953	5,849
Total	329,444	267,803	327,470	328,846	364,369	349,646	408,929	365,714	284,224	215,834	309,531	275,318	132,988	104,859	176,075	171,966	48.361	42.016	156,518	189,871

TABLE VII.

Ages by Religions.—Part (C).

MUSALMAN.

TABLE VII.—Ages by Religions.—Part (C). MUSALMAN.

AGENCY.	TOTAL MUSALMANS.			AGE PERIODS.															
				UNDER 1 YEAR.		1 YEAR.		2 YEARS.		3 YEARS.		4 YEARS.		TOTAL 0—4.		5—9.		10—14.	
	Total.	Males.	Females.	Males.	Females.	Males.	Females.	Males.	Females.	Males.	Females.	Males.	Females.	Males.	Females.	Males.	Females.	Males.	Females.
1	2	3	4	5	6	7	8	9	10	11	12	13	14	15	16	17	18	19	20
INDORE	45,828	25,019	20,809	604	649	323	328	563	601	534	604	536	558	2,560	2,740	2,550	2,451	2,323	1,920
GWALIOR	77,673	42,252	35,421	964	888	430	408	746	831	913	920	967	941	4,020	3,988	4,798	4,366	4,129	3,005
BHOPAL	161,354	85,635	75,719	2,509	2,532	971	1,054	1,933	2,011	2,058	2,363	2,108	2,110	9,579	10,070	10,635	10,090	9,331	6,963
BUNDELKHAND	54,722	28,533	26,189	778	748	841	379	543	650	744	814	731	763	3,137	3,354	3,841	3,806	3,391	2,459
BAGHELKHAND	43,723	22,377	21,346	611	590	877	369	543	629	630	754	626	731	2,787	3,073	3,316	3,216	2,901	2,032
WESTERN MALWA	126,311	66,226	60,085	1,831	1,772	969	982	1,448	1,567	1,535	1,736	1,590	1,592	7,373	7,649	8,113	7,619	6,828	5,365
BHOPAWAR	46,388	24,199	22,189	811	870	818	322	503	618	547	632	583	577	2,762	3,019	2,919	2,984	2,742	2,151
GUNA	12,641	6,874	5,767	173	159	77	82	121	160	191	187	153	188	715	776	891	796	694	478
Total	568,640	301,115	267,525	8,281	8,208	5,306	3,924	6,400	7,067	7,152	8,010	7,294	7,460	32,933	34,669	37,063	35,328	32,339	24,373

AGENCY.	AGE PERIODS.																			
	15—19.		20—24.		25—29.		30—34.		35—39.		40—44.		45—49.		50—54.		55—59.		60 AND OVER.	
	Males.	Females.	Males.	Females.	Males.	Females.	Males.	Females.	Males.	Females.	Males.	Females.	Males.	Females.	Males.	Females.	Males.	Females.	Males.	Females.
	21	22	23	24	25	26	27	28	29	30	31	32	33	34	35	36	37	38	39	40
INDORE	1,911	1,771	2,300	2,290	2,512	2,082	2,955	2,087	1,671	941	2,195	1,597	780	423	1,463	1,031	287	194	1,512	1,282
GWALIOR	3,733	2,883	4,012	3,691	4,252	3,557	4,609	3,839	2,561	1,712	3,764	2,924	1,442	821	2,279	1,904	595	406	2,058	2,325
BHOPAL	6,290	5,043	7,024	7,271	8,320	7,632	9,107	7,653	5,637	4,137	7,297	5,747	2,890	1,839	4,272	3,985	1,135	883	4,118	4,406
BUNDELKHAND	2,338	1,908	2,357	2,168	2,536	2,316	2,966	2,683	1,652	1,477	2,307	2,102	988	785	1,421	1,232	369	372	1,230	1,527
BAGHELKHAND	1,700	1,216	1,625	1,727	2,143	1,949	2,280	2,174	1,360	1,257	1,575	1,688	697	647	925	956	251	289	817	1,122
WESTERN MALWA	5,203	4,777	5,699	6,109	5,856	5,740	6,923	6,127	4,441	3,407	5,652	4,775	2,206	1,534	3,623	3,077	807	555	3,502	3,351
BHOPAWAR	1,794	1,597	2,040	2,335	2,251	2,161	2,719	2,278	1,530	1,079	2,037	1,654	806	537	1,243	1,056	260	184	1,096	1,154
GUNA	541	411	580	510	739	559	772	604	484	334	510	464	243	158	349	260	78	74	278	343
Total	23,510	19,606	25,637	26,101	28,609	25,996	32,331	27,445	19,336	14,344	25,337	20,951	10,052	6,744	15,575	13,501	3,782	2,957	14,611	15,510

TABLE VII.

Ages by Religions.—Part (D).

JAIN.

TABLE VII.—Ages by Religions.—Part (D). JAIN.

AGENCY.	TOTAL JAINS.			AGE PERIODS.															
	Total.	Males.	Females.	Under 1 year.		1 year.		2 years.		3 years.		4 years.		Total 0—4.		5—9.		10—14.	
				Males.	Females.	Males.	Females.	Males.	Females.	Males.	Females.	Males.	Females.	Males.	Females.	Males.	Females.	Males.	Females.
1	2	3	4	5	6	7	8	9	10	11	12	13	14	15	16	17	18	19	20
Indore	5,659	3,090	2,569	90	75	29	22	47	47	48	40	45	65	259	249	222	244	278	215
Gwalior	10,056	5,340	4,716	123	122	69	49	94	86	103	125	112	101	501	483	595	512	576	407
Bhopal	10,828	5,570	5,258	149	148	60	47	104	105	109	129	111	119	533	548	578	620	588	455
Bundelkhand . . .	12,530	6,369	6,161	166	132	98	96	132	119	152	135	143	158	691	640	881	763	834	646
Baghelkhand . . .	474	250	224	13	6	...	6	5	...	3	10	6	3	27	25	18	34	32	20
Western Malwa . .	33,408	17,685	15,723	403	453	259	250	369	366	332	363	320	375	1,683	1,807	1,818	1,836	1,752	1,363
Bhopawar . . .	12,222	6,333	5,889	192	193	67	47	101	142	119	137	121	125	600	644	643	652	668	571
Guna	4,807	2,603	2,204	44	60	28	37	63	59	53	58	76	51	264	265	298	281	259	199
Total .	89,984	47,240	42,744	1,180	1,189	610	554	915	924	919	997	934	997	4,558	4,661	5,058	4,942	4,987	3,876

AGENCY.	AGE PERIODS.																			
	15—19.		20—24.		25—29.		30—34.		35—39.		40—44.		45—49.		50—54.		55—59.		60 and over.	
	Males.	Females.	Males.	Females.	Males.	Females.	Males.	Females.	Males.	Females.	Males.	Females.	Males.	Females.	Males.	Females.	Males.	Females.	Males.	Females.
	21	22	23	24	25	26	27	28	29	30	31	32	33	34	35	36	37	38	39	40
Indore	253	243	274	251	323	254	340	285	246	146	280	232	170	82	214	164	69	38	162	166
Gwalior	484	389	474	453	503	446	517	497	386	290	441	432	220	152	274	276	102	70	267	309
Bhopal	465	420	508	552	568	501	596	510	355	328	481	444	256	173	294	309	90	76	258	322
Bundelkhand . . .	613	470	513	487	555	530	560	566	400	384	426	536	254	269	258	328	124	124	260	418
Baghelkhand . . .	16	15	26	20	24	18	26	20	7	14	24	17	12	7	12	11	6	3	20	20
Western Malwa . .	1,483	1,330	1,753	1,576	1,600	1,440	1,840	1,472	1,335	1,043	1,404	1,326	837	591	1,057	908	354	240	769	791
Bhopawar . . .	545	500	603	536	628	510	620	600	447	340	523	521	331	214	331	349	128	99	266	353
Guna	222	191	245	195	283	222	253	195	167	149	177	167	111	85	132	97	54	29	138	129
Total .	4,081	3,558	4,396	4,070	4,484	3,921	4,752	4,145	3,343	2,694	3,756	3,675	2,191	1,573	2,572	2,442	927	679	2,140	2,508

TABLE VII.

Ages by Religions.—Part (E).

ABORIGINAL.

TABLE VII.—Ages by Religions—Part (E). ABORIGINAL.

AGENCY.	TOTAL ABORIGINALS.			AGE PERIODS.															
	Total.	Males.	Females.	UNDER 1 YEAR.		1 YEAR.		2 YEARS.		3 YEARS.		4 YEARS.		TOTAL 0—4.		5—9.		10—14.	
				Males.	Females.	Males.	Females.	Males.	Females.	Males.	Females.	Males.	Females.	Males.	Females.	Males.	Females.	Males.	Females.
1	2	3	4	5	6	7	8	9	10	11	12	13	14	15	16	17	18	19	20
INDORE	33,341	17,337	16,004	536	504	260	304	419	437	506	542	524	512	2,245	2,299	2,422	2,272	1,881	1,302
GWALIOR	121,699	64,150	57,549	1,873	1,862	795	834	1,713	1,767	2,156	2,296	2,472	2,456	9,009	9,215	10,461	9,302	7,714	5,364
BHOPAL	322,766	167,150	155,616	4,409	4,833	2,291	2,316	4,336	4,571	4,560	5,119	5,090	5,171	20,686	22,010	23,265	21,747	18,948	14,232
BUNDELKHAND	94,974	47,926	47,048	1,219	1,221	682	886	1,218	1,453	1,622	1,947	1,736	2,005	6,477	7,512	8,456	8,147	6,144	4,869
BAGHELKHAND	522,033	259,355	262,678	7,738	8,241	4,631	5,227	7,715	9,216	10,101	12,482	10,121	11,130	40,306	46,296	48,579	46,528	35,774	27,696
WESTERN MALWA	295,730	155,937	139,793	3,852	3,941	2,241	2,366	3,610	3,731	4,159	4,606	4,478	4,254	18,340	18,898	22,749	19,932	17,482	12,412
BHOPAWAR	484,282	248,755	235,527	8,667	9,185	3,563	3,899	6,974	7,783	8,374	9,465	8,576	8,941	36,154	39,273	41,303	38,311	28,608	24,314
GUNA	41,384	21,949	19,435	479	465	346	329	536	584	729	818	796	782	2,886	2,978	3,597	3,040	2,481	1,678
Total	1,916,209	982,559	933,650	28,773	30,252	14,809	16,161	26,521	29,542	32,207	37,275	33,793	35,251	136,103	148,481	160,832	149,279	119,032	91,867

AGENCY.	AGE PERIODS.																			
	15—19.		20—24.		25—29.		30—34.		35—39.		40—44.		45—49.		50—54.		55—59.		60 AND OVER.	
	Males.	Females.	Males.	Females.	Males.	Females.	Males.	Females.	Males.	Females.	Males.	Females.	Males.	Females.	Males.	Females.	Males.	Females.	Males.	Females.
	21	22	23	24	25	26	27	28	29	30	31	32	33	34	35	36	37	38	39	40
INDORE	1,273	1,143	1,385	1,672	1,749	1,737	1,930	1,712	1,032	745	1,386	1,225	398	329	870	734	109	91	657	743
GWALIOR	4,643	3,804	4,503	4,750	5,555	5,556	6,416	5,769	3,627	3,122	4,918	4,026	1,820	1,366	2,635	2,305	658	596	2,191	2,334
BHOPAL	12,163	10,350	13,137	14,908	15,918	16,152	17,285	15,735	10,813	9,453	13,879	10,986	5,176	4,001	7,396	6,718	1,628	1,644	6,856	7,680
BUNDELKHAND	3,609	2,775	2,818	3,304	3,516	3,989	4,481	4,535	2,632	2,881	3,780	3,481	1,677	1,392	2,040	1,748	525	499	1,771	1,916
BAGHELKHAND	16,908	14,112	14,288	16,621	17,816	20,568	23,029	25,254	14,140	15,958	19,228	17,627	7,226	6,958	9,939	9,479	2,456	2,967	9,666	12,614
WESTERN MALWA	13,474	11,144	14,501	14,644	13,050	12,567	16,283	14,326	10,628	8,604	11,300	10,430	4,714	3,616	6,360	6,296	1,530	1,146	5,526	5,778
BHOPAWAR	19,543	18,348	19,658	22,288	23,087	23,256	25,555	22,412	14,167	11,164	16,940	14,273	6,088	5,045	8,996	8,130	1,864	1,463	6,792	7,250
GUNA	1,657	1,357	1,573	1,778	1,985	2,072	2,184	1,881	1,466	1,276	1,651	1,172	668	512	804	669	237	221	760	801
Total	73,270	63,033	71,863	80,005	82,676	85,897	97,163	91,624	58,505	53,203	73,062	[illegible]	27,767	22,219	30,040	36,079	9,007	8,627	24,219	30,116

TABLE VII.

Ages by Religions.—Part (F).

CHRISTIAN.

TABLE VII.—Ages by Religions—Part (F). CHRISTIAN.

Agency.	Total Christians: Total.	Total Christians: Males.	Total Christians: Females.	Under 1 year: Males.	Under 1 year: Females.	1 year: Males.	1 year: Females.	2 years: Males.	2 years: Females.	3 years: Males.	3 years: Females.	4 years: Males.	4 years: Females.	Total 0–4: Males.	Total 0–4: Females.	5–9: Males.	5–9: Females.	10–14: Males.	10–14: Females.
1	2	3	4	5	6	7	8	9	10	11	12	13	14	15	16	17	18	19	20
Indore	3,513	2,696	817	43	38	27	26	36	26	46	33	19	31	171	154	102	91	72	63
Gwalior	392	252	140	4	4	2	3	2	2	2	3	4	4	14	16	10	12	8	13
Bhopal	304	156	148	6	3	2	4	1	4	1	3	4	4	14	18	14	13	15	13
Bundelkhand	677	576	101	4	4	4	3	5	4	7	3	3	5	23	19	14	14	6	5
Baghelkhand	227	128	99	2	3	1	2	2	5	2	4	7	4	14	18	10	12	8	11
Western Malwa	844	611	233	7	10	10	6	10	3	8	9	9	17	44	45	36	33	17	22
Bhopawar	24	18	6	...	...	...	...	...	...	...	...	...	...	...	...	...	2	1	...
Guna	18	15	3	...	1	...	...	...	...	...	...	...	...	...	1	1	...	...	...
Total	**5,999**	**4,452**	**1,547**	**66**	**63**	**46**	**44**	**56**	**44**	**66**	**55**	**46**	**65**	**280**	**271**	**187**	**177**	**127**	**127**

Agency.	15–19: Males.	15–19: Females.	20–24: Males.	20–24: Females.	25–29: Males.	25–29: Females.	30–34: Males.	30–34: Females.	35–39: Males.	35–39: Females.	40–44: Males.	40–44: Females.	45–49: Males.	45–49: Females.	50–54: Males.	50–54: Females.	55–59: Males.	55–59: Females.	60 and over: Males.	60 and over: Females.
	21	22	23	24	25	26	27	28	29	30	31	32	33	34	35	36	37	38	39	40
Indore	93	69	990	110	717	108	222	75	105	57	90	32	44	11	33	17	20	8	37	22
Gwalior	5	11	53	19	91	12	12	14	14	10	13	10	10	1	8	13	3	1	11	8
Bhopal	12	21	22	12	14	17	20	12	11	4	9	11	13	4	5	10	3	4	4	9
Bundelkhand	12	4	283	15	163	18	35	8	14	6	12	7	11	2	1	1	1	...	1	2
Baghelkhand	12	5	11	13	16	12	18	9	6	4	8	8	8	2	10	1	4	2	3	2
Western Malwa	34	18	166	26	148	34	61	11	41	14	26	11	21	4	12	4	5	5	...	6
Bhopawar	1	1	...	2	3	...	3	...	4	...	1	...	3	...	2	1	...	...	...	...
Guna	1	...	3	...	3	...	3	1	1	...	2	...	...	...	...	1	...	...	1	...
Total	**170**	**129**	**1,528**	**197**	**1,155**	**201**	**374**	**130**	**196**	**95**	**161**	**79**	**110**	**24**	**71**	**48**	**36**	**20**	**57**	**49**

TABLE VII.

Ages by Religions.—Part (G).

PARSI.

Table VII.—Ages by Religions—Parsi—Central India.

TABLE VII.—Ages by Religions.—Part (G). PARSI.

AGENCY.	TOTAL PARSIS.			AGE PERIODS.															
	Total.	Males.	Females.	Under 1 year.		1 year.		2 years.		3 years.		4 years.		Total 0–4.		5–9.		10–14.	
				Males.	Females.	Males.	Females.	Males.	Females.	Males.	Females.	Males.	Females.	Males.	Females.	Males.	Females.	Males.	Females.
1	2	3	4	5	6	7	8	9	10	11	12	13	14	15	16	17	18	19	20
Indore	583	298	285	12	11	6	5	5	13	7	10	6	8	36	47	38	38	34	33
Gwalior	2	2	...	...	...	...	...	...	...	...	...	...	...	...	...	...	...	...	...
Bhopal	36	16	20	...	2	...	...	...	2	1	1	1	2	2	7	1	2	...	3
Bundelkhand	2	2	...	...	...	...	...	...	...	...	...	...	...	...	...	...	...	...	...
Baghelkhand	...	...	...	...	...	...	...	...	...	...	...	...	...	...	...	...	...	...	...
Western Malwa	191	104	87	5	1	2	1	...	5	2	4	3	2	12	13	11	15	16	9
Bhopawar	23	15	8	...	...	...	...	...	...	...	...	...	...	...	...	1	3	1	1
Guna	...	...	...	...	...	...	...	...	...	...	...	...	...	...	...	...	...	...	...
Total	**837**	**437**	**400**	**17**	**14**	**8**	**6**	**5**	**20**	**10**	**15**	**10**	**12**	**50**	**67**	**51**	**58**	**51**	**46**

AGENCY.	AGE PERIODS.																			
	15–19.		20–24.		25–29.		30–34.		35–39.		40–44.		45–49.		50–54.		55–59.		60 and over.	
	Males.	Females.	Males.	Females.	Males.	Females.	Males.	Females.	Males.	Females.	Males.	Females.	Males.	Females.	Males.	Females.	Males.	Females.	Males.	Females.
	21	22	23	24	25	26	27	28	29	30	31	32	33	34	35	36	37	38	39	40
Indore	41	23	38	29	22	21	14	20	23	19	13	9	6	11	15	13	6	6	12	16
Gwalior	...	...	...	...	1	...	...	...	...	...	...	...	1	...	...	...	...	...	...	...
Bhopal	...	...	2	1	3	2	4	1	...	1	2	...	1	...	1	...	...	2	...	1
Bundelkhand	...	...	1	...	...	...	...	...	...	...	...	...	...	...	...	...	...	...	1	...
Baghelkhand	...	...	...	...	...	...	...	...	...	...	...	...	...	...	...	...	...	...	...	...
Western Malwa	7	10	5	5	3	6	13	12	9	4	9	6	4	2	7	...	5	2	3	3
Bhopawar	...	1	...	...	2	...	3	2	3	1	1	...	2	...	1	...	...	...	1	...
Guna	...	...	...	...	...	...	...	...	...	...	...	...	...	...	...	...	...	...	...	...
Total	**48**	**34**	**46**	**35**	**31**	**29**	**34**	**35**	**35**	**25**	**25**	**15**	**14**	**13**	**24**	**13**	**11**	**10**	**17**	**20**

TABLE VII.

Ages by Religions.—Part (H).

SIKH.

TABLE VII.—Ages by Religions.—Part (H). SIKH.

AGENCY.	TOTAL SIKHS.			AGE PERIODS.															
				UNDER 1 YEAR.		1 YEAR.		2 YEARS.		3 YEARS.		4 YEARS.		TOTAL 0—4.		5—9.		10—14.	
	Total.	Males.	Females.	Males.	Females.	Males.	Females.	Males.	Females.	Males.	Females.	Males.	Females.	Males.	Females.	Males.	Females.	Males.	Females.
1	2	3	4	5	6	7	8	9	10	11	12	13	14	15	16	17	18	19	20
INDORE	321	205	116	...	...	1	3	4	5	2	4	1	2	8	14	7	10	13	9
GWALIOR	4	4	...	...	...	...	...	...	...	...	...	...	...	...	...	...	...	...	...
BHOPAL	455	308	147	9	5	3	3	4	7	6	2	3	3	25	20	15	14	15	8
BUNDELKHAND	325	298	27	1	2	...	...	...	...	3	1	1	...	5	3	6	3	8	2
BHAGHELKHAND	61	44	17	3	...	...	...	...	...	...	...	...	...	3	...	3	1	7	2
WESTERN MALWA	303	231	72	6	4	...	...	3	...	1	2	2	2	12	8	10	3	5	8
BHOPAWAR	8	4	4	...	...	...	...	...	...	...	...	...	...	...	...	...	...	1	...
GUNA	348	264	84	2	3	2	1	3	4	3	3	2	3	12	14	16	8	16	9
Total	1,825	1,358	467	21	14	6	7	14	16	15	12	9	10	65	59	57	39	65	38

AGENCY.	AGE PERIODS.																			
	15—19.		20—24.		25—29.		30—34.		35—39.		40—44.		45—49.		50—54.		55—59.		60 AND OVER.	
	Males.	Females.	Males.	Females.	Males.	Females.	Males.	Females.	Males.	Females.	Males.	Females.	Males.	Females.	Males.	Females.	Males.	Females.	Males.	Females.
	21	22	23	24	25	26	27	28	29	30	31	32	33	34	35	36	37	38	39	40
INDORE	22	15	50	16	34	8	28	8	9	2	12	14	5	6	8	3	1	2	8	9
GWALIOR	...	...	1	...	...	...	1	...	...	...	1	...	...	...	1	...	...	...	...	...
BHOPAL	24	15	64	26	55	14	40	18	22	3	18	8	9	3	7	9	2	2	12	7
BUNDELKHAND	82	3	77	8	30	4	32	1	27	...	17	1	5	1	4	1	...	...	5	...
BAGHELKHAND	1	2	7	2	6	4	6	2	...	...	...	...	2	1	2	1	2	2	5	...
WESTERN MALWA	12	9	56	12	56	10	31	15	13	1	13	2	11	1	4	2	2	...	6	1
BHOPAWAR	...	...	1	1	...	...	...	1	...	...	1	1	...	...	1	...	..	...	...	1
GUNA	14	6	55	21	69	9	30	5	22	1	13	4	8	...	7	2	2	2	...	3
Total	155	50	311	86	250	49	168	50	98	7	75	30	40	12	34	18	9	8	36	21

TABLE VII.

Ages by Religions.—Part (I).

JEW.

TABLE VII.—Ages by Religions, Part (I).—JEW.

AGENCY.	TOTAL JEWS.			AGE PERIODS.																
				UNDER 1 YEAR.		1 YEAR.		2 YEARS.		3 YEARS.		4 YEARS.		TOTAL 0–4.		5–9.		10–14.	
	Total.	Males.	Females.	Males.	Females.	Males.	Females.	Males.	Females.	Males.	Females.	Males.	Females.	Males.	Females.	Males.	Females.	Males.	Females.
1	2	3	4	5	6	7	8	9	10	11	12	13	14	15	16	17	18	19	20
INDORE	54	33	21	1	...	2	2	3	1	1	...	2	...	9	3	4	3	3	1
GWALIOR	...	...	...	...	...	...	...	...	...	...	...	...	...	...	...	...	...	...	...
BHOPAL	...	...	...	...	...	...	...	...	...	...	...	...	...	...	...	...	...	...	...
BUNDELKHAND	...	...	...	...	...	...	...	...	...	...	...	...	...	...	...	...	...	...	...
BAGHELKHAND	...	...	...	...	...	...	...	...	...	...	...	...	...	...	...	...	...	...	...
WESTERN MALWA	18	11	7	...	...	...	...	...	...	1	...	...	...	1	...	1	1	2	1
BHOPAWAR	...	...	...	...	...	...	...	...	...	...	...	...	...	...	...	...	...	...	...
GUNA	...	...	...	...	...	...	...	...	...	...	...	...	...	...	...	...	...	...	...
Total	72	44	28	1	...	2	2	3	1	2	...	2	...	10	3	5	4	5	2

AGENCY.	AGE PERIODS.																			
	15–19.		20–24.		25–29.		30–34.		35–39.		40–44.		45–49.		50–54.		55–59.		60 AND OVER.	
	Males.	Females.	Males.	Females.	Males.	Females.	Males.	Females.	Males.	Females.	Males.	Females.	Males.	Females.	Males.	Females.	Males.	Females.	Males.	Females.
	21	22	23	24	25	26	27	28	29	30	31	32	33	34	35	36	37	38	39	40
INDORE	1	4	6	5	2	4	4	...	2	...	1	...	...	...	1	...	...	...	...	1
GWALIOR	...	...	...	...	...	...	...	...	...	...	...	...	...	...	...	...	...	...	...	...
BHOPAL	...	...	...	...	...	...	...	...	...	...	...	...	...	...	...	...	...	...	...	...
BUNDELKHAND	...	...	...	...	...	...	...	...	...	...	...	...	...	...	...	...	...	...	...	...
BAGHELKHAND	...	...	...	...	...	...	...	...	...	...	...	...	...	...	...	...	...	...	...	...
WESTERN MALWA	1	1	...	...	...	1	3	...	...	1	2	1	...	...	...	...	...	...	1	1
BHOPAWAR	...	...	...	...	...	...	...	...	...	...	...	...	...	...	...	...	...	...	...	...
GUNA	...	...	...	...	...	...	...	...	...	...	...	...	...	...	...	...	...	...	...	...
Total	2	5	6	5	2	5	7	...	[illegible]	1	[illegible]	[illegible]			[illegible]				[illegible]	[illegible]

TABLE VIII.

Total Population by Age and Civil Condition.

ALL CONDITIONS.

NOTE.—This Table applies only to persons enumerated on the British India Schedule.

Table VIII.—Total population by Civil Condition—Central India.

TABLE VIII.—Total Population by Age and Civil Condition.

AGENCY.	ALL CONDITIONS.																												
	TOTAL POPULATION.			AGE PERIODS.																									
				0—4.		5—9.		10—14.		15—19.		20—24.		25—29.		30—34.		35—39.		40—44.		45—49.		50—54.		55—59.		60 AND OVER.	
	Total.	Males.	Females.	Males.	Females.	Males.	Females.	Males.	Females.	Males.	Females.	Males.	Females.	Males.	Females.	Males.	Females.	Males.	Females.	Males.	Females.	Males.	Females.	Males.	Females.	Males.	Females.	Males.	Females.
1	2	3	4	5	6	7	8	9	10	11	12	13	14	15	16	17	18	19	20	21	22	23	24	25	26	27	28	29	30
INDORE	43,358	25,854	17,504	2,397	2,474	2,266	2,220	2,031	1,580	1,763	1,549	3,427	1,942	3,543	1,771	3,057	1,539	1,882	818	1,986	1,114	878	443	1,138	740	320	226	1,166	1,088
GWALIOR	4,703	2,782	1,921	244	255	262	222	258	173	210	175	323	205	390	200	327	202	199	101	202	130	105	43	120	98	62	30	80	87
BHOPAL	11,881	6,647	5,234	757	743	633	699	599	453	506	417	732	505	782	557	787	498	475	267	480	377	278	162	310	233	87	49	221	274
BUNDELKHAND	11,079	7,077	4,002	620	592	617	561	534	369	618	313	1,114	402	943	413	821	412	482	186	507	295	255	84	308	171	73	34	185	170
BAGHELKHAND	6,426	4,437	1,989	255	294	217	257	260	154	356	173	647	259	893	278	723	207	363	88	332	98	129	42	156	66	41	23	65	50
WESTERN MALWA	21,734	12,979	8,755	1,254	1,284	1,164	1,119	975	736	1,024	663	1,697	872	1,859	883	1,577	850	962	556	952	599	449	296	468	360	180	122	418	415
BHOPAWAR	3,152	1,760	1,392	214	216	176	200	139	119	152	124	164	147	211	164	264	150	180	81	122	107	51	16	22	20	5	3	60	45
GUNA	4,693	2,729	1,964	269	257	264	247	239	161	252	186	334	179	356	194	304	202	188	97	192	158	88	62	119	102	36	29	88	90
Total	107,026	64,265	42,761	6,010	6,115	5,599	5,525	5,035	3,745	4,881	3,600	8,438	4,511	8,977	4,460	7,860	4,060	4,731	2,194	4,772	2,878	2,233	1,148	2,641	1,790	804	516	2,283	2,219

TABLE VIII.

Civil Condition by Religion and Age.— Part (A).

TOTAL POPULATION.

(1) UNMARRIED

(2) MARRIED.

(3) WIDOWED.

NOTE.—This Table applies only to persons enumerated on the British India Schedule.

TABLE VIII.—Civil Condition by Religion and Age.—Part (A). TOTAL POPULATION.

AGENCY.	Total Unmarried. Total.	Total Unmarried. Males.	Total Unmarried. Females.	0–4 Males.	0–4 Females.	5–9 Males.	5–9 Females.	10–14 Males.	10–14 Females.	15–19 Males.	15–19 Females.	20–24 Males.	20–24 Females.	25–29 Males.	25–29 Females.	30–34 Males.	30–34 Females.	35–39 Males.	35–39 Females.	40–44 Males.	40–44 Females.	45–49 Males.	45–49 Females.	50–54 Males.	50–54 Females.	55–59 Males.	55–59 Females.	60 and over. Males.	60 and over. Females.
1	2	3	4	5	6	7	8	9	10	11	12	13	14	15	16	17	18	19	20	21	22	23	24	25	26	27	28	29	30
(1) UNMARRIED.																													
Indore	17,275	11,602	5,673	2,389	2,445	2,232	2,091	1,845	838	1,132	143	1,830	59	1,237	30	456	16	158	14	161	14	62	...	46	6	13	6	41	11
Gwalior	1,749	1,193	556	241	253	249	199	207	70	106	12	138	4	131	4	52	6	30	2	11	1	13	1	9	3	3	...	3	1
Bhopal	4,689	2,918	1,771	756	739	627	671	544	271	311	37	306	13	171	13	92	7	36	3	43	8	13	3	8	2	3	1	8	3
Bundelkhand	4,433	3,048	1,385	620	590	606	533	456	202	363	25	520	12	291	9	98	6	36	...	17	4	15	...	13	3	6	...	7	1
Baghelkhand	1,953	1,306	647	252	293	214	237	216	90	168	12	173	9	150	3	74	2	26	1	22	...	6	...	2	...	1	...	2	...
Western Malwa	8,151	5,373	2,778	1,250	1,267	1,114	1,017	806	360	599	60	707	19	468	21	209	10	92	5	57	9	34	3	19	7	4	...	14	...
Bhopawar	1,236	738	498	213	213	175	193	129	77	84	9	56	1	30	2	22	1	13	2	9	...	6	...	1	...	...	...	...	...
Guna	1,629	1,078	551	247	237	235	200	178	86	135	19	102	4	63	2	55	2	28	...	17	...	7	...	9	...	...	...	2	1
Total	**41,115**	**27,256**	**18,859**	**5,968**	**6,087**	**5,452**	**5,141**	**4,881**	**1,994**	**2,898**	**317**	**3,832**	**121**	**2,541**	**84**	**1,058**	**50**	**419**	**27**	**337**	**36**	**156**	**7**	**107**	**21**	**30**	**7**	**77**	**17**
(2) MARRIED.																													
Indore	21,797	12,774	9,023	5	22	31	122	180	730	610	1,363	1,544	1,797	2,179	1,603	2,434	1,313	1,580	634	1,602	688	721	252	893	272	235	71	760	156
Gwalior	2,371	1,391	980	3	2	13	23	51	101	102	156	176	184	239	166	247	156	153	72	158	67	75	19	79	23	44	1	51	10
Bhopal	5,854	3,280	2,574	1	4	6	27	54	174	190	368	405	464	570	499	620	418	396	208	384	230	226	77	240	78	52	13	136	14
Bundelkhand	5,754	3,686	2,068	...	2	11	28	77	166	249	282	570	368	618	371	676	354	410	159	449	196	210	51	248	56	52	12	116	23
Baghelkhand	3,994	2,931	1,063	3	1	3	20	42	63	186	145	457	232	714	241	609	167	319	71	280	63	104	21	128	25	34	8	52	6
Western Malwa	11,621	6,930	4,691	4	16	46	101	164	372	414	585	953	816	1,317	807	1,286	744	811	450	792	383	362	158	356	139	144	45	281	75
Bhopawar	1,706	936	770	1	3	1	7	10	41	68	115	103	144	177	159	234	139	157	69	88	70	41	8	17	8	4	...	35	7
Guna	2,446	1,420	1,026	...	3	5	23	38	70	106	160	214	169	275	177	224	162	145	73	158	98	71	30	92	39	30	13	62	9
Total	**55,543**	**33,348**	**22,195**	**17**	**58**	**116**	**351**	**616**	**1,717**	**1,925**	**3,174**	**4,422**	**4,174**	**6,089**	**4,028**	**6,330**	**3,453**	**3,971**	**1,736**	**3,911**	**1,795**	**1,810**	**616**	**2,058**	**640**	**595**	**168**	**1,493**	**300**
(3) WIDOWED.																													
Indore	4,286	1,478	2,808	3	7	3	7	6	12	21	43	53	86	127	138	167	210	144	170	223	412	95	191	199	462	72	149	365	921
Gwalior	583	198	385	...	...	...	...	...	2	2	7	9	17	20	30	28	49	16	27	33	62	17	23	32	72	15	29	26	76
Bhopal	1,338	449	889	...	...	...	1	1	8	5	12	21	28	41	45	75	73	43	56	53	139	39	82	62	153	32	35	77	257
Bundelkhand	892	343	549	...	...	...	...	1	1	6	6	24	22	34	33	47	53	36	27	41	95	30	33	47	112	15	22	62	146
Baghelkhand	479	200	279	...	...	...	...	2	1	2	16	17	18	29	34	40	38	18	16	30	35	19	21	26	41	6	15	11	44
Western Malwa	1,962	676	1,286	...	1	4	1	5	4	11	18	37	37	74	55	82	96	59	101	103	207	53	135	93	214	32	77	123	340
Bhopawar	210	86	124	...	...	...	...	...	1	...	...	5	2	4	3	8	10	10	10	25	37	4	8	4	12	1	3	25	38
Guna	618	231	387	22	17	24	24	23	5	11	7	18	6	18	15	25	38	15	24	17	60	10	32	18	63	6	16	24	80
Total	**10,368**	**3,661**	**6,707**	**25**	**25**	**31**	[illegible]	**38**	**34**	**58**	**109**	**184**	**216**	**347**	**353**	**472**	**557**	**341**	**431**	**525**	**1,047**	**267**	**525**	**481**	**1,129**	**179**	**346**	**713**	**1,902**

TABLE VIII.

Civil Condition by Religion and Age.— Part (B).

HINDU.

(1) UNMARRIED.

(2) MARRIED.

(3) WIDOWED.

NOTE.—This Table applies only to persons enumerated on the British India Schedule.

TABLE VIII.—Civil Condition by Religion and Age.—Part (B). HINDU.

AGENCY.	Total Unmarried.			Age Period. 0–4		5–9		10–14		15–19		20–24		25–29		30–34		35–39		40–44		45–49		50–54		55–59		60 and over.	
	Total.	Males.	Females.	Males.	Females.	Males.	Females.	Males.	Females.	Males.	Females.	Males.	Females.	Males.	Females.	Males.	Females.	Males.	Females.	Males.	Females.	Males.	Females.	Males.	Females.	Males.	Females.	Males.	Females.
1	2	3	4	5	6	7	8	9	10	11	12	13	14	15	16	17	18	19	20	21	22	23	24	25	26	27	28	29	30
(1) UNMARRIED.																													
Indore	10,071	6,486	3,585	1,533	1,608	1,491	1,388	1,209	456	677	57	579	31	454	13	241	7	82	10	112	6	41	...	32	2	7	2	28	5
Gwalior	1,193	799	394	190	187	185	155	147	42	80	4	67	1	45	2	36	2	23	1	8	...	8	...	6	...	2	...	2	...
Bhopal	3,418	2,122	1,296	578	561	481	512	409	196	228	15	180	5	105	2	64	1	23	...	32	2	8	1	4	...	3	...	7	1
Bundelkhand	2,495	1,610	885	408	404	410	349	294	108	189	11	116	4	81	3	53	3	21	...	13	...	9	...	11	2	1	...	4	1
Baghelkhand	1,349	932	417	185	203	133	152	150	55	115	5	130	1	116	...	61	1	18	...	15	...	5	...	2	...	...	...	2	...
Western Malwa	5,231	3,424	1,807	835	837	740	685	546	225	391	30	372	6	254	7	139	5	50	1	47	5	21	2	14	4	3	...	12	...
Bhopawar	611	384	227	87	87	96	99	74	36	48	3	28	...	14	...	18	1	9	1	5	...	5	...	...	...	...	...	...	...
Guna	1,144	740	404	177	171	172	152	124	59	95	15	67	3	35	1	28	2	15	...	14	...	6	...	6	...	...	...	1	1
Total	**25,512**	**16,497**	**9,015**	**3,993**	**4,058**	**3,708**	**3,492**	**2,953**	**1,177**	**1,823**	**140**	**1,539**	**51**	**1,104**	**28**	**640**	**22**	**241**	**18**	**246**	**18**	**103**	**8**	**75**	**8**	**16**	**2**	**56**	**8**
(2) MARRIED.																													
Indore	15,256	9,175	6,081	5	16	24	88	136	542	453	963	1,177	1,193	1,641	1,052	1,759	886	1,126	400	1,128	450	496	166	597	179	142	46	491	100
Gwalior	1,840	1,082	758	2	1	12	18	49	80	87	129	142	149	185	125	203	110	111	53	113	52	52	12	58	19	28	1	40	9
Bhopal	4,474	2,473	2,001	...	3	4	22	42	142	150	285	306	363	412	388	456	314	312	159	288	184	168	60	195	60	33	10	107	11
Bundelkhand	3,714	2,356	1,358	...	1	7	20	55	125	169	173	370	250	397	243	403	222	253	99	274	127	136	36	157	37	34	10	81	15
Baghelkhand	3,014	2,256	758	3	...	2	14	34	47	160	115	373	166	577	174	443	107	239	51	212	41	74	17	87	19	17	3	35	4
Western Malwa	8,070	4,858	3,212	3	8	34	65	121	266	302	388	671	570	917	539	919	522	575	298	560	267	238	111	241	94	93	30	184	54
Bhopawar	763	419	344	...	3	1	5	9	33	26	54	49	44	59	56	85	50	59	36	60	42	28	8	10	7	4	...	29	6
Guna	1,676	911	765	...	3	5	22	26	52	71	121	126	122	154	135	143	118	92	57	114	78	51	16	66	30	18	6	45	5
Total	**38,807**	**23,530**	**15,277**	**13**	**35**	**89**	**254**	**472**	**1,287**	**1,418**	**2,228**	**3,214**	**2,857**	**4,342**	**2,712**	**4,431**	**2,329**	**2,767**	**1,158**	**2,749**	**1,241**	**1,243**	**426**	**1,411**	**445**	**369**	**106**	**1,012**	**204**
(3) WIDOWED.																													
Indore	3,002	1,014	1,988	2	7	3	7	4	9	14	31	32	69	89	99	110	151	100	121	177	307	71	138	127	315	49	94	236	649
Gwalior	472	165	307	...	...	...	...	...	2	2	4	9	12	15	25	25	31	13	24	23	54	13	19	28	52	15	24	22	60
Bhopal	1,039	333	706	...	...	...	1	...	6	4	8	15	25	30	36	56	70	32	44	38	110	28	66	39	118	26	26	65	196
Bundelkhand	579	236	343	...	...	...	...	1	1	5	5	13	10	28	22	28	32	18	21	31	64	23	21	33	70	13	8	43	89
Baghelkhand	358	148	210	...	...	...	...	...	1	2	12	14	16	24	34	30	28	13	9	24	24	15	12	15	32	4	10	7	32
Western Malwa	1,389	481	908	...	...	3	...	2	4	8	14	30	30	49	39	60	65	47	69	75	155	36	92	62	153	21	55	88	232
Bhopawar	153	64	89	...	...	...	...	...	...	...	...	2	2	4	3	5	7	8	9	21	24	3	6	3	7	...	2	18	29
Guna	501	184	317	19	17	22	23	17	4	8	7	13	6	13	12	21	31	13	20	11	47	7	25	14	46	5	10	21	69
Total	**7,493**	**2,625**	**4,868**	**21**	**24**	**28**	**31**	**24**	**27**	**43**	**81**	**128**	**161**	**252**	**270**	**335**	**415**	**244**	**317**	**400**	**785**	**196**	**379**	**3 1**	**793**	**133**	**229**	**500**	**1,356**

TABLE VIII.

Civil Condition by Religion and Age.
Part (C).

MUSALMAN.

(1) UNMARRIED.

(2) MARRIED.

(3) WIDOWED.

NOTE.—This Table applies only to persons enumerated on the British India Schedule.

TABLE VIII.—Civil Condition by Religion and Age.—Part (C). MUSALMAN.

AGENCY.	Total Unmarried.			Age Period. 0—4		5—9		10—14		15—19		20—24		25—29		30—34		35—39		40—44		45—49		50—54		55—59		60 and over.	
	Total.	Males.	Females.	Males.	Females.	Males.	Females.	Males.	Females.	Males.	Females.	Males.	Females.	Males.	Females.	Males.	Females.	Males.	Females.	Males.	Females.	Males.	Females.	Males.	Females.	Males.	Females.	Males.	Females.
1	2	3	4	5	6	7	8	9	10	11	12	13	14	15	16	17	18	19	20	21	22	23	24	25	26	27	8	29	30
(1) UNMARRIED.																													
Indore	4,215	2,648	1,567	634	620	583	571	511	291	321	38	233	9	148	11	101	9	48	1	32	5	13	...	12	4	3	2	9	6
Gwalior	344	225	119	43	51	57	33	47	19	24	5	22	...	11	2	10	3	2	...	2	1	3	1	2	3	1	...	1	1
Bhopal	1,053	632	421	152	152	133	145	123	73	70	16	75	8	39	9	18	4	11	3	5	4	2	2	3	2	...	1	1	2
Bundelkhand	1,266	817	449	180	167	180	166	150	89	109	11	97	6	56	3	25	3	5	...	4	3	3	...	1	1	4	...	3	...
Baghelkhand	408	262	146	44	62	62	56	43	16	42	4	33	5	22	1	8	1	5	1	3	...	...	...	...	...	...	...	...	...
Western Malwa	2,153	1,350	803	348	369	307	281	217	107	163	13	155	9	82	9	34	4	27	3	6	4	6	1	2	3	1	...	2	...
Bhopawar	74	48	26	5	10	13	9	9	7	7	...	6	...	5	...	2	...	1	...	...	...	...	...	...	...	...	...	...	...
Guna	345	235	110	57	49	45	36	43	20	30	3	19	1	9	1	17	...	10	...	3	...	1	...	1	...	...	...	...	...
Total	9,858	6,217	3,641	1,463	1,480	1,380	1,297	1,143	622	766	90	640	38	372	36	215	24	109	8	55	17	28	4	21	13	9	3	16	9
(2) MARRIED.																													
Indore	5,248	2,894	2,354	...	6	7	33	39	164	138	340	319	473	412	420	531	327	345	174	379	207	176	70	249	79	72	16	227	45
Gwalior	424	252	172	1	1	1	5	2	16	10	21	32	30	43	32	38	34	31	15	35	12	21	4	16	1	15	...	7	1
Bhopal	1,138	647	491	...	...	1	5	10	31	25	69	75	80	133	94	130	87	58	47	86	42	44	15	40	16	16	2	29	3
Bundelkhand	1,749	1,110	639	...	1	4	7	21	40	54	105	154	96	184	110	212	120	129	56	150	63	62	12	89	19	17	2	34	8
Baghelkhand	805	573	232	...	1	1	6	7	13	22	25	79	52	117	48	140	42	67	15	55	16	22	3	32	6	15	4	16	1
Western Malwa	2,913	1,664	1,249	1	5	11	34	43	98	97	175	219	206	319	216	289	183	186	125	187	94	89	40	94	40	40	13	89	20
Bhopawar	108	65	43	...	...	...	2	...	1	4	9	7	12	13	8	11	6	14	1	9	4	3	...	...	...	...	...	4	...
Guna	519	322	197	...	...	...	1	6	13	29	31	43	24	67	30	57	37	34	14	29	16	12	12	20	9	11	6	14	4
Total	12,904	7,527	5,377	2	14	25	98	128	376	379	775	928	978	1,288	958	1,408	836	864	447	980	454	429	156	540	170	186	48	420	82
(3) WIDOWED.																													
Indore	1,068	393	675	...	...	...	...	1	3	5	10	21	23	31	29	51	48	38	37	35	82	18	44	62	123	16	43	115	233
Gwalior	82	24	58	...	...	...	...	...	...	...	3	...	5	4	3	2	7	3	2	8	5	2	3	2	14	...	2	3	14
Bhopal	254	88	166	...	...	...	...	1	2	1	4	5	3	8	9	14	3	8	10	12	26	8	15	15	30	5	6	11	58
Bundelkhand	290	94	196	...	...	...	...	...	...	1	1	6	12	5	11	16	19	16	6	9	31	7	11	14	38	2	14	18	53
Baghelkhand	90	36	54	...	...	...	...	1	...	...	2	3	2	4	...	6	6	4	7	2	9	2	6	10	8	1	4	3	10
Western Malwa	503	173	330	...	...	1	1	3	...	3	4	7	7	25	12	21	27	8	30	22	46	13	38	28	52	9	17	33	96
Bhopawar	24	9	15	...	...	...	...	...	1	...	...	...	...	...	...	1	2	1	...	1	3	...	1	1	2	1	...	4	6
Guna	83	36	47	3	...	2	1	5	1	3	...	2	...	3	...	1	5	1	1	5	11	3	5	4	11	1	4	3	8
Total	2,394	853	1,541	3	...	3	2	11	7	13	24	44	52	80	6	112	117	79	93	94	213	53	123	186	278	85	90	190	478

TABLE VIII.

Civil Condition by Religion and Age.
Part (D).

JAIN.

(1) UNMARRIED.

(2) MARRIED.

(3) WIDOWED.

NOTE.—This Table applies only to persons enumerated on the British India Schedule.

Table VIII.—Civil Condition by Religion—Jain—Central India.

TABLE VIII.—Civil Condition by Religion and Age.—Part (D). JAIN.

AGENCY.	Total Unmarried.			Age Period.																									
				0—4		5—9		10—14		15—19		20—24		25—29		30—34		35—39		40—44		45—49		50—54		55—59		60 and over.	
	Total.	Males.	Females.	Males.	Females.	Males.	Females.	Males.	Females.	Males.	Females.	Males.	Females.	Males.	Females.	Males.	Females.	Males	Females.	Males.	Females.	Males.	Females.	Males.	Females.	Males.	Females.	Males.	Females.
1	2	3	4	5	6	7	8	9	10	11	12	13	14	15	16	17	18	19	20	21	22	23	24	25	26	27	28	29	30
(1) UNMARRIED.																													
Indore	104	78	26	11	15	16	5	16	6	4	...	12	...	6	...	6	...	3	...	2	...	1	...	...	...	1	...	...	...
Gwalior	55	35	20	3	6	4	7	12	6	2	...	4	1	2	...	5	...	3	...	...	...	...	...	...	...	...	...	...	...
Bhopal	49	33	16	8	8	3	5	6	...	3	...	3	...	2	...	2	2	...	...	5	1	...	...	1	...	...	...	...	...
Bundelkhand	14	12	2	5	...	4	2	2	...	1	...	...	...	...	...	...	...	...	...	...	...	...	...	...	...	...	...	...	...
Baghelkhand	...	...	...	...	...	...	...	...	...	...	...	...	...	...	...	...	...	...	...	...	...	...	...	...	...	...	...	...	...
Western Malwa	84	60	24	9	13	17	9	9	2	5	...	6	...	6	...	4	...	1	...	1	...	1	...	1	...	...	...	...	...
Bhopawar	...	...	...	...	...	...	...	...	...	...	...	...	...	...	...	...	...	...	...	...	...	...	...	...	...	...	...	...	...
Guna	27	17	10	2	3	3	4	3	2	1	1	3	...	2	...	1	...	1	...	...	...	...	...	1	...	...	...	...	...
Total	**333**	**235**	**98**	**38**	**45**	**47**	**32**	**48**	**16**	**16**	**1**	**28**	**1**	**18**	...	**18**	**2**	**8**	...	**8**	**1**	**2**	...	**3**	...	**1**	...	...	...
(2) MARRIED.																													
Indore	176	100	76	...	...	...	...	5	14	9	15	6	7	14	13	14	10	12	2	13	7	8	2	8	1	1	3	10	2
Gwalior	67	34	33	...	...	...	...	...	5	5	4	1	4	5	5	4	9	8	...	5	2	...	3	4	1	...	...	2	...
Bhopal	71	43	28	...	1	1	...	2	1	5	7	6	4	4	8	11	3	7	1	1	2	3	...	2	1	1	...	...	...
Bundelkhand	27	16	11	...	...	...	1	...	1	1	1	3	3	3	...	3	4	2	...	1	...	1	1	1	...	1	...	...	...
Baghelkhand	...	...	...	...	...	...	...	...	...	...	...	...	...	...	...	...	...	...	...	...	...	...	...	...	...	...	...	...	...
Western Malwa	180	109	71	...	1	1	2	...	3	9	6	15	10	13	13	14	14	14	9	14	6	11	4	8	3	5	...	5	...
Bhopawar	...	...	...	...	...	...	...	...	...	...	...	...	...	...	...	...	...	...	...	...	...	...	...	...	...	...	...	...	...
Guna	31	15	16	...	...	...	...	...	1	...	2	3	4	3	4	3	1	...	1	2	1	...	2	1	...	1	...	2	...
Total	**552**	**317**	**235**	...	**2**	**2**	**8**	**7**	**25**	**29**	**35**	**34**	**32**	**42**	**43**	**49**	**41**	**43**	**18**	**36**	**18**	**23**	**12**	**24**	**6**	**9**	**8**	**19**	**2**
(3) WIDOWED.																													
Indore	68	21	47	...	...	...	...	...	...	1	1	...	2	...	3	3	6	...	...	4	11	4	1	3	8	3	6	3	9
Gwalior	27	9	18	...	...	...	...	...	...	...	...	...	...	1	2	1	2	...	1	2	3	2	1	2	6	...	2	1	1
Bhopal	27	13	14	...	...	...	...	...	...	...	...	...	...	1	...	...	...	2	2	...	2	2	1	6	3	1	3	1	3
Bundelkhand	10	1	9	...	...	...	...	...	...	...	...	...	...	...	...	...	1	...	...	...	...	...	1	...	3	...	...	1	4
Baghelkhand	...	...	...	...	...	...	...	...	...	...	...	...	...	...	...	...	...	...	...	...	...	...	...	...	...	...	...	...	...
Western Malwa	33	6	27	...	1	...	...	...	...	...	...	...	...	...	2	...	3	1	1	1	6	2	2	...	5	2	3	...	4
Bhopawar	...	...	...	...	...	...	...	...	...	...	...	...	...	...	...	...	...	...	...	...	...	...	...	...	...	...	...	...	...
Guna	18	3	15	...	...	...	...	1	...	...	...	...	...	1	3	...	2	1	3	...	1	...	2	...	3	...	1	...	...
Total	**183**	**53**	**130**	...	**1**	...	...	**1**	...	**1**	**1**	...	**2**	**3**	**10**	**4**	**14**	**4**	**7**	**7**	**23**	**10**	**8**	**11**	**28**	**6**	**15**	**6**	**21**

TABLE VIII.

Civil Condition by Religion and Age.
Part (E).

ABORIGINAL.

(1) UNMARRIED.

(2) MARRIED.

(3) WIDOWED.

NOTE.—This Table applies only to persons enumerated on the British India Schedule.

TABLE VIII.—Civil Condition by Religion and Age.—Part (E). ABORIGINAL.

AGENCY.	Total Unmarried. Total.	Total Unmarried. Males.	Total Unmarried. Females.	0—4 Males.	0—4 Females.	5—9 Males.	5—9 Females.	10—14 Males.	10—14 Females.	15—19 Males.	15—19 Females.	20—24 Males.	20—24 Females.	25—29 Males.	25—29 Females.	30—34 Males.	30—34 Females.	35—39 Males.	35—39 Females.	40—44 Males.	40—44 Females.	45—49 Males.	45—49 Females.	50—54 Males.	50—54 Females.	55—59 Males.	55—59 Females.	60 and over. Males.	60 and over. Females.
1	2	3	4	5	6	7	8	9	10	11	12	13	14	15	16	17	18	19	20	21	22	23	24	25	26	27	28	29	30
(1) UNMARRIED.																													
Indore	2	2	...	...	...	...	...	...	...	...	...	1	...	1	...	...	...	...	...	...	...	...	...	...	...	...	...	...	...
Gwalior	...	...	...	...	...	...	...	...	...	...	...	...	...	...	...	...	...	...	...	...	...	...	...	...	...	...	...	...	...
Bhopal	...	...	...	...	...	...	...	...	...	...	...	...	...	...	...	...	...	...	...	...	...	...	...	...	...	...	...	...	...
Bundelkhand	...	...	...	...	...	...	...	...	...	...	...	...	...	...	...	...	...	...	...	...	...	...	...	...	...	...	...	...	...
Baghelkhand	83	47	36	9	10	9	17	16	9	3	...	2	...	5	...	2	...	...	...	1	...	...	...	...	...	...	...	...	...
Western Malwa	...	...	...	...	...	...	...	...	...	...	...	...	...	...	...	...	...	...	...	...	...	...	...	...	...	...	...	...	...
Bhopawar	453	300	243	121	116	66	83	45	34	29	6	22	1	10	2	1	...	2	1	4	...	...	...	...	...	...	...	...	...
Guna	...	...	...	...	...	...	...	...	...	...	...	...	...	...	...	...	...	...	...	...	...	...	...	...	...	...	...	...	...
Total	**628**	**349**	**279**	**130**	**126**	**75**	**100**	**61**	**43**	**32**	**6**	**25**	**1**	**16**	**2**	**3**	...	**2**	**1**	**5**	...	...	...	...	...	...	...	...	...
(2) MARRIED.																													
Indore	...	...	...	...	...	...	...	...	...	...	...	...	...	...	...	...	...	...	...	...	...	...	...	...	...	...	...	...	...
Gwalior	...	...	...	...	...	...	...	...	...	...	...	...	...	...	...	...	...	...	...	...	...	...	...	...	...	...	...	...	...
Bhopal	...	...	...	...	...	...	...	...	...	...	...	...	...	...	...	...	...	...	...	...	...	...	...	...	...	...	...	...	...
Bundelkhand	...	...	...	...	...	...	...	...	...	...	...	...	...	...	...	...	...	...	...	...	...	...	...	...	...	...	...	...	...
Baghelkhand	90	58	32	...	...	...	...	1	3	3	3	3	4	11	10	15	9	10	2	11	...	2	1	2	...	...	...	...	...
Western Malwa	...	...	...	...	...	...	...	...	...	...	...	...	...	...	...	...	...	...	...	...	...	...	...	...	...	...	...	...	...
Bhopawar	823	444	379	1	...	...	...	1	7	37	51	47	86	104	95	136	83	81	32	19	24	10	...	6	...	...	...	2	1
Guna	...	...	...	...	...	...	...	...	...	...	...	...	...	...	...	...	...	...	...	...	...	...	...	...	...	...	...	...	...
Total	**913**	**502**	**411**	**1**	...	...	...	**2**	**10**	**40**	**54**	**50**	**90**	**115**	**105**	**151**	**92**	**91**	**34**	**30**	**24**	**12**	**1**	**8**	...	...	...	**2**	**1**
(3) WIDOWED.																													
Indore	...	...	...	...	...	...	...	...	...	...	...	...	...	...	...	...	...	...	...	...	...	...	...	...	...	...	...	...	...
Gwalior	...	...	...	...	...	...	...	...	...	...	...	...	...	...	...	...	...	...	...	...	...	...	...	...	...	...	...	...	...
Bhopal	...	...	...	...	...	...	...	...	...	...	...	...	...	...	...	...	...	...	...	...	...	...	...	...	...	...	...	...	...
Bundelkhand	...	...	...	...	...	...	...	...	...	...	...	...	...	...	...	...	...	...	...	...	...	...	...	...	...	...	...	...	...
Baghelkhand	16	7	9	...	...	...	...	1	...	...	2	...	...	1	...	2	4	1	...	1	...	1	1	...	...	...	1	...	1
Western Malwa	...	...	...	...	...	...	...	...	...	...	...	...	...	...	...	...	...	...	...	...	...	...	...	...	...	...	...	...	...
Bhopawar	33	13	20	...	...	...	...	...	...	...	...	3	...	...	...	2	1	1	1	3	10	1	1	...	3	...	1	3	3
Guna	...	...	...	...	...	...	...	...	...	...	...	...	...	...	...	...	...	...	...	...	...	...	...	...	...	...	...	...	...
Total	**49**	**20**	**29**	...	...	...	...	**1**	...	...	**2**	**3**	...	**1**	...	**4**	**5**	**2**	**1**	**4**	**10**	**2**	**2**	...	**3**	...	**2**	**3**	**4**

Table VIII.—Civil Condition by Religion—Aborigina—Central India.

TABLE VIII.

Civil Condition by Religion and Age.

Part (F).

CHRISTIAN.

(1) UNMARRIED.

(2) MARRIED.

(3) WIDOWED.

NOTE.—This Table applies only to persons enumerated on the British India Schedule.

TABLE VIII.—Civil Condition by Religion and Age.—Part (F). CHRISTIAN.

AGENCY.	Total Unmarried.			Age Period. 0—4.		5—9.		10—14.		15—19.		20—24.		25—29.		30—34.		35—39.		40—44.		45—49.		50—54.		55—59.		60 and over.	
	Total.	Males.	Females.	Males.	Females.	Males.	Females.	Males.	Females.	Males.	Females.	Males.	Females.	Males.	Females.	Males.	Females.	Males.	Females.	Males.	Females.	Males.	Females.	Males.	Females.	Males.	Females.	Males.	Females.
1	2	3	4	5	6	7	8	9	10	11	12	13	14	15	16	17	18	19	20	21	22	23	24	25	26	27	28	29	30
(1) UNMARRIED.																													
Indore	2,527	2,173	354	167	152	99	86	70	57	90	31	967	15	621	5	106	...	25	3	15	3	7	...	1	...	2	2	3	...
Gwalior	157	134	23	5	9	3	4	1	3	...	3	45	2	73	...	1	1	2	1	1	...	2	...	1	...	...	...	...	...
Bhopal	50	28	22	8	6	3	5	3	2	3	6	6	...	2	2	2	...	1	...	...	1	...	...	...	...	...	...	...	...
Bundelkhand	552	507	45	23	17	9	14	5	5	11	3	275	2	150	3	19	...	10	...	...	1	3	...	1	...	1	...	...	...
Baghelkhand	113	65	48	14	18	10	12	7	10	8	3	8	3	7	2	3	...	3	...	3	...	1	...	...	...	1	...	...	...
Western Malwa	535	439	96	38	33	32	27	15	17	27	11	154	2	120	4	31	1	13	1	2	...	5	...	2	...	...	...	...	...
Bhopawar	8	6	2	...	...	...	2	1	...	...	...	...	...	1	...	1	...	1	...	...	...	1	...	1	...	...	...	...	...
Guna	14	13	1	...	1	1	...	...	...	1	...	3	...	3	...	3	...	1	...	...	...	...	...	...	...	...	...	1	...
Total	**3,956**	**3,365**	**591**	**255**	**236**	**157**	**150**	**102**	**94**	**140**	**57**	**1,458**	**24**	**977**	**16**	**166**	**2**	**56**	**5**	**21**	**5**	**19**	...	**6**	...	**4**	**2**	**4**	...
(2) MARRIED.																													
Indore	833	455	378	...	...	...	1	...	3	...	34	20	92	85	95	109	70	75	40	66	19	35	8	26	6	15	4	24	6
Gwalior	40	23	17	...	...	...	...	...	...	...	2	1	1	6	4	2	3	3	4	5	1	2	...	1	2	1	...	2	...
Bhopal	44	23	21	...	...	...	...	...	...	1	4	2	4	3	3	3	5	5	1	1	2	6	1	1	1	1	...	...	...
Bundelkhand	95	49	46	...	...	...	...	...	...	...	1	6	13	11	14	12	7	2	4	10	5	8	2	...	...	...	...	...	...
Baghelkhand	85	44	41	...	...	...	...	...	...	1	2	2	10	9	9	11	9	3	3	2	6	6	...	7	...	2	1	1	1
Western Malwa	199	114	85	...	1	...	...	...	2	1	6	8	17	17	26	26	7	21	13	17	9	12	1	9	2	3	1	...	...
Bhopawar	12	8	4	...	...	...	...	...	...	1	1	...	2	1	...	2	...	3	...	...	...	...	...	1	1	...	...	...	...
Guna	2	1	1	...	...	...	...	...	...	...	...	...	...	...	...	...	1	...	...	1	...	...	...	...	...	...	...	...	...
Total	**1,310**	**717**	**593**	...	**1**	...	**1**	...	**5**	**4**	**50**	**39**	**189**	**182**	**151**	**165**	**102**	**112**	**65**	**102**	**42**	**69**	**12**	**45**	**12**	**22**	**6**	**27**	**7**
(3) WIDOWED.																													
Indore	92	34	58	...	...	...	...	...	...	...	...	...	...	6	6	3	3	3	11	6	8	2	3	4	10	2	2	8	15
Gwalior	2	...	2	...	...	...	...	...	...	...	...	...	...	...	...	...	...	...	...	...	...	...	...	...	...	...	1	...	1
Bhopal	4	3	1	...	...	...	...	...	...	...	...	...	...	...	...	2	...	...	...	...	...	...	...	1	1	...	...	...	...
Bundelkhand	5	4	1	...	...	...	...	...	...	...	...	...	...	1	...	2	...	1	...	...	...	...	...	...	1	...	...	—	...
Baghelkhand	15	9	6	...	...	...	...	...	...	...	...	...	...	...	...	2	...	...	...	3	2	1	2	1	1	1	...	1	1
Western Malwa	17	6	11	...	...	...	...	...	...	...	...	...	...	...	...	...	...	2	...	3	...	1	3	...	2	...	1	...	5
Bhopawar	...	...	...	...	...	...	...	...	...	...	...	...	...	...	...	...	...	...	...	...	...	...	...	...	...	...	...	...	...
Guna	2	1	1	...	...	...	...	...	...	...	...	...	...	...	...	...	...	...	...	1	...	...	...	...	1	...	...	...	...
Total	**137**	**57**	**80**	...	...	...	...	...	...	...	...	...	...	**7**	**6**	**9**	**3**	**6**	**11**	**13**	**10**	**4**	**8**	**6**	**16**	**3**	**4**	**9**	**22**

TABLE VIII.

Civil Condition by Religion and Age.— Part (G).

PARSI.

(1) UNMARRIED.

(2) MARRIED.

(3) WIDOWED.

NOTE.—This Table applies only to persons enumerated on the British India Schedule.

Table VIII.—Civil Condition by Religion—Parsi—Central India.

TABLE VIII.—Civil Condition by Religion and Age.—Part (G). PARSI.

AGENCY.	Total Unmarried.			0—4		5—9		10—14		15—19		20—24		25—29		30—34		35—39		40—44		45—49		50—54		55—59		60 and over.	
	Total.	Males.	Females.	Males.	Females.	Males.	Females.	Males.	Females.	Males.	Females.	Males.	Females.	Males.	Females.	Males.	Females.	Males.	Females.	Males.	Females.	Males.	Females.	Males.	Females.	Males.	Females.	Males.	Females.
1	2	3	4	5	6	7	8	9	10	11	12	13	14	15	16	17	18	19	20	21	22	23	24	25	26	27	28	29	30
(1) UNMARRIED.																													
Indore	308	174	134	35	47	38	38	33	28	35	16	28	4	2	1	1	...	...	...	...	...	...	...	1	...	...	...	1	...
Gwalior	...	...	...	...	...	...	...	...	...	...	...	...	...	...	...	...	...	...	...	...	...	...	...	...	...	...	...	...	...
Bhopal	6	2	4	1	4	...	...	...	...	...	...	...	...	...	...	...	...	...	...	...	...	1	...	...	...	...	...	...	...
Bundelkhand	...	...	...	...	...	...	...	...	...	...	...	...	...	...	...	...	...	...	...	...	...	...	...	...	...	...	...	...	...
Baghelkhand	...	...	...	...	...	...	...	...	...	...	...	...	...	...	...	...	...	...	...	...	...	...	...	...	...	...	...	...	...
Western Malwa	69	35	34	7	8	8	11	12	6	5	6	3	2	...	1	...	...	...	...	...	...	...	...	...	...	...	...	...	...
Bhopawar	...	...	...	...	...	...	...	...	...	...	...	...	...	...	...	...	...	...	...	...	...	...	...	...	...	...	...	...	...
Guna	...	...	...	...	...	...	...	...	...	...	...	...	...	...	...	...	...	...	...	...	...	...	...	...	...	...	...	...	...
Total	**383**	**211**	**172**	**43**	**59**	**46**	**49**	**45**	**34**	**40**	**22**	**31**	**6**	**2**	**2**	**1**	...	...	...	...	...	**1**	...	**1**	...	...	...	**1**	...
(2) MARRIED.																													
Indore	221	108	113	...	...	...	...	...	5	5	6	10	24	19	19	13	18	20	18	12	5	6	6	11	7	4	2	8	3
Gwalior	...	...	...	...	...	...	...	...	...	...	...	...	...	...	...	...	...	...	...	...	...	...	...	...	...	...	...	...	...
Bhopal	5	3	2	1	...	...	...	...	...	...	...	...	1	1	...	1	1	...	...	...	...	...	...	...	...	...	...	...	...
Bundelkhand	2	2	...	...	...	...	...	...	...	...	...	1	...	...	...	...	...	...	...	...	...	...	...	...	...	...	...	1	...
Baghelkhand	...	...	...	...	...	...	...	...	...	...	...	...	...	...	...	...	...	...	...	...	...	...	...	...	...	...	...	...	...
Western Malwa	50	27	23	...	...	...	...	...	...	...	2	2	1	3	4	7	7	5	3	3	4	2	1	2	...	2	1	1	...
Bhopawar	...	...	...	...	...	...	...	...	...	...	...	...	...	...	...	...	...	...	...	...	...	...	...	...	...	...	...	...	...
Guna	...	...	...	...	...	...	...	...	...	...	...	...	...	...	...	...	...	...	...	...	...	...	...	...	...	...	...	...	...
Total	**278**	**140**	**138**	**1**	...	...	...	...	**5**	**5**	**8**	**13**	**26**	**23**	**23**	**21**	**26**	**25**	**21**	**15**	**9**	**8**	**7**	**13**	**7**	**6**	**3**	**10**	**3**
(3) WIDOWED.																													
Indore	54	16	38	1	...	...	...	1	...	1	1	...	1	1	1	...	2	3	1	1	4	...	5	3	6	2	4	3	13
Gwalior	...	...	...	...	...	...	...	...	...	...	...	...	...	...	...	...	...	...	...	...	...	...	...	...	...	...	...	...	...
Bhopal	...	...	...	...	...	...	...	...	...	...	...	...	...	...	...	...	...	...	...	...	...	...	...	...	...	...	...	...	...
Bundelkhand	...	...	...	...	...	...	...	...	...	...	...	...	...	...	...	...	...	...	...	...	...	...	...	...	...	...	...	...	...
Baghelkhand	...	...	...	...	...	...	...	...	...	...	...	...	...	...	...	...	...	...	...	...	...	...	...	...	...	...	...	...	...
Western Malwa	10	4	6	...	...	...	...	...	...	...	...	...	...	...	...	...	1	...	1	1	...	1	...	1	...	...	1	1	3
Bhopawar	...	...	...	...	...	...	...	...	...	...	...	...	...	...	...	...	...	...	...	...	...	...	...	...	...	...	...	...	...
Guna	...	...	...	...	...	...	...	...	...	...	...	...	...	...	...	...	...	...	...	...	...	...	...	...	...	...	...	...	...
Total	**64**	**20**	**44**	**1**	...	...	...	**1**	...	**1**	**1**	...	**1**	**1**	**1**	...	**3**	**3**	**2**	**2**	**4**	**1**	**5**	**4**	**6**	**2**	**5**	**4**	**16**

Table VIII.

Civil Condition by Religion and Age.— Part (H).

SIKH.

(1) UNMARRIED.

(2) MARRIED.

(3) WIDOWED.

NOTE.—This Table applies only to persons enumerated on the British India Schedule.

TABLE VIII.—Civil Condition by Religion and Age.—Part (H). SIKH.

AGENCY.	Total Unmarried. Total.	Total Unmarried. Males.	Total Unmarried. Females.	0–4 Males.	0–4 Females.	5–9 Males.	5–9 Females.	10–14 Males.	10–14 Females.	15–19 Males.	15–19 Females.	20–24 Males.	20–24 Females.	25–29 Males.	25–29 Females.	30–34 Males.	30–34 Females.	35–39 Males.	35–39 Females.	40–44 Males.	40–44 Females.	45–49 Males.	45–49 Females.	50–54 Males.	50–54 Females.	55–59 Males.	55–59 Females.	60 and over. Males.	60 and over. Females.
1	2	3	4	5	6	7	8	9	10	11	12	13	14	15	16	17	18	19	20	21	22	23	24	25	26	27	28	29	30
(1) UNMARRIED.																													
Indore	21	21	...	...	...	1	...	3	...	4	...	7	...	5	...	1	...	...	...	...	...	...	...	...	...	...	...	...	...
Gwalior	...	...	...	...	...	...	...	...	...	...	...	...	...	...	...	...	...	...	...	...	...	...	...	...	...	...	...	...	...
Bhopal	113	101	12	9	8	7	4	3	...	7	...	42	...	23	—	6	...	1	...	1	...	2	...	...	...	...	...	...	...
Bundelkhand	106	102	4	4	2	3	2	5	...	53	...	32	...	4	...	1	...	...	...	...	...	...	...	...	...	...	...	...	...
Baghelkhand	...	...	...	...	...	...	...	...	...	...	...	...	...	...	...	...	...	...	...	...	...	...	...	...	...	...	...	...	...
Western Malwa	72	60	12	12	7	9	3	5	2	7	...	17	...	6	...	1	...	1	...	1	...	1	...	...	...	...	...	...	...
Bhopawar	...	...	...	...	...	...	...	...	...	...	...	...	...	...	...	...	...	...	...	...	...	...	...	...	...	...	...	...	...
Guna	99	73	26	11	13	14	8	8	5	8	...	10	...	14	...	6	...	1	...	...	...	...	...	1	...	...	...	...	...
Total	**411**	**357**	**54**	**36**	**30**	**34**	**17**	**24**	**7**	**79**	...	**108**	...	**52**	...	**15**	...	**3**	...	**2**	...	**3**	...	**1**	...	...	...	...	...
(2) MARRIED.																													
Indore	37	29	8	...	...	...	...	...	1	5	2	9	3	6	...	4	2	...	...	3	...	...	...	1	...	1	...	...	...
Gwalior	...	...	...	...	...	...	...	...	...	...	...	...	...	...	...	...	...	...	...	...	...	...	...	...	...	...	...	...	...
Bhopal	122	91	31	...	...	...	...	...	...	9	3	16	12	17	6	19	8	14	...	8	...	5	1	2	...	1	1	...	...
Bundelkhand	167	153	14	...	...	...	...	1	...	25	2	36	6	23	4	26	1	24	...	14	1	3	...	1	...	...	...	...	...
Baghelkhand	...	...	...	...	...	...	...	...	...	...	...	...	...	...	...	...	...	...	...	...	...	...	...	...	...	...	...	...	...
Western Malwa	199	153	46	...	1	...	...	...	3	5	7	38	12	48	8	29	11	10	1	9	2	10	1	2	...	1	...	1	...
Bhopawar	...	...	...	...	...	...	...	...	...	...	...	...	...	...	...	...	...	...	...	...	...	...	...	...	...	...	...	...	...
Guna	218	171	47	...	...	...	...	6	4	6	6	42	19	51	8	21	5	19	1	12	3	8	...	5	...	...	1	1	...
Total	**748**	**597**	**146**	...	**1**	...	...	**7**	**8**	**50**	**20**	**141**	**52**	**145**	**26**	**99**	**27**	**67**	**2**	**46**	**6**	**26**	**2**	**11**	...	**3**	**2**	**2**	...
(3) WIDOWED.																													
Indore	1	...	1	...	...	...	...	...	...	...	...	...	...	...	...	...	...	...	...	...	...	...	...	...	...	...	...	...	1
Gwalior	...	...	...	...	...	...	...	...	...	...	...	...	...	...	...	...	...	...	...	...	...	...	...	...	...	...	...	...	...
Bhopal	14	12	2	...	...	...	...	...	...	...	...	1	...	2	...	3	...	1	...	3	1	1	...	1	1	...	...	...	...
Bundelkhand	8	8	...	...	...	...	...	...	...	...	...	5	...	...	...	1	...	1	...	1	...	...	...	...	...	...	...	...	...
Baghelkhand	...	...	...	...	...	...	...	...	...	...	...	...	...	...	...	...	...	...	...	...	...	...	...	...	...	...	...	...	...
Western Malwa	9	5	4	...	...	...	...	...	...	...	...	...	...	...	2	...	...	1	...	1	...	...	...	2	2	...	...	1	...
Bhopawar	...	...	...	...	...	...	...	...	...	...	...	...	...	...	...	...	...	...	...	...	...	...	...	...	...	...	...	...	...
Guna	14	7	7	...	...	...	...	...	...	...	...	3	...	1	...	3	...	...	...	...	1	...	...	...	2	...	1	...	3
Total	**46**	**32**	**14**	...	...	...	...	...	...	...	...	**9**	...	**3**	**2**	**7**	...	[illegible]	...	**5**	**2**	**1**	...	**3**	**5**	...	**1**	**1**	**4**

Table VIII.—Civil Condition by Religion—Sikh—Central India.

TABLE VIII.

Civil Condition by Religion and Age.— Part (I).

JEW.

(1) UNMARRIED.

(2) MARRIED.

(3) WIDOWED.

NOTE.—This Table applies only to persons enumerated on the British India Schedule.

TABLE VIII.—Civil Condition by Religion and Age.—Part (I). JEW.

AGENCY.	TOTAL UNMARRIED.			AGE PERIOD.																									
				0—4		5—9		10—14		15—19		20—24		25—29		30—34		35—39		40—44		45—49		50—54		55—59		60 AND OVER.	
	Total.	Males.	Females.	Males.	Females.	Males.	Females.	Males.	Females.	Males.	Females.	Males.	Females.	Males.	Females.	Males.	Females.	Males.	Females.	Males.	Females.	Males.	Females.	Males.	Females.	Males.	Females.	Males.	Females.
1	2	3	4	5	6	7	8	9	10	11	12	13	14	15	16	17	18	19	20	21	22	23	24	25	26	27	28	29	30
(1) UNMARRIED.																													
INDORE	27	20	7	9	3	4	3	3	...	1	1	3	...	...	...	...	...	...	...	...	...	...	...	...	...	...	...	...	...
GWALIOR	...	...	...	...	...	...	...	...	...	...	...	...	...	...	...	...	...	...	...	...	...	...	...	...	...	...	...	...	...
BHOPAL	...	...	...	...	...	...	...	...	...	...	...	...	...	...	...	...	...	...	...	...	...	...	...	...	...	...	...	...	...
BUNDELKHAND	...	...	...	...	...	...	...	...	...	...	...	...	...	...	...	...	...	...	...	...	...	...	...	...	...	...	...	...	...
BAGHELKHAND	...	...	...	...	...	...	...	...	...	...	...	...	...	...	...	...	...	...	...	...	...	...	...	...	...	...	...	...	...
WESTERN MALWA	7	5	2	1	...	1	1	2	1	1	...	...	...	...	...	...	...	...	...	...	...	...	...	...	...	...	...	...	...
BHOPAWAR	...	...	...	...	...	...	...	...	...	...	...	...	...	...	...	...	...	...	...	...	...	...	...	...	...	...	...	...	...
GUNA	...	...	...	...	...	...	...	...	...	...	...	...	...	...	...	...	...	...	...	...	...	...	...	...	...	...	...	...	...
Total	34	25	9	10	8	5	4	5	1	2	1	3	...	...	...	...	...	...	...	...	...	...	...	...	...	...	...	...	...
(2) MARRIED.																													
INDORE	26	13	13	...	...	...	...	...	1	...	3	3	5	2	4	4	...	2	...	1	...	...	...	1	...	...	...	...	...
GWALIOR	...	...	...	...	...	...	...	...	...	...	...	...	...	...	...	...	...	...	...	...	...	...	...	...	...	...	...	...	...
BHOPAL	...	...	...	...	...	...	...	...	...	...	...	...	...	...	...	...	...	...	...	...	...	...	...	...	...	...	...	...	...
BUNDELKHAND	...	...	...	...	...	...	...	...	...	...	...	...	...	...	...	...	...	...	...	...	...	...	...	...	...	...	...	...	...
BAGHELKHAND	...	...	...	...	...	...	...	...	...	...	...	...	...	...	...	...	...	...	...	...	...	...	...	...	...	...	...	...	...
WESTERN MALWA	10	5	5	...	...	...	...	...	...	...	1	...	...	...	1	2	...	...	1	2	1	...	...	...	...	...	...	1	1
BHOPAWAR	...	...	...	...	...	...	...	...	...	...	...	...	...	...	...	...	...	...	...	...	...	...	...	...	...	...	...	...	...
GUNA	...	...	...	...	...	...	...	...	...	...	...	...	...	...	...	...	...	...	...	...	...	...	...	...	...	...	...	...	...
Total	36	18	18	...	...	...	...	...	1	...	4	3	5	2	5	6	...	2	1	3	1	...	...	1	...	...	...	1	1
(3) WIDOWED.																													
INDORE	1	...	1	...	...	...	...	...	...	...	...	...	...	...	...	...	...	...	...	...	...	...	...	...	...	...	...	...	1
GWALIOR	...	...	...	...	...	...	...	...	...	...	...	...	...	...	...	...	...	...	...	...	...	...	...	...	...	...	...	...	...
BHOPAL	...	...	...	...	...	...	...	...	...	...	...	...	...	...	...	...	...	...	...	...	...	...	...	...	...	...	...	...	...
BUNDELKHAND	...	...	...	...	...	...	...	...	...	...	...	...	...	...	...	...	...	...	...	...	...	...	...	...	...	...	...	...	...
BAGHELKHAND	...	...	...	...	...	...	...	...	...	...	...	...	...	...	...	...	...	...	...	...	...	...	...	...	...	...	...	...	...
WESTERN MALWA	1	1	...	...	...	...	...	...	...	...	...	...	...	...	...	1	...	...	...	...	...	...	...	...	...	...	...	...	...
BHOPAWAR	...	...	...	...	...	...	...	...	...	...	...	...	...	...	...	...	...	...	...	...	...	...	...	...	...	...	...	...	...
GUNA	...	...	...	...	...	...	...	...	...	...	...	...	...	...	...	...	...	...	...	...	...	...	...	...	...	...	...	...	...
Total	2	1	1	...	...	...	...	...	...	...	...	...	...	...	...	1	...	...	...	...	...	...	...	...	...	...	...	...	1

Table IX.

Education by Religion and Age.—Part (A).

TOTAL POPULATION.

NOTE.—This Table applies only to persons enumerated on the British India Schedule.

TABLE IX.—Education by Religion and Age.—Part (A). TOTAL POPULATION.

AGENCY.	TOTAL POPULATION.			TOTAL BY EDUCATION.						AGE PERIODS. 0–14							
				Learning.		Literate.		Illiterate.		Total.		Learning.		Literate.		Illiterate.	
	Total.	Males.	Females.	Males.	Females.	Males.	Females.	Males.	Females.	Males.	Females.	Males.	Females.	Males.	Females.	Males.	Females.
1	2	3	4	5	6	7	8	9	10	11	12	13	14	15	16	17	18
Indore	43,358	25,854	17,504	1,075	167	7,107	644	17,672	16,693	6,694	6,274	824	161	215	69	5,655	6,044
Gwalior	4,703	2,782	1,921	57	7	698	32	2,027	1,882	764	650	47	7	41	2	676	641
Bhopal	11,881	6,647	5,234	295	20	1,277	50	5,075	5,164	1,989	1,895	184	18	32	5	1,773	1,872
Bundelkhand	11,079	7,077	4,002	236	17	1,606	89	5,235	3,896	1,771	1,522	133	11	25	10	1,613	1,501
Baghelkhand	6,426	4,437	1,989	62	13	619	79	3,756	1,897	732	705	50	13	17	12	665	680
Western Malwa	21,734	12,979	8,755	400	44	3,367	240	9,212	8,471	3,393	3,139	271	35	172	48	2,950	3,056
Bhopawar	3,152	1,760	1,392	98	...	301	3	1,361	1,389	529	535	43	...	14	...	472	535
Guna	4,693	2,729	1,964	68	5	557	11	2,104	1,948	772	665	44	4	48	4	680	657
Total	**107,026**	**64,265**	**42,761**	**2,291**	**278**	**15,532**	**1,148**	**46,442**	**41,840**	**16,644**	**15,885**	**1,596**	**249**	**564**	**150**	**14,484**	**14,986**

AGENCY.	AGE PERIODS. 15–24								25 AND OVER.							
	Total.		Learning.		Literate.		Illiterate.		Total.		Learning.		Literate.		Illiterate.	
	Males.	Females.	Males.	Females.	Males.	Females.	Males.	Females.	Males.	Females.	Males.	Females.	Males.	Females.	Males.	Females.
	19	20	21	22	23	24	25	26	27	28	29	30	31	32	33	34
Indore	5,190	3,491	223	4	2,142	224	2,825	3,263	13,970	7,739	28	2	4,750	351	9,192	7,386
Gwalior	533	380	10	...	161	9	362	371	1,485	891	...	..	496	21	989	870
Bhopal	1,238	922	106	1	364	20	768	901	3,420	2,417	5	1	881	25	2,534	2,391
Bundelkhand	1,732	715	67	3	537	28	1,128	684	3,574	1,765	36	3	1,044	51	2,494	1,711
Baghelkhand	1,003	432	7	...	156	27	840	405	2,702	852	5	...	446	40	2,251	812
Western Malwa	2,721	1,535	76	5	949	75	1,696	1,457	6,865	4,081	53	4	2,246	119	4,566	3,958
Bhopawar	316	271	14	...	72	2	230	269	915	586	41	...	215	1	659	585
Guna	586	365	18	1	145	1	423	363	1,371	[illegible]	6	...	364	6	1,001	928
Total	**13,319**	**8,111**	**521**	**14**	**4,526**	**384**	**8,272**	**7,718**	**34,302**	**19,265**	**174**	**10**	**10,442**	**614**	**23,686**	**18,641**

TABLE IX.

Education by Religion and Age.—Part (B).

HINDU.

NOTE.—This table applies only to persons enumerated on the British India Schedule.

Table IX.—Education by Religion and Age.—Part (B). HINDU.

AGENCY.	TOTAL POPULATION.			TOTAL BY EDUCATION.						AGE PERIODS. 0–14							
				Learning.		Literate.		Illiterate.		Total.		Learning.		Literate.		Illiterate.	
	Total.	Males.	Females.	Males.	Females.	Males.	Females.	Males.	Females.	Males.	Females.	Males.	Females.	Males.	Females.	Males.	Females.
1	2	3	4	5	6	7	8	9	10	11	12	13	14	15	16	17	18
Indore	28,329	16,675	11,654	621	39	3,667	118	12,387	11,497	4,407	4,121	484	37	120	10	3,803	4,074
Gwalior	3,505	2,046	1,459	38	...	449	3	1,559	1,456	585	485	31	...	29	...	525	485
Bhopal	8,931	4,928	4,003	180	7	906	8	3,842	3,988	1,514	1,443	103	6	25	...	1,386	1,437
Bundelkhand	6,788	4,202	2,586	135	2	640	16	3,427	2,568	1,175	1,008	71	2	12	1	1,092	1,005
Baghelkhand	4,721	3,336	1,385	30	3	429	16	2,877	1,366	507	472	21	3	13	1	473	468
Western Malwa	14,690	8,763	5,927	225	3	1,966	47	6,572	5,877	2,284	2,090	144	1	100	12	2,040	2,077
Bhopawar	1,527	867	660	36	...	188	...	643	660	267	263	23	...	6	...	238	263
Guna	3,321	1,835	1,486	20	...	268	5	1,547	1,481	562	503	14	...	24	2	524	501
Total	**71,812**	**42,652**	**29,160**	**1,285**	**54**	**8,518**	**218**	**32,854**	**28,893**	**11,301**	**10,385**	**891**	**49**	**329**	**26**	**10,081**	**10,810**

AGENCY.	AGE PERIODS. 15–24								25 and over.							
	Total.		Learning.		Literate.		Illiterate.		Total.		Learning.		Literate.		Illiterate.	
	Males.	Females.	Males.	Females.	Males.	Females.	Males.	Females.	Males.	Females.	Males.	Females.	Males.	Females.	Males.	Females.
	19	20	21	22	23	24	25	26	27	28	29	30	31	32	33	34
Indore	2,932	2,335	126	1	834	36	1,972	1,298	9,336	5,198	11	1	2,713	72	6,612	5,125
Gwalior	387	299	7	...	102	1	278	298	1,074	675	...	...	318	2	756	673
Bhopal	883	701	72	...	205	5	606	696	2,531	1,859	5	1	676	3	1,850	1,855
Bundelkhand	862	453	42	...	135	5	685	448	2,165	1,125	22	...	493	10	1,650	1,115
Baghelkhand	794	315	5	...	117	9	672	306	2,035	598	4	...	299	6	1,732	592
Western Malwa	1,774	1,038	42	2	510	17	1,222	1,019	4,705	2,799	39	...	1,356	18	3,310	2,781
Bhopáwar	153	103	6	...	47	...	100	103	447	294	7	...	135	...	305	294
Guňa	380	274	6	...	72	...	302	274	893	709	...	...	172	3	721	706
Total	**8,165**	**5,518**	**306**	**3**	**2,022**	**78**	**5,887**	**5,442**	**23,186**	**18,257**	**88**	**2**	**6,162**	**114**	**16,936**	**13,141**

TABLE IX.

Education by Religion and Age.—Part (C).

MUSALMAN.

NOTE.—This Table applies only to persons enumerated on the British India Schedule.

Table IX.—Education by Religion and Age.—Part (C). MUSALMAN.

AGENCY.	TOTAL POPULATION.			TOTAL BY EDUCATION.						AGE PERIODS. 0—14							
	Total.	Males.	Females.	Learning.		Literate.		Illiterate.		Total.		Learning.		Literate.		Illiterate.	
				Males.	Females.	Males.	Females.	Males.	Females.	Males.	Females.	Males.	Females.	Males.	Females.	Males.	Females.
1	2	3	4	5	6	7	8	9	10	11	12	13	14	15	16	17	18
Indore	10,531	5,935	4,596	241	23	981	43	4,713	4,530	1,775	1,688	195	21	34	7	1,546	1,660
Gwalior	850	501	349	9	...	74	...	418	349	151	125	7	...	3	...	141	125
Bhopal	2,445	1,367	1,078	105	13	200	14	1,062	1,051	420	408	71	12	5	3	344	393
Bundelkhand	3,305	2,021	1,284	55	2	359	15	1,607	1,267	535	470	42	1	4	2	489	467
Baghelkhand	1,303	871	432	19	1	104	6	748	425	158	154	17	1	2	1	139	152
Western Malwa	5,569	3,187	2,382	102	6	696	58	2,389	2,318	931	895	74	6	41	8	816	881
Bhopawar	206	122	84	2	...	22	...	98	84	27	30	2	...	1	...	24	30
Guna	947	593	354	35	5	117	6	441	343	161	121	20	4	13	2	128	115
Total	**25,156**	**14,597**	**10,559**	**568**	**50**	**2,553**	**142**	**11,476**	**10,367**	**4,158**	**3,891**	**428**	**45**	**108**	**23**	**3,627**	**3,823**

AGENCY.	AGE PERIODS. 15—24								25 AND OVER.							
	Total.		Learning.		Literate.		Illiterate.		Total.		Learning.		Literate.		Illiterate.	
	Males.	Females.	Males.	Females.	Males.	Females.	Males.	Females.	Males.	Females.	Males.	Females.	Males.	Females.	Males.	Females.
	19	20	21	22	23	24	25	26	27	28	29	30	31	32	33	34
Indore	1,037	893	37	1	222	17	778	875	3,123	2,015	9	1	725	19	2,389	1,995
Gwalior	88	64	2	...	18	...	68	64	262	160	...	...	53	...	209	160
Bhopal	251	180	34	1	87	4	130	175	696	490	...	...	108	7	588	483
Bundelkhand	421	231	11	...	88	7	322	224	1,065	583	2	1	267	6	796	576
Baghelkhand	179	90	1	...	21	3	157	87	534	188	1	...	81	2	452	186
Western Malwa	644	414	20	...	192	18	432	396	1,612	1,073	8	...	463	32	1,141	1,041
Bhopawar	24	21	...	...	9	...	15	21	71	33	...	...	12	...	59	33
Guna	126	59	10	1	35	1	81	57	306	174	5	...	69	3	232	171
Total	**2,770**	**1,952**	**115**	**3**	**672**	**50**	**1,988**	**1,899**	**7,669**	**4,716**	**25**	**2**	**1,778**	**69**	**5,866**	**4,646**

TABLE IX.

Education by Religion and Age.—Part (D).

JAIN.

NOTE.—This Table applies only to persons enumerated on the British India Schedule.

TABLE IX.—Education by Religion and Age.—Part (D). JAIN.

AGENCY.	TOTAL POPULATION.			TOTAL BY EDUCATION.						AGE PERIODS.																							
										0—14								15—24								25 AND OVER.							
				Learning.		Literate.		Illiterate.		Total.		Learning.		Literate.		Illiterate.		Total.		Learning.		Literate.		Illiterate.		Total.		Learning.		Literate.		Illiterate.	
	Total.	Males.	Females.	Males.	Females.	Males.	Females.	Males.	Females.	Males.	Females.	Males.	Females.	Males.	Females.	Males.	Females.	Males.	Females.	Males.	Females.	Males.	Females.	Males.	Females.	Males.	Females.	Males.	Females.	Males.	Females.	Males.	Females.
1	2	3	4	5	6	7	8	9	10	11	12	13	14	15	16	17	18	19	20	21	22	23	24	25	26	27	28	29	30	31	32	33	34
Indore . . .	348	199	149	13	...	135	...	51	149	48	40	13	...	12	...	23	40	32	25	...	...	28	...	4	25	119	84	...	...	95	...	24	84
Gwalior . . .	149	78	71	7	...	52	1	19	70	19	24	6	...	7	...	6	24	12	9	1	...	8	...	3	9	47	38	...	...	37	1	10	37
Bhopal . . .	147	89	58	6	...	48	...	35	58	20	15	6	...	2	...	12	15	17	11	...	...	7	...	10	11	52	32	...	...	39	...	13	32
Bundelkhand . .	51	29	22	4	...	13	...	12	22	11	4	4	...	...	...	7	4	5	4	...	...	2	...	3	4	13	14	...	...	11	...	2	14
Baghelkhand . .	...	...	...	...	...	...	...	...	...	...	...	...	...	...	...	...	...	...	...	...	...	...	...	...	...	...	...	...	...	...	...	...	...
Western Malwa .	297	175	122	13	...	118	...	44	122	36	31	12	...	11	...	13	31	35	16	1	...	27	...	7	16	104	75	...	...	80	...	24	75
Bhopawar . . .	...	...	...	...	...	...	...	...	...	...	...	...	...	...	...	...	...	...	...	...	...	...	...	...	...	...	...	...	...	...	...	...	...
Guna . . .	76	35	41	...	...	27	...	8	41	9	10	...	...	6	...	3	10	7	7	...	...	5	...	2	7	19	24	...	...	16	...	3	24
Total	1,068	605	463	43	...	393	1	169	462	143	124	41	...	38	...	64	124	108	72	2	...	77	...	29	72	354	267	...	...	278	1	76	266

TABLE IX.

Education by Religion and Age.—Part (E).

ABORIGINAL.

NOTE.—This Table applies only to persons enumerated on the British India Schedule.

TABLE IX.—Education by Religion and Age.—Part (E). ABORIGINAL.

Agency.	Total Population. Total.	Total Population. Males.	Total Population. Females.	Total by Education. Learning. Males.	Total by Education. Learning. Females.	Total by Education. Literate. Males.	Total by Education. Literate. Females.	Total by Education. Illiterate. Males.	Total by Education. Illiterate. Females.	0–14 Total. Males.	0–14 Total. Females.	0–14 Learning. Males.	0–14 Learning. Females.	0–14 Literate. Males.	0–14 Literate. Females.	0–14 Illiterate. Males.	0–14 Illiterate. Females.	15–24 Total. Males.	15–24 Total. Females.	15–24 Learning. Males.	15–24 Learning. Females.	15–24 Literate. Males.	15–24 Literate. Females.	15–24 Illiterate. Males.	15–24 Illiterate. Females.	25 and over Total. Males.	25 and over Total. Females.	25 and over Learning. Males.	25 and over Learning. Females.	25 and over Literate. Males.	25 and over Literate. Females.	25 and over Illiterate. Males.	25 and over Illiterate. Females.
1	2	3	4	5	6	7	8	9	10	11	12	13	14	15	16	17	18	19	20	21	22	23	24	25	26	27	28	29	30	31	32	33	34
Indore	2	2	...	...	...	...	...	2	...	...	...	...	...	...	...	...	...	1	...	...	...	...	...	1	...	1	...	...	...	...	...	1	...
Gwalior	...	...	...	...	...	...	...	...	...	...	...	...	...	...	...	...	...	...	...	...	...	...	...	...	...	...	...	...	...	...	...	...	...
Bhopal	...	...	...	...	...	...	...	...	...	...	...	...	...	...	...	...	...	...	...	...	...	...	...	...	...	...	...	...	...	...	...	...	...
Bundelkhand	...	...	...	...	...	...	...	...	...	...	...	...	...	...	...	...	...	...	...	...	...	...	...	...	...	...	...	...	...	...	...	...	...
Baghelkhand	189	112	77	...	...	...	...	112	77	36	39	...	...	...	...	36	39	11	9	...	...	...	...	11	9	65	29	...	...	...	...	65	29
Western Malwa	...	...	...	...	...	...	...	...	...	...	...	...	...	...	...	...	...	...	...	...	...	...	...	...	...	...	...	...	...	...	...	...	...
Bhopawar	1,399	757	642	60	...	81	...	616	642	234	240	18	...	7	...	209	240	138	144	8	...	15	...	115	144	385	258	34	...	59	...	292	258
Guna	...	...	...	...	...	...	...	...	...	...	...	...	...	...	...	...	...	...	...	...	...	...	...	...	...	...	...	...	...	...	...	...	...
Total	1,590	871	719	60	...	81	...	730	719	270	279	18	...	7	...	245	279	150	153	8	...	15	...	127	153	451	287	34	...	59	...	358	287

TABLE IX.

Education by Religion and Age.—Part (F).

CHRISTIAN.

NOTE.—This Table applies only to persons enumerated on the British India Schedule.

TABLE IX.—Education by Religion and Age.—Part (F). CHRISTIAN.

AGENCY.	TOTAL POPULATION.			TOTAL BY EDUCATION.						AGE PERIODS.																							
				Learning.		Literate.		Illiterate.		0–14								15–24								25 and over.							
										Total.		Learning.		Literate.		Illiterate.		Total.		Learning.		Literate.		Illiterate.		Total.		Learning.		Literate.		Illiterate.	
	Total.	Males.	Females.	Males.	Females.	Males.	Females.	Males.	Females.	Males.	Females.	Males.	Females.	Males.	Females.	Males.	Females.	Males.	Females.	Males.	Females.	Males.	Females.	Males.	Females.	Males.	Females.	Males.	Females.	Males.	Females.	Males.	Females.
1	2	3	4	5	6	7	8	9	10	11	12	13	14	15	16	17	18	19	20	21	22	23	24	25	26	27	28	29	30	31	32	33	34
Indore	3,452	2,662	790	71	58	2,144	342	447	390	336	299	52	57	48	34	236	208	1,077	172	13	1	1,008	118	56	53	1,249	319	6	...	1,088	190	155	129
Gwalior	199	157	42	3	7	123	28	31	7	9	16	3	7	2	2	4	7	46	8	...	...	33	8	13	...	102	18	...	...	88	18	14	...
Bhopal	98	54	44	4	...	29	26	21	18	14	13	4	...	...	2	10	11	12	14	...	...	8	10	4	4	28	17	...	...	21	14	7	3
Bundelkhand	652	560	92	32	13	460	55	68	24	37	36	9	8	9	7	19	21	292	19	11	3	256	15	25	1	231	37	12	2	195	33	24	2
Baghelkhand	213	118	95	13	9	86	57	19	29	31	40	12	9	2	10	17	21	19	18	1	...	18	15	...	3	68	37	...	...	66	32	2	5
Western Malwa	751	559	192	35	31	423	101	101	60	85	80	23	24	11	21	51	35	190	36	7	3	172	29	11	4	284	76	5	4	240	51	39	21
Bhopawar	20	14	6	...	...	10	3	4	3	1	2	...	...	...	...	1	2	1	3	...	...	1	2	...	1	12	1	...	...	9	1	3	...
Guna	18	15	3	1	...	11	...	3	3	1	1	1	...	...	...	...	1	4	...	...	...	4	...	...	...	10	2	...	...	7	...	3	2
Total	5,403	4,139	1,264	159	118	3,286	612	694	534	514	487	104	105	72	76	338	306	1,641	270	32	7	1,500	197	109	66	1,984	507	28	6	1,714	339	247	162

TABLE IX.

Education by Religion and Age.—Part (G).

PARSI.

NOTE.—This Table applies only to persons enumerated on the British India Schedule.

TABLE IX.—Education by Religion and Age.—Part (G). PARSI.

AGENCY.	TOTAL POPULATION.			TOTAL BY EDUCATION.						AGE PERIODS.																							
										0—14								15—24								25 AND OVER.							
				Learning.		Literate.		Illiterate.		Total.		Learning.		Literate.		Illiterate.		Total.		Learning.		Literate.		Illiterate.		Total.		Learning.		Literate.		Illiterate.	
	Total.	Males.	Females.	Males.	Females.	Males.	Females.	Males.	Females.	Males.	Females.	Males.	Females.	Males.	Females.	Males.	Females.	Males.	Females.	Males.	Females.	Males.	Females.	Males.	Females.	Males.	Females.	Males.	Females.	Males.	Females.	Males.	Females.
1	2	3	4	5	6	7	8	9	10	11	12	13	14	15	16	17	18	19	20	21	22	23	24	25	26	27	28	29	30	31	32	33	34
Indore . . .	583	298	285	117	47	141	133	40	105	108	118	72	46	1	18	35	54	79	52	43	1	35	48	1	3	111	115	2	...	105	67	4	48
Gwalior . . .	...	...	...	...	...	...	...	...	...	...	...	...	...	...	...	...	...	...	...	...	...	...	...	...	...	...	...	...	...	...	...	...	...
Bhopal . . .	11	5	6	...	...	3	2	2	4	2	4	...	...	...	...	2	4	...	1	...	...	...	1	...	...	3	1	...	...	3	1	...	...
Bundelkhand . .	2	2	...	...	...	2	...	...	...	...	...	...	...	...	...	...	...	1	...	...	...	1	...	...	...	1	...	...	...	1	...	...	...
Baghelkhand . .	...	...	...	...	...	...	...	...	...	...	...	...	...	...	...	...	...	...	...	...	...	...	...	...	...	...	...	...	...	...	...	...	...
Western Malwa .	129	66	63	16	4	37	30	13	29	27	25	13	4	5	5	9	16	10	11	3	...	7	9	...	2	29	27	...	...	25	16	4	11
Bhopawar . . .	...	...	...	...	...	...	...	...	...	...	...	...	...	...	...	...	...	...	...	...	...	...	...	...	...	...	...	...	...	...	...	...	...
Guna	...	...	...	...	...	...	...	...	...	...	...	...	...	...	...	...	...	...	...	...	...	...	...	...	...	...	...	...	...	...	...	...	...
Total .	725	371	354	133	51	183	165	55	138	137	147	85	50	6	23	46	74	90	64	46	1	43	58	1	5	144	143	2	...	134	84	8	59

TABLE IX.

Education by Religion and Age.— Part (H).

SIKH.

NOTE.—This Table applies only to persons enumerated on the British India Schedule.

TABLE IX.—Education by Religion and Age.—Part (H). SIKH.

AGENCY.	TOTAL POPULATION.			TOTAL BY EDUCATION.						AGE PERIODS.																							
										0—14								15—24								25 AND OVER.							
				Learning.		Literate.		Illiterate.		Total.		Learning.		Literate.		Illiterate.		Total.		Learning.		Literate.		Illiterate.		Total.		Learning.		Literate.		Illiterate.	
	Total.	Males.	Females.	Males.	Females.	Males.	Females.	Males.	Females.	Males.	Females.	Males.	Females.	Males.	Females.	Males.	Females.	Males.	Females.	Males.	Females.	Males.	Females.	Males.	Females.	Males.	Females.	Males.	Females.	Males.	Females.	Males.	Females.
1	2	3	4	5	6	7	8	9	10	11	12	13	14	15	16	17	18	19	20	21	22	23	24	25	26	27	28	29	30	31	32	33	34
Indore	59	50	9	6	...	24	3	20	6	4	1	3	...	...	...	1	1	25	5	3	...	9	2	13	3	21	3	...	...	15	1	6	2
Gwalior	...	...	...	...	...	...	...	...	...	...	...	...	...	...	...	...	...	...	...	...	...	...	...	...	...	...	...	...	...	...	...	...	...
Bhopal	249	204	45	...	...	91	...	113	45	19	12	...	...	...	...	19	12	75	15	...	...	57	...	18	15	110	18	...	...	34	...	76	18
Bundelkhand	281	263	18	10	...	132	3	121	15	13	4	7	...	...	...	6	4	151	8	3	...	55	1	93	7	99	6	...	...	77	2	22	4
Baghelkhand	...	...	...	...	...	...	...	...	...	...	...	...	...	...	...	...	...	...	...	...	...	...	...	...	...	...	...	...	...	...	...	...	...
Western Malwa	280	218	62	9	...	118	...	91	62	26	16	5	...	1	...	20	16	67	19	3	...	40	...	24	19	125	27	1	...	77	...	47	27
Bhopawar	...	...	...	...	...	...	...	...	...	...	...	...	...	...	...	...	...	...	...	...	...	...	...	...	...	...	...	...	...	...	...	...	...
Guna	331	251	80	12	...	134	...	105	80	39	30	9	...	5	...	25	30	69	25	2	...	29	...	38	25	143	25	1	...	100	...	42	25
Total	1,200	986	214	37	...	499	6	450	208	101	68	24	...	6	...	71	68	387	72	11	...	190	3	186	69	498	79	2	...	303	3	193	76

TABLE IX.

Education by Religion and Age.—Part (I).

JEW.

Table IX.—Education by Religion and Age.—Part (I). JEW.

AGENCY.	TOTAL POPULATION.			TOTAL BY EDUCATION.						AGE—PERIODS.																							
										0—14								15—24								25 AND OVER.							
				Learning.		Literate.		Illiterate.		Total.		Learning.		Literate.		Illiterate.		Total.		Learning.		Literate.		Illiterate.		Total.		Learning.		Literate.		Illiterate.	
	Total.	Males.	Females.	Males.	Females.	Males.	Females.	Males.	Females.	Males.	Females.	Males.	Females.	Males.	Females.	Males.	Females.	Males.	Females.	Males.	Females.	Males.	Females.	Males.	Females.	Males.	Females.	Males.	Females.	Males.	Females.	Males.	Females.
1	2	3	4	5	6	7	8	9	10	11	12	13	14	15	16	17	18	19	20	21	22	23	24	25	26	27	28	29	30	31	32	33	34
Indore	54	33	21	6	...	15	5	12	16	16	7	5	...	...	...	11	7	7	9	1	...	6	3	...	6	10	5	...	...	9	2	1	3
Gwalior	...	...	...	...	...	...	...	...	...	...	...	...	...	...	...	...	...	...	...	...	...	...	...	...	...	...	...	...	...	...	...	...	...
Bhopal	...	...	...	...	...	...	...	...	...	...	...	...	...	...	...	...	...	...	...	...	...	...	...	...	...	...	...	...	...	...	...	...	...
Bundelkhand	...	...	...	...	...	...	...	...	...	...	...	...	...	...	...	...	...	...	...	...	...	...	...	...	...	...	...	...	...	...	...	...	...
Baghelkhand	...	...	...	...	...	...	...	...	...	...	...	...	...	...	...	...	...	...	...	...	...	...	...	...	...	...	...	...	...	...	...	...	...
Western Malwa	18	11	7	...	...	9	4	2	3	4	2	...	...	3	2	1	...	1	1	...	...	1	...	...	1	6	4	...	...	5	2	1	2
Bhopawar	...	...	...	...	...	...	...	...	...	...	...	...	...	...	...	...	...	...	...	...	...	...	...	...	...	...	...	...	...	...	...	...	...
Guna	...	...	...	...	...	...	...	...	...	...	...	...	...	...	...	...	...	...	...	...	...	...	...	...	...	...	...	...	...	...	...	...	...
Total	72	44	28	6	...	24	9	14	19	20	9	5	...	3	2	12	7	8	10	1	...	7	3	...	7	16	9	...	...	14	4	2	5

TABLE X.

Parent-tongue.

NOTE.—This Table applies only to persons enumerated on the British India Schedule.

TABLE X.—Parent-tongue.

AGENCY.	Total Population.			Malvi.			Rangri.			Hindi.			Marathi.			Dekhani.			Nimari.		
	Total.	Males.	Females.	Total.	Males.	Females.	Total.	Males.	Females.	Total.	Males.	Females.	Total.	Males.	Females.	Total.	Males.	Females.	Total.	Males.	Females.
1	2	3	4	5	6	7	8	9	10	11	12	13	14	15	16	17	18	19	20	21	22
Indore	43,358	25,854	17,504	536	322	214	19	17	2	6,260	3,915	2,345	5,533	3,169	2,364	...	...	...	21	19	2
Gwalior	4,703	2,782	1,921	1,812	1,037	775	...	...	...	45	33	12	17	15	2	...	...	...	...	...	...
Bhopal	11,881	6,647	5,234	...	...	...	...	...	...	...	...	...	182	114	68	...	...	...	...	...	...
Bundelkhand	11,079	7,077	4,002	...	...	...	...	...	...	2,041	1,491	550	19	9	10	...	...	...	...	...	...
Baghelkhand	6,426	4,437	1,989	...	...	...	...	...	...	4,285	3,010	1,275	28	16	12	...	...	...	...	...	...
Western Malwa	21,734	12,979	8,755	1,041	803	238	...	...	...	2,292	1,917	375	4,928	4,503	425	182	91	91	11	11	...
Bhopawar	3,152	1,760	1,392	975	516	459	...	...	...	6	6	...	...	...	...	90	55	35	...	...	...
Guna	4,693	2,729	1,964	1,337	693	644	...	...	...	...	...	...	9	9	...	8	...	8	...	...	...
Total	107,026	64,265	42,761	5,701	3,371	2,330	19	17	2	14,929	10,372	4,557	10,716	7,835	2,881	280	146	134	32	30	2

AGENCY.	Bhilwari.			Dhundari.			Marwari.			Mewari.			Hindustani.			Urdu.			Gujrati.		
	Total.	Males.	Females.	Total.	Males.	Females.	Total.	Males.	Females.	Total.	Males.	Females.	Total.	Males.	Females.	Total.	Males.	Females.	Total.	Males.	Females.
	23	24	25	26	27	28	29	30	31	32	33	34	35	36	37	38	39	40	41	42	43
Indore	...	...	...	33	17	16	4,043	2,275	1,768	78	48	30	20,205	11,566	8,639	...	...	...	1,334	763	571
Gwalior	...	...	...	236	123	113	155	82	73	...	...	...	1,957	1,177	780	...	...	...	2	2	...
Bhopal	...	...	...	...	...	...	625	292	333	40	40	...	10,568	5,821	4,747	...	...	...	11	9	2
Bundelkhand	...	...	...	...	...	...	...	...	...	...	...	...	7,940	4,632	3,308	...	...	...	15	8	7
Baghelkhand	...	...	...	...	...	...	...	...	...	...	...	...	1,088	745	343	638	425	213	55	41	14
Western Malwa	...	...	...	637	527	110	1,064	161	903	310	137	173	8,458	3,070	5,388	...	...	...	457	256	201
Bhopawar	759	418	341	1	1	...	255	142	113	188	105	83	762	448	314	...	...	...	99	54	45
Guna	...	...	...	113	72	41	47	26	21	2	2	...	2,809	1,632	1,177	...	...	...	1	1	...
Total	759	418	341	1,020	740	280	6,189	2,978	3,211	618	332	286	53,787	29,091	24,696	638	425	213	1,974	1,134	840

Table X.—Parent-tongue—Central India.

AGENCY.	Purbi.			Kachhi.			Gandi.			Banjari.			Tamil.			Telingi.			Karnataki.		
	Total.	Males.	Females.	Total.	Males.	Females.	Total.	Males.	Females.	Total.	Males.	Females.	Total.	Males.	Females.	Total.	Males.	Females.	Total.	Males.	Females.
	44	45	46	47	48	49	50	51	52	53	54	55	56	57	58	59	60	61	62	63	64
Indore	715	403	312	12	10	2	...	...	...	...	...	...	241	125	116	325	173	152	1	1	...
Gwalior	13	10	3	...	...	...	...	...	...	...	...	...	...	...	...	4	2	2	...	...	...
Bhopal	...	...	...	...	...	...	...	...	...	...	...	...	9	4	5	...	...	...	...	...	...
Bundelkhand	4	3	1	...	...	...	...	...	...	...	...	...	2	1	1	...	...	...	...	...	...
Baghelkhand	...	...	...	11	11	...	21	19	2	3	3	...	22	9	13	44	23	21	...	...	...
Western Malwa	952	537	415	...	...	...	...	...	...	...	...	...	23	17	6	108	57	51	2	2	...
Bhopawar	...	...	...	...	...	...	...	...	...	...	...	...	...	...	...	...	...	...	...	...	...
Guna	...	...	...	...	...	...	...	...	...	...	...	...	...	...	...	...	...	...	...	...	...
Total	**1,684**	**953**	**731**	**23**	**21**	**2**	**21**	**19**	**2**	**3**	**3**	...	**297**	**156**	**141**	**481**	**255**	**226**	**3**	**3**	...

AGENCY.	Madrasi.			Kamati.			Bengali.			Punjabi.			Kashmiri.			Pushtu.			Narnoli.		
	Total.	Males.	Females.	Total.	Males.	Females.	Total.	Males.	Females.	Total.	Males.	Females.	Total.	Males.	Females.	Total.	Males.	Females.	Total.	Males.	Females.
	65	66	67	68	69	70	71	72	73	74	75	76	77	78	79	80	81	82	83	84	85
Indore	482	262	220	139	65	74	120	78	42	195	174	21	18	12	6	61	59	2	29	14	15
Gwalior	...	...	...	...	...	...	3	3	...	263	143	120	2	1	1	1	1	...	...	...	...
Bhopal	1	...	1	...	...	...	13	6	7	349	311	38	...	...	...	4	4	...	...	...	...
Bundelkhand	5	2	3	...	...	...	16	7	9	385	356	29	...	...	...	9	9	...	...	...	...
Baghelkhand	1	1	...	...	...	...	31	19	12	4	4	...	...	...	...	...	...	...	...	...	...
Western Malwa	45	29	16	42	21	21	...	...	...	436	291	145	...	...	...	49	36	13	...	...	...
Bhopawar	...	...	...	...	...	...	...	...	...	1	1	...	...	...	...	...	...	...	...	...	...
Guna	...	...	...	...	...	...	4	2	2	326	266	60	...	...	...	26	16	10	...	...	...
Total	**534**	**294**	**240**	**181**	**86**	**95**	**187**	**115**	**72**	**1,959**	**1,546**	**413**	**20**	**13**	**7**	**150**	**125**	**25**	**29**	**14**	**15**

TABLE X.—Parent-tongue—(contd.)

AGENCY.	Sindhi.			Goanese.			Persian.			Arabic.			Bokhari.			English.			Welsh.		
	Total.	Males.	Females.	Total.	Males.	Females.	Total.	Males.	Females.	Total.	Males.	Females.	Total.	Males.	Females.	Total.	Males.	Females.	Total.	Males.	Females.
	86	87	88	89	90	91	92	93	94	95	96	97	98	99	100	101	102	103	104	105	106
Indore	1	1	...	84	59	25	26	26	...	18	5	13	...	...	...	2,600	2,135	465	1	1	...
Gwalior	...	...	...	...	...	...	1	1	...	...	...	...	...	...	...	181	148	33	...	...	...
Bhopal	1	1	...	1	1	...	10	6	4	1	...	1	1	1	...	59	31	28	...	...	...
Bundelkhand	...	...	...	...	...	...	6	3	3	1	1	...	...	...	...	633	552	81	...	...	...
Baghelkhand	...	...	...	...	...	...	5	1	4	...	...	...	...	...	...	189	109	80	...	...	...
Western Malwa	...	...	...	19	16	3	15	8	7	35	...	35	...	...	...	586	450	136	...	...	...
Bhopawar	...	...	...	1	1	...	...	...	...	...	...	...	...	...	...	10	8	2	...	...	...
Guna	...	...	...	...	...	...	...	...	...	...	...	...	...	...	...	11	10	1	...	...	...
Total	2	2	...	105	77	28	63	45	18	55	6	49	1	1	...	4,269	3,443	826	1	1	...

AGENCY.	Irish.			French.			Portuguese.			Spanish.			German.			Swiss.			Italian.		
	Total.	Males.	Females.	Total.	Males.	Females.	Total.	Males.	Females.	Total.	Males.	Females.	Total.	Males.	Females.	Total.	Males.	Females.	Total.	Males.	Females.
	107	108	109	110	111	112	113	114	115	116	117	118	119	120	121	122	123	124	125	126	127
Indore	27	6	21	9	9	...	176	116	60	1	1	...	9	3	6	1	1	...	5	4	1
Gwalior	1	...	1	7	1	6	...	...	...	...	...	...	1	1	...	...	...	...	2	2	...
Bhopal	...	...	...	...	6	...	...	...	...	...	...	...	...	...	...	...	...	...	...	...	...
Bundelkhand	...	...	...	1	1	...	...	...	...	...	...	...	...	...	...	...	...	...	2	2	...
Baghelkhand	...	...	...	...	...	...	...	...	...	...	...	...	1	1	...	...	...	...	...	...	...
Western Malwa	...	...	...	1	1	...	41	38	3	...	...	...	...	...	...	...	...	...	...	...	...
Bhopawar	...	...	...	...	...	...	5	5	...	...	...	...	...	...	...	...	...	...	...	...	...
Guna	...	...	...	...	...	...	...	...	...	...	...	...	...	...	...	...	...	...	...	...	...
Total	28	6	22	24	18	6	222	159	63	1	1	...	11	5	6	1	1	...	9		

TABLE XI.

Birth-place.

TABLE XI.—

A.—States within Central India. B.—Provinces or States in India beyond Central India.

STATE, PROVINCE, OR COUNTRY OF BIRTH.	TOTAL OF PROVINCE OR STATE.			AGENCIES.								
				INDORE.			GWALIOR.			BHOPAL.		
	TOTAL.	Males.	Females.	TOTAL.	Males.	Females.	TOTAL.	Males.	Females.	TOTAL.	Males.	Females.
1	2	3	4	5	6	7	8	9	10	11	12	13
A.—												
INDORE	995,866	519 743	476,123	181,318	93,595	87,723	2,034	516	1,518	137,026	72,808	64,218
GWALIOR	3,278,939	1,758,689	1,520,250	60,854	30,346	30,508	1,607,747	884,918	722,829	451,045	235,822	215,223
DEWAS	122,295	66,052	56,243	51,868	28,829	23,039	25	13	12	23,859	12,722	10,867
BAGLI	9,128	5,297	3,831	9,126	5,296	3,830	...	...	...	...	...	...
DHAR	172,384	86,292	86,092	2,627	1,047	1,580	9	6	3	1,515	924	591
JHABUA	135,952	61,150	74,802	14	4	10	...	...	...	...	...	...
BARWANI	31,754	23,986	7,768	9	5	4	...	...	...	...	...	...
ALI RAJPUR	84,317	43,819	40,498	7	7	...	1	...	1	...	...	...
JOBAT	14,019	7,463	6,556	...	...	...	...	...	...	...	...	...
KATHIWARA	2,365	1,203	1,162	...	...	...	...	...	...	...	...	...
MATHWAR	2,371	1,375	996	...	...	...	...	...	...	...	...	...
RATANMAL	1,103	569	534	...	...	...	...	...	...	...	...	...
MANPUR (BRITISH)	2,848	1,576	1,272	45	21	24	1	1	...	4	2	2
BHOPAWAR AGENCY (UNSPECIFIED)	3,777	1,918	1,829	...	...	...	...	...	...	...	...	...
JAORA	109,074	57,697	51,377	619	355	264	...	...	...	97	53	44
RATLAM	86,623	44,190	42,433	899	426	473	3	2	1	195	84	111
SITAMAU	28,180	15,735	12,445	35	14	21	...	...	...	3	1	2
SAILANA	28,001	15,099	12,902	71	1	70	..	...	...			
PIPLAUDA	8,023	4,790	3,233	...	...	...	...	...	...	...	...	...
PANTH PIPLAUDA	2,303	1,499	804	...	...	...	...	...	...	...	...	...
BHOPAL	873,178	449,819	423,359	3,549	1,586	1,963	222	113	109	866,052	446,506	419,546
RAJGARH	104,684	56,204	48,390	41	23	18	6	4	2	102,437	55,426	47,011
NARSINGHGARH	101,471	54,268	47,203	92	53	39	3	1	2	98,061	52,919	45,142
KHILCHIPUR	33,463	19,106	14,357	2	2	...	2	...	2	32,885	18,857	14,028
KURWAI	15,851	8,530	7,321	...	...	...	...	...	...	15,845	8,526	7,319
MAKSUDANGHAR	10,605	5,802	4,803	...	...	...	...	...	...	9,923	5,578	4,345
AGRA BARKHERA	4,271	2,605	1,666	...	...	...	...	...	...	4,271	2,605	1,666
BASODA	5,226	2,714	2,512	...	...	...	...	...	...	5,226	2,714	2,512
SUTHALIA	2,868	1,698	1,170	...	...	...	...	...	...	2,830	1,689	1,141
PATHARI	3,530	1,986	1,544	...	...	...	...	...	...	3,530	1,986	1,544
MAHOMADGARH	3,432	1,849	1,583	...	...	...	...	...	...	3,432	1,849	1,583
RAGHOGARH	14,922	8,390	6,532	1	1	...	9	2	7	114	73	41
GURRAH	7,548	4,203	3,345	...	...	...	...	...	...	65	38	27
PARONE	3,958	2,345	1,613	...	...	...	...	...	...	...	...	...
DHARNAODA	3,203	1,792	1,411	...	...	...	...	..	...	...	...	...
SIRSI	3,377	1,874	1,503	...	...	...	...	...	...	...	...	...
BHADAURA	1,993	1,172	821	...	...	...	...	...	...	...	...	...
UMRI	1,983	1,205	778	...	...	...	...	...	...	...	...	...
KHIAODA	528	299	229	...	...	...	...	...	...	...	...	...
KHANIADHANA	12,195	6,882	5,313	...	...	...	12,054	6,836	5,218	...	...	...
BARAUDA	7,455	4,511	2,944	...	...	...	7,455	4,511	2,944	...	...	...
PAHARGARH	10,725	5,625	5,100	...	...	...	10,725	5,625	5,100	...	...	...
KATHAUN	2,810	1,527	1,283	...	...	...	2,810	1,527	1,283	..	...	...
REWA	1,452,567	728 726	723,841	13	11	2	22	8	14	1,168	654	514
NAGODE	77,989	39,384	38,605	...	...	...	...	...	...	...	...	...
MAIHAR	65,267	33,728	31,539	...	...	...	...	...	...	...	...	...
SOHAWAL	37,675	19,670	17,996	...	...	...	...	...	...	...	...	...
KOTHI	19,424	10,030	9,394	...	...	...	...	...	...	...	...	...
BAGHELKHAND (UNSPECIFIED.)	18	12	6	8	4	4	..	...	...	10	8	2
URCHHA	321,497	171,474	150,023	1	1	...	1,076	342	734	3,545	2,011	1,534
PANNA	221,075	115,049	106,026	6	5	1	142	60	82	529	148	381
DATIA	182,580	99,936	82,644	365	213	152	18,813	5,653	13,160	2,606	1,568	1,038
CHHATARPUR	171,892	91 620	80,272	3	1	2	736	361	375	970	933	37
CHARKHARI	117,471	66,251	51.220	10	3	7	44	25	19	47	19	28
BIJAWAR	127,575	67,648	59,927	...	...	...	104	49	55	18	8	10
AJAIGARH	82,708	43,216	39.492	...	...	...	...	...	...	...	...	...
SAMTHAR	33,573	18,981	14,592	...	...	...	2,326	588	1,738	1,078	93	985
BARAUNDHA	15,580	8,468	7,112	...	...	...	...	...	...	...	...	...
BAONI	12,387	7,330	5,057	...	...	...	...	...	...	...	...	...
ALIPURA	11,276	7,003	4,273	...	...	...	...	...	...	...	...	...
GAURIHAR	7,457	4,344	3,113	...	...	...	...	...	...	...	...	...
TORI FATEHPUR	6,959	4,382	2,627	...	...	...	...	...	...	...	...	...
PALDEV	6,419	3,747	2,672	...	...	...	...	...	...	...	...	...
JASSO	7,946	4,068	3,878	...	...	...	...	...	...	...	...	...
LUGASI	5,445	3,237	2,208	...	...	...	...	...	...	...	...	...
SARILA	3,586	2,174	1,412	...	...	...	...	...	...	...	...	...
GARAULI	3,863	2,269	1,594	...	...	...	...	...	...	...	...	...
BHAISONDHA	3,365	1,897	1,468	...	...	...	...	...	...	...	...	...
BERI	3,341	2,069	1,272	...	...	...	...	...	...	...	...	...
BIHAT	3,085	2,005	1,080	...	...	...	...	...	...	...	...	...

Birth-place.

C.—Countries in Asia beyond India. D.—Countries beyond Asia.

AGENCIES.														
BUNDELKHAND.			BAGHELKHAND.			WESTERN MALWA.			BHOPAWAR.			GUNA.		
TOTAL.	Males.	Females.	TOTAL.	Males.	Females.	TOTAL.	Males.	Females.	TOTAL.	Males.	Females.	TOTAL.	Males.	Females.
14	15	16	17	18	19	20	21	22	23	24	25	26	27	28
13,222	8,043	5,179	31	15	16	372,241	196,499	175,742	289,786	148,168	141,618	208	99	109
23,673	5,532	18,141	251	157	94	764,995	409,405	355,590	142,505	71,206	71,299	227,869	121,303	106,566
2	...	2	...	...	...	43,324	22,668	20,656	3,470	1,805	1,665	17	15	2
...	...	...	...	...	...	1	1	...	1	...	1	...	...	...
...	...	...	...	...	...	6,353	2,211	4,142	161,859	82,003	79,766	21	11	10
...	...	...	...	...	...	1,326	564	762	134,612	60,582	74,030	...	...	...
...	...	...	...	...	...	...	...	...	31,745	21,981	7,764	...	...	...
...	...	...	...	...	...	1	1	...	84,308	43,811	4,0497	...	...	...
...	...	...	...	...	...	...	...	...	14,019	7,463	6,556	...	...	...
...	...	...	...	...	...	...	...	...	2,365	1,203	1,162	...	...	...
...	...	...	...	...	...	...	...	...	2,371	1,375	996	...	...	...
...	...	...	...	...	...	...	...	...	1,103	569	534	...	...	...
...	...	...	...	...	...	...	...	...	2,798	1,552	1,246	...	...	...
...	...	...	...	...	...	...	...	...	3,777	1,048	1,829	...	...	...
4	2	2	...	...	...	107,381	56,734	50,647	972	553	419	1	...	1
1	...	1	11	10	1	79,688	40,676	39,012	5,790	2,908	2,822	36	24	12
...	...	...	...	...	...	28,018	15,671	12,347	123	48	75	1	1	...
...	...	...	...	...	...	25,442	13,785	11,657	2,488	1,313	1,175	...	...	...
...	...	...	...	...	...	8,023	4,700	3,233	...	...	...	...	...	...
...	...	...	...	...	...	2,303	1,499	804	...	...	...	...	...	...
185	78	107	19	13	6	1,900	875	1,025	652	367	285	599	281	318
...	...	...	...	...	...	659	235	424	...	...	...	1,541	606	935
3	1	2	...	...	...	2,554	950	1,604	87	71	16	671	273	398
...	...	...	...	...	...	431	182	249	...	...	...	143	65	78
...	...	...	...	...	...	...	...	...	...	...	...	6	4	2
...	...	...	...	...	...	...	...	...	...	...	...	682	224	458
...	...	...	...	...	...	...	...	...	...	...	...	...	...	...
...	...	...	...	...	...	...	...	...	...	...	...	...	...	...
...	...	...	...	...	...	...	...	...	...	...	...	38	9	29
...	...	...	...	...	...	...	...	...	...	...	...	...	...	...
...	...	...	...	...	...	...	...	...	...	...	...	...	...	...
...	...	...	...	...	...	3	1	2	2	2	...	14,793	8,311	6,482
...	...	...	...	...	...	...	...	...	...	...	...	7,483	4,165	3,318
...	...	...	...	...	...	...	...	...	...	...	...	3,958	2,345	1,613
...	...	...	...	...	...	...	...	...	...	...	...	3,203	1,792	1 411
...	...	...	...	...	...	...	...	...	...	...	...	3,377	1,874	1,503
...	...	...	...	...	...	...	...	...	...	...	...	1,993	1,172	821
...	...	...	...	...	...	...	...	...	...	...	...	1,983	1,205	778
...	...	...	...	...	...	...	...	...	...	...	...	528	299	229
103	27	76	...	...	...	...	...	...	...	...	...	38	19	19
...	...	...	...	...	...	...	...	...	...	...	...	...	...	...
...	...	...	...	...	...	...	...	...	...	...	...	...	...	...
...	...	...	...	...	...	...	...	...	...	...	...	...	...	...
4,791	1,047	2,844	1,446,509	726,066	720 443	4	3	1	58	35	23	2	2	...
4,439	1,551	2,888	73,544	37,828	35,716	...	...	...	6	5	1	...	...	...
1,356	543	813	63,911	33,185	30,726	...	...	...	...	...	...	...	...	...
2,290	964	1,326	35,385	18,715	16,670	...	...	...	...	...	...	...	...	...
872	343	529	18,552	9,687	8,865	...	...	...	...	...	...	...	...	...
...	...	...	...	...	...	...	...	...	...	...	...	...	...	...
316,804	169,063	147 741	20	14	6	33	33	...	...	...	...	18	10	8
209,836	111,121	98,715	10,559	3,713	6,846	...	...	...	...	...	...	3	2	1
160,525	92,328	68,197	1	6	5	37	25	12	114	73	41	109	70	39
169,821	90,135	79,686	362	190	172	...	...	...	...	...	...	...	...	...
117,158	66,107	51,051	212	97	115	...	...	...	...	...	...	...	...	...
127,127	67,425	59,702	326	166	160	...	...	...	...	...	...	...	...	...
79,810	42,328	37,491	2,889	888	2,001	...	...	...	...	...	...	...	...	...
30,168	18,300	11,868	...	...	...	...	...	...	...	...	...	1	...	1
14,415	7,083	6,432	1,165	485	680	...	...	...	...	...	...	...	...	...
12,387	7,330	5,057	...	...	...	...	...	...	...	...	...	...	...	...
11,275	7,002	4,273	1	1	...	...	...	...	...	...	...	...	...	...
7,457	4,344	3,113	...	...	...	...	...	...	...	...	...	...	...	...
6,959	4,332	2,627	...	...	...	...	...	...	...	...	...	...	...	...
6,413	3,743	2,670	6	4	2	...	...	...	...	...	...	...	...	...
7,223	3,809	3,414	723	259	464	...	...	...	...	...	...	...	...	...
5,445	3,237	2,208	...	...	...	...	...	...	...	...	...	...	...	...
3,536	2,174	1,412	...	...	...	...	...	...	...	...	...	...	...	...
3,863	2,269	1,594	...	...	...	...	...	...	...	...	...	...	...	...
3,365	1,897	1,468	...	...	...	...	...	...	...	...	...	...	...	...
3,341	2,069	1,272	...	...	...	...	...	...	...	...	...	...	...	...
3,085	2,005	1,080	...	...	...	...	...	...	...	...	...	...	...	...

TABLE XI.—

A.—States within Central India. B.—Provinces or States in India beyond Central India.

STATE, PROVINCE, OR COUNTRY OF BIRTH.	TOTAL OF PROVINCE OR STATE.			AGENCIES. INDORE.			GWALIOR.			BHOPAL.		
	Total.	Males.	Females.	Total.	Males.	Females.	Total.	Males.	Females.	Total.	Males.	Females.
1	2	3	4	5	6	7	8	9	10	11	12	13
A.—contd.												
Pahra	2,757	1,593	1,164	...	...	...	...	...	...	...	...	...
Jioni	2,709	1,703	1,006	...	...	...	...	...	...	...	...	...
Taraon	2,170	1,213	957	...	...	...	...	...	...	...	...	...
Rebai	2,157	1,325	832	...	...	...	...	...	...	...	...	...
Belhari	1,615	951	664	...	...	...	...	...	...	...	...	...
Bijna	1,471	955	516	...	...	...	...	...	...	...	...	...
Dharwai	1,103	677	426	...	...	...	...	...	...	...	...	...
Kamta Rajaula	849	521	328	...	...	...	...	...	...	...	...	...
Banka Pahari	701	438	263	...	...	...	...	...	...	...	...	...
Bundelkhand (unspecified)	1,670	1,071	653	701	434	267	48	28	20	463	259	204
Tonk	163,369	87,864	75,505	155	105	50	514	293	221	85,210	46,167	39,043
Central India (unspecified)	33,443	14,931	18,512	1,804	999	805	40	34	6	18,464	8,731	9,733
B.—												
Banswara	4,396	2,312	2,084	62	50	12	...	...	...	...	...	...
Partabgarh	10,408	4,094	6,314	300	233	67	15	10	5	35	28	7
Jhallawar	55,434	22,961	32,473	205	120	85	2,375	1,022	1,353	8,855	4,103	4,752
Udaipur	42,231	18,153	24,078	1,411	847	564	465	264	201	3,553	2,009	1,544
Dongarpur	122	56	66	3	2	1	...	...	...	...	...	...
Kotah	14,652	6,752	7,900	244	154	90	5,364	2,051	3,313	1,641	918	723
Jesulmer	672	397	275	5	3	2	58	29	29	361	221	140
Bundi	1,279	606	673	70	42	28	322	141	181	195	92	103
Jaipur	37,015	21,814	15,201	4,585	2,974	1,611	7,332	3,593	3,739	11,390	6,859	4,531
Jodhpur	31,631	17,937	13,694	3,400	2,053	1,347	1,366	772	594	8,050	4,679	3,371
Nagaur	19	6	13	17	5	12	...	...	...	...	...	...
Bharatpur	7,095	4,160	2,935	403	255	148	773	476	297	3,006	1,704	1,302
Karauli	5,690	2,827	2,863	174	114	60	3,972	1,839	2,133	813	410	403
Kishangarh	408	198	210	37	19	18	11	4	7	172	61	111
Bikanir	761	400	361	151	91	60	58	29	29	242	122	120
Dholpur	8,080	3,914	4,166	24	19	5	4,969	1,929	3,040	2,009	1,281	728
Alwar	3,452	2,109	1,343	194	137	57	314	208	106	730	441	289
Sirohi	9	7	2	...	...	...	...	...	...	9	7	2
Kusalgarh	2,190	1,126	1,064	...	...	...	...	...	...	...	...	...
Rajputana (unspecified)	12 016	7,352	4,664	4,837	3,083	1,754	265	137	128	1,683	988	695
Ajmere	2,757	1,660	1,097	463	272	191	375	207	168	323	196	127
Central Provinces	117,878	52,895	64,983	1,787	965	822	106	55	51	56,611	25,754	30,857
Makrai	2	...	2	...	...	...	...	...	...	2	...	4
Bombay	55,984	30,766	25,218	12,810	7,401	5,409	1,963	13,10	653	4,780	2,408	2,372
Bhor	2	1	1	2	1	1	...	...	...	...	...	...
Vinchur	2	1	1	1	...	1	1	1	...	...	...	...
Kolhapur	5	2	3	1	...	1	3	1	2	...	...	...
Akalkot	22	7	15	22	7	15	...	...	...	...	...	...
Baria	459	264	195	...	...	...	...	...	...	...	...	...
Hirawal	3	...	3	...	...	...	...	...	...	...	...	...
Rajpiplia	16	6	10	...	...	...	...	...	...	...	...	...
Chhota Udaipur	3,661	1,755	1,906	...	...	...	...	...	...	...	...	...
Lunawara	43	36	7	...	...	...	...	...	...	...	...	...
Sawantwadi	6	1	5	...	...	...	6	1	5	...	...	...
Jamkhandi	4	2	2	...	...	...	...	...	...	...	...	...
Junagarh	1	1	...	...	...	...	...	...	...	...	...	...
Baroda	4,357	2,239	2,118	292	173	119	73	42	31	209	134	75
N.-W. Provinces	260,678	105,440	155,238	9,163	6,302	2,861	53,311	18,467	34,844	20,577	12,264	8,313
Oudh	28,254	19,937	8,317	11,341	8,298	3,043	2,287	1,597	690	3,950	2,661	1,289
Rampur	584	371	213	26	18	8	210	146	64	2	2	...
Garhwal	15	15	...	...	...	...	2	2	...	...	...	...
Kashmir	44	38	6	6	6	...	12	12	...	16	11	5
Panjab	12,094	8,635	3,459	1,781	1,243	538	2,506	1,560	946	2,279	1,655	624
Patiala	422	257	165	9	9	...	261	151	110	118	77	41
Nabha	45	39	6	...	...	...	45	39	6	...	...	...
Kapurthala	14	14	...	...	...	...	14	14	...	...	...	...
Jhind	1	1	...	...	...	...	...	...	...	...	...	...
Nepal	140	91	49	8	5	3	3	2	1	21	18	3
Assam	35	24	11	3	2	1	29	21	8	3	1	2
Manipur	4	1	3	...	...	...	1	...	1	3	1	2
Calcutta	1,009	749	260	850	637	213	10	...	10	...	...	...
Bengal	17,467	10,698	6,769	295	200	95	1,067	679	388	2,102	1,340	762
Haidarabad	1,028	697	331	378	247	131	121	109	12	190	102	88
Mysore	12	7	5	3	1	2	...	...	...	1	1	...
Madras	1,478	876	602	583	323	260	192	132	60	232	116	116

Birth-place—*continued.*

—Countries in Asia beyond India. D.—Countries beyond Asia—*continued.*

AGENCIES.

Bundelkhand.			Baghelkhand.			Western Malwa.			Bhopawar.			Guna.		
Total.	Males.	Females.	Total.	Males.	Females.	Total.	Males.	Females.	Total.	Males.	Females.	Total.	Males.	Females.
14	15	16	17	18	19	20	21	22	23	24	25	26	27	28
2,757	1,593	1,164	...	...	...	...	...	...	...	...	...	...	...	...
2,709	1,703	1,005	...	...	...	...	...	...	...	...	...	...	...	...
2,170	1,213	957	...	...	...	...	...	...	...	...	...	...	...	...
2;157	1,325	832	...	...	...	...	...	...	...	...	...	...	...	...
1,615	951	664	...	...	...	...	...	...	...	...	...	...	...	...
1,471	955	516	...	...	...	...	...	...	...	...	...	...	...	...
1,103	677	426	...	...	...	...	...	...	...	...	...	...	...	...
849	521	328	...	...	...	...	...	...	...	...	...	...	...	...
701	438	263	...	...	...	...	...	...	...	...	...	...	...	...
103	57	46	192	135	57	105	72	33	2	1	1	56	31	25
52	43	9	32	17	15	38,153	20,800	17,353	34	26	8	39,219	20,413	18,806
880	469	411	200	126	74	6,986	2,376	4,610	124	48	76	4,945	2,148	2,797
...	...	...	...	...	...	2,862	1,433	1,429	1,472	829	643	...	...	...
11	5	6	6	1	5	8,922	3,085	5,837	1,117	730	387	2	2	...
5	1	4	...	...	...	35,066	13,302	21,764	170	156	14	8,758	4,257	4,501
7	2	5	42	18	24	28,607	10,638	17,969	7,937	4,251	3,686	209	124	85
...	...	...	...	...	...	79	31	48	40	23	17	...	...	...
7	5	2	96	52	44	2,410	1,160	1,250	594	461	133	4,296	1,951	2,345
1	...	1	1	...	1	204	115	89	12	8	4	30	21	9
2	1	1	61	30	31	543	250	293	23	14	9	63	36	27
108	72	36	503	300	194	5,914	3,659	2,255	4,603	2,797	1,806	2,580	1,551	1,029
113	98	15	251	160	91	10,208	5,713	4,495	7,447	4,052	3,395	796	410	385
...	...	...	...	...	...	2	1	1	...	...	...	...	...	...
28	21	7	4	3	1	1,569	889	680	416	303	113	856	509	387
3	...	3	1	1	...	207	149	58	...	...	...	520	314	206
...	...	...	...	...	...	136	77	59	40	28	12	12	9	3
3	1	2	30	14	16	234	116	118	1	1	...	42	26	16
67	20	47	...	...	...	251	105	56	2	2	...	758	468	290
10	7	3	24	16	8	1,457	888	569	284	164	120	439	248	191
...	...	...	...	...	...	...	...	...	...	...	...	...	...	...
...	...	...	...	...	...	576	295	281	1,614	831	783	...	...	...
473	295	178	38	28	10	4,029	2,405	1,624	89	57	32	602	359	243
...	...	...	3	2	1	1,344	836	508	170	94	76	79	53	26
11,467	3,701	7,766	29,458	13,002	16,456	258	152	106	18,162	9,258	8,904	29	8	21
...	...	...	...	...	...	...	...	...	...	...	...	...	...	...
333	214	119	293	152	141	5,439	3,185	2,254	30,186	15,074	14,212	178	122	56
...	...	...	...	...	...	...	...	...	...	...	...	...	...	...
...	...	...	...	...	...	...	...	...	...	...	...	...	...	...
...	...	...	...	...	...	1	1	...	...	...	...	...	...	...
...	...	...	...	...	...	...	...	...	...	...	...	...	...	...
...	...	...	...	...	...	...	...	...	459	264	195	...	...	...
...	...	...	...	...	...	...	...	...	3	...	3	...	...	...
...	...	...	...	...	...	...	...	...	16	6	10	...	...	...
...	...	...	...	...	...	...	...	...	3,661	1,755	1,906	...	...	...
...	...	...	...	...	...	...	...	...	43	36	7	...	...	...
...	...	...	...	...	...	...	...	...	...	...	...	...	...	...
...	...	...	...	...	...	4	2	2	...	...	...	...	...	...
...	...	...	...	...	...	1	1	...	...	...	...	...	...	...
8	6	2	28	8	20	810	444	366	2,905	1,418	1,487	32	14	18
122,526	38,746	83,780	41,363	20,626	20,737	6,833	4,631	2,202	5,531	3,508	2,023	1,374	896	478
1,893	1,399	494	3,210	2,046	1,164	2,470	1,816	654	2,849	1,940	909	254	180	74
...	...	...	...	...	...	338	200	138	...	...	...	8	5	3
...	...	...	...	...	...	...	...	...	...	...	...	13	13	...
...	...	...	3	3	...	4	3	1	2	2	...	1	1	...
1,207	983	224	250	228	62	2,460	1,758	702	860	641	219	711	567	144
5	3	2	5	3	2	20	11	9	...	...	...	4	3	1
...	...	...	...	...	...	...	...	...	...	...	...	...	...	...
...	...	...	...	...	...	...	...	...	...	...	...	...	...	...
...	...	...	1	1	...	...	...	...	...	...	...	...	...	...
5	5	...	27	18	9	65	36	29	8	5	3	3	2	1
...	...	...	...	...	...	...	...	...	...	...	...	...	...	...
...	...	...	...	...	...	...	...	...	...	...	...	...	...	...
...	...	...	22	13	9	127	90	28	...	...	...	...	...	...
1,535	760	775	6,781	3,606	3.175	3,074	2,262	812	2,468	1,743	725	145	108	37
15	11	4	23	15	8	193	138	55	101	72	29	7	3	4
...	...	...	8	5	3	...	...	...	...	...	...	...	...	...
34	19	15	55	31	24	305	207	98	66	39	27	11	9	2

Table XI.—Birth-place—Central India.

TABLE XI.—

A.—States within Central India. B.—Provinces or States in India beyond Central India.

State, Province, or Country of Birth.	Total of Province or State.			Agencies.								
				Indore.			Gwalior.			Bhopal.		
	Total.	Males.	Females.	Total.	Males.	Females.	Total.	Males.	Females.	Total.	Males.	Females.
1	2	3	4	5	6	7	8	9	10	11	12	13
B.—*contd.*												
Travancore	2	1	1	1	1	...	1	...	1	...	...	...
British India (unspecified)	2,194	1,451	743	296	196	100	62	56	6	22	7	15
Goa	25	22	3	23	22	1	...	...	...	2	...	2
C.—												
Burma	33	25	8	13	9	4	19	15	4	1	1	...
Ceylon	31	19	12	17	9	8	...	...	...	3	3	...
Afghanistan	798	657	141	58	55	3	47	28	19	293	239	54
Baluchistan	21	18	3	3	2	1	...	...	...	...	...	...
China	9	5	4	1	1	...	...	...	...	8	4	4
Persia	22	19	3	2	2	...	1	1	...	12	12	...
Arabia	117	65	52	48	25	23	2	2	...	42	24	18
Turkey in Asia	3	2	1	2	1	1	...	...	...	1	1	...
Turkestan	4	3	1	...	...	...	1	1	...	3	2	1
At sea	1	1	...	...	...	...	1	1	...	...	...	...
D.—												
Australia	5	2	3	4	2	2	...	...	...	1	...	1
Africa	14	8	6	9	5	4	...	...	...	...	...	...
England	2,768	2,566	202	1,864	1,721	143	127	123	4	23	16	7
Wales	18	13	5	16	12	4	...	...	...	1	...	1
Scotland	52	41	11	41	34	7	...	...	...	4	2	2
Ireland	206	152	54	151	111	40	...	...	...	...	...	...
Isle of Man	7	6	1	7	6	1	...	...	...	...	...	...
Europe	170	149	21	22	20	2	19	10	9	22	19	3
America	24	13	11	15	7	8	1	...	1	...	...	...
Not returned	1,570	1,058	512	10	5	5	...	...	...	3	2	1
Total	10,318,812	5,395,536	4,923,276	372,792	201,944	170,848	1,757,509	948,805	808,704	2,006,859	1,052,777	958,042

irth-place—*concluded.*

.—Countries in Asia beyond India. D.—Countries beyond Central Asia—*concluded.*

AGENCIES.														
Bundelkhand.			Baghelkhand.			Western Malwa.			Bhopawar.			Guna.		
Total.	Males.	Females.	Total.	Males.	Females.	Total.	Males.	Females.	Total.	Males.	Females.	Total.	Males.	Females.
14	15	16	17	18	19	20	21	22	23	24	25	26	27	28
...	...	...	...	...	...	...	...	...	...	...	...	...	...	...
10	*6*	4	...	...	...	1,785	*1,170*	615	6	*5*	1	13	*11*	2
...	...	...	...	...	...	...	...	...	...	...	...	...	...	...
...	...	...	...	...	...	...	...	...	...	...	...	...	...	...
1	...	1	3	*3*	...	7	*4*	3	...	...	...	...	...	...
17	*17*	...	19	*19*	...	241	*199*	42	99	*76*	23	24	*24*	...
...	...	...	1	...	1	...	...	...	17	*16*	1	...	...	...
...	...	...	...	...	...	...	...	...	...	...	...	...	...	...
1	*1*	...	...	...	...	3	...	3	3	*3*	...	...	...	...
7	*4*	3	1	...	1	16	*9*	7	...	...	...	1	*1*	...
...	...	...	...	...	...	...	...	...	...	...	...	...	...	...
...	...	...	...	...	...	...	...	...	...	...	...	...	...	...
...	...	...	...	...	...	...	...	...	...	...	...	...	...	...
...	...	...	...	...	...	...	...	...	...	...	...	...	...	...
5	*3*	2	...	...	...	...	...	...	...	...	...	...	...	...
490	*465*	25	32	*24*	8	227	*213*	14	4	*3*	1	1	*1*	...
...	...	...	...	...	...	...	...	...	...	...	...	1	*1*	...
3	*3*	...	4	*2*	2	...	...	...	...	...	...	...	...	...
47	*35*	12	7	*5*	2	...	...	...	...	...	...	1	*1*	...
...	...	...	...	...	...	...	...	...	...	...	...	...	...	...
1	*1*	...	1	*1*	...	104	*97*	7	1	*1*	...	...	...	...
6	*4*	2	...	...	...	2	*2*	...	...	...	...	...	...	...
19	*15*	4	...	...	...	...	...	...	...	...	...	1,538	*1,036*	502
08,053	**784,906**	**723,147**	**1,787,606**	**872,222**	**865,384**	**1,619,368**	**851,933**	**767,435**	**978,652**	**502,832**	**4'5,820**	**337,973**	**180,117**	**157,856**

TABLE XI.—Birth-place.

SUMMARY.

AGENCY.	A.—Born in States where enumerated.			B.—Born in remote parts of India.			C.—Born in other countries of Asia.						D.—Born in other Continents.			E.—Born at sea.			F.—Birth-place unspecified.			TOTAL.		
							a.—Contiguous to India.			b.—Remote from India.														
	TOTAL.	Males.	Females.	TOTAL.	Males.	Females.	Total.	Males.	Females.	Total.	Males.	Females.	TOTAL.	Males.	Females.	TOTAL.	Males.	Females.	TOTAL.	Males.	Females.	TOTAL.	Males.	Females.
1	2	3	4	5	6	7	8	9	10	11	12	13	14	15	16	17	18	19	20	21	22	23	24	25
INDORE . . .	314,243	163,387	150,856	56,271	36,534	19.737	87	72	15	52	28	24	2,129	1,918	211	...	...	...	10	5	5	372,792	201,944	170,848
GWALIOR . . .	1,666,971	911,516	755,455	90,336	37,121	53,215	51	31	20	3	3	...	147	133	14	1	1	...	...	...	...	1,757,509	948,805	808,704
BHOPAL . . .	1,872,253	981,781	890,472	134,169	70,654	63,515	328	266	62	55	37	18	51	37	14	...	...	...	3	2	1	2,006,859	1,052,777	954,082
BUNDELKHAND . .	1,367,595	737,992	629,603	139,856	46,361	93,495	23	22	1	8	5	3	552	511	41	...	...	...	19	15	4	1,508,053	784,906	723,147
BAGHELKHAND . .	1,654,911	831,777	823,134	82,600	40,373	42,227	50	40	10	1	...	1	44	32	12	...	...	...	...	...	...	1,737,606	872,222	865,384
WESTERN MALWA .	1,489,961	790,056	699,905	128,742	61,317	67,425	313	239	74	19	9	10	333	312	21	...	...	...	...	...	...	1,619,368	851,933	767 3 5
BHOPAWAR . .	885,171	451,266	433,905	93,349	51,462	41,887	124	97	27	3	3	...	5	4	1	...	...	...	...	...	...	978,652	502,832	475,820
GONA . . .	313,524	166,755	146,769	22,880	12,296	10,584	27	26	1	1	1	...	3	3	...	...	...	...	1,538	1,036	502	337,973	180,117	157,856
TOTAL .	9,564,629	5,034,530	4,530,099	746,203	356,118	392,085	1,003	793	210	142	86	56	3,264	2,950	314	1	1	...	1,570	1,058	512	10,318,812	5,395,536	4,923,276

TABLE XII.

Persons of Unsound Mind, by Age.

NOTE.—This Table applies only to persons enumerated on the British India Schedule.

TABLE XII.—Persons of Unsound Mind, by Age.

AGENCY.	TOTAL AFFLICTED.			DISTRIBUTION BY AGE.																									
				0—4		5—9		10—14		15—19		20—24		25—29		30—34		35—39		40—44		45—49		50—54		55—59		60 AND OVER.	
	Total.	Males.	Females.	Males.	Females.	Males.	Females.	Males.	Females.	Males.	Females.	Males.	Females.	Males.	Females.	Males.	Females.	Males.	Females.	Males.	Females.	Males.	Females.	Males.	Females.	Males.	Females.	Males.	Females.
1	2	3	4	5	6	7	8	9	10	11	12	13	14	15	16	17	18	19	20	21	22	23	24	25	26	27	28	29	30
Indore	5	2	3	...	...	1	1	...	...	...	...	1	...	...	...	...	2	...	...	...	...	...	...	...	...	...	...	...	...
Gwalior	...	...	...	...	...	...	...	...	...	...	...	...	...	...	...	...	...	...	...	...	...	...	...	...	...	...	...	...	...
Bhopal	15	11	4	...	...	...	...	...	...	...	...	2	1	4	...	2	...	2	...	1	3	...	...	...	...	...	...	...	...
Bundelkhand	1	1	...	...	...	...	...	...	...	...	...	...	...	...	...	...	...	...	...	...	...	...	...	1	...	...	...	...	...
Baghelkhand	1	...	1	...	...	...	...	...	1	...	...	...	...	...	...	...	...	...	...	...	...	...	...	...	...	...	...	...	...
Western Malwa	30	18	12	...	...	3	1	...	...	3	1	1	2	2	2	1	1	...	1	2	1	1	...	3	3	...	...	2	...
Bhopawar	...	...	...	...	...	...	...	...	...	...	...	...	...	...	...	...	...	...	...	...	...	...	...	...	...	...	...	...	...
Guna	17	8	9	1	...	1	1	1	...	2	1	...	...	2	1	...	...	...	1	...	1	...	1	1	1	...	...	...	2
Total	69	40	29	1	...	5	3	1	1	5	2	4	3	8	3	3	3	2	2	3	5	1	1	5	4	...	...	2	2

TABLE XIIA.

Persons of Unsound Mind, by Caste, Tribe or Race.

NOTE.—This Table applies only to persons enumerated on the British India Schedule.

TABLE XIIA.—Persons of Unsound Mind, by Caste, Tribe or Race.

Class.	Group.	Caste, Tribe, etc.	Religion.	TOTAL.			DISTRIBUTION BY AGENCIES.															
							INDORE.		GWALIOR.		BHOPAL.		BUNDELKHAND.		BAGHELKHAND.		WESTERN MALWA.		BHOPAWAR.		GUNA.	
				Total.	Males.	Females.	Males.	Females.	Males.	Females.	Males.	Females.	Males.	Females.	Males.	Females.	Males.	Females.	Males.	Females.	Males.	Females.
1	2	3	4	5	6	7	8	9	10	11	12	13	14	15	16	17	18	19	20	21	22	23
A.—AGRICULTURAL.	1. MILITARY AND DOMINANT.	RAJPUT	Hindu	1	1	...	...	...	...	...	...	...	...	...	...	...	1	...	...	...	...	...
		JAT	"	4	3	1	...	...	...	...	...	...	...	...	...	...	2	...	...	...	1	1
		GUJAR	"	2	1	1	...	...	...	...	...	...	...	...	...	...	1	1	...	...	...	...
	2. MINOR AGRICULTURAL.	MALI	"	7	3	4	...	...	...	...	...	...	...	...	...	...	1	1	...	...	2	3
		KACHHI	"	3	2	1	...	...	...	...	2	1	...	...	...	...	...	...	...	...	...	...
		AHIR	"	2	1	1	...	...	...	...	1	...	...	...	...	...	...	1	...	...	...	...
		KURMI	"	4	1	3	...	...	...	...	...	...	...	...	...	...	1	3	...	...	...	...
		DANGI	"	4	3	1	...	...	...	...	...	...	...	...	...	...	3	1	...	...	...	...
		DHAKARA	"	1	1	...	...	...	...	...	...	...	...	...	...	...	1	...	...	...	...	...
		BALAI	"	1	1	...	...	...	...	...	...	...	...	...	...	...	1	...	...	...	...	...
	4. FOREST AND HILL TRIBES.	MINA	"	1	1	...	...	...	...	...	1	...	...	...	...	...	...	...	...	...	...	...
B.—PROFESSIONAL.	5. PRIESTS	BRAHMAN	"	2	1	1	...	...	...	...	1	1	...	...	...	...	...	...	...	...	...	...
		SAIYAD	Musalman	1	...	1	...	1	...	...	...	...	...	...	...	...	...	...	...	...	...	...
	6. DEVOTEES	GOSAIN	Hindu	1	1	...	...	...	...	...	...	...	...	...	...	...	1	...	...	...	...	...
C.—COMMERCIAL	14. TRADERS	BANIA	"	1	...	1	...	...	...	...	...	...	...	...	...	1	...	...	...	...	...	...
		MAHAJAN	"	5	4	1	...	...	...	...	2	...	...	...	...	...	1	...	...	...	1	1
D.—ARTISAN AND VILLAGE MENIAL.	18. BARBERS	NAI	"	1	...	1	...	1	...	...	...	...	...	...	...	...	...	...	...	...	...	...
	19. BLACKSMITHS	LOHAR	"	2	2	...	...	...	...	...	...	...	...	...	...	...	1	...	...	...	1	...
	23. WEAVERS	KUNDERA	"	2	2	...	...	...	...	...	1	...	...	...	...	...	...	...	...	...	1	...
	26. SHEPHERDS	DHANGAR	"	2	2	...	...	...	...	...	...	...	...	...	...	...	...	...	...	...	2	...
	28. POTTERS	KUMHAR	"	1	...	1	...	...	...	...	...	...	...	...	...	...	...	...	...	...	...	1
	38. LEATHER WORKERS	CHAMAR	"	5	2	3	...	...	...	...	1	...	1	...	...	...	...	2	...	...	...	1
E.—VAGRANT, MINOR ARTISANS AND PERFORMERS, ETC.	44. HUNTERS AND FOWLERS, ETC.	BAGRI	"	1	1	...	...	...	...	...	...	...	...	...	...	...	1	...	...	...	...	...
	45. MISCELLANEOUS AND DISREPUTABLE LIVERS.	HINDU (UNSPECIFIED).	"	1	...	1	...	1	...	...	...	...	...	...	...	...	...	...	...	...	...	...
		MUSALMAN (UNSPECIFIED).	Musalman	2	...	2	...	...	...	...	...	...	...	...	...	...	...	...	...	...	...	2
		SONDHIA	Hindu	3	1	2	...	...	...	...	...	...	...	...	...	...	1	2	...	...	...	...
F.—RACES AND NATIONALITIES.	48. NON-INDIAN ASIATIC RACES.	PATHAN	Musalman	4	3	1	1	...	...	...	1	1	...	...	...	...	1	...	...	...	...	...
		SHEKH	"	5	3	2	1	...	...	...	1	1	...	...	...	...	1	1	...	...	...	...
		Total	......	69	40	29		3	...	...	11	4	1	...	...	1	18	12	...	...	8	9

Table XIIA.—Persons of Unsound Mind, by Caste, etc.—Central India.

TABLE XIII.

Deaf Mutes, by Age.

NOTE.—This Table applies only to persons enumerated on the British India Schedule.

TABLE XIII.—Deaf Mutes, by Age.

AGENCY.	TOTAL AFFLICTED.			DISTRIBUTION BY AGE.																									
				0—4		5—9		10—14		15—19		20—24		25—29		30—34		35—39		40—44		45—49		50—54		55—59		60 AND OVER.	
	Total.	Males.	Females.	Males.	Females.	Males.	Females.	Males.	Females.	Males.	Females.	Males.	Females.	Males.	Females.	Males.	Females.	Males.	Females.	Males.	Females.	Males.	Females.	Males.	Females.	Males.	Females.	Males.	Females.
1	2	3	4	5	6	7	8	9	10	11	12	13	14	15	16	17	18	19	20	21	22	23	24	25	26	27	28	29	30
INDORE	12	6	6	...	...	...	...	1	...	...	1	1	1	1	...	...	1	...	1	2	1	1	...	...	...	...	...	...	1
GWALIOR	2	2	...	...	...	...	...	1	...	1	...	...	...	...	...	...	...	...	...	...	...	...	...	...	...	...	...	...	...
BHOPAL	7	3	4	...	...	1	...	...	...	...	...	1	...	...	...	...	...	...	...	...	1	...	...	1	2	...	1	...	...
BUNDELKHAND	6	4	2	...	...	...	...	1	...	2	1	...	1	...	...	...	...	...	...	...	...	...	...	1	...	...	...	...	...
BAGHELKHAND	5	2	3	...	...	...	...	...	...	...	...	1	...	...	1	1	...	...	1	...	1	...	...	...	...	...	...	...	...
WESTERN MALWA	9	4	5	...	1	1	...	...	1	...	...	...	...	...	...	...	1	...	1	2	...	...	...	1	...	...	...	...	1
BHOPAWAR	...	...	...	...	...	...	...	...	...	...	...	...	...	...	...	...	...	...	...	...	...	...	...	...	...	...	...	...	...
GUNA	8	5	3	...	...	...	...	...	...	2	...	1	...	...	...	1	...	1	1	...	...	...	...	...	1	...	...	...	1
Total	49	26	23	...	1	2	...	3	1	5	2	4	2	1	1	2	2	1	4	4	2	1	...	3	3	...	1	...	3

TABLE XIIIA.

Deaf Mutes, by Caste, Tribe or Race.

NOTE.—This Table applies only to persons enumerated on the British India Schedule.

TABLE XIIIA.—Deaf Mutes, by Caste, Tribe or Race.

Class.	Group.	Caste, Tribe, etc.	Religion.	TOTAL.			DISTRIBUTION BY AGENCIES.															
							Indore.		Gwalior.		Bhopal.		Bundelkhand.		Baghelkhand.		Western Malwa.		Bhopawar.		Guna.	
				Total.	Males.	Females.	Males.	Females.	Males.	Females.	Males.	Females.	Males.	Females.	Males.	Females.	Males.	Females.	Males.	Females.	Males.	Females.
1	2	3	4	5	6	7	8	9	10	11	12	13	14	15	16	17	18	19	20	21	22	23
A.—Agricultural.	2. Minor Agricultural	Mali	Hindu	1	1	...	...	...	...	...	...	...	...	...	...	...	1	...	...	...	...	...
		Ahir	"	3	2	1	1	...	...	...	...	...	...	...	...	...	...	...	...	...	1	1
		Dhakar	"	1	...	1	...	...	...	...	...	...	...	...	...	...	...	1	...	...	...	...
B.—Professional.	11. Musicians and ballad-reciters	Dholi	"	1	...	1	...	...	...	...	...	...	...	...	...	...	...	...	...	...	...	1
		Katia	"	1	...	1	...	...	...	...	...	...	...	...	...	1	...	...	...	...	...	...
C.—Commercial	14. Traders	Bania	"	1	...	1	...	1	...	...	...	...	...	...	...	...	...	...	...	...	...	...
		Mahajan	"	1	1	...	...	...	...	...	...	...	...	...	...	...	...	...	...	...	1	...
		Oswal	"	1	...	1	...	...	...	...	...	1	...	...	...	...	...	...	...	...	...	...
D.—Artisan and Village Menials.	17. Goldsmiths	Sonar	"	2	1	1	...	...	...	...	1	...	...	...	...	1	...	...	...	...	...	...
	27. Oil-pressers	Teli	"	1	1	...	...	...	...	...	...	...	1	...	...	...	...	...	...	...	...	...
	37. Butchers	Khatik	"	1	1	...	...	...	...	...	...	...	...	...	...	...	1	...	...	...	...	...
	38. Leather-workers	Chamar	"	5	1	4	...	...	...	...	...	1	...	...	...	1	1	2	...	...	...	...
	39. Scavengers	Bhangi	"	2	...	2	...	...	...	...	...	...	...	...	...	...	...	2	...	...	...	...
E.—Vagrant, Minor Artisans and Performers, etc.	45. Miscellaneous and disreputable livers	Hindu (unspecified).	"	11	6	5	2	2	...	...	1	2	...	1	...	...	1	...	...	...	2	...
		Khangar	"	1	1	...	...	...	...	...	...	...	...	...	1	...	...	...	...	...	...	...
F.—Races and Nationalities.	48. Non-Indian Asiatic Races	Pathan	Musalman	6	4	2	2	1	1	...	...	...	...	1	...	...	...	...	...	...	1	...
		Shekh	"	9	6	3	...	2	1	...	1	...	3	...	1	...	...	...	...	...	...	1
	52. Christian Converts	Christian	Christian	1	1	...	1	...	...	...	...	...	...	...	...	...	...	...	...	...	...	...
		Total		49	26	23	6	6	2	...	3	4	4	2	2	3	4	5	...	...	5	3

TABLE XIV.

Blind, by Age.

NOTE.—This Table applies only to persons enumerated on the British India Schedule.

TABLE XIV.—Blind, by Age.

AGENCY.	TOTAL AFFLICTED.			DISTRIBUTION BY AGE.																									
				0—4		5—9		10—14		15—19		20—24		25—29		30—34		35—39		40—44		45—49		50—54		55—59		60 AND OVER.	
	Total	Males.	Females.	Males.	Females.	Males.	Females.	Males.	Females.	Males.	Females.	Males.	Females.	Males.	Females.	Males.	Females.	Males.	Females.	Males.	Females.	Males.	Females.	Males.	Females.	Males.	Females.	Males.	Females.
1	2	3	4	5	6	7	8	9	10	11	12	13	14	15	16	17	18	19	20	21	22	23	24	25	26	27	28	29	30
Indore	19	14	5	...	...	2	...	...	1	2	...	2	...	1	...	1	1	...	...	...	1	...	...	2	1	1	...	3	1
Gwalior	...	...	...	...	...	...	...	...	...	...	...	...	...	...	...	...	...	...	...	...	...	...	...	...	...	...	...	...	...
Bhopal	128	78	50	1	...	7	...	3	2	3	2	4	1	3	6	7	3	1	5	11	6	3	2	8	10	4	...	23	13
Bundelkhand	9	6	3	...	...	2	...	2	...	...	1	...	...	1	...	1	...	...	...	...	...	...	...	...	2	...	...	...	..
Baghelkhand	16	7	9	...	1	.	1	...	...	2	...	2	1	...	1	...	...	...	1	...	...	...	1	1	1	...	1	2	1
Western Malwa	157	81	76	1	1	12	3	8	1	6	1	7	4	1	1	4	3	3	4	7	10	3	3	7	6	4	3	18	36
Bhopawar	...	...	...	...	...	...	...	...	...	...	...	...	...	...	...	...	...	...	...	...	...	...	...	...	...	...	...	...	...
Guna	102	59	43	...	1	2	1	3	...	2	1	3	1	8	2	6	5	3	...	8	3	5	1	4	7	...	4	15	17
Total	431	245	186	2	3	25	5	16	4	15	5	18	7	14	10	19	12	7	10	26	20	11	7	22	27	9	8	61	68

TABLE XIVA.

Blind, by Caste, Tribe or Race.

NOTE.—This Table applies only to persons enumerated on the British India Schedule.

TABLE XIVA.—Blind, by Caste, Tribe or Race.

Class.	Group.	Caste, Tribe, etc.	Religion.	TOTAL. Total.	TOTAL. Males.	TOTAL. Females.	Indore. Males.	Indore. Females.	Gwalior. Males.	Gwalior. Females.	Bhopal. Males.	Bhopal. Females.	Bundelkhand. Males.	Bundelkhand. Females.	Baghelkhand. Males.	Baghelkhand. Females.	Western Malwa. Males.	Western Malwa. Females.	Bhopawar. Males.	Bhopawar. Females.	Guna. Males.	Guna. Females.
1	2	3	4	5	6	7	8	9	10	11	12	13	14	15	16	17	18	19	20	21	22	23
A.—AGRICULTURAL	1. MILITARY AND DOMINANT	RAJPUT	Hindu	12	5	7	...	...	...	...	3	2	...	...	...	...	2	5	...	...	...	...
		JAT	"	1	...	1	...	...	...	...	...	...	...	...	...	...	...	...	...	...	...	1
		GUJAR	"	9	6	3	...	...	...	...	1	...	...	...	...	...	3	2	...	...	2	1
	2. MINOR AGRICULTURAL	MALI	"	9	6	3	...	...	...	...	2	...	...	...	...	...	2	2	...	...	2	1
		KACHHI	"	7	...	7	...	...	...	...	...	7	...	...	...	...	...	...	...	...	...	...
		AHIR	"	12	8	4	1	...	...	...	5	2	...	...	...	...	1	...	...	...	1	2
		KURMI	"	13	3	10	...	...	...	...	2	2	...	...	...	...	1	8	...	...	...	...
		DANGI	"	3	1	2	...	...	...	...	1	2	...	...	...	...	...	...	...	...	...	...
		DHAKARA	"	10	8	2	...	...	...	...	...	...	...	...	...	...	2	1	...	...	6	1
		BALAI	"	12	5	7	...	...	...	...	...	...	...	...	...	...	5	7	...	...	...	...
		KOL	"	3	1	2	...	...	...	...	...	...	...	...	1	2	...	...	...	...	...	...
		TAMBOLI	"	3	2	1	...	...	...	...	...	1	...	...	...	...	1	...	...	...	1	...
		LODHA	"	5	4	1	...	...	...	...	3	...	...	...	...	...	...	...	...	...	1	1
		KOLI	"	11	4	7	...	...	...	...	1	4	...	...	...	...	1	...	...	...	2	3
	4. FOREST AND HILL TRIBES.	MINA	"	7	6	1	...	...	...	...	...	...	...	...	...	...	...	...	...	...	6	1
		SAHARIYA	"	9	4	5	...	...	...	...	...	...	...	...	...	...	...	...	...	...	4	5
		MER	"	1	1	...	...	...	...	...	...	...	...	...	...	...	...	...	...	...	1	...
		CHARAR	"	3	1	2	...	...	...	...	1	2	...	...	...	...	...	...	...	...	...	...
		KARAR	"	2	1	1	...	...	...	...	...	...	...	...	...	...	...	...	...	...	1	1
B.—PROFESSIONAL	5. PRIESTS	BRAHMAN	"	25	17	8	1	...	...	...	6	1 [4]	1	...	...	...	2	1	...	...	7	...
		SAIYAD	Musalman	1	...	1	...	...	...	...	...	1	...	...	...	...	...	...	...	...	...	...
	6. DEVOTEES	GOSAIN	Hindu	6	4	2	...	...	...	...	1	...	...	...	...	...	1	1	...	...	2	1
		BAIRAGI	"	9	7	2	1	...	...	...	1	2	...	...	...	...	4	...	...	...	1	...
	9. WRITERS	KAYASTH	"	4	3	1	...	...	...	...	1	...	...	...	...	...	2	1	...	...	...	...
	11. MUSICIANS AND BALLAD-RECITERS	BHAT	"	1	1	...	...	...	...	...	1	...	...	...	...	...	...	...	...	...	...	...
C.—COMMERCIAL.	14. TRADERS	OSWAL	Jain	3	3	...	...	...	...	...	2	...	...	...	...	...	1	...	...	...	...	...
		PORWAL	"	3	2	1	...	...	...	...	2	...	...	...	...	...	...	...	...	...	...	1
		BANIA	Hindu	5	3	2	...	...	...	...	3	2	...	...	...	...	...	...	...	...	...	...
		MAHAJAN	"	7	2	5	...	...	...	...	...	...	...	...	...	...	1	2	...	...	1	3
D.—ARTISAN AND VILLAGE MENIALS.	17. GOLDSMITHS	SONAR	"	3	1	2	...	...	...	...	...	1	...	...	...	...	1	1	...	...	...	...
	18. BARBERS	NAI	"	6	3	3	...	...	...	...	1	...	...	...	...	...	1	1	...	...	1	2

Table XIVA.—Blind, by Caste, etc.—Central India.

Class.	Group.	Caste, Tribe, etc.	Religion.	Total.	Males.	Females.	Indore. Males.	Indore. Females.	Gwalior. Males.	Gwalior. Females.	Bhopal. Males.	Bhopal. Females.	Bundelkhand. Males.	Bundelkhand. Females.	Baghelkhand. Males.	Baghelkhand. Females.	Western Malwa. Males.	Western Malwa. Females.	Bhopawar. Males.	Bhopawar. Females.	Guna. Males.	Guna. Females.
1	2	3	4	5	6	7	8	9	10	11	12	13	14	15	16	17	18	19	20	21	22	23
D.—Artisan and Village Menials	19. Blacksmiths	Lohar	Hindu	4	2	2	...	...	...	...	...	...	...	...	1	2	1	...	...	...	...	...
	20. Carpenters and Turners	Khati	"	9	6	3	...	...	...	...	4	2	...	...	...	...	...	1	...	...	2	...
	22. Tailors	Darzi	"	13	11	2	...	...	...	...	...	...	...	...	...	...	11	2	...	...	...	...
	23. Weavers, Calenderers and Dyers	Kori	"	1	1	...	...	...	...	...	...	...	...	...	1	...	...	...	...	...	...	...
		Chhipa	"	1	1	...	...	...	...	...	1	...	...	...	...	...	...	...	...	...	...	...
		Kander	"	1	...	1	...	...	...	...	...	1	...	...	...	...	...	...	...	...	...	...
	24. Washerman	Dhobi	"	2	1	1	...	...	...	...	...	...	...	...	...	...	1	...	...	...	...	1
	26. Shepherds and Wool-weavers	Gadaria	"	1	1	...	...	...	...	...	1	...	...	...	...	...	...	...	...	...	...	...
	27. Oil Pressers	Teli	"	7	4	3	...	...	...	...	1	2	...	...	...	...	3	...	...	...	...	1
	28. Potters	Kumhar	"	8	6	2	...	...	...	...	1	...	...	...	...	...	4	...	...	...	1	2
	30. Salt, etc., workers	Lunia	"	1	1	...	...	...	...	...	...	...	...	...	1	...	...	...	...	...	...	...
	35. Fishermen, Cooks, etc.	Kewat	"	1	...	1	...	...	...	...	...	...	...	...	...	1	...	...	...	...	...	...
		Bharbhunja	"	1	1	...	...	...	...	...	...	...	...	...	1	...	...	...	...	...	...	...
	36. Distillers and Toddy drawers	Kalal	"	3	1	2	...	...	...	...	...	...	...	...	...	...	1	1	...	...	...	1
	38. Leather-workers	Chamar	"	61	30	31	2	3	...	...	14	10	2	...	...	...	1	11	...	...	11	7
		Mochi	"	3	1	2	...	...	...	...	1	...	...	...	...	...	...	2	...	...	...	...
		Do.	Musalman	1	1	...	1	...	...	...	...	...	...	...	...	...	...	...	...	...	...	...
	39. Scavengers	Bhangi	Hindu	1	...	1	...	...	...	...	...	...	...	...	...	...	...	...	...	...	...	1
E.—Vagrant, Minor Artisans and Performers, etc.	42. Knife grinders	Sikligar	"	3	2	1	...	...	...	...	...	...	...	...	...	...	2	1	...	...	...	...
	44. Hunters and Fowlers	Bagri	"	2	1	1	...	...	...	...	...	...	...	...	...	...	1	1	...	...	...	...
	45. Miscellaneous and Disreputable Livers	Hindu (unspecified)	"	15	8	7	4	...	...	...	2	2	...	1	...	...	1	4	...	...	1	...
		Daroga	"	1	1	...	...	...	...	...	...	...	...	...	...	...	1	...	...	...	...	...
		Khangar	"	1	1	...	...	...	...	...	...	...	...	...	...	...	...	...	...	...	1	...
		Sondhia	"	25	11	14	...	...	...	...	...	...	...	...	...	...	11	14	...	...	...	...
F.—Races and Nationalities	48. Races and Nationalities	Pathan	Musalman	13	9	4	...	1	...	...	3	1	...	...	...	1	5	1	...	...	1	...
		Shekh	"	35	24	11	3	...	...	...	11	3	2	2	2	1	4	5	...	...	2	...
		Moghul	"	1	...	1	...	...	...	...	...	...	...	...	...	1	...	...	...	...	...	...
		Others	"	9	7	2	1	1	...	...	2	...	1	...	...	...	2	1	...	...	1	...
	50. Non-Asiatic Races	European	Christian	1	...	1	...	...	...	...	...	...	...	—	...	1	...	...	...	...	...	...
	52. Christian Convert	Native Christian	Do.	1	1	...	...	...	...	...	...	...	...	...	...	...	1	...	...	...	...	...
			Total	481	245	186	14	5	...	...	78	50	6	8	7	9	81	76	...	...	59	48

TABLE XV.

Lepers, by Age.

NOTE.—This Table applies only to persons enumerated on the British India Schedule.

TABLE XV.—Lepers, by Age.

AGENCY.	TOTAL AFFLICTED.			DISTRIBUTION BY AGE.																									
				0—4		5—9		10—14		15—19		20—24		25—29		30—34		35—39		40—44		45—49		50—54		55—59		60 AND OVER.	
	Total.	Males.	Females.	Males.	Females.	Males.	Females.	Males.	Females.	Males.	Females.	Males.	Females.	Males.	Females.	Males.	Females.	Males.	Females.	Males.	Females.	Males.	Females.	Males.	Females.	Males.	Females.	Males.	Females.
1	2	3	4	5	6	7	8	9	10	11	12	13	14	15	16	17	18	19	20	21	22	23	24	25	26	27	28	29	30
INDORE	1	1	...	...	...	...	...	1	...	...	...	...	...	...	...	...	...	...	...	...	...	...	...	...	...	...	...	...	...
GWALIOR	1	...	1	...	...	...	...	...	...	...	...	...	...	...	...	...	...	...	1	...	...	...	...	...	...	...	...	...	...
BHOPAL	16	12	4	...	...	...	...	...	1	1	1	...	...	6	...	...	1	...	...	1	1	...	...	3	...	...	...	1	...
BUNDELKHAND	3	2	1	...	...	...	...	...	...	...	...	...	...	...	...	...	...	...	...	1	...	1	...	...	...	...	...	...	1
BAGHELKHAND	...	...	...	...	...	...	...	...	...	...	...	...	...	...	...	...	...	...	...	...	...	...	...	...	...	...	...	...	...
WESTERN MALWA	36	28	8	...	...	...	...	...	...	2	...	2	1	3	...	3	...	1	4	4	1	4	...	5	...	1	3	3	2
BHOPAWAR	1	...	1	...	...	...	...	...	...	...	...	...	...	...	...	...	1	...	...	...	...	...	...	...	...	...	...	...	...
GUNA	22	16	6	...	...	...	...	1	1	...	...	1	1	3	2	2	...	2	1	1	1	...	...	4	...	1	...	1	...
Total	80	59	21	...	...	...	...	2	2	3	1	3	2	12	2	5	2	3	6	7	3	5	...	12	...	2	3	5	3

TABLE XVA.

Lepers, by Caste, Tribe, or Race.

NOTE.—This Table applies only to persons enumerated on the British India Schedule.

Table XVA.—Lepers, by Caste, etc.—Central India.

TABLE XVA.—Lepers, by Caste, Tribe or Race.

Class.	Group.	Caste, Tribe, etc.	Religion.	TOTAL.			DISTRIBUTION BY AGENCIES.															
							Indore.		Gwalior.		Bhopal.		Bundelkhand.		Baghelkhand.		Western Malwa.		Bhopawar.		Guna.	
				Total.	Males.	Females.	Males.	Females.	Males.	Females.	Males.	Females.	Males.	Females.	Males.	Females.	Males.	Females.	Males.	Females.	Males.	Females.
1	2	3	4	5	6	7	8	9	10	11	12	13	14	15	16	17	18	19	20	21	22	23
A.—Agricultural.	1. Military and Dominant.	Rajput	Hindu	4	3	1	...	...	...	...	...	1	...	...	...	...	3	...	...	...	...	...
		Gujar	"	1	...	1	...	...	...	...	...	...	...	...	...	...	...	1	...	...	...	...
	2. Minor Agricultural.	Mali	"	3	2	1	...	...	...	...	...	...	...	...	...	...	2	...	...	...	...	1
		Ahir	"	1	1	...	...	...	...	...	...	...	...	...	...	...	...	...	...	...	1	...
		Ghosi	"	1	1	...	...	...	...	...	1	...	...	...	...	...	...	...	...	...	...	...
		Kurmi	"	4	4	...	...	...	...	...	...	...	...	...	...	...	4	...	...	...	...	...
		Dangi	"	3	3	...	...	...	...	...	1	...	...	...	...	...	2	...	...	...	...	...
		Balai	"	6	2	4	...	...	...	...	...	...	...	...	...	...	2	4	...	...	...	...
		Koli	"	2	2	...	...	...	...	...	2	...	...	...	...	...	...	...	...	...	...	...
		Tamboli	"	1	1	...	...	...	...	...	1	...	...	...	...	...	...	...	...	...	...	...
		Lodha	"	1	1	...	...	...	...	...	...	...	...	...	...	...	...	...	...	...	1	...
	4. Forest and Hill Tribes.	Bhil	Aboriginal	1	...	1	...	...	...	...	...	...	...	...	...	...	...	...	...	1	...	...
		Mina	Hindu	8	6	2	...	...	...	...	...	...	...	...	...	...	...	...	...	...	6	2
		Sahariya	"	2	2	...	...	...	...	...	...	...	...	...	...	...	...	...	...	...	2	...
B.—Professional	5. Priests	Brahman	"	4	3	1	...	...	...	1	...	...	...	...	...	...	2	...	...	...	1	...
C.—Commercial	14. Traders	Mahajan	"	2	2	...	...	...	...	...	1	...	...	...	...	...	1	...	...	...	...	...
D.—Artisan and Village Menials.	16. Carriers	Banjara	"	1	1	...	...	...	...	...	...	...	...	...	...	...	...	...	...	...	1	...
	17. Goldsmiths	Sonar	"	2	2	...	...	...	...	...	...	...	...	...	...	...	1	...	...	...	1	...
	18. Barbers	Nai	"	2	1	1	...	...	...	...	1	...	...	...	...	...	...	1	...	...	...	...
	20. Carpenters and Turners.	Khati	"	1	1	...	...	...	...	...	...	...	...	...	...	...	...	...	...	...	1	...
	24. Washermen	Dhobi	"	3	3	...	...	...	...	...	...	...	...	...	...	...	2	...	...	...	1	...
	26. Distillers and Toddy-drawers.	Kalal	"	1	1	...	...	...	...	...	...	...	...	...	...	...	1	...	...	...	...	...
	37. Butchers	Khatik	"	1	...	1	...	...	...	...	...	...	...	...	...	...	...	...	...	...	...	1
	38. Leather workers	Chamar	"	10	6	4	1	...	...	...	2	...	...	1	...	...	2	2	...	...	1	1
	39 Scavengers	Bhangi	"	2	1	1	...	...	...	...	...	1	1	...	...	...	...	...	...	...	...	...
E.—Vagrant Minor Artisan and Performers.	45. Miscellaneous and Disreputable Livers.	Hindu (unspecified).	"	3	2	1	...	...	...	...	1	...	1	...	...	...	...	...	...	...	...	1
		Sondhia	"	5	5	...	...	...	...	...	...	...	...	...	...	...	5	...	...	...	...	...
F.—Races and Nationalities.	48. Non-Indian Asiatic Races.	Shekh	Musalman	5	3	2	...	...	...	...	2	2	...	...	...	...	1	...	...	...	...	...
			Total	80	59	1	1	...	...	1	12	4	2	1	...	...	28	8	...	1	16	6

TABLE XVI.

Castes, Tribes and Races, by Nationality or traditional Occupation.

TABLE XVI.—Castes, Tribes and Races, by Nationality or traditional Occupation.

NAME AND CLASSIFICATION.				PROVINCIAL TOTAL.			DISTRIBUTION BY AGENCIES.								
							INDORE.			GWALIOR.			BHOPAL.		
Class.	Group.	Caste.	Religion.	Total.	Males.	Females.	Total.	Males.	Females.	Total.	Males.	Females.	Total.	Males.	Females.
1	2	3	4	5	6	7	8	9	10	11	12	13	14	15	16
A.—AGRICULTURAL.	I.—MILITARY AND DOMINANT.	BUNDELA	Hindu	104	58	46	41	20	21	...	...	...	...	...	...
		BHAISAUNGHYA	Do.	33	33	...	...	...	...	...	...	...	...	...	...
		BHATTI	Do.	2	2	...	2	2	...	...	...	...	...	...	...
		BASORI	Do.	3,377	1,676	1,701	...	...	...	...	...	...	...	...	...
		BHAIYA	Do.	1	1	...	...	...	...	...	...	...	...	...	...
		BHADAURIYA	Do.	5	3	2	...	...	...	...	...	...	...	...	...
		BHAGDAWAT	Do.	92	48	44	...	...	...	...	...	...	...	...	...
		BHAYAR	Aboriginal	1,206	622	584	...	...	...	...	...	...	...	...	...
		BHUMIA	Do.	2,647	1,338	1,309	...	...	...	...	...	...	...	...	...
		CHOHAN	Hindu	9	6	3	5	2	3	...	...	...	...	...	...
		Do.	Musalman	22	9	13	5	2	3	...	...	...	...	...	...
		CHHATTRI	Hindu	84,231	44,303	39,928	...	...	...	...	...	...	...	...	...
		CHAROT	Do.	2	...	2	...	...	...	...	...	...	...	...	...
		DESWALI	Musalman	4,630	2,547	2,083	...	...	...	...	...	...	2,780	1,616	1,164
		Do.	Aboriginal	33,127	17,053	16,074	1,120	601	519	...	...	...	30,610	15,727	14,883
		DUSADH	Hindu	5	2	3	...	...	...	...	...	...	...	...	...
		DHANKAR	Do.	55	55	...	...	...	...	...	...	...	...	...	...
		GARKWAR	Do.	1	1	...	...	...	...	...	...	...	...	...	...
		GUJAR	Do.	204,501	113,966	90,535	2,593	1,459	1,134	74,643	43,114	31,529	38,747	21,164	17,583
		Do.	Musalman	10	4	6	3	1	2	...	...	...	7	3	4
		GOLANDAJ	Hindu	19	11	8	...	...	...	...	...	...	19	11	8
		JAT	Do.	56,529	30,255	26,274	2,888	1,590	1,298	12,012	6,804	5,208	17,263	9,472	7,791
		Do.	Musalman	1	1	...	1	1	...	...	...	...	...	...	...
		JANGHARA	Hindu	4	...	4	4	...	4	...	...	...	...	...	...
		JODHA	Do.	13	8	5	...	...	...	...	...	...	12	7	5
		JAIS	Do.	150	41	109	...	...	...	...	...	...	150	41	109
		JADHAVA	Do.	11	7	4	7	3	4	...	...	...	...	...	...
		KACHHWA	Do.	352	225	127	307	199	108	42	23	19	3	3	...
		KUNTEL	Aboriginal	35	31	4	...	...	...	...	...	...	...	...	...
		KHARE	Hindu	1	1	...	1	1	...	...	...	...	...	...	...
		KHODGAR	Do.	2	2	...	...	...	...	...	...	...	...	...	...
		MARATHA	Do.	35,608	18,508	17,100	9,749	5,092	4,657	10,243	5,293	4,950	2,564	1,251	1,313
		MIRDHA	Do.	83	52	31	4	4	...	...	...	...	...	...	...
		Do.	Aboriginal	15,657	8,151	7,506	...	...	...	10,011	5,266	4,745	3,297	1,683	1,614
		NANAKSAI	Hindu	25	7	18	4	...	4	...	...	...	21	7	14
		PAMAR	Do.	9,975	4,993	4,982	92	38	54	1	1	...	9,867	4,944	4,923
		Do.	Musalman	24	24	...	...	...	...	...	...	...	...	...	...
		PURBIA	Hindu	2,973	1,564	1,409	1,600	869	731	...	...	...	912	455	457
		PARIHAR	Do.	2	2	...	...	...	...	...	...	...	...	...	...
		PARMAR	Do.	1	1	...	...	...	...	...	...	...	...	1	...

NAME AND CLASSIFICATION.

Class.	Group.	Caste.	Religion.	Bundelkhand. Total.	Bundelkhand. Males.	Bundelkhand. Females.	Baghelkhand. Total.	Baghelkhand. Males.	Baghelkhand. Females.	Western Malwa. Total.	Western Malwa. Males.	Western Malwa. Females.	Bhopawar. Total.	Bhopawar. Males.	Bhopawar. Females.	Guna. Total.	Guna. Males.	Guna. Females.
				17	18	19	20	21	22	23	24	25	26	27	28	29	30	31
A.—AGRICULTURAL.	I.—MILITARY AND DOMINANT.	BUNDELA	Hindu	...	...	...	...	...	...	58	35	23	2	1	1	3	2	1
		BHAISAUNDHYA	Do.	33	33	...	...	...	...	...	...	...	...	...	...	...	...	...
		BHATTI	Do.	...	...	...	...	...	...	...	...	...	...	...	...	...	...	...
		BASORI	Do.	...	...	...	3,377	1,676	1,701	...	...	...	...	...	...	...	...	...
		BHAIYA	Do.	...	...	...	1	1	...	...	...	...	...	...	...	...	...	...
		BHADAURIYA	Do.	...	...	...	...	...	...	4	2	2	1	1	...	...	...	...
		BHAGDAWAT	Do.	...	...	...	...	...	...	92	48	44	...	...	...	...	...	...
		BHAYAR	Aboriginal	...	...	...	1,206	622	584	...	...	...	...	...	...	...	...	...
		BHUMIA	Do.	...	...	...	2,647	1,338	1,309	...	...	...	...	...	...	...	...	...
		CHOHAN	Hindu	...	...	...	4	4	...	...	...	...	...	...	...	...	...	...
		Do.	Musalman	...	...	...	...	...	...	17	7	10	...	...	...	...	...	...
		CHHATTRI	Hindu	84	57	27	84,147	44,246	39,901	...	...	...	...	...	...	...	...	...
		CHAROT	Do.	...	...	...	...	...	...	2	...	2	...	...	...	...	...	...
		DESWALI	Musalman	...	...	...	...	...	...	840	423	417	...	...	...	1,010	508	502
		Do.	Aboriginal	68	39	29	...	...	...	352	189	163	977	497	480	...	...	...
		DUSADH	Hindu	5	2	3	...	...	...	...	...	...	...	...	...	...	...	...
		DHANKAR	Do.	...	...	...	...	...	...	55	55	...	...	...	...	...	...	...
		GAEKWAR	Do.	...	...	...	...	...	...	1	1	...	...	...	...	...	...	...
		GUJAR	Do.	7,617	4,276	3,341	208	102	106	60,071	32,466	27,605	12,636	6,829	5,807	7,986	4,556	3,430
		Do.	Musalman	...	...	...	...	...	...	...	...	...	...	...	...	...	...	...
		GOLANDAJ	Hindu	...	...	...	...	...	...	...	...	...	...	...	...	...	...	...
		JAT	Do.	1,364	813	551	27	17	10	14,695	7,177	7,518	6,676	3,446	3,230	1,604	936	668
		Do.	Musalman	...	...	...	...	...	...	...	...	...	...	...	...	...	...	...
		JANGHARA	Hindu	...	...	...	...	...	...	...	...	...	...	...	...	...	...	...
		JODHA	Do.	...	...	...	1	1	...	...	...	...	...	...	...	...	...	...
		JAIS	Do.	...	...	...	...	...	...	...	...	...	...	...	...	...	...	...
		JADHAVA	Do.	...	...	...	...	...	...	4	4	...	...	...	...	...	...	...
		KACHHWA	Do.	...	...	...	...	...	...	...	...	...	...	...	...	...	...	...
		KUNTEL	Aboriginal	...	...	...	...	...	...	...	...	...	35	31	4	...	...	...
		KHARB	Hindu	...	...	...	...	...	...	...	...	...	...	...	...	...	...	...
		KHODGAR	Do.	...	...	...	...	...	...	...	...	...	2	2	...	...	...	...
		MARATHA	Do.	53	28	25	11	10	1	4,908	2,710	2,198	7,828	3,971	3,857	252	153	99
		MIRDHA	Do.	...	...	...	...	...	...	24	20	4	...	...	...	55	28	27
		Do.	Aboriginal	3	1	2	22	12	10	...	...	...	...	...	...	2,324	1,189	1,135
		NANAKSAI	Hindu	...	...	...	...	...	...	...	...	...	...	...	...	...	...	...
		PAMAR	Do.	...	...	...	...	...	...	5	3	2	10	7	3	...	...	...
		Do.	Musalman	...	...	...	...	...	...	24	24	...	...	...	...	...	...	...
		PURBIA	Hindu	...	...	...	...	...	...	461	240	221	...	...	...	...	...	...
		PARIHAR	Do.	...	...	...	3	2	1	...	...	...	...	...	...	...	...	...
		PARMAR	Do.	...	...	...	...	...	...	...	...	...	...	...	...	...	...	...

TABLE XVI.—Castes, Tribes and Races, by Nationality or traditional Occupation—*contd.*

NAME AND CLASSIFICATION.				PROVINCIAL TOTAL.			DISTRIBUTION BY AGENCIES.								
							INDORE.			GWALIOR.			BHOPAL.		
Class.	Group.	Caste.	Religion.	Total.	Males.	Females.	Total.	Males.	Females.	Total.	Males.	Females.	Total.	Males.	Females.
1	2	3	4	5	6	7	8	9	10	11	12	13	14	15	16
A.—AGRICULTURAL—*contd.*	1.—MILITARY AND DOMINANT—*contd.*	RAJPUT	Hindu	601,972	331,428	270,544	28,174	15,771	12,403	142,835	83,090	59,745	142,343	76,113	66,230
		RAWAT	Do.	24,241	13,307	10,934	333	178	155	20,196	10,712	9,484	927	459	468
		RANA	Do.	2	2	...	2	2	...	...	...	...	...	...	...
		RAWALIA	Do.	62	35	27	...	...	...	...	...	...	...	...	...
		RAGHUBANSI	Do.	14,359	7,591	6,808	...	...	...	...	...	...	2,786	1,461	1,325
		RATHI	Do.	152	74	78	...	...	...	152	74	78	...	...	...
		RATHOR	Do.	2,258	1,237	1,021	...	...	...	...	...	...	2,258	1,237	1,021
		Do.	Musalman	6	...	6	...	...	...	...	...	...	...	...	...
		RAWAL	Hindu	2	2	...	1	1	...	...	...	...	...	...	...
		RANGRA	Musalman	2	1	1	...	...	...	...	...	...	...	...	...
		SIKARWAR	Hindu	3	3	...	3	3	...	...	...	...	...	...	...
		SURAJBANSI	Do.	3	3	...	3	3	...	...	...	...	...	...	...
		SOLANKI	Do.	9	7	2	3	1	2	...	...	...	...	...	...
		Do.	Musalman	4	3	1	...	...	...	...	...	...	...	...	...
		SAMAR	Hindu	1	1	...	...	...	...	...	...	...	...	...	...
		SIKH	Sikh	1,825	1,358	467	321	205	116	4	4	...	455	308	147
		THAKUR	Hindu	14,724	7,895	6,829	474	305	169	...	...	...	8,611	4,549	4,062
		Total Group I	......	1,115,191	608558	506,633	47,740	26,353	21,387	270,139	154,381	115,758	263,633	140,512	123,121
	2. MINOR AGRICULTURAL.	ARAKH	Hindu	216	126	90	...	...	...	...	...	...	...	...	...
		Do.	Aboriginal	2,375	1,149	1,226	...	...	...	...	...	...	...	...	...
		ALIA	Hindu	1,388	677	711	310	150	160	...	...	...	...	...	...
		AJNA	Do.	18,692	9,598	9,094	313	159	154	...	...	...	807	413	394
		AHIR	Do.	373,591	198,064	175,527	8,423	5,155	3,268	62,588	34,173	28,415	52,769	27,821	24,948
		BALAI	Do.	346,546	175,709	170,837	34,270	17,301	16,969	6,599	3,457	3,142	103,238	53,000	50,238
		BHADAR	Do.	1,787	896	891	1	1	...	...	...	...	1	1	...
		BHAGWAT	Do.	2	...	2	...	...	...	...	...	...	...	...	...
		BARAI	Do.	4,980	2,594	2,386	...	...	...	...	...	...	...	...	...
		BARGAH	Do.	4,651	2,243	2,408	...	...	...	...	...	...	...	...	...
		BARWAR	Do.	388	198	190	...	...	...	—	...	...	...	...	...
		BHUIYAR	Aboriginal	1,677	793	884	...	...	...	...	...	...	...	...	...
		CHOBDAR	Hindu	21	11	10	21	11	10	...	...	...	...	...	...
		CHINDAR	Do.	1,706	553	1,153	17	7	10	1,683	545	1,138	...	...	...
		CHANDER	Do.	200	...	200	...	...	...	...	...	...	...	...	...
		CHIRAR	Do.	9,225	4,837	4,388	...	...	...	...	...	...	4,441	2,400	2,041
		CHHAPARBANDHA	Do.	29	25	4	...	...	...	...	...	...	...	...	...
		DANGI	Do.	58,691	38,002	[illegible]	840	427	413	[illegible]	[illegible]	[illegible]	39,030	21,757	17,273
		DAGI	Do.	[illegible]	1,234	1,383	...	...	...	...	...	...	[illegible]	...	...

Table XVI.—Castes, Tribes and Races, etc.—Central India.

A—AGRICULTURAL—contd.

NAME AND CLASSIFICATION.			DISTRIBUTION BY AGENCIES.														
			Bundelkhand.			Baghelkhand.			Western Malwa.			Bhopawar.			Guna.		
Group.	Caste.	Religion.	Total.	Males.	Females.	Total.	Males.	Females.	Total.	Males.	Females.	Total.	Males.	Females.	Total.	Males.	Females.
			17	18	19	20	21	22	23	24	25	26	27	28	29	30	31
1.—Military and Dominant—*contd.*	Rajput	Hindu	73,775	*40,649*	33,126	37	*30*	7	147,644	*80,811*	66,833	59,367	*30,503*	28,864	7,797	*4,461*	3,336
	Rawat	Do.	1,999	*1,511*	488	9	*6*	3	56	*31*	25	229	*137*	92	492	*273*	219
	Rana	Do.	...	...	...	...	...	...	...	...	...	...	...	...	...	...	...
	Rawalia	Do.	...	...	...	...	...	...	...	...	...	...	...	...	62	*35*	27
	Raghubansi	Do.	...	...	...	...	...	...	3	...	3	...	...	...	11,610	*6,130*	5,480
	Rathi	Do.	...	...	...	...	...	...	...	...	...	...	...	...	...	...	...
	Rathor	Do.	...	...	...	...	...	...	...	...	...	...	...	...	...	...	...
	Do.	Musalman	...	...	...	...	...	...	6	...	6	...	...	...	...	...	...
	Rawal	Hindu	...	...	...	1	*1*	...	...	...	...	...	...	...	...	...	...
	Rangra	Musalman	...	...	...	...	...	...	2	*1*	1	...	...	...	...	...	...
	Sikarwar	Hindu	...	...	...	...	...	...	...	...	...	...	...	...	...	...	...
	Surajbansi	Do.	...	...	...	...	...	...	...	...	...	...	...	...	...	...	...
	Solanki	Do.	...	...	...	...	...	...	6	*6*	...	...	...	...	...	...	...
	Do.	Musalman	...	...	...	...	...	...	4	*3*	1	...	...	...	...	...	...
	Samar	Hindu	1	*1*	...	...	...	...	...	...	...	...	...	...	...	...	...
	Sikh	Sikh	325	*298*	27	61	*44*	17	303	*231*	72	8	*4*	4	348	*264*	84
	Thakur	Hindu	...	...	...	307	*246*	61	5,332	*2,795*	2,537	...	...	...	...	...	...
		Total Group I	85,327	47,708	37,619	92,069	48,358	43,711	234,969	127,282	107,687	87,771	45,429	42,342	33,543	18,535	15,008
2. Minor Agricultural.	Arakh	Hindu	...	...	...	216	*126*	90	...	...	...	...	...	...	...	...	...
	Do.	Aboriginal	2,375	*1,149*	1,226	...	...	...	...	...	...	...	...	...	...	...	...
	Alia	Hindu	...	...	...	...	...	...	...	...	...	1,078	*527*	551	...	...	...
	Ajna	Do.	...	...	...	...	...	...	17,572	*9,026*	8,546	...	...	...	...	...	...
	Ahir	Do.	111,005	*58,774*	52,231	78,514	*39,938*	38,576	14,745	*7,774*	6,971	20,905	*10,972*	9,933	24,642	*13,457*	11,185
	Balai	Do.	...	...	...	...	...	...	155,670	*79,139*	76,531	46,763	*22,807*	23,956	6	*5*	1
	Bhadar	Do.	...	...	...	...	...	...	...	...	...	1,329	*638*	691	456	*256*	200
	Bhagwat	Do.	...	...	...	...	...	...	...	...	...	...	...	...	2	...	2
	Barai	Do.	1,371	*701*	670	3,579	*1,878*	1,701	...	...	...	...	...	...	30	*15*	15
	Bargah	Do.	...	...	...	4,651	*2,243*	2,408	...	...	...	...	...	...	...	...	...
	Barwar	Do.	...	...	...	377	*194*	183	...	...	...	...	...	...	11	*4*	
	Bhuiyar	Aboriginal	...	...	...	1,677	*793*	884	...	...	...	...	...	...	...	...	...
	Chobdar	Hindu	...	...	...	...	...	...	...	...	...	...	...	...	...	...	...
	Chindar	Do.	...	...	...	...	...	...	6	*1*	5	...	...	...	...	...	...
	Chander	Do.	...	...	...	...	...	...	...	...	...	...	...	...	200	...	207
	Chirar	Do.	...	...	...	...	...	...	...	...	...	1	*1*	...	4,783	*2,436*	2,340
	Chhaparbandha	Do.	...	...	...	...	...	...	29	*25*	4	...	...	...	...	...	...
	Dangi	Do.	8,582	*4,497*	4,085	...	...	...	8,604	*4,557*	4,047	1,635	*764*	871	...	...	...
	Dagi	Do.	...	...	...	...	...	...	...	...	...	...	...	...	989	*408*	581
	Dodhar	Do.	38	*38*	...	...	...	...	...	...	...	...	...	...	...	...	...

Table XIV.—Castes, Tribes and Races, by Nationality or traditional Occupation.

NAME AND CLASSIFICATION.				PROVINCIAL TOTAL.			DISTRIBUTION BY AGENCIES.								
							Indore.			Gwalior.			Bhopal.		
Class.	Group.	Caste.	Religion.	Total.	Males.	Females.	Total.	Males.	Females.	Total.	Males.	Females.	Total.	Males.	Females.
1	2	3	4	5	6	7	8	9	10	11	12	13	14	15	16
	2.—Minor Agricultural—contd.	Dhakar	Hindu	4,957	2,787	2,170	57	57	...	...	...	...	81	42	39
		Do.	Aboriginal	47,260	24,143	23,117	2,077	1,033	1,044	2,671	1,249	1,422	7,568	4,055	3,513
		Dhanuk	Hindu	358	107	251	19	19	...	3	3	...	20	10	10
		Do.	Aboriginal	14,516	7,745	6,771	646	313	333	5,195	2,972	2,223	5,144	2,525	2,619
		Damar	Hindu	9,827	4,875	4,952	...	...	...	...	...	...	...	...	...
		Gwal	Do.	1,092	535	557	...	...	...	...	...	...	...	...	...
		Gaoli	Do.	10,042	5,325	4,717	155	117	38	4,214	2,206	2,008	815	525	290
		Gaddi	Do.	3	3	...	...	...	...	...	...	...	...	...	...
		Do.	Musalman	722	391	331	...	...	...	...	...	...	719	388	331
		Ghosi	Hindu	22,764	12,246	10,518	2	...	2	5,432	2,930	2,502	2,842	1,502	1,340
		Do.	Musalman	180	89	91	25	10	15	...	...	...	64	32	32
		Gotia	Hindu	22	12	10	...	...	...	...	...	...	22	12	10
		Golapurab	Do.	407	213	194	...	...	...	...	...	...	407	213	194
		Jadoi	Do.	37	19	18	...	...	...	...	...	...	37	19	18
		Kachhi	Do.	472,124	245,777	226,347	2,284	1,232	1,052	123,372	66,082	57,290	68,630	35,882	32,748
		Do.	Musalman	10	6	4	10	6	4	...	...	...	...	...	...
		Kalota	Hindu	20,703	10,167	10,536	6,839	3,399	3,440	...	...	...	5,565	2,741	2,824
		Kunbi	Do.	57,884	29,551	28,333	7,384	4,025	3,359	...	...	...	11,768	6,175	5,593
		Kulambi	Do.	42	42	...	10	10	...	...	...	...	...	...	...
		Kurmi	Do.	164,117	85,434	78,683	94	94	...	2,070	1,137	933	15,600	7,895	7,705
		Do.	Musalman	1	...	1	...	...	...	...	...	...	1	...	1
		Kunjra	Hindu	5	5	...	1	1	...	...	...	...	2	2	...
		Do.	Musalman	1,219	632	587	36	19	17	...	...	...	364	185	179
		Kumawat	Hindu	7,621	3,870	3,751	3,188	1,623	1,565	...	...	...	144	75	69
		Do.	Aboriginal	14	7	7	...	...	...	...	...	...	14	7	7
		Kachbandhiya	Hindu	263	139	124	...	...	...	13	13	...	...	...	...
		Do.	Aboriginal	603	293	310	...	...	...	...	...	...	250	86	164
		Khairwar	Hindu	8,197	4,077	4,120	...	...	...	...	...	...	25	12	13
		Do.	Aboriginal	37	20	17	...	...	...	...	...	...	...	...	...
		Kamariya	Hindu	4,007	2,076	1,931	...	...	...	1,656	844	812	...	...	...
		Karar	Do.	40	23	17	...	...	...	...	...	...	40	23	17
		Kamar	Do.	376	213	163	...	...	...	...	...	...	356	204	152
		Kisan	Do.	39	21	18	...	...	...	...	...	...	...	...	...
		Kawari	Do.	29	23	6	...	...	...	...	...	...	...	...	...
		Koli	Do.	123,455	65,257	58,198	2,262	1,621	641	63,014	33,178	29,836	37,577	19,410	18,167
		Lodha	Do.	252,658	132,278	120,380	3,446	2,059	1,387	59,109	31,389	27,720	73,776	38,759	35,070
		Lunariya	Do.	725	654	71	...	...	...	725	654	71	...	...	...
		Loda	Do.	13,971	7,789	6,182	589	301	288	...	...	...	12,773	7,074	5,699
		Mali	Do.	91,365	47,306	44,059	6,875	3,665	3,210	8,565	4,472	4,093	27,080	14,345	12,735
		Murati		2	1	1	2	1	1	...	...	...	...	...	...

Table XVI.—Castes, Tribes and Races, by Nationality or traditional Occupation—*contd.*

NAME AND CLASSIFICATION.				PROVINCIAL TOTAL.			DISTRIBUTION BY AGENCIES.								
							INDORE.			GWALIOR.			BHOPAL.		
Class.	Group.	Caste.	Religion.	Total.	Males.	Females.	Total.	Males.	Females.	Total.	Males.	Females.	Total.	Males.	Females.
1	2	3	4	5	6	7	8	9	10	11	12	13	14	15	16
A.—AGRICULTURAL—*contd.*	2.—MINOR AGRICULTURAL—*contd.*	MURAI	Hindu	1,417	936	481	665	475	190	4	4	...	7	3	4
		MODIYA	Do.	53	29	24	...	...	...	...	...	...	...	...	...
		MAR	Do.	2	2	...	...	...	...	...	...	...	...	...	...
		MOTIYA	Do.	273	164	109	...	...	...	...	...	...	118	116	2
		MANKAR	Do.	54	24	30	8	...	8	...	...	...	...	...	...
		Do.	Aboriginal	19,766	10,064	9,702	282	152	130	...	...	...	40	19	21
		NENAWAT	Hindu	6	3	3	6	3	3	...	...	...	...	...	...
		NANDBANSI	Do.	2	1	1	2	1	1	...	...	...	...	...	...
		NAYTA	Do.	1	1	...	...	...	...	...	...	...	...	...	...
		Do.	Musalman	6,167	3,360	2,807	2,967	1,536	1,431	...	...	...	282	147	135
		PATEL	Hindu	103	103	...	1	1	...	...	...	...	...	...	...
		Do.	Aboriginal	507	507	...	...	...	...	...	...	...	...	...	...
		PASBAN	Hindu	170	135	35	...	...	...	...	...	...	...	...	...
		SIRVI	Do.	7	7	...	7	7	...	...	...	...	...	...	...
		SONKAR	Do.	1,413	705	708	4	3	1	...	...	...	24	17	7
		Do.	Aboriginal	20,550	10,506	10,044	...	...	...	...	...	...	2,238	1,277	961
		SONDLIA	Do.	10,097	4,676	5,421	3,416	1,206	2,240	...	...	...	6,651	3,470	3,181
		TAMBOLI	Hindu	24,398	12,666	11,732	966	566	400	4,579	2,449	2,130	4,200	2,139	2,061
		TODIYA	Do.	10	6	4	10	6	4	...	...	...	...	...	...
		TUTAKAR	Do.	24	11	13	24	11	13	...	...	...	...	...	...
		TAGOLI	Do.	21	21	...	21	21	...	...	...	...	...	...	...
		THORI	Do.	590	240	350	...	...	...	...	...	...	157	69	88
		Do.	Aboriginal	61	45	16	...	...	...	...	...	...	61	45	16
		TAMKHERA	Hindu	62	37	25	...	...	...	...	...	...	62	37	25
		TAMAKIYA	Aboriginal	148	34	114	8	5	3	...	...	...	1	1	...
		VISHNOI	Hindu	34	18	16	...	...	...	...	...	...	22	11	11
			Total Group 2	2,246,451	1,169,200	1,077,251	88,613	46,809	41,804	353,121	188,584	164,537	485,833	254,941	230,892
	4.—FOREST AND HILL TRIBES.	BHIL	Hindu	2,612	1,423	1,189	46	46	...	...	...	...	701	380	321
		Do.	Aboriginal	351,565	178,675	172,890	6,908	3,585	3,323	2,174	943	1,231	16,835	8,377	8,458
		BHARUD	Hindu	11,444	5,873	5,571	...	...	...	...	...	...	...	...	...
		BHILALA	Musalman	4	...	4	...	...	...	...	...	...	...	...	...
		Do.	Aboriginal	159,362	82,530	76,832	35	8	27	...	...	...	849	461	388
		BERNAHA	Do.	3,342	1,696	1,646	...	...	...	...	...	...	...	...	...
		BHILLA	Do.	29	29	...	...	...	...	...	...	...	...	...	...
		BHALIA	Do.	2,880	1,444	1,436	...	...	...	...	...	...	...	...	...
		BHUJAR	Do.	295	278	17	...	...	...	...	...	...	...	...	...
		CHARAD	Hindu	4	4	...	...	...	...	...	...	...	...	...	...

Table XVI.—Castes, Tribes and Races, by Nationality or traditional Occupation—*contd.*

Class.	Group.	Caste.	Religion.	Provincial Total. Total.	Provincial Total. Males.	Provincial Total. Females.	Indore. Total.	Indore. Males.	Indore. Females.	Gwalior. Total.	Gwalior. Males.	Gwalior. Females.	Bhopal. Total.	Bhopal. Males.	Bhopal. Females.
1	2	3	4	5	6	7	8	9	10	11	12	13	14	15	16
A.—AGRICULTURAL—*contd.*	2.—Minor Agricultural—*contd.*	Murai	Hindu	1,417	936	481	665	475	190	4	4	...	7	3	4
		Modiya	Do.	53	29	24	...	...	...	...	...	...	...	...	...
		Mal	Do.	2	2	...	...	...	...	...	...	...	...	...	...
		Motiya	Do.	273	164	109	...	...	...	...	...	...	118	116	2
		Mankar	Do.	54	24	30	8	...	8	...	...	...	...	...	...
		Do.	Aboriginal	19,766	10,064	9,702	282	152	130	...	...	...	40	19	21
		Nenawat	Hindu	6	3	3	6	3	3	...	...	...	...	...	...
		Nandbansi	Do.	2	1	1	2	1	1	...	...	...	...	...	...
		Natya	Do.	1	1	...	...	...	...	...	...	...	...	...	...
		Do.	Musalman	6,167	3,360	2,807	2,967	1,536	1,431	...	...	...	282	147	135
		Patel	Hindu	103	103	...	1	1	...	...	...	...	...	...	...
		Do.	Aboriginal	507	507	...	...	...	...	...	...	...	...	...	...
		Pasban	Hindu	170	135	35	...	...	...	...	...	...	...	...	...
		Sirvi	Do.	7	7	...	7	7	...	...	...	...	...	...	...
		Sonkar	Do.	1,413	705	708	4	3	1	...	...	...	24	17	7
		Do.	Aboriginal	20,550	10,506	10,044	...	...	...	...	...	...	2,238	1,277	961
		Sondlia	Do.	10,097	4,676	5,421	3,446	1,206	2,240	...	...	...	6,651	3,470	3,181
		Tamboli	Hindu	24,398	12,666	11,732	966	566	400	4,579	2,449	2,130	4,200	2,139	2,061
		Todiya	Do.	10	6	4	10	6	4	...	...	...	...	...	...
		Tutakar	Do.	24	11	13	24	11	13	...	...	...	...	...	...
		Tagoli	Do.	21	21	...	21	21	...	...	...	...	...	...	...
		Thori	Do.	590	240	350	...	...	...	...	...	...	157	69	88
		Do.	Aboriginal	61	45	16	...	...	...	...	...	...	61	45	16
		Tamkhera	Hindu	62	37	25	...	...	...	...	...	...	62	37	25
		Tamakiya	Aboriginal	148	34	114	8	5	3	...	...	...	1	1	...
		Vishnoi	Hindu	34	18	16	...	...	...	...	...	...	22	11	11
			Total Group 2	2,246,451	1,169,200	1,077,251	88,613	46,809	41,804	353,121	188,584	164,537	485,833	254,941	230,892
	4.—Forest and Hill Tribes.	Bhil	Hindu	2,612	1,423	1,189	46	46	...	...	...	...	701	380	321
		Do.	Aboriginal	351,565	178,675	172,890	6,908	3,585	3,323	2,174	943	1,231	16,835	8,377	8,458
		Bharud	Hindu	11,444	5,873	5,571	...	...	...	...	...	...	...	...	...
		Bhilala	Musalman	4	...	4	...	...	...	...	...	...	...	...	...
		Do.	Aboriginal	159,362	82,530	76,832	35	8	27	...	...	...	849	461	388
		Bernaha	Do.	3,342	1,696	1,646	...	...	...	...	...	...	...	...	...
		Bhilla	Do.	29	29	...	...	...	...	...	...	...	...	...	...
		Bhalia	Do.	2,880	1,444	1,436	...	...	...	...	...	...	...	...	...
		Bhujar	Hindu	295	278	17	...	...	...	...	...	...	...	...	...
		Charad		4	4	...	...	...	...	...	...	...	...	...	...

Class.	Group.	Caste.	Religion.	Bundelkhand. Total.	Bundelkhand. Males.	Bundelkhand. Females.	Baghelkhand. Total.	Baghelkhand. Male.	Baghelkhand. Females.	Western Malwa. Total.	Western Malwa. Males.	Western Malwa. Females.	Bhopawar. Total.	Bhopawar. Males.	Bhopawar. Females.	Guna. Total.	Guna. Males.	Guna. Females.
				17	18	19	20	21	22	23	24	25	26	27	28	29	30	31
A.—AGRICULTURAL—*contd.*	2.—Minor Agricultural—*contd.*	Murai	Hindu	135	70	65	443	251	192	19	16	3	144	117	27	...	...	...
		Modiya	Do.	...	...	...	...	...	—	...	...	...	53	29	24	...	...	...
		Mal	Do.	...	...	...	...	...	...	...	...	...	2	2	...	...	—	...
		Motiya	Do.	...	...	...	...	...	...	...	...	...	133	34	99	...	14	8
		Mankar	Do.	...	...	...	...	...	..	46	24	22	...	...	...	...	...	...
		Do.	Aboriginal	...	...	...	...	...	...	...	...	...	19,444	9,893	9,551	...	...	...
		Nenawat	Hindu	...	..	...	...	...	...	...	...	...	...	...	...	...	...	...
		Nandbansi	Do.	...	...	...	...	...	...	...	...	...	...	...	...	...	...	...
		Nayta	Hindu	...	...	...	...	...	...	...	...	...	1	1	...	...	...	...
		Do.	Musalman	...	...	...	...	...	...	2,910	1,676	1,234	...	...	...	8	1	7
		Patel	Hindu	...	...	...	...	...	...	...	...	...	102	102	...	...	...	...
		Do.	Aboriginal	...	...	...	...	...	...	...	...	...	507	507	...	...	...	...
		Pasban	Hindu	...	...	...	...	...	...	18	...	18	...	...	...	152	135	17
		Sirvi	Do.	...	...	...	...	...	...	...	...	...	...	...	...	...	...	...
		Sonkir	Do.	1,302	663	639	6	2	4	...	...	...	77	20	57	...	...	...
		Do.	Aboriginal	18,312	9,229	9,083	...	...	...	...	...	...	...	...	...	...	...	...
		Sondlia	Do.	...	...	...	...	...	...	...	...	...	...	...	...	...	...	...
		Tamboli	Hindu	8,147	4,132	4,015	...	...	...	3,425	1,838	1,587	2,267	1,146	1,121	814	396	418
		Todiya	Do.	...	...	...	...	...	...	...	...	...	...	...	...	...	...	...
		Tutakar	Do.	...	...	...	...	...	...	...	...	...	...	...	...	...	...	...
		Tagoli	Do.	...	...	...	...	...	...	...	...	...	...	...	...	...	...	...
		Thori	Do.	...	...	...	...	...	...	413	156	257	7	7	...	13	8	5
		Do.	Aboriginal	...	...	...	...	...	...	...	...	...	...	...	...	...	...	...
		Tamkhera	Hindu	...	...	...	...	...	...	...	...	...	...	...	...	...	...	...
		Tamakiya	Aboriginal	...	...	...	...	...	...	139	28	111	...	...	...	...	...	...
		Vishnoi	Hindu	...	...	...	...	...	...	12	7	5	...	...	...	...	...	...
			Total Group 2	415,976	218,129	197,847	279,134	140,795	138,339	362,792	186,126	176,666	173,871	87,743	86,128	87,111	46,073	41,038
	4. Forest and Hill Tribes—*contd.*	Bhil	Hindu	...	...	...	...	...	...	1,432	748	684	...	...	...	433	249	184
		Do.	Aboriginal	216	112	104	203	101	102	77,605	39,822	37,783	244,347	123,967	120,380	3,277	1,768	1,509
		Bharud	Hindu	...	...	...	...	...	...	...	...	...	11,444	5,873	5,571	...	...	...
		Bhilala	Musalman	...	...	...	...	...	...	4	...	4	...	...	...	...	...	...
		Do.	Aboriginal	...	...	...	...	...	...	...	...	...	158,478	82,061	76,417	...	...	...
		Bernaha	Do.	...	...	...	3,342	1,696	1,646	...	...	...	...	...	...	...	...	...
		Bhilla	Do.	...	...	...	...	...	...	29	29	...	...	...	...	...	...	...
		Bhalia	Do.	2,880	1,444	1,436	...	...	...	...	...	...	...	...	...	...	...	...
		Bhujar	Do.	295	278	17	...	...	...	...	...	...	...	...	...	...	...	...
		Charad	Hindu	4	4	...	...	...	...	...	...	...	...	...	...	...	...	...

TABLE XVI.—Castes, Tribes and Races by Nationality or traditional Occupation—*contd.*

NAME AND CLASSIFICATION.				PROVINCIAL TOTAL.			DISTRIBUTION BY AGENCIES.								
							INDORE.			GWALIOR.			BHOPAL.		
Class.	Group.	Caste.	Religion.	TOTAL.	Males.	Females.	TOTAL.	Males.	Females.	TOTAL.	Males.	Females.	TOTAL.	Males.	Females.
1	2	3	4	5	6	7	8	9	10	11	12	13	14	15	16
	3—FOREST AND HILL TRIBES—*contd.*	DANGAR	Hindu	178	91	87	12	8	4	...	...	...	166	83	83
		DEDWA	Do.	3	1	2	3	1	2	...	...	...	...	...	...
		GOND	Do.	26	21	5	...	...	...	...	...	...	...	...	...
		Do.	Musalman	4	2	2	4	2	2	...	...	...	...	...	...
		Do.	Aboriginal	254,419	126,695	127,724	10	8	2	1,046	530	516	94,326	46,709	47,617
		GANERA	Hindu	45	20	25	...	...	...	...	...	...	...	...	...
		KHARGOND	Do.	11	6	5	...	...	...	...	...	...	...	...	...
		KIRAR	Do.	113,831	59,947	53,884	5	5	...	55,509	29,781	25,728	34,338	17,741	16,597
		KOTWAR	Do.	28,335	14,046	14,289	...	...	...	...	...	...	1,246	650	596
		KORKU	Aboriginal	20,631	10,493	10,138	768	399	369	...	...	...	18,877	9,600	9,277
		Do.	Hinu	500	306	194	...	...	...	...	...	...	...	...	...
		KOL	Musalman	1	...	1	...	...	...	...	...	...	...	...	...
		Do.	Aboriginal	217,273	106,706	110,567	292	162	130	52	22	30	...	...	...
		MEWATI	Hindu	53	53	...	...	...	...	...	...	...	53	53	...
		Do.	Musalman	21,340	11,198	10,142	909	494	415	4,205	2,255	1,950	7,652	3,971	3,681
		MINA	Hindu	6,815	3,673	3,142	18	18	...	1	1	...	1,404	717	687
		Do.	Musalman	5	5	...	...	...	...	...	...	...	...	...	...
		Do.	Aboriginal	111,518	60,140	51,378	223	137	86	35,558	19,342	16,216	31,968	17,276	14,692
		MEO MEWATI	Musalman	12	3	9	...	...	...	...	...	...	...	...	...
		MAWASI	Hindu	4	2	2	...	...	...	...	...	...	...	...	...
		Do.	Aboriginal	2,820	1,400	1,420	...	...	...	...	...	...	...	...	...
		MANGHOLIA	Do.	7,845	4,038	3,807	162	87	75	142	67	75	2,219	1,143	1,076
		MAWAYA	Do.	1,416	635	781	...	...	...	...	...	...	...	...	...
		MODHA	Do.	19	17	2	...	...	...	...	...	...	...	...	...
		NIHAL	Do.	7,436	3,823	3,613	1	1	...	...	...	...	513	342	171
		NAYAK	Hindu	936	438	498	9	9	...	...	...	...	313	113	200
		Do.	Aboriginal	9,803	5,257	4,546	1,075	563	512	...	...	...	517	298	219
		PAHARI	Hindu	4	2	2	4	2	2	...	...	...	...	...	...
		PULAKRA	Musalman	7	...	7	...	...	...	...	...	...	...	...	...
		PARMAR	Aboriginal	16	7	9	...	...	...	...	...	...	...	...	...
		RAJ-GOND	Hindu	131	63	68	...	...	...	...	...	...	...	...	...
		Do.	Aboriginal	1	1	...	...	...	...	...	...	...	1	1	...
		SARGARA	Hindu	1,997	966	1,031	340	157	183	...	...	...	35	20	15
		Do.	Aboriginal	25	24	1	...	...	...	...	...	...	25	24	1
		SEHERIYA	Hindu	3,685	1 894	1,791	...	...	...	...	...	...	1,129	618	511
		Do.	Aboriginal	66,319	34,478	31,841	...	...	...	41,117	21,491	19,626	11,202	5,642	5,560
		SOR	Hindu	1	1	...	...	...	...	...	...	...	—	...	...
		Do.	Aboriginal	866	422	444	...	...	...	...	...	...	866	422	444
			Total Group 4	1,409,868	718,826	691,042	10,824	5,692	5,132	139,804	74,432	65,372	225,235	114,641	110,594
			Total Class A	4,771,510	2,496,584	2,274,926	7177	78,854	68,323	763,064	417,897	345,667	974,701	4	464,607

Table XVI.—Castes, Tribes and Races, etc.—Central India.

Class.	Group.	Caste.	Religion.	Bundelkhand. Total.	Bundelkhand. Males.	Bundelkhand. Females.	Baghelkhand. Total.	Baghelkhand. Males.	Baghelkhand. Females.	Western Malwa. Total.	Western Malwa. Males.	Western Malwa. Females.	Bhopawar. Total.	Bhopawar. Males.	Bhopawar. Females.	Guna. Total.	Guna. Males.	Guna. Females.
				17	18	19	20	21	22	23	24	25	26	27	28	29	30	31
A.—AGRICULTURAL—contd.	4.—Forest and Hill Tribes—contd.	Dangar	Hindu	...	...	...	...	...	...	...	...	...	...	...	...	...	...	...
		Dedwa	Do.	...	...	...	...	...	...	...	...	...	...	...	...	...	...	...
		Gond	Do.	...	...	...	19	*18*	1	4	*1*	3	...	...	...	3	*2*	1
		Do.	Musalman	...	...	...	...	...	...	...	...	...	...	...	...	...	...	...
		Do.	Aboriginal	15,487	*7,834*	7,653	143,313	*71,545*	71,768	151	*26*	125	86	*43*	43	...	...	...
		Ganera	Hindu	...	...	...	...	...	...	...	...	...	45	*20*	25	...	...	...
		Khargond	Do.	11	*6*	5	...	...	...	...	...	...	...	...	...	...	...	...
		Kirar	Do.	6,843	*3,476*	3,367	...	...	...	224	*123*	101	...	...	...	16,912	*8,821*	8,091
		Kotwar	Do.	20	*7*	13	27,069	*13,389*	13,680	...	...	...	...	...	...	...	...	...
		Korku	Aboriginal	...	...	...	746	*371*	375	...	...	...	240	*123*	117	...	...	...
		Do.	Hindu	...	...	...	500	*306*	194	...	...	...	...	...	...	...	...	...
		Kol	Musalman	...	...	...	1	...	1	...	...	...	...	...	...	...	...	...
		Do.	Aboriginal	6,730	*3,362*	3,368	210,045	*103,080*	106,965	6	*3*	3	148	*77*	71	...	...	...
		Mewati	Hindu	...	...	...	...	...	...	...	...	...	...	...	...	...	...	...
		Do.	Musalman	...	...	...	1	*1*	...	8,129	*4,205*	3,924	13	*10*	3	431	*262*	169
		Mina	Hindu	...	...	...	...	...	...	95	*60*	35	...	...	...	5,297	*2,877*	2,420
		Do.	Musalman	...	...	...	...	...	...	5	*5*	...	...	...	...	...	...	...
		Do.	Aboriginal	45	*22*	23	871	*435*	436	25,470	*13,459*	12,011	1,057	*559*	498	16,326	*8,910*	7,416
		Meo Mewati	Musalman	...	...	...	...	...	...	...	...	...	...	...	...	12	*3*	9
		Mawasi	Hindu	...	...	...	4	*2*	2	...	...	...	...	...	...	...	...	...
		Do.	Aboriginal	2,820	*1,400*	1,420	...	...	...	...	...	...	...	...	...	...	...	...
		Mangholia	Do.	196	*96*	100	...	...	...	3,786	*1,955*	1,831	937	*475*	462	403	*215*	188
		Mawaya	Do.	1,326	*590*	736	9	*45*	45	...	...	...	...	...	...	...	...	...
		Modha	Do.	19	*17*	2	...	...	...	...	...	...	...	...	...	...	...	...
		Nihal	Do.	...	...	...	...	...	...	1	*1*	...	6,921	*3,479*	3,442	...	...	...
		Nayak	Hindu	...	...	...	...	...	...	142	*63*	79	379	*201*	178	93	*52*	41
		Do.	Aboriginal	37	*18*	19	606	*339*	267	5,698	*3,014*	2,684	1,870	*1,025*	845	...	...	...
		Pahari	Hindu	...	...	...	...	...	...	...	...	...	...	...	...	...	...	...
		Pulakra	Musalman	...	...	...	...	...	...	7	...	7	...	...	...	...	...	...
		Parmar	Aboriginal	...	...	...	...	...	...	16	*7*	9	...	...	...	...	...	...
		Raj-gond	Hindu	131	*63*	68	...	...	...	...	...	...	...	...	...	...	...	...
		Do.	Aboriginal	...	...	...	...	...	...	...	...	...	...	...	...	...	...	...
		Sargara	Hindu	...	...	...	...	...	...	1,170	*593*	577	452	*196*	256	...	...	...
		Do.	Aboriginal	...	...	...	...	...	...	...	...	...	...	...	...	...	...	...
		Seheriya	Hindu	...	...	...	...	...	...	7	6	1	...	...	...	2,549	*1,270*	1,279
		Do.	Aboriginal	606	*316*	290	...	...	...	...	...	...	...	...	...	13,394	*7,029*	6,365
		Sor	Hindu	...	...	...	1	*1*	...	...	...	...	...	...	...	...	...	...
		Do.	Aboriginal	...	...	...	...	...	...	...	...	...	...	...	...	...	...	...
			Total Group 4	**37,666**	**19,045**	**18,621**	**386,811**	**191,329**	**195,482**	**123,981**	**64,120**	**59,861**	**426,417**	**218,109**	**208,308**	**59,130**	**31,458**	**27,672**
			Total Class A	**538,969**	**284,882**	**254,087**	**758,014**	**380,482**	**377,532**	**721,742**	**377,528**	**344,214**	**688,059**	**351,281**	**336,778**	**179,784**	**96,066**	**83,718**

TABLE XVI.—Castes, Tribes and Races, by Nationality or traditional Occupation—*contd.*

NAME AND CLASSIFICATION.				PROVINCIAL TOTAL.			DISTRIBUTION BY AGENCIES.								
							INDORE.			GWALIOR.			BHOPAL.		
Class.	Group.	Caste.	Religion.	Total.	Males.	Females.	Total.	Males.	Females.	Total.	Males.	Females.	Total.	Males.	Females.
1	2	3	4	5	6	7	8	9	10	11	12	13	14	15	16
B.—PROFESSIONAL.	5.—PRIESTS.	ATITHA	Hindu	3	3	...	...	...	...	...	...	...	...	...	...
		BRAHMAN	Do.	945,475	503,140	442,335	32,503	19,190	13,313	244,428	133,497	110,931	93,803	50,218	43,585
		BHADÁRIYA	Do.	38	...	38	...	...	...	...	...	...	...	...	...
		BIÁS	Do.	13	4	9	...	...	...	...	...	...	...	...	...
		BHADRI	Do.	26	14	12	...	...	...	26	14	12	...	...	...
		BAKSARIYA	Do.	2	...	2	...	...	...	2	...	2	...	...	...
		BHOJAK	Do.	387	217	170	2	...	2	...	...	...	...	...	...
		Do.	Jain	32	22	10	...	...	...	...	...	...	...	...	...
		BAJPAI	Hindu	1	1	...	...	...	...	...	...	...	...	...	...
		CHOBE	Do.	16	14	2	6	5	1	...	...	...	...	...	...
		DAKSHANI	Do.	7	5	2	3	3	...	...	...	...	4	2	...
		GURYA	Do.	2	2	...	2	2	...	...	...	...	...	...	...
		GAUR	Do.	4	3	1	...	...	...	...	...	...	...	...	...
		GODE	Do.	1	1	...	...	...	...	...	...	...	...	...	...
		GORA	Do.	1	1	...	...	...	...	...	...	...	...	...	...
		GURUJI	Jain	36	18	18	...	...	...	...	...	...	...	...	...
		HARDAS	Hindu	3	1	2	...	...	...	...	...	...	...	...	...
		KANAUJIA	Do.	6	6	...	5	5	...	...	...	...	...	...	...
		KAZI	Musalman	106	62	44	...	...	...	...	...	...	30	22	8
		MISRA	Hindu	6	5	1	...	...	...	...	...	...	...	...	...
		MAHABRAHMAN	Do.	8	3	5	...	...	...	...	...	...	...	...	...
		MEHTAJI	Do.	2	...	2	...	...	...	...	...	...	...	...	...
		MAULVI	Musalman	1	1	...	1	1	...	...	...	...	...	...	...
		MULLA	Do.	60	30	30	...	...	...	...	...	...	...	...	...
		NAGAR	Hindu	50	10	40	6	4	2	...	...	...	...	...	...
		OLIYA	Do.	1,019	540	479	...	...	...	...	...	...	...	...	...
		OJA	Aboriginal	267	154	113	...	...	...	...	...	...	267	154	113
		PATHAK	Hindu	1	1	...	...	...	...	...	...	...	...	...	...
		PANDE	Do.	4	3	1	...	...	...	...	...	...	...	...	...
		PUROHIT	Do.	17	10	7	7	...	7	...	...	...	...	...	...
		PIR	Musalman	5	3	2	...	...	...	...	...	...	5	3	2
		SHENWI	Hindu	58	34	24	53	30	23	...	...	...	...	...	...
		SANADH	Do.	1	1	...	...	...	...	...	...	...	...	...	...
		SHRIMALI	Do.	16	6	10	...	...	...	...	...	...	...	...	...
		TAILANGI	Do.	50	44	6	40	40	...	...	...	...	...	...	...
		TEWARI	Do.	15	8	7	...	...	...	...	...	...	...	...	...
		YUDHISHTIR	Do.	2	2	...	...	...	...	...	...	...	...	...	...
			Total Group 5	947,741	504,369	443,372	32,628	19,280	13,348	244,456	133,511	110,945	94,109	50,399	43,710

Table XIV.—Castes, Tribes and Races, etc.—Central India.

NAME AND CLASSIFICATION.				DISTRIBUTION BY AGENCIES.														
				Bundelkhand.			Baghelkhand.			Western Malwa.			Bhopawar.			Guna.		
Class.	Group.	Caste.	Religion.	Total.	Males.	Females.	Total.	Males.	Females.	Total.	Males.	Females.	Total.	Males.	Females.	Total.	Males.	Females.
				17	18	19	20	21	22	23	24	25	26	27	28	29	30	31
B.—PROFESSIONAL.	5.—Priests.	Atitha	Hindu	...	...	...	3	3	...	...	...	...	...	...	...	...	...	...
		Brahman	Do.	178,403	94,559	83,844	252,384	127,511	124,873	91,564	49,270	42,294	32,058	17,623	14,435	20,332	11,272	9,060
		Bhadariya	Do.	...	...	...	...	...	...	38	...	38	...	...	...	...	...	...
		Bias	Do.	...	...	...	4	4	...	9	...	9	...	...	...	...	...	...
		Bhadri	Do.	...	...	...	...	...	...	...	...	...	...	...	...	...	...	...
		Baksariya	Do.	...	...	...	...	...	...	...	...	...	...	...	...	...	...	...
		Bhojak	Do.	...	...	...	...	...	...	333	192	141	52	25	27	...	...	...
		Do.	Jain	...	...	...	...	...	...	32	22	10	...	...	...	...	...	...
		Bajpai	Hindu	1	1	...	...	...	...	...	...	...	...	...	...	...	...	...
		Chobe	Do.	...	...	...	2	1	1	8	8	...	...	...	...	...	...	...
		Dakshani	Do.	...	...	...	...	...	...	...	...	...	...	...	...	...	...	...
		Gurya	Do.	...	...	...	...	...	...	...	...	...	...	...	...	...	...	...
		Gaur	Do.	4	3	1	...	...	...	...	...	...	...	...	...	...	...	...
		Gode	Do.	...	...	...	1	1	...	...	...	...	...	...	...	...	...	...
		Gora	Do.	...	...	...	1	1	...	...	...	...	...	...	...	...	...	...
		Guruji	Jain	...	...	...	...	...	...	36	18	18	...	...	...	...	...	...
		Hardas	Hindu	...	...	...	...	...	...	...	...	...	3	1	2	...	...	...
		Kanaujia	Do.	...	...	...	1	1	...	...	...	...	...	...	...	...	...	...
		Kazi	Musalman	...	...	...	...	...	...	76	40	36	...	...	...	...	...	...
		Misra	Hindu	...	...	...	6	5	1	...	...	...	...	...	...	...	...	...
		Mahabrahman	Do.	8	3	5	...	...	...	...	...	...	...	...	...	...	...	...
		Mehtaji	Do.	...	...	...	...	...	...	2	...	2	...	...	...	...	...	...
		Maulvi	Musalman	...	...	...	...	...	...	...	...	...	...	...	...	...	...	...
		Mulla	Do.	...	...	...	...	...	...	60	30	30	...	...	...	...	...	...
		Nagar	Hindu	...	...	...	...	...	...	44	6	38	...	...	...	...	...	...
		Oliya	Do.	...	...	...	...	...	...	1,029	540	479	...	...	...	...	...	...
		Oja	Aboriginal	...	...	...	...	...	...	...	...	...	...	...	...	...	...	...
		Pathak	Hindu	...	...	...	1	1	...	...	...	...	...	...	...	...	...	...
		Pande	Do.	...	...	...	4	3	1	...	...	...	...	...	...	...	...	...
		Purohit	Do.	...	...	...	...	...	...	7	7	...	3	3	...	...	...	...
		Pir	Musalman	...	...	...	...	...	...	...	...	...	...	...	...	...	...	...
		Shenwi	Hindu	...	...	...	...	...	...	...	...	...	5	4	1	...	...	...
		Sanadh	Do.	...	...	...	1	1	...	...	...	...	...	...	...	...	...	...
		Shrimali	Do.	...	...	...	...	...	...	...	...	...	...	...	...	16	6	10
		Tailangi	Do.	...	...	...	...	...	...	10	4	6	...	...	...	...	...	...
		Tewari	Do.	...	...	...	15	8	7	...	...	...	...	...	...	...	...	...
		Yudhishtir	Do.	...	...	...	2	2	...	...	...	...	...	...	...	...	...	...
			Total Group 5	178,416	94,566	83,850	252,425	127,542	124,883	93,238	50,137	43,101	32,121	17,656	14,465	20,348	11,278	9,070

Table XVI.—Castes, Tribes and Races, by Nationality or traditional Occupation—*contd.*

B.—PROFESSIONAL—*contd.*

Class.	Group.	Caste.	Religion.	Provincial Total: Total.	Provincial Total: Males.	Provincial Total: Females.	Indore: Total.	Indore: Males.	Indore: Females.	Gwalior: Total.	Gwalior: Males.	Gwalior: Females.	Bhopal: Total.	Bhopal: Males.	Bhopal: Females.
1	2	3	4	5	6	7	8	9	10	11	12	13	14	15	16
	6.—Devotees.	Aghori	Hindu	84	50	34	...	...	...	...	...	...	...	...	...
		Appapanthi	Do.	2	2	...	...	...	...	...	...	...	2	2	...
		Bairagi	Do.	58,986	33,203	25,783	2,390	1,443	947	4,636	2,778	1,858	15,417	8,396	7,021
		Brahmachari	Do.	9	6	3	...	...	...	...	...	...	1	1	...
		Bhartari	Do.	54	54	...	...	...	...	...	...	...	...	...	...
		Babaji	Do.	223	144	79	...	...	...	223	144	79	...	...	...
		Baba	Do.	17	7	10	...	...	...	...	...	...	15	5	10
		Brahmdandi	Do.	122	68	54	...	...	...	...	...	...	...	...	...
		Dhanakdhari	Do.	1	1	...	...	...	...	...	...	...	...	...	...
		Dadopanthi	Do.	79	58	21	35	24	11	19	13	6	17	17	...
		Fakir	Musalman	12,759	6,863	5,896	735	390	345	...	...	...	4,683	2,453	2,230
		Gosain	Hindu	35,950	19,736	16,214	1,644	951	693	5,253	2,937	2,316	10,583	5,603	4,980
		Gelot	Do.	20,879	10,800	10,079	...	...	...	...	...	...	20,879	10,800	10,079
		Jangam	Do.	198	101	97	111	53	58	...	...	...	77	41	36
		Jogi	Do.	10,274	5,116	5,158	47	37	10	3,555	1,800	1,755	564	260	304
		Jati	Do.	15	12	3	5	5	...	...	...	...	6	4	2
		Do.	Jain	352	230	122	9	7	2	...	...	...	2	1	1
		Jogda	Hindu	551	420	131	...	...	...	...	...	...	...	...	...
		Kabirpanthi	Do.	193	82	111	12	9	3	10	4	6	41	15	26
		Khaki	Do.	41	29	12	...	...	...	...	...	...	...	...	...
		Kankata Baba	Do.	10	3	7	...	...	...	...	...	...	...	...	...
		Largar	Do.	1	1	...	1	1	...	...	...	...	...	...	...
		Mahant	Do.	23	21	2	...	...	...	...	...	...	17	17	...
		Madari	Do.	3	3	...	...	...	...	...	...	...	...	...	...
		Do.	Musalman	15	7	8	14	6	8	...	...	...	...	...	...
		Naga	Hindu	11	9	2	...	...	...	3	3	...	8	6	2
		Nath Baba	Do.	178	178	...	...	...	...	...	...	...	...	...	...
		Nanak Panthi	Do.	2	1	1	...	...	...	...	...	...	...	...	...
		Oghad	Do.	11	6	5	11	6	5	...	...	...	...	...	...
		Do.	Aboriginal	1	1	...	...	...	...	...	...	...	1	1	...
		Puri	Hindu	2	1	1	2	1	1	...	...	...	...	...	...
		Paramhans	Do.	3	3	...	...	...	...	...	...	...	...	...	...
		Ramsnehi	Do.	54	42	12	2	2	...	8	7	1	...	...	...
		Raida	Do.	2	2	...	2	2	...	...	...	...	...	...	...
		Ramanuji	Do.	3	3	...	...	...	...	3	3	...	...	...	...
		Radha	Musalman	24	4	20	...	...	...	...	...	...	...	...	...
		Sadhu	Hindu	621	473	138	48	48	...	[illegible]	58	...	328	222	106
		Do.	Jain	37	9	28	6	3	[illegible]	32	[illegible]	18	...	...	...
		Sannyasi	Hindu	[illegible]	[illegible]	[illegible]	...	...	...	...	...	...	...	...	...
		Swami	Do.												

Table XVI.—Castes, Tribes and Races, etc.—Central India.

Class.	Group.	Caste.	Religion.	Bundelkhand. Total.	Bundelkhand. Males.	Bundelkhand. Females.	Baghelkhand. Total.	Baghelkhand. Males.	Baghelkhand. Females.	Western Malwa. Total.	Western Malwa. Males.	Western Malwa. Females.	Bhopawar. Total.	Bhopawar. Males.	Bhopawar. Females.	Guna. Total.	Guna. Males.	Guna. Females.
				17	18	19	20	21	22	23	24	25	26	27	28	29	30	31
B.—PROFESSIONAL—*contd.*	6.—DEVOTEES—*contd.*	AGHORI	Hindu	...	...	...	84	50	34	...	...	...	...	...	...	...	...	...
		APPAPANTHI	Do.	...	...	...	...	...	...	...	...	...	...	...	...	...	...	...
		BAIRAGI	Do.	2,200	1,540	660	1,123	621	502	26,042	14,246	11,796	4,014	2,477	1,537	3,164	1,702	1,462
		BRAHMACHARI	Do.	...	...	...	8	5	3	...	...	...	...	...	...	...	...	...
		BHARTARI	Do.	...	...	...	54	54	...	...	...	...	...	...	...	...	...	...
		BABAJI	Do.	...	...	...	...	...	...	...	...	...	...	...	...	...	...	...
		BABA	Do.	2	2	...	...	...	...	...	...	...	...	...	...	...	...	...
		BRAHMDANDI	Do.	6	6	...	...	...	...	116	62	54	...	...	...	...	...	...
		DHANAKDHARI	Do.	...	...	...	...	...	...	...	...	...	...	...	...	1	1	...
		DADOPANTHI	Do.	...	...	...	...	...	...	...	...	...	8	4	4	...	...	...
		FAKIR	Musalman	...	...	...	10	5	5	6,773	3,721	3,052	...	...	...	558	294	264
		GOSAIN	Hindu	1,451	849	602	1,610	902	708	10,798	5,816	4,982	2,995	1,741	1,254	1,616	937	679
		GELOT	Do.	...	...	...	...	...	...	...	...	...	...	...	...	...	...	...
		JANGAM	Do.	...	...	...	...	...	...	10	7	3	...	...	...	...	...	...
		JOGI	Do.	2,461	1,155	1,306	2,414	1,221	1,193	31	26	5	...	...	...	1,202	617	585
		JATI	Do.	...	...	...	...	...	...	4	3	1	...	...	...	...	...	...
		Do.	Jain	...	...	...	...	...	...	335	216	119	6	6	...	...	...	...
		JOGDA	Hindu	337	321	16	214	99	115	...	...	...	...	...	...	...	...	...
		KABIRPANTHI	Do.	17	8	9	44	15	29	45	20	25	23	11	12	1	...	1
		KHAKI	Do.	...	...	...	9	9	...	32	20	12	...	...	...	...	...	...
		KANKATA BABA	Do.	...	...	...	...	...	...	10	3	7	...	...	...	...	...	...
		LARGAR	Do.	...	...	...	...	...	...	...	...	...	...	...	...	...	...	...
		MAHANT	Do.	...	...	...	...	...	...	...	...	...	...	...	...	...	...	...
		MADARI	Do.	...	...	...	...	...	...	5	4	1	1	...	1	...	...	...
		Do.	Musalman	...	...	...	...	...	...	3	3	...	...	...	...	1	1	...
		NAGA	Hindu	...	...	...	...	...	...	...	...	...	...	...	...	...	...	...
		NATH BABA	Do.	...	...	...	...	...	...	178	178	...	...	...	...	...	...	...
		NANAK PANTHI	Do.	2	1	1	...	...	...	...	...	...	...	...	...	...	...	...
		OGHAD	Do.	...	...	...	...	...	...	...	...	...	...	...	...	...	...	...
		Do.	Aboriginal	...	...	...	...	...	...	...	...	...	...	...	...	...	...	...
		PURI	Hindu	...	...	...	...	...	...	...	...	...	...	...	...	...	...	...
		PARAMHANS	Do.	...	...	...	...	...	...	...	...	...	...	...	...	...	...	...
		RAMSNEHI	Do.	...	...	...	3	3	...	...	...	...	...	...	...	...	...	...
		RAIDA	Do.	...	...	...	...	...	...	44	33	11	...	...	...	...	...	...
		RAMANUJI	Do.	...	...	...	...	...	...	...	...	...	...	...	...	...	...	...
		RADHA	Musalman	...	...	...	...	...	...	24	4	20	...	...	...	...	...	...
		SADHU	Hindu	...	...	...	133	101	32	44	44	...	...	...	...	...	...	...
		Do.	Jain	...	...	...	...	...	...	37	9	28	...	...	...	...	...	...
		SANNYASI	Hindu	15	10	5	403	199	204	3	3	...	10	1	9	...	...	...
		SWAMI	Do.	...	...	...	...	...	...	...	...	...	...	...	...	...	...	...

TABLE XVI.—Castes, Tribes and Races, by Nationality or traditional Occupation—*contd.*

NAME AND CLASSIFICATION.				PROVINCIAL TOTAL.			DISTRIBUTION BY AGENCIES.								
							INDORE.			GWALIOR.			BHOPAL.		
Class.	Group.	Caste.	Religion.	TOTAL.	Males.	Females.	TOTAL.	Males.	Females.	TOTAL.	Males.	Females.	TOTAL.	Males.	Females.
1	2	3	4	5	6	7	8	9	10	11	12	13	14	15	16
B.—PROFESSIONAL—*contd.*	6.—DEVOTEES—*contd.*	SANJOGI	Hindu	325	162	163	...	...	...	...	...	...	...	...	...
		SODHI	Do.	3	1	2	3	1	2	...	...	...	...	...	...
		UDASI	Do.	18	11	7	1	1	...	...	...	...	...	...	...
		VASUDEO	Do.	310	153	157	...	...	...	...	...	...	...	...	...
			Total Group 6	142,917	78,358	64,559	5,079	2,991	2,088	13,811	7,772	6,039	52,641	27,844	24,797
	7.—TEMPLE SERVANTS	BHOPA	Hindu	1,519	1,109	410	30	18	12	...	...	...	691	670	21
		GURAV	Do.	1,179	559	620	216	99	117	27	16	11	5	5	...
		LINGAIT	Do.	4	4	...	3	3	...	1	1	...	...	...	...
		MANBHAO	Do.	66	38	28	63	35	28	...	...	...	...	...	...
		PUJARI	Do.	269	147	122	...	...	...	...	...	...	269	147	122
		MUJAWAR	Musulman	47	23	24	2	...	2	...	...	...	7	5	2
			Total Group 7	3,084	1,880	1,204	314	155	159	28	17	11	972	827	145
	8.—GENEALOGISTS	BHAT	Hindu	38,335	20,852	17,483	1,201	672	529	5,017	2,629	2,388	8,952	4,684	4,268
		Do.	Musalman	260	137	123	9	7	2	...	...	...	169	85	84
		Do.	Aboriginal	57	32	25	...	...	...	...	...	...	52	32	20
		BHAROT	Hindu	20	12	8	...	...	...	...	...	...	...	...	...
		CHARAN	Do.	6,166	3,067	3,099	...	...	...	...	...	...	381	210	171
			Total Group 8	44,838	24,100	20,738	1,210	679	531	5,017	2,629	2,388	9,554	5,012	4,543
	9.—WRITERS	BANGALI	Hindu	5	5	...	5	5	...	...	...	...	...	...	...
		GOLAK	Do.	169	10	159	...	...	...	...	...	...	...	...	...
		KAYASTH	Do.	74,471	39,530	34,941	887	570	317	19,813	10,564	9,249	16,593	8,617	7,966
		KHATRI	Do.	4,100	2,221	1,879	145	111	34	739	408	331	872	504	368
		LALA	Do.	2	2	...	...	...	...	2	2	...	...	...	...
		PARBHU	Do.	783	419	364	285	147	138	15	6	9	10	6	4
		NIGAM	Do.	181	84	97	...	...	...	...	...	...	...	...	...
		PANCHOLI	Do.	558	296	262	541	293	249	1	...	1	10	3	7
		VIDUR	Do.	527	291	236	102	51	50	[illegible]	14	7	189	119	70
			Total Group 9	80,796	42,858	37,937	1,965	1,177	788	20,591	10,994	9,597	17,674	9,259	8,415

Table XVI.—Castes, Tribes and Races, etc.—Central India.

Class.	Group.	Caste.	Religion.	Bundelkhand. Total.	Bundelkhand. Males.	Bundelkhand. Females.	Baghelkhand. Total.	Baghelkhand. Males.	Baghelkhand. Females.	Western Malwa. Total.	Western Malwa. Males.	Western Malwa. Females.	Bhopawar. Total.	Bhopawar. Males.	Bhopawar. Females.	Guna. Total.	Guna. Males.	Guna. Females.
				17	18	19	20	21	22	23	24	25	26	27	28	29	30	31
B.—PROFESSIONAL—*contd.*	6.—Devotees—*contd.*	Sanjogi	Hindu	325	162	163	...	...	...	...	...	...	...	...	...	...	...	...
		Sodhi	Do.	...	...	...	...	...	...	...	...	...	...	...	...	...	...	...
		Udasi	Do.	...	...	...	...	...	...	6	6	...	11	4	7	...	...	...
		Vasudeo	Do.	...	...	...	...	...	...	256	125	131	54	28	26	...	...	...
			Total Group 6	**6,816**	**4,054**	**2,762**	**6,109**	**3,284**	**2,825**	**44,796**	**24,549**	**20,247**	**7,122**	**4,272**	**2,850**	**6,543**	**3,552**	**2,991**
	7.—Temple Servants	Bhopa	Hindu	...	...	...	...	...	...	640	331	309	100	58	42	58	32	26
		Gurav	Do.	...	...	...	...	...	...	28	23	5	903	416	487	...	...	...
		Lingait	Do.	...	...	...	...	...	...	...	...	...	...	...	...	...	...	...
		Manbhao	Do.	...	...	...	...	...	...	...	...	...	3	3	...	...	...	...
		Pujari	Do.	...	...	...	...	...	...	...	...	...	...	...	...	...	...	...
		Mujawar	Musalman	...	...	...	...	...	...	38	18	20	...	...	...	...	...	...
			Total Group 7	...	...	...	...	...	...	**706**	**372**	**334**	**1,006**	**477**	**529**	**58**	**32**	**26**
	8.—Genealogists	Bhat	Hindu	5,857	2,999	2,858	4,278	2,156	2,122	10,222	6,222	4,000	2,211	1,198	1,013	597	292	305
		Do.	Musalman	...	...	...	...	...	...	41	18	23	...	...	...	41	27	14
		Do.	Aboriginal	...	...	...	...	...	...	...	...	...	...	...	...	5	...	5
		Bharot	Hindu	...	...	...	...	...	...	...	...	...	...	...	...	20	12	8
		Charan	Do.	...	...	...	...	...	...	3,030	1,449	1,581	2,750	1,403	1,347	5	5	...
			Total Group 8	**5,857**	**2,999**	**2,858**	**4,278**	**2,156**	**2,122**	**13,293**	**7,689**	**5,604**	**4,961**	**2,601**	**2,360**	**668**	**336**	**332**
	9.—Writers	Bangali	Hindu	...	...	...	...	...	...	...	...	...	...	...	...	...	...	...
		Golak	Do.	...	...	...	...	...	...	...	...	...	169	10	150	...	...	...
		Kayasth	Do.	20,204	10,594	9,610	8,200	4,392	3,808	5,088	2,758	2,330	1,137	630	507	2,519	1,395	1,154
		Khatri	Do.	836	450	386	57	34	23	1,013	524	489	404	156	248	34	34	...
		Lala	Do.	...	...	...	...	...	...	...	...	...	...	...	...	...	...	...
		Parbhu	Do.	...	...	...	...	...	...	27	7	20	444	252	192	2	1	1
		Nigam	Do.	...	...	...	...	...	...	...	...	...	...	...	...	181	84	97
		Pancholi	Do.	...	...	...	...	...	...	5	...	5	...	...	...	...	...	...
		Vidur	Do.	...	...	...	...	...	...	148	71	77	68	36	32	...	...	...
			Total Group 9	**21,040**	**11,044**	**9,996**	**8,257**	**4,426**	**3,831**	**6,281**	**3,360**	**2,921**	**2,222**	**1,084**	**1,138**	**2,766**	**1,514**	**1,252**

TABLE XVI.—Castes, Tribes and Races, by Nationality or traditional Occupation—*contd.*

NAME AND CLASSIFICATION.				PROVINCIAL TOTAL.			DISTRIBUTION BY AGENCIES.								
							INDORE.			GWALIOR.			BHOPAL.		
Class.	Group.	Caste.	Religion.	Total.	Males.	Females.	Total.	Males.	Females.	Total.	Males.	Females.	Total.	Males.	Females.
1	2	3	4	5	6	7	8	9	10	11	12	13	14	15	16
	10.—ASTROLOGERS	DAKOT	Hindu	1,789	888	901	160	82	78	...	...	...	...	...	...
		DAKOTRA	Do.	65	31	34	...	...	...	...	...	...	65	31	34
		Do.	Aboriginal	1	1	...	...	...	...	...	...	...	1	1	...
		DARIA	Hindu	713	357	356	...	...	...	...	...	...	...	...	...
		JOSHI	Do.	12,204	6,237	5,967	266	97	169	6,910	3,542	3,368	1,707	907	800
		RAMMAL	Musalman	1	1	...	...	...	...	...	...	...	...	...	...
			Total Group 10	14,773	7,515	7,258	426	179	247	6,910	3,542	3,368	1,773	939	834
	11.—MUSICIANS AND BALLAD-RECITERS.	CHADAR	Hindu	4	4	...	...	...	...	...	...	...	...	...	...
		CHHADI	Do.	12	9	3	12	9	3	...	...	...	...	...	...
		DAMAMI	Do	98	62	36	48	35	13	...	...	...	...	...	...
		Do.	Aboriginal	1,540	843	697	...	...	...	...	...	...	...	...	...
		DHOLI	Hindu	423	192	231	8	8	...	...	...	...	34	9	25
		Do.	Musalman	21	15	6	...	...	...	...	...	...	13	13	...
		Do.	Aboriginal	16,194	8,178	8,016	1,231	615	616	...	...	...	1,707	836	871
		DASODI	Hindu	2	1	1	...	...	...	...	...	...	...	...	...
		DHORI	Musalman	76	37	39	1	1	...	...	...	...	75	36	39
		JAOGAO	Hindu	2	2	...	2	2	...	...	...	...	...	...	...
		JAGA	Do.	279	138	141	...	...	...	279	138	141	...	...	...
		JAGI	Do.	72	31	41	...	...	...	...	...	...	...	...	...
		KANARCHI	Do.	875	428	447	5	2	3	...	...	...	...	...	...
		Do.	Musalman	19	19	...	...	...	...	...	...	...	...	...	...
		KOTUIRH	Aboriginal	38	8	30	...	...	...	...	...	...	...	...	...
		MIRASI	Hindu	91	43	48	3	3	...	75	37	38	...	...	...
		Do.	Musalman	1,250	545	705	53	27	26	...	...	...	518	221	297
		MAHAPATRA	Hindu	18	6	12	...	...	...	...	...	...	...	...	...
		RAI	Do.	803	429	374	...	...	...	803	429	374	...	...	...
		RAO	Do.	5,635	2,999	2,636	1	1	...	...	...	...	4,218	2,175	2,043
			Total Group 11	27,452	13,989	13,463	1,364	703	661	1,157	604	553	6,565	3,290	3,275
	12.—DANCERS AND SINGERS	BHADUA	Hindu	133	79	54	...	...	...	...	...	...	...	...	...
		BRIJBASI	Do.	18	9	9	...	...	...	...	...	...	...	...	...
		BERI	Aboriginal	184	86	98	...	...	—	...	...	...	...	...	...
		BHIMA	Do.	36	17	19	...	...	...	...	...	...	...	...	...
		DAPHALI	Hindu	8	4	4	1	1	...	7	3	4	...	...	...
		DOM	Do.	747	369	378	...	...	...	229	101	128	18	11	7
		Do.	Musalman	34	14	20	...	...	...	...	...	...	28	12	16
		DAHRI	Do.	1	1	...	1	1	...	...	...	...	...	...	...
		HIJRA	Hindu	135	70	65	...	...	...	7	7	...	128	63	65
		Do.	Musalman	60	35	25	...	...	...	...	...	...	60	35	25

Table XVI.—Castes, Tribes and Races, etc.—Central India.

NAME AND CLASSIFICATION.				DISTRIBUTION BY AGENCIES.														
				BUNDELKHAND.			BAGHELKHAND.			WESTERN MALWA.			BHOPAWAR.			GUNA.		
Class.	Group.	Caste.	Religion.	TOTAL.	Males.	Females.	TOTAL.	Males.	Females.	TOTAL.	Males.	Females.	TOTAL.	Males.	Females.	TOTAL.	Males.	Females.
				17	18	19	20	21	22	23	24	25	26	27	28	29	30	31
B.—PROFESSIONAL—*contd.*	10.—ASTROLOGERS	DAKOT	Hindu	...	...	...	...	...	...	1,503	*762*	741	126	*44*	82	...	...	...
		DAKOTRA	Do.	...	...	...	...	...	...	...	...	...	...	...	...	...	...	...
		Do.	Aboriginal	...	...	...	...	...	...	...	...	...	...	...	...	...	...	...
		DARIA	Hindu	713	*357*	356	...	...	...	...	...	...	...	...	...	...	...	...
		JOSHI	Do.	3,031	*1,528*	1,503	14	*8*	6	...	...	...	...	...	...	276	*155*	121
		RAMMAL	Musalman	...	...	...	...	...	...	1	*1*	...	...	...	...	...	...	...
			Total Group 10.	3,744	1,885	1,859	14	8	6	1,504	763	741	126	44	82	276	155	121
	11.—MUSICIANS AND BALLÁD-RECITERS.	CHADAR	Hindu	...	...	...	4	4	...	...	...	...	...	...	...	...	...	...
		CHHADI	Do.	...	...	...	...	...	...	...	...	...	...	...	...	...	...	...
		DAMAMI	Do.	...	...	...	...	...	...	50	*27*	23	...	...	...	...	...	...
		Do.	Aboriginal	...	...	...	...	...	...	...	...	...	1,540	*843*	697	...	...	...
		DHOLI	Hindu	...	...	...	...	...	...	22	*15*	7	...	...	...	359	*160*	199
		Do.	Musalman	...	...	...	...	...	...	8	*2*	6	...	...	...	...	...	...
		Do.	Aboriginal	38	*8*	30	...	...	...	13,218	*6,719*	6,499	...	...	...	...	...	...
		DASODI	Hindu	...	...	...	4	*1*	1	...	...	...	...	...	...	...	...	...
		DHORI	Musalman	...	...	...	...	...	...	...	...	...	...	...	...	...	...	...
		JAOGAO	Hindu	...	...	...	...	...	...	...	...	...	...	...	...	...	...	...
		JAGA	Do.	...	...	...	...	...	...	...	...	...	...	...	...	...	...	...
		JAGI	Do.	61	*26*	35	...	...	...	...	...	...	...	...	...	11	*5*	6
		KANARCHI	Do.	...	...	...	...	...	...	870	*426*	444	...	...	...	...	...	...
		Do.	Musalman	...	...	...	...	...	...	19	*19*	...	...	...	...	...	...	...
		KOTUIRE	Aboriginal	38	*8*	30	...	...	...	...	...	...	...	...	...	...	...	...
		MIRASI	Hindu	...	...	...	...	...	...	8	...	8	...	...	...	5	*3*	2
		Do.	Musalman	...	...	...	...	...	...	650	*277*	373	...	...	...	29	*20*	9
		MAHAPATRA	Hindu	18	*6*	12	...	...	...	...	...	...	...	...	...	...	...	...
		RAI	Do.	...	...	...	...	...	...	...	...	...	...	...	...	...	...	...
		RAO	Do.	...	...	...	...	...	...	190	*124*	66	7	*7*	...	1,219	*692*	527
			Total Group 11	155	48	107	6	5	1	15,035	7,609	7,426	1,547	850	697	1,623	880	743
	12.—DANCERS AND SINGERS	BHADUA	Hindu	...	...	...	...	...	...	133	*79*	54	...	...	...	...	...	...
		BRIJBASI	Do.	18	*9*	9	...	...	...	...	...	...	...	...	...	...	...	...
		BERI	Aboriginal	...	...	...	184	*86*	98	...	...	...	...	...	...	...	...	...
		BHIMA	Do.	...	...	...	36	*17*	19	...	...	...	...	...	...	...	...	...
		DAPHALI	Hindu	...	...	...	...	...	...	...	...	...	...	...	...	...	...	...
		DOM	Do.	500	*257*	243	...	...	...	...	...	...	...	...	...	...	...	...
		Do.	Musalman	...	...	...	...	...	...	6	*2*	4	...	...	...	...	...	...
		DAHRI	Do.	...	...	...	...	...	...	...	...	...	...	...	...	...	...	...
		HIJRA	Hindu	...	...	...	...	...	...	...	...	...	...	...	...	...	...	...
		Do.	Musalman	...	...	...	...	...	...	...	...	...	...	...	...	...	...	...

TABLE XVI.—Castes, Tribes and Races, by Nationality or traditional Occupation—*contd.*

NAME AND CLASSIFICATION.				PROVINCIAL TOTAL.			DISTRIBUTION BY AGENCIES.								
							Indore.			Gwalior.			Bhopal.		
Class.	Group.	Caste.	Religion.	Total.	Males.	Females.	Total.	Males.	Females.	Total.	Males.	Females.	Total.	Males.	Females.
1	2	3	4	5	6	7	8	9	10	11	12	13	14	15	16
	12.—Dancers and Singers—*contd.*	Hela	Musalman	121	...	121	...	...	...	...	...	...	...	...	...
		Gavai	Hindu	4	3	1	2	1	1	...	...	...	...	...	...
		Gondhali	Do.	283	132	151	154	69	85	14	9	5	95	41	54
		Gandharb	Do.	16	8	8	...	...	...	...	...	...	...	...	...
		Gavaiya	Do.	4	4	...	...	...	...	...	...	...	4	4	...
		Jasodia	Aboriginal	888	16	472	...	...	...	365	155	210	58	37	21
		Jasodi	Do.	152	41	111	115	25	90	...	...	...	...	...	...
		Kathak	Hindu	95	55	40	12	8	4	...	...	...	...	...	...
		Kalawat	Do.	354	178	176	...	...	...	236	125	111	...	...	...
		Do.	Musalman	26	20	6	...	...	...	...	...	...	26	20	6
		Ramjani	Hindu	445	235	210	...	...	...	...	...	...	2	...	2
		Do.	Musalman	115	12	103	...	...	...	...	...	...	6	...	6
		Saphardai	Hindu	15	9	6	...	...	...	...	...	...	...	...	...
		Do.	Musalman	6	4	2	5	3	2	...	...	—	...	...	...
		Sarangia	Hindu	282	137	145	...	...	...	...	...	—	...	...	...
		Tawaif	Musalman	27	6	21	...	...	...	...	...	...	...	...	...
			Total Group 12.	4,189	1,944	2,245	290	108	182	858	400	458	425	223	202
	13.—Actors and Mimes.	Bhavai	Hindu	708	321	387	9	4	5	...	...	...	...	...	...
		Bhand	Do.	326	202	124	10	3	7	70	43	27	49	24	25
		Do.	Musalman	92	47	45	4	3	1	...	...	...	88	44	44
		Bairupya	Hindu	428	10	418	...	...	...	6	3	3	15	7	8
		Bhanmati	Do.	189	105	84	13	6	7	...	...	...	113	67	46
		Do.	Musalman	13	9	4	...	...	...	...	...	...	...	...	...
		Do.	Aboriginal	2,191	1,130	1,061	...	...	...	...	...	...	321	297	24
		Baria	Hindu	32	13	19	32	13	19	...	...	...	...	...	...
		Do.	Aboriginal	685	380	305	1	1	...	...	...	...	...	...	...
		Bharia	Do.	24,539	12,279	12,260	...	...	...	...	...	...	...	...	...
		Dodhi	Hindu	8	3	5	8	3	5	...	...	...	...	...	...
		Karnatic	Do.	39	13	26	—	...	...	...	...	...	32	9	23
		Natakshahi	Do.	1	1	...	1	1	...	...	...	...	...	...	...
		Nakarchi	Do.	259	129	130	...	...	...	...	...	...	222	119	103
		Rangibhand	Do.	4	3	1	...	...	...	...	...	...	...	...	...
			Total Group 13.	29,514	14,645	14,869	78	34	44	76	46	30	840	567	273
			Total Class B.	1,295,304	689,618	605,686	43,354	25,306	18,048	292,904	159,515	133,389	184,553	98,359	86,194

Class.	Group.	Caste.	Religion.	Bundelkhand. Total.	Males.	Females.	Baghelkhand. Total.	Males.	Females.	Western Malwa. Total.	Males.	Females.	Bhopawar. Total.	Males.	Females.	Guna. Total.	Males.	Females.
				17	18	19	20	21	22	23	24	25	26	27	28	29	30	31
B.—PROFESSIONAL—concld.	12.—Dancers and Singers—contd.	Hela	Musalman	...	...	...	...	...	...	121	...	121	...	...	...	...	...	...
		Gavai	Hindu	...	...	...	...	...	...	2	2	...	...	...	...	...	...	...
		Gondhali	Do.	...	...	...	...	...	...	5	2	3	15	11	4	...	...	...
		Gandharb	Do.	...	...	...	16	8	8	...	...	...	...	...	...	...	...	...
		Gavaiya	Do.	...	...	...	...	...	...	...	...	...	...	...	...	...	...	...
		Jasodia	Aboriginal	446	217	229	4	2	2	...	...	...	15	5	10	...	...	...
		Jasodi	Do.	...	...	...	...	...	...	...	...	...	37	16	21	...	...	...
		Kathak	Hindu	...	...	...	83	47	36	...	...	...	...	...	...	...	...	...
		Kalawat	Do.	42	22	20	...	...	...	1	1	...	...	...	...	75	30	45
		Do.	Musalman	...	...	...	...	...	...	...	...	...	...	...	...	...	...	...
		Ramjani	Hindu	...	...	...	293	108	185	150	127	23	...	...	...	...	...	...
		Do.	Musalman	...	...	...	...	...	...	109	12	97	...	...	...	...	...	...
		Saphardai	Hindu	...	...	...	...	...	...	15	9	6	...	...	...	...	...	...
		Do.	Musalman	...	...	...	...	...	...	1	1	...	...	...	...	...	...	...
		Sarangia	Hindu	...	...	...	282	137	145	...	...	...	...	...	...	...	...	...
		Tawaif	Musalman	...	...	...	...	...	...	27	6	21	...	...	...	...	...	...
			Total Group 12	1,006	505	501	898	405	493	570	241	329	67	32	35	75	30	45
	13.—Actors and Mimes.	Bhavai	Hindu	...	...	...	...	...	...	699	317	382	...	...	...	...	...	...
		Bhand	Do.	...	...	...	...	...	...	177	127	50	8	5	3	12	...	12
		Do.	Musalman	...	...	...	...	...	...	...	...	...	...	...	...	...	...	...
		Bairupya	Hindu	...	...	...	...	...	...	2	...	2	405	...	405	...	...	...
		Bhanmati	Do.	...	...	...	...	...	...	63	32	31	...	...	...	...	...	...
		Do.	Musalman	...	...	...	...	...	...	13	9	4	...	...	...	...	...	...
		Do.	Aboriginal	1,870	833	1,037	...	...	...	...	...	...	...	...	...	...	...	...
		Baria	Hindu	...	...	...	...	...	...	...	...	...	...	...	...	...	...	...
		Do.	Aboriginal	638	358	280	...	...	...	...	...	...	46	21	25	...	...	...
		Bharia	Do.	1,114	541	573	23,425	11,738	11,687	...	...	...	...	...	...	...	...	...
		Dodhi	Hindu	...	...	...	...	...	...	...	...	...	...	...	...	...	...	...
		Karnatic	Do.	...	...	...	7	4	3	...	...	...	...	...	...	...	...	...
		Natakshahi	Do.	...	...	...	...	...	...	...	...	...	...	...	...	...	...	...
		Nakarchi	Do.	...	...	...	...	...	...	37	10	27	...	...	...	...	...	...
		Rangibhand	Do.	...	...	...	...	...	...	...	...	...	...	...	...	4	3	1
			Total Group 13	3,622	1,732	1,890	23,432	11,742	11,690	991	495	496	459	26	433	16	3	13
			Total Class B	220,656	116,833	103,823	295,419	149,568	145,851	176,414	95,215	81,199	49,631	27,042	22,589	32,378	17,780	14,593

TABLE XVI.—Castes, Tribes and Races, by Nationality or traditional Occupation—*contd.*

C.—COMMERCIAL.

NAME AND CLASSIFICATION.				PROVINCIAL TOTAL.			DISTRIBUTION BY AGENCIES.								
							Indore.			Gwalior.			Bhopal.		
Class.	Group.	Caste.	Religion.	Total.	Males.	Females.	Total.	Males.	Females.	Total.	Males.	Females	Total.	Males.	Females.
1	2	3	4	5	6	7	8	9	10	11	12	13	14	15	16
	14.—Traders	Audhya	Hindu	2,519	1,273	1,246	...	...	...	...	...	...	...	...	...
		Agarwal	Do.	2,070	1,087	983	...	...	...	...	...	...	...	...	...
		Do.	Jain	68	54	14	14	9	5	8	5	3	...	...	...
		Alota	Do.	12	5	7	...	...	...	...	...	...	...	...	...
		Bania	Hindu	243,091	127,602	115,489	9,953	5,528	4,425	63,552	34,125	29,427	26,977	14,283	12,694
		Do.	Jain	17,693	9,276	8,417	36	19	17	9,907	5,262	4,645	3,283	1,681	1,602
		Bakal	Hindu	10	4	6	...	...	...	...	...	...	...	...	...
		Do.	Jain	193	87	106	...	...	...	...	...	...	...	...	...
		Bijawargi	Hindu	182	55	127	...	...	...	...	...	...	...	...	...
		Do.	Jain	6	2	4	...	...	...	...	...	...	...	...	...
		Bhatera	Hindu	25	18	7	...	...	...	...	...	...	...	...	...
		Do.	Jain	464	237	227	192	100	92	...	...	...	...	...	...
		Bhatia	Hindu	34	21	13	...	...	...	...	...	...	...	...	...
		Bania Dasora	Do.	937	494	443	...	...	...	...	...	...	...	...	...
		Bania Harsora	Do.	54	30	24	...	...	...	...	...	...	...	...	...
		Baiswar	Do.	4,147	3,159	988	...	...	...	...	...	...	...	...	...
		Bania Mahesri	Do.	111	82	29	...	...	...	...	...	...	111	82	29
		Bohra	Musalman	14,930	7,745	7,185	1,158	726	432	156	79	77	1,626	939	687
		Bagdia	Jain	133	74	59	...	...	...	...	...	...	...	...	...
		Dhusar	Hindu	201	116	85	...	...	...	20	9	11	123	72	51
		Dhami	Do.	598	323	275	...	...	...	...	...	...	...	...	...
		Darugar	Do.	71	20	51	...	...	...	62	19	43	...	...	...
		Do.	Musalman	3	2	1	...	...	...	...	...	...	...	...	...
		Damda	Jain	230	94	136	...	...	...	...	...	...	...	...	...
		Digambari	Do.	68	34	34	...	...	...	...	...	...	...	...	...
		Fatehpura	Hindu	3	...	3	...	...	...	...	...	...	...	...	...
		Gujrati	Do.	1,761	997	764	263	126	137	...	...	...	1,485	863	622
		Ghoi	Do.	22	10	12	...	...	...	...	...	...	...	...	...
		Gawoi	Jain	1	1	...	...	...	...	...	...	...	...	...	...
		Galaparcha	Do.	786	421	365	...	...	...	...	...	...	...	...	...
		Galalari	Do.	587	289	298	...	...	...	...	...	...	...	...	...
		Harbar	Do.	81	81	...	...	...	...	...	...	...	...	...	...
		Jalanbali	Hindu	1	1	...	1	1	...	...	...	...	...	...	...
		Jaiswal	Do.	13	11	2	12	10	2	...	...	...	...	...	...
		Jaiswar	Do.	32	21	11	...	...	...	...	...	...	...	...	...
		Do.	Jain	2,652	1,374	1,278	...	...	...	9	3	6	1,891	979	912
		Javeri	Hindu	62	62	...	58	58	...	...	...	...	...	...	...
		Jaghad	Jain	3	3	...	...	...	...	...	...	...	...	...	...
		Kand	Hindu	3	1	2	3	1	2	...	...	...	...	...	...
		Khandelwal	Do.	1	...	1	...	...	...	...	...	...	...	...	...

C.—COMMERCIAL—*contd.*

NAME AND CLASSIFICATION.				DISTRIBUTION BY AGENCIES.														
				Bundelkhand.			Baghelkhand.			Western Malwa.			Bhopawar.			Guna.		
Class.	Group.	Caste.	Religion.	Total.	Males.	Females.	Total.	Males.	Females.	Total.	Males.	Females.	Total.	Males.	Females.	Total.	Males.	Females.
				17	18	19	20	21	22	23	24	25	26	27	28	29	30	31
	14.—Traders	Audhya	Hindu	...	...	...	1,654	781	873	865	492	373	...	...	...	...	...	...
		Agarwal	Do.	...	...	...	4	4	...	...	...	...	2,066	1,083	983	...	...	...
		Do.	Jain	...	...	...	...	...	...	33	33	...	11	6	5	2	1	1
		Alota	Do.	...	...	...	...	...	...	12	5	7	...	...	...	...	...	...
		Bania	Hindu	37,158	19,218	17,940	37,562	18,327	19,235	52,495	27,951	24,544	10,582	5,673	4,909	4,812	2,497	2,315
		Do.	Jain	51	29	22	...	...	...	4,169	2,143	2,026	...	...	...	247	142	105
		Bakal	Hindu	...	...	...	...	...	...	10	4	6	...	...	...	...	...	...
		Do.	Jain	...	...	...	...	...	...	193	87	106	...	...	...	...	...	...
		Bijawargi	Hindu	...	...	...	...	...	...	111	30	81	71	25	46	...	...	...
		Do.	Jain	...	...	...	...	...	...	...	...	...	6	2	4	...	...	...
		Bhatera	Hindu	...	...	...	...	...	...	18	18	...	7	...	7	...	...	...
		Do.	Jain	...	...	...	...	...	...	244	122	122	28	15	13	...	...	...
		Bhatia	Hindu	...	...	...	...	...	...	3	2	1	31	19	12	...	...	...
		Bania Dasora	Do.	...	...	...	...	...	...	...	...	...	937	494	443	...	...	...
		Bania Harsora	Do.	...	...	...	...	...	...	...	...	...	54	30	24	...	...	...
		Baiswar	Do.	...	...	...	4,147	3,159	988	...	...	...	...	...	...	...	...	...
		Bania Mahesri	Do.	...	...	...	...	...	...	...	...	...	...	...	...	...	...	...
		Bohra	Musalman	...	...	...	...	...	...	10,897	5,643	5,254	1,093	358	735	...	...	...
		Bagdia	Jain	...	...	...	...	...	...	130	74	56	...	...	...	3	...	3
		Dhusar	Hindu	...	...	...	...	...	...	43	28	15	...	...	...	15	7	8
		Dhami	Do.	598	323	275	...	...	...	...	...	...	...	...	...	...	...	...
		Darugar	Do.	...	...	...	...	...	...	...	...	...	...	...	...	...	...	...
		Do.	Musalman	...	...	...	...	...	...	9	1	8	...	...	...	...	...	...
		Damda	Jain	...	...	...	...	...	...	...	...	...	...	...	...	3	2	1
		Digambari	Do.	68	34	34	...	...	...	19	5	14	211	89	122	...	...	...
		Fatehpura	Hindu	...	...	...	...	...	...	...	...	...	...	...	...	...	...	...
		Gujrati	Do.	...	...	...	...	...	...	3	...	3	...	...	...	...	...	...
		Ghoi	Do.	...	...	...	4	4	...	9	4	5	...	...	...	...	...	...
		Gawoi	Jain	...	...	...	...	...	...	...	...	...	...	...	...	22	10	12
		Galaparcha	Do.	786	421	365	...	...	...	...	...	...	...	...	...	1	1	...
		Galalari	Do.	587	289	298	...	...	...	...	...	...	...	...	...	...	...	...
		Harbar	Do.	...	...	...	...	...	...	...	...	...	...	...	...	...	...	...
		Jalanbali	Hindu	...	...	...	...	...	...	81	81	...	...	...	...	...	...	...
		Jaiswal	Do.	...	...	...	...	...	...	...	...	...	...	...	...	...	...	...
		Jaiswar	Do.	4	4	...	...	...	...	1	1	...	...	...	...	...	...	...
		Do.	Jain	2	2	...	...	...	...	26	15	11	2	2	...	...	...	...
		Javeri	Hindu	...	...	...	...	...	...	...	...	...	...	...	...	750	390	360
		Jaghad	Jain	...	...	...	...	...	...	...	...	...	4	4	...	...	...	...
		Kand	Hindu	...	...	...	...	...	...	3	3	...	...	...	...	...	...	...
		Khandelwal	Do.	...	...	...	...	...	...	1	...	1	...	...	...	...	...	...

TABLE XVI.—Castes, Tribes and Races, by Nationality or traditional Occupation—*contd.*

C.—COMMERCIAL—*contd.*

NAME AND CLASSIFICATION.				PROVINCIAL TOTAL.			DISTRIBUTION BY AGENCIES.								
							Indore.			Gwalior.			Bhopal.		
Class.	Group.	Caste.	Religion.	Total.	Males.	Females.	Total.	Males.	Females.	Total.	Males.	Females.	Total.	Males.	Females.
1	2	3	4	5	6	7	8	9	10	11	12	13	14	15	16
	14.—Traders—*contd.*	Khandelwal	Jain	72	25	47	1	1	...	...	...	...	1	...	1
		Kandwah	Hindu	570	280	290	...	...	...	...	...	...	...	...	...
		Kagdi	Musalman	65	22	43	...	...	...	...	...	...	...	...	...
		Khoja	Do.	6	2	4	...	...	...	...	...	...	...	...	...
		Lohia	Hindu	5	5	...	...	...	...	...	...	...	...	...	...
		Lad	Do.	118	51	67	...	...	...	...	...	...	...	...	...
		Do.	Jain	4	2	2	...	...	...	...	...	...	...	...	...
		Mahajan	Hindu	4,133	2,909	1,224	1,668	1,668	...	...	...	...	2,019	1,105	914
		Do.	Jain	198	118	80	4	4	...	...	...	...	33	29	4
		Marwari	Hindu	107	58	49	23	14	9	...	...	...	...	...	...
		Do.	Musalman	29	13	16	7	4	3	...	...	...	...	...	...
		Mahesri	Do.	648	233	415	...	...	...	...	...	...	...	...	...
		Mod	Do.	113	...	113	...	...	...	...	...	...	113	...	113
		Megwal	Do.	2,147	1,019	1,128	4	4	...	...	...	...	...	...	...
		Malwi	Hindu	3	3	...	3	3	...	...	...	...	...	...	...
		Do.	Jain	8	7	1	...	...	...	...	...	...	...	...	...
		Mangelia	Do.	9	9	...	9	9	...	...	...	...	...	...	...
		Mertmal	Do.	98	56	42	...	...	...	...	...	...	98	56	42
		Nandwani	Hindu	273	241	32	...	...	...	...	...	...	28	14	14
		Nima	Do.	366	82	284	...	...	...	...	...	...	...	...	...
		Narsingpur	Jain	449	215	234	47	22	25	...	...	...	...	...	...
		Oswal	Do.	35,857	18,759	17,098	1,961	1,048	913	81	40	41	1,467	770	697
		Parwari	Hindu	257	257	...	256	256	...	...	...	...	...	...	...
		Porwal	Do.	44	18	26	...	...	...	...	...	...	44	18	26
		Do.	Jain	9,262	4,914	4,348	327	164	163	...	...	...	2,528	1,313	1,215
		Paliwal	Hindu	106	64	42	...	...	...	...	...	...	...	...	...
		Do.	Jain	10	6	4	...	...	...	10	6	4	...	...	...
		Parmar	Do.	11,427	5,712	5,715	...	...	...	...	...	...	405	126	279
		Sigwar	Hindu	39	21	18	15	7	8	...	...	...	...	...	...
		Saraogi	Jain	8,496	4,761	3,735	2,568	1,481	1,087	41	24	17	1,119	614	505
		Srimal	Do.	94	54	40	...	...	...	...	...	...	...	...	...
		Sitambari	Do.	55	55	...	...	...	...	...	...	...	...	...	...
		Samia	Do.	6	3	3	...	...	...	...	...	...	...	...	...
		Seoda	Do.	8	6	2	...	...	...	...	...	...	...	...	...
		Terwa	Hindu	24	14	10	...	...	...	...	...	...	...	...	...
		Unchwal	Do.	8	4	4	8	4	4	...	...	...	...	...	...
		Umat	Do.	18	9	9	18	9	9	...	...	...	...	...	...
		Vishnao	Do.	16	12	4	...	...	...	...	...	...	...	...	...
		Wani	Jain	491	226	265	491	226	265	...	...	...	...	...	...
			Total Group 14	269,497	195,411	174,086	19,100	11,502	7,598	73,846	39,572	34,274	43,351	22,944	20,407

Class.	Group.	Caste.	Religion.	Bundelkhand. Total.	Males.	Females.	Baghelkhand. Total.	Males.	Females.	Western Malwa. Total.	Males.	Females.	Bhopawar. Total.	Males.	Females.	Guna. Total.	Males.	Females.
				17	18	19	20	21	22	23	24	25	26	27	28	29	30	31
	14.—Traders—*contd.*	Khandelwal	Jain	...	...	...	...	...	...	...	...	...	64	18	46	6	6	...
		Kandwah	Hindu	...	...	...	570	289	290	...	...	...	...	...	...	...	...	...
		Kagdi	Musalman	...	...	...	...	...	...	65	22	43	...	...	...	...	...	...
		Khoja	Do.	...	...	...	...	...	...	6	2	4	...	...	...	...	...	...
		Lohia	Hindu	...	...	...	...	...	...	5	5	...	...	...	...	...	...	...
		Lad	Do.	...	...	...	...	...	...	...	...	...	118	51	67	...	...	...
		Do.	Jain	...	...	...	...	...	...	...	...	...	4	2	2	...	...	...
		Mahajan	Hindu	255	8	247	1	1	...	190	127	63	...	...	...	...	...	...
		Do.	Jain	...	...	...	...	...	...	161	85	76	...	...	...	...	...	...
		Marwari	Hindu	80	42	38	...	...	...	4	2	2	...	...	...	...	...	...
		Do.	Musalman	...	...	...	...	...	...	22	9	13	...	...	...	...	...	...
		Mahesri	Do.	...	...	...	...	...	...	...	...	...	648	233	415	...	...	...
		Mod	Musalman	...	...	...	...	...	...	...	...	...	...	...	...	...	...	...
		Megwal	Do.	...	...	...	...	...	...	...	...	...	2,143	1,015	1,128	...	...	...
		Malwi	Hindu	...	...	...	...	...	...	...	...	...	...	...	...	...	...	...
		Do.	Jain	...	...	...	...	...	...	...	...	...	8	7	1	...	...	...
		Mangelia	Do.	...	...	...	...	...	...	...	...	...	...	...	...	...	...	...
		Mertmal	Do.	...	...	...	...	...	...	...	...	...	...	...	...	...	...	...
		Nandwani	Hindu	...	...	...	...	...	...	4	2	2	241	225	16	...	...	...
		Nima	Do.	...	...	...	...	...	...	...	...	...	366	82	284	...	...	...
		Narsingpur	Jain	...	...	...	...	...	...	402	193	209	...	...	...	...	...	...
		Oswal	Do.	...	...	...	...	...	...	24,002	12,573	11,429	8,126	4,212	3,914	220	116	104
		Parwari	Hindu	...	...	...	...	...	...	...	...	...	1	1	...	...	...	...
		Porwál	Do.	...	...	...	...	...	...	...	...	...	...	...	...	...	...	...
		Do.	Jain	...	...	...	474	250	224	588	349	239	2,050	1,039	1,011	3,295	1,799	1,496
		Paliwal	Hindu	...	...	...	...	...	...	106	64	42	...	...	...	...	...	...
		Do.	Jain	...	...	...	...	...	...	...	...	...	...	...	...	...	...	...
		Parmar	Do.	11,022	5,586	5,436	...	...	...	...	...	...	...	...	...	...	...	...
		Segwar	Hindu	...	...	...	...	...	...	24	14	10	...	...	...	...	...	...
		Saraogi	Jain	8	5	3	...	...	...	2,905	1,652	1,253	1,653	882	771	202	103	99
		Shrimal	Do.	...	...	...	...	...	...	13	9	4	...	...	...	81	45	36
		Sitambari	Do.	...	...	...	...	...	...	...	...	...	55	55	...	...	...	...
		Samia	Do.	6	3	3	...	...	...	...	...	...	...	...	...	...	...	...
		Seoda	Do.	...	...	...	...	...	...	8	6	2	...	...	...	...	...	...
		Terwa	Hindu	...	...	...	...	...	...	24	14	10	...	...	...	...	...	...
		Unchwal	Do.	...	...	...	...	...	...	...	...	...	...	...	...	...	...	...
		Umat	Do.	...	...	...	...	...	...	...	...	...	...	...	...	...	...	...
		Vishnao	Do.	...	...	...	16	12	4	...	...	...	...	...	...	...	...	...
		Wani	Jain	...	...	...	...	...	...	...	...	...	...	...	...	...	...	...
			Total Group 14	50,625	25,964	24,661	44,432	22,818	21,614	97,904	51,870	46,034	30,580	15,622	14,958	9,659	5,119	4,540

TABLE XVI.—Castes, Tribes and Races, by Nationality or traditional Occupation—*contd.*

NAME AND CLASSIFICATION.				PROVINCIAL TOTAL.			DISTRIBUTION BY AGENCIES.								
							INDORE.			GWALIOR.			BHOPAL.		
Class.	Group.	Caste.	Religion.	Total.	Males.	Females.	Total.	Males.	Females.	Total.	Males.	Females.	Total.	Males.	Females.
1	2	3	4	5	6	7	8	9	10	11	12	13	14	15	16
C.—COMMERCIAL—concld.	15.—PEDLARS	DHIRKAR	Hindu	4,224	2,111	2,113	...	...	...	...	...	...	...	...	...
		GHANDHI	Do.	225	128	97	47	26	21	...	...	...	41	26	15
		Do.	Musalman	36	20	16	...	...	...	...	...	...	32	19	13
		KOMATI	Hindu	72	33	39	59	26	33	13	7	6	...	...	...
		PASARI	Do.	14	7	7	2	2	...	...	...	...	12	5	7
			Total Group 15	4,571	2,299	2,272	108	54	54	13	7	6	85	50	35
	16.—CARRIERS	BANJARA	Hindu	1,396	855	541	...	...	...	...	...	...	879	531	348
		Do.	Musalman	30	13	17	...	...	...	...	...	...	8	3	5
		Do.	Aboriginal	37,478	21,071	16,407	1,416	859	557	1,640	857	783	11,878	6,616	5,262
		BULDALIYA	Hindu	21	21	...	...	...	...	...	...	...	...	...	...
		HAMAL	Do.	1	...	1	...	...	...	...	...	...	...	...	...
		Do.	Musalman	50	31	19	...	...	...	...	...	...	33	22	11
		LOBHANA	Hindu	2,111	1,145	966	...	...	...	...	...	...	...	...	...
		MUKERI	Do.	15	8	7	...	...	...	15	8	7	...	...	...
		Do.	Musalman	71	36	35	...	...	...	...	...	...	63	31	32
			Total Group 16	41,173	23,180	17,993	1,416	859	557	1,655	865	790	12,861	7,203	5,658
			Total Class C.	415,241	220,890	194,351	20,624	12,415	8,209	75,514	40,444	35,070	56,297	30,197	26,100
D.—ARTISAN AND VILLAGE MENIAL.	17.—GOLDSMITHS	JARGAR	Hindu	5	2	3	...	...	...	...	...	...	...	...	...
		JARIA	Do.	128	64	64	...	...	...	...	...	...	...	...	...
		SONAR	Do.	73,862	38,583	35,279	2,787	1,602	1,185	10,977	5,910	5,067	15,424	7,957	7,467
			Total Group 17	73,995	38,649	35,346	2,787	1,602	1,185	10,977	5,910	5,067	15,424	7,957	7,467
	18.—BARBERS	BARI	Hindu	11,194	5,164	6,030	21	21	...	1,537	779	758	343	160	183
		NAI	Do.	170,393	88,619	81,774	5,166	2,927	2,239	33,038	17,551	15,487	35,541	18,406	17,135
		Do.	Musalman	257	143	114	19	10	9	...	...	...	132	62	70
		SIRNAI	Do.	628	325	303	...	...	...	...	...	...	...	...	...
			Total Group 18	182,472	94,251	88,221	5,206	2,958	2,248	34,575	18,330	16,245	36,016	18,628	17,388

Table XVI.—Castes, Tribes and Races, etc.—Central India.

Class.	Group.	Caste.	Religion.	Bundelkhand. Total.	Bundelkhand. Males.	Bundelkhand. Females.	Baghelkhand. Total.	Baghelkhand. Males.	Baghelkhand. Females.	Western Malwa. Total.	Western Malwa. Males.	Western Malwa. Females.	Bhopawar. Total.	Bhopawar. Males.	Bhopawar. Females.	Guna. Total.	Guna. Males.	Guna. Females.
				17	18	19	20	21	22	23	24	25	26	27	28	29	30	31
C.—COMMERCIAL · *concld.*	15.—Pedlars.	Dhirkar	Hindu	...	...	...	4,219	*2,109*	2,110	...	...	...	...	...	...	5	*2*	3
		Ghandhi	Do.	...	...	...	...	...	...	106	*54*	52	31	*22*	9	...	...	...
		Do.	Musalman	...	...	...	...	...	...	4	*1*	3	...	...	...	...	...	...
		Komati	Hindu	...	...	...	...	...	...	...	...	...	...	...	...	...	...	...
		Pasari	Do.	...	...	...	...	...	...	...	...	...	...	...	...	...	...	...
			Total Group 15	...	...	...	4,219	2,109	2,110	110	55	55	31	22	9	5	2	3
	16.—Carriers.	Banjara	Hindu	...	...	...	...	...	...	5	*4*	1	36	*21*	15	476	*299*	177
		Do.	Musalman	...	...	...	...	...	...	22	*10*	12	...	...	...	...	...	...
		Do.	Aboriginal	7	*5*	2	42	*22*	20	1,106	*621*	485	20,015	*11,327*	8,688	1,374	*764*	610
		Buldaliya	Hindu	...	...	...	...	...	...	21	*21*	...	...	...	...	...	...	...
		Hamal	Do.	...	...	...	...	...	...	1	...	1	...	...	...	...	...	...
		Do.	Musalman	...	...	...	...	...	...	11	*7*	4	...	...	...	6	*2*	4
		Lobhana	Hindu	...	...	...	...	...	...	164	*154*	10	1,947	*991*	956	...	...	...
		Mukeri	Do.	...	...	...	...	...	...	...	...	...	...	...	...	...	...	...
		Do.	Musalman	...	...	...	...	...	...	8	5	3	...	...	...	...	...	...
			Total Group 16	7	5	2	42	22	20	1,338	822	516	21,998	12,339	9,659	1,856	1,065	791
			Total Class C.	50,632	25,969	24,663	48,693	24,949	23,744	99,352	52,747	46,605	52,609	27,983	24,626	11,520	6,186	5,334
D.—ARTISAN AND VILLAGE MENIAL.	17.—Goldsmiths.	Jargar	Hindu	...	...	...	...	...	...	5	*2*	3	...	...	...	...	...	...
		Iaria	Do.	99	*46*	53	...	...	...	29	*18*	11	...	...	...	...	...	...
		Sonar	Do.	12,287	*6,444*	5,843	12,842	*6,484*	6,358	12,600	*6,473*	6,127	4,686	*2,511*	2,175	2,259	*1,202*	1,057
			Total Group 17	12,386	6,490	5,896	12,842	6,484	6,358	12,634	6,493	6,141	4,686	2,511	2,175	2,259	1,202	1,057
	18.—Barbers.	Bari	Hindu	2,964	*1,055*	1,909	6,265	*3,115*	3,150	8	*3*	5	...	...	...	56	*31*	25
		Nai	Do.	32,116	*16,593*	15,523	24,265	*12,226*	12,039	27,057	*14,124*	12,933	6,979	*3,507*	3,472	6,231	*3,285*	2,946
		Do.	Musalman	...	...	...	...	...	...	103	*68*	35	...	...	...	3	*3*	...
		Sirnai	Do.	...	...	...	...	...	...	628	*325*	303	...	...	...	...	...	...
			Total Group 18	35,080	17,648	17,432	30,530	15,341	15,189	27,796	14,520	13,276	6,979	3,507	3,472	6,290	3,319	2,971

TABLE XVI.—Castes, Tribes and Races, by Nationality or traditional Occupation—*contd.*

NAME AND CLASSIFICATION.				PROVINCIAL TOTAL.			DISTRIBUTION BY AGENCIES.								
							INDORE.			GWALIOR.			BHOPAL.		
Class.	Group.	Caste.	Religion.	TOTAL.	Males.	Females.	TOTAL.	Males.	Females.	TOTAL.	Males.	Females.	TOTAL.	Males.	Females.
1	2	3	4	5	6	7	8	9	10	11	12	13	14	15	16
	19.—BLACKSMITHS	JOTIA	Hindu	1	1	...	...	...	...	...	...	...	...	...	...
		KAMAR	Do.	4	3	1	4	3	1	...	...	...	...	...	...
		LOHAR	Do.	106,472	55,544	50,928	2,162	1,146	1,016	16,370	8,706	7,664	18,209	9,346	8,863
		Do.	Musalman	599	291	308	60	27	33	...	...	...	433	216	217
			Total Group 19	107,076	55,839	51,237	2,226	1,176	1,050	16,370	8,706	7,664	18,642	9,562	9,080
	20.—CARPENTERS AND TURNERS.	BARHAI	Hindu	43,789	25,868	17,921	...	...	...	27,126	14,389	12,737	6,107	3,131	2,976
		JAUGAR	Do.	6,214	...	6,214	...	...	...	...	...	...	...	...	...
		KHATI	Do.	85,410	44,639	40,771	22,490	11,908	10,582	...	...	...	41,265	21,461	19,804
		Do.	Musalman	20	10	10	...	...	...	...	...	...	20	10	10
		KAMANGAR	Hindu	94	51	43	11	7	4	15	6	9	33	12	21
		Do.	Musalman	3	3	...	...	...	...	...	...	...	3	3	...
		KHARADI	Hindu	569	213	356	24	17	7	...	...	...	325	184	141
		Do.	Musalman	57	24	33	...	...	...	...	...	...	...	...	...
		KARIGAR	Hindu	3	3	...	3	3	...	...	...	...	...	...	...
		KARKHAR	Do.	305	168	137	...	...	...	...	...	...	...	...	...
		LAKHERA	Do.	3,215	1,642	1,573	148	76	72	...	...	...	...	...	...
		SUTAR	Do.	83,987	44,749	39,238	4,133	2,157	1,976	...	...	...	24,482	12,947	11,535
		SILAWAT	Do.	4,428	2,144	2,284	42	21	21	1,138	580	558	1,187	519	668
		Do.	Musalman	12	8	4	...	...	...	...	...	...	...	...	...
		TARKHAN	Hindu	2	2	...	1	1	...	...	...	...	...	...	...
			Total Group 20	228,108	119,524	108,584	26,852	14,190	12,662	28,279	14,975	13,304	73,422	38,267	35,155
	21.—BRASS AND COPPER SMITHS.	BHAREWA	Hindu	635	344	291	16	6	10	...	...	...	151	81	70
		KASEGAR	Do.	2	2	...	...	...	...	...	...	...	...	...	...
		KASERA	Do.	4,151	2,361	1,790	536	289	247	15	8	7	1,637	923	714
		Do.	Musalman	3	3	...	...	...	...	...	...	...	3	3	...
		KALAIGAR	Hindu	20	11	9	...	...	...	...	...	...	...	...	...
		Do.	Musalman	53	21	32	...	...	...	...	...	...	...	...	...
		TAMBAT	Hindu	70	40	30	8	5	3	...	...	...	62	35	27
		THATHERA	Do.	538	272	266	1	1	...	366	198	168	136	50	86
		TAMER	Do.	1,013	541	472	...	...	...	...	...	...	...	...	...
			Total Group 21	6,485	3,595	2,890	561	301	260	381	206	175	1,989	1,092	897

D.—ARTISAN AND VILLAGE MENIAL—*contd.*

NAME AND CLASSIFICATION.				DISTRIBUTION BY AGENCIES														
				BUNDELKHAND.			BAGHELKHAND.			WESTERN MALWA.			BHOPAWAR.			GUNA.		
Class.	Group.	Caste.	Religion.	Total.	Males.	Females.	Total.	Males.	Females.	Total.	Males.	Females.	Total.	Males.	Females.	Total.	Males.	Females.
				17	18	19	20	21	22	23	24	25	26	27	28	29	30	31
	19.—BLACKSMITHS	JOTIA	Hindu	...	...	...	...	...	...	...	...	...	1	*1*	...	...	...	...
		KAMAR	Do.	...	...	...	...	...	...	...	...	...	...	...	...	...	...	...
		LOHAR	Do.	24,064	*12,571*	11,493	22,939	*11,491*	11,448	15,949	*8,780*	7,169	4,081	*2,060*	2,021	2,698	*1,444*	1,254
		Do.	Musalman	...	...	...	...	...	...	106	*48*	58	...	...	...	...	...	...
			Total Group 19	24,064	12,571	11,493	22,939	11,491	11,448	16,055	8,828	7,227	4,082	2,061	2,021	2,698	1,444	1,254
	20.—CARPENTERS AND TURNERS.	BARHAI	Hindu	...	...	...	5,863	*5,863*	...	...	...	...	...	...	...	4,693	*2,485*	2,208
		JAUGAR	Do.	...	...	...	6,214	...	6,214	...	...	...	...	...	...	...	...	...
		KHATI	Do.	32	*32*	...	...	...	...	16,957	*8,775*	8,182	3,028	*1,583*	1,445	1,638	*880*	758
		Do.	Musalman	...	...	...	...	...	...	...	...	...	...	...	...	...	...	...
		KAMANGAR	Hindu	...	...	...	...	...	...	25	*19*	6	...	...	...	10	*7*	3
		Do.	Musalman	...	...	...	...	...	...	...	...	...	...	...	...	...	...	...
		KHARADI	Hindu	...	...	...	...	...	...	211	*7*	204	9	*5*	4	...	...	...
		Do.	Musalman	...	...	...	...	...	...	57	*24*	33	...	...	...	...	...	...
		KARIGAR	Hindu	...	...	...	...	...	...	...	...	...	...	...	...	...	...	...
		KAKBHAR	Do.	...	...	...	305	*168*	137	...	...	...	...	...	...	...	...	...
		LAKHERA	Do.	1,783	*921*	862	1,284	*645*	639	...	...	...	...	...	...	...	...	...
		SUTAR	Do.	20,951	*10,993*	9,958	...	...	...	27,624	*15,191*	12,433	6,797	*3,461*	3,336	...	...	...
		SILAWAT	Do.	...	...	...	...	...	...	1,685	*816*	869	54	*28*	26	322	*180*	142
		Do.	Musalman	...	...	...	...	...	...	12	*8*	4	...	...	...	...	...	...
		TARKHAN	Hindu	1	*1*	...	...	...	...	...	...	...	...	...	...	...	...	...
			Total Group 20	22,767	11,947	10,820	13,666	6,676	6,990	46,571	24,840	21,731	9,888	5,077	4,811	6,663	3,552	3,111
	21.—BRASS AND COPPER SMITHS.	BHAREWA	Hindu	1	*1*	...	13	*8*	5	265	*147*	118	189	*101*	88	...	...	...
		KASEGAR	Do.	2	*2*	...	...	...	...	...	...	...	...	...	...	...	...	...
		KASERA	Do.	43	*25*	18	...	...	...	1,578	*906*	672	287	*181*	106	55	*29*	26
		Do.	Musalman	...	...	...	...	...	...	...	...	...	...	...	...	...	...	...
		KALAIGAR	Hindu	2	...	2	...	...	...	...	...	...	...	...	...	...	...	...
		Do.	Musalman	...	...	...	...	...	...	11	*6*	5	...	...	...	7	*5*	2
		TAMBAT	Hindu	...	...	...	...	...	...	53	*21*	32	...	...	...	...	...	...
		THATERA	Do.	4	*3*	1	...	...	...	...	...	...	...	...	...	31	*20*	11
		TAMER	Do.	1,008	*540*	468	...	...	...	5	*1*	4	...	...	...	...	...	...
			Total Group 21	1,060	571	489	13	8	5	1,912	1,081	831	476	282	194	93	54	39

TABLE XVI.—Castes, Tribes and Races, by Nationality or traditional Occupation—*contd.*

NAME AND CLASSIFICATION.				PROVINCIAL TOTAL.			DISTRIBUTION BY AGENCIES.								
							INDORE.			GWALIOR.			BHOPAL.		
Class.	Group.	Caste.	Religion.	TOTAL.	Males.	Females.	TOTAL.	Males.	Females.	TOTAL.	Males.	Females.	TOTAL.	Males.	Females.
1	2	3	4	5	6	7	8	9	10	11	12	13	14	15	16
D.—ARTISAN AND VILLAGE MENIAL—*contd.*	22.—TAILORS	BORA	Hindu	10	*10*	...	...	...	...	...	...	...	...	...	...
		DARZI	Do.	66,256	*33,818*	32,438	3,821	*2,076*	1,745	7,204	*3,811*	3,393	15,758	*7,604*	8,154
		Do.	Musalman	55	*17*	38	26	*12*	14	...	...	...	23	...	23
		KHALIFA	Do.	1	*1*	...	...	...	...	...	...	...	...	...	...
			Total Group 22.	66,322	33,846	32,476	3,847	2,088	1,759	7,204	3,811	3,393	15,781	7,604	8,177
	23.—WEAVERS, CALENDERERS AND DYERS.	BUNKAR	Hindu	3,021	*1,568*	1,453	...	...	...	...	...	...	...	...	...
		CHHIPA	Do.	16,890	*8,630*	8,260	323	*169*	154	3,691	*1,953*	1,738	5,722	*2,923*	2,799
		Do.	Musalman	3,763	*1,841*	1,922	348	*159*	189	...	...	...	214	*179*	35
		GANDI	Hindu	198	*98*	100	14	*9*	5	...	...	...	87	*53*	34
		JULLAHA	Do.	8	*6*	2	...	...	...	...	...	...	...	...	...
		Do.	Musalman	428	*166*	262	...	...	...	...	...	...	237	*70*	167
		KOD	Hindu	20	*12*	8	20	*12*	8	...	...	...	...	...	...
		KORI	Do.	91,594	*45,846*	45,748	488	*419*	69	34	*22*	12	7,377	*4,064*	3,313
		KOSHTI	Do.	1,593	*807*	786	630	*332*	298	517	*252*	265	321	*155*	166
		KASSI	Do.	75	*44*	31	...	...	...	...	...	...	75	*44*	31
		KUSHTA	Do.	395	*187*	208	...	...	...	...	...	...	...	...	...
		LILGAR	Do.	443	*179*	264	15	*6*	9	...	...	...	366	*143*	223
		MARU	Do.	5,300	*2,439*	2,861	63	*32*	31	...	...	...	...	...	...
		MOMIN	Do.	2	*1*	1	...	...	...	...	...	...	...	...	...
		Do.	Musalman	2,345	*1,230*	1,115	326	*183*	143	...	...	...	588	*292*	296
		NILGAR	Hindu	2	*2*	...	2	*2*	...	...	...	...	...	...	...
		Do	Musalman	908	*458*	450	...	...	...	...	...	...	144	*71*	73
		PATWA	Hindu	5,915	*3,103*	2,812	21	*16*	5	866	*445*	421	2,198	*1,189*	1,009
		Do.	Musalman	5	*5*	...	...	...	...	...	...	...	...	...	...
		PANIKA	Aboriginal	33,522	*16,980*	16,542	...	...	...	...	...	...	...	...	...
		RANGARA	Hindu	4,783	*2,372*	2,411	646	*345*	301	...	...	...	648	*356*	292
		Do.	Musalman	245	*139*	106	...	...	...	...	...	...	...	...	...
		RANGREZ	Hindu	23	*10*	13	...	...	...	20	*8*	12	...	...	...
		Do.	Musalman	882	*448*	434	8	*4*	4	...	...	...	402	*224*	178
		RANGAR	Hindu	29	*7*	22	...	...	...	...	...	...	29	*7*	22
		RAWALIA	Do.	5	*3*	2	5	*3*	2	...	...	...	...	...	...
		SALVI	Do.	322	*212*	110	...	...	...	...	...	...	...	...	...
		Do.	Aboriginal	307	*167*	140	292	*159*	133	...	...	...	15	*8*	7
		SALI	Hindu	13,691	*7,208*	6,483	...	...	...	...	...	...	...	...	...
			Total Group 23	186,724	94,168	92,546	3,201	1,850	1,351	5,128	2,680	2,448	18,423	9,778	8,645

Table XVI.—Castes, Tribes and Races, etc.—Central India.

NAME AND CLASSIFICATION.				DISTRIBUTION BY AGENCIES.														
				BUNDELKHAND.			BAGHELKHAND.			WESTERN MALWA.			BHOPAWAR.			GUNA.		
Class.	Group.	Caste.	Religion.	TOTAL.	Males.	Females.	TOTAL.	Males.	Females.	TOTAL.	Males.	Females.	TOTAL.	Males.	Females.	TOTAL.	Males.	Females.
				17	18	19	20	21	22	23	24	25	26	27	28	29	30	31
D.—ARTISAN AND VILLAGE MENIAL—contd.	22.—TAILORS	BORA	Hindu	...	...	...	...	...	...	10	10	...	...	...	...	...	...	...
		DARZI	Do.	9,251	4,657	4,594	8,388	4,206	4,182	15,815	8,285	7,530	3,982	2,000	1,982	2,037	1,179	858
		Do.	Musalman	...	...	...	...	...	...	...	...	...	...	...	...	6	5	1
		KHALIFA	Do.	...	...	...	...	...	...	1	1	...	...	...	...	...	...	...
			Total Group 22.	9,251	4,657	4,594	8,388	4,206	4,182	15,826	8,296	7,530	3,982	2,000	1,982	2,043	1,184	859
	23.—WEAVERS, CALENDERERS AND DYERS.	BUNKAR	Hindu	3,021	1,568	1,453	...	...	...	...	...	...	...	...	...	...	...	...
		CHHIPA	Do.	1,279	621	658	...	...	...	4,432	2,157	2,275	412	293	119	1,031	514	517
		Do.	Musalman	...	...	...	...	...	...	3,166	1,481	1,685	...	...	...	35	22	13
		GANDI	Hindu	...	...	...	...	...	...	97	36	61	...	...	...	...	...	...
		JULLAHA	Do.	...	...	...	...	...	...	8	6	2	...	...	...	...	...	...
		Do.	Musalman	...	...	...	...	...	...	190	95	95	...	...	...	1	1	...
		KOD	Hindu	...	...	...	...	...	...	...	...	...	...	...	...	...	...	...
		KORI	Do.	51,863	25,517	26,346	31,573	15,644	15,929	76	76	...	183	104	79	...	...	...
		KOSHTI	Do.	...	...	...	3	2	1	122	66	56	...	...	...	...	...	...
		KASSI	Do.	...	...	...	...	...	...	...	...	...	...	...	...	...	...	...
		KUSHTA	Do.	395	187	208	...	...	...	...	...	...	...	...	...	...	...	...
		LILGAR	Do.	...	...	...	...	...	...	62	30	32	...	...	...	...	...	...
		MARU	Do.	...	...	...	...	...	...	56	40	16	5,181	2,367	2,814	...	...	...
		MOMIN	Do.	...	...	...	...	...	...	2	1	1	...	...	...	...	...	...
		Do.	Musalman	...	...	...	2	2	...	1,429	753	676	...	...	...	...	...	...
		NILGAR	Hindu	...	...	...	...	...	...	...	...	...	...	...	...	...	...	...
		Do.	Musalman	...	...	...	...	...	...	760	385	375	...	...	...	4	2	2
		PATWA	Hindu	1,163	626	537	1,340	649	691	56	31	25	26	20	6	245	127	118
		Do.	Musalman	...	...	...	...	...	...	5	5	...	...	...	...	...	...	...
		PANIKA	Aboriginal	...	...	...	32,243	16,356	15,887	1,279	624	655	...	...	...	...	...	...
		RANGARA	Hindu	...	...	...	...	...	...	1,965	902	1,063	1,524	769	755	...	...	...
		Do.	Musalman	...	...	...	...	...	...	245	139	106	...	...	...	...	...	...
		RANGREZ	Hindu	...	...	...	...	...	...	...	...	...	...	...	...	3	2	1
		Do.	Musalman	...	...	...	...	...	...	453	213	240	...	...	...	19	7	12
		RANGAR	Hindu	...	...	...	...	...	...	...	...	...	...	...	...	...	...	...
		RAWALIA	Do.	...	...	...	...	...	...	...	...	...	...	...	...	...	...	...
		SALVI	Do.	...	...	...	...	...	...	29	2	27	293	210	83	...	...	...
		Do.	Aboriginal	...	...	...	...	...	...	...	...	...	...	...	...	...	...	...
		SALI	Hindu	...	...	...	...	...	...	361	198	163	13,330	7,010	6,320	...	...	...
			Total Group 23.	57,721	28,519	29,202	65,161	32,653	32,508	14,793	7,240	7,553	20,949	10,773	10,176	1,338	675	663

Table XVI.—Castes, Tribes and Races, by Nationality or traditional Occupation—*contd.*

NAME AND CLASSIFICATION.				PROVINCIAL TOTAL.			DISTRIBUTION BY AGENCIES.								
							INDORE.			GWALIOR.			BHOPAL.		
Class.	Group.	Caste.	Religion.	TOTAL.	Males.	Females.	TOTAL.	Males.	Females.	TOTAL.	Males.	Females.	TOTAL.	Males.	Females.
1	2	3	4	5	6	7	8	9	10	11	12	13	14	15	16
D.—ARTISAN AND VILLAGE MENIAL—*contd.*	24.—WASHERMEN	DHOBI	Hindu	94,607	49,577	45,030	2,274	1,366	908	21,301	11,326	9,975	21,119	11,409	9,710
		Do.	Musalman	177	84	93	14	8	6	...	...	...	27	14	13
		Do.	Aboriginal	1,813	911	902	...	...	...	...	...	...	...	...	...
			Total Group 24	96,597	50,572	46,025	2,288	1,374	914	21,301	11,326	9,975	21,146	11,423	9,723
	25.—COTTON CLEANERS	KANDERA	Hindu	22,047	11,874	10,173	12	9	3	14,382	8,089	6,293	5,068	2,434	2,634
		Do.	Aboriginal	6,998	3,567	3,431	...	...	...	...	...	...	...	...	...
		PINJARA	Hindu	430	88	342	1	...	1	...	...	...	...	...	...
		Do.	Musalman	21,500	11,213	10,287	704	398	306	...	...	...	7,491	3,936	3,555
			Total Group 25	50,975	26,742	24,233	717	407	310	14,382	8,089	6,293	12,559	6,370	6,189
	26.—SHEPHERDS AND WOOL WEAVERS.	DHANGAR	Hindu	4,532	2,004	2,528	3,111	1,472	1,619	...	...	...	...	...	...
		GADARIA	Do.	171,332	89,435	81,897	3,543	2, 29	1,5 4	50,827	26,776	24,051	16,501	8,903	7,598
		GARI	Do.	3,226	1,750	1,476	3,226	1,750	1,476	...	...	...	...	...	...
		GARHI	Do.	14	?	11	...	...	...	...	...	...	...	...	...
		GARARIA	Do.	158	158	...	...	...	...	...	...	...	158	158	...
		GADRI	Do.	803	16	787	...	...	...	...	...	...	...	...	...
		GWARA	Do.	139	139	...	...	...	...	...	...	...	...	...	...
		KOLBKAR	Do.	2	...	2	...	...	...	...	...	...	...	...	...
		REBARI	Do.	1,882	1,001	881	19	19	...	74	55	19	349	235	114
		Do.	Musalman	1	1	...	...	...	...	...	...	...	...	...	...
			Total Group 26.	182,089	94,507	87,582	9,899	5,290	4,609	50,901	26,831	24,070	17,008	9,296	7,712
	27.—OIL-PRESSERS	TELI	Hindu	210,813	108,476	102,337	3,589	1,874	1,715	31,992	16,670	15,322	43,051	22,142	20,909
		Do.	Musalman	471	248	223	45	28	17	...	...	...	342	182	160
		Do.	Jain	1	1	...	...	...	...	...	...	...	1	1	...
			Total Group 27.	211,285	108,725	102,560	3,634	1,902	1,732	31,992	16,670	15,322	43,394	22,325	21,069
	28.—POTTERS	KUMHAR	Hindu	166,698	86,309	80,389	5,067	2,741	2,326	26,921	14,247	12,674	32,629	16,971	15,658
			Total Group 28.	166,698	86,309	80,389	5,067	2,741	2,326	26,921	14,247	12,674	32,629	16,971	15,658

Table XVI.—Castes, Tribes and Races, etc.— Central India.

NAME AND CLASSIFICATION.				DISTRIBUTION BY AGENCIES.														
				BUNDELKHAND.			BAGHELKHAND.			WESTERN MALWA.			BHOPAWAR.			GUNA.		
Class.	Group.	Caste.	Religion.	TOTAL.	Males.	Females.	TOTAL.	Males.	Females.	TOTAL.	Males.	Females.	TOTAL.	Males.	Females.	TOTAL.	Males.	Females.
				17	18	19	20	21	22	23	24	25	26	27	28	29	30	31
	24.—WASHERMEN	DHOBI	Hindu	22,490	11,600	10,890	10,273	5,119	5,154	10,991	5,568	5,423	2,367	1,205	1,162	3,792	1,984	1,808
		Do.	Musalman	...	...	...	...	...	...	136	62	74	...	...	...	...	...	...
		Do.	Aboriginal	...	...	...	1,813	911	902	...	...	...	...	...	...	...	...	...
			Total Group 24.	22,490	11,600	10,890	12,086	6,030	6,056	11,127	5,630	5,497	2,367	1,205	1,162	3,792	1,984	1,808
	25.—COTTON CLEANERS	KANDERA	Hindu	453	223	230	498	250	248	225	119	106	14	11	3	1,395	739	656
		Do.	Aboriginal	6,998	3,567	3,431	...	...	...	...	...	...	...	...	...	...	...	...
		PINJARA	Hindu	...	...	...	...	...	...	283	12	271	146	76	70	...	...	...
		Do.	Musalman	...	...	...	5	5	...	12,943	6,688	6,255	...	...	...	357	186	171
			Total Group 25.	7,451	3,790	3,661	503	255	248	13,451	6,819	6,632	160	87	73	1,752	925	827
	26.—SHEPHERDS AND WOOL WEAVERS.	DHANGAR	Hindu	...	...	...	1	1	...	226	96	130	1,194	415	779	...	...	...
		GADARIA	Do.	40,314	20,870	19,444	15,716	7,952	7,764	36,221	18,346	17,875	4,182	2,410	1,772	4,028	2,149	1,879
		GARI	Do.	...	...	...	...	...	...	...	...	...	...	...	...	...	...	...
		GARHI	Do	...	...	...	...	...	...	...	...	...	...	...	...	14	3	11
		GARARIA	Do.	...	...	...	...	...	...	...	...	...	...	...	...	...	...	...
		GADRI	Do.	...	...	...	...	...	...	...	...	...	...	...	...	803	16	787
		GWARA	Do.	...	...	...	...	...	...	139	139	...	...	...	...	...	...	...
		KOLEKAR	Do.	...	...	...	...	...	...	2	...	2	...	...	...	...	...	...
		REBARI	Do.	54	32	22	...	...	...	1,317	601	716	16	16	...	53	43	10
		Do.	Musalman	...	...	...	...	...	...	1	1	...	...	...	...	...	...	...
			Total Group 26.	40,368	20,902	19,466	15,717	7,953	7,764	37,906	19,183	18,723	5,392	2,841	2,551	4,898	2,211	2,687
	27.—OIL-PRESSERS	TELI	Hindu	35,784	18,457	17,327	52,031	26,330	25,701	28,025	14,682	13,343	9,987	5,080	4,907	6,354	3,241	3,113
		Do.	Musalman	...	...	...	...	...	...	84	38	46	...	...	...	...	...	...
		Do.	Jain	...	...	...	...	...	...	...	...	...	...	...	...	...	...	...
			Total Group 27.	35,784	18,457	17,327	52,031	26,330	25,701	28,109	14,720	13,389	9,987	5,080	4,907	6,354	3,241	3,113
	28.—POTTERS	KUMHAR	Hindu	24,889	12,878	12,011	22,474	11,217	11,257	42,154	21,759	20,395	7,432	3,788	3,644	5,132	2,708	2,424
			Total Group 28.	24,889	12,878	12,011	22,474	11,217	11,257	42,154	21,759	20,395	7,432	3,788	3,644	5,132	2,708	2,424

TABLE XVI.—Castes, Tribes and Races, by Nationality or traditional Occupation—*contd.*

NAME AND CLASSIFICATION.				PROVINCIAL TOTAL.			DISTRIBUTION BY AGENCIES.								
							Indore.			Gwalior.			Bhopal.		
Class.	Group.	Caste.	Religion.	Total.	Males.	Females.	Total.	Males.	Females.	Total.	Males.	Females.	Total.	Males.	Females.
1	2	3	4	5	6	7	8	9	10	11	12	13	14	15	16
	29.—Glass Workers	Churiwala	Hindu	5	5	...	...	...	...	...	...	...	...	...	...
		Churigar	Do.	9	9	...	...	...	...	...	...	...	...	...	...
		Do.	Musalman	140	73	67	...	...	...	...	...	...	...	...	...
		Churihar	Do.	1	...	1	...	...	...	...	...	...	1	...	1
		Kachera	Hindu	731	380	351	...	...	...	...	...	...	...	...	...
		Do.	Musalman	26	7	19	...	...	...	...	...	...	23	7	16
		Manihar	Hindu	328	207	121	39	11	28	...	...	...	23	13	10
		Do.	Musalman	160	71	89	...	...	...	...	...	...	121	53	68
		Sisgar	Hindu	23	14	9	...	...	...	...	...	...	...	...	...
		Do.	Musalman	123	73	50	...	...	...	...	...	...	69	39	30
		Lakhera	Hindu	7,835	3,967	3,868	...	...	...	1,355	691	664	1,169	626	543
		Do.	Musalman	1,098	578	520	21	12	9	...	...	...	267	132	135
			Total Group 29.	10,479	5,384	5,095	60	23	37	1,355	691	664	1,673	870	803
	30.—Salt, &c., Workers	Agariya	Hindu	5,295	2,702	2,593	...	...	...	...	...	...	...	...	...
		Baria	Do.	45	30	15	...	...	...	...	...	...	...	...	...
		Kharol	Do.	4,056	2,209	1,847	286	146	140	...	...	...	...	...	...
		Luniya	Do.	7,461	4,095	3,366	620	471	149	...	...	...	135	66	69
		Nunya	Do.	292	151	141	...	...	...	...	...	...	...	...	...
			Total Group 30.	17,149	9,187	7,962	906	617	289	...	...	...	135	66	69
	31.—Lime Burners	Chunekar	Hindu	9	9	...	9	9	...	...	...	...	...	...	...
		Chuneri	Do.	1	1	...	...	...	...	...	...	...	...	...	...
		Kedda	Do.	116	59	57	46	20	26	...	...	...	...	...	...
			Total Group 31.	126	69	57	55	29	26	...	...	...	...	...	...
	32.—Goldsmiths' Refuse Collectors	Dhuldhoya	Hindu	5	3	2	...	...	...	...	...	...	...	...	...
		Do.	Musalman	37	21	16	...	...	...	...	...	...	...	...	...
			Total Group 32.												

D.—ARTISAN AND VILLAGE MENIAL—*contd.*

NAMES AND CLASSIFICATION.				DISTRIBUTION BY AGENCIES.														
				BUNDELKHAND.			BAGHELKHAND.			WESTERN MALWA.			BHOPAWAR.			GUNA.		
Class.	Group.	Caste.	Religion.	Total.	Males.	Females.	Total.	Males.	Females.	Total.	Males.	Females.	Total.	Males.	Females.	Total.	Males.	Females.
				17	18	19	20	21	22	23	24	25	26	27	28	29	30	31
	29.—Glass Workers	Churiwala	Hindu	...	...	...	...	...	...	...	...	...	...	...	...	5	5	...
		Churigar	Do.	...	...	...	...	...	...	9	9	...	...	...	...	...	...	...
		Do.	Musalman	...	...	...	...	...	...	140	73	67	...	...	...	...	...	...
		Churihar	Do.	...	...	...	...	...	...	...	...	...	...	...	...	...	...	...
		Kachera	Hindu	724	377	347	...	...	...	...	...	...	...	...	...	7	3	4
		Do.	Musalman	...	...	...	...	...	...	...	...	...	...	...	...	3	...	3
		Manihar	Hindu	...	...	...	...	...	...	139	109	30	127	74	53	...	...	...
		Do.	Musalman	...	...	...	...	...	...	1	1	...	...	...	...	38	17	21
		Sisgar	Hindu	...	...	...	...	...	...	1	...	1	...	...	...	22	14	8
		Do.	Musalman	...	...	...	...	...	...	54	34	20	...	...	...	...	...	...
		Lakhera	Hindu	...	...	...	2,804	1,396	1,408	1,943	974	969	483	233	250	81	47	34
		Do.	Musalman	...	...	...	...	...	...	784	417	367	...	...	...	26	17	9
			Total Group 29.	724	377	347	2,804	1,396	1,408	3,071	1,617	1,454	610	307	303	182	103	79
	30.—Salt, etc., Workers.	Agariya	Hindu	...	...	...	5,293	2,700	2,593	...	...	...	...	...	...	2	2	...
		Baria	Do.	...	...	...	...	...	...	...	...	...	45	30	15	...	...	...
		Kharol	Do.	...	...	...	...	...	...	2,713	1,436	1,277	1,057	627	430	...	...	...
		Luniya	Do.	...	...	...	6,074	3,194	2,880	148	86	62	395	201	194	89	77	12
		Nunya	Do.	281	141	140	11	10	1	...	...	...	...	...	...	...	...	...
			Total Group 30.	281	141	140	11,378	5,904	5,474	2,861	1,522	1,339	1,497	858	639	91	79	12
	31.—Lime Burners	Chunekar	Hindu	...	...	...	...	...	...	...	...	...	...	...	...	...	...	...
		Chuneri	Do.	1	1	...	...	...	...	...	...	...	...	...	...	...	...	...
		Kedda	Do.	70	39	31	...	...	...	...	...	...	...	...	...	...	...	...
			Total Group 31.	71	40	31	...	...	...	...	...	...	...	...	...	...	...	...
	32.—Goldsmiths' Refuse Collectors.	Dhuldhoya	Hindu	...	...	...	...	...	...	5	3	2	...	...	...	...	...	...
		Do.	Musalman	...	...	...	...	...	...	37	21	16	...	...	...	...	...	...
			Total Group 32.	...	...	...	...	...	...	42	24	18	...	...	...	...	...	...

TABLE XVI.—Castes, Tribes and Races, by Nationality or traditional Occupation—*contd.*

NAME AND CLASSIFICATION.				PROVINCIAL TOTAL.			DISTRIBUTION BY AGENCIES.								
							INDORE.			GWALIOR.			BHOPAL.		
Class.	Group.	Caste.	Religion.	Total.	Males.	Females.	Total.	Males.	Females.	Total.	Males.	Females.	Total.	Males.	Females.
1	2	3	4	5	6	7	8	9	10	11	12	13	14	15	16
D.—ARTISAN AND VILLAGE MENIAL—*contd.*	33.—GOLDWASHERS.	NIYARIA	Hindu	46	22	24	27	13	14	...	...	...	...	...	...
		Do.	Musalman	11	9	2	...	...	...	...	...	...	11	9	2
			Total Group 33	57	31	26	27	13	14	...	...	...	11	9	2
	35.—FISHERMEN, BOATMEN, PALKIBEARERS, COOKS, ETC.	ACHARI	Hindu	2	2	...	...	...	...	...	...	...	...	...	...
		BHISHTI	Do.	1	1	...	1	1	...	...	...	...	...	...	...
		Do.	Musalman	1,105	570	535	67	38	29	2	2	271	193	99	94
		BHARBHUNJA	Hindu	5,930	3,083	2,847	250	154	96	995	328	...	...	...	...
		Do.	Musalman	131	56	75	...	...	...	...	...	...	...	...	...
		BHUNJWA	Hindu	1,177	785	392	145	132	13	...	...	...	622	417	205
		BHUJARI	Do.	10	10	...	8	8	...	...	...	...	...	...	...
		BHOI	Do.	16,488	8,355	8,133	2,203	1,220	983	...	...	...	6,709	3,348	3,361
		Do.	Musalman	13	9	4	...	...	...	...	...	...	13	9	4
		Do.	Aboriginal	286	142	144	...	...	...	...	...	...	...	...	...
		BHATIARA	Hindu	2	1	1	...	...	...	...	...	...	2	1	1
		Do.	Musalman	57	42	15	...	...	...	...	...	...	48	38	10
		BHATTI	Do.	57	37	20	...	...	...	...	...	...	...	...	...
		CHAKAR	Hindu	2,082	1,012	1,070	4	4	...	...	...	...	...	...	...
		Do.	Musalman	39	1	38	...	...	...	...	...	...	...	...	...
		Do.	Jain	5	...	5	...	...	...	...	...	...	...	...	...
		CHEROA	Aboriginal	81	38	43	...	...	...	...	...	...	...	...	...
		DHIMAR	Hindu	69,429	35,335	34,094	1	1	...	6	5	1	8,752	4,419	4,333
		DUTYA	Do.	44	44	...	35	35	...	...	...	...	...	...	...
		DARBARI	Do.	1	1	...	...	...	...	...	...	...	...	...	...
		GHARUK	Do.	1	1	...	...	...	...	...	...	...	...	...	...
		GHUSIA	Aboriginal	3,596	1,884	1,712	...	...	...	...	...	...	310	228	82
		GERIA	Do.	5	3	2	...	...	...	...	...	...	5	3	2
		HALWAI	Hindu	365	213	152	9	5	4	1	1	...	284	168	116
		Do.	Musalman	7	3	4	...	...	...	...	...	...	7	3	4
		HUZURIYA	Hindu	2,799	1,311	1,488	31	17	14	...	...	...	...	...	...
		KATIYA	Do.	453	226	227	39	12	27	...	...	...	71	38	33
		Do.	Musalman	3	...	3	...	...	...	...	...	...	...	...	...
		KAMATHI	Hindu	148	81	67	39	39	...	...	...	...	...	...	...
		KAHAR	Do.	81,321	41,480	39,841	250	249	1	25,523	13,479	12,044	16,007	8,301	7,706

NAME AND CLASSIFICATION.				DISTRIBUTION BY AGENCIES.														
				Bundelkhand.			Baghelkhand.			Western Malwa.			Bhopawar.			Guna.		
Class.	Group.	Caste.	Religion.	Total.	Males.	Females.	Total.	Males.	Females.	Total.	Males.	Females.	Total.	Males.	Females.	Total.	Males.	Females.
				17	18	19	20	21	22	23	24	25	26	27	28	29	30	31
	33.—Goldwashers	Niyaria	Hindu	14	9	5	...	...	...	...	...	...	...	...	...	...	...	5
		Do.	Musalman	...	...	...	...	...	...	...	...	...	...	...	...	...	...	...
			Total Group 33	14	9	5	...	...	...	...	...	...	...	...	...	5	—	5
	35.—Fishermen, Boatmen, Palkibearers, Cooks, etc.	Achari	Hindu	...	...	...	...	...	...	2	2	...	...	...	...	...	...	...
		Bhishti	Do.	...	...	...	...	...	...	...	...	...	...	...	...	—	...	...
		Do.	Musalman	...	...	...	...	...	...	821	422	399	...	...	...	22	9	13
		Bharbhunja	Hindu	2,064	1,039	1,025	2,736	1,375	1,361	237	160	77	...	...	...	44	27	17
		Do.	Musalman	...	...	...	...	...	...	131	56	75	...	...	...	...	...	...
		Bhunjwa	Hindu	...	...	...	...	...	...	2	2	...	408	234	174	...	...	...
		Bhujari	Do.	...	...	...	...	...	...	2	2	...	...	...	...	...	...	...
		Bhoi	Do.	...	...	...	...	...	...	4,541	2,338	2,203	2,615	1,371	1,244	420	78	342
		Do.	Musalman	...	...	...	...	...	...	...	...	...	...	...	...	...	...	...
		Do.	Aboriginal	...	...	...	286	142	144	...	...	...	...	...	...	...	...	...
		Bhatiara	Hindu	...	...	...	...	...	...	...	...	...	...	...	...	...	...	...
		Do.	Musalman	...	...	...	...	...	...	9	4	5	...	...	...	...	...	...
		Bhatti	Do.	...	...	...	...	...	...	57	37	20	...	...	...	...	...	...
		Chakar	Hindu	...	...	...	...	...	...	2,074	1,008	1,066	...	...	...	4	...	4
		Do.	Musalman	...	...	...	...	...	...	39	1	38	...	...	...	...	...	...
		Do.	Jain	...	...	...	...	...	...	5	...	5	...	...	...	...	...	...
		Cheroa	Aboriginal	...	...	...	81	38	43	...	...	...	...	...	...	...	...	...
		Dhimar	Hindu	56,046	28,468	27,578	...	...	...	2	2	...	...	...	...	4,622	2,440	2,182
		Dutya	Do.	...	...	...	...	...	...	9	9	...	...	...	...	...	...	...
		Darbari	Do.	...	...	...	...	...	...	...	...	...	...	...	...	1	1	...
		Gharuk	Do.	...	...	...	...	...	...	...	...	...	1	1	...	...	...	...
		Ghusia	Aboriginal	3,230	1,658	1,592	2	1	1	...	...	...	...	...	...	54	17	37
		Geria	Do.	...	...	...	...	...	...	...	...	...	...	...	...	...	...	...
		Halwai	Hindu	11	4	7	9	6	3	47	29	18	...	...	...	4	...	4
		Do.	Musalman	...	...	...	...	...	...	...	...	...	...	...	...	...	...	...
		Huzuriya	Hindu	...	...	...	...	...	...	2,768	1,294	1,474	...	...	...	...	...	...
		Katiya	Do.	...	...	...	40	25	15	89	36	53	214	115	99	...	...	...
		Do.	Musalman	...	...	...	...	...	...	3	...	3	...	...	...	...	...	...
		Kamathi	Hindu	...	...	...	...	...	...	109	42	67	...	...	...	...	...	...
		Kahar	Do.	459	285	174	32,687	15,959	16,728	1,505	818	687	4,875	2,382	2,493	15	7	8

TABLE XVI.—Castes, Tribes and Races, by Nationality or traditional Occupation—*contd.*

NAME AND CLASSIFICATION.				PROVINCIAL TOTAL.			DISTRIBUTION BY AGENCIES.								
							INDORE.			GWALIOR.			BHOPAL.		
Class.	Group.	Caste.	Religion.	TOTAL.	Males.	Females.	TOTAL.	Males.	Females.	TOTAL.	Males.	Females.	TOTAL.	Males.	Females.
1	2	3	4	5	6	7	8	9	10	11	12	13	14	15	16
D.—ARTISAN AND VILLAGE MENIAL—*contd.*	35.—FISHERMEN, BOATMEN, PALKI BEARERS, COOKS, ETC.—*contd.*	KEWAT	Hindu	8	4	4	6	4	2	...	...	...	...	...	...
		KUNWAR	Do.	126	48	78	126	48	78	...	...	...	...	...	...
		KHIDMATGAR	Do.	64	9	55	...	...	...	...	...	...	...	...	...
		KIR	Do.	9,202	5,005	4,197	930	495	435	...	...	...	3,350	1,811	1,539
		Do.	Musalman	2	...	2	...	...	...	...	...	...	...	...	...
		Do.	Aboriginal	2	1	1	...	...	...	...	...	...	...	...	...
		KAMKER	Musalman	231	...	231	...	...	...	...	...	...	...	...	...
		MADRASI	Hindu	44	37	7	32	32	...	...	...	...	...	...	...
		MALLAH	Do.	31,988	16,042	15,946	...	...	...	...	...	...	...	...	...
		MACHHIYA	Do.	6	2	4	...	...	...	...	...	...	...	...	...
		NAWAR	Do.	982	427	555	...	...	...	...	...	...	...	...	...
		SEVAK	Do.	144	60	84	...	...	...	...	...	...	...	...	...
			Total Group 35	**228,437**	**116,361**	**112,076**	**4,176**	**2,494**	**1,682**	**26,131**	**13,815**	**12,316**	**36,373**	**18,883**	**17,490**
	36.—DISTILLERS AND TODDY DRAWERS.	BHANDARI	Hindu	20	5	15	...	...	...	...	...	...	...	...	...
		KATAL	Do.	62,452	31,719	30,733	1,348	756	592	9,426	4,958	4,468	15,976	7,918	8,058
		KALAR	Do.	12,098	6,073	6,025	...	...	...	...	...	...	...	...	...
		KALWAR	Do.	3	1	2	...	...	...	3	1	2	...	...	...
			Total Group 36	**74,573**	**37,798**	**36,775**	**1,348**	**756**	**592**	**9,429**	**4,959**	**4,470**	**15,976**	**7,918**	**8,058**
	37.—BUTCHERS	CHIKWA	Hindu	857	430	418	...	...	...	...	...	...	...	...	...
		KHATIK	Do.	18,165	9,389	8,776	942	649	203	6,025	3,144	2,881	2,279	1,116	1,163
		Do.	Musalman	48	24	24	37	20	17	...	...	...	7	2	5
		Do.	Aboriginal	29	29	...	...	...	...	29	29	...	...	...	...
		KASAI	Hindu	65	22	43	34	17	17	...	...	...	...	...	...
		Do.	Musalman	1,591	834	757	49	22	27	...	...	...	702	383	319
			Total Group 37	**20,755**	**10,737**	**10,018**	**1,062**	**708**	**354**	**6,054**	**3,173**	**2,881**	**2,988**	**1,501**	**1,487**
	38.—LEATHER WORKERS	BHAMBI	Hindu	20	20	...	7	7	...	...	...	...	...	...	...
		BHAMI	Aboriginal	13,444	6,711	6,733	1,582	826	756	...	...	...	1,284	498	786
		CHAMAR	Hindu	888,018	458,139	429,879	14,463	7,863	6,600	223,294	117,122	106,172	189,520	99,380	90,140
		CHAMCHISI	Do.	18	7	11	...	...	...	...	...	...	18	7	11
		DABGAR	Do.	201	106	95	30	12	18	...	...	...	...	...	...

NAME AND CLASSIFICATION.				DISTRIBUTION BY AGENCIES.														
				BUNDELKHAND.			BAGHELKHAND.			WESTERN MALWA.			BHOPAWAR.			GUNA.		
Class.	Group.	Caste.	Religion.	TOTAL.	Males.	Females.	TOTAL.	Males.	Females.	TOTAL.	Males.	Females.	TOTAL.	Males.	Females.	TOTAL.	Males.	Females.
				17	18	19	20	21	22	23	24	25	26	27	28	29	30	31
	35.—FISHERMEN, BOATMEN, PALKI BEARERS, COOKS, ETC.—*contd.*	KEWAT	Hindu	...	...	...	2	...	2	...	...	...	...	...	...	...	...	...
		KUNWAR	Do.	...	...	...	...	...	...	...	...	...	...	...	...	...	...	...
		KHIDMATGAR	Do.	...	...	...	...	...	...	64	*9*	55	...	...	...	...	...	...
		KIR	Do.	...	...	...	...	...	...	3,111	*1,634*	1,477	1,520	*774*	746	291	*291*	...
		Do.	Musalman	...	...	...	...	...	...	2	...	2	...	...	...	...	...	...
		Do.	Aboriginal	2	*1*	1	...	...	...	...	...	...	...	...	...	...	...	...
		KAMKER	Musalman	...	...	...	...	...	...	231	...	231	...	...	...	...	...	...
		MADRASI	Hindu	...	...	...	...	...	...	12	*5*	7	...	...	...	...	...	...
		MALLAH	Do.	6	*2*	4	31,977	*16,035*	15,942	5	*5*	...	...	...	...	...	...	...
		MACHHIYA	Do.	...	...	...	...	...	...	6	*2*	4	...	...	...	...	...	...
		NAWAR	Do.	...	...	...	...	...	...	...	...	...	982	*427*	555	...	...	...
		SEVAK	Do.	...	...	...	...	...	...	137	*55*	82	7	*5*	2	...	...	...
			Total Group 35	61,818	31,437	30,381	67,820	33,581	34,239	16,020	7,972	8,048	10,622	5,309	5,313	5,477	2,870	2,607
	36.—DISTILLERS AND TODDY DRAWERS.	BHANDARI	Hindu	...	...	...	...	...	...	20	*5*	15	...	...	...	...	...	...
		KATAL	Do.	...	...	...	21,492	*10,572*	10,920	6,291	*3,339*	2,952	5,573	*2,933*	2,640	2,346	*1,243*	1,103
		KALAR	Do.	12,098	*6,073*	6,025	...	...	...	...	...	...	...	...	...	...	...	...
		KALWAR	Do.	...	...	...	...	...	...	...	...	...	...	...	...	...	...	...
			Total Group 36	12,098	6,073	6,025	21,492	10,572	10,920	6,311	3,344	2,967	5,573	2,933	2,640	2,346	1,243	1,103
	37.—BUTCHERS	CHIKWA	Hindu	58	*29*	29	799	*410*	389	...	...	...	...	...	...	...	...	...
		KHATIK	Do.	3,004	*1,469*	1,535	1,798	*903*	895	3,519	*1,787*	1,732	198	*101*	97	400	*220*	180
		Do.	Musalman	...	...	...	...	...	...	...	...	...	...	...	...	4	*2*	2
		Do.	Aboriginal	...	...	...	...	...	...	...	...	...	...	...	...	...	...	...
		KASAI	Hindu	...	...	...	...	...	...	5	*5*	...	...	...	...	26	...	26
		Do.	Musalman	...	...	...	...	...	...	834	*427*	407	...	...	...	6	*2*	4
			Total Group 37	3,062	1,498	1,564	2,597	1,313	1,284	4,358	2,219	2,139	198	101	97	436	224	212
	38—LEATHER WORKERS	BHAMBI	Hindu	...	...	...	...	...	...	13	*13*	...	...	...	...	...	...	...
		BHAMI	Aboriginal	...	...	...	777	*377*	400	8,086	*4,148*	3,938	1,715	*862*	853	...	...	...
		CHAMAR	Hindu	200,509	*132,555*	97,954	115,492	*56,370*	59,122	90,689	*46,447*	44,242	12,961	*5,916*	7,045	41,090	*22,486*	18,604
		CHAMCHISI	Do.	...	...	...	...	...	...	...	...	...	...	...	...	...	...	...
		DABGAR	Do.	...	...	...	...	...	...	74	*41*	33	97	*53*	44	...	...	...

TABLE XVI.—Castes, Tribes and Races, by Nationality or traditional Occupation—*contd.*

NAME AND CLASSIFICATION.				PROVINCIAL TOTAL.			DISTRIBUTION BY AGENCIES.								
							INDORE.			GWALIOR.			BHOPAL.		
Class.	Group.	Caste.	Religion.	Total.	Males.	Females.	Total.	Males.	Females.	Total.	Males.	Females.	Total.	Males.	Females.
1	2	3	4	5	6	7	8	9	10	11	12	13	14	15	16
D.—ARTISAN AND VILLAGE MENIAL—*contd.*	38.—LEATHER WORKERS—*contd.*	GHASIA	Aboriginal	770	375	395	...	...	...	...	...	...	...	...	...
		JATIYA	Hindu	10	5	5	10	5	5	...	...	...	...	...	...
		JATHA	Do.	22	11	11	...	...	...	...	...	...	...	...	...
		JINGAR	Do.	642	357	285	127	63	64	61	38	23	137	69	68
		KHARWAL	Do.	57	31	26	...	...	...	...	...	...	...	...	...
		KOYALA	Do.	72	34	38	...	...	...	...	...	...	52	25	27
		MOCHI	Do.	6,209	3,519	2,690	1,272	954	318	933	487	446	870	501	369
		Do.	Musalman	138	65	73	3	2	1	...	...	...	...	...	...
		MANGI	Aboriginal	48,474	24,212	24,262	...	...	...	...	...	...	...	...	...
		ORI	Hindu	26	14	12	26	14	12	...	...	...	...	...	...
			Total Group 38	958,121	493,606	464,515	17,520	9,746	7,774	224,288	117,647	106,641	191,881	100,480	91,401
	38A.—LOW CASTES NOT INCLUDED IN GROUP 38.	DHER	Hindu	69	61	8	41	41	...	...	...	...	5	1	4
		Do.	Aboriginal	1	1	...	...	...	...	...	...	...	...	...	...
		MANG	Hindu	375	261	114	156	156	...	...	...	...	173	80	93
		Do.	Aboriginal	1,662	820	842	786	399	387	80	40	40	...	...	...
		MAHAR	Hindu	1,600	1,353	247	1,064	1,064	...	5	3	2	12	7	5
		Do.	Aboriginal	13,041	6,543	6,498	...	...	...	337	153	184	3,685	1,861	1,824
		RAMOSI	Hindu	19	10	9	...	...	...	...	...	...	...	...	...
		SURTI	Do.	8	8	...	8	8	...	...	...	...	...	...	...
			Total Group 38A	16,775	9,057	7,718	2,055	1,668	387	422	196	226	3,875	1,949	1,926
	39.—SCAVENGERS	BHANGI	Hindu	35,523	18,652	16,871	2,040	1,060	980	13,358	7,164	6,194	8,411	4,292	4,119
		Do.	Musalman	2,475	1,252	1,223	291	150	141	...	...	...	559	273	286
		BEDIYA	Hindu	10	7	3	...	...	...	...	...	...	...	...	...
		BELAHAR	Do.	726	364	362	...	...	...	726	364	362	...	...	...
		CHANDAL	Do.	38	24	14	...	...	...	...	...	...	...	...	...
		MEHTAR	Do.	7,129	3,953	3,176	719	719	...	...	...	...	141	73	68
		SARBHANGI	Do.	43	29	14	20	18	2	5	...	5	13	6	7
			Total Group 39	45,944	24,281	21,663	3,070	1,947	1,123	14,089	7,528	6,561	9,124	4,644	4,480
			Total Class D.	2,931,274	1,513,262	1,418,012	96,564	53,880	42,684	530,179	279,790	250,389	568,469	295,593	272,876

D.—ARTISAN AND VILLAGE MENIAL—*concld.*

NAME AND CLASSIFICATION.				DISTRIBUTION BY AGENCIES.														
				BUNDELKHAND.			BAGHELKHAND.			WESTERN MALWA.			BHOPAWAR.			GUNA.		
Class.	Group.	Caste.	Religion.	Total.	Males.	Females.	Total.	Males.	Females.	Total.	Males.	Females.	Total.	Males.	Females.	Total.	Males.	Females.
				17	18	19	20	21	22	23	24	25	26	27	28	29	30	31
D.—Artisan and Village Menial—*concld.*	38.—Leather Workers—*contd.*	Ghasia	Aboriginal	...	...	...	770	*375*	395	...	...	...	...	...	...	...	...	...
		Jatiya	Hindu	...	...	...	...	...	...	...	...	...	...	...	...	...	...	...
		Jatha	Do.	...	...	...	...	...	...	22	*11*	11	...	...	...	...	...	...
		Jingar	Do.	...	...	...	...	...	...	166	*100*	66	151	*87*	64	...	...	...
		Kharwal	Do.	...	...	...	...	...	...	...	...	...	...	...	...	57	*31*	26
		Koyala	Do.	...	...	...	...	...	...	1	...	1	19	*9*	10	...	...	...
		Mochi	Do.	626	*338*	288	419	*222*	197	1,633	*782*	851	228	*132*	96	228	*103*	125
		Do.	Musalman	...	...	...	...	...	...	135	*63*	72	...	...	...	...	...	...
		Mangi	Aboriginal	...	...	...	48,474	*24,212*	24,262	...	...	...	...	...	...	...	...	...
		Ori	Hindu	...	...	...	...	...	...	...	...	...	...	...	...	...	...	...
			Total Group 38.	201,135	102,893	98,242	165,932	81,556	84,376	100,819	51,605	49,214	15,171	7,059	8,112	41,375	22,620	18,755
	38A.—Low Castes not included in Group 38.	Dher	Hindu	...	...	...	...	...	...	23	*19*	4	...	...	...	...	...	...
		Do.	Aboriginal	...	...	...	...	...	...	...	...	...	1	*1*	...	...	...	...
		Mang	Hindu	...	...	...	...	...	...	46	*25*	21	...	...	...	...	...	...
		Do.	Aboriginal	23	*10*	13	2	*1*	1	447	*205*	242	324	*165*	159	...	...	...
		Mahar	Hindu	...	...	...	26	*18*	8	470	*248*	222	11	*7*	4	12	*6*	6
		Do.	Aboriginal	...	...	...	7,429	*3,730*	3,699	19	*8*	11	873	*421*	452	698	*370*	328
		Ramosi	Hindu	...	...	...	...	...	...	12	*7*	5	7	*3*	4	...	...	...
		Surti	Do.	...	...	...	...	...	...	...	...	...	...	...	...	...	...	...
			Total Group 38 A.	23	10	13	7,457	3,749	3,708	1,017	512	505	1,216	597	619	710	376	334
	39.—Scavengers	Bhangi	Hindu	...	...	...	...	...	...	7,243	*3,804*	3,439	1,595	*854*	741	2,876	*1,478*	1,398
		Do.	Musalman	...	...	...	1	*1*	...	1,346	*699*	647	176	*83*	93	102	*46*	56
		Bediya	Hindu	...	...	...	10	*7*	3	...	...	...	...	...	...	...	...	...
		Balahar	Do.	...	...	...	...	...	...	...	...	...	...	...	...	...	...	...
		Chandal	Do.	26	*14*	12	...	...	...	12	*10*	2	...	...	...	...	...	...
		Mehtar	Do.	5,412	*2,758*	2,654	173	*97*	76	684	*306*	378	...	...	...	...	...	...
		Sarbhangi	Do.	...	...	...	...	...	...	...	...	...	...	...	...	5	*5*	...
			Total Group 39.	5,438	2,772	2,666	184	105	79	9,285	4,819	4,466	1,771	937	834	2,983	1,529	1,454
			Total Class D.	577,975	295,280	282,695	536,014	266,820	269,194	412,118	213,043	199,075	113,038	57,313	55,725	96,917	51,543	45,514

TABLE XVI.—Castes, Tribes and Races, by Nationality or traditional Occupation—*contd.*

NAME AND CLASSIFICATION.				PROVINCIAL TOTAL.			DISTRIBUTION BY AGENCIES.								
							INDORE.			GWALIOR.			BHOPAL.		
Class.	Group.	Caste.	Religion.	Total.	Males.	Females.	Total.	Males.	Females.	Total.	Males.	Females.	Total.	Males.	Females.
1	2	3	4	5	6	7	8	9	10	11	12	13	14	15	16
	40.—Grindstone makers and Stone quarriers.	Bind	Aboriginal	478	235	243	...	...	...	...	...	...	...	...	...
			Total Group 40	478	235	243	...	...	...	...	...	...	...	...	...
	41.—Earth workers and Stone dressers.	Beldar	Hindu	7,734	4,003	3,731	540	302	238	10	6	4	2,282	1,325	957
		Do.	Musalman	333	171	162	...	...	...	...	...	...	333	171	162
		Bhathphod	Hindu	59	30	29	...	...	...	...	...	...	...	...	...
		Od	Do.	146	88	58	...	...	...	146	88	58	...	...	...
		Odya	Do.	59	32	27	...	...	...	...	...	...	59	32	27
		Raj	Do.	74	38	36	...	...	...	...	...	...	...	...	...
		Tankara	Do.	380	306	74	...	...	...	...	...	...	...	...	...
			Total Group 41	8,785	4,668	4,117	540	302	238	156	94	62	2,674	1,528	1,146
	42.—Knife grinders	Sikalgar	Hindu	3,608	2,196	1,412	126	63	63	215	105	110	1,351	889	462
		Do.	Musalman	42	23	19	...	...	...	...	...	...	41	23	18
			Total Group 42	3,650	2,219	1,431	126	63	63	215	105	110	1,392	912	480
	43.—Mat makers, Cane splitters.	Barudia	Hindu	122	50	72	91	46	45	...	...	...	...	...	...
		Bansphod	Do.	43,890	22,332	21,558	277	175	102	...	...	...	13,620	6,651	6,969
		Do.	Musalman	5	1	4	4	1	3	...	...	...	...	...	...
		Basor	Aboriginal	343	156	187	...	...	...	343	156	187	...	...	...
		Chitodya	Hindu	36	21	15	...	...	...	...	...	...	36	21	15
		Bargunda	Aboriginal	3,841	1,960	1,881	473	234	239	...	...	...	647	351	296
		Ganchha	Hindu	25	10	15	...	...	...	...	...	...	...	...	...
		Do.	Aboriginal	903	479	424	91	42	49	...	...	...	14	5	9
		Kurur	Hindu	75	38	37	...	...	...	...	...	...	...	...	...
			Total Group 43	49,240	25,047	24,193	936	408	428	343	156	187	14,317	7,028	7,289

Table XVI.—Castes, Tribes and Races, etc.—Central India.

NAME AND CLASSIFICATION.				DISTRIBUTION BY AGENCIES.														
				BUNDELKHAND.			BAGHELKHAND.			WESTERN MALWA.			BHOPAWAR.			GUNA.		
Class.	Group.	Caste.	Religion.	Total.	Males.	Females.	Total.	Males.	Females.	Total.	Males.	Females.	Total.	Males.	Females.	Total.	Males.	Females.
				17	18	19	20	21	22	23	24	25	26	27	28	29	30	31
E.—VAGRANT MINOR ARTISANS AND PERFORMERS, ETC.	40.—GRINDSTONE MAKERS AND STONE QUARRIERS.	BIND	Aboriginal	...	...	..	450	220	230	...	...	...	28	15	13	...	...	...
			Total Group 40	...	...	...	450	220	230	...	...	...	28	15	13	...	...	...
	41.—EARTH WORKERS AND STONE DRESSERS.	BELDAR	Hindu	1,868	912	956	1,070	515	555	704	369	335	937	413	524	323	161	162
		Do.	Musalman	...	...	...	...	...	...	...	...	...	...	...	...	...	...	...
		BHATHEPHOD	Hindu	...	...	...	...	...	...	...	...	...	...	...	...	59	30	29
		OD	Do.	...	...	...	...	...	...	...	...	...	...	...	...	...	...	...
		ODYA	Do.	...	...	...	...	...	...	...	...	...	...	...	...	...	...	...
		RAJ	Do.	...	...	...	...	...	...	74	38	36	...	...	...	...	...	...
		TANKARA	Do.	...	...	...	...	...	...	225	216	9	155	90	65	...	...	...
			Total Group 41	1,868	912	956	1,070	515	555	1,003	623	380	1,092	503	589	382	191	191
	42.—KNIFE GRINDERS	SIKALGAR	Hindu	...	...	...	...	...	...	1,217	759	458	587	322	265	112	58	54
		Do.	Musalman	...	...	...	...	...	...	1	...	1	...	...	...	...	...	...
			Total Group 42	...	...	...	...	...	...	1,218	759	459	587	322	265	112	58	54
	43.—MAT MAKERS, CANE SPLITTERS.	BARUDIA	Hindu	...	...	...	...	...	...	4	4	...	27	...	27	...	...	...
		BANSPHOD	Do.	28,905	14,934	13,971	...	...	...	23	16	7	...	...	.	1,065	556	509
		Do.	Musalman	...	...	...	...	...	...	1	...	1	...	...	...	...	...	...
		BASOR	Aboriginal	...	...	...	...	...	...	...	...	...	...	...	...	...	...	...
		CHITODYA	Hindu	...	...	...	...	...	...	...	..	...	...	...	...	...	...	...
		BARGUNDA	Aboriginal	...	...	...	...	...	...	1,889	949	940	832	426	406	...	...	...
		GANCHHA	Hindu	...	...	...	...	...	...	25	10	15	...	...	...	...	...	...
		Do.	Aboriginal	...	...	...	...	...	...	89	58	31	709	374	335	...	...	...
		KURUR	Hindu	...	...	...	75	38	37	...	...	...	...	...	...	...	...	...
			Total Group 43	28,905	14,934	13,971	75	38	37	2,031	1,037	994	1,568	800	768	1,065	556	509

TABLE XVI.—Castes, Tribes and Races, by Nationality or traditional Occupation—*contd.*

NAME AND CLASSIFICATION.				PROVINCIAL TOTAL.			DISTRIBUTION BY AGENCIES.								
							INDORE.			GWALIOR.			BHOPAL.		
Class.	Group.	Caste.	Religion.	Total.	Males.	Females.	Total.	Males.	Females.	Total.	Males.	Females.	Total.	Males.	Females.
1	2	3	4	5	6	7	8	9	10	11	12	13	14	15	16
	44.—Hunters, Fowlers, etc.	Bahelya	Hindu	58	50	8	...	...	...	55	48	7	...	...	...
		Gachia	Do.	12	10	2	...	...	...	...	...	...	...	...	...
		Bediya	Do.	1	1	...	1	1	...	...	...	...	...	...	...
		Do.	Aboriginal	4,697	1,993	2,704	...	...	...	1,349	584	765	2,351	1,043	1,308
		Bahalia	Hindu	2,351	1,171	1,180	...	...	...	...	...	...	...	...	...
		Bhairia	Do.	2	2	...	...	...	...	...	...	...	...	...	...
		Do.	Aboriginal	174	66	108	...	...	...	...	...	...	...	...	...
		Bhar	Do.	15	3	12	...	...	...	...	...	...	...	...	...
		Bagri	Do.	57,406	30,234	27,172	4,642	2,402	2,240	2,469	1,321	1,148	7,222	3,919	3,303
		Kanjar	Hindu	332	198	134	64	64	...	...	...	...	30	8	22
		Do.	Muslaman	256	256	...	...	...	...	...	...	...	...	...	...
		Do.	Aboriginal	1,604	725	879	157	75	82	399	200	199	210	113	97
		Moghya	Hindu	131	82	49	18	18	...	...	...	...	22	12	10
		Do.	Aboriginal	110,784	63,362	47,422	1,343	1,332	11	...	...	...	36,572	21,247	15,325
		Pasi	Hindu	2,459	1,611	848	708	506	202	6	3	3	129	85	44
		Do.	Aboriginal	110	56	54	...	...	...	...	...	...	...	...	...
		Pardhi	Hindu	2	2	...	...	...	...	...	...	...	...	...	...
		Do.	Aboriginal	6,291	2,594	3,697	...	...	...	71	36	35	4,701	1,717	2,984
		Sansi	Hindu	13	10	3	...	...	...	...	...	...	...	...	...
		Do.	Aboriginal	977	502	475	2	1	1	906	446	460	...	...	...
		Shikari	Do.	39	19	20	...	...	...	...	...	...	...	...	...
			Total Group 44.	187,714	102,947	84,767	6,935	4,399	2,536	5,255	2,638	2,617	51,237	28,144	23,093
	45.—Miscellaneous and Disreputable Livers.	Asauda	Hindu	282	155	127	...	...	...	...	...	...	...	...	...
		Aiknath	Do.	10	10	...	10	10	...	...	...	...	...	...	...
		Ajnavia	Do.	16	5	11	...	...	...	...	...	...	...	...	...
		Adirval	Do.	4	2	2	...	...	...	...	...	...	...	...	...
		Ajmeri	Musalman	252	252	...	...	...	...	...	...	...	...	...	...
		Baori	Hindu	4	4	...	4	4	...	...	...	...	...	...	...
		Bijara	Do.	36	19	17	36	19	17	...	...	...	...	...	...
		Bhelsia	Do.	61	24	37	...	...	...	...	...	...	...	...	...
		Baldia	Do.	10	7	3	...	...	...	...	...	...	...	...	...
		Bagrawad	Do.	1	...	1	...	...	...	...	...	...	...	...	...
		Babar	Do.	587	295	292	...	...	...	1	1	...	12	10	2
		Balungai	Do.	2	1	1	...	...	...	...	...	...	...	...	...
		Baljabu	Do.	3	1	2	...	...	...	...	...	...	...	...	...
		Bhoai	Do.	7	4	3	...	...	...	...	...	...	...	...	...
		[illegible]	Do.	2	1	2	...	...	...	...	...	...	...	...	...

NAME AND CLASSIFICATION.				DISTRIBUTION BY AGENCIES.														
				BUNDELKHAND.			BAGHELKHAND.			WESTERN MALWA.			BHOPAWAR.			GUNA.		
Class.	Group.	Caste.	Religion.	TOTAL.	Males.	Females.	TOTAL.	Males.	Females.	TOTAL.	Males.	Females.	TOTAL.	Males.	Females.	TOTAL.	Males.	Females.
				17	18	19	20	21	22	23	24	25	26	27	28	29	30	31
E.—VAGRANT MINOR ARTISANS AND PERFORMERS, ETC.—contd.	44.—HUNTERS, FOWLERS, ETC.	BAHELYA	Hindu	...	...	...	...	...	...	...	...	...	...	...	...	3	2	1
		GACHIA	Do.	...	...	...	...	...	...	...	...	...	12	10	2	...	...	...
		BEDIYA	Do.	...	...	...	...	...	...	...	...	...	...	...	...	...	...	...
		Do.	Aboriginal	...	...	...	...	...	...	39	17	22	...	...	...	958	349	609
		BAHALIA	Hindu	30	12	18	2,321	1,159	1,162	...	...	...	...	...	...	...	...	...
		BHAIRIA	Do.	2	2	...	...	...	...	...	...	...	...	...	...	...	...	...
		Do.	Aboriginal	...	...	...	174	66	108	...	...	...	...	...	...	...	...	...
		BHAR	Do.	...	...	...	15	3	12	...	...	...	...	...	...	...	...	...
		BAGRI	Do.	...	...	...	2,831	1,410	1,421	36,129	19,097	17,032	3,601	1,797	1,804	512	288	224
		KANJAR	Hindu	82	81	11	...	...	...	190	91	99	...	...	...	16	14	2
		Do.	Musalman	...	...	...	...	...	...	256	256	...	...	...	...	...	...	...
		Do.	Aboriginal	9	3	6	29	12	17	677	268	409	115	51	64	8	3	5
		MOGHYA	Hindu	...	...	...	...	...	...	42	26	16	1	1	...	48	25	23
		Do.	Aboriginal	...	...	...	...	...	...	72,787	40,730	32,057	7	6	1	75	47	28
		PASI	Hindu	44	32	12	773	451	322	308	233	75	491	301	190	...	...	...
		Do.	Aboriginal	110	56	54	...	...	...	...	...	...	...	...	...	...	...	...
		PARDHI	Hindu	...	...	...	...	...	...	2	2	...	...	...	...	...	...	...
		Do.	Aboriginal	...	...	...	...	...	...	644	370	274	871	469	402	4	2	2
		SANSI	Hindu	...	...	...	...	...	...	...	...	...	...	...	...	13	10	3
		Do.	Aboriginal	...	...	...	2	2	...	62	50	12	5	3	2	...	...	...
		SHIKARI	Do.	...	...	...	...	...	...	...	...	...	...	...	...	39	19	20
			Total Group 44.	227	126	101	6,145	3,103	3,042	111,136	61,140	49,996	5,103	2,638	2,465	1,676	759	917
	45.—MISCELLANEOUS AND DISREPUTABLE LIVERS.	ASAUDA	Hindu	...	...	...	...	...	...	...	...	...	282	155	127	...	...	...
		AIKNATH	Do.	...	...	...	...	...	...	...	...	...	...	...	...	...	...	...
		AJNAVIA	Do.	...	...	...	...	...	...	...	...	...	16	5	11	...	...	...
		ADIRVAL	Do.	4	2	2	...	...	...	...	...	...	...	...	...	...	...	...
		AJMERI	Musalman	...	...	...	...	...	...	252	252	...	...	...	...	...	...	...
		BAORI	Hindu	...	...	...	...	...	...	...	...	...	...	...	...	...	...	...
		BIJARA	Do.	...	...	...	...	...	...	...	...	...	...	...	...	...	...	...
		BHELSIA	Do.	...	...	...	...	...	...	...	...	...	61	24	37	...	...	...
		BALDIA	Do.	...	...	...	...	...	...	...	...	...	...	...	...	10	7	3
		BAGRAWAD	Do.	...	...	...	...	...	...	1	...	1	...	...	...	...	...	...
		BABAR	Do.	...	...	...	...	...	...	574	284	290	...	...	...	...	...	...
		BALUNGAI	Do.	...	...	...	2	1	1	...	...	...	...	...	...	...	...	...
		BALJABU	Do.	...	...	...	3	1	2	...	...	...	...	...	...	...	...	...
		BEGAI	Do.	...	...	...	7	4	3	...	...	...	...	...	...	...	...	...
		BAWARASI	Do.	...	...	...	3	1	2	...	...	...	...	...	...	...	...	...

TABLE XVI.—Castes, Tribes and Races, by Nationality or traditional Occupation—*contd.*

Class.	Group.	Caste.	Religion.	Provincial Total. Total.	Provincial Total. Males.	Provincial Total. Females.	Indore. Total.	Indore. Males.	Indore. Females.	Gwalior. Total.	Gwalior. Males.	Gwalior. Females.	Bhopal. Total.	Bhopal. Males.	Bhopal. Females.
1	2	3	4	5	6	7	8	9	10	11	12	13	14	15	16
	45.—Miscellaneous and Disreputable Livers—*contd.*	Balji	Hindu	5	4	1	...	...	...	...	...	...	...	...	...
		Borat	Do.	181	113	68								...	...
		Baraundi	Do.	10	10	...	...	...	...	56	42	14	10	10	...
		Burara	Do.	4	3	1	...	...	...	...	...	...	...	...	...
		Bhagor	Do.	7	4	3	...	...	...	...	...	...	7	4	3
		Badedewli	Do.	3	1	2	...	...	...	...	...	...	3	1	2
		Banswi	Do.	2	2	...	...	...	...	...	...	...			
		Bunyar	Do.	3	2	1	...	...	...	...	...	...	...	...	
		Barori	Do.	2	2	...	...	...	...	...	...	...	...	...	...
		Bansli	Do.	24	16	8	...	...	...	...	...	...	...	...	...
		Balduja	Do.	5	...	5	...	...	...	...	...	...	...	...	...
		Badami	Do.	4	3	1	...	...	...	...	...	...	...	...	...
		Bayate	Do.	70	42	28	...	...	...	...	...	...	...	...	...
		Bagadia	Do	63	39	24	...	...	...	...	...	...	63	39	24
		Bhujawal	Do.	34	...	34	...	...	...	...	...	...	...	...	...
		Bagar	Do.	2,669	1,405	1,264	1	1	...	...	...	...	1,295	651	644
		Bhapshah	Musalman	1	1	...	1	1	...	...	...	...			
		Bhulwar	Do.	3	1	2	3	1	2	...	...	...	...	...	...
		Belim	Do.	3	...	3	...	...	...	...	...	...	...	...	...
		Bonis	Do.	4	...	4	...	...	...	...	...	...	...	...	...
		Baiga	Aboriginal	15,968	8,058	7,910	...	...	...	...	...	...	...	...	...
		Bagaria	Do.	105	48	57	...	...	...	...	...	...	...	...	...
		Bedni	Do.	74	62	12	...	...	...	...	...	...	74	62	12
		Basudev	Do.	62	26	36	...	...	...	...	...	...	...	...	...
		Bawari	Do.	95	40	55	...	...	...	...	...	...	...	...	...
		Chora	Hindu	20	12	8	...	...	...	...	...	...	20	12	8
		Chingar	Do.	5	5	...	...	...	...	...	...	...	...	...	...
		Chhangar	Do.	3	2	1	...	...	...	...	...	...	3	2	1
		Chalpuriya	Do.	4	3	1	...	...	...	...	...	...	4	3	1
		Chandi	Do.	2	...	2	...	...	...	...	...	...	...	...	...
		Darahi	Do.	25	25	...	1	1	...	...	...	...	...	...	...
		Daksh	Do.	27	27	...	...	...	...	...	...	...	...	...	...
		Dhodi	Do.	3	...	3	...	...	...	...	...	...	...	...	...
		Do.	Musalman	53	25	28	...	...	...	...	...	...	...	...	...
		[illegible]	Hindu	[illegible]	[illegible]	[illegible]	...	...	...	...	...	...	...	...	...

E—VAGRANT MINOR ARTISANS AND PERFORMERS, Etc.—*contd.*

E.—VAGRANT MINOR ARTISANS AND PERFORMERS, Etc.—contd.

NAME AND CLASSIFICATION.				DISTRIBUTION BY AGENCIES.														
				BUNDELKHAND.			BAGHELKHAND.			WESTERN MALWA.			BHOPAWAR.			GUNA.		
Class.	Group.	Caste.	Religion.	Total.	Males.	Females.	Total.	Males.	Females.	Total.	Males.	Females.	Total.	Males.	Females.	Total.	Males.	Females.
				17	18	19	20	21	22	23	24	25	26	27	28	29	30	31
	45.—Miscellaneous and Disreputable Livers—contd.	Balji	Hindu	...	...	...	5	4	1	...	...	...	...	...	...	...	...	...
		Borat	Do.	...	...	...	...	...	...	125	71	54	...	...	...	...	...	...
		Baraundi	Do.	...	...	...	...	...	...	...	...	...	...	...	...	...	...	...
		Burara	Do.	...	...	...	...	...	...	4	3	1	...	...	...	...	...	...
		Bhagor	Do.	...	...	...	...	...	...	...	...	...	...	...	...	...	...	...
		Badedewli	Do.	...	...	...	...	...	...	...	...	...	...	...	...	...	...	...
		Banswi	Do.	...	...	...	...	...	...	...	...	...	2	2	...	...	...	...
		Bunyar	Do.	...	...	...	3	2	1	...	...	...	...	...	...	...	...	...
		Barori	Do.	2	2	...	...	...	...	...	...	...	...	...	...	...	...	...
		Bansli	Do.	24	16	8	...	...	...	...	...	...	...	...	...	...	...	...
		Balduja	Do.	...	...	...	...	...	...	5	...	5	...	...	...	...	...	...
		Badami	Do.	4	3	1	...	...	...	...	...	...	...	...	...	...	...	...
		Bayate	Do.	...	...	...	...	...	...	70	42	28	...	...	...	...	...	...
		Bagadia	Do.	...	...	...	...	...	...	...	...	...	...	...	...	...	...	...
		Bhujawal	Do.	...	...	...	...	...	...	34	...	34	...	...	...	...	...	...
		Bagar	Do.	423	215	208	...	...	...	911	509	402	...	...	...	39	29	10
		Bhapseah	Musalman	...	...	...	...	...	...	...	...	...	...	...	...	...	...	...
		Bhulwar	Do.	...	...	...	...	...	...	...	...	...	...	...	...	...	...	...
		Belim	Do.	...	...	...	...	...	...	3	...	3	...	...	...	...	...	...
		Bonis	Do.	...	...	...	...	...	...	4	...	4	...	...	...	...	...	...
		Baiga	Aboriginal	...	...	...	15,968	8,058	7,910	...	...	...	...	...	...	...	...	...
		Bagaria	Do.	...	...	...	...	...	...	...	...	...	...	...	...	105	48	57
		Bedni	Do.	...	...	...	...	...	...	...	...	...	...	...	...	...	...	...
		Basudev	Do.	...	...	...	...	...	...	62	26	36	...	...	...	...	...	...
		Bawari	Do	37	12	25	58	28	30	...	...	...	...	...	...	...	...	...
		Chora	Hindu	...	...	...	...	...	...	...	...	...	...	...	...	...	...	...
		Chingar	Do.	...	...	...	...	...	...	5	5	...	...	...	...	...	...	...
		Chhangar	Do.	...	...	...	...	...	...	...	...	...	...	...	...	...	...	...
		Chalpuriya	Do.	...	...	...	...	...	...	...	...	...	...	...	...	...	...	...
		Chandi	Do.	...	...	...	...	...	...	2	...	2	...	...	...	...	...	...
		Darahi	Do.	...	...	...	...	...	...	...	...	...	...	...	...	24	24	...
		Daksh	Do.	...	...	...	...	...	...	...	...	...	...	...	...	27	27	...
		Dhodi	Do.	...	...	...	...	...	...	3	...	3	...	...	...	...	...	...
		Do.	Musalman	...	...	...	...	...	...	53	25	28	...	...	...	...	...	...
		Dhopa	Hindu	...	...	...	...	...	...	8	8	...	...	...	...	...	...	...

TABLE XVI.—Castes, Tribes and Races, by Nationality or traditional Occupation—*contd.*

NAME AND CLASSIFICATION.				PROVINCIAL TOTAL.			DISTRIBUTION BY AGENCIES.								
							INDORE.			GWALIOR.			BHOPAL.		
Class.	Group.	Caste.	Religion.	Total.	Males.	Females.	Total.	Males.	Females.	Total.	Males.	Females.	Total.	Males.	Females.
1	2	3	4	5	6	7	8	9	10	11	12	13	14	15	16
	45.—Miscellaneous and Disreputable Livers—*contd.*	Dhaoli Pawal	Hindu	8	8	...	...	...	...	...	...	...	...	...	...
		Dhonkula	Do.	74	73	1	...	...	...	...	...	...	...	...	...
		Dahar	Do.	42	...	42	...	...	...	...	...	...	...	...	...
		Dhanipurab	Do.	145	74	71	...	...	...	...	...	...	...	...	...
		Dedhari	Musalman	4	2	2	4	2	2	...	...	...	...	...	...
		Dasugar	Do.	58	21	37	...	...	...	...	...	...	58	21	37
		Dharam	Do.	1	1	...	...	...	...	...	...	...	1	1	...
		Dewada	Do.	1	...	1	1	...	1	...	...	...	...	...	...
		Danuhar	Aboriginal	4,034	2,009	2,025	...	...	...	...	...	...	...	...	...
		Dayet	Do.	70	32	38	...	...	...	..	...	...	..	...	...
		Dhalpulya	Do.	14	7	7	...	...	...	...	...	...	...	...	...
		Eshan	Hindu	4	...	4	...	...	...	...	...	...	...	...	...
		Farakabadi	Musalman	15	10	5	...	...	...	...	...	...	...	...	...
		Farsi	Do.	9	5	4	...	...	...	...	...	...	...	...	...
		Gangoria	Hindu	88	49	39	...	...	...	...	...	...	88	49	39
		Goyer	Do.	63	56	7	...	...	...	...	...	...	63	56	7
		Ghori	Do.	186	1	185	...	...	...	...	...	...	166	...	166
		Gokar	Do.	2	2	...	...	...	...	...	...	...	...	...	...
		Gaya	Do.	25	24	1	...	...	...	...	...	...	...	...	...
		Gayari	Do.	13	13	...	...	...	...	...	...	...	...	...	...
		Ghodawi	Do.	4	4	...	...	...	...	...	...	...	...	...	...
		Gujrathi	Musalman	7	7	...	...	...	...	...	...	...	...	...	...
		Hatola	Hindu	2	1	1	2	1	1	...	...	...	...	...	...
		Hatkar	Do.	48	26	22	...	...	...	...	...	...	...	...	...
		Harbola	Do.	412	76	336	...	...	...	...	...	...	...	...	...
		Do.	Aboriginal	171	105	66	...	...	...	13	8	5	9	7	2
		Japosi	Hindu	95	31	64	...	...	...	...	...	...	...	...	...
		Jokhan	Do.	1	1	...	...	...	...	...	...	...	...	...	...
		Jankera	Do.	13	5	8	...	...	...	...	...	...	13	5	8
		Jugawat	Do.	321	4	317	...	...	...	...	...	...	...	...	...
		Jamrol	Aboriginal	801	405	396	...	...	...	...	...	...	...	...	...
		Kutnora	Hindu	2	2	...	...	...	...	...	...	...	2	2	...
		Kaparia	Do.	10	4	6	...	...	...	...	...	...	...	...	...
		Do.	Aboriginal	19	10	9	...	...	...	...	...	...	...	...	...
		Kawari	Hindu	1,756	873	883	...	...	...	...	...	...	...	...	...
		Kodar	Do.	42	24	18	...	...	...	...	...	...	...	...	...
		Khangar	Do.	77	60	17	4	4	...	...	...	...	...	...	...
		Do.	Aboriginal	38,121	19,664	18,457	117	74	43	13,445	7,002	6,443	3,919	2,017	1,902
		Khebria	Hindu	171	87	84	...	...	...	...	...	...	171	87	84
		Kerba	Do.	[illegible]	54	38	...	...	...	...	...	...	[illegible]	54	38

NAME AND CLASSIFICATION.				DISTRIBUTION BY AGENCIES.																
				BUNDELKHAND.			BAGHELKHAND.			WESTERN MALWA.			BHOPAWAR.			GUNA.				
Class.	Group.	Caste.	Religion.	TOTAL.	Males.	Females.	TOTAL.	Males.	Females.	TOTAL.	Males.	Females.	TOTAL.	Males.	Females.	TOTAL.	Males.	Females.		
				17	18	19	20	21	22	23	24	25	26	27	28	29	30	31		
	45.—MISCELLANEOUS AND DISREPUTABLE LIVERS—contd.	DHAOLI PAWAL	Hindu	...	...	...	...	...	...	8	8	...	...	...	...	...	...	...		
		DHONKULA	Do.	...	...	...	...	...	...	74	73	1	...	...	...	...	...	...		
		DAHAR	Do.	42	...	42	...	...	...	...	...	...	...	...	...	...	...	...		
		DHANIPURAB	Do.	45	74	71	...	...	...	...	...	...	...	...	...	...	...	...		
		DIDHARI	Musalman	...	...	...	...	...	...	...	...	...	...	...	...	...	...	...		
		DASUGAR	Do.	...	...	...	...	...	...	...	...	...	...	...	...	...	...	...		
		DHARAM	Do.	...	...	...	...	...	...	...	...	...	...	...	...	...	...	...		
		DEWADA	Do.	...	...	...	...	...	...	...	...	...	...	...	...	...	...	...		
		DANUHAR	Aboriginal	4,034	2,009	2,025	...	...	...	...	...	...	...	...	...	...	...	...		
		DAYET	Do.	...	...	...	70	32	38	...	...	...	...	...	...	...	...	...		
		DHALPULYA	Do.	...	...	...	14	7	7	...	...	...	...	...	...	...	...	...		
		ESHAN	Hindu	...	...	...	...	...	...	4	...	4	...	...	...	...	...	...		
		FARAKABADI	Musalman	...	...	...	...	...	...	15	10	5	...	...	...	...	...	...		
		FARSI	Do.	...	...	...	...	...	...	9	5	4	...	...	...	...	...	...		
		GANGORIA	Hindu	...	...	...	...	...	...	...	...	...	...	...	...	...	...	...		
		GOYEE	Do.	...	...	...	...	...	...	...	...	...	...	...	...	...	...	...		
		GHORI	Do.	20	1	19	...	...	...	...	...	...	...	...	...	...	...	...		
		GOKAR	Do.	...	...	...	...	...	...	1	1	...	...	...	...	1	1	...		
		GAYA	Do.	...	...	...	...	...	...	23	23	...	2	1	1	...	...	...		
		GAYARI	Do.	...	...	...	...	...	...	13	13	...	...	...	...	...	...	...		
		GHODAWI	Do.	...	...	...	1	1	...	3	3	...	...	...	...	...	...	...		
		GUJRATHI	Musalman	...	...	...	...	...	...	7	7	...	...	...	...	...	...	...		
		HATOLA	Hindu	...	...	...	...	...	...	...	...	...	...	...	...	...	...	...		
		HATKAR	Do.	...	...	...	...	...	...	...	...	...	48	26	22	...	...	...		
		HARBOLA	Do.	...	...	...	...	...	...	412	76	336	...	...	...	...	...	...		
		Do.	Aboriginal	21	14	7	61	36	25	...	...	...	67	40	27	...	...	...		
		JAPOSI	Hindu	...	...	...	...	...	...	...	...	...	...	...	...	95	31	64		
		JOKHAN	Do.	1	1	...	...	...	...	...	...	...	...	...	...	...	...	...		
		JANKERA	Do.	...	...	...	...	...	...	...	...	...	...	...	...	...	...	...		
		JUGAWAT	Do.	316	2	314	...	...	...	5	2	3	...	...	...	...	...	...		
		JAMROL	Aboriginal	...	...	...	...	...	...	...	...	...	801	405	396	...	...	...		
		KUTNORA	Hindu	...	...	...	...	...	...	...	...	...	...	...	...	...	...	...		
		KAPARIA	Do.	...	...	...	8	2	6	...	...	...	...	...	...	2	2	...		
		Do.	Aboriginal	19	10	9	...	...	...	...	...	...	...	...	...	...	...	...		
		KAWARI	Hindu	...	...	...	1,756	873	883	...	...	...	...	...	...	...	...	...		
		KODAR	Do.	...	...	...	42	24	18	...	...	...	...	...	...	...	...	...		
		KHANGAR	Do.	14	14	...	46	32	14	13	10	3	...	...	...	...	...	...		
		Do.	Aboriginal	20,142	10,308	9,834	125	67	58	37	36	1	267	120	147	69	40	29		
		KHERIA	Hindu	...	...	...	...	...	...	...	...	...	...	...	...	...	...	...		
		KERBA	Do.	...	...	...	...	...	...	...	...	...	...	...	...	...	...	...		

TABLE XVI.—Castes, Tribes and Races, by Nationality or traditional Occupation—*contd.*

E.—VAGRANT MINOR ARTISANS AND PERFORMERS, Etc.—*contd.*

NAME AND CLASSIFICATION.				PROVINCIAL TOTAL.			DISTRIBUTION BY AGENCIES.								
							Indore.			Gwalior.			Bhopal.		
Class.	Group.	Caste.	Religion.	Total.	Males.	Females.	Total.	Males.	Females.	Total.	Males.	Females.	Total.	Males.	Females.
1	2	3	4	5	6	7	8	9	10	11	12	13	14	15	16
	45.—Miscellaneous and Disreputable Livers—*contd.*	Koril	Hindu	9	9	...	...	...	...	...	...	...	...	...	...
		Kakera	Do.	461	154	307	...	...	...	...	...	...	...	...	...
		Kananra	Do.	2,634	1,396	1,238	...	...	...	...	...	...	...	...	...
		Khanazai	Do.	390	179	211	...	...	...	301	133	168	...	...	...
		Do.	Musalman	9	9	...	...	...	...	...	...	...	...	...	...
		Kantora	Hindu	15	7	8	...	...	...	...	...	...	3	3	...
		Karel	Do.	34	17	17	...	...	...	34	17	17	...	...	...
		Karar	Do.	21	...	21	...	...	...	...	...	...	...	...	...
		Kalakar	Do.	2	2	...	...	...	...	...	...	...	...	...	...
		Kanjak	Do.	74	36	38	...	...	...	...	...	...	...	...	...
		Khedawat	Do.	8	4	4	...	...	...	...	...	...	...	...	...
		Kalingar	Musalman	5	2	3	5	2	3	...	...	...	...	...	...
		Kaswa	Aboriginal	2	1	1	...	...	...	...	...	...	...	...	...
		Kingaria	Do.	254	115	139	...	...	...	...	...	...	...	...	...
		Kanphora	Do.	15	10	5	...	...	...	...	...	...	...	...	...
		Langar	Hindu	1	1	...	...	...	...	1	1	...	...	...	...
		Lahagiri	Do.	238	114	124	...	...	...	...	...	...	...	...	...
		Ladia	Do.	35	19	16	...	...	...	...	...	...	35	19	16
		Laria	Do.	50	22	28	...	...	...	...	...	...	...	...	...
		Lochia	Do.	5	2	3	...	...	...	...	...	...	...	...	...
		Lopala	Do.	2	...	2	...	...	...	...	...	...	...	...	...
		Laktora	Aboriginal	58	36	22	...	...	...	58	36	22	...	...	...
		Math	Hindu	35	17	18	35	17	18	...	...	...	...	...	...
		Mutha	Do.	4,466	2,235	2,231	...	...	...	...	...	...	...	...	...
		Mavi	Do.	120	37	83	...	...	...	...	...	...	...	...	...
		Marimart	Do.	431	198	233	...	...	...	...	...	...	...	...	...
		Monat	Do.	88	36	52	...	...	...	...	...	...	88	36	52
		Mashhar	Do.	76	44	32	...	...	...	...	...	...	...	...	...
		Miraha	Do.	7,376	3,663	3,713	...	...	...	...	...	...	...	...	...
		Musawar	Do.	3	1	2	...	...	...	...	...	...	3	1	2
		Makdai	Do.	6	4	2	...	...	...	...	...	...	2	1	1
		Mawel	Do.	83	83	...	...	...	...	...	...	...	...	...	...
		Mohada	Do.	11	8	3	...	...	...	...	...	...	...	...	...
		Metwal	Do.	78	...	78	...	...	...	...	...	...	...	...	...
		Multani	Musalman	1,714	821	893	116	63	53	...	...	...	124	70	54
		Manania	Do.	18	13	5	...	...	...	...	...	...	18	13	5
		Mhair	Aboriginal	2,588	1,287	1,301	1,118	502	616	...	...	...	...	...	...

Table XVI.—Castes, Tribes and Races, etc.—Central India.

E.—VAGRANT MINOR ARTISANS AND PERFORMERS, ETC.—contd.

Class.	Group.	Caste.	Religion.	Bundelkhand. Total.	Bundelkhand. Males.	Bundelkhand. Females.	Baghelkhand. Total.	Baghelkhand. Males.	Baghelkhand. Females.	Western Malwa. Total.	Western Malwa. Males.	Western Malwa. Females.	Bhopawar. Total.	Bhopawar. Males.	Bhopawar. Females.	Guna. Total.	Guna. Males.	Guna. Females.
				17	18	19	20	21	22	23	24	25	26	27	28	29	30	31
	45.—Miscellaneous and Disreputable Livers—contd.	Koril	Hindu	9	9	...	...	...	...	...	...	...	...	...	...	...	...	...
		Kakera	Do.	458	154	304	...	...	...	3	...	3	...	...	...	...	...	...
		Kananra	Do.	2,578	1,367	1,211	...	...	...	56	29	27	...	...	...	...	...	...
		Khanazad	Do.	...	...	...	...	...	...	...	...	...	...	...	...	89	46	43
		Do.	Musalman	...	...	...	...	...	...	6	6	...	...	...	...	...	...	...
		Kantora	Hindu	...	...	...	...	...	...	15	7	8	...	...	...	...	...	...
		Kakel	Do.	...	...	...	...	...	...	...	...	...	...	...	...	...	...	...
		Karar	Do.	...	...	...	...	...	...	21	...	21	...	...	...	...	...	...
		Kalakar	Do.	...	...	...	...	...	...	2	2	...	...	...	...	...	...	...
		Kanjak	Do.	...	...	...	...	...	...	74	36	38	...	...	...	...	...	...
		Khedawat	Do.	...	...	...	...	...	...	8	4	4	...	...	...	...	...	...
		Kalingar	Musalman	...	...	...	...	...	...	...	...	...	...	...	...	...	...	...
		Kaswa	Aboriginal	...	...	...	2	1	1	...	...	...	...	...	...	...	...	...
		Kingaria	Do.	254	115	139	...	...	...	...	...	...	...	...	...	...	...	...
		Kanphora	Do.	15	10	5	...	...	...	...	...	...	...	...	...	...	...	...
		Langar	Do.	...	...	...	...	...	...	...	...	...	...	...	...	...	...	...
		Lahagiri	Do.	...	...	...	238	114	124	...	...	...	...	...	...	...	...	...
		Ladia	Do.	...	...	...	...	...	...	...	...	...	...	...	...	...	...	...
		Laria	Do.	50	22	28	...	...	...	...	...	...	...	...	...	...	...	...
		Lochia	Do.	...	...	...	...	...	...	5	2	3	...	...	...	...	...	...
		Lopala	Do.	...	...	...	...	...	...	2	...	2	...	...	...	...	...	...
		Laktora	Aboriginal	...	...	...	...	...	...	...	...	...	...	...	...	...	...	...
		Math	Hindu	...	...	...	...	...	...	...	...	...	...	...	...	...	...	...
		Mutha	Do.	...	...	...	...	...	...	...	...	...	4,466	2,235	2,231	...	...	...
		Mavi	Do.	...	...	...	...	...	...	...	...	...	120	37	83	...	...	...
		Marimart	Do.	...	...	...	...	...	...	...	...	...	...	...	...	431	198	233
		Monat	Do.	...	...	...	...	...	...	...	...	...	...	...	...	...	...	...
		Mashhar	Do.	...	...	...	76	44	32	...	...	...	...	...	...	...	...	...
		Miraha	Do.	...	...	...	7,376	3,663	3,713	...	...	...	...	...	...	...	...	...
		Musawar	Do.	...	...	...	...	...	...	...	...	...	...	...	...	...	...	...
		Makdai	Do.	...	...	...	...	...	...	4	3	1	...	...	...	...	...	...
		Mawel	Do.	1	1	...	...	...	...	82	82	...	...	...	...	...	...	...
		Mohada	Do.	...	...	...	...	...	...	11	8	3	...	...	...	...	...	...
		Metwal	Do.	...	...	...	...	...	...	78	...	78	...	...	...	...	...	...
		Multani	Musalman	...	...	...	...	...	...	1,474	688	786	...	...	...	...	...	...
		Mahania	Do.	...	...	...	...	...	...	...	...	...	...	...	...	...	...	...
		Mbair	Aboriginal	...	...	...	3	1	2	198	150	48	2	2	...	1,267	632	635

TABLE XVI.—Castes, Tribes and Races, by Nationality or traditional Occupation—*contd.*

NAME AND CLASSIFICATION.				PROVINCIAL TOTAL.			DISTRIBUTION BY AGENCIES.								
							INDORE.			GWALIOR.			BHOPAL.		
Class.	Group.	Caste.	Religion.	TOTAL.	Males.	Females.	TOTAL.	Males.	Females.	TOTAL.	Males.	Females.	TOTAL.	Males.	Females.
1	2	3	4	5	6	7	8	9	10	11	12	13	14	15	16
	45.—MISCELLANEOUS AND DISREPUTABLE LIVERS—*contd.*	MAHOJI	Aboriginal	27	13	14	...	...	...	...	...	...	...	...	...
		MAHIA	Do.	72	40	32	...	...	...	...	...	...	...	...	...
		NAYAD	Hindu	1	1	...	...	...	...	...	...	...	...	...	...
		NAMDA	Do.	85	43	42	...	...	...	...	...	...	85	43	42
		NIGROL	Do.	95	11	84	...	...	...	...	...	...	95	11	84
		NURI	Do.	42	2	40	...	...	...	...	...	...	37	2	35
		NANGAR	Do.	17	17	...	...	...	...	...	...	...	...	...	...
		NONACHAMARI	Do.	27	8	19	...	...	...	...	...	...	...	...	...
		NAHARGARH	Do.	25	8	17	...	...	...	...	...	...	...	...	...
		Do.	Musalman	131	75	56	...	...	...	...	...	...	...	...	...
		NAO MUSLIM	Do.	1,253	590	663	...	...	...	...	...	...	29	14	15
		NAL	Do.	22	14	8	...	...	...	...	...	...	22	14	8
		Do.	Aboriginal	1,832	918	914	600	321	279	...	...	...	1,232	597	635
		NALGAR	Musalman	6	6	...	...	...	...	...	...	...	...	...	...
		NANGOND	Aboriginal	3,042	1,475	1,567	...	...	...	...	...	...	...	...	...
		PINDHARA	Hindu	170	102	68	...	...	...	...	...	...	...	...	...
		Do.	Musalman	3,186	1,648	1,538	46	18	28	...	...	...	3,125	1,615	1,508
		PUNJABI	Hindu	1	1	...	1	1	...	...	...	...	...	...	...
		PARDESI	Do.	48	14	34	6	6	...	...	...	...	...	...	...
		PINGAN	Do.	6	5	1	...	...	...	...	...	...	...	...	...
		PANIGAR	Do.	4	2	2	...	...	...	...	...	...	...	...	...
		PIDARA	Do.	6	5	1	...	...	...	1	...	1	...	...	...
		PARDHAN	Do.	114	57	57	...	...	...	...	...	...	108	61	57
		PATIA	Do.	110	18	92	...	...	...	...	...	...	...	...	...
		PAVAK	Do.	170	56	114	...	...	...	...	...	...	...	...	...
		PINARA	Do.	4	4	...	...	...	...	...	...	...	...	...	...
		PIROWADI	Do.	204	105	99	...	...	...	...	...	...	...	...	...
		PUTATA	Do.	2	...	2	...	...	...	...	...	...	...	...	...
		POKHAR	Musalman	2	...	2	...	...	...	...	...	...	...	...	...
		PAWA	Aboriginal	15,077	7,545	7,532	...	...	...	...	...	...	...	...	...
		PALIHAR	Do.	218	115	103	...	...	...	...	...	...	...	...	...
		PUTHARI	Do.	3,571	1,791	1,780	...	...	...	...	...	...	...	...	...
		POKKA	Do.	32	14	18	...	...	...	...	...	...	...	...	...
		PATHLA	Do.	12,088	5,862	6,226	...	...	...	...	...	...	...	...	...
		PORKIA	Do.	595	294	301	511	257	254	...	...	...	84	37	47
		PAL	Do.	2,824	1,693	1,131	...	...	...	...	...	...	2,604	1,578	1,026
		PADIYAL	Do.	145	125	20	...	...	...	...	...	...	145	125	20

E.—VAGRANT MINOR ARTISANS AND PERFORMERS, ETC.—*contd.*

NAME AND CLASSIFICATION.				DISTRIBUTION BY AGENCIES.														
				BUNDELKHAND.			BAGHELKHAND.			WESTERN MALWA.			BHOPAWAR.			GUNA.		
Class.	Group.	Caste.	Religion.	Total.	Males.	Females.	Total.	Males.	Females.	Total.	Males.	Females.	Total.	Males.	Females.	Total.	Males.	Females.
				17	18	19	20	21	22	23	24	25	26	27	28	29	30	31
	45.—MISCELLANEOUS AND DISREPUTABLE LIVERS—*contd.*	MAHOJI	Aboriginal	...	...	...	...	...	...	...	...	...	...	...	...	27	13	14
		MAHIA	Do.	72	40	32	...	...	...	...	...	...	...	...	...	...	...	...
		NAYAD	Hindu	...	...	...	1	1	...	...	...	...	...	...	...	...	...	...
		NAMDA	Do.	...	...	...	...	...	...	...	...	...	...	...	...	...	...	...
		NIGROL	Do.	...	...	...	...	...	...	...	...	...	...	...	...	...	...	...
		NURI	Do.	...	...	...	...	...	...	5	...	5	...	...	...	...	...	...
		NANGAR	Do.	17	17	...	...	...	...	...	...	...	...	...	...	...	...	...
		NONACHAMARI	Do.	27	8	19	...	...	...	...	...	...	...	...	...	...	...	...
		NAHARGARH	Do.	...	...	...	...	...	...	25	8	17	...	...	...	...	...	...
		Do.	Musalman	...	...	...	...	...	...	131	75	56	...	...	...	...	...	...
		NAO MUSLIM	Do.	...	...	...	3	3	...	1,221	573	648	...	...	...	...	...	...
		NAL	Do.	...	...	...	...	...	...	...	...	...	...	...	...	...	...	...
		Do.	Aboriginal	...	...	...	...	...	...	...	...	...	...	...	...	...	...	...
		NALGAR	Musalman	...	...	...	...	...	...	6	6	...	...	...	...	...	...	...
		NANGOND	Aboriginal	3,042	1,475	1,567	...	...	...	...	...	...	...	...	...	...	...	...
		PINDHARA	Hindu	...	...	...	...	...	...	...	...	...	...	...	...	170	102	68
		Do.	Musalman	...	...	...	...	...	...	...	...	...	13	13	...	4	2	2
		PUNJABI	Hindu	...	...	...	...	...	...	...	...	...	...	...	...	...	...	...
		PARDESI	Do.	...	...	...	...	...	...	...	...	...	42	8	34	...	...	...
		PINGAN	Do.	...	...	...	...	...	...	...	...	...	6	5	1	...	...	...
		PANIGAR	Do.	...	...	...	...	...	...	...	...	...	...	...	...	4	2	2
		PIDARA	Do.	5	5	...	...	...	...	...	...	...	...	...	...	...	...	...
		PARDHAN	Do.	...	...	...	...	...	...	6	6	...	...	...	...	...	...	...
		PATIA	Do.	110	18	92	...	...	...	...	...	...	...	...	...	...	...	...
		PAYAK	Do.	...	...	...	...	...	...	170	56	114	...	...	...	...	...	...
		PINARA	Do.	...	...	...	...	...	...	4	4	...	...	...	...	...	...	...
		PIROWADI	Do.	...	...	...	...	...	...	204	105	99	...	...	...	...	...	...
		PUTATA	Do.	...	...	...	...	...	...	2	...	2	...	...	...	...	...	...
		POKHAR	Musalman	...	...	...	...	...	...	2	...	2	...	...	...	...	...	...
		PAWA	Aboriginal	...	...	...	15,077	7,545	7,532	...	...	...	...	...	...	...	...	...
		PALIHAR	Do.	...	...	...	218	115	103	...	...	...	...	...	...	...	...	...
		PUTHARI	Do.	...	...	...	3,571	1,791	1,780	...	...	...	...	...	...	...	...	...
		POKKA	Do.	...	...	...	32	14	18	...	...	...	...	...	...	...	...	...
		PATHLA	Do.	...	...	...	...	...	...	...	...	...	12,088	5,862	6,226	...	...	...
		PORKIA	Do.	...	...	...	...	...	...	...	...	...	...	...	...	...	...	...
		PAL	Do.	...	...	...	3	2	1	217	113	104	...	...	...	...	...	...
		PADIYAL	Do.	...	...	...	...	...	...	...	...	...	...	...	...	...	...	...

TABLE XVI.—Castes, Tribes and Races, by Nationality or traditional Occupation—*contd.*

NAME AND CLASSIFICATION.				PROVINCIAL TOTAL.			DISTRIBUTION BY AGENCIES.								
							INDORE.			GWALIOR.			BHOPAL.		
Class.	Group.	Caste.	Religion.	Total.	Males.	Females.	Total.	Males.	Females.	Total.	Males.	Females.	Total.	Males.	Females.
1	2	3	4	5	6	7	8	9	10	11	12	13	14	15	16
	45.—Miscellaneous and Disreputable Livers—*contd.*	Randi	Hindu	23	3	20	...	...	...	19	...	19	4	3	1
		Do.	Musalman	36	19	17	...	...	...	...	...	...	36	19	17
		Rajbangar	Hindu	59	59	...	...	...	...	...	...	...	...	...	...
		Rarboni	Do.	3	3	...	3	3	...	...	...	...	...	...	...
		Rasab	Musalman	5	2	3	...	...	...	...	...	...	5	2	3
		Rijata	Do.	6	6	...	...	...	...	...	...	...	...	...	...
		Rajbhar	Aboriginal	10	9	1	...	...	...	...	...	...	...	...	...
		Sondhia	Hindu	8,044	4,447	3,597	...	...	...	...	...	...	...	...	...
		Sornas	Do.	1	1	...	1	1	...	...	...	...	...	...	...
		Saran	Do.	1	1	...	1	1	...	...	...	...	...	...	...
		Sikhi	Do.	13	8	5	...	...	...	...	...	...	9	5	4
		Sameya	Do.	19	19	...	...	...	...	...	...	...	...	...	...
		Satia	Do.	16	11	5	...	...	...	...	...	...	...	...	...
		Simpi	Do.	6	3	3	...	...	...	...	...	...	...	...	...
		Silod	Do.	6	1	5	...	...	...	...	...	...	...	...	...
		Selani	Do.	2	2	...	...	...	...	...	...	...	...	...	...
		Sejari	Do.	2	1	1	...	...	...	...	...	...	...	...	...
		Sumeria	Do.	101	28	73	...	...	...	...	...	...	97	24	73
		Sagwar	Do.	56	26	30	...	...	...	...	...	...	...	...	...
		Sathia	Do.	18	10	8	...	...	...	...	...	...	...	...	...
		Sukora	Do.	7	...	7	...	...	...	...	...	...	7	...	7
		Shankar	Do.	32	...	32	...	...	...	...	...	...	...	...	...
		Shekhawati	Do.	49	49	...	...	...	...	...	...	...	...	...	...
		Sasari	Do.	11	9	2	...	...	...	...	...	...	...	...	...
		Silligal	Do.	6	6	...	...	...	...	...	...	...	...	...	...
		Shudra	Do.	7	3	4	2	2	...	...	...	...	...	...	...
		Sigori	Do.	1	1	...	...	...	...	...	...	...	...	...	...
		Sethbax	Do.	6	6	...	6	6	...	...	...	...	...	...	...
		Savaya	Do.	1,286	2	1,284	2	...	2	...	...	...	...	...	...
		Sabgar	Musalman	5	4	1	...	...	...	...	...	...	5	4	1
		Sabsarnia	Do.	1	...	1	...	...	...	...	...	...	...	...	...
		Surbdi	Do.	9	...	9	...	...	...	...	...	...	9	...	9
		Saota	Aboriginal	214	125	89	...	...	...	...	...	...	...	...	...
		Sabranga	Do.	17	7	10	...	...	...	...	...	...	17	7	10
		Tilo	Hindu	9	4	5	9	4	5	...	...	...	...	...	...
		Tramor	Do.	19	...	19	...	...	...	...	...	...	...	...	...

E.—VAGRANT MINOR ARTISANS AND PERFORMERS, ETC.—*contd.*

NAME AND CLASSIFICATION.				DISTRIBUTION BY AGENCIES.														
Class.	Group.	Caste.	Religion.	Bundelkhand.			Baghelkhand.			Western Malwa.			Bhopawar.			Guna.		
				Total.	Males.	Females.	Total.	Males.	Females.	Total.	Males.	Females.	Total.	Males.	Females.	Total.	Males.	Females.
				17	18	19	20	21	22	23	24	25	26	27	28	29	0	31
	45.—MISCELLANEOUS AND DISREPUTABLE LIVERS—*contd.*	RANDI	Hindu	...	...	...	...	...	...	...	...	...	...	...	...	...	...	...
		Do.	Musalman	...	...	...	...	...	...	...	...	...	...	...	...	...	...	...
		RAJBANGAR	Hindu	...	...	...	...	...	...	59	59	...	...	...	...	...	...	...
		RARBONI	Do.	...	...	...	...	...	...	...	...	...	...	...	...	...	...	...
		RASAB	Musalman	...	...	...	...	...	...	...	...	...	...	...	...	...	...	...
		RIJATA	Do.	...	...	...	...	...	...	6	6	...	...	...	...	...	...	...
		RAJBHAR	Aboriginal	...	...	...	10	9	1	...	...	...	...	...	...	...	...	...
		SONDHIA	Hindu	12	...	12	...	...	...	7,963	4,417	3,546	67	30	37	2	...	2
		SORNAS	Do.	...	...	...	...	...	...	...	...	...	...	...	...	...	...	...
		SARAN	Do.	...	...	...	...	...	...	...	...	...	...	...	...	...	...	...
		SIKHI	Do.	...	...	...	...	...	...	...	...	...	4	3	1	...	...	...
		SAMEYA	Do.	...	...	...	...	...	...	...	...	...	...	...	...	19	19	...
		SATIA	Do.	...	...	...	...	...	...	9	8	1	...	...	...	7	3	4
		SIMPI	Do.	...	...	...	6	3	3	...	...	...	...	...	...	...	...	...
		SILOD	Do.	...	...	...	1	1	...	5	...	5	...	...	...	...	...	...
		SELANI	Do.	...	...	...	...	...	...	2	2	...	...	...	...	...	...	...
		SEJARI	Do.	2	1	1	...	...	...	...	...	...	...	...	...	...	...	...
		SUMERIA	Do.	4	4	...	...	...	...	...	...	...	...	...	...	...	...	...
		SAGWAR	Do.	56	26	30	...	...	...	...	...	...	...	...	...	...	...	...
		SATHIA	Do.	18	10	8	...	...	...	...	...	...	...	...	...	...	...	...
		SUKORA	Do.	...	...	...	...	...	...	...	...	...	...	...	...	...	...	...
		SHANKAR	Do.	...	...	...	13	...	13	19	...	19	...	...	...	...	...	...
		SHEKHAWATI	Do.	...	...	...	...	...	...	49	49	...	...	...	...	...	...	...
		SASARI	Do.	...	...	...	...	...	...	11	9	2	...	...	...	...	...	...
		SILLIGAL	Do.	...	...	...	...	...	...	6	6	...	...	...	...	...	...	...
		SHUDRA	Do.	...	...	...	5	1	4	...	...	...	...	...	...	...	...	...
		SIGORI	Do.	...	...	...	...	...	...	1	1	...	...	...	...	...	...	...
		SETHBAX	Do.	...	...	...	...	...	...	...	...	...	...	...	...	...	...	...
		SAVAYA	Do.	5	2	3	...	...	...	...	...	...	...	...	...	1,279	...	1,279
		SABGAR	Musalman	...	...	...	...	...	...	...	...	...	...	...	...	...	...	...
		SABSARNIA	Do.	...	...	...	...	...	...	1	...	1	...	...	...	...	...	...
		SUREDI	Do.	...	...	...	...	...	...	...	...	...	...	...	...	...	...	...
		SAOTA	Aboriginal	...	...	...	214	125	89	...	...	...	...	...	...	...	...	...
		SABRANGA	Do.	...	...	...	...	...	...	...	...	...	...	...	...	...	...	...
		TILO	Hindu	...	...	...	...	...	...	...	...	...	...	...	...	...	...	...
		THAMOR	Do.	19	...	19	...	...	...	...	...	...	...	...	...	...	...	...

TABLE XVI.—Castes, Tribes and Races, by Nationality or traditional Occupation—*contd.*

NAME AND CLASSIFICATION.				PROVINCIAL TOTAL.			DISTRIBUTION BY AGENCIES.								
							INDORE.			GWALIOR.			BHOPAL.		
Class.	Group.	Caste.	Religion.	TOTAL.	Males.	Females.	TOTAL.	Males.	Females.	TOTAL.	Males.	Females.	TOTAL.	Males.	Females.
1	2	3	4	5	6	7	8	9	10	11	12	13	14	15	16
E.—VAGRANT MINOR ARTISANS AND PERFORMERS, Etc.—*concld.*	45.—MISCELLANEOUS AND DISREPUTABLE LIVERS—*concld.*	TARKIHAR	Hindu	499	228	271	...	...	...	...	...	...	...	...	...
		TIHUR	Do.	3	2	1	...	...	...	3	2	1	...	...	...
		TAPPA	Do.	13	9	4	...	...	...	...	...	...	13	9	4
		TAKOCH	Do.	3	1	2	...	...	...	...	...	...	3	1	2
		TAMERA	Do.	1,299	638	661	...	...	...	...	...	...	137	76	61
		TANWAR	Do.	2	2	...	...	...	...	...	...	...	...	...	...
		TELUKI	Musalman	1	...	1	...	...	...	...	...	...	...	...	...
		TAWAR	Do.	2	...	2	...	...	...	...	...	...	...	...	...
		TAPORKI	Aboriginal	25	12	13	...	...	...	...	...	...	...	...	...
		UMRAO	Do.	646	326	320	...	...	...	...	...	...	...	...	...
		VED	Hindu	1	1	...	...	...	...	...	...	...	...	...	...
		VARAT	Do.	2	1	1	...	...	...	...	...	...	2	1	1
		VEDNI	Do.	12	4	8	...	...	...	...	...	...	12	4	8
		WABAR	Do.	105	63	42	...	...	...	...	...	...	105	63	42
		WIRJA	Do.	173	132	41	...	...	...	...	...	...	173	132	41
		WARDA	Do.	8	4	4	...	...	...	...	...	...	8	4	4
		WALI	Musalman	7	...	7	...	...	...	...	...	...	...	...	...
		OTHERS	Hindu	14,163	3,079	11,084	10,205	286	9,919	14	9	5	2,225	1,347	878
		Do.	Musalman	2,311	1,385	926	545	340	205	9	5	4	1,346	724	622
			Total Group 45	163,900	78,620	85,280	13,396	1,948	11,448	13,955	7,256	6,699	18,123	9,748	8,375
	46.—TUMBLERS AND ACROBATS.	BANCHRA	Aboriginal	2,919	1,490	1,429	453	250	203	...	...	...	...	...	...
		NAT	Hindu	532	63	469	...	...	...	...	...	...	408	3	405
		Do.	Musalman	20	14	6	...	...	...	...	...	...	6	2	4
		Do.	Aboriginal	8,501	4,399	4,102	450	235	215	1,100	634	466	2,652	1,289	1,363
		NATH	Hindu	160	7	153	...	...	...	...	...	...	...	...	...
		Do.	Aboriginal	15,059	7,615	7,444	795	410	385	1,129	611	518	5,937	2,940	2,997
			Total Group 46.	27,191	13,588	13,603	1,698	895	803	2,229	1,245	984	9,003	4,234	4,769
	47.—JUGGLERS, SNAKE CHARMERS AND ANIMAL EXHIBITORS.	BAZIGAR	Hindu	427	206	221	44	21	23	...	...	...	257	109	148
		Do.	Musalman	15	11	4	...	...	...	...	...	...	10	6	4
		Do.	Aboriginal	764	396	368	113	58	55	...	...	...	...	...	...

E.—VAGRANT MINOR ARTISANS AND PERFORMERS, Etc.—concld.

NAME AND CLASSIFICATION.				DISTRIBUTION BY AGENCIES.														
				Bundelkhand.			Baghelkhand.			Western Malwa.			Bhopawar.			Guna.		
Class.	Group.	Caste.	Religion.	Total.	Males.	Females.	Total.	Males.	Females.	Total.	Males.	Females.	Total.	Males.	Females.	Total.	Males.	Females.
				16	17	18	19	20	21	22	23	24	26	27	28	29	30	31
	45.—Miscellaneous and Disreputable Livers—*concld.*	Tarkihar	Hindu	...	...	...	...	...	...	499	228	271	...	...	...	...	...	...
		Tihur	Do.	...	...	...	...	...	...	...	...	...	...	...	...	...	...	...
		Tappa	Do.	...	...	...	...	...	...	...	...	...	...	...	...	...	...	...
		Takoch	Do.	...	...	...	...	...	...	...	...	...	...	...	...	...	...	...
		Tamera	Do.	...	...	...	...	...	...	1,162	562	600	...	...	...	...	...	...
		Tanwar	Do.	...	...	...	...	...	...	2	2	—	...	...	...	...	...	...
		Teluki	Musalman	...	...	...	...	...	...	1	...	1	...	...	...	...	...	...
		Tawar	Do.	...	...	...	...	...	...	2	...	2	...	...	...	...	...	...
		Taporki	Aboriginal	25	12	13	...	...	...	...	...	...	...	...	...	...	...	...
		Umrao	Do.	...	...	...	646	326	320	...	...	...	...	...	...	...	...	...
		Ved	Hindu	...	...	...	...	...	...	1	1	...	...	...	...	...	...	...
		Varat	Do.	...	...	...	...	...	...	...	...	...	...	...	...	...	—	...
		Vedni	Do.	...	...	...	...	...	...	...	...	...	...	...	...	...	...	...
		Wabar	Do.	...	...	...	...	...	...	...	...	...	...	...	...	...	...	...
		Wirja	Do.	...	...	...	...	...	...	...	...	...	...	...	...	...	...	...
		Warda	Do.	...	...	...	...	...	...	...	...	—	...	...	...	...	...	...
		Wali	Musalman	...	...	...	...	...	...	7	...	7	...	...	...	...	...	...
		Others	Hindu	445	378	67	11	9	2	252	53	199	1,011	997	14	...	...	...
		Do.	Musalman	253	193	60	...	...	...	...	...	...	14	11	3	144	112	32
			Total Group 45	32,725	16,550	16,175	45,678	22,941	22,737	16,829	8,858	7,971	19,379	9,981	9,398	3,815	1,338	2,477
	46.—Tumblers and Acrobats.	Banchar	Aboriginal	...	...	...	...	...	...	2,466	1,240	1,226	...	...	...	...	...	...
		Nat	Hindu	...	...	...	...	...	...	79	30	49	...	...	...	45	30	15
		Do.	Musalman	...	...	...	...	...	...	2	...	2	...	...	...	12	12	...
		Do.	Aboriginal	901	467	434	1,198	646	552	1,825	946	879	270	118	152	105	64	41
		Nath	Hindu	...	...	...	...	...	...	160	7	153	...	...	...	...	...	...
		Do.	Aboriginal	30	30	...	...	...	...	5,244	2,636	2,608	1,606	828	778	318	160	158
			Total Group 46	931	497	434	1,198	646	552	9,776	4,859	4,917	1,876	946	930	480	266	214
	47.—Jugglers, Snake Charmers and Animal Exhibitors.	Bazigar	Hindu	...	...	...	...	...	...	...	...	...	9	9	...	117	67	50
		Do.	Musalman	...	...	...	...	...	...	5	5	...	...	...	...	...	...	...
		Do.	Aboriginal	...	...	...	651	338	313	...	...	...	...	...	...	...	...	...

TABLE XVI.—Castes, Tribes and Races, by Nationality or traditional Occupation—*contd.*

Name and Classification.				Provincial Total.			Distribution by Agencies.								
							Indore.			Gwalior.			Bhopal.		
Class.	Group.	Caste.	Religion.	Total.	Males.	Females.	Total.	Males.	Females.	Total.	Males.	Females.	Total.	Males.	Females.
1	2	3	4	5	6	7	8	9	10	11	12	13	14	15	16
E.—*contd.*	47.—Jugglers, Snake Charmers and Animals Exhibitors—*contd.*	Garudi	Hindu	245	40	205	...	...	...	...	...	..	...	...	...
		Kalbelya	Aboriginal	1,701	896	805	...	...	...	...	...	...	720	334	386
		Kalbhotia	Do.	272	114	158	...	...	...	...	...	...	...	...	...
			Total Group 47	3,424	1,663	1,761	157	79	78	...	...	...	987	449	538
			Total Class E.	444,382	228,987	215,395	23,788	8,184	15,604	22,153	11,494	10,659	97,733	52,043	45,690
F.—Races and Nationalities.	48.—Tribal Communities of Foreign Asiatic origin or reputed descent.	Arab	Musalman	134	17	117	...	...	...	1	1	...	100	3	97
		Agwan	Do.	2	2	...	...	...	...	...	...	...	...	...	...
		Fadali	Do.	10	4	6	7	4	3	...	...	...	...	...	...
		Ghori	Do.	47	19	28	...	...	...	...	...	...	...	...	...
		Habshi	Do.	1	1	...	...	...	...	...	...	...	1	1	...
		Jew	Jew	72	44	28	54	33	21	...	...	...	...	...	...
		Khan	Musalman	3	3	...	...	...	...	...	...	...	3	3	...
		Korbishi	Do.	2	...	2	...	...	...	...	...	...	2	...	2
		Khokhar	Do.	6	...	6	...	...	...	...	...	...	...	...	...
		Khilji	Do.	13	4	9	...	...	...	...	...	...	...	...	...
		Kaym Khani	Do.	3	...	3	...	...	...	...	...	...	3	...	3
		Khatri	Do.	2	...	2	2	...	2	...	...	...	...	...	...
		Mirza	Do.	376	204	172	...	...	...	...	...	...	125	63	62
		Makrani	Do.	315	238	77	5	3	2	...	...	...	...	...	...
		Mir	Do.	14	8	6	13	7	6	...	...	...	1	1	...
		Moghal	Do.	10,124	5,361	4,763	368	216	152	2,277	1,172	1,105	2,663	1,418	1,245
		Pathan	Do.	170,020	90,787	79,233	11,514	6,437	5,077	28,600	15,948	12,652	52,086	27,347	24,739
		Parsi	Parsi	837	437	400	583	298	285	2	2	...	36	16	20
		Rabzi	Musalman	2	1	1	2	1	1	...	...	...	...	...	...
		Sayyid	Do.	34,877	19,177	15,700	3,610	2,013	1,597	5,650	3,270	2,380	12,032	6,667	5,365
		Sheikh	Do.	234,789	123,248	111,541	21,273	11,417	9,856	36,773	19,520	17,253	57,586	30,702	26,884
		Sunni	Do.	28	24	4	23	22	1	...	...	...	...	...	...
		Sidi	Do.	475	192	283	255	121	134	...	...	...	14	7	7
		Shiah	Do.	1,838	1,290	548	...	...	...	...	...	...	...	...	...
		Sunat Jamat	Do.	370	220	150	...	...	...	...	...	..	...	...	...
		Turki	Do.	2	...	2	...	..	...	...	...	...	...	...	...
		Vilaiti	Do.	740	462	278	63	37	26	...	...	...	150	107	43
			Total Group 48.	455,100	241,743	213,359	37,779	20,609	17,163	[illegible]303	39,913	33,390	124,800	66,335	58,467

Table XVI.- Castes, Tribes and Races, etc.—Central India.

NAME AND CLASSIFICATION.				DISTRIBUTION BY AGENCIES.														
Class.	Group.	Caste.	Religion.	Bundelkhand.			Baghelkhand.			Western Malwa.			Bhopawar.			Guna.		
				Total.	Males.	Females.	Total.	Males.	Females.	Total.	Males.	Females.	Total.	Males.	Females.	Total.	Males.	Females.
				17	18	19	20	21	22	23	24	25	26	27	28	29	30	31
E—*contd.*	47.—Jugglers, Snake Charmers and Animals Exhibitors—*contd.*	Garudi	Hindu	...	...	...	...	...	...	63	5	58	182	35	147	...	...	...
		Kalbelya	Aboriginal	17	5	12	...	...	...	599	350	249	365	207	158	...	...	...
		Kalbhotia	Do.	...	...	...	272	114	158	...	...	...	...	...	...	...	...	...
			Total Group 47	17	5	12	923	452	471	667	360	307	556	251	395	117	67	50
			Total Class E	64,673	33,024	31,649	55,539	27,915	27,624	142,660	77,636	65,024	30,189	15,456	14,733	7,647	3,235	4,412
F.—Races and Nationalities.	48.—Tribal Communities of Foreign Asiatic Origin or Reputed Descent.	Arab	Musalmn	...	...	...	...	...	...	32	12	20	...	...	...	1	1	...
		Agwan	Do.	...	...	...	...	...	...	2	2	...	...	...	...	...	...	...
		Fadali	Do.	...	...	...	...	...	...	3	...	3	...	...	...	...	...	...
		Ghori	Do.	...	...	...	...	...	...	47	19	28	...	...	...	...	...	...
		Habshi	Do.	...	...	...	...	...	...	...	...	...	...	...	...	...	...	...
		Jew	Jew	...	...	...	...	...	...	18	11	7	...	...	...	...	...	...
		Khan	Musalman	...	...	...	...	...	...	...	...	...	...	...	...	...	...	...
		Koreishi	Do.	...	...	...	...	...	...	...	...	...	...	...	...	...	...	...
		Kh okhar	Do.	...	...	...	...	...	...	6	...	6	...	...	...	...	...	...
		Khilji	Do.	...	...	...	...	...	...	13	4	9	...	...	...	...	...	...
		Kayam Khani	Do.	...	...	...	...	...	...	...	...	...	...	...	...	...	...	...
		Khatri	Do.	...	...	...	...	...	...	...	...	...	...	...	...	...	...	...
		Mirza	Do.	...	...	...	...	...	...	240	136	104	...	...	...	11	5	6
		Makrani	Do.	...	...	...	...	...	...	313	[illegible]	75	...	...	...	...	...	...
		Mir	Do.	...	...	...	...	...	...	...	...	...	...	...	...	...	...	...
		Moghal	Do.	1,100	571	529	42	226	198	2,197	1,148	1,049	87	468	404	223	142	81
		Pathan	Do.	20,559	10,754	9,805	9,256	4,796	4,460	26,822	14,276	12,546	15,754	8,240	7,514	5,429	2,989	2,440
		Parsi	Parsi	2	2	...	...	...	...	191	104	87	23	15	8	...	...	...
		Rabzi	Musalman	...	...	...	...	...	...	...	...	...	...	...	...	...	...	...
		Sayyid	Do.	3,541	1,842	1,699	1,046	588	458	4,999	2,745	2,254	3,148	1,575	1,573	851	477	374
		Sheikh	Do.	29,269	15,173	14,096	32,974	16,750	16,224	30,254	15,860	14,394	23,467	12,151	11,316	193	1,675	1,518
		Sunni	Do.	...	...	...	...	...	...	...	...	...	...	...	...	5	2	3
		Sidi	Do.	...	...	...	...	...	...	206	64	142	...	...	...	...	...	...
		Shiah	Do.	...	...	...	...	...	...	...	...	...	1,838	1,290	548	...	...	...
		Sunat Jamat	Do.	...	...	...	...	...	...	370	220	150	...	...	...	...	...	...
		Turki	Do.	...	...	...	...	...	...	2	...	2	...	...	...	...	...	...
		Vilaiti	Do.	...	...	...	...	...	...	526	317	209	...	...	...	1	1	...
			Total Group 48	54,471	28,342	26,129	43,700	22,360	21,340	66,238	35,153	31,085	45,102	23,739	21,363	9,714	5,292	4,422

Y

TABLE XVI.—Castes, Tribes and Races, by Nationality or traditional Occupation—*contd.*

NAME AND CLASSIFICATION.				PROVINCIAL TOTAL,			DISTRIBUTION BY AGENCIES.								
							INDORE.			GWALIOR.			BHOPAL.		
Class.	Group.	Caste.	Religion.	Total.	Males.	Females.	Total.	Males.	Females.	Total.	Males.	Females.	Total.	Males.	Females.
1	2	3	4	5	6	7	8	9	10	11	12	13	14	15	16
	50.—Non-Asiatic Races	African	Christian	2	...	2	1	...	1	1	...	1	...	...	...
		American	Do.	2	...	2	2	...	2	...	...	...	...	...	...
		Canadian	Do.	2	2	...	2	2	...	...	...	...	...	...	...
		European, unspecified	Do.	1,288	1,045	243	5	4	1	5	4	1	13	5	6
		English	Do.	2,361	2,004	357	2,172	1,854	318	166	134	32	11	5	6
		French	Do.	139	68	71	9	8	1	2	...	2	128	60	68
		German	Do.	4	2	2	2	2	...	...	...	...	2	...	2
		Irish	Do.	239	176	63	225	166	59	4	2	2	6	5	1
		Italian	Do.	6	6	...	4	4	...	2	2	...	...	...	...
		Scotch	Do.	94	68	26	79	57	22	8	7	1	5	2	3
		Swiss	Do.	4	4	...	3	3	...	1	1	...	...	...	...
		Welsh	Do.	13	12	1	12	12	...	...	...	...	1	...	1
			Total Group 50	4,154	3,387	767	2,516	2,112	404	189	150	39	166	78	88
	51.—Eurasians	Eurasian, unspecified	Christian	839	470	369	128	64	64	203	102	101	70	39	31
		East Indian, do.	Do.	135	74	61	135	74	61	...	...	...	...	...	...
		Goanese	Do.	176	129	47	176	129	47	...	...	...	...	...	...
		Madrasi	Do.	212	115	97	212	115	97	...	...	...	...	...	...
		Portuguese	Do.	167	101	66	151	92	59	...	...	...	13	6	7
		Spanish	Do.	6	4	2	6	4	2	...	...	...	...	...	...
			Total Group 51	1,535	893	642	808	478	330	203	102	101	83	45	38
	52.—Christian Converts	Native Christians	Christian	310	172	138	189	106	83	...	...	...	55	33	22
			Total Group 52	310	172	138	189	106	83	...	...	...	55	33	22
			Total Class F	461,101	246,195	214,906	41,285	23,305	17,980	78,695	40,165	38,530	125,106	66,491	58,615
			Total of all Classes	10,218,812	5,295,536	4,923,276	372,792	201,944	170,848	1,77,309	948,805	806,704	2,006,859	1,052,777	954,082

Table XVI.—Castes, Tribes and Races, etc.—Central India.

F.—RACES AND NATIONALITIES—contd.

NAME AND CLASSIFICATION.				DISTRIBUTION BY AGENCIES.														
				[illegible]ELKHAND.			BAGHELKHAND.			WESTERN MALWA.			BHOPAWAR.					
Class.	Group.	Caste.	Religion.	TOTAL.	Males.	Females.	TOTAL.	Males.	Females.	TOTAL.	Males.	Females	TOTAL.	Males.	Females.	TOTAL.	Males.	Females.
				17	18	19	20	21	22	23	24	25	26	27	28	29	30	31
	50.—Non-Asiatic Races.	African	Christian	...	...	...	...	...	...	...	...	...	...	...	...	...	...	...
		American	Do.	...	...	...	...	...	...	...	...	...	...	...	...	...	...	...
		Canadian	Do.	...	...	...	...	...	...	...	...	...	...	...	...	...	...	...
		European, unspecified	Do.	632	552	80	102	52	50	527	423	104	1	1	...	3	3	...
		English	Do.	...	...	...	...	...	...	...	...	...	6	5	1	6	6	...
		French	Do.	...	...	...	...	...	...	...	...	...	...	...	...	...	...	...
		German	Do.	...	...	...	...	...	...	...	...	...	...	...	...	...	...	...
		Irish	Do.	...	...	...	...	...	...	...	...	...	3	2	1	1	1	...
		Italian	Do.	...	...	...	...	...	...	...	...	...	...	...	...	...	...	...
		Scotch	Do.	...	...	...	...	...	...	...	...	...	...	...	...	2	2	...
		Swiss	Do.	...	...	...	...	...	...	...	...	...	...	...	...	...	...	...
		Welsh	Do.	...	...	...	...	...	...	...	...	...	...	...	...	...	...	...
			Total Group 50	632	552	80	102	52	50	527	423	104	10	8	2	12	12	...
	51.—Eurasians	Eurasian, unspecified	Christian	29	19	10	100	66	34	298	172	126	5	5	...	6	3	3
		East Indian	Do.	...	...	...	...	...	...	...	...	...	...	...	...	...	...	...
		Goanese	Do.	...	...	...	...	...	...	...	...	...	...	...	...	...	...	...
		Madrasi	Do.	...	...	...	...	...	...	...	...	...	...	...	...	...	...	...
		Portuguese	Do.	...	...	...	...	...	...	...	...	...	3	3	...	...	...	...
		Spanish	Do.	...	...	...	...	...	...	...	...	...	...	...	...	...	...	...
			Total Group 51	29	19	10	100	66	34	298	172	126	8	8	...	6	3	3
	52.—Christian Converts.	Native Christians	Christian	16	5	11	25	10	15	19	16	3	6	2	4	...	...	...
			Total Group 52	16	5	11	25	10	15	19	16	3	6	2	4	...	...	...
			Total Class F	55,148	28,918	26,230	48,927	22,488	21,439	67,082	35,764	31,318	45,126	23,757	21,369	9,732	5,307	4,425
			Total of all Classes	1,508,053	784,906	723,147	1,737,606	872,222	865,384	1,619,368	851,933	767,435	978,652	502,832	475,820	337,973	180,117	157,856

TABLE XVII.

Occupations by Age.

Part A.—(PROVINCIAL SUMMARY.)

Table XVII A.—Occupations—Central India.

TABLE XVII.—Occupations by Age.—Part A.—PROVINCIAL SUMMARY.

OCCUPATION AND CLASS.			PROVINCIAL TOTAL.											
			TOTAL.				MALES.				FEMALES.			
Class.	Order.	Sub-order, Group and Occupation.	Total.	0—4	5—14	15 and over.	Total.	0—4	5—14	15 and over.	Total.	0—4	5—14	15 and over.
1	2	3	4	5	6	7	8	9	10	11	12	13	14	15
		1.—Service of Imperial and Provincial Governments.												
	I.—ADMINISTRATION	Political service	54	4	12	38	24	3	6	15	30	...	6	23
		Magistrates	5	...	...	5	2	...	...	2	3	...	...	3
		Assistant Superintendents of Police	3	2	1	...	3	2	1	...	...	...	...	...
		Deputy Collector	1	...	...	1	...	...	...	...	1	...	...	1
		Office Superintendents	5	2	1	2	2	1	...	1	3	1	1	1
		Clerical Establishments	378	54	76	248	167	20	29	118	211	34	47	130
		Police Inspectors	28	2	2	24	20	2	1	17	8	...	1	7
		Peons	284	29	42	213	241	20	33	188	43	9	9	25
		Police Constables	958	100	123	735	618	47	65	506	340	53	58	229
		Menials	124	12	30	82	81	9	15	57	43	3	15	25
		Bailiffs	1	...	...	1	...	...	...	...	1	...	...	1
		Subordinate Government service unspecified	354	44	72	238	176	19	33	124	178	25	39	114
		Total 1	2,195	249	359	1,587	1,334	123	183	1,028	861	126	176	559
		2.—Service of Local and Municipal Bodies.												
		Octroi Darogahs	8	2	1	5	5	1	...	4	3	1	1	1
		" Clerks	25	2	3	20	13	1	2	10	12	1	1	10
		" Menials	56	5	7	44	32	3	4	25	24	2	3	19
		Total 2	89	9	11	69	50	5	6	39	39	4	5	30
		3.—Village Service.												
		Headmen of Villages, Kanungoes, etc.	19,486	2,197	4,443	12,846	10,383	1,089	2,409	6,884	9,103	1,107	2,034	5,962
		Watchmen, menials, etc.	54,192	7,253	12,959	33,980	26,769	3,280	6,573	16,916	27,423	3,973	6,386	17,064
		Total 3	73,678	9,450	17,402	46,826	37,152	4,370	8,982	23,800	36,526	5,080	8,420	23,026
		Total I.—Administration	75,962	9,708	17,772	48,488	38,537	4,498	9,171	24,868	37,426	5,210	8,601	23,615
		4.—Army.												
	II.—DEFENCE	Officers	397	48	43	306	274	32	22	220	123	16	21	86
		Non-Commissioned Officers and Privates	14,392	1,362	1,444	11,586	10,966	690	790	9,486	3,426	672	654	2,100
		Followers	2,277	293	429	1,555	1,199	119	217	863	1,078	174	212	692
		Administrative Establishments	87	23	16	48	58	16	10	32	29	7	6	16
		Total 4	17,153	1,726	1,932	13,495	12,497	857	1,039	10,601	4,656	869	893	2,894

CLASS A.

Table XVII A.—Occupations—Central India.

NAME AND CLASSIFICATION.			DISTRIBUTION BY AGENCIES.											
OCCUPATION AND CLASS.			TOWN.											
			TOTAL.				MALES.				FEMALES.			
Class.	Order.	Sub-order, Group and Occupation.	Total.	0—4	5—14	15 and over.	Total.	0—4	5—14	15 and over.	Total.	0—4	5—14	15 and over.
			16	17	18	19	20	21	22	23	24	25	26	27
		1.—Service of Imperial and Provincial Governments.												
	I.—Administration	Political Service	41	4	10	27	23	3	6	14	18	1	4	13
		Magistrates	3	...	...	3	2	...	...	2	1	...	...	1
		Assistant Superintendents of Police	3	2	1	...	3	2	1	...	...	...	...	...
		Deputy Collector	1	...	...	1	...	...	...	...	1	...	...	1
		Office Superintendents	5	2	1	2	2	1	...	1	3	1	1	1
		Clerical Establishments	343	52	71	220	134	19	24	91	209	33	47	129
		Police Inspectors	26	2	2	22	19	2	1	16	7	...	1	6
		Peons	284	29	42	213	241	20	33	188	43	9	9	25
		Police Constables	806	96	115	595	583	45	62	476	223	51	53	119
		Menials	111	12	29	70	71	9	15	47	40	3	14	23
		Bailiffs	1	...	...	1	...	...	...	...	1	...	...	1
		Subordinate Government service unspecified	208	20	38	150	135	11	24	100	73	9	14	50
		Total 1	1,833	219	309	1,305	1,214	112	166	936	619	107	143	369
		2.—Service of Local and Municipal Bodies.												
		Octroi Darogahs	8	2	1	5	5	1	...	4	3	1	1	1
		" Clerks	23	2	3	18	11	1	2	8	12	1	1	10
		" Menials	49	4	5	40	26	2	2	22	23	2	3	18
		Total 2	80	8	9	63	42	4	4	34	38	4	5	29
		3.—Village Service.												
		Headmen of Villages, Kanungoes, etc.	1,171	124	253	794	88	71	171	446	483	53	82	348
		Watchmen, menials, etc.	2,240	224	417	1,599	1,077	84	192	801	1,163	140	225	798
		Total 3	3,411	340	670	2,393	1,765	155	363	1,247	1,646	193	307	1,146
		Total I.—Administration	**5,324**	**575**	**988**	**3,761**	**3,021**	**271**	**583**	**2,217**	**2,808**	**804**	**455**	**1,544**
		4.—Army.												
	II.—Defence	Officers	344	46	39	259	235	32	19	184	109	14	20	75
		Non-Commissioned Officers and Privates	11,408	988	1,039	9,381	9,041	501	580	79,60	2,367	487	459	1,421
		Followers	1,565	221	291	1,053	750	87	132	531	815	134	159	522
		Administrative Establishments	87	23	16	48	58	16	10	32	29	7	6	16
		Total 4	13,403	1,278	1,385	10,740	10,083	636	741	8,706	3,320	642	644	2,034

Table XVII A.—Occupations—Central India.

TABLE XVII.—Occupations by Age.—Part A.—PROVINCIAL SUMMARY—*contd.*

OCCUPATION AND CLASS.			COUNTRY.											
			TOTAL.				MALES.				FEMALES.			
Class.	Order.	Sub-order, Group and Occupation.	Total.	0—4	5—14	15 and over.	Total.	0—4	5—14	15 and over.	Total.	0—4	5—14	15 and over.
			28	29	30	31	32	33	34	35	36	37	38	39
		1.—Service of Imperial and Provincial Governments.												
CLASS A.	I.—ADMINISTRATION	Political Service	13	...	2	11	1	...	...	1	12	...	2	10
		Magistrates	2	...	...	2	...	...	...	...	2	...	...	2
		Assistant Superintendents of Police	...	...	...	...	...	...	...	...	...	...	...	...
		Deputy Collector	...	...	...	...	...	...	...	...	...	...	...	...
		Office Superintendents	...	...	...	...	...	...	...	...	...	...	...	...
		Clerical Establishments	16	2	3	11	14	1	3	10	2	1	...	1
		Police Inspectors	2	...	...	2	1	...	...	1	1	...	...	1
		Peons	...	...	...	...	...	...	...	...	...	...	...	...
		Police Constables	152	4	8	140	35	2	3	30	117	2	5	110
		Menials	13	...	1	12	10	...	...	10	3	...	1	2
		Bailiffs	...	...	...	...	...	...	...	...	...	...	...	...
		Subordinate Government service unspecified	146	24	34	88	41	8	9	24	105	16	25	59
		Total 1	363	30	50	283	121	11	17	93	142	19	33	190
		2.—Service of Local and Municipal Bodies.												
		Octroi Darogahs	...	...	...	...	...	...	...	...	...	...	...	...
		" Clerks	2	...	...	2	2	...	...	2	...	...	...	...
		" Menials	7	1	2	4	6	1	2	3	1	...	...	1
		Total 2	9	1	2	6	8	1	2	5	1	...	...	1
		3.—Village Service.												
		Headmen of Villages, Kanungoes, etc.	18,315	2,073	4,190	12,052	9,695	1,019	2,238	6,438	8,620	1,054	1,952	5,614
		Watchmen, menials, etc.	51,952	7,029	12,542	32,381	25,692	3,196	6,381	16,115	26,260	2,833	6,161	16,266
		Total 3	70,267	9,102	16,732	44,433	35,387	4,215	8,619	22,553	34,880	4,887	8,113	21,880
		Total I.—Administration	**70,639**	**9,133**	**16,784**	**44,722**	**35,516**	**4,227**	**8,638**	**22,651**	**35,123**	**4,906**	**8,146**	**22,071**
		4.—Army.												
	II.—DEFENCE	Officers	53	2	4	47	39	...	3	36	14	2	1	11
		Non-Commissioned Officers and Privates	2,984	374	405	2,205	1,925	189	210	1,526	1,059	185	195	679
		Followers	712	72	138	502	449	32	85	332	263	40	53	170
		Administrative Establishments	...	...	...	...	...	...	...	...	...	...	...	...
		Total 4	3,749	448	547	2,754	2,413	221	298	1,894	1,336	227	249	860

Class.	Order.	Sub-Order, Group and Occupation.	Total: Total.	Total: 0–4	Total: 5–14	Total: 15 and over.	Males: Total.	Males: 0–4	Males: 5–14	Males: 15 and over.	Females: Total.	Females: 0–4	Females: 5–14	Females: 15 and over.
1	2	3	4	5	6	7	8	9	10	11	12	13	14	15
CLASS A—contd.		**5.—Navy and Marine**												
	II.—Defence—contd.	Officer, Royal Navy	1	...	...	1	1	...	...	1	...	...	...	...
		Total 5	1	...	...		1	...	...	1	...	...	...	...
		Total II.—Defence	**17,154**	**1,726**	**1,932**	**13,496**	**12,498**	**857**	**1,089**	**10,602**	**4,656**	**869**	**898**	**2,894**
		6.—Administrative Service.												
	III.—Foreign and Feudatory State Service.	Chiefs	503	28	88	387	195	12	47	136	308	16	41	251
		Officers	10,761	1,363	2,078	7,320	7,797	829	1,527	5,441	2,964	534	551	1,879
		Clerical Establishments	29,192	3,016	5,820	20,356	13,732	1,233	2,547	9,952	15,460	1,783	3,273	10,404
		Menials, etc.	191,759	20,203	37,349	134,207	105,202	9,641	19,287	76,274	86,557	10,562	18,062	57,933
		Total 6	232,215	24,610	45,335	162,270	126,926	11,715	23,408	91,803	105,289	12,895	21,927	70,467
		7.—Army.												
		State soldiers	112,807	10,638	20,660	81,509	71,214	5,712	11,878	53,624	41,593	4,926	8,782	27,885
		Total 7	112,807	10,638	20,660	81,509	71,214	5,712	11,878	53,624	41,593	4,926	8,782	27,885
		Total III.—Feudatory State Service	**345,022**	**35,248**	**65,995**	**243,779**	**198,140**	**17,427**	**35,286**	**145,427**	**146,882**	**17,821**	**30,709**	**98,352**
		Total Class A.	**438,188**	**46,682**	**85,699**	**305,757**	**249,174**	**22,782**	**45,496**	**180,896**	**188,964**	**23,900**	**40,208**	**124,861**
CLASS B.		**8.—Stock breeding and dealing.**												
		(a) Horses and horned cattle.												
	IV.—Live Stock	Horse breeders and dealers	176	21	36	119	98	11	20	67	78	10	16	52
		Cattle " "	21,950	2,363	6,777	12,810	13,144	1,166	4,581	7,397	8,806	1,197	2,196	5413
		Cattle ground keepers and grazers	113	11	19	83	104	8	17	79	9	3	2	4
		Herdsmen	40,067	4,713	15,751	19,603	25,649	2,481	11,052	12,116	14,418	2,232	4,699	7,487
		Total 8 (a)	*62,306*	*7,108*	*22,583*	*32,615*	*38,995*	*3,666*	*15,670*	*19,659*	*23,311*	*3,442*	*6,913*	*12,956*
		(b) Other draught, etc., animals.												
		Elephant catchers	9	1	2	6	5	1	1	3	4	...	1	3
		Camel breeders and dealers	501	73	107	321	272	32	56	184	229	41	51	137
		Total 8 (b)	*510*	*74*	*109*	*327*	*277*	*33*	*57*	*187*	*233*	*41*	*52*	*140*

Table XVII A.—Occupations—Central India.

TABLE XVII.—Occupations by Age.—Part A.—PROVINCIAL SUMMARY—*contd.*

Class.	Order.	Sub-order, Group and Occupation.	Town. Total. Total.	Town. Total. 0–4	Town. Total. 5–14	Town. Total. 15 and over.	Town. Males. Total.	Town. Males. 0–4	Town. Males. 5–14	Town. Males. 15 and over.	Town. Females. Total.	Town. Females. 0–4	Town. Females. 5–14	Town. Females. 15 and over.
			16	17	18	19	20	21	22	23	24	25	26	27
CLASS A—*contd.*		**5.—Navy and Marine.**												
	II.—Defence—*contd.*	Officer, Royal Navy	1	...	...	1	1	...	...	1	...	...	...	...
		Total 5	1	...	...	1	1	...	...	1	...	...	...	...
		Total II.—Defence	**13,404**	**1,278**	**1,385**	**10,741**	**10,084**	**636**	**741**	**8,707**	**3,320**	**642**	**644**	**2,034**
		6.—Administrative Service.												
	III.—Feudatory State Service.	Chiefs	158	13	31	114	60	6	12	42	98	7	19	72
		Officers	926	97	207	622	381	36	77	268	545	61	130	354
		Clerical Establishments	16,599	1,713	3,239	11,647	6,409	593	1,204	4,612	10,190	1,120	2,035	7,035
		Menials, etc.	86,918	8,842	16,907	61,169	50,510	4,875	10,034	35,601	36,408	3,967	6,873	25,568
		Total 6	104,601	10,665	20,384	73,552	57,360	5,510	11,327	40,523	47,241	5,155	9,057	33,029
		7.—Army.												
		State soldiers	57,782	5,049	9,742	42,991	36,294	2,662	5,432	28,200	21,488	2,387	4,310	14,791
		Total 7	57,782	5,049	9,742	42,991	36,294	2,662	5,432	28,200	21,488	2,387	4,310	14,791
		Total III.—Feudatory State Service	**162,383**	**15,714**	**30,126**	**116,543**	**93,654**	**8,172**	**16,759**	**68,723**	**68,729**	**7,542**	**13,367**	**47,820**
		Total Class A	**181,111**	**17,567**	**32,499**	**131,045**	**106,759**	**9,079**	**18,033**	**79,647**	**74,352**	**8,488**	**14,466**	**51,398**

Class.	Order.	Sub-order, Group and Occupation.	Town. Total. Total.	Town. Total. 0–4	Town. Total. 5–14	Town. Total. 15 and over.	Town. Males. Total.	Town. Males. 0–4	Town. Males. 5–14	Town. Males. 15 and over.	Town. Females. Total.	Town. Females. 0–4	Town. Females. 5–14	Town. Females. 15 and over.
CLASS B.		**8.—Stock breeding and dealing.**												
		(a) Horse and horned cattle.												
	IV.—Live Stock	Horse breeders and dealers	45	5	7	33	45	5	7	33	1	...	...	...
		Cattle " " "	1,298	177	311	810	862	83	228	551	436	94	83	259
		Cattle ground keepers and grazers	3	...	2	1	3	...	2	1	...	...	...	...
		Herdsmen	765	83	198	484	501	52	132	317	264	31	66	167
		Total 8 (a)	*2,111*	*265*	*518*	*1,328*	*1,411*	*140*	*369*	*902*	*700*	*125*	*149*	*426*
		(b) Other draught, etc., animals.												
		Elephant catchers	1	...	...	1	1	...	...	1	...	...	...	...
		Camel breeders and dealers	430	57	95	278	204	17	45	142	226	40	50	136
		Total 8 (b)	*431*	*57*	*95*	*279*	*205*	*17*	*45*	*143*	*226*	*40*	*50*	*136*

Class.	Order.	Sub-order, Group and Occupation.	Town. Total. Total.	Total. 0—4	Total. 5—14	Total. 15 and over.	Males. Total.	Males. 0—4	Males. 5—14	Males. 15 and over.	Females. Total.	Females. 0—4	Females. 5—14	Females. 15 and over.
			28	29	30	31	32	33	34	35	36	37	38	39
CLASS A—contd.		5.—Navy and Marine.												
	II.—Defence—contd.	Officer, Royal Navy	...	...	...	...	...	...	...	...	...	...	...	...
		Total 5	...	...	...	...	...	...	...	...	...	...	...	...
		Total II.—Defence	**3,749**	**448**	**547**	**2,754**	**2,413**	**221**	**298**	**1,894**	**1,336**	**227**	**249**	**860**
		6.—Administrative Service.												
	III.—Feudatory State Service.	Chiefs	345	15	57	273	135	6	35	94	210	9	22	179
		Officers	9,835	1,266	1,871	2,500	7,416	793	1,450	5,173	2,419	473	421	1,525
		Clerical Establishments	12,593	1,303	2,581	8,709	7,323	640	1,343	5,340	5,270	663	1,238	3,369
		Menials, etc.	104,841	11,361	20,442	73,038	54,692	4,766	9,253	40,673	50,149	6,595	11,189	32,365
		Total 6	127,614	13,945	24,951	88,718	69,566	6,205	12,081	51,280	58,048	7,740	12,870	37,438
		7.—Army.												
		State soldiers	55,025	5,589	10,918	38,518	34,920	3,050	6,446	25,424	20,105	2,539	4,472	13,094
		Total 7	55,025	5,589	10,918	38,518	34,920	3,050	6,446	25,424	20,105	2,539	4,472	13,094
		Total III.—Feudatory State Service	**182,639**	**19,534**	**35,869**	**127,236**	**144,486**	**9,255**	**18,527**	**76,704**	**78,153**	**10,279**	**17,842**	**50,532**
		Total Class A.	**257,027**	**29,115**	**53,200**	**174,712**	**142,415**	**18,708**	**27,463**	**101,249**	**114,612**	**15,412**	**25,737**	**78,463**
CLASS B.		8.—Stock breeding and dealing.												
		(a) Horse and horned cattle.												
	IV.—Live Stock	Horse breeders and dealers	131	16	29	86	53	6	13	34	78	10	16	52
		Cattle " "	20,652	2,186	6,466	12,000	12,282	1,083	4,353	6,846	8,370	1,103	2,113	5,154
		Cattle ground keepers and grazers	110	11	17	82	101	8	15	78	9	3	2	4
		Herdsmen	39,302	4,630	15,553	19,119	25,148	2,429	10,920	11,799	14,154	2,201	4,633	7,320
		Total 8 (a)	*60,105*	*6,843*	*22,065*	*31,287*	*37,584*	*3,526*	*15,301*	*18,757*	*22,611*	*3,317*	*6,764*	*12,530*
		(b) Other draught, etc., animals.												
		Elephant catchers	8	1	2	5	4	1	1	2	4	...	1	3
		Camel breeders and dealers	71	16	12	43	68	15	11	42	3	1	1	1
		Total 8 (b)	*79*	*17*	*14*	*48*	*72*	*16*	*12*	*44*	*7*	*1*	*2*	*4*

TABLE XVII.—Occupations by Age.—Part A.—PROVINCIAL SUMMARY—*contd.*

Class.	Order.	Sub-order, Group and Occupation.	Total: Total.	Total: 0–4	Total: 5–14	Total: 15 and over.	Males: Total.	Males: 0–4	Males: 5–14	Males: 15 and over.	Females: Total.	Females: 0–4	Females: 5–14	Females: 15 and over.
1	2	3	4	5	6	7	8	9	10	11	12	13	14	15
		8.—Stock breeding and dealing—*contd.* (*c*) *Small Stock.*												
	IV.—Live Stock—*contd.*	Sheep and goat breeders and dealers	31,535	4,176	9,148	18,211	17,269	2,110	5,179	9,980	14,266	2,066	3,969	8,231
		Pig breeders and dealers	48	8	14	26	32	5	11	16	16	3	3	10
		Total 8 (c)	*31,583*	*4,184*	*9,162*	*18,237*	*17,301*	*2,115*	*5,190*	*9,996*	*14,282*	*2,069*	*3,972*	*8,241*
		9.—Subsidiary Services to Stock.												
		(*a*) *Training and doctoring Live Stock.*												
		Veterinary Surgeons	39	1	9	29	25	...	6	19	14	1	3	10
		Farriers	408	55	100	253	213	26	60	127	195	29	40	126
		Horse breakers and trainers	508	47	84	377	357	28	46	283	151	19	38	94
		Elephant breakers and trainers	1,182	139	310	733	646	68	170	408	536	71	140	325
		Total 9 (a)	*1,372*	*242*	*503*	*1,392*	*1,241*	*122*	*282*	*837*	*896*	*120*	*221*	*555*
		Total IV.—Live Stock	**96,536**	**11,608**	**32,357**	**52,571**	**57,814**	**5,936**	**21,199**	**30,679**	**38,722**	**5,672**	**11,158**	**21,892**
		10.—Interest in Land.												
	V.—Agricultural	Land occupants not cultivating	137,223	15,553	33,091	88,579	77,928	8,958	19,974	48,996	59,295	6,595	13,117	39,583
		Land occupants cultivating	4,530,861	612,508	1,181,523	2,736,830	2,383,304	303,594	649,643	1,430,067	2,147,557	308,914	531,880	1,306,763
		Lessees of villages, etc.	8,891	1,122	2,129	5,640	4,685	571	1,141	2,973	4,206	551	988	2,667
		Total 10	**4,676,975**	**629,183**	**1,216,743**	**2,831,049**	**2,465,917**	**313,123**	**670,758**	**1,482,036**	**2,211,058**	**316,060**	**545,985**	**1,349,013**
		11.—Agricultural Labourers.												
		Farm servants	187,016	32,822	56,048	98,146	120,088	17,706	35,149	67,233	66,928	15,116	20,899	30,913
		Field labourers	3,048	415	751	1,882	1,971	226	468	1,277	1,077	189	283	605
		Total 11	**190,064**	**33,237**	**56,799**	**100,028**	**122,059**	**17,932**	**35,617**	**68,510**	**68,005**	**15,305**	**21,182**	**31,518**

CLASS B—*contd.*

Class.	Order.	Sub-order, Group and Occupation.	TOWN. Total. Total.	Total. 0—4	Total. 5—14	Total. 15 and over.	Males. Total.	Males. 0—4	Males. 5—14	Males. 15 and over.	Females. Total.	Females. 0—4	Females. 5—14	Females. 15 and over.
			16	17	18	19	20	21	22	23	24	25	26	27
	IV.—Live Stock—*contd.*	**8.—Stock breeding and dealing—*contd.***												
		(c) Small Stock.												
		Sheep and goat breeders and dealers	1,190	161	312	717	764	98	209	457	426	63	103	260
		Pig breeders and dealers	19	3	5	11	16	3	4	9	3	...	1	2
		Total 8 (c)	*1,209*	*164*	*317*	*728*	*780*	*101*	*213*	*466*	*429*	*63*	*104*	*262*
		9.—Subsidiary Services to Stock.												
		(a) Training and doctoring Live Stock.												
		Veterinary Surgeons	17	1	2	14	12	...	2	10	5	1	...	4
		Farriers	177	28	34	115	97	14	22	61	80	14	12	54
		Horse breakers and trainers	375	34	53	288	319	20	43	250	56	8	10	38
		Elephant breakers and trainers	654	78	168	408	392	45	101	246	262	33	67	162
		Total 9 (a)	*1,223*	*141*	*257*	*825*	*820*	*85*	*168*	*567*	*403*	*56*	*89*	*258*
		Total IV.—Live Stock	**4,974**	**627**	**187**	**8,160**	**3,216**	**848**	**795**	**2,078**	**1,758**	**284**	**892**	**1,082**
	V.—Agricultural.	**10.—Interest in Lands.**												
		Land occupants not cultivating	3,984	362	908	2,714	1,116	92	207	807	2,878	270	701	1,907
		Land occupants cultivating	84,295	11,030	22,598	50,667	42,914	5,359	13,127	24,428	41,381	5,671	9,471	26,239
		Lessees of villages, etc.	1,304	136	270	898	923	81	182	660	381	55	88	238
		Total 10	89,583	11,528	23,776	54,279	44,943	5,532	13,516	25,895	44,640	5,996	10,260	28,384
		11.—Agricultural Labourers.												
		Farm servants	422	22	36	364	422	22	36	364	...	...	...	...
		Field labourers	571	71	86	414	147	14	26	107	424	57	60	307
		Total 11	993	93	122	778	569	36	62	471	424	57	60	307

TABLE XVII.—Occupations by Age.—Part A.—PROVINCIAL SUMMARY—*contd.*

Class.	Order.	Sub-order, Group and Occupation.	Country. Total. Total.	Total. 0–4	Total. 5–14	Total. 15 and over.	Males. Total.	Males. 0–4	Males. 5–14	Males. 15 and over.	Females. Total.	Females. 0–4	Females. 5–14	Females. 15 and over.
			28	29	30	31	32	33	34	35	36	37	38	39
		8.—Stock breeding and dealing—*contd.*												
		(c) Small Stock.												
	IV.—Live Stock—*contd.*	Sheep and goat breeders and dealers	30,345	4,015	8,836	12,494	16,505	2,012	4,970	9,523	13,840	2,003	3,866	7,971
		Pig breeders and dealers	29	5	9	15	16	2	7	7	13	3	2	8
		Total 8 (c)	*30,374*	*4,020*	*8,845*	*17,509*	*16,521*	*2,014*	*4,977*	*9,530*	*13,853*	*2,006*	*3,868*	*7,979*
		9.—Subsidiary Services to Stock.												
		(a) Training and doctoring Live Stock.												
		Veterinary Surgeons	22	...	7	15	13	...	4	9	9	...	3	6
		Farriers	231	27	66	138	116	12	38	66	115	15	28	72
		Horse breakers and trainers	133	13	31	89	38	2	3	33	95	11	28	56
		Elephant breakers and trainers	528	61	142	325	254	23	69	162	274	38	73	103
		Total 9 (a)	*914*	*101*	*246*	*567*	*421*	*37*	*114*	*270*	*493*	*64*	*132*	*297*
		Total IV.—Live Stock.	**91,562**	**10,981**	**31,170**	**49,411**	**54,598**	**5,598**	**20,404**	**28,601**	**36,964**	**5,388**	**10,766**	**20,810**
		10.—Interest in Land.												
	V.—Agricultural	Land occupants not cultivating	133,239	15,191	32,183	85,865	76,82	8 866	19,767	48,189	56,417	6,325	12,416	37,676
		Land occupants cultivating	4,446,566	601,478	1,158,925	2,686,163	2,340,390	298,235	636,516	1,405,639	2,106,176	303,243	522,409	1,280,524
		Lessees of villages, etc.	7,587	986	1,859	4,742	3,762	490	959	2,313	3,825	496	900	2,429
		Total 10	4,587,392	617,655	1,192,967	2,776,770	2,420,974	307,591	657,242	1,456,141	2,166,418	310,064	535,725	1,320,629
		11.—Agricultural Labourers.												
		Farm servants	186,594	32,800	56,012	97,782	119,666	17,684	35,113	66,869	66,928	15,116	20,899	30,913
		Field labourers	2,477	344	665	1,468	1,824	212	442	1,170	653	132	223	298
		Total 11.	189,071	33,144	56,677	99,250	121,490	17,896	35,555	68,039	67,581	5,248	21,122	31,211

OCCUPATION AND CLASS.			PROVINCIAL TOTAL.											
			TOTAL.				MALES.				FEMALES.			
Class.	Order.	SUB-ORDER, GROUP AND OCCUPATION.	TOTAL.	0—4	5—14	15 and over.	TOTAL.	0—4	5—14	15 and over.	TOTAL.	0—4	5—14	15 and over.
1	2	3	4	5	6	7	8	9	10	11	12	13	14	15
CLASS B—concld.		**12.—Growers of Special Products and Trees.**												
	V.—AGRICULTURAL—contd.	Betel-vine, etc., growers	3,083	453	711	1,919	1,285	179	324	782	1,798	274	387	1,137
		Waternut growers	3,256	506	921	1,829	1,401	185	407	809	1,855	321	514	1,020
		Water melon growers	352	47	86	219	192	19	51	122	160	28	35	97
		Market gardeners	706	115	191	400	359	55	104	200	347	60	87	200
		Gardeners	3,866	474	832	2,560	2,165	226	461	1,478	1,701	248	371	1,082
		Forest officers	2	...	...	2	1	...	...	1	1	...	...	1
		Forest rangers, etc.	57	6	12	39	39	3	8	28	18	3	4	11
		Total 12	11,322	1,601	2,753	6,963	5,442	667	1,355	3,420	5,880	934	1,398	3,548
		13.—Agricultural Training and Supervision.												
		Agents and Managers of landed estates	8,573	989	2,049	5,535	4,947	496	1,151	3,300	3,626	493	898	2,235
		Total 13	8,573	989	2,049	5,535	4,947	496	1,151	3,300	3,626	493	898	2,235
		Total V.—Agricultural	**4,886,934**	**665,010**	**1,278,844**	**2,943,580**	**2,598,365**	**332,218**	**708,881**	**1,557,266**	**2,288,569**	**332,792**	**569,463**	**1,386,314**
		Total Class B	**4,983,470**	**676,618**	**1,310,701**	**2,996,151**	**2,656,179**	**338,154**	**730,080**	**1,587,945**	**2,327,291**	**338,464**	**580,621**	**1,408,206**
CLASS C.		**14.—Personal and Domestic Services.**												
	VI.—PERSONAL AND HOUSEHOLD SERVICES.	Barbers	110,475	14,122	26,545	69,808	59,054	6,977	14,834	37,243	51,421	7,145	11,711	32,565
		Ear-pickers	53	5	17	31	1	...	...	1	52	5	17	30
		Washermen	53,210	7,080	13,397	32,733	28,059	3,587	7,426	17,046	25,151	3,593	5,971	15,687
		Water-carriers	26,679	3,691	6,861	16,127	13,704	1,827	3,689	8,188	12,975	1,864	3,172	7,939
		Cooks	2,341	251	431	1,659	1,468	127	246	1,095	873	124	185	564
		Indoor servants	204,263	23,146	43,868	137,249	117,697	12,042	25,122	80,533	86,566	11,104	18,746	56,716
		Grooms, etc.	5,671	694	1,157	3,820	3,439	371	647	2,421	2,232	323	510	1,399
		Doorkeepers	2,000	266	538	1,196	1,227	150	330	747	773	116	208	449
		Domestic service, unspecified	78,488	7,860	14,540	56,088	41,588	3,482	7,175	30,931	36,900	4,378	7,365	25,157
		Total 14	483,180	57,115	107,354	318,711	266,237	28,563	59,469	178,205	216,943	28,552	47,885	140,506
		15.—Non-domestic Establishment.												
		Hotel and refreshment-room keepers, etc.	80	9	6	65	73	6	4	63	7	3	2	2
		Rest-house, sarai keepers, etc.	45	5	12	28	26	1	9	16	19	4	3	12
		Total 15	125	14	18	93	99	7	13	79	26	7	5	14

TABLE XVII.—Occupations by Age.—Part A.—PROVINCIAL SUMMARY—*contd.*

Class.	Order.	Sub-order, Group and Occupation.	TOWN. Total. Total.	Total. 0—4	Total. 5—14	Total. 15 and over.	Males. Total.	Males. 0—4	Males. 5—14	Males. 15 and over.	Females. Total.	Females. 0—4	Females. 5—14	Females. 15 and over.
			16	17	18	19	20	21	22	23	24	25	26	27
CLASS B—*contd.*	V.—Agricultural—*contd.*	**12.—Growers of Special Products and Trees.**												
		Betel-vine, etc., growers	...	...	...	...	...	...	...	...	...	...	...	...
		Waternut growers	377	39	70	268	14	2	5	7	363	37	65	261
		Water-melon growers	...	...	...	...	...	...	...	...	...	...	...	...
		Market gardeners	...	...	...	...	...	...	...	...	...	...	...	...
		Gardeners	3,058	346	663	2,049	1,858	169	405	1,284	1,200	177	258	765
		Forest officers	2	...	...	2	1	...	...	1	1	...	...	1
		Forest rangers, etc.	5	...	...	5	4	...	...	4	1	...	...	1
		Total 12	3,442	385	733	2,324	1,877	171	410	1,296	1,565	214	323	1,028
		13.—Agricultural Training and Supervision.												
		Agents and Managers of landed estates	169	11	39	119	115	5	26	84	54	6	13	35
		Total 13	169	11	39	119	115	5	26	84	54	6	13	35
		Total V.—Agricultural	**94,187**	**12,017**	**24,670**	**57,500**	**47,504**	**5,744**	**14,014**	**27,746**	**46,683**	**6,273**	**10,656**	**29,754**
		Total Class B	**99,161**	**12,644**	**25,857**	**60,660**	**50,720**	**6,087**	**14,809**	**29,824**	**48,441**	**6,557**	**11,048**	**30,836**
CLASS C.	VI.—Personal and Household Services.	**14.—Personal and Domestic Services.**												
		Barbers	11,080	1,206	2,089	7,785	6,107	611	1,141	4,355	4,973	595	948	3,430
		Ear-pickers	53	5	17	31	1	...	...	1	52	5	17	30
		Washermen	8,265	987	1,931	5,347	4,385	507	1,084	2,794	3,880	480	847	2,553
		Water-carriers	6,422	730	1,394	4,298	3,566	403	755	2,408	2,856	327	639	1,890
		Cooks	1,898	227	418	1,253	1,059	115	240	704	839	112	178	549
		Indoor servants	65,064	6,812	12,926	45,326	35,250	3,344	7,059	24,847	29,814	3,468	5,867	20,479
		Grooms, etc.	4,103	518	803	2,782	2,182	253	383	1,546	1,921	265	420	1,236
		Doorkeepers	120	12	21	87	110	11	20	79	10	1	1	8
		Domestic service, unspecified	12,668	954	1,761	9,953	11,144	781	1,462	8,901	1,524	173	299	1,052
		Total 14	109,673	11,451	21,360	76,862	63,804	6,025	12,144	45,635	45,869	5,426	9,216	31,227
		15.—Non-domestic Establishment.												
		Hotel and refreshment-room keepers, etc.	5	...	...	5	5	...	...	5	...	...	...	...
		Rest-house, sarai keepers, etc.	6	...	...	6	3	...	...	3	3	...	...	3
		Total 15	11	...	...	11	8	...	...	8	3	...	...	3

Table XVII A.—Occupations—Central India.

Class.	Order.	Sub-order, Group and Occupation.	Country. Total. Total.	Total. 0—4	Total. 5—14	Total. 15 and over.	Males. Total.	Males. 0—4	Males. 5—14	Males. 15 and over.	Females. Total.	Females. 0—4	Females. 5—14	Females. 15 and over.
			28	29	30	31	32	33	34	35	36	37	38	39
CLASS B—concld.	V.—Agricultural—contd.	**12.—Growers of Special Products and Trees.**												
		Betel-vine, etc., growers	3,083	453	711	1,919	1,285	179	324	782	1,798	274	387	1,137
		Waternut growers	2,879	467	851	1,561	1,387	183	402	802	1,492	284	449	759
		Water-melon growers	352	47	86	219	192	19	51	122	160	28	35	97
		Market gardeners	706	115	191	400	359	55	104	200	347	60	87	200
		Gardeners	808	128	169	511	307	57	56	194	501	71	113	317
		Forest officers	...	...	...	...	...	...	...	...	...	...	...	...
		Forest rangers, etc.	52	6	12	34	35	3	8	24	17	3	4	10
		Total 12	7,880	1,216	2,020	4,644	3,565	496	945	2,124	4,315	720	1,075	2,520
		13.—Agricultural Training and Supervision.												
		Agents and Managers of landed estates	8,404	978	2,010	5,416	4,832	491	1,125	3,216	3,572	487	885	2,200
		Total 13	8,404	978	2,010	5,416	4,832	491	1,125	3,216	3,572	487	885	2,200
		Total V.—Agricultural	792,747	652,998	1,253,674	2,886,080	2,550,861	826,474	694,867	1,529,520	2,241,886	826,519	558,807	1,356,560
		Total Class B	4,834,309	663,974	1,284,844	2,935,491	2,605,459	382,067	715,271	1,558,121	2,278,850	331,907	569,573	1,877,370
CLASS C.	VI.—Personal and Household Services.	**14.—Personal and Domestic Services.**												
		Barbers	99,395	12,916	24,456	62,023	52,947	6,366	13,693	32,888	46,448	6,550	10,763	29,135
		Ear-pickers	...	...	...	...	...	...	...	...	...	...	...	...
		Washermen	44,945	6,093	11,466	27,386	23,674	3,080	6,342	14,252	21,271	3,013	5,124	13,134
		Water-carriers	20,257	2,961	5,467	11,829	10,138	1,424	2,934	5,780	10,119	1,537	2,533	6,049
		Cooks	443	24	13	406	409	12	6	391	34	12	7	15
		Indoor servants	139,199	16,334	30,942	91,923	82,447	8,698	18,063	55,686	56,752	7,636	12,879	36,237
		Grooms, etc.	1,568	176	354	1,038	1,257	118	264	875	311	58	90	163
		Doorkeepers	1,880	214	517	1,109	1,117	139	310	668	763	115	207	441
		Domestic service, unspecified	65,820	6,906	12,779	46,135	30,444	2,701	5,713	22,030	35,376	4,205	7,066	24,105
		Total 14	373,507	45,664	35,994	241,849	202,433	22,538	47,325	132,570	171,074	23,126	38,669	109,279
		15.—Non-domestic Establishment.												
		Hotel and refreshment-room-keepers, etc.	75	9	6	60	68	6	4	58	7	3	2	2
		Rest-house, sarai keepers, etc.	39	5	12	22	23	1	9	13	16	4	3	9
		Total 15	114	14	18	32	91	7	13	71	23	7	5	11

TABLE XVII.—Occupations by Age.—Part A.—PROVINCIAL SUMMARY—*contd.*

Class	Order.	Sub-order, Group and Occupation.	Total: Total.	Total: 0—4	Total: 5—14	Total: 15 and over.	Males: Total.	Males: 0—4	Males: 5—14	Males: 15 and over.	Females: Total.	Females: 0—4	Females: 5—14	Females: 15 and over.
1	2	3	4	5	6	7	8	9	10	11	12	13	14	15
CLASS C—*contd.*	VI.—Personal and Household Services—*contd*	**16.—Sanitation.**												
		Sanitary inspectors	21	...	8	13	7	...	2	5	14	...	6	8
		Sweepers and scavengers	34,361	4,393	8,547	21,421	18,186	2,159	4,677	11,350	16,175	2,234	3,870	10,071
		Total 16	34,382	4,393	8,555	21,434	18,193	2,159	4,679	11,355	16,189	2,234	3,876	10,079
		Total VI.—Personal and Household Services	517,687	61,522	115,927	340,238	284,529	30,729	64,161	189,639	238,158	30,798	51,766	150,599
		Total Class C	517,687	61,522	115,927	340,238	284,529	30,729	64,161	189,639	238,158	30,798	51,766	150,599
CLASS D.—PREPARATION AND SUPPLY OF MATERIAL SUBSTANCES.	VII.—Food and Drink.	**17.—Animal Food.**												
		Milk and butter sellers	17,034	2,081	4,403	10,550	8,526	996	2,355	5,175	8,508	1,085	2,048	5,375
		Ghee preparers and sellers	2,044	224	491	1,329	1,122	108	275	739	922	116	216	590
		Cheese sellers	4	...	1	3	3	...	1	2	1	...	...	1
		Butchers	17,072	2,171	4,359	10,542	10,838	1,244	2,777	6,817	6,234	927	1,582	3,725
		Fowl and egg sellers	246	30	68	148	127	10	39	78	119	20	29	70
		Fish dealers	4,348	711	1,190	2,447	2,165	300	646	1,219	2,183	411	544	1,228
		Total 17	40,748	5,217	10,512	25,019	22,781	2,658	6,093	14,030	17,967	2,559	4,419	10,989
		18.—Vegetable Food.												
		Grain dealers	26,031	3,089	5,788	17,154	8,133	824	1,686	5,623	17,898	2,265	4,102	11,531
		Grain parchers	5,392	670	1,230	3,492	3,021	308	739	1,974	2,371	362	491	1,518
		Pulse and flour preparers and sellers	47,084	5,000	10,703	31,381	24,157	2,426	5,810	15,921	22,927	2,574	4,893	15,460
		Flour mill service	88	14	25	49	88	14	25	49	...	...	...	...
		Bakers	1,220	124	282	814	777	73	186	518	443	51	96	296
		Bread sellers	519	65	126	328	482	60	117	303	37	5	9	23
		Bran sellers	23	1	8	14	14	1	...	13	9	...	8	1
		Vegetable sellers	16,888	2,341	4,426	10,121	8,449	1,158	2,320	4,971	8,439	1,183	2,106	5,150
		Fruit sellers	791	74	185	532	369	35	81	253	422	39	104	279
		Cocoanut sellers	521	80	170	271	519	80	169	270	2	...	1	1
		Confectioners	6,424	623	1,342	4,459	3,651	341	760	2,550	2,773	282	582	1,909
		Sweetmeat sellers	2,771	289	636	1,846	1,708	174	377	1,157	1,063	115	259	689
		Total 18	107,752	12,370	24,921	70,461	51,368	5,494	12,270	33,604	56,384	6,876	12,651	36,857

Table XVII A.—Occupations—Central India.

Class.	Order.	Sub-order, Group and Occupation.	TOWN. Total. Total.	Total. 0–4	Total. 5–14	Total. 15 and over.	Males. Total.	Males. 0–4	Males. 5–14	Males. 15 and over.	Females. Total.	Females. 0–4	Females. 5–14	Females. 15 and over.
			16	17	18	19	20	21	22	23	24	25	26	27
CLASS C—*contd.*	VI.—Personal and Household Services.—*contd.*	**16.—Sanitation.**												
		Sanitary inspectors	9	...	2	7	2	...	...	2	7	...	2	5
		Sweepers and scavengers	7,253	898	1,692	4,663	4,861	609	1,146	3,106	2,392	289	546	1,557
		Total 16	7,262	898	1,694	4,670	4,863	609	1,146	3,108	2,399	289	548	1,562
		Total VI.—Personal and Household Services	**116,946**	**12,849**	**23,054**	**81,543**	**68,675**	**6,684**	**13,290**	**48,751**	**48,271**	**5,715**	**9,764**	**32,792**
		Total Class C	**116,946**	**12,349**	**23,054**	**81,543**	**68,675**	**6,684**	**13,290**	**48,751**	**48,271**	**5,715**	**9,764**	**32,792**
CLASS D.—PREPARATION AND SUPPLY OF MATERIAL SUBSTANCES.	VII.—Food and Drink.	**17.—Animal Food.**												
		Milk and butter sellers	5,884	743	1,399	3,742	3,204	384	789	2,031	2,680	359	610	1,711
		Ghee preparers and sellers	510	50	114	346	272	25	63	184	238	25	51	162
		Cheese sellers	...	...	...	...	...	...	...	...	...	...	...	...
		Butchers	5,505	692	1,399	3,414	2,973	343	790	1,840	2,532	349	609	1,574
		Fowl and egg sellers	163	19	41	103	89	9	28	52	74	10	13	51
		Fish dealers	757	120	195	442	367	54	98	215	390	66	97	227
		Total 17	12,819	1,624	3,148	8,047	6,905	815	1,768	4,322	5,914	809	1,380	3,725
		18.—Vegetable Food.												
		Grain dealers	5,742	595	1,202	3,945	3,761	378	785	2,598	1,981	217	417	1,347
		Grain parchers	1,711	181	314	1,216	877	70	159	648	834	111	155	568
		Pulse and flour preparers and sellers	20,361	2,180	3,947	14,234	7,333	695	1,501	5,137	13,028	1,485	2,446	9,097
		Flour mill service	69	13	25	31	69	13	25	31	...	...	...	...
		Bakers	429	36	85	308	260	16	39	205	169	20	46	103
		Bread sellers	110	9	22	79	110	9	22	79	...	...	...	...
		Bran sellers	15	1	...	14	14	1	...	13	1	...	...	1
		Vegetable sellers	4,172	511	1,008	2,653	2,098	265	540	1,293	2,074	246	468	1,360
		Fruit sellers	509	37	118	354	243	14	57	172	266	23	61	182
		Cocoanut sellers	3	...	3	...	3	...	3	...	...	...	...	...
		Confectioners	1,271	95	231	945	1,260	95	227	938	11	...	4	7
		Sweetmeat sellers	2,164	213	492	1,459	1,335	123	291	921	829	90	201	538
		Total 18	36,556	3,871	7,447	25,238	17,363	1,679	3,649	12,035	19,193	2,192	3,798	13,203

TABLE XVII.—Occupations by Age.—Part A.—PROVINCIAL SUMMARY—*contd.*

OCCUPATION AND CLASS.			COUNTRY.											
			TOTAL.				MALES.				FEMALES.			
Class.	Order.	Sub-order, Group and Occupation.	TOTAL.	0—4	5—14	15 and over.	TOTAL.	0—4	5—14	15 and over.	TOTAL.	0—4	5—14	15 and over.
			28	29	30	31	32	33	34	35	36	37	38	39
CLASS C—*contd.*	VI.—PERSONAL AND HOUSEHOLD SERVICES—*contd.*	**16.—Sanitation.**												
		Sanitary inspectors	12	...	6	6	5	...	2	3	7	...	4	
		Sweepers and scavengers	27,108	3,495	6,855	16,738	13,325	1,550	3,531	8,244	13,783	1,945	3,324	8,5143
		Total 16	27,120	3,495	6,861	16,764	13,330	1,550	3,533	8,247	13,790	1,945	3,328	8,517
		Total VI.—Personal and Household Services	**400,741**	**49,178**	**92,878**	**258,695**	**215,854**	**24,095**	**50,871**	**140,888**	**184,887**	**25,078**	**42,002**	**117,807**
		Total Class C	**400,741**	**49,178**	**9,878**	**258,695**	**215,854**	**24,095**	**50,871**	**140,888**	**184,887**	**25,078**	**42,002**	**117,807**
CLASS D.—PREPARATION AND SUPPLY OF MATERIAL SUBSTANCES.	VII.—FOOD AND DRINK.	**17.—Animal Food**												
		Milk sellers	11,150	1,338	3,004	6,808	5,322	612	1,566	3,144	5,828	726	1,438	3,664
		Ghee preparers and sellers	1,534	174	377	983	850	83	212	555	684	91	165	428
		Cheese sellers	4	...	1	3	3	...	1	2	1	...	...	1
		Butchers	11,567	1,479	2,960	7,128	7,865	901	1,987	4,977	3,702	578	973	2,151
		Fowl and egg sellers	83	11	27	45	38	1	11	26	45	10	16	19
		Fish dealers	3,591	591	995	2,005	1,798	246	548	1,004	1,793	345	447	1,001
		Total 17	27,529	3,593	7,364	16,972	15,876	1,843	4,325	9,708	12,053	1,750	3,039	7,264
		18.—Vegetable F.od.												
		Grain dealers	20,289	2,494	4,586	13,209	4,372	446	901	3,025	15,917	2,048	3,685	10,184
		Grain parchers	3,681	489	916	2,276	2,144	238	580	1,326	1,537	251	336	950
		Pulse and flour preparers and sellers	26,723	2,820	6,756	17,147	1,824	1,731	4,309	10,784	9,899	1,089	2,447	6,363
		Flour mill service	19	1	...	18	19	1	...	18	...	...	...	...
		Bakers	791	88	197	506	517	57	147	313	274	31	50	193
		Bread sellers	409	56	104	249	372	51	95	226	37	5	9	23
		Bran sellers	8	...	8	...	...	...	...	...	8	...	8	...
		Vegetable sellers	12,716	1,830	3,418	7,468	6,351	893	1,780	3,678	6,365	937	1,638	3,790
		Fruit sellers	282	37	67	178	126	21	24	81	156	16	43	97
		Cocoanut sellers	518	80	167	271	516	80	166	270	2	...	1	1
		Confectioners	5,153	528	1,111	3,514	2,319	246	533	1,612	2,762	282	578	1,902
		Sweetmeat sellers	607	76	144	387	373	51	86	236	234	25	58	151
		Total 18	71,196	8,499	17,474	45,223	34,005	3,815	8,621	21,569	37,191	4,684	8,853	23,654

OCCUPATION AND CLASS.			PROVINCIAL TOTAL.											
			TOTAL.				MALES.				FEMALES.			
Class.	Order.	SUB-ORDER, GROUP AND OCCUPATION.	TOTAL.	0—4	5—14	15 and over.	TOTAL.	0—4	5—14	15 and over.	TOTAL.	0—4	5—14	15 and over.
1	2	3	4	5	6	7	8	9	10	11	12	13	14	15
		19.—Drink, Condiments and Narcotics.												
	VII.—FOOD AND DRINK	Ice manufacturers and sellers	5	...	...	5	3	...	...	3	2	...	...	2
		Soda-water manufacturers	51	3	11	37	15	...	2	13	36	3	9	24
		Country spirit distillers and sellers	34,534	4,206	8,109	22,219	17,979	2,077	4,355	11,547	16,555	2,129	3,754	10,672
		Toddy drawers and sellers	45	10	8	27	9	1	2	6	36	9	6	21
		Tea sellers	21	2	3	16	19	2	2	15	2	...	1	1
		Sugar manufacturers and sellers	2	...	...	2	1	...	...	1	1	...	...	1
		Jaggery sellers	302	32	70	200	203	24	42	137	99	8	28	63
		Salt preparers and sellers	3,540	517	950	2,073	1,897	265	530	1,102	1,643	252	420	971
		Assafœtida, etc., sellers	4	...	...	4	3	...	...	3	1	...	...	1
		Pickle makers and sellers	35	5	11	19	10	2	3	5	25	3	8	14
		Grocers and general condiment dealers	26,297	2,943	5,745	17,609	14,053	1,403	3,124	9,526	12,244	1,540	2,621	8,083
		Betel-leaf sellers	14,328	1,696	3,481	9,151	8,171	939	2,055	5,177	6,157	757	1,426	3,974
		Tobacco manufacturers and sellers	6,582	720	1,671	4,191	3,312	389	871	2,052	3,270	331	800	2,139
		Snuff manufacturers and sellers	29	4	3	22	2	...	...	2	27	4	3	20
		Opium, etc., manufacturers and sellers	188	17	35	136	104	6	19	79	84	11	16	57
		Bhang and ganja preparers and sellers	297	32	71	194	215	22	49	144	82	10	22	50
														1
		Total 19	**86,260**	**10,187**	**20,168**	**55,905**	**45,996**	**5,130**	**11,054**	**29,812**	**40,264**	**5,057**	**9,114**	**26,093**
		Total VII.-Food and Drink	**234,760**	**27,774**	**55,601**	**151,385**	**120,145**	**13,282**	**29,417**	**77,446**	**114,615**	**14,492**	**26,184**	**78,989**
		20.-Lighting.												
	VIII.—LIGHT, FIRING AND FORAGE.	Oil pressers and sellers	85,582	11,368	21,782	52,432	47,059	6,075	12,508	28,476	38,523	5,293	9,274	23,956
		Candle makers and sellers	5	...	1	4	2	...	...	2	3	...	1	2
		Torch makers and sellers	92	6	18	68	56	3	14	39	36	3	4	29
		Match makers and sellers	2	...	...	2	2	...	...	2	...	...	...	...
		Total 20	**85,681**	**11,374**	**21,801**	**52,506**	**47,119**	**6,078**	**12,522**	**28,519**	**38,562**	**5,296**	**9,279**	**23,987**
		21.-Fuel and Forage.												
		Firewood and grass gatherers and sellers	19,439	2,232	4,880	12,327	15,911	1,733	4,059	10,119	3,528	499	821	2,208
		Coal dealers	611	102	178	331	318	41	91	186	293	61	87	145
		Cowdung fuel preparers and sellers	570	74	138	358	250	36	76	138	320	38	62	220
		Hay contractors, etc.	9	1	3	5	6	...	3	3	3	1	...	2
		Total 21	**20,629**	**2,409**	**5,199**	**13,021**	**16,485**	**1,810**	**4,229**	**10,446**	**4,144**	**599**	**970**	**2,575**
		Total VIII.-Light, Firing and Forage	**106,310**	**13,783**	**27,000**	**65,527**	**63,604**	**7,888**	**16,751**	**38,965**	**42,706**	**5,895**	**10,249**	**26,562**

TABLE XVII.—Occupations by Age.—Part A.—PROVINCIAL SUMMARY—*contd.*

Class.	Order.	Sub-order, Group and Occupation.	Town. Total. Total.	Total. 0–4	Total. 5–14	Total. 15 and over.	Males. Total.	Males. 0–4	Males. 5–14	Males. 15 and over.	Females. Total.	Females. 0–4	Females. 5–14	Females. 15 and over.
			16	17	18	19	20	21	22	23	24	25	26	27
		19.—Drink, Condiments and Narcotics.												
	VII.—Food and Drink—*contd.*	Ice manufacturers and sellers	5	...	...	5	3	...	...	3	2	...	...	2
		Soda-water maufacturers	23	1	6	16	9	...	2	7	14	1	4	9
		Country spirit distillers and sellers	2,965	344	640	1,981	1,615	195	334	1,086	1,350	149	306	895
		Toddy drawers and sellers	1	...	...	1	...	...	...	...	1	...	...	1
		Tea sellers	5	1	2	2	3	1	1	1	2	...	...	1
		Sugar manufacturers and sellers	...	...	...	...	...	...	...	...	...	...	...	...
		Jaggery sellers	6	...	...	6	1	...	...	1	5	...	...	5
		Salt preparers and sellers	279	45	60	174	49	5	14	30	230	40	46	144
		Assafœtida, etc., sellers	...	...	...	...	...	...	...	...	...	...	...	...
		Pickle makers and sellers	30	4	10	16	7	2	2	3	23	2	8	13
		Grocers and general condiment dealers	4,070	461	845	2,764	1,815	180	378	1,257	2,255	281	467	1,507
		Betel-leaf sellers	3,777	423	793	2,561	2,115	252	452	1,411	1,662	171	341	1,150
		Tobacco manufacturers and sellers	1,195	127	288	780	708	73	154	481	487	54	134	299
		Snuff manufacturers and sellers	29	4	3	22	2	...	...	2	27	4	3	20
		Opium, etc., manufacturers and sellers	84	6	15	63	84	6	15	63	...	...	...	...
		Bhang and ganja preparers and sellers	128	10	18	100	89	6	6	77	39	4	12	23
		Total 19	12,597	1,426	2,680	8,491	6,500	720	1,358	4,422	6,097	706	1,322	4,069
		Total VII.—Food and Drink	**61,972**	**6,921**	**1,375**	**41,776**	**30,768**	**3,214**	**6,775**	**20,779**	**31,204**	**3,707**	**6,500**	**20,997**
		20.—Lighting.												
	VIII.—Light, Firing and Forage.	Oil pressers and sellers	10,721	1,346	2,436	6,939	5,453	692	1,308	3,453	5,268	654	1,128	3,486
		Candle makers and sellers	4	...	1	3	2	...	...	2	2	...	1	1
		Torch makers and sellers	77	6	16	55	47	3	13	31	30	3	3	24
		Match makers and sellers	...	...	...	...	...	...	...	...	...	...	...	...
		Total 20	10,802	1,352	453	6,997	5,502	695	1,321	3,486	5,300	657	1,132	3,511
		21.—Fuel and Forage.												
		Firewood and grass gatherers and sellers	2,910	361	679	1,870	1,541	182	389	970	1,369	179	290	900
		Coal dealers	86	12	22	52	62	8	13	41	24	4	9	11
		Cowdung fuel preparers and sellers	77	8	17	52	30	1	12	17	47	7	5	35
		Hay contractors, etc.	6	...	3	3	6	...	3	3	...	...	...	...
		Total 21	3,079	381	721	1,977	1,639	191	417	1,031	1,440	190	304	946
		Total VIII.—Light, Firing and Forage	**13,881**	**1,733**	**3,174**	**8,974**	**7,141**	**886**	**1,738**	**4,517**	**6,740**	**847**	**1,436**	**4,457**

OCCUPATION AND CLASS.			COUNTRY.											
Class.	Order.	Sub-order, Group and Occupation.	Total.				Males.				Females.			
			Total.	0—4	5—14	15 and over.	Total.	0—4	5—14	15 and over.	Total.	0—4	5—14	15 and over.
			28	29	30	31	32	33	34	35	36	37	38	39
		19.—Drink, Condiments and Narcotics.												
	VII.—Food and Drink—contd.	Ice manufactures and sellers	...	...	...	...	...	...	...	...	...	...	...	...
		Soda-water manufacturers	28	2	5	21	6	...	...	6	22	2	5	15
		Country spirit distillers and sellers	31,569	3,862	7,469	20,238	16,364	1,882	4,021	10,461	15,205	1,980	3,448	9,777
		Toddy drawers and sellers	44	10	8	26	9	1	2	6	35	9	6	20
		Tea sellers	16	1	1	14	16	1	1	14	...	...	...	...
		Sugar manufacturers and sellers	2	...	...	2	1	...	...	1	1	...	...	1
		Jaggery sellers	296	32	70	194	202	24	42	136	94	8	28	58
		Salt preparers and sellers	3,261	472	890	1,899	1,848	260	516	1,072	1,413	212	374	827
		Assafœtida, etc., sellers	4	...	...	4	3	...	...	3	1	...	...	1
		Pickle makers and sellers	5	1	1	3	3	...	1	2	2	1	...	1
		Grocers and general condiment dealers	22,227	2,482	4,900	14,845	12,238	1,223	2,746	8,269	9,989	1,259	2,154	6,576
		Betel-leaf sellers	10,551	1,273	2,688	6,590	6,056	687	1,603	3,766	4,495	586	1,085	2,824
		Tobacco manufacturers and sellers	5,387	593	1,383	3,411	2,604	316	717	1,571	2,783	277	666	1,840
		Snuff manufacturers and sellers	...	...	...	...	...	...	...	...	...	...	...	...
		Opium, etc., manufacturers and sellers	104	11	20	73	20	...	4	16	84	11	16	57
		Bhang and ganja preparers and sellers	169	22	53	94	126	16	43	67	43	6	10	27
		Total 19	73,663	8,761	17,488	47,414	39,496	4,410	9,696	25,390	34,167	4,351	7,792	22,024
		Total VII.—Food and Drink.	**172,788**	**20,853**	**42,326**	**109,609**	**89,377**	**10,068**	**22,642**	**56,667**	**83,411**	**10,785**	**19,684**	**52,942**
		20.—Lighting.												
	VIII.—Light, Firing and Forage.	Oil pressers and sellers	74,861	10,622	19,346	45,493	41,606	5,383	11,200	25,023	33,255	4,639	8,146	20,470
		Candle makers and sellers	1	...	...	1	...	...	...	...	1	...	...	1
		Torch makers and sellers	15	...	2	13	9	...	1	8	6	...	1	5
		Match makers and sellers	2	...	...	2	2	...	...	2	...	...	...	...
		Total 20	74,879	10,622	19,348	45,509	41,617	5,383	11,201	25,033	33,262	4,639	8,147	20,476
		21.—Fuel and Forage.												
		Firewood and grass gatherers and sellers	16,529	1,871	4,201	10,457	14,370	1,551	3,670	9,149	2,159	320	531	1,308
		Coal dealers	525	90	156	279	256	33	78	145	269	57	78	134
		Cowdung fuel preparers and sellers	493	66	121	306	220	35	64	121	273	31	57	185
		Hay contractors, etc.	3	1	...	2	...	...	...	...	3	1	...	2
		Total 21	17,550	2,028	4,478	11,044	14,846	1,619	3,812	9,415	2,704	409	666	1,629
		Total VIII.—Light, Firing and Forage.	**92,429**	**12,050**	**28,826**	**56,585**	**56,463**	**7,002**	**16,018**	**34,448**	**35,966**	**5,048**	**8,813**	**22,105**

TABLE XVII.—Occupations by Age—Part A.—PROVINCIAL SUMMARY—*contd.*

OCCUPATION AND CLASS.			PROVINCIAL TOTAL.											
			TOTAL.				MALES.				FEMALES.			
Class.	Order.	SUB-ORDER, GROUP AND OCCUPATION.	TOTAL.	0—4	5—14	15 and over.	TOTAL.	0—4	5—14	15 and over.	TOTAL.	0—4	5—14	15 and over.
1	2	3	4	5	6	7	8	9	10	11	12	13	14	15
		22.—Building Materials.												
	IX.—BUILDINGS	Brick and tile makers and sellers	41,744	5,826	11,326	24,592	21,268	2,838	5,974	12,456	20,476	2,988	5,352	12,136
		Lime, chunam and shell burners and sellers	3,568	515	1,032	2,021	1,924	248	563	1,113	1,644	267	469	908
		Stone quarry owners, contractors, etc.	2,564	357	604	1,603	1,245	153	298	794	1,319	204	306	809
		Total 22	47,876	6,698	12,962	28,216	24,437	3,239	6,835	14,363	23,439	3,459	6,127	13,853
		23.—Artificers in Building.												
		Building contractors	213	17	32	164	213	17	32	164	...	...	...	...
		Stone and marble workers	9,022	1,084	2,057	5,881	5,271	577	1,247	3,447	3,751	507	810	2,434
		Masons	16,035	2,090	3,741	10,204	8,825	1,094	2,112	5,619	7,210	996	1,629	4,585
		Mud wall builders	1,807	278	409	1,120	717	87	171	459	1,090	191	238	661
		Total 23	27,077	3,469	6,239	17,369	15,026	1,775	3,562	9,689	12,051	1,694	2,677	7,680
		Total IX.—Buildings	**74,953**	**10,167**	**19,201**	**45,585**	**39,463**	**5,014**	**10,897**	**24,052**	**35,490**	**5,158**	**8,804**	**21,533**
		24.—Railway Plant.												
	X.—VEHICLES	Fitters	149	23	27	99	101	16	19	66	48	7	8	33
		Painters	17	...	...	17	17	...	...	17	...	...	...	...
		Plate-layers	4	...	...	4	3	...	...	3	1	...	...	1
		Inspectors	83	13	15	55	51	7	8	36	32	6	7	19
		Lorrymen	162	12	17	133	93	3	4	86	69	9	13	47
		Trollymen	86	4	11	71	74	2	7	65	12	2	4	6
		Total 24	501	52	70	379	33	28	38	273	162	24	32	106
		25.—Carts, Carriages, etc.												
		Carriage makers and sellers	8	...	3	5	8	...	3	5	...	...	...	...
		Total 25	8	...		5	8	...	3	5	...	...	...	...
		Total X.—Vehicles	**509**	**52**	**73**	**384**	**347**	**28**	**41**	**278**	**162**	**24**	**32**	**106**

OCCUPATION AND CLASS.			TOWN.											
			TOTAL.				MALES.				FEMALES.			
Class.	Order.	Sub-order, Group and Occupation.	Total.	0—4	5—14	15 and over.	Total.	0—4	5—14	15 and over.	Total.	0—4	5—14	15 and over.
			16	17	18	19	20	21	22	23	24	25	26	27
		22.—Building Materials.												
	IX.—BUILDINGS	Brick and tile makers and sellers	4,826	591	1,159	3,076	2,546	289	640	1,617	2,280	302	519	1,459
		Lime, chunam and shell burners and sellers	411	56	106	249	151	24	42	85	260	32	64	164
		Stone quarry owners, contractors, etc.	657	80	131	446	72	7	22	43	585	73	109	403
		Total 22	5,894	727	1,396	3,771	2,769	320	704	1,745	3,125	407	692	2,026
		23.—Artificers in Building.												
		Building contractors	198	17	28	153	169	17	28	153	...	...	...	...
		Stone and marble workers	5,829	689	1,292	3,848	2,817	328	683	1,806	3,012	361	609	2,042
		Masons	5,240	668	1,122	3,450	2,925	365	630	1,930	2,315	303	492	1,520
		Mudwall builders	382	56	67	259	76	10	13	53	306	46	54	206
		Total 23	11,649	1,430	2,509	7,710	6,016	720	1,354	3,942	5,633	710	1,155	3,768
		Total IX.—Buildings	17,543	2,15	3,905	11,481	6,785	1,040	2,058	5,687	8,758	1,117	1,847	5,794
		24.—Railway Plant.												
	X.—VEHICLES	Fitters	127	19	22	86	101	16	19	66	26	3	3	20
		Painters	17	...	...	17	17	...	...	17	...	...	...	...
		Plate-layers	3	...	...	3	3	...	...	3	...	...	...	...
		Inspectors	47	4	6	37	40	3	4	33	7	1	2	4
		Lorrymen	162	12	17	133	93	3	4	36	69	9	13	47
		Trollymen	86	4	11	71	74	2	7	65	12	2	4	6
		Total 24	442	39	56	347	328	24	34	270	114	15	22	77
		25.—Carts, Carriages, etc.												
		Carriage makers and sellers	...	...	...	...	...	...	...	...	...	...	...	...
		Total 25	...	...	...	...	...	...	...	...	...	...	...	...
		Total X.—Vehicles	442	39	56	347	328	24	34	270	114	15	22	77

TABLE XVII.—Occupations, by Age.—Part A.—PROVINCIAL SUMMARY—*contd.*

Class.	Order.	Sub-order, Group and Occupation.	Country. Total. Total.	Total. 0—4	Total. 5—14	Total. 15 and over.	Males. Total.	Males. 0—4	Males. 5—14	Males. 15 and over.	Females. Total.	Females. 0—4	Females. 5—14	Females. 15 and over.
			28	29	30	31	32	33	34	35	36	37	38	39
		22.—Building Materials.												
	IX.—Buildings	Brick and tile makers and sellers	36,918	5,235	10,167	21,516	18,722	2,549	5,334	10,839	18,196	2,686	4,833	10,677
		Lime, chunam and shell burners and sellers	3,157	459	926	1,772	1,773	224	521	1,028	1,384	235	405	744
		Stone quarry owners, etc.	1,507	277	473	1,157	1,173	146	276	751	734	131	197	406
		Total 22	41,982	5,971	11,566	24,445	21,668	2,919	6,131	12,618	20,314	3,052	5,435	11,827
		23.—Artificers in Building.												
		Building contractors	15	...	4	11	15	...	4	11	...	...	...	...
		Stone and marble workers	3,193	395	765	2,033	2,454	249	564	1,641	739	146	201	392
		Masons	10,795	1,422	2,619	6,754	5,900	729	1,482	3,689	4,895	693	1,137	3,065
		Mud wall builders	1,425	222	342	861	641	77	158	406	784	145	184	455
		Total 23	15,428	2,039	3,730	9,659	9,010	1,055	2,208	5,747	6,418	984	1,522	3,912
		Total IX.—Buildings	**57,410**	**8,010**	**15,296**	**34,104**	**30,678**	**3,974**	**8,339**	**18,365**	**26,782**	**4,036**	**6,957**	**15,739**
		24.—Railway Plant.												
	X.—Vehicles	Fitters	22	4	5	13	...	...	...	...	22	4	5	13
		Painters	...	...	...	...	...	...	...	...	...	...	...	...
		Plate-layers	1	...	...	1	...	...	...	...	1	...	...	1
		Inspectors	36	9	9	18	11	4	4	3	25	5	5	15
		Lorrymen	...	...	...	...	...	...	...	...	...	...	...	...
		Trollymen	...	...	...	...	...	...	...	...	...	...	...	...
		Total 24	59	13	14	32	11	4	4	3	48	9	10	29
		25.—Carts, Carriages, etc.												
		Carriage makers and sellers	8	...	3	5	8	...	3	5	...	...	...	...
		Total 25	8	...	3	5	8	...	3	5	...	...	...	...
		Total X.—Vehicles	**67**	**13**	**17**	**37**	**19**	**4**	**7**	**8**	**48**	**9**	**10**	**29**

CLASS D.—PREPARATION AND SUPPLY OF MATERIAL SUBSTANCES—*contd.*

Class.	Order.	Sub-order, Group, and Occupation.	Provincial Total. Total. Total.	Total. 0—4	Total. 5—14	Total. 15 and over.	Males. Total.	Males. 0—4	Males. 5—14	Males. 15 and over.	Females. Total.	Females. 0—4	Females. 5—14	Females. 15 and over.
1	2	3	4	5	6	7	8	9	10	11	12	13	14	15
		27.—Paper, etc.												
		Paper makers and sellers	953	83	173	697	479	22	74	383	474	61	99	314
		Stationers	970	122	213	635	564	73	125	366	406	49	88	269
		Total 27	1,923	205	386	1,332	1,043	95	199	749	880	110	187	588
		28.—Books and Prints, etc.												
		Printers	30	3	3	24	20	1	1	18	10	2	2	6
		Book-binders	71	10	22	39	43	7	11	25	28	3	11	14
		Book-sellers	77	4	15	58	44	2	9	33	33	2	6	25
		Total 28	178	17	40	121	107	10	21	76	71	7	19	45
		29.—Watches, Clocks and Scientific Instruments.												
		Watch and clock repairers and sellers	186	32	31	123	124	26	16	82	62	6	15	41
		Total 29	186	32	31	123	124	26	16	82	62	6	15	41
		30.—Carving, Engraving, etc.												
		Turners	572	62	136	374	366	33	90	243	206	29	46	131
		Die-sinkers	15	3	4	8	11	2	4	5	4	1	...	3
		Total 30	587	65	140	382	377	35	94	248	210	30	46	134
		31.—Toys, Curiosities, etc.												
	XI.—Supplementary Requirements.	Toy makers and sellers	557	76	159	322	315	43	98	174	242	33	61	148
		Kite makers and sellers	19	2	6	11	9	1	3	5	10	1	3	6
		Hukka stem makers and sellers	454	54	107	293	283	32	70	181	171	22	37	112
		Tabut and tazia makers and sellers	23	2	6	15	9	1	3	5	14	1	3	10
		Curiosity dealers	60	7	10	43	27	3	3	21	33	4	7	22
		Total 31	1,113	141	288	684	643	80	177	386	470	61	111	298
		32.—Music and Musical Instruments.												
		Music and musical instrument dealers	66	10	18	38	39	5	13	21	27	5	5	17
		Drum makers	92	14	21	57	39	7	9	23	53	7	12	34
		Total 32	158	24	39	95	78	12	22	44	80	12	17	51

TABLE XVII.—Occupations, by Age.—Part A.—PROVINCIAL SUMMARY—*contd.*

OCCUPATION AND CLASS.			TOWN.											
			TOTAL.				MALES.				FEMALES.			
Class.	Order.	Sub-order, Group and Occupation.	Total.	0—4	5—14	15 and over.	Total.	0—4	5—14	15 and over.	Total.	0—4	5—14	15 and over.
			16	17	18	19	20	21	22	23	24	25	26	27
		27.—Paper, etc.												
	XI.—Supplementary Requirements.	Paper makers and sellers	339	29	72	238	150	13	45	132	149	16	27	106
		Stationers	462	55	99	308	293	30	61	202	169	25	38	106
		Total 27	801	84	171	546	483	43	106	334	318	41	65	212
		28.—Books and Prints, etc.												
		Printers	23	2	3	18	14	1	1	12	9	1	2	6
		Book-binders	54	7	19	28	31	5	10	16	23	2	9	12
		Book-sellers	54	4	6	44	32	2	2	28	22	2	4	16
		Total 28	131	13	28	90	77	8	13	56	54	5	15	34
		29.—Watches, Clocks and Scientific Instruments.												
		Watch and clock repairers and sellers	150	29	25	96	102	23	13	66	48	6	12	30
		Total 29	150	29	25	96	102	23	13	66	48	6	12	30
		30.—Carving, Engraving, etc.												
		Turners	169	15	30	124	90	6	13	71	79	9	17	53
		Die sinkers	...	...	...	...	...	...	...	...	...	...	...	...
		Total 30	169	15	30	124	90	6	13	71	79	9	17	53
		31.—Toys, Curiosities, etc.												
		Toy makers and sellers	110	15	25	70	38	9	6	23	72	6	19	47
		Kite makers and sellers	...	...	...	...	...	...	...	...	...	...	...	...
		Hukka stem makers and sellers	290	23	55	212	203	20	42	141	87	3	13	71
		Tabut and tazia makers and sellers	7	1	1	5	...	...	...	...	7	1	1	5
		Curiosity dealers	3	...	...	3	3	...	...	3	...	...	...	...
		Total 31	410	39	81	290	244	29	48	167	166	10	33	123
		32.—Music and Musical Instruments.												
		Music and musical instrument dealers	...	...	...	...	...	...	...	...	...	...	...	...
		Drum makers	61	8	15	38	38	7	9	22	23	1	6	16
		Total 32	61	8	15	38	38	7	9	22	23	1	6	16

Class.	Order.	Sub-order, Group and Occupation.	Total. Total.	Total. 0—4	Total. 5—14	Total. 15 and over.	Males. Total.	Males. 0—4	Males. 5—14	Males. 15 and over.	Females. Total.	Females. 0—4	Females. 5—14	Females. 15 and over.
			28	29	30	31	32	33	34	35	36	37	38	39
		27.—Paper, etc.												
	XI.—Supplementary Requirements.	Paper makers and sellers	614	54	101	459	289	9	29	251	325	45	72	208
		Stationers	508	67	114	327	271	43	64	164	237	24	50	163
		Total 27	1,122	121	215	786	560	52	93	415	562	69	122	371
		28.—Books and Prints, etc.												
		Printers	7	1	...	6	6	...	...	6	1	1	...	...
		Book-binders	17	3	3	11	12	2	1	9	5	1	2	2
		Book-sellers	23	...	9	14	12	...	7	5	11	...	2	9
		Total 28	47	4	12	31	30	2	8	20	17	2	4	11
		29.—Watches, Clocks, and Scientific Instruments.												
		Watch makers and sellers	36	3	6	27	22	3	3	16	14	...	3	11
		Total 29	36	3	6	27	22	3	3	16	14	...	3	11
		30.—Carving, Engraving, etc.												
		Turners	403	47	106	250	276	27	77	172	127	20	29	78
		Die sinkers	15	3	4	8	11	2	4	5	4	1	...	3
		Total 30	418	50	110	258	287	29	81	177	131	21	29	81
		31.—Toys, Curiosities, etc.												
		Toy makers and sellers	447	61	134	252	277	34	92	151	170	27	42	101
		Kite makers and sellers	19	2	6	11	9	1	3	5	10	1	3	6
		Hukka stem makers and sellers	164	31	52	81	80	12	28	40	84	19	24	41
		Tabut and tazia makers and sellers	16	1	5	10	9	1	3	5	7	...	2	5
		Curiosity dealers	57	7	10	40	24	3	3	18	33	4	7	22
		Total 31	703	102	207	394	399	51	129	219	304	51	78	175
		32.—Music and Musical Instruments.												
		Music and musical instrument dealers	66	10	18	38	39	5	13	21	27	5	5	17
		Drum makers	31	6	6	19	1	...	...	1	30	6	6	18
		Total 32	97	16	24	57	40	5	13	22	57	11	11	35

TABLE XVII.—Occupations, by Age.—Part A.—PROVINCIAL SUMMARY—*contd.*

CLASS D.—PREPARATION AND SUPPLY OF MATERIAL SUBSTANCES—*contd.*

OCCUPATION AND CLASS.			PROVINCIAL TOTAL.											
			TOTAL.				MALES.				FEMALES.			
Class.	Order.	Sub-order, Group and Occupation.	Total.	0–4	5–15	15 and over.	Total.	0–4	5–14	15 and over.	Total.	0–4	5–14	15 and over.
1	2	3	4	5	6	7	8	9	10	11	12	13	14	15
	XI.—SUPPLEMENTARY REQUIREMENTS—*concld.*	**33.—Necklaces, Bracelets, Beads, Sacred Threads, etc.**												
		Bangle makers and sellers	16,889	2,021	4,079	10,789	8,693	974	2,254	5,465	8,196	1,047	1,825	5,324
		Imitation jewellery makers and sellers	1,662	194	414	1,054	841	93	221	527	821	101	893	527
		Necklace makers and sellers	34	4	8	22	18	4	4	10	16	...	4	12
		Flower garland makers and sellers	1,313	147	335	831	793	92	215	486	520	55	120	345
		Sacred thread makers and sellers	12	2	1	9	7	1	1	5	5	1	...	4
		Total 33	19,910	2,368	4,837	12,705	10,352	1,164	2,695	6,493	9,558	1,204	2,142	6,212
		34.—Furniture.												
		Bed-stead makers	18	3	2	13	12	2	2	8	6	1	...	5
		Furniture makers	13	3	4	6	7	2	3	2	6	1	1	4
		Looking-glass makers and sellers	19	2	6	11	14	2	4	8	5	...	2	3
		Total 34	50	8	12	30	33	6	9	18	17	2	3	12
		35.—Harness.												
		Saddlery makers and sellers	1,580	197	349	1,034	769	79	209	481	811	118	140	553
		Total 35	1,580	197	349	1,034	769		209	481	811	118	140	553
		36.—Tools and Machinery.												
		Knife grinders	3,135	371	733	2,031	1,748	187	444	1,117	1,387	184	289	914
		Tool grinders	128	10	32	86	75	3	20	52	53	7	12	34
		Mechanics	72	13	13	46	44	9	7	28	28	4	6	18
		Artisans, unspecified	2,167	279	497	1,391	1,126	139	254	733	1,041	140	243	658
		Total 36	5,502	673	1,275	3,554	2,993	338	725	1,930	2,509	335	550	1,624
		37.—Arms and Ammunition.												
		Gun menders and sellers	124	31	22	71	65	20	10	35	59	11	12	36
		Gunpowder makers and sellers	1,411	174	353	884	759	97	203	459	652	77	150	425
		Fire-work makers and sellers	1,154	121	303	730	623	60	182	381	531	61	121	349
		Sword makers and sellers	73	13	19	41	33	7	6	20	40	6	13	21
		Scabbard makers and sellers	263	24	56	183	147	17	26	104	116	7	30	79
		Bow and arrow makers and sellers	52	7	18	27	18	1	10	7	34	6	8	20
		Total 37	3,077	370	771	1,936	1,645	202	437	1,006	1,432	168	334	930
		Total XI.—Supplementary Requirements	84,264	4,100	8,168	21,996	18,164	2,047	4,604	11,518	16,100	2,05	8,564	10,483

OCCUPATION AND CLASS.			TOWN.											
			TOTAL.				MALES.				FEMALES.			
Class.	Order.	Sub-order, Group and Occupation.	Total.	0—4	5—14	15 and over.	Total.	0—4	5—14	15 and over.	Total.	0—4	5—14	15 and over.
			16	17	18	19	20	21	22	23	24	25	26	27
		33.—Necklaces, Bracelets, Beads, Sacred Threads, etc.												
	XI.—SUPPLEMENTARY REQUIREMENTS—concld.	Bangle makers and sellers	3,928	486	835	2,607	1,962	260	422	1,280	1,966	226	413	1,327
		Imitation jewellery makers and sellers	105	11	19	75	37	4	7	26	68	7	12	49
		Necklace makers and sellers	9	...	3	6	...	...	...	...	9	...	3	6
		Flower garland makers and sellers	371	35	70	266	189	21	41	127	182	14	29	139
		Sacred thread makers and sellers	9	1	1	7	4	...	1	3	5	1	...	4
		Total 33	4,422	533	928	2,961	2,192	285	471	1,436	2,230	248	457	1,525
		34.—Furniture.												
		Bed-stead makers	4	...	1	3	4	...	1	3	...	...	...	...
		Furniture makers	...	...	...	...	...	...	...	...	...	...	...	...
		Looking-glass makers and sellers	14	2	4	8	14	2	4	8	...	...	...	...
		Total 34	18	2	5	11	18	2	5	11	...	...	...	...
		35.—Harness.												
		Saddlery makers and sellers	734	71	152	511	422	41	94	287	312	30	58	224
		Total 35	734	71	152	511	422	41	94	287	312	30	58	224
		36.—Tools and Machinery.												
		Knife grinders	1,334	132	534	668	841	65	433	343	493	67	101	325
		Tool grinders	...	...	...	...	...	...	...	...	...	...	...	...
		Mechanics	...	...	...	...	...	...	...	...	...	...	...	...
		Artisans, unspecified	418	57	86	275	230	28	43	59	188	29	43	116
		Total 36	1,752	189	620	943	1,071	93	476	502	681	96	144	441
		37.—Arms and Ammunition.												
		Gun menders and sellers	41	3	3	35	23	1	2	20	18	2	1	15
		Gunpowder makers and sellers	120	7	29	84	47	3	11	33	73	4	18	51
		Fire-work makers and sellers	622	75	153	394	324	46	90	188	298	29	63	206
		Sword makers and sellers	...	...	...	...	...	...	...	...	...	...	...	...
		Scabbard makers and sellers	145	16	28	101	74	11	12	51	71	5	16	50
		Bow and arrow makers and sellers	17	1	11	5	13	1	9	3	4	...	2	2
		Total 37	945	102	224	619	481	62	124	295	464	40	100	324
		Total XI.—Supplementary Requirements	9,593	1,085	2,279	6,229	5,218	599	1,872	3,247	375	486	907	2,982

TABLE XVII.—Occupations by Age.—Part A.—PROVINCIAL SUMMARY—*contd.*

OCCUPATION AND CLASS.			COUNTRY.											
Class.	Order.	Sub-order, Group and Occupation.	Total.				Males.				Females.			
			Total.	0—4	5—14	15 and over.	Total.	0—4	5—14	15 and over.	Total.	0—4	5—14	15 and over.
			28	29	30	31	32	33	34	35	36	37	38	39
CLASS D.—PREPARATION AND SUPPLY OF MATERIAL SUBSTANCES—*contd.*	XI.—Supplementary Requirements—*concld.*	**33.—Necklaces, Bracelets, Beads, Sacred Threads, etc.**												
		Bangle makers and sellers	12,961	1,535	3,244	8,182	6,731	714	1,832	4,185	6,230	821	1,412	3,997
		Imitation jewellery makers and sellers	1,557	183	395	979	804	89	214	501	753	94	181	478
		Necklace makers and sellers	25	4	5	16	18	4	4	10	7	...	1	6
		Flower garland makers and sellers	942	112	265	565	604	71	174	359	338	41	91	206
		Sacred thread makers and sellers	3	1	...	2	3	1	...	2	...	...	...	...
		Total 33	15,488	1,835	3,909	9,744	8,160	879	2,224	5,057	7,328	956	1,685	4,687
		34.—Furniture.												
		Bed-stead makers	14	3	1	10	8	2	1	5	6	1	...	5
		Furniture makers	13	3	2	6	7	2	3	2	6	1	1	4
		Looking-glass makers and sellers	5	...	2	3	...	...	...	...	5	...	2	3
		Total 34	32	6	7	19	15	4	4	7	17	2	3	12
		35.—Harness.												
		Saddlery makers and sellers	846	126	197	523	347	38	115	194	499	88	82	329
		Total 35	846	126	197	523	347	38	115	194	499	88	82	329
		36.—Tools and Machinery.												
		Knife grinders	1,801	239	199	1,363	907	122	11	774	894	117	188	589
		Tool grinders	128	10	32	86	75	3	20	52	53	7	12	34
		Mechanics	72	13	13	46	44	9	7	28	28	4	6	18
		Artisans, unspecified	1,749	222	411	1,116	896	111	211	574	853	111	200	542
		Total 36	3,750	484	655	2,611	1,922	245	249	1,428	1,828	239	406	1,183
		37.—Arms and Ammunition.												
		Gun menders and sellers	83	28	19	36	42	19	8	15	41	9	11	21
		Gun-powder makers and sellers	1,291	167	324	800	712	94	192	426	579	73	132	374
		Fire-work makers and sellers	532	46	150	336	299	14	92	193	233	32	58	143
		Sword makers and sellers	73	13	19	41	33	7	6	20	40	6	13	21
		Scabbard makers and sellers	118	8	28	82	73	6	14	53	45	2	14	29
		Bow and arrow makers and sellers	35	6	7	22	5	...	1	4	30	6	6	18
		Total 37	2,132	268	547	1,317	1,164	140	313	711	968	128	234	606

CLASS D.—PREPARATION AND SUPPLY OF MATERIAL SUBSTANCES—*contd.*

Class.	Order.	Sub-order, Group and Occupation.	Total.				Provincial Total. Males.				Females.			
			Total.	0–4	5–14	15 and over.	Total.	0–4	5–14	15 and over.	Total.	0–4	5–14	15 and over.
1	2	3	4	5	6	7	8	9	10	11	12	13	14	15
	XII.—Textile Fabrics and Dress.	**38.—Wool and Fur.**												
		Shawl weavers and sellers	46	3	6	37	31	1	4	26	15	2	2	11
		Felt workers and sellers	133	13	37	83	71	8	22	41	62	5	15	42
		Blanket weavers and sellers	6,322	839	1,748	3,735	3,596	442	1,022	2,131	2,726	397	725	1,604
		Woollen cloth manufacturers and sellers	124	18	28	78	51	8	14	29	73	10	14	49
		Fur dealers	21	5	3	13	9	2	...	7	12	3	3	6
		Total 38	6,646	878	1,822	3,946	3,758	461	1,063	2,234	2,888	417	759	1,712
		39.—Silk.												
		Silk weavers	3,513	399	722	2,392	1,962	204	394	1,364	1,551	195	328	1,028
		Braid makers and sellers	757	87	175	495	385	45	87	253	372	42	88	242
		Total 39	4,270	486	897	2,887	2,347	249	481	1,617	1,923	237	416	1, 270
		40.—Cotton.												
		Cotton cleaners	45,970	6,194	11,451	28,334	23,983	3,119	6,133	14,731	21,996	3,075	5,318	13,603
		Cotton pressers	1,290	165	301	824	216	14	51	151	1,074	151	250	673
		Cotton carpet makers and sellers	236	30	68	138	230	29	68	133	6	1	...	5
		Cotton spinners	5,310	462	872	3,976	935	162	260	513	4,375	300	612	3,463
		Yarn beaters	17	4	5	8	5	...	1	4	12	4	4	4
		Cotton weavers	152,032	21,440	37,897	93,595	80,425	10,700	20,352	49,373	72,507	10,740	17,545	44,222
		Calenderers	1,690	194	470	1,026	897	96	211	590	793	98	259	436
		Cotton dyers	26,892	3,303	6,235	17,354	13,767	1,626	3,320	8,821	13,125	1,677	2,915	8,533
		Tape makers and sellers	9	1	3	5	3	...	1	2	6	1	2	3
		Total 40	234,355	31,793	57,302	145,260	120,461	15,746	30,397	74,318	113,894	16,047	26,905	70,942
		41.—Jute, Flax, Coir, etc.												
		Hemp rope makers and sellers	514	63	128	323	273	25	66	182	241	38	62	141
		Jute manufacturers	145	21	45	79	76	9	20	47	69	12	25	32
		Sacking and gunny makers and sellers	107	19	24	64	98	17	21	60	9	2	3	4
		Net makers and sellers	5	1	2	2	2	...	1	1	3	1	1	1
		Coir preparers and sellers	681	112	148	421	398	58	91	249	283	54	57	172
		Total 41	1,452	216	347	889	847	109	199	539	605	107	148	350

TABLE XVII.—Occupations, by Age.—Part A.—PROVINCIAL SUMMARY—*contd.*

OCCUPATION AND CLASS.			TOWN.											
			Total.				Males.				Females.			
Class.	Order.	Sub-order, Group and Occupation.	Total.	0–4	5–14	15 and over.	Total.	0–4	5–14	15 and over.	Total.	0–4	5–14	15 and over.
			16	17	18	19	20	21	22	23	24	25	26	27
		38.—Wool and Fur.												
	XII.—Textile Fabrics and Dress.	Shawl weavers and sellers	14	...	3	11	11	...	3	8	3	...	...	3
		Felt workers and sellers	74	8	22	44	36	5	13	18	38	3	9	26
		Blanket weavers and sellers	688	79	157	452	295	30	69	196	393	49	88	256
		Woollen cloth manufacturers and sellers	25	2	7	16	23	2	6	15	2	...	1	1
		Fur dealers	...	...	...	...	...	...	...	...	...	...	...	...
		Total 38	801	89	189	523	365	37	91	237	436	52	98	286
		39.—Silk.												
		Silk weavers	2,395	261	446	1,688	1,342	134	238	970	1,053	127	208	718
		Braid makers and sellers	493	47	112	33	271	28	66	177	222	19	46	157
		Total 39	2,888	308	558	2,022	1,613	162	304	1,147	1,275	146	254	875
		40.—Cotton.												
		Cotton cleaners	4,095	498	916	2,681	2,269	281	531	1,457	1,826	217	385	1,224
		Cotton pressers	125	16	27	82	6	...	1	5	119	16	26	77
		Cotton carpet makers and sellers	24	2	10	12	20	2	10	8	4	...	...	4
		Cotton spinners	1,392	154	298	940	456	70	106	280	936	84	192	660
		Yarn beaters	2	...	1	1	2	...	1	1	...	...	...	...
		Cotton weavers	21,051	2,532	4,790	13,729	9,183	1,017	2,102	6,064	11,868	1,515	2,688	7,665
		Calenderers	675	76	144	455	421	51	92	278	254	25	52	177
		Cotton dyers	9,324	1,093	1,960	6,271	5,184	590	1,109	3,485	4,140	503	851	2,786
		Tape makers and sellers	9	1	3	5	3	...	1	2	6	1	2	3
		Total 40	36,697	4,373	8,148	24,176	17,544	2,011	3,953	11,580	19,153	2,361	4,196	12,596
		41.—Jute, Flax, Coir, etc.												
		Hemp rope makers and sellers	135	18	48	69	35	8	13	14	100	10	35	55
		Jute manufacturers	43	4	12	27	34	2	9	23	9	2	3	4
		Sacking and gunny makers and sellers	...	...	...	...	...	...	...	...	...	...	...	...
		Net makers and sellers	...	...	...	...	...	...	...	...	...	...	...	...
		Coir preparers and sellers	234	12	40	182	188	7	27	154	46	5	13	28
		Total 41	412	34	100	278	257	17	49	191	155	17	51	[illegible]

CLASS D.—PREPARATION AND SUPPLY OF MATERIAL SUBSTANCES—*contd.*

Class.	Order.	Sub-order, Group, and Class.	Country. Total. Total.	Total. 0–4	Total. 5–14	Total. 15 and over.	Males. Total	Males. 0–4	Males. 5–14	Males. 15 and over.	Females. Total.	Females. 0–4	Females. 5–14	Females. 15 and ovr.
			28	29	30	31	32	33	34	35	36	37	38	39
		38.—Wool and Fur.												
	XII.—Textile Fabrics and Dress.	Shawl weavers and sellers	32	3	3	26	20	1	1	18	12	2	2	8
		Felt workers and sellers	59	5	15	39	35	3	9	23	24	2	6	16
		Blanket weavers and sellers	5,634	760	1,591	3,283	3,301	412	954	1,935	2,333	348	637	1,348
		Woollen cloth manufacturers and sellers	99	16	21	62	28	6	8	14	71	10	13	48
		Fur dealers	21	5	3	13	9	2	...	7	12	3	3	6
		Total 38	5,845	789	1,633	3,423	3,303	424	972	1,997	2,452	365	661	1,426
		39.—Silk.												
		Silk weavers	1,118	138	276	704	620	70	156	394	498	68	120	310
		Braid makers and sellers	264	40	63	161	114	17	21	76	150	23	42	85
		Total 39	1,382	178	339	865	734	87	177	470	648	91	162	395
		40.—Cotton.												
		Cotton cleaners	41,884	5,696	10,535	25,653	21,714	2,838	5,602	13,274	20,170	2,858	4,933	12,379
		Cotton pressers	1,165	149	274	742	210	14	50	146	955	135	224	596
		Cotton carpet makers and sellers	212	28	58	126	210	27	58	125	2	1	...	1
		Cotton spinners	3,918	308	574	3,036	479	92	154	233	3,439	216	420	2,803
		Yarn beaters	15	3	5	7	3	...	...	3	12	4	4	4
		Cotton weavers	131,881	18,908	33,107	79,866	71,242	9,683	18,250	43,309	60,639	9,225	14,857	36,557
		Calenderers	1,015	118	326	571	476	45	119	312	539	73	207	259
		Cotton dyers	17,568	2,210	4,275	11,033	8,583	1,036	2,211	5,336	8,985	1,174	2,064	5,747
		Tape makers and sellers	...	...	...	...	...	...	...	...	...	...	...	...
		Total 40	197,658	27,420	49,154	121,084	102,917	13,735	26,444	62,698	94,741	13,686	22,709	58,346
		41.—Jute, Flax, Coir, etc.												
		Hemp rope makers and sellers	379	45	80	254	238	17	53	168	141	28	27	86
		Jute manufacturers	102	17	33	52	42	7	11	24	60	10	32	28
		Sacking and gunny makers and sellers	107	19	24	64	98	17	21	60	9	2	3	4
		Net makers and sellers	5	1	2	2	2	...	1	1	3	1	1	1
		Coir preparers and sellers	447	100	108	239	210	51	64	95	237	49	44	144
		Total 41	1,040	182	247	611	590	92	150	348	450	90	97	263

TABLE XVII.—Occupations, by Age.—Part A.—PROVINCIAL SUMMARY—*contd.*

Class.	Order.	Sub-order, Group and Occupation.	Provincial Total. Total. Total.	Total. 0–4	Total. 5–14	Total. 15 and over.	Males. Total.	Males. 0–4	Males. 5–14	Males. 15 and over.	Females. Total.	Females. 0–4	Females. 5–14	Females. 15 and over.
1	2	3	4	5	6	7	8	9	10	11	12	13	14	15
CLASS D.—PREPARATION AND SUPPLY OF MATERIAL SUBSTANCES—*contd.*		**42.—Dress.**												
	XII.—Textile Fabrics and Dress—*contd.*	Tailors	56,319	6,961	12,846	36,512	29,954	3,452	7,039	19,463	26,365	3,509	5,807	17,049
		Darners	112	9	26	77	61	5	15	41	51	4	11	36
		Haberdashers	4,677	528	1,147	3,002	2,581	270	663	1,648	2,096	258	484	1,354
		Hat and cap makers and sellers	3	...	1	2	2	...	1	1	1	...	...	1
		Turban binders	50	5	11	34	30	2	4	24	20	3	7	10
		Umbrella makers and sellers	17	2	5	10	4	1	1	2	13	1	4	8
		Embroiderers	35	2	7	26	5	...	2	3	30	2	5	23
		Lace makers and sellers	3	...	...	3	2	...	...	2	1	...	...	1
		Fringe makers and sellers	1,591	181	384	1,026	488	54	141	293	1,103	127	243	733
		False plait makers and sellers	257	34	66	157	139	18	34	87	118	16	32	70
		Piece goods merchants	2,052	274	453	1,325	1,149	116	211	822	903	158	242	503
		Cloth merchants	11,675	1,262	2,460	7,953	6,240	617	1,271	4,352	5,435	645	1,189	3,601
		Total 42	76,791	9,258	17,406	50,127	40,655	4,535	9,382	26,738	36,136	4,723	8,024	23,389
		Total XII.—Textile Fabrics and Dress	**328,514**	**42,631**	**77,774**	**208,109**	**168,068**	**21,100**	**41,522**	**105,446**	**155,446**	**21,581**	**36,252**	**97,663**
		43.—Gold, Silver and Precious Stones.												
	XIII.—Metals and Precious Stones.	Gold and silver dealers	551	68	143	340	541	67	140	334	10	1	3	6
		Assayers	9	2	2	5	7	2	1	4	2	...	1	1
		Mint servants	76	6	12	58	33	...	4	29	43	6	8	29
		Gold and silver workers	52,372	6,189	11,884	34,299	27,631	2,968	6,421	18,242	24,741	3,221	5,463	16,057
		Jewellery makers	469	62	98	309	250	35	58	157	219	27	40	152
		Gold beaters	37	5	10	22	37	5	10	22	...	...	...	...
		Goldsmiths' dust washers	1,001	133	233	635	352	41	82	229	649	92	151	406
		Enamellers	14	1	2	11	7	...	1	6	7	1	1	5
		Electroplaters	31	1	3	27	24	...	2	22	7	1	1	5
		Gilders	19	1	6	12	10	...	2	8	9	1	4	4
		Diamond dealers	46	11	14	21	15	4	6	5	31	7	8	16
		Diamond diggers	272	34	70	168	139	10	38	91	133	24	32	77
		Pearl dealers	24	1	8	15	19	1	8	10	5	...	...	5
		Ring stone dealers	90	14	18	58	47	8	11	28	43	6	7	30
		Total 43	55,011	6,528	12,503	35,980	29,112	3,141	6,784	19,187	25,899	3,387	5,719	16,793

CLASS D.—PREPARATION AND SUPPLY OF MATERIAL SUBSTANCES—*contd.*

Class.	Order.	Sub-order, Group and Occupation.	Town. Total. Total.	Total. 0–4	Total. 5–14	Total. 15 and over.	Males. Total.	Males. 0–4	Males. 5–14	Males. 15 and over.	Females. Total.	Females. 0–4	Females. 5–14	Females. 15 and over.
			16	17	18	19	20	21	22	23	24	25	26	27
	XII.—Textile Fabrics and Dress—*contd.*	**42.—Dress.**												
		Tailors	11,647	1,222	2,210	8,215	6,546	660	1,260	4,626	5,101	562	950	3,589
		Darners	95	8	22	65	54	5	14	35	41	3	8	30
		Haberdashers	2,427	306	561	1,560	908	113	215	580	1,519	193	346	980
		Hat and cap makers and sellers	...	...	...	...	...	...	...	...	...	...	...	...
		Turban binders	46	5	9	32	29	2	3	24	17	3	6	8
		Umbrella makers and sellers	...	...	...	...	...	...	...	...	...	...	...	...
		Embroiderers	25	2	6	17	3	...	1	2	22	2	5	15
		Lace makers and sellers	...	...	...	...	...	...	...	...	...	...	...	...
		Fringe makers and sellers	163	12	36	115	80	6	15	59	83	6	21	56
		False plait makers and sellers	...	...	...	...	...	...	...	...	...	...	...	...
		Piece goods merchants	...	...	...	...	...	...	...	...	...	...	...	...
		Cloth merchants	5,486	560	1,104	3,822	3,114	310	595	2,209	2,372	250	509	1,613
		Total 42	19,889	2,115	3,948	13,826	1 0,734	1,096	2,103	7,535	9,155	1,019	1,845	6,291
		Total XII.—Textile Fabrics and Dress.	**60,687**	**6,918**	**12,944**	**40,825**	**30,518**	**3,323**	**6,500**	**20,690**	**30,174**	**3,595**	**6,444**	**20,185**
	XIII.—Metals and Precious Stones.	**43.—Gold, Silver, and Precious Stones.**												
		Gold and silver dealers	58	5	17	36	53	5	15	33	5	...	2	3
		Assayers	3	1	...	2	2	1	...	1	1	...	...	1
		Mint servants	48	...	10	38	32	...	4	28	16	...	6	10
		Gold and silver workers	12,518	1,340	2,483	8,695	6,649	677	1,308	4,664	5,869	663	1,175	4,031
		Jewellery makers	269	18	55	196	122	9	24	89	147	9	31	107
		Gold beaters	5	1	...	4	5	1	...	4	...	...	...	...
		Goldsmiths' dust washers	256	30	65	161	167	22	42	103	89	8	23	58
		Enamellers	14	1	2	11	7	...	1	6	7	1	1	5
		Electroplaters	31	1	3	27	24	...	2	22	7	1	1	5
		Gilders	2	...	...	2	1	...	...	1	1	...	...	1
		Diamond dealers	30	2	7	21	9	1	3	5	21	1	4	16
		Diamond diggers	53	3	17	33	53	3	17	33	...	...	...	...
		Pearl dealers	14	...	4	10	14	...	4	10	...	...	...	...
		Ring stone dealers	29	5	6	18	27	5	6	16	2	...	...	2
		Total 43	13,330	1,407	2,669	9,254	7,165	724	1,426	5,015	6,165	683	1,243	4,239

TABLE XVII.—Occupations, by Age.—Part A.—PROVINCIAL SUMMARY—*concld.*

Class.	Order.	Sub-order, Group, and Occupation.	Country: Total. Total.	Total. 0–5	Total. 5–14	Total. 15 and over.	Males. Total.	Males. 0–4	Males. 5–14	Males. 15 and over.	Females. Total.	Females. 0–4	Females. 5–14	Females. 15 and over.
			28	29	30	31	32	33	34	35	36	37	38	39
		42.—Dress.												
	XII.—Textile Fabrics and Dress—*contd.*	Tailors	44,672	5,739	10,636	28,297	23,408	2,792	5,779	14,837	21,264	2,947	4,857	13,460
		Darners	17	1	4	12	7	...	1	6	10	1	3	6
		Harberdashers	2,250	222	586	1,442	1,673	157	448	1,068	577	65	138	374
		Hat and cap makers and sellers	3	...	1	2	2	...	1	1	1	...	...	1
		Turban binders	4	...	2	2	1	...	1	...	3	...	1	2
		Umbrella makers and sellers	17	2	5	10	4	1	1	2	13	1	4	8
		Embroiderers	10	...	1	9	2	...	1	1	8	...	...	8
		Lace makers and sellers	3	...	...	3	2	...	...	2	1	...	...	1
		Fringe makers and sellers	1,428	169	348	911	408	48	126	234	1,020	121	222	677
		False plait makers and sellers	257	34	66	157	139	18	34	87	118	16	32	70
		Piece goods merchants	2,052	274	453	1,325	1,149	116	211	822	903	158	242	503
		Cloth merchants	6,189	702	1,356	4,131	3,126	307	676	2,143	3,063	395	680	1,988
		Total 42	56,902	7,143	13,458	36,301	29,921	3,439	7,279	19,203	26,981	3,704	6,179	17,098
		Total XII.—Textile Fabrics and Dress.	**262,827**	**85,718**	**64,880**	**162,284**	**187,555**	**17,777**	**85,022**	**84,756**	**125,272**	**17,986**	**29,808**	**77,528**
		43.—Gold, Silver and Precious Stones.												
	XIII.—Metals and Precious Stones.	Gold and silver dealers	493	63	126	304	488	62	125	301	5	1	1	3
		Assayers	6	1	2	3	5	1	1	3	1	...	1	...
		Mint servants	28	6	2	20	1	...	...	1	27	6	2	19
		Gold and silver workers	39,854	4,849	9,401	25,604	20,982	2,291	5,113	13,578	18,872	2,558	4,288	21,026
		Jewellery makers	200	44	43	113	128	26	34	68	72	18	9	45
		Gold beaters	32	4	10	18	32	4	10	18	...	...	...	...
		Goldsmiths' dust washers	745	103	168	474	185	19	40	126	560	84	128	348
		Enamellers	...	...	...	...	...	...	...	...	...	...	...	...
		Electroplaters	...	...	...	...	...	...	...	...	...	...	...	...
		Gilders	17	1	6	10	9	...	2	7	8	1	4	3
		Diamond dealers	16	9	7	...	6	3	3	...	10	6	4	...
		Diamond diggers	219	31	53	135	86	7	21	58	133	24	32	77
		Pearl dealers	10	1	4	5	5	1	4	...	5	...	...	5
		Ring stone dealers	61	9	13	40	20	3	5	12	41	6	7	28
		Total 43	41,681	5,121	9,834	26,726	21,947	2,417	5,358	14,172	19,734	2,704	4,476	12,554

OCCUPATION AND CLASS.			PROVINCIAL.											
			TOTAL.				MALES.				FEMALES.			
Class.	Order.	Sub-order, Group and Occupation.	Total.	0–4	5–14	15 and over.	Total.	0–4	5–14	15 and over.	Total.	0–4	5–14	15 and over.
1	2	3	4	5	6	7	8	9	10	11	12	13	14	15
		44.—Brass, Copper and Bell-metal.												
	XIII.—METALS AND PRECIOUS STONES—*contd.*	Brass pot makers and sellers	2,452	278	567	1,607	1,210	124	289	797	1,242	154	278	810
		Brass and copper wire drawers and sellers	19	4	2	13	5	1	...	4	14	3	2	9
		Bell-metal workers and sellers	1,496	160	345	991	765	73	193	499	731	87	152	492
		General workers in brass	3,558	454	820	2,284	1,943	234	458	1,251	1,615	220	362	1,033
		Total 44	7,525	896	1,734	4,895	3,923	432	940	2,551	3,602	464	794	2,344
		45.—Tin, Zinc, Mercury, and Lead.												
		284. Tin workers and sellers	705	97	158	450	374	44	76	254	331	53	82	196
		287. Lead workers and sellers	205	30	47	128	103	16	27	60	102	14	20	68
		288. General workers in tin, zinc, lead, etc.	602	65	143	394	307	35	63	209	295	30	80	185
		Total 45	1,512	192	348	972	784	95	166	523	728	97	182	449
		46.—Iron and Steel.												
		Blacksmiths	59,573	8,046	15,285	36,242	31,250	3,972	8,251	19,027	28,323	4,074	7,034	17,215
		Iron dealers	5,957	776	1,562	3,619	3,312	405	896	2,011	2,645	371	666	1,608
		Nail makers and sellers	136	16	25	95	69	6	15	48	67	10	10	47
		Total 46	65,666	8,838	16,872	39,956	34,631	4,383	9,162	21,086	31,035	4,455	7,710	18,870
		Total XIII.—Metals and Precious Stones.	**129,714**	**16,454**	**31,457**	**81,808**	**68,450**	**8,051**	**17,052**	**43,847**	**61,264**	**8,408**	**14,405**	**38,456**
		47.—Glass and Chinaware.												
	XIV.—GLASS, POTTERY, AND STONE WARE.	Bottle dealers	40	6	8	26	...	...	...	...	40	6	8	26
		Chinaware dealers	18	1	4	13	18	1	4	13	...	...	...	...
		Total 47	58	7	12	39	18	1	4	13	40	6	8	26
		48.—Earthen and Stoneware.												
		Potters	61,578	8,679	15,705	37,194	32,162	4,283	8,426	19,453	29,416	4,396	7,279	17,741
		Grindstone and millstone makers and sellers	1,260	138	258	864	436	53	123	260	824	85	135	604
		Soapstone powder preparers and sellers	30	7	8	15	30	7	8	15	...	...	...	...
		Total 48	62,868	8,824	15,971	38,073	32,628	4,343	8,557	19,728	30,240	4,481	7,414	18,345
		Total XIV.—Glass, Pottery, and Stoneware.	**62,926**	**8,831**	**15,983**	**38,112**	**32,646**	**4,344**	**8,561**	**19,741**	**30,280**	**4,487**	**7,422**	**18,871**

TABLE XVII.—Occupations, by Age.—Part A.—PROVINCIAL SUMMARY—*contd.*

Class.	Order.	Sub-order, Group and Occupation.	Town. Total. Total.	Total. 0–4	Total. 5–14	Total. 15 and over.	Males. Total.	Males. 0–4	Males. 5–14	Males. 15 and over.	Females. Total.	Females. 0–4	Females. 5–14	Females. 15 and over.
			16	17	18	19	20	21	22	23	24	25	26	27
CLASS D.—PREPARATION AND SUPPLY OF MATERIAL SUBSTANCES—*contd.*	XIII.—Metals and Precious Stones—*contd.*	**44.—Brass, Copper, and Bell-metal.**												
		Brass pot makers and sellers	1,688	209	382	1,097	913	112	209	592	775	97	173	505
		Brass and copper wire drawers and sellers	...	...	...	...	...	...	...	...	...	...	...	...
		Bell-metal workers and sellers	130	10	30	90	32	...	8	24	98	10	22	66
		General workers in brass	1,222	116	267	839	868	75	189	604	354	41	78	235
		Total 44	3,040	335	679	2,026	1,813	187	406	1,220	1,227	148	273	806
		45.—Tin, Zinc, Mercury, and Lead.												
		Tin workers and sellers	531	61	119	351	311	33	66	212	220	28	53	139
		Lead workers and sellers	65	7	18	40	36	3	11	22	29	4	7	18
		General workers in tin, zinc, lead, etc.	117	12	36	69	50	10	17	23	67	2	19	46
		Total 45	713	80	173	460	397	46	94	257	316	34	79	203
		46.—Iron and Steel.												
		Blacksmiths	5,381	606	1,168	3,607	2,958	329	646	1,983	2,423	277	522	1,624
		Iron-dealers	794	89	199	506	419	46	105	268	375	43	94	238
		Nail makers and sellers	109	13	19	77	53	4	12	37	56	9	7	40
		Total 46	6,284	708	1,386	4,190	3,430	379	763	2,288	2,854	329	623	1,902
		Total XIII.—Metal and Precious Stones.	**28,367**	**2,580**	**4,907**	**15,930**	**12,805**	**1,836**	**2,689**	**8,780**	**10,562**	**1,194**	**2,218**	**7,150**
	XIV.—Glass, Pottery, and Stoneware.	**47.—Glass and Chinaware.**												
		Bottle dealers	22	3	8	11	...	...	...	...	22	3	8	11
		Chinaware dealers	18	1	4	13	18	1	4	13	...	...	...	...
		Total 47	40	4	12	24	18	1	4	13	22	3	8	11
		48.—Earthen and Stoneware.												
		Potters	4,214	537	909	2,768	1,618	204	371	1,043	2,596	333	538	1,725
		Grindstone and millstone makers and sellers	504	33	91	380	75	3	36	36	429	30	55	344
		Soapstone powder preparers and sellers	12	1	5	6	12	1	5	6	...	...	...	...
		Total 48	4,730	571	1,005	3,154	1,705	208	412	1,085	3,025	363	593	2,069
		Total XIV.—Glass, Pottery, and Stoneware	**4,770**	**575**	**1,017**	**3,178**	**1,723**	**209**	**416**	**1,098**	**3,047**	**366**	**601**	**2,080**

Class.	Order.	Sub-order, Group and Occupation.	Country. Total. Total.	0—4	5—14	15 and over.	Males. Total.	0—4	5—14	15 and over.	Females. Total.	0—4	5—14	15 and over.
			28	29	30	31	32	33	34	35	36	37	38	39
		44.—Brass, Copper, and Bell-metal.												
	XIII.—Metals and Precious Stones—*contd.*	Brass pot makers and sellers	761	69	185	510	297	12	80	205	467	57	105	305
		Brass and copper wire drawers and sellers	19	4	2	13	5	1	...	4	14	3	2	9
		Bell-metal workers and sellers	1,366	150	315	901	733	73	185	475	633	77	130	426
		General workers in brass	2,336	338	553	1,445	1,075	159	269	647	1,261	179	284	798
		Total 44	4,485	561	1,055	2,869	2,110	245	534	1,331	2,375	316	521	1,538
		45.—Tin, Zinc, Mercury, and Lead.												
		Tin workers and sellers	174	36	39	99	63	11	10	42	111	25	29	57
		Lead workers and sellers	140	23	29	88	67	13	16	38	73	10	13	50
		General workers in tin, zinc, lead, etc.	485	53	107	325	257	25	46	186	228	28	61	139
		Total 45	799	112	175	512	387	49	72	266	412	63	103	246
		46.—Iron and Steel.												
		Blacksmiths	54,192	7,440	14,117	32,635	28,292	3,643	7,605	17,044	25,900	3,797	6,512	15,591
		Iron dealers	5,163	687	1,363	3,113	2,893	359	791	1,743	2,270	328	572	1,370
		Nail makers and sellers	27	3	6	18	16	2	3	11	11	1	3	7
		Total 46	59,382	8,130	15,486	35,766	31,201	4,004	8,399	18,798	28,181	4,126	7,087	16,968
		Total XIII.—Metal and Precious Stones.	**106,347**	**18,924**	**26,550**	**65,878**	**55,645**	**6,715**	**14,868**	**34,567**	**50,702**	**7,209**	**12,187**	**31,306**
		47.—Glass and Chinaware.												
	XIV.—Glass, Pottery, and Stone-wares.	Bottle dealers	18	3	...	15	...	...	...	...	18	3	...	15
		Chinaware dealers	...	...	...	...	...	...	...	...	...	...	...	...
		Total 47	18	3	...	15	...	...	...	...	18	3	...	15
		48.—Earthen and Stoneware.												
		Potters	57,364	8,142	14,796	34,426	30,544	4,079	8,055	18,410	26,820	4,063	6,741	16,016
		Grind stone and mill stone makers and sellers	756	105	167	484	361	50	87	224	395	55	80	260
		Soapstone powder preparers and sellers	18	6	3	9	18	6	3	9	...	...	...	...
		Total 48	58,138	8,253	14,966	34,919	30,923	4,135	8,145	18,643	27,215	4,118	6,821	16,276
		Total XIV.—Glass, Pottery, and Stoneware.	**58,156**	**8,256**	**14,966**	**34,934**	**30,928**	**4,135**	**8,145**	**18,643**	**27,233**	**4,121**	**6,821**	**16,291**

TABLE XVII.—Occupations, by Age.—Part A.—PROVINCIAL SUMMARY—*contd.*

OCCUPATION AND CLASS.			PROVINCIAL TOTAL.											
Class.	Order.	Sub-order, Group and Occupation.	Total.				Males.				Females.			
			Total.	0—4	5—14	15 and over.	Total.	0—4	5—14	15 and over.	Total.	0—4	5—14	15 and over.
1	2	3	4	5	6	7	8	9	10	11	12	13	14	15
CLASS D.—PREPARATION AND SUPPLY OF MATERIAL SUBSTANCES—*contd.*		**49.—Timber and Wood.**												
	XV.—Wood, Cane, and Leaves, etc.	Timber dealers	595	62	124	409	319	26	62	231	276	36	62	178
		Bamboo dealers	2,650	352	658	1,640	1,602	200	411	991	1,048	152	247	649
		Wood cutters	3,343	403	825	2,115	1,926	254	497	1,175	1,417	149	328	940
		Wood sawyers	73	7	13	53	46	4	9	33	27	3	4	20
		Carpenters	88,864	11,448	21,331	56,085	47,616	5,673	11,749	30,194	41,248	5,775	9,582	25,891
		Total 49	95,525	12,272	22,951	60,302	51,509	6,157	12,728	32,624	44,016	6,115	10,223	27,678
		50.—Canework, Matting and Leaves, etc.												
		Bamboo splitters, etc.	15,408	2,409	4,562	8,437	7,957	1,147	2,515	4,295	7,451	1,262	2,047	4,142
		Basket weavers	34,390	5,257	9,766	19,367	18,206	2,608	5,446	10,152	16,184	2,649	4,320	9,215
		Mat makers and sellers	2,886	399	719	1,768	1,218	164	292	762	1,668	235	427	1,006
		Screen makers and sellers	46	9	12	25	14	2	5	7	32	7	7	18
		Leaf plate makers and sellers	2,698	354	707	1,637	1,242	177	355	710	1,456	177	352	927
		Comb makers and sellers	812	83	212	517	375	32	99	244	437	51	113	273
		Broom makers and sellers	229	24	47	158	139	16	30	93	90	8	17	65
		Pith and bark collectors	266	44	61	161	125	22	40	63	141	22	21	98
		Total 50	56,735	8,579	16,086	32,070	29,276	4,168	8,782	16,326	27,459	4,411	7,304	15,744
		Total XV.—Wood, Cane and Leaves.	**152,260**	**20,851**	**39,087**	**92,372**	**80,785**	**10,325**	**21,510**	**48,950**	**71,475**	**10,526**	**17,527**	**48,422**
		51.—Gums, Wax and similar Forest Produce.												
	XVI.—Drugs, Gums, Dyes, etc.	Gum collectors	5,291	932	1,638	2,721	2,578	388	816	1,374	2,713	544	822	1,347
		Catechu preparers and sellers	2,903	472	867	1,564	1,613	236	490	887	1,290	236	377	677
		Lac collectors	200	29	48	123	200	29	48	123	...	...	...	...
		Sealing wax makers and sellers	1,632	211	402	1,019	649	86	157	406	983	125	245	613
		Honey collectors and sellers	22	2	8	12	15	1	6	8	7	1	2	4
		Total 51	10,048	1,646	2,963	5,439	5,055	740	1,517	2,798	4,993	906	1,446	2,641

Table XVII A.—Occupations—Central India.

CLASS D.—PREPARATION AND SUPPLY OF MATERIAL SUBSTANCES—contd.

Class.	Order.	Sub-order, Group and Occupation.	Town. Total. Total.	Total. 0–4	Total. 5–14	Total. 15 and over.	Males. Total.	Males. 0–4	Males. 5–14	Males. 15 and over.	Females. Total.	Females. 0–4	Females. 5–14	Females. 15 and over.
			16	17	18	19	20	21	22	23	24	25	26	27
		49.—Timber and Wood.												
	XV.—Wood, Cane, and Leaves, etc.	Timber dealers	255	21	55	179	225	19	51	155	30	2	4	24
		Bamboo dealers	396	41	64	291	155	10	14	131	241	31	50	160
		Wood cutters	125	14	28	83	114	13	26	75	11	1	2	8
		Wood sawyers	58	4	10	44	38	2	6	30	20	2	4	14
		Carpenters	9,087	985	1,845	6,257	5,335	538	1,110	3,687	3,752	447	735	2,570
		Total 49	9,921	1,065	2,002	6,854	5,867	582	1,207	4,078	4,054	483	795	2,776
		50.—Canework, Matting and Leaves, etc.												
		Bamboo splitters, etc.	162	22	40	100	76	10	21	45	86	12	19	55
		Basket weavers	3,271	453	792	2,026	1,879	262	484	1,133	1,392	191	308	893
		Mat makers and sellers	14	1	3	10	8	...	2	6	6	1	1	4
		Screen makers and sellers	22	4	4	14	12	2	3	7	10	2	1	7
		Leaf plate makers and sellers	435	52	79	304	192	20	40	132	243	32	39	172
		Comb makers and sellers	45	3	19	23	18	...	7	11	27	3	12	12
		Broom makers and sellers	125	10	28	87	53	5	13	35	72	5	15	52
		Pith and bark collectors	...	...	...	...	...	...	...	...	...	...	...	...
		Total 50	4,074	545	965	2,564	2,238	299	570	1,369	1,836	246	395	1,195
		Total XV.—Wood, Cane and Leaves	18,995	1,610	2,967	9,418	8,105	881	1,777	5,447	5,890	729	1,190	3,971
		51.—Gums, Wax and similar Forest Produce.												
	XVI.—Drugs, Gums, Dyes, etc.	Gum collectors	196	38	49	109	57	7	14	36	139	31	35	73
		Catechu preparers and sellers	...	...	...	...	...	...	...	...	...	...	...	...
		Lac collectors	...	...	...	...	...	...	...	...	...	...	...	...
		Sealing wax makers and sellers	2	...	1	1	2	...	1	1	...	...	...	...
		Honey collectors and sellers	2	...	...	2	2	...	...	2	...	...	...	...
		Total 51	200	38	50	112	61	7	15	39	139	31	35	73

TABLE XVII—Occupations, by Age.—Part A.—PROVINCIAL SUMMARY—*contd.*

CLASS D.—PREPARATION AND SUPPLY OF MATERIAL SUBSTANCES—*contd.*

Class.	Order.	Sub-order, Group and Occupation.	Country. Total. Total.	Total. 0—4	Total. 5—14	Total. 15 and over.	Males. Total.	Males. 0—4	Males. 5—14	Males. 15 and over.	Females. Total.	Females. 0—4	Females. 5—14	Females. 15 and over.
			28	29	30	31	32	33	34	35	36	37	38	39
		49.—Timber and Wood.												
	XV.—Wood, Cane, and Leaves, etc.	Timber dealers	340	41	69	230	94	7	11	76	246	34	58	154
		Bamboo dealers	2,254	311	514	1,349	1,447	190	397	860	807	121	197	489
		Wood cutters	3,218	389	797	2,032	1,812	241	471	1,100	1,406	148	326	932
		Wood sawyers	15	3	3	9	8	2	3	3	7	1	...	6
		Carpenters	79,777	10,463	19,486	49,828	42,281	5,135	10,639	26,507	37,496	5,328	8,847	23,321
		Total 49	85,604	11,207	20,949	53,448	45,642	5,575	11,521	28,546	39,962	5,632	9,428	24,902
		50.—Canework, Matting and Leaves, etc.												
		Bamboo splitters, etc.	15,246	2,387	4,522	8,337	7,881	1,137	2,494	4,250	7,365	1,250	2,028	4,087
		Basket weavers	31,119	4,804	8,974	17,341	16,327	2,346	4,962	9,019	14,792	2,458	4,012	8,322
		Mat makers and sellers	2,872	398	716	1,758	1,210	164	290	756	1,662	234	426	1,002
		Screen makers and sellers	24	5	8	11	2	...	2	...	22	5	6	11
		Leaf plate makers and sellers	2,263	302	628	1,333	1,050	157	315	578	1,213	145	313	755
		Comb makers and sellers	767	80	193	494	571	32	92	233	410	48	101	261
		Broom makers and sellers	104	14	19	71	863	11	17	58	18	3	2	13
		Pith and bark collectors	266	44	61	161	25	22	40	63	141	22	21	98
		Total 50	52,661	8,034	15,121	29,506	27,038	3,869	8,212	14,957	25,623	4,165	6,909	14,549
		Total XV.—Wood, Cane and Leaves	**188,265**	**19,241**	**36,070**	**82,954**	**72,680**	**9,444**	**19,738**	**48,508**	**65,585**	**9,797**	**16,337**	**39,451**
	XVI.—Drugs, Gums, Dyes, etc.	51.—Gums, Wax and similar Forest Produce.												
		Gum collectors	5,095	894	1,589	2,612	2,521	381	802	1,338	2,574	513	787	1,274
		Catechu preparers and sellers	2,903	472	867	1,564	1,613	236	490	887	1,290	236	377	677
		Lac collectors	200	29	48	123	200	29	48	123	...	...	...	...
		Sealing wax makers and sellers	1,630	211	401	1,018	647	86	156	405	983	125	245	613
		Honey collectors and sellers	20	2	8	10	13	1	6	6	7	1	2	4
		Total 51	9,848	1,608	2,913	5,327	4,994	733	1,502	2,759	4,854	875	1,411	2,568

Class.	Order.	Sub-order, Group and Occupation.	Total.	0–4	5–14	15 and over.	Total.	0–4	5–14	15 and over.	Total.	0–4	5–14	15 and over.
			PROVINCIAL TOTAL.											
			Total.				Males.				Females.			
1	2	3	4	5	6	7	8	9	10	11	12	13	14	15
CLASS D.—PREPARATION AND SUPPLY OF MATERIAL SUBSTANCES—concld.		52.—Drugs, Dyes, Pigments, etc.												
	XVI.—Drugs, Gums, Dyes, etc.—contd.	Chemists and druggists	4,250	504	898	2,848	2,262	231	486	1,545	1,988	273	412	1,303
		Soap makers and sellers	82	14	20	48	42	8	13	21	40	6	7	27
		Indigo workers, etc.	16	2	2	12	4	...	...	4	12	2	2	8
		Ink makers and sellers	34	5	4	25	25	4	4	17	9	1	...	8
		Antimony preparers and sellers	16	3	3	10	6	1	1	4	10	2	2	6
		Perfume preparers and sellers	1,273	115	290	868	779	62	167	550	494	53	123	318
		Total 52	5,671	643	1,217	3,811	3,118	306	671	2,141	2,553	337	546	1,670
		Total XVI.—Drugs, Gums, Dyes, etc.	**15,719**	**2,289**	**4,180**	**9,250**	**8,178**	**1,046**	**2,188**	**4,939**	**7,546**	**1,248**	**1,992**	**4,311**
		53.—Leather, etc.												
	XVII.—Leather, Horns, Bones and Grease.	Tanners, curriers, etc.	78,727	11,297	20,545	46,885	41,706	5,407	10,760	25,539	37,021	5,890	9,785	21,346
		Shoe makers and sellers	142,179	22,386	39,827	79,966	78,966	11,353	22,466	45,147	63,213	11,033	17,361	34,819
		Leather dyers	632	82	149	401	224	22	51	151	408	60	98	250
		Ghee pot makers and sellers	32	3	9	20	22	1	5	16	10	2	4	4
		Hide and bone dealers	3,482	489	828	2,165	1,882	241	441	1,200	1,600	248	387	965
		Total 53	225,052	34,257	61,358	129,437	122,800	17,024	33,723	72,053	102,252	17,233	27,635	57,384
		Total XVII.—Leather, Horns, Bones and Grease	**225,052**	**34,257**	**61,358**	**129,437**	**122,800**	**17,024**	**33,723**	**72,053**	**102,252**	**17,233**	**27,635**	**57,384**
		Total Class D	**1,359,981**	**181,189**	**339,832**	**838,960**	**722,645**	**90,149**	**185,766**	**446,730**	**637,336**	**91,040**	**154,066**	**392,230**
CLASS E.—COMMERCE, TRANSPORT, STORAGE.		54.—Dealers in Money and Securities.												
	Commerce	Bankers	16,733	1,743	3,564	11,426	8,689	895	1,880	5,914	8,044	848	1,684	5,512
		Money lenders	17,423	2,010	4,124	11,289	8,764	1,007	2,146	5,611	8,659	1,003	1,978	5,678
		Money changers and testers	7,268	748	1,484	5,036	3,831	371	795	2,665	3,437	377	689	2,371
		Total 54	41,424	4,501	9,172	27,751	21,284	2,273	4,821	14,190	20,140	2,228	4,351	13,561

TABLE XVII.—Occupations, by Age.—Part A.—PROVINCIAL SUMMARY—*contd.*

OCCUPATION AND CLASS.			TOWN.											
			TOTAL.				MALES.				FEMALES.			
Class.	Order.	Sub-order, Group and Occupation.	Total.	0—4	5—14	15 and over.	Total.	0—4	5—14	15 and over.	Total.	0—4	5—14	15 and over.
			16	17	18	19	20	21	22	23	24	25	26	27
CLASS D.—PREPARATION AND SUPPLY OF MATERIAL SUBSTANCES—*concld.*		52.—Drugs, Dyes, Pigments, etc.												
	XVI.—Drugs, Gums, Dyes, etc.—*contd.*	Chemists and druggists	2,370	273	512	1,585	1,270	135	249	886	1,100	138	263	699
		Soap makers and sellers	73	11	18	44	42	8	13	21	31	3	5	23
		Indigo workers, etc.	2	...	...	2	...	...	...	...	2	...	...	2
		Ink makers and sellers	15	2	2	11	10	2	2	6	5	...	...	5
		Antimony preparers and sellers	16	3	3	10	6	1	1	4	10	2	2	6
		Perfume preparers and sellers	996	88	226	682	632	47	140	445	364	41	86	237
		Total 52	3,472	377	761	2,334	1,960	193	405	1,362	1,512	184	356	972
		Total XVI.—Drugs, Gums, Dyes, etc.	3,672	415	811	2,446	2,021	200	420	1,401	1,651	215	391	1,045
		53.—Leather, etc.												
	XVII.—Leather, Horns, Bones and Grease.	Tanners, curriers, etc.	6,008	793	1,351	3,864	2,861	341	617	1,903	3,147	452	734	2,061
		Shoe makers and sellers	9,168	1,248	2,243	5,677	5,383	713	1,304	3,366	3,785	535	939	2,311
		Leather dyers	175	28	49	98	70	11	18	41	105	17	31	57
		Ghee pot makers and sellers	9	1	2	6	9	1	2	6	...	...	...	...
		Hide and bone dealers	1,571	192	325	1,054	833	86	168	579	738	106	157	475
		Total 53	16,931	2,262	3,970	10,699	9,156	1,152	2,109	5,895	7,775	1,110	1,861	4,804
		Total XVII.—Leather, Horns, Bones and Grease.	16,981	2,262	3,970	10,699	9,156	1,152	2,109	5,895	7,775	1,110	1,861	4,804
		Total Class D	226,858	26,245	49,805	151,808	116,568	12,864	25,888	77,811	110,290	18,384	23,417	73,492
CLASS E.—COMMERCE, TRANSPORT, STORAGE.		54.—Dealers in Money and Securities.												
	Commerce	Bankers	4,566	397	881	3,288	2,674	237	48	1,948	1,892	160	392	1,340
		Money lenders	3,097	296	678	2,123	1,606	144	366	1,096	1,491	152	312	1,027
		Money changers and testers	4,835	474	913	3,448	2,579	233	507	1,839	2,256	241	406	1,609
		Total 54	12,498	1,167	2,472	8,859	6,859	614	1,362	4,883	5,639	553	1,110	3,976

Class.	Order.	Sub-order, Group and Occupation.	Country. Total. Total.	Total. 0—4	Total. 5—14	Total. 15 and over.	Males. Total.	Males. 0—4	Males. 5—14	Males. 15 and over.	Females. Total.	Females. 0—4	Females. 5—14	Females. 15 and over.
			28	29	30	31	32	33	34	35	36	37	38	39
CLASS D.—PREPARATION AND SUPPLY OF MATERIAL SUBSTANCES—*concld.*	XVI.—Drugs, Gums, Dyes, etc.—*contd.*	**52.—Drugs, Dyes, Pigments, etc.**												
		Chemists and druggists	1,880	231	385	1,263	992	96	237	659	888	135	149	604
		Soap makers and sellers	9	3	2	4	...	...	...	...	9	3	2	4
		Indigo workers	14	2	2	10	4	...	...	4	10	2	2	6
		Ink makers and sellers	19	3	2	14	15	2	2	11	4	1	...	3
		Antimony preparers and sellers	...	...	...	...	...	...	...	...	...	...	...	...
		Perfume preparers and sellers	277	27	64	186	147	15	27	105	130	12	37	81
		Total 52	2,199	266	456	1,477	1,158	113	266	779	1,041	153	190	698
		Total XVI.—Drugs, Gums, Dyes, etc.	**12,047**	**1,874**	**3,869**	**6,804**	**6,152**	**846**	**1,768**	**3,538**	**5,895**	**1,028**	**1,601**	**3,266**
	XVII.—Leather, Horns, Bones and Grease.	**53.—Leather, etc.**												
		Tanners, curriers, etc.	72,719	10,504	19,194	43,021	38,845	5,066	10,143	23,636	33,874	5,438	9,051	19,385
		Shoe makers and sellers	133,011	21,138	37,584	74,289	73,583	10,640	21,162	41,781	59,428	10,498	16,422	32,508
		Leather dyers	457	54	100	303	154	11	33	110	303	43	67	193
		Ghee pot makers and sellers	23	2	7	14	13	...	3	10	10	2	4	4
		Hide and bone dealers	1,911	297	503	1,111	1,049	155	273	621	862	142	230	490
		Total 53	208,121	31,995	57,388	118,738	113,644	15,872	31,614	66,158	94,477	16,123	25,774	52,580
		Total XVII.—Leather, Horns, Bones and Grease.	**208,121**	**31,995**	**57,388**	**118,738**	**113,644**	**15,872**	**31,614**	**66,158**	**94,477**	**16,123**	**25,774**	**52,580**
		Total Class D	**1,133,128**	**154,944**	**290,527**	**687,657**	**606,082**	**77,285**	**159,878**	**368,919**	**527,046**	**77,659**	**130,649**	**318,738**
CLASS E.—COMMERCE, TRANSPORT, STORAGE.	XVIII.—Commerce	**54.—Dealers in Money and Securities.**												
		Bankers	12,167	1,346	2,683	8,138	6,015	658	1,391	3,966	6,152	688	1,292	4,172
		Money lenders	14,326	1,714	3,446	9,166	7,158	863	1,780	4,515	7,168	851	1,666	4,651
		Money changers and testers	2,433	274	571	1,588	1,252	138	288	826	1,181	136	283	762
		Total 54	28,926	3,334	6,700	18,892	14,425	1,659	3,459	9,307	14,501	1,675	3,241	9,585

TABLE XVII.—Occupations, by Age.—Part A.—PROVINCIAL SUMMARY—*contd.*

OCCUPATION AND CLASS.			PROVINCIAL TOTAL.											
			TOTAL.				MALES.				FEMALES.			
Class.	Order.	Sub-order, Group and Occupation.	Total.	0—4	5—14	15 and over.	Total.	0—4	5—14	15 and over.	Total.	0—4	5—14	15 and over.
1	2	3	4	5	6	7	8	9	10	11	12	15	14	15
		55.—General Merchandise.												
	XVIII.—Commerce—*contd.*	General merchants	11,598	1,348	2,579	7,671	6,849	701	1,555	4,593	4,749	647	1,024	3,078
		Merchants, unspecified	54,482	6,158	11,897	36,427	27,844	2,865	6,029	18,950	26,638	3,293	5,868	17,477
		Merchants' clerks	1,336	128	263	945	764	76	136	552	572	52	127	393
		Total 55	67,416	7,634	14,739	45,043	35,457	3,642	7,720	24,095	31,959	3,992	7,019	20,948
		56.—Dealing, Unspecified.												
		Shop-keepers, otherwise unspecified	136,101	15,696	30,703	89,702	70,703	7,404	15,941	47,358	65,398	8,292	14,762	42,344
		Pedlars	10,663	1,122	2,340	7,197	6,272	628	1,403	4,241	4,391	498	937	2,956
		Total 56	146,764	16,822	33,043	96,899	76,975	8,032	17,344	51,599	69,789	8,790	15,699	45,300
		57.—Middlemen, etc.												
		(a) Brokers, etc.												
		Brokers and Agents	8,404	833	1,665	5,906	4,019	360	765	2,894	4,385	473	900	3,012
		Auctioneers	2	...	...	2	1	...	...	1	1	...	...	1
		Total 57(a)	*8,406*	*833*	*1,665*	*5,908*	*4,020*	*360*	*765*	*2,895*	*4,386*	*473*	*900*	*3,013*
		(b) Contractors and Farmers.												
		Farmers of ferries	1	...	...	1	1	...	...	1	...	...	...	...
		Farmers of liquor and opium	14	2	3	9	10	2	2	6	4	...	1	3
		Contractors	4,146	475	909	2,762	2,316	228	487	1,601	1,830	247	422	1,161
		Total 57.(b)	*4,161*	*477*	*912*	*2,772*	*2,327*	*230*	*489*	*1,608*	*1,834*	*247*	*423*	*1,164*
		Total XVIII.—Commerce	**268,171**	**80,267**	**59,581**	**178,878**	**140,068**	**14,587**	**31,189**	**94,887**	**128,108**	**15,730**	**28,392**	**83,986**

OCCUPATION AND CLASS.			TOWN.											
			TOTAL.				MALES.				FEMALES.			
Class.	Order.	Sub-order, Group and Occupation.	Total.	0–4	5–14	15 and over.	Total.	0–4	5–14	15 and over.	Total.	0–4	5–14	15 and over.
			16	17	18	19	20	21	22	23	24	25	26	27
		55.—General Merchandise.												
	XVIII.—Commerce—contd.	General merchants	2,122	177	381	1,564	1,299	100	220	979	823	77	161	585
		Merchants, unspecified	2,265	205	466	1,594	1,309	144	266	899	956	61	200	695
		Merchants' clerks	1,119	105	210	804	630	58	125	447	489	47	85	357
		Total 55	5,506	487	1,057	3,962	3,238	302	611	2,325	2,268	185	446	1,637
		56.—Dealing, Unspecified.												
		Shop-keepers, otherwise unspecified	42,388	4,602	28,762	29,024	26,257	2,705	5,491	18,061	16,131	1,897	3,271	10,963
		Pedlars	1,753	179	390	1,184	1,055	96	235	724	698	83	155	460
		Total 56	44,141	4,781	9,152	30,208	27,312	2,801	5,726	18,785	16,829	1,980	3,426	11,423
		57.—Middlemen, etc.												
		(a) Brokers, etc.												
		Brokers and Agents	5,677	497	1,049	4,131	3,022	252	520	2,250	2,655	245	529	1,881
		Auctioneers	2	...	...	2	1	...	...	1	1	...	...	1
		Total 57 (a)	*5,679*	*497*	*1,049*	*4,133*	*3,023*	*252*	*520*	*2,251*	*2,656*	*245*	*529*	*1,882*
		(b) Contractors and Farmers.												
		Farmers of ferries	...	...	...	...	...	...	...	...	...	...	...	...
		Farmers of liquor and opium	...	...	...	...	...	...	...	...	...	...	...	...
		Contractors	809	87	175	547	215	22	59	134	594	65	116	413
		Total 57 (b)	*809*	*87*	*175*	*547*	*215*	*22*	*59*	*134*	*594*	*65*	*116*	*413*
		Total XVIII.—Commerce	68,688	7,028	18,901	47,709	40,647	8,991	8,278	28,878	27,986	3,028	5,627	19,331

TABLE XVII.—Occupations, by Age.—Part A.—PROVINCIAL SUMMARY—*contd.*

OCCUPATION AND CLASS.			COUNTRY.											
			TOTAL.				MALES.				FEMALES.			
Class.	Order.	SUB-ORDER, GROUP AND OCCUPATION.	TOTAL.	0—4	5—14	15 and over.	TOTAL.	0—4	5—14	15 and over.	TOTAL.	0—4	5—14	15 and over.
			28	29	30	31	32	33	34	35	36	37	38	39
		55.—General Merchandise.												
	XVIII.—COMMERCE—*contd.*	General merchants	9,476	1,171	2,198	6,107	5,550	601	1,335	3,614	3,926	570	863	2,493
		Merchants, unspecified	2,217	5,953	11,431	34,833	26,535	2,721	5,763	18,051	25,682	3,232	5,668	16,782
		Merchants' clerks	5,217	23	53	141	134	18	11	105	83	5	42	36
		Total 55	61,910	7,147	13,682	41,081	32,219	3,340	7,109	21,770	29,691	3,807	6,573	19,311
		56.—Dealing, Unspecified.												
		Shop-keepers, otherwise unspecified	93,713	11,094	21,941	60,678	44,446	4,699	10,450	29,297	49,267	6,395	11,491	31,381
		Pedlars	8,910	947	1,950	6,013	5,217	532	1,168	3,517	3,693	415	782	2,496
		Total 56	102,623	12,041	23,891	66,691	49,663	5,231	11,616	32,814	52,960	6,810	12,273	33,877
		57.—Middlemen, etc.												
		(a) Brokers, etc.												
		Brokers and Agents	2,727	336	616	1,775	997	108	245	644	1,730	228	371	1,131
		Auctioneers	...	...	...	...	...	...	...	...	...	...	...	...
		Total 57 (*a*)	2,727	336	616	1,775	997	108	245	644	1,730	228	371	1,131
		(b) Contractors and Farmers.												
		Farmers of ferries	1	...	...	1	1	...	...	1	...	...	...	...
		Farmers of liquor and opium	14	2	3	9	10	2	2	6	4	...	1	3
		Contractors	3,337	388	734	2,215	2,101	206	428	1,467	1,236	182	306	748
		Total 57 (*b*)	3,352	390	737	2,225	2,112	208	430	1,474	1,240	182	307	751
		Total XVIII.—Commerce	**199,588**	**23,248**	**45,626**	**130,664**	**99,416**	**10,546**	**22,861**	**66,009**	**100,122**	**12,702**	**22,765**	**64,655**

OCCUPATION AND CLASS.			PROVINCIAL TOTAL.											
			TOTAL.				MALES.				FEMALES.			
Class.	Order.	Sub-order, Group and Occupation.	Total.	0—4	5—14	15 and over.	Total.	0—4	5—14	15 and over.	Total.	0—4	5—14	15 and over.
1	2	3	4	5	6	7	8	9	10	11	12	13	14	15
		58.—Railway.												
		(a) Administration.												
	XIX.—Transport and Storage.	Officers	4	1	...	3	4	1	...	3	...	...	...	...
		Locomotive Superintendents	1	...	...	1	1	...	...	1	...	...	...	...
		Store-keepers	87	16	18	53	42	8	7	27	45	8	11	26
		Auditors	4	1	...	3	1	...	...	1	3	1	...	2
		Clerical staff, railway	548	58	84	406	332	25	49	258	216	33	35	148
		Total 58(a)	*644*	*76*	*102*	*466*	*380*	*34*	*56*	*290*	*264*	*42*	*46*	*176*
		(b) Working Staff.												
		Station masters and assistants	289	35	46	208	146	13	20	113	143	22	26	95
		Guards, drivers, etc.	250	41	54	155	613	15	18	75	12	26	36	80
		Pointsmen, etc.	1,014	105	154	755	108	40	84	489	461	65	70	266
		Total 58(b)	*1,553*	*181*	*254*	*1,118*	*867*	*68*	*122*	*677*	*686*	*113*	*132*	*441*
		59.—Road.												
		(a) Cart and Carriage Owners and Drivers.												
		Cart owners and drivers	5,732	516	978	4,238	3,746	281	550	2,915	1,986	235	428	1,323
		Drivers, stable servants, etc.	2,015	165	401	1,449	1,876	145	374	1,357	139	20	27	92
		Palki bearers	1,875	263	493	1,119	1,124	147	308	609	751	116	185	450
		Total 59(a)	*9,622*	*944*	*1,872*	*6,806*	*6,746*	*573*	*1,232*	*4,941*	*2,876*	*371*	*640*	*1,865*
		(b) Carriers by Pack Animals.												
		Pack bullock owners and drivers	9,274	988	2,196	6,090	5,291	503	1,260	3,528	3,983	485	936	2,562
		Camel drivers	65	9	17	39	65	9	17	39	...	...	...	...
		Total 59(b)	*9,339*	*997*	*2,213*	*6,129*	*5,356*	*512*	*1,277*	*3,567*	*3,983*	*485*	*936*	*2,562*
		60.—Water.												
		(b) Working Staff of Vessels.												
		Boatmen	874	102	233	539	485	43	133	309	389	59	100	230
		Total 60(b)	*874*	*102*	*233*	*539*	*485*	*43*	*133*	*309*	*389*	*59*	*100*	*230*

TABLE XVII.—Occupations, by Age.—Part A.—PROVINCIAL SUMMARY—*contd.*

CLASS E.—COMMERCE, TRANSPORT, STORAGE—*contd.*

OCCUPATION AND CLASS.			TOWN.											
			TOTAL.				MALES.				FEMALES.			
Class.	Order.	Sub-order, Group and Occupation.	Total.	0—4	5—14	15 and over.	Total.	0—4	5—14	15 and over.	Total.	0—4	5—14	15 and over.
			16	17	18	19	20	21	22	23	24	25	26	27
		58.—Railway.												
		(a) Administration.												
	XIX.—Transport and Storage.	Officers	4	1	...	3	4	1	...	3	...	...	...	...
		Locomotive Superintendents	1	...	...	1	1	...	...	1	...	...	...	...
		Store-keepers	41	9	6	26	38	8	6	24	3	1	...	2
		Auditor	4	1	...	3	1	...	...	1	3	1	...	2
		Clerical staff, railway	354	32	57	265	199	15	34	150	155	17	23	115
		Total 58 (a)	*404*	*43*	*63*	*298*	*243*	*24*	*40*	*179*	*161*	*19*	*23*	*119*
		(b) Working Staff.												
		Station masters and assistants	193	16	21	156	136	7	16	113	57	9	5	43
		Guards, drivers, etc.	241	38	54	149	108	15	18	75	133	23	36	74
		Pointsmen, etc.	613	43	85	485	576	40	79	457	37	3	6	28
		Total 58 (b)	*1,047*	*97*	*160*	*790*	*820*	*62*	*113*	*645*	*227*	*35*	*47*	*145*
		59.—Road.												
		(a) Cart and Carriage Owners and Drivers.												
		Cart owners and drivers	3,547	379	638	2,530	2,118	210	341	1,567	1,429	169	297	963
		Drivers, stable servants, etc.	131	13	13	95	90	7	18	65	41	6	5	30
		Palki bearers	847	103	183	561	658	79	141	438	189	24	42	123
		Total 59 (a)	*4,525*	*495*	*844*	*3,186*	*2,866*	*296*	*500*	*2,070*	*1,659*	*199*	*344*	*1,116*
		(b) Carriers by Pack Animals.												
		Pack bullock owners and drivers	1,615	180	307	1,128	1,265	121	212	932	350	59	95	196
		Camel drivers	15	1	3	11	15	1	3	11	...	...	...	...
		Total 59 (b)	*1,630*	*181*	*310*	*1,139*	*1,280*	*122*	*215*	*943*	*350*	*59*	*95*	*196*
		60.—Water.												
		(b) Working Staff of Vessels.												
		Boatmen	213	29	47	137	53	6	12	35	160	23	35	102
		Total 60 (b)	*213*	*29*	*47*	*137*	*53*	*6*	*12*	*35*	*160*	*23*	*35*	*102*

Class.	Order.	Sub-order, Group and Occupation.	COUNTRY. Total. Total.	Total. 0–4	Total. 5–14	Total. 15 and over.	Males. Total.	Males. 0–4	Males. 5–14	Males. 15 and over.	Females. Total.	Females. 0–4	Females. 5–14	Females. 15 and over.
			28	29	30	31	32	33	34	35	36	37	38	39
		58.—Railway.												
		(a) Administration.												
	XIX.—Transport and Storage.	Officers	...	...	...	...	...	...	...	...	...	...	...	...
		Locomotive Superintendents	...	...	...	...	...	...	...	...	...	...	...	...
		Store-keepers	46	7	12	27	4	...	1	3	42	7	11	24
		Auditors	...	...	...	...	...	...	...	...	...	...	...	...
		Clerical staff, railway	194	26	27	141	133	10	15	108	61	16	12	33
		Total 58 (a)	*240*	*33*	*39*	*168*	*137*	*10*	*16*	*111*	*103*	*23*	*23*	*57*
		(b) Working Staff.												
		Station masters and assistants	96	19	25	52	10	6	4	...	86	13	21	52
		Guards, drivers, etc.	9	3	...	6	...	...	...	...	9	3	...	6
		Pointsmen, etc.	401	62	69	270	37	...	5	32	364	62	64	238
		Total 58 (b)	*506*	*84*	*94*	*328*	*47*	*6*	*9*	*32*	*459*	*78*	*85*	*296*
		59.—Road.												
		(a) Cart and Carriage Owners and Drivers.												
		Cart owners and drivers	2,185	137	340	1,708	1,628	71	209	1,348	557	66	131	360
		Drivers, stable servants, etc.	1,884	152	378	1,354	1,786	138	356	1,292	98	14	22	62
		Palki bearers	1,028	160	310	558	466	68	167	231	562	92	143	327
		Total 59 (a)	*5,097*	*449*	*1,028*	*3,620*	*3,880*	*277*	*732*	*2,871*	*1,217*	*172*	*296*	*749*
		(b) Carriers by Pack Animals.												
		Pack bullock owners and drivers	7,659	808	1,889	4,962	4,026	382	1,048	2,596	3,633	426	841	2,366
		Camel drivers	50	8	14	28	50	8	14	28	...	...	...	...
		Total 59 (b)	*7,709*	*816*	*1,903*	*4,990*	*4,076*	*390*	*1,062*	*2,624*	*3,633*	*426*	*841*	*2,366*
		60.—Water.												
		(b) Working Staff of Vessels.												
		Boatmen	661	73	186	402	432	37	121	274	229	36	65	128
		Total 60 (b)	*661*	*73*	*186*	*402*	*432*	*37*	*121*	*274*	*229*	*36*	*65*	*128*

TABLE XVII.—Occupations by Age.—Part A.—PROVINCIAL SUMMARY—*contd.*

OCCUPATION AND CLASS.			PROVINCIAL TOTAL.											
			TOTAL.				MALES.				FEMALES.			
Class.	Order.	SUB-ORDER, GROUP AND OCCUPATION.	TOTAL.	0—4	5—14	15 and over.	TOTAL.	0—4	5—14	15 and over.	TOTAL.	0—4	5—14	15 and over.
1	2	3	4	5	6	7	8	9	10	11	12	13	14	15
CLASS E.—COMMERCE, TRANSPORT, STORAGE—*contd.*		**61.—Messengers.**												
		(a) Post, etc.												
	XIX.—TRANSPORT AND STORAGE—*contd.*	Postmasters and clerks	183	22	29	132	125	12	18	95	58	10	11	37
		Postal messengers and postmen	425	41	70	314	287	25	34	228	138	16	36	86
		Messengers, unspecified	8	...	4	4	2	...	...	2	6	...	4	2
		Total 61(a)	*616*	*63*	*103*	*450*	*414*	*37*	*52*	*325*	*202*	*26*	*51*	*125*
		(b) Telegraph.												
		Telegraph officers	2	...	...	2	2	...	...	2	...	...	...	...
		Signallers and messengers	166	9	30	127	90	4	15	71	76	5	15	56
		Total 61(b)	*168*	*9*	*30*	*129*	*92*	*4*	*15*	*73*	*76*	*5*	*15*	*56*
		62.—Storage and Weighing.												
		Porters, general	2,895	337	577	1,981	1,669	144	303	1,222	1,226	193	274	759
		Weighmen	4,220	485	969	2,766	2,966	313	706	1,947	1,254	172	263	819
		Watchmen (not village)	4,130	527	929	2,674	2,221	241	472	1,508	1,909	286	457	1,166
		Total 62	11,245	1,349	2,475	7,421	6,856	698	1,481	4,677	4,389	651	994	2,744
		Total XIX.—Transport and Storage	**34,061**	**3,721**	**7,282**	**23,058**	**21,196**	**1,969**	**4,368**	**14,859**	**12,865**	**1,752**	**2,914**	**8,199**
		Total Class E	**302,232**	**38,988**	**66,818**	**201,431**	**161,259**	**16,506**	**35,507**	**109,246**	**140,973**	**1,482**	**31,306**	**92,185**
CLASS F.—PROFESSIONS.		**63.—Religion.**												
		(a) Priests, Ministers, etc.												
	XX.—LEARNED AND ARTISTIC PROFESSIONS.	Priests, preachers, etc.	29,740	3,298	6,586	19,856	16,428	1,674	3,776	10,978	13,312	1,624	2,810	8,878
		Hail averters	140	16	39	85	94	11	28	55	46	5	11	30
		Arruletiers, etc.	61	11	13	37	41	6	9	26	20	5	4	11
		Total 63(a)	*29,941*	*3,325*	*6,638*	*19,978*	*16,563*	*1,691*	*3,813*	*11,059*	*13,378*	*1,634*	*2,825*	*8,919*

Class.	Order.	Sub-order, Group and Occupation.	Town. Total. Total.	Total. 0—4	Total. 5—14	Total. 15 and over.	Males. Total.	Males. 0—4	Males. 5—14	Males. 15 and over.	Females. Total.	Females. 0—4	Females. 5—14	Females. 15 and over.
			16	17	18	19	20	21	22	23	24	25	26	27
CLASS E.—COMMERCE, TRANSPORT, STORAGE—contd.		**61.—Messengers.**												
		(a) Post, etc.												
	XIX.—Transport and Storage—contd.	Postmasters and clerks	126	15	26	85	96	10	18	68	30	5	8	17
		Postal messengers and postmen	135	18	24	93	44	2	4	38	91	16	20	55
		Messengers, unspecified	...	...	...	...	...	...	...	...	...	...	...	...
		Total 61 (a)	*261*	*33*	*50*	*178*	*140*	*12*	*22*	*106*	*121*	*21*	*28*	*72*
		(b) Telegraph.												
		Telegraph officers	2	...	...	2	2	...	...	2	...	...	...	...
		Signallers and messengers	138	9	24	105	8	4	15	69	50	5	9	36
		Total 61 (b)	*140*	*9*	*24*	*107*	*90*	*4*	*15*	*71*	*50*	*5*	*9*	*36*
		62.—Storage and Weighing.												
		Porters, general	2,291	259	471	1,561	1,475	140	300	1,035	816	119	171	526
		Weighmen	1,164	138	231	795	772	91	150	531	392	47	81	264
		Watchmen (not village)	888	83	66	639	412	29	65	318	476	54	101	321
		Total 62	**4,343**	**480**	**868**	**2,995**	**2,659**	**260**	**515**	**1,884**	**1,684**	**220**	**353**	**1,111**
		Total XIX.—Transport and Storage	**12,568**	**1,868**	**2,870**	**8,830**	**8,151**	**786**	**1,432**	**5,933**	**4,412**	**581**	**984**	**2,897**
		Total Class E	**81,196**	**8,386**	**16,321**	**56,539**	**48,798**	**4,777**	**90,710**	**34,311**	**32,398**	**3,609**	**6,561**	**22,228**
CLASS F.—PROFESSIONS.		**63.—Religion.**												
		(a) Priests, Ministers, etc.												
	XX.—Learned and Artistic Professions.	Priests, preachers, etc.	3,785	372	782	2,631	1,961	194	449	1,318	1,824	178	333	1,313
		Hail averters	12	4	3	5	10	3	3	4	2	1	...	1
		Amuletiers, etc.	...	...	...	...	...	...	...	...	...	...	...	...
		Total 63 (a)	*3,797*	*376*	*785*	*2,636*	*1,971*	*197*	*452*	*1,322*	*1,826*	*179*	*333*	*1,314*

TABLE XVII.—Occupations, by Age.—Part A.—PROVINCIAL SUMMARY—*contd.*

Class.	Order.	Sub-order, Group and Occupation.	Country. Total. Total.	Total. 0—4	Total. 5—14	Total. 15 and over.	Males. Total.	Males. 0—4	Males. 5—14	Males. 15 and over.	Females. Total.	Females. 0—4	Females. 5—14	Females. 15 and over.
			28	29	30	31	32	33	34	35	36	37	38	39
CLASS E.—COMMERCE, TRANSPORT, STORAGE—*contd.*	XIX.—TRANSPORT AND STORAGE—*contd.*	**61.—Messengers.**												
		(a) *Post, etc.*												
		Postmasters and clerks	57	7	3	47	29	2	...	27	28	5	3	20
		Postal messengers and postmen	190	23	46	221	243	23	30	190	47	...	16	31
		Messengers, unspecified	8	...	4	4	2	...	...	2	6	...	4	2
		Total 61 (a)	*355*	*30*	*53*	*272*	*274*	*25*	*30*	*219*	*81*	*5*	*23*	*53*
		(b) *Telegraph.*												
		Telegraph officers	...	...	...	...	...	...	...	...	...	...	...	...
		Signallers and messengers	28	...	6	22	2	...	...	2	26	...	6	20
		Total 61 (b)	*28*	...	*6*	*22*	*2*	...	...	*2*	*26*	...	*6*	*20*
		62.—Storage and Weighing.												
		Porters, general	604	78	106	420	192	4	3	187	410	74	103	233
		Weighmen	3,056	347	738	1,971	2,194	222	556	1,416	862	125	182	555
		Watchmen (not village)	3,242	444	763	2,035	1,809	212	407	1,190	1,433	232	356	845
		Total 62	6,902	869	1,607	4,426	4,197	438	966	2,793	2,705	431	441	1,633
		Total XIX.—Transport and Storage	**21,498**	**2,354**	**4,916**	**14,228**	**13,045**	**1,183**	**2,936**	**8,926**	**8,458**	**1,171**	**1,980**	**5,302**
		Total Class E	**221,036**	**25,602**	**50,542**	**144,892**	**112,461**	**11,729**	**25,797**	**74,935**	**108,575**	**13,878**	**24,745**	**69,957**
CLASS F.—PROFESSIONS.	XX.—LEARNED AND ARTISTIC PROFESSIONS.	**63.—Religion.**												
		(a) *Priests, Ministers, etc.*												
		Priests, preachers, etc.	25,955	2,926	5,804	17,225	14,467	1,480	3,327	9,660	11,488	1,446	2,477	7,565
		Hail averters	128	12	36	80	84	8	25	51	44	4	11	29
		Amuletiers, etc.	61	11	13	37	41	6	9	26	20	5	4	11
		Total 63 (a)	*26,144*	*2,949*	*5,853*	*17,342*	*14,592*	*1,494*	*3,361*	*9,737*	*11,552*	*1,455*	*2,492*	*7,605*

Table XVII A.—Occupations—Central India.

OCCUPATION AND CLASS.			PROVINCIAL TOTAL.											
			Total.				Males.				Females.			
Class.	Order.	Sub-order, Group and Occupation.	Total.	0—4	5—14	15 and over.	Total.	0—4	5—14	15 and over.	Total.	0—4	5—14	15 and over.
1	2	3	4	5	6	7	8	9	10	11	12	13	14	15
		63.—Religion—*contd.*												
		(b) Subsidiary Religious Services.												
	XX.—Learned and Artistic Professions—*contd.*	Religious mendicants	11,094	1,111	2,273	7,710	7,803	731	1,586	5,485	3,291	380	687	2,224
		Devotees	644	32	105	507	415	8	58	349	229	24	47	158
		Temple servants	26,220	2,469	5,322	18,429	15,256	1,204	2,902	11,150	10,964	1,265	2,420	7,279
		Burial ground servants	10	...	4	6	5	...	3	2	5	...	1	4
		Pilgrim conductors	184	5	8	171	167	3	5	159	17	2	3	12
		Total 63 (b)	*38,152*	*3,617*	*7,712*	*26,823*	*23,646*	*1,946*	*4,554*	*17,146*	*14,506*	*1,671*	*3,158*	*9,677*
		64.—Education.												
		Teachers, schoolmasters, etc.	1,992	203	407	1,382	1,226	116	254	856	766	87	153	526
		Total 64	**1,992**	**203**	**407**	**1,382**	**1,226**	**116**	**254**	**856**	**766**	**87**	**153**	**526**
		65.—Literature.												
		Authors and ballad-makers	12	1	4	7	7	...	3	4	5	1	1	3
		Private secretaries and clerks	837	77	165	595	460	36	88	336	377	41	77	259
		Public scribes	9,885	1,106	2,647	6,072	5,807	607	1,331	3,809	4,078	559	1,316	2,203
		Total 65	**10,734**	**1,244**	**2,816**	**6,674**	**6,274**	**643**	**1,422**	**4,209**	**4,460**	**601**	**1,394**	**2,465**
		66.—Law.												
		Pleaders and law agents	3,208	357	700	2,151	1,459	140	324	995	1,749	217	376	1,156
		Lawyers' clerks	33	3	6	24	27	2	5	20	6	1	1	4
		Stamp vendors	10	1	3	6	10	1	3	6	...	...	...	...
		Petition-writers	206	22	38	146	120	11	17	92	86	11	21	54
		Total 66	**3,457**	**383**	**747**	**2,327**	**1,616**	**154**	**349**	**1,113**	**1,841**	**229**	**398**	**1,214**
		67.—Medicine.												
		(a) Practitioners.												
		Practitioners by diploma	644	63	88	493	287	36	30	221	357	27	8	272
		Practitioners without diploma	846	82	183	581	456	39	98	319	390	43	85	262
		Hakims, baids, etc.	2,924	326	610	1,988	1,453	149	289	1,015	1,471	177	321	973
		Dentists	1	...	...	1	1	...	...	1	...	...	...	...
		Vaccinators	38	2	9	27	26	...	6	20	12	2	3	7
		Midwifery	295	26	37	232	47	4	9	34	248	22	28	198
		Total 67 (a)	*4,748*	*499*	*927*	*3,322*	*2,270*	*228*	*432*	*1,610*	*2,478*	*271*	*495*	*1,712*

TABLE XVII.—Occupations, by Age.—Part A.—PROVINCIAL SUMMARY—*contd.*

Class.	Order.	Sub-order, Group and Occupation.	Town. Total. Total.	Total. 0–4	Total. 5–14	Total. 15 and over.	Males. Total.	Males. 0–4	Males. 5–14	Males. 15 and over.	Females. Total.	Females. 0–4	Females. 5–14	Females. 15 and over.
			16	17	18	19	20	21	22	23	24	25	26	27
		63.—Religion—*contd.*												
		(b) Subsidiary Religious Services.												
	XX.—Learned and Artistic Professions—*contd.*	Religious mendicants	5,427	424	967	4,036	3,402	246	590	2,566	2,025	178	377	1,470
		Devotees	79	2	9	68	45	1	5	39	34	1	4	29
		Temple servants	6,986	562	1,356	5,068	4,008	294	730	2,984	2,978	268	626	2,084
		Burial ground servants	...	...	...	...	...	...	...	...	...	...	...	...
		Pilgrim conductors	...	...	...	...	...	...	...	...	...	...	...	...
		Total 63 (b)	*12,492*	*988*	*2,332*	*9,172*	*7,455*	*541*	*1,325*	*5,589*	*5,937*	*447*	*1,007*	*3,583*
		64.—Education.												
		Teachers, schoolmasters, etc.	1,228	125	238	865	715	67	149	499	513	58	89	366
		Total 64	1,228	125	238	865	715	67	149	499	513	58	89	366
		65.—Literature.												
		Authors and ballad-makers	7	...	3	4	6	...	3	3	1	...	...	1
		Private secretaries and clerks	...	...	...	...	...	...	...	...	...	...	...	...
		Public scribes	3,622	372	775	2,475	2,284	239	551	1,494	1,338	133	224	981
		Total 65	3,629	372	778	2,479	2,290	239	554	1,497	1,339	33	224	982
		66.—Law.												
		Pleaders and law agents	1,549	164	341	1,044	891	87	203	601	658	77	138	443
		Lawyers' clerks	...	...	...	...	...	...	...	...	...	...	...	...
		Stamp vendors	10	1	3	6	10	1	3	6	...	...	...	...
		Petition-writers	105	9	27	69	45	3	10	32	60	6	17	37
		Total 66	1,664	174	371	1,119	946	91	216	639	718	83	155	480
		67.—Medicine.												
		(a) Practitioners.												
		Practitioners by diploma	208	36	56	116	85	12	19	54	123	24	37	62
		Practitioners without diploma	724	66	146	512	425	34	85	306	299	32	61	206
		Hakims, baids, etc.	1,642	143	293	1,206	863	81	152	630	779	62	141	576
		Dentists	1	...	...	1	1	...	...	1	...	...	...	...
		Vaccinators	37	2	8	27	26	...	6	20	11	2	2	7
		Midwifery	18	2	4	12	4	...	2	2	14	2	2	10
		Total 67 (a)	*2,630*	*249*	*507*	*1,874*	*1,404*	*127*	*264*	*1,013*	*1,226*	*122*	*243*	*861*

Table XVII A.—Occupations—Central India.

OCCUPATION AND CLASS.			COUNTRY.											
			TOTAL.				MALES.				FEMALES.			
Class.	Order.	Sub-order, Group and Occupation.	TOTAL.	0—4	5—14	15 and over.	TOTAL.	0—4	5—14	15 and over.	TOTAL.	0—4	5—14	15 and over.
			28	29	30	31	32	33	34	35	36	37	38	39
		63.—Religion—*contd.*												
	XX.—LEARNED AND ARTISTIC PROFESSIONS—*contd.*	*(b) Subsidiary Religious Services.*												
		Religious mendicants	5,667	687	1,306	3,674	4,401	485	996	2,920	1,266	202	310	754
		Devotees	565	30	96	439	370	7	53	310	195	23	43	129
		Temple servants	19,234	1,907	3,966	13,361	11,248	910	2,172	8,166	7,986	997	1,794	5,195
		Burial ground servants	10	...	4	6	5	...	3	2	5	...	1	4
		Pilgrim conductors	184	5	8	171	167	3	5	159	17	2	3	12
		Total 63 (b)	*25,660*	*2,629*	*5,380*	*17,651*	*16,191*	*1,405*	*3,229*	*11,557*	*9,469*	*1,224*	*2,151*	*6,094*
		64.—Education.												
		Teachers, schoolmasters, etc.	764	78	169	527	511	49	105	357	253	29	64	160
		Total 64	764	78	169	527	511	49	105	357	253	29	64	160
		65.—Literature.												
		Authors and ballad-makers	5	1	1	3	1	...	...	1	4	1	1	2
		Private secretaries and clerks	837	77	165	595	460	36	88	336	377	41	77	259
		Public scribes	6,263	794	1,872	3,597	3,523	368	780	2,375	2,740	426	1,092	1,222
		Total 65	7,105	872	2,038	4,195	3,984	404	868	2,712	3,121	468	1,170	1,483
		66.—Law.												
		Pleaders and law agents	1,659	193	359	1,107	568	53	121	394	1,091	140	238	713
		Lawyers' clerks	33	3	6	24	27	2	5	20	6	1	1	4
		Stamp vendors	...	...	...	...	...	...	...	...	...	...	...	...
		Petition-writers	101	13	11	77	75	8	7	60	26	5	4	17
		Total 66	1,793	209	376	1,208	670	63	133	474	1,123	146	243	734
		67.—Medicine.												
		(a) Practitioners.												
		Practitioners by diploma	436	27	32	377	202	24	11	167	234	3	21	210
		Practitioners without diploma	122	16	37	69	31	5	13	13	91	11	24	56
		Hakims, baids, etc.	1,282	183	317	782	590	68	137	385	692	115	180	397
		Dentists	...	...	...	...	...	...	...	...	...	...	...	...
		Vaccinators	1	...	1	...	...	...	...	...	1	...	1	...
		Midwifery	277	24	33	220	43	4	7	32	234	20	26	188
		Total 67 (a)	*2,118*	*250*	*420*	*1,448*	*866*	*101*	*168*	*597*	*1,252*	*149*	*252*	*851*

TABLE XVII.—Occupations, by Age.—Part A.—PROVINCIAL SUMMARY—*contd.*

Class.	Order.	Sub-order, Group and Occupation.	Total: Total.	Total: 0—4	Total: 5—14	Total: 15 and over.	Males: Total.	Males: 0—4	Males: 5—14	Males: 15 and over.	Females: Total.	Females: 0—4	Females: 5—14	Females: 15 and over.
1	2	3	4	5	6	7	8	9	10	11	12	13	14	15
		(b) Subsidiary Medical Services.												
	XX.—Learned and Artistic Professions—*contd.*	Hospital assistants	40	4	10	26	20	1	6	13	20	3	4	13
		Asylum servants	5	...	1	4	1	...	...	1	4	...	1	3
		Apothecaries	59	10	16	33	51	10	12	29	8	...	4	4
		Compounders	99	15	26	58	51	8	13	30	48	7	13	28
		Dispensary servants	672	73	138	461	608	68	127	413	64	5	11	48
		Total 67 (b)	*875*	*102*	*191*	*582*	*731*	*87*	*158*	*486*	*144*	*15*	*33*	*96*
		68.—Engineering and Surveying.												
		(a) Engineers, Architects and Surveyors.												
		Administrative staff	42	3	8	31	31	2	5	24	11	1	3	7
		Civil Engineers	71	10	9	52	40	5	5	30	31	5	4	22
		Total 68 (a)	*113*	*13*	*17*	*83*	*71*	*7*	*10*	*54*	*42*	*6*	*7*	*29*
		(b) Subsidiary Staff.												
		Draughtsmen, etc.	124	10	25	89	67	3	12	52	57	7	13	37
		Total 68 (b)	*124*	*10*	*25*	*89*	*67*	*3*	*12*	*52*	*57*	*7*	*13*	*37*
		69.—Other Sciences.												
		(b) Minor Sciences.												
		Astrologers and horoscope casters	1,387	183	305	899	630	57	140	433	757	126	165	466
		Total 69 (b)	*1,387*	*183*	*305*	*899*	*630*	*57*	*140*	*433*	*757*	*126*	*165*	*466*
		70.—Pictorial Art and Sculpture.												
		Painters	2,299	309	498	1,492	1,164	153	285	726	1,135	156	213	766
		Photographers	44	1	12	31	26	...	6	20	18	1	6	11
		Total 70	**2,343**	**310**	**510**	**1,523**	**1,190**	**153**	**291**	**746**	**1,153**	**157**	**219**	**777**

Class.	Order.	Sub-order, Group and Occupation.	Town. Total. Total.	Total. 0—4	Total. 5—14	Total. 15 and over.	Males. Total.	Males. 0—4	Males. 5—14	Males. 15 and over.	Females. Total.	Females. 0—4	Females. 5—14	Females. 15 and over.
			16	17	18	19	20	21	22	23	24	25	26	27
	XX.—Learned and Artistic Professions—*contd.*	*(b) Subsidiary Medical Services.*												
		Hospital assistants	20	1	6	13	13	...	3	10	7	1	3	3
		Asylum servants	1	...	...	1	1	...	...	1	...	...	...	...
		Apothecaries	31	4	14	13	23	4	10	9	8	...	4	4
		Compounders	66	11	20	35	40	6	13	21	26	5	7	14
		Dispensary servants	102	13	20	69	49	9	11	29	53	4	9	40
		Total 67 (b)	*220*	*29*	*60*	*131*	*126*	*19*	*37*	*70*	*94*	*10*	*23*	*61*
		68.—Engineering and Surveying.												
		(a) Engineers, Architects and Surveyors.												
		Administrative staff	29	2	6	21	27	2	5	20	2	...	1	1
		Civil Engineers	64	8	8	48	35	3	4	28	29	5	4	20
		Total 68 (a)	*93*	*10*	*14*	*69*	*62*	*5*	*9*	*48*	*31*	*5*	*5*	*21*
		(b) Subsidiary Staff.												
		Draughtsmen, etc.	108	10	25	73	51	3	12	36	57	7	13	37
		Total 68 (b)	*108*	*10*	*25*	*73*	*51*	*3*	*12*	*36*	*57*	*7*	*13*	*37*
		69.—Other Sciences.												
		(b) Minor Sciences.												
		Astrologers and horoscope casters	441	41	99	301	255	23	56	176	186	18	43	125
		Total 69 (b)	*441*	*41*	*99*	*301*	*255*	*23*	*56*	*176*	*186*	*18*	*43*	*125*
		70.—Pictorial Art and Sculpture.												
		Painters	45	57	100	228	140	16	37	87	305	41	63	201
		Photographers	38	1	7	30	21	...	1	20	17	1	6	10
		Total 70	483	58	107	318	161	16	38	107	322	42	69	211

TABLE XVII.—Occupations, by Age.—Part A.—PROVINCIAL SUMMARY—*contd.*

Class.	Order.	Sub-order, Group and Occupation.	Country. Total. Total.	Total. 0—4	Total. 5—14	Total. 15 and over.	Males. Total.	Males. 0—4	Males. 5—14	Males. 15 and over.	Females. Total.	Females. 0—4	Females. 5—14	Females. 15 and over.
			28	29	30	31	32	33	34	35	36	37	38	39
		(b) Subsidiary Medical Services.												
	XX.—Learned and Artistic Professions—*contd.*	Hospital assistants	20	3	4	13	7	1	3	3	13	2	1	10
		Asylum servants	4	...	1	3	...	...	...	...	4	...	1	3
		Apothecaries	28	6	2	20	28	6	2	20	...	...	...	...
		Compounders	33	4	6	23	11	2	...	9	22	2	6	14
		Dispensary servants	570	60	118	392	559	59	116	384	11	1	2	8
		Total 67 (b)	*655*	*73*	*131*	*451*	*605*	*68*	*121*	*416*	*50*	*5*	*10*	*35*
		68.—Engineering and Surveying.												
		(a) Engineers, Architects and Surveyors.												
		Administrative staff	13	1	2	10	4	...	...	4	9	1	2	6
		Civil Engineers	7	2	1	4	5	2	1	2	2	...	...	2
		Total 68 (a)	*20*	*3*	*3*	*14*	*9*	*2*	*1*	*6*	*11*	*1*	*2*	*8*
		(b) Subsidiary Staff.												
		Draughtsmen, etc.	16	...	...	16	16	...	...	16	...	...	...	...
		Total 68 (b)	*16*	...	...	*16*	*16*	...	...	*16*	...	...	...	...
		69.—Other Sciences.												
		(b) Minor Sciences.												
		Astrologers and horoscope casters	946	142	206	598	375	34	84	257	571	108	122	341
		Total 69 (b)	*946*	*142*	*206*	*598*	*375*	*34*	*84*	*257*	*571*	*108*	*122*	*341*
		70.—Pictorial Art and Sculpture.												
		Painters	1,854	252	398	1,204	1,024	137	248	639	830	115	150	565
		Photographers	6	...	5	1	5	...	5	...	1	...	...	1
		Total 70	**1,860**	**252**	**403**	**1,205**	**1,029**	**137**	**253**	**639**	**831**	**115**	**150**	**566**

OCCUPATION AND CLASS.			PROVINCIAL TOTAL.											
			TOTAL.				MALES.				FEMALES.			
Class.	Order.	Sub-order, Group and Occupation.	Total.	0—4	5—14	15 and over.	Total.	0—4	5—14	15 and over.	Total.	0—4	5—14	15 and over.
1	2	3	4	5	6	7	8	9	10	11	12	13	14	15
		71.—Music, Acting, Dancing.												
	XX.—LEARNED AND ARTISTIC PROFESSIONS.—*concld.*	Musicians (not military)	2,059	241	440	1,378	982	107	202	673	1,077	134	238	705
		Drummers	8,174	965	1,824	5,385	4,481	513	949	3,019	3,693	452	875	2,366
		Actors	958	108	189	661	508	50	99	359	450	58	90	302
		Singers and dancers	8,056	741	1,681	5,634	3,702	346	871	2,485	4,354	395	810	3,149
		Total 71	19,247	2,055	4,134	13,058	9,673	1,016	2,121	6,536	9,574	1,039	2,013	6,522
		Total XX.—Learned and Artistic Professions	**118,113**	**11,944**	**24,429**	**76,740**	**68,957**	**6,101**	**18,556**	**44,800**	**49,156**	**5,848**	**10,878**	**82,440**
		72.—Sport.												
	XXI.—SPORTS AND AMUSEMENTS.	Shikaris and bird catchers	970	145	258	567	581	73	162	346	389	72	96	221
		Total 72	970	145	258	567	581	73	162	346	389	72	96	221
		73.—Exhibitions and Games.												
		(a) Catching, training and exhibiting Animals.												
		Snake charmers	17	3	5	9	10	2	5	3	7	1	...	6
		Circus performers	13	2	2	9	7	2	...	5	6	...	2	4
		Total 73 (a)	*30*	*5*	*7*	*18*	*17*	*4*	*5*	*8*	*13*	*1*	*2*	*10*
		(b) Conjuring, Fortune-telling and other Exhibitions.												
		Buffoons	292	47	89	156	184	25	55	104	108	22	34	52
		Ballad reciters	870	90	211	569	384	39	92	253	486	51	119	316
		Exhibitors of puppets	55	5	13	37	...	...	...	...	55	5	13	37
		Conjurors	449	52	105	292	265	21	64	180	184	31	41	112
		Fortune-tellers	330	33	79	218	175	21	50	104	155	12	29	114
		Total 73 (b)	*1,996*	*227*	*497*	*1,272*	*1,008*	*106*	*261*	*641*	*988*	*121*	*236*	*631*
		(c) Acrobatics and Athletics.												
		Tumblers, acrobats and wrestlers	3,745	414	782	2,549	3,337	350	671	2,316	408	64	111	233
		Total 73 (c)	*3,745*	*414*	*782*	*2,549*	*3,337*	*350*	*671*	*2,316*	*408*	*64*	*111*	*233*

TABLE XVII.—Occupations, by Age.—Part A.—PROVINCIAL SUMMARY—*contd.*

OCCUPATION AND CLASS.			TOWN.											
			TOTAL.				MALE.				FEMALES.			
Class.	Order.	Sub-order, Group and Occupation.	Total.	0—4	5—14	15 and over.	Total.	0—4	5—14	15 and over.	Total.	0—4	5—14	15 and over.
			16	17	18	19	20	21	22	23	24	25	26	27
		71.—Music, Acting, Dancing.												
	XX.—Learned and Artistic Professions—*concld.*	Musicians (not military)	253	29	49	175	140	11	30	99	113	18	19	76
		Drummers	1,608	215	313	1,080	925	131	178	616	683	84	135	464
		Actors	11	1	1	9	8	...	1	7	3	1	...	2
		Singers and dancers	3,379	254	581	2,544	1,232	101	252	879	2,147	153	329	1,665
		Total 71	5,251	499	944	3,808	2,305	243	461	1,601	2,946	256	483	2,207
		Total XX.—Learned and Artistic Professions	**32,086**	**2,931**	**6,260**	**22,845**	**17,741**	**1,571**	**3,573**	**12,597**	**14,295**	**1,360**	**2,687**	**10,248**
		72.—Sport.												
	XXI.—Sports and Amusements.	Shikaris and bird catchers	150	15	32	103	67	4	10	53	83	11	22	50
		Total 72	150	15	32	103	67	4	10	53	83	11	22	50
		73.—Exhibitions and Games.												
		(a) Catching, training and exhibiting Animals.												
		Snake charmers	4	...	...	4	...	...	...	...	4	...	...	4
		Circus performers	1	...	...	1	1	...	...	1	...	...	...	...
		Total 73 (a)	*5*	...	...	*5*	*1*	...	...	*1*	*4*	...	..	*4*
		(b) Conjuring, Fortune-telling and other Exhibitions.												
		Buffoons	33	7	10	16	33	7	10	16	...	...	...	...
		Ballad reciters	242	28	88	126	124	10	31	83	118	18	57	43
		Exhibitors of puppets	...	...	...	...	...	...	...	...	...	...	...	...
		Conjurors	134	4	26	104	98	1	17	80	36	3	9	24
		Fortune-tellers	137	12	30	95	62	9	16	37	75	3	14	58
		Total 73 (b)	*546*	*51*	*154*	*341*	*317*	*27*	*74*	*216*	*229*	*24*	*80*	*125*
		(c) Acrobatics and Athletics.												
		Tumblers, acrobats and wrestlers	392	35	71	286	206	16	25	165	186	19	46	121
		Total 73 (c)	*392*	*35*	*71*	*286*	*206*	*16*	*25*	*165*	*186*	*19*	*46*	*121*

Class.	Order.	Sub-order, Group and Occupation.	Total				Males				Females			
			Total.	0—4	5—14	15 and over.	Total.	0—4	5—14	15 and over.	Total.	0—4	5—14	15 and over.
			28	29	30	31	32	33	34	35	36	37	38	39
	XX.—Learned and Artistic Professions—*concld.*	**71.—Music, Acting, Dancing.**												
		Musicians (not military)	1,806	212	391	1,203	842	96	172	574	964	116	219	629
		Drummers	6,566	750	1,511	4,305	3,556	382	771	2,403	3,010	368	740	1,902
		Actors	947	108	188	652	500	50	98	352	447	57	90	300
		Singers and dancers	4,677	487	1,100	3,090	2,470	245	619	1,606	2,207	242	481	1,484
		Total 71	13,996	1,556	3,190	9,250	7,368	773	1,660	4,935	6,628	783	1,530	4,315
		Total XX.—Learned and Artistic Professions	**81,077**	**9,018**	**18,169**	**53,895**	**46,216**	**4,530**	**9,988**	**31,703**	**34,861**	**4,483**	**8,186**	**22,192**
	XXI.—Sports and Amusements.	**72.—Sport.**												
		Shikaris and bird catchers	820	130	226	464	514	69	152	293	306	61	74	171
		Total 72	820	130	226	464	514	69	152	293	306	61	74	171
		73.—Exhibitions and Games.												
		(a) Catching, training and exhibiting Animals.												
		Snake charmers	13	3	5	5	10	2	5	3	3	1	...	2
		Circus performers	12	2	2	8	6	2	...	4	6	...	2	4
		Total 73 (a)	*25*	*5*	*7*	*13*	*16*	*4*	*5*	*7*	*9*	*1*	*2*	*6*
		(b) Conjuring, Fortune-telling and other Exhibitions.												
		Buffoons	259	40	79	140	151	18	45	88	108	22	34	52
		Ballad reciters	628	62	123	443	260	29	61	170	368	33	62	273
		Exhibitors of puppets	55	5	13	37	...	...	...	...	55	5	13	37
		Conjurors	315	48	79	188	167	20	47	100	148	28	32	88
		Fortune-tellers	193	21	49	123	113	12	34	67	80	9	15	56
		Total 73 (b)	*1,450*	*176*	*343*	*931*	*691*	*79*	*187*	*425*	*759*	*97*	*156*	*506*
		(c) Acrobatics and Athletics.												
		Tumblers, acrobats and wrestlers	3,353	379	711	2,263	3,131	334	646	2,151	222	45	65	112
		Total 73 (c)	*3,353*	*379*	*711*	*2,263*	*3,131*	*334*	*646*	*2,151*	*222*	*45*	*65*	*112*

TABLE XVII.—Occupations, by Age.—Part A.—PROVINCIAL SUMMARY—*contd.*

Class.	Order.	Sub-order, Group and Occupation.	Provincial Total. Total. Total.	Total. 0—4	Total. 5—14	Total. 15 and over.	Males. Total.	Males. 0—4	Males. 5—14	Males. 15 and over.	Females. Total.	Females. 0—4	Females. 5—14	Females. 15 and over.
1	2	3	4	5	6	7	8	9	10	11	12	13	14	15
CLASS F.—PROFESSIONS —*concld.*		*(d) Service of places of entertainments.*												
	XXI.—Sports and Amusements—*contd*	Billiard-room managers	35	3	8	24	15	1	5	9	20	2	3	15
		Total 73 (d)	*35*	*3*	*8*	*24*	*15*	*1*	*5*	*9*	*20*	*2*	*3*	*15*
		Total XXI.—Sports and Amusements	**6,776**	**794**	**1,552**	**4,430**	**4,958**	**534**	**1,104**	**3,320**	**1,818**	**260**	**448**	**1,110**
		Total Class F	**119,889**	**12,788**	**25,981**	**81,170**	**68,915**	**6,635**	**14,660**	**47,620**	**50,974**	**6,103**	**11,821**	**33,550**
CLASS G.—INDEFINITE AND INDEPENDENT.		74.—Unskilled Labour.												
		(a) Special Branches.												
	XXIII.—Indefinite.	Well-sinkers	19	1	4	14	17	1	4	12	2	...	...	2
		Road labourers	492	24	69	399	365	10	49	306	127	14	20	93
		Railway labourers	785	99	96	590	477	45	46	386	308	54	50	204
		Gangmen	562	43	66	453	540	41	62	437	22	2	4	16
		Miners (unspecified)	1,128	116	167	845	742	58	90	594	386	58	77	251
		Total 74 (a)	*2,986*	*283*	*402*	*2,301*	*2,141*	*155*	*231*	*1,735*	*845*	*128*	*151*	*566*
		(b) General.												
		General labour	139,545	280,180	551,148	1,308,217	1,006,526	129,091	286,909	590,526	1,133,019	151,089	264239	717,691
		Total 74 (b)	*2,139,545*	*280,180*	*551,148*	*1,308,217*	*1,006,526*	*129,091*	*286,909*	*590,526*	*1,133,019*	*151,089*	*264,239*	*717,691*
		75.—Undefined, etc.												
		Undefined and disreputable means of livelihood	4,004	401	843	2,760	1,444	173	354	917	2,560	228	489	1,843
		Total 75	**4,004**	**401**	**843**	**2,760**	**1,444**	**173**	**354**	**917**	**2,560**	**228**	**489**	**1,843**
		Total XXIII.—Indefinite	**2,146,585**	**280,864**	**552,808**	**1,818,278**	**1,010,111**	**129,419**	**287,514**	**593,178**	**1,136,424**	**151,445**	**24,8 79**	**720,100**

Class.	Order.	Sub-order, Group and Occupation.	Town. Total. Total.	Total. 0—4	Total. 5—14	Total. 15 and over.	Males. Total.	Males. 0—4	Males. 5—14	Males. 15 and over.	Females. Total.	Females. 0—4	Females. 5—14	Females. 15 and over.
			16	17	18	19	20	21	22	23	24	25	26	27
Class F.—Professions—concld.	XXI.—Sports and Amusements—contd.	*(d) Service of places of entertainments.*												
		Billiard-room managers	29	2	8	19	15	1	5	9	14	1	3	10
		Total 73 (d)	*29*	*2*	*8*	*19*	*15*	*1*	*5*	*9*	*14*	*1*	*3*	*10*
		Total XXI.—Sports and Amusements	**1,122**	**108**	**265**	**754**	**606**	**48**	**114**	**444**	**516**	**55**	**151**	**310**
		Total Class F	**33,158**	**3,034**	**525**	**23,599**	**18,347**	**1,619**	**3,687**	**13,041**	**14,811**	**1,415**	**2,838**	**10,558**
Class G.—Indefinite and Independent.	XXIII.—Indefinite	**74.—Unskilled Labour.**												
		(a) Special Branches.												
		Well-sinkers	4	...	6	4	4	...	...	4	...	...	...	...
		Road labourers	65	7	16	42	42	3	15	24	23	4	1	18
		Railway labourers	686	87	77	522	448	41	41	366	238	46	36	156
		Gangmen	485	38	60	387	482	38	60	384	3	...	...	3
		Miners (unspecified)	27	...	3	24	27	...	3	24	...	...	...	...
		Total 74 (a)	*1,267*	*132*	*156*	*979*	*1,003*	*82*	*119*	*802*	*264*	*50*	*37*	*177*
		(b) General.												
		General labour	151,060	17,096	32,907	101,057	69,913	7,584	16,723	45,606	81,147	9,512	16,184	55,451
		Total 74 (b)	*151,060*	*17,096*	*32,907*	*101,057*	*69,913*	*7,584*	*16,723*	*45,606*	*81,147*	*9,512*	*16,184*	*55,451*
		75.—Undefined, etc.												
		Undefined and disreputable means of livelihood	1,514	96	245	1,173	428	39	80	309	1,086	57	165	864
		Total 75	1,154	96	245	1,173	428	39	80	309	1,086	57	165	864
		Total XXIII.—Indefinite	**153,841**	**17,824**	**33,308**	**103,209**	**71,344**	**7,705**	**16,922**	**46,717**	**82,497**	**9,619**	**16,386**	**56,492**

TABLE XVII A.—Occupations, by Age.—Part A.—PROVINCIAL SUMMARY—*contd.*

OCCUPATION AND CLASS.			COUNTRY.											
			Total.				Males.				Females.			
Class.	Order.	Sub-order, Group and Occupation.	Total.	0—4	5—14	15 and over.	Total.	0—4	5—14	15 and over.	Total.	0—4	5—14	15 and over.
			28	29	30	31	32	33	34	35	36	37	38	39
CLASS F.—PROFESSIONS—*concld.*	XXI.—Sports and Amusements—*contd.*	*(d) Service of places of entertainments.*												
		Billiard-room managers	6	1	...	5	...	...	...	...	6	1	...	5
		Total 73 (d)	*6*	*1*	...	*5*	...	...	...	...	*6*	*1*	...	*5*
		Total XXI.—Sports and Amusements	**5,654**	**691**	**1,287**	**3,676**	**4,352**	**486**	**990**	**2,876**	**1,302**	**205**	**297**	**800**
		Total Class F	**86,731**	**9,704**	**19,456**	**57,571**	**50,568**	**5,016**	**10,973**	**34,579**	**36,163**	**4,688**	**8,483**	**22,992**
CLASS G.—INDEFINITE AND INDEPENDENT.	XXIII.—Indefinite.	**74.—Unskilled Labour.**												
		(a) Special Branches.												
		Well-sinkers	15	1	4	10	13	1	4	8	2	...	...	2
		Road labourers	427	17	53	357	323	7	34	282	104	10	19	75
		Railway labourers	99	12	19	68	29	4	5	20	70	8	14	48
		Gangmen	77	5	6	66	58	3	2	53	19	2	4	13
		Miners (unspecified)	1,101	116	164	821	715	58	87	570	386	58	77	251
		Total 74 (a)	*1,719*	*151*	*246*	*1,322*	*1,138*	*73*	*132*	*933*	*581*	*78*	*114*	*389*
		(b) General.												
		General labour	1,988,485	263,084	518,241	1,207,160	936,613	121,507	270,186	544,920	1,051,872	141,577	248,055	662,240
		Total 74 (b)	*1,988,485*	*263,084*	*518,241*	*1,207,160*	*936,613*	*121,507*	*270,186*	*544,920*	*1,051,872*	*141,577*	*248,055*	*662,240*
		75.—Undefined, etc.												
		Undefined and disreputable means of livelihood	2,490	305	598	1,587	1,016	134	274	608	1,474	171	324	979
		Total 75	**2,490**	**305**	**598**	**1,587**	**1,016**	**134**	**274**	**608**	**1,474**	**171**	**324**	**979**
		Total XXIII.—Indefinite	**1,992,694**	**263,540**	**519,085**	**1,210,069**	**988,767**	**121,714**	**270,592**	**54,641**	**1,058,927**	**141,826**	**248,498**	**663,608**

OCCUPATION AND CLASS.			PROVINCIAL TOTAL.											
			TOTAL.				MALES.				FEMALES.			
Class.	Order.	Sub-order, Group and Occupation.	Total.	0—4	5—14	15 and over.	Total.	0—4	5—14	15 and over.	Total.	0—4	5—14	15 and over.
1	2	3	4	5	6	7	8	9	10	11	12	13	14	15
		76.—Property and Alms.												
		(a) Property and Allowance.												
	XXIV.—Independent of work.	House-rent, shares, etc.	624	58	156	410	327	30	82	215	297	28	74	195
		Allowances from patrons	1,107	79	217	811	336	21	87	228	771	58	130	583
		Total 76 (a)	*1,731*	*137*	*373*	*1,221*	*663*	*51*	*169*	*443*	*1,068*	*86*	*204*	*778*
		(b) Charity and Endowment.												
		Scholarship	234	33	77	124	207	30	75	102	27	3	2	22
		Mendicancy (not religious)	262,327	27,843	57,096	177,388	142,265	14,683	34,104	93,478	120,062	13,160	22,992	83,910
		Total 76 (b)	*262,561*	*27,876*	*57,173*	*177,512*	*142,472*	*14,713*	*34,179*	*93,580*	*120,089*	*13,163*	*22,994*	*83,932*
		77.—Supported at the Public Charge.												
		(a) Pension.												
		Pensioners, civil	1,369	112	289	968	708	62	158	488	661	50	131	480
		Ditto military	1,276	99	256	921	683	58	162	463	593	41	94	458
		Ditto (unspecified)	1,260	97	257	906	583	46	137	400	677	51	120	506
		Total 77 (a)	*3,905*	*308*	*802*	*2,795*	*1,974*	*166*	*457*	*1,351*	*1,931*	*142*	*345*	*1,444*
		(b) Prisoners.												
		Prisoners	1,548	31	65	1,452	1,270	5	10	1,255	278	26	55	197
		Total 77 (b)	*1,548*	*31*	*65*	*1,452*	*1,270*	*5*	*10*	*1,255*	*278*	*26*	*55*	*197*
		Total XXIV.—Independent of work	**269,745**	**28,352**	**58,418**	**182,980**	**146,879**	**14,935**	**134,815**	**96,629**	**123,866**	**13,417**	**23,598**	**86,351**
		Total Class G	**2,416,280**	**809,216**	**610,806**	**1,496,258**	**1,156,490**	**144,354**	**322,329**	**689,807**	**1,259,790**	**164,862**	**288,477**	**806,451**
		Total of all Classes	**10,137,677**	**1,821,958**	**2,555,759**	**6,259,965**	**5,299,191**	**649,309**	**1,397,999**	**3,251,883**	**4,838,486**	**672,444**	**157,760**	**3,008,082**

TABLE XVII.—Occupations, by Age.—Part A.—PROVINCIAL SUMMARY—*contd.*

OCCUPATION AND CLASS.			TOWN.											
			TOTAL.				MALES.				FEMALES.			
Class.	Order.	SUB-ORDER, GROUP AND OCCUPATION.	TOTAL.	0–4	5–14	15 and over.	TOTAL.	0–4	5–14	15 and over.	TOTAL.	0–4	5–14	15 and over.
			16	17	18	19	20	21	22	23	24	25	26	27
		76.—Property and Alms.												
		(a) Property and Allowance.												
	XXIV.—INDEPENDENT OF WORK.	House-rent, shares, etc.	313	24	70	219	177	17	40	120	136	7	30	99
		Allowances from patrons	388	45	87	256	80	6	24	50	308	39	63	206
		Total 76 (a)	*701*	*69*	*157*	*475*	*257*	*23*	*64*	*170*	*444*	*46*	*93*	*305*
		(b) Charity and Endowment.												
		Scholarship	106	2	29	75	94	2	28	64	12	...	1	11
		Mendicancy (not religious)	42,882	3,542	99	32,241	17,285	1,721	3,812	11,752	25,597	1,821	3,287	20,489
		Total 76 (b)	*42,988*	*3,544*	*128*	*32,316*	*17,379*	*1,723*	*3,840*	*11,816*	*25,609*	*1,821*	*3,288*	*20,500*
		77.—Supported at the Public Charge.												
		(a) Pension.												
		Pensioners, civil	1,210	84	254	872	615	37	126	452	595	47	128	420
		Ditto military	934	84	174	676	460	54	104	302	474	30	70	374
		Ditto (unspecified)	903	73	202	628	427	23	93	311	476	50	109	317
		Total 77 (a)	*3,047*	*241*	*630*	*2,176*	*1,502*	*114*	*323*	*1,065*	*1,545*	*127*	*307*	*1,111*
		(b) Prisoners.												
		Prisoners	746	3	6	737	720	3	5	712	26	...	1	25
		Total 77 (b)	*746*	*3*	*6*	*737*	*720*	*3*	*5*	*712*	*26*	...	*1*	*25*
		Total XXIV.—Independent of work	**47,482**	**3,857**	**921**	**35,704**	**19,858**	**1,863**	**4,232**	**13,763**	**27,624**	**1,994**	**3,589**	**21,941**
		Total Class G	**201,823**	**21,181**	**41,229**	**138,918**	**91,202**	**9,568**	**21,154**	**60,480**	**110,121**	**11,613**	**20,075**	**78,433**
		Total of all Classes	**939,748**	**101,406**	**194,740**	**643,602**	**501,064**	**50,628**	**106,571**	**343,865**	**438,684**	**50,778**	**88,169**	**299,787**

OCCUPATION AND CLASS.			COUNTRY.											
			TOTAL.				MALES.				FEMALES.			
Class.	Order.	Sub-order, Group and Occupation.	TOTAL.	0—4	5—14	15 and over.	TOTAL.	0—4	5—14	15 and over.	TOTAL.	0—4	5—14	15 and over.
			28	29	30	31	32	33	34	35	36	37	38	39
		76.—Property and Alms.												
		(a) Property and Allowance.												
	XXIV.—INDEPENDENT OF WORK.	House-rent, shares, etc.	311	34	86	191	150	13	42	95	161	21	44	96
		Allowances from patrons	719	34	130	555	256	15	63	178	463	19	67	377
		Total 76 (a)	*1,030*	*68*	*216*	*746*	*406*	*28*	*105*	*273*	*624*	*40*	*111*	*473*
		(b) Charity and Endowment.												
		Scholarship	128	31	48	49	113	28	47	38	15	3	1	11
		Mendicancy (not religious)	219,445	24,301	49,997	145,147	124,980	12,962	30,292	81,717	94,465	11,339	19,705	63,421
		Total 76 (b)	*219,573*	*24,332*	*50,045*	*145,196*	*125,093*	*12,990*	*30,339*	*81,755*	*94,980*	*11,342*	*19,706*	*63,432*
		77.—Supported at the Public Charge.												
		(a) Pension.												
		Pensioners, civil	159	28	35	96	93	25	32	36	66	3	3	60
		Ditto military	342	15	82	245	223	4	58	161	119	11	24	84
		Ditto (unspecified)	357	24	55	278	156	23	44	89	201	1	11	189
		Total 77 (a)	*858*	*67*	*172*	*619*	*472*	*52*	*134*	*286*	*386*	*15*	*38*	*333*
		(b) Prisoners.												
		Prisoners	802	28	59	715	550	2	5	543	252	26	54	172
		Total 77 (b)	*802*	*28*	*59*	*715*	*550*	*2*	*5*	*543*	*252*	*26*	*54*	*172*
		Total XXIV.—Independent of work	**222,263**	**24,495**	**50,492**	**147,276**	**126,521**	**13,072**	**30,583**	**82,866**	**95,742**	**11,423**	**19,909**	**64,410**
		Total Class G	**2,214,957**	**288,035**	**569,577**	**1,357,345**	**1,065,288**	**184,786**	**301,175**	**629,327**	**1,149,669**	**153,249**	**268,402**	**728,018**
		Total of all Classes	**9,197,929**	**1,220 547**	**2,361,019**	**5,616,363**	**4,798,127**	**598,681**	**1,291,428**	**2,908,018**	**4,399,802**	**621,866**	**1,069,591**	**2,708,345**

TABLE XVII.—Occupations.—Part B.—(Provincial Distribution).

TABLE XVII.—Occupations.—Part B.—(Provincial Distribution).

Class.	Order.	Sub-order Group and Occupation.	Provincial Total. Total.	Provincial Total. Males.	Provincial Total. Females.	Indore. Total.	Indore. Males.	Indore. Females.	Gwalior. Total.	Gwalior. Males.	Gwalior. Females.	Bhopal. Total.	Bhopal. Males.	Bhopal. Females.
1	2	3	4	5	6	7	8	9	10	11	12	13	14	15
CLASS A.		1.—Service of the Imperial and Provincial Governments.												
	I.—Administration	Political service	116	65	51	34	19	15	6	1	5	20	13	7
		Magistrates	5	2	3	1	1	...	4	1	3	...	...	...
		Assistant superintendents of police	3	3	...	...	...	...	3	3	...	...	...	...
		Deputy Collector	1	...	1	...	...	...	...	...	...	...	...	...
		Office superintendents	5	2	3	5	2	3	...	...	...	...	...	...
		Clerical establishments	378	167	211	197	49	148	38	38	...	42	13	29
		Police inspectors	28	20	8	16	10	6	4	4	...	...	...	...
		Peons	284	241	43	205	179	26	...	...	...	68	51	17
		Police constables	958	618	340	223	154	69	144	114	30	99	48	51
		Menials	124	81	43	30	18	12	90	62	28	...	...	...
		Bailiffs	1	...	1	1	...	1	...	...	...	...	...	...
		Subordinate Government service unspecified.	354	176	178	134	86	48	49	37	12	29	21	8
		Total 1	2,257	1,375	882	846	518	328	338	260	78	258	146	112
		2.—Service of Local or Municipal Bodies.												
		Octroi darogahs	8	5	3	4	1	3	...	...	...	...	...	...
		" Clerks	25	13	12	6	3	3	...	...	...	...	...	...
		" Menials	56	32	24	5	2	3	51	30	21	...	...	...
		Total 2	89	50	39	15	6	9	51	30	21	...	...	...
		3.—Village Service.												
		Headmen of villages, Kanungoes, etc.	19,486	10,383	9,103	117	62	55	9,364	5,117	4,247	5,264	2,543	2,721
		Watchmen, menials, etc.	54,192	26,769	27,423	1,698	897	801	7,875	4,707	3,168	13,891	7,508	6,383
		Total 3	73,678	37,152	36,526	1,815	959	856	17,239	9,824	7,415	19,155	10,051	9,104
		Total I.—Administration	76,025	38,578	37,447	2,677	1,484	1,193	17,628	10,114	7,514	19,418	10,197	9,216
		4.—Army.												
	II.—Defence	Officers	397	274	123	188	121	67	47	46	1	6	4	2
		Non-commissioned officers and privates	14,392	10,966	3,426	5,392	4,287	1,105	162	135	27	1,431	1,099	332
		Followers	2,277	1,199	1,078	1,183	510	673	10	6	4	18	10	8
		Administrative establishments	87	58	29	45	27	18	...	...	...	1	1	...
		Total 4	17,153	12,497	4,656	6,808	4,945	1,863	219	187	32	1,456	1,114	342

Table XVII—B.—Occupations—(Provincial Distribution).

CLASS A.

Class.	Order.	Sub-order, Group and Occupation.	Bundelkhand. Total.	Bundelkhand. Males.	Bundelkhand. Females.	Baghelkhand. Total.	Baghelkhand. Males.	Baghelkhand. Females.	Western Malwa. Total.	Western Malwa. Males.	Western Malwa. Females.	Bhopawar. Total.	Bhopawar. Males.	Bhopawar. Females.	Guna. Total.	Guna. Males.	Guna. Females.
			16	17	18	19	20	21	22	23	24	25	26	27	28	29	30
		1.—Service of the Imperial and Provincial Governments.															
	I.—Administration	Political service	1	...	1	2	1	1	44	29	15	...	...	...	9	2	7
		Magistrates	...	...	...	...	...	...	...	...	...	...	...	...	...	...	...
		Assistant superintendents of police	...	...	...	...	...	...	...	...	...	...	...	...	...	...	...
		Deputy Collector	1	...	1	...	...	...	...	...	...	...	...	...	...	...	...
		Office superintendents	...	...	...	...	...	...	...	...	...	...	...	...	...	...	...
		Clerical establishments	59	32	27	19	19	...	21	15	6	2	1	1	...	...	...
		Police inspectors	...	...	...	...	...	...	6	5	1	2	1	1	...	...	...
		Peons	...	...	...	...	...	...	...	...	...	7	7	...	4	4	...
		Police constables	229	157	72	54	30	24	209	115	94	...	...	...	...	...	...
		Menials	...	...	...	...	...	...	...	...	...	...	...	...	4	1	3
		Bailiffs	...	...	...	...	...	...	...	...	...	...	...	...	...	...	...
		Subordinate Government service unspecified.	44	32	12	...	...	...	...	...	...	98	...	98	...	...	...
		Total 1	334	221	113	75	50	25	280	164	116	109	9	100	17	7	10
		2.—Service of Local or Municipal Bodies.															
		Octroi darogahs	3	3	...	...	...	...	1	1	...	...	...	...	...	...	...
		" Clerks	19	10	9	...	...	...	...	...	...	...	...	...	...	...	...
		" Menials	...	...	...	...	...	...	...	...	...	...	...	...	...	...	...
		Total 2	22	13	9	...	...	...	1	1	...	...	...	...	...	...	...
		3.—Village Service.															
		Headmen of villages, Kanungoes, etc.	2,053	1,153	900	611	411	200	2,002	1,059	943	...	...	...	75	38	37
		Watchmen, menials, etc.	3,924	2,260	1,664	7,884	2,306	5,578	16,674	7,962	8,712	2,058	1,035	1,023	188	94	94
		Total 3	5,977	3,413	2,564	8,495	2,717	5,778	18,676	9,021	9,655	2,058	1,035	1,023	263	132	131
		Total I.—Administration	**6,333**	**3,647**	**2,686**	**8,570**	**2,767**	**5,803**	**18,957**	**9,186**	**9,771**	**2,167**	**1,044**	**1,123**	**280**	**139**	**141**
		4.—Army.															
	II.—Defence	Officers	41	30	11	...	...	...	32	13	19	77	54	23	6	6	...
		Non-commissioned officers and privates	1,853	1,634	219	11	11	...	3,484	2,597	887	1,663	941	722	396	262	134
		Followers	146	108	38	...	...	...	902	547	355	2	2	...	16	16	...
		Administrative establishments	28	17	11	...	...	...	13	13	...	...	...	...	...	...	...
		Total 4	2,068	1,789	279	11	11	...	4,431	3,170	1,261	1,742	997	745	418	284	134

TABLE XVII.—Occupations.—PART B.—(Provincial Distribution)—*contd.*

Class.	Order.	Sub-order, Group and Occupation.	Provincial Total. Total.	Provincial Total. Males.	Provincial Total. Females.	Indore. Total.	Indore. Males.	Indore. Females.	Gwalior. Total.	Gwalior. Males.	Gwalior. Females.	Bhopal. Total.	Bhopal. Males.	Bhopal. Females.
1	2	3	4	5	6	7	8	9	10	11	12	13	14	15
CLASS A—*contd.*		**5—Navy and Marine.**												
	II.—Defence—*contd.*	Officer, royal navy	1	1	...	1	1	...	...	...	...	...	...	...
		Total 5	1	1	...	1	1	...	...	...	...	...	...	...
		Total II.—Defence	**17,154**	**12,498**	**4,656**	**6,809**	**4,946**	**1,863**	**219**	**187**	**32**	**1,456**	**1,114**	**342**
		6.—Administrative Service.												
	III.—Feudatory State Service.	Chiefs	503	195	308	14	4	10	52	33	19	46	14	32
		Officers	12,318	8,624	3,694	611	216	395	887	507	380	6,089	5,400	689
		Clerical establishments	29,192	13,732	15,460	3,748	1,987	1,761	9,932	5,473	4,459	128	54	74
		Menials, etc.	191,759	105,202	86,557	23,038	13,053	9,985	58,658	30,446	28,212	48,189	27,207	20,982
		Total 6	233,772	127,753	106,019	27,411	15,260	12,151	69,529	36,459	33,070	54,452	32,675	21,777
		7.—Army.												
		State soldiers	115,581	72,775	42,806	3,203	2,458	745	27,288	19,203	8,085	11,241	6,417	4,824
		Total 7	115,581	72,775	42,806	3,203	2,458	745	27,288	19,203	8,085	11,241	6,417	4,824
		Total III.—Feudatory State Service	**349,353**	**200,528**	**148,825**	**30,614**	**17,718**	**12,896**	**96,817**	**55,662**	**41,155**	**65,693**	**39,092**	**26,601**
		Total Class A	**442,531**	**251,603**	**190,928**	**40,099**	**24,147**	**15,952**	**114,664**	**65,963**	**48,701**	**86,562**	**50,403**	**36,159**
CLASS B.		**8.—Stock Breeding and Dealing.**												
		(a) Horses and Horned Cattle.												
	IV.—Live-Stock	Horse breeders and dealers	176	98	78	109	66	43	...	...	...	...	...	...
		Cattle breeders and dealers	22,093	13,238	8,855	645	534	111	183	163	20	8,231	5,117	3,114
		Cattle ground keepers and graziers	113	104	9	...	...	...	...	...	...	6	6	...
		Herdsmen	40,560	25,963	14,597	699	465	234	5,295	2,892	2,403	278	193	85
		Total 8 (a)	62,942	39,403	23,539	1,453	1,065	388	5,478	3,055	2,423	8,515	5,316	3,199
		(b) Other Draught, etc., Animals.												
		Elephant catchers	9	5	4	...	...	...	...	...	...	...	...	...
		Camel breeders and dealers	501	272	229	14	...	14	...	...	...	5	...	5
		Total 8 (b)	510	277	233	14	...	14	...	...	...	5	...	5

Table XVII—B.—Occupations—(Provincial Distribution).

Class.	Order.	Sub-order, Group and Occupation.	DISTRIBUTION BY AGENCIES. Bundelkhand. Total.	Bundelkhand. Males.	Bundelkhand. Females.	Baghelkhand. Total.	Baghelkhand. Males.	Baghelkhand. Females.	Western Malwa. Total.	Western Malwa. Males.	Western Malwa. Females.	Bhopawar. Total.	Bhopawar. Males.	Bhopawar. Females.	Guna. Total.	Guna. Males.	Guna. Females.
			16	17	18	19	20	21	22	23	24	25	26	27	28	29	30
CLASS A—contd.		**5.—Navy and Marine.**															
	II.—Defence—contd.	Officer, royal navy	...	...	...	...	...	...	...	...	...	...	...	...	...	...	...
		Total 5	...	...	...	...	...	...	...	...	...	...	...	...	...	...	...
		Total II.—Defence	**2,068**	**1,789**	**279**	**11**	**11**	...	**4,431**	**3,170**	**1,261**	**1,742**	**997**	**745**	**418**	**284**	**184**
		6.—Administrative Service.															
	III.—Feudatory State Service.	Chiefs	176	100	76	45	16	29	150	14	136	10	4	6	10	10	...
		Officers	115	91	24	186	50	136	4,042	2,163	1,879	...	...	...	388	197	191
		Clerical establishments	6,365	1,033	5,332	3,598	1,773	1,825	3,684	2,103	1,581	1,443	1,165	278	294	144	150
		Menials, etc.	1,938	287	1,651	6,954	6,306	648	25,698	15,432	10,266	26,448	11,977	14,471	836	494	342
		Total 6	8,594	1,511	7,083	10,783	8,145	2,638	33,574	19,712	13,862	27,901	13,146	14,755	1,528	845	683
		7.—Army.															
		State soldiers	58,780	35,142	23,638	4,639	3,134	1,505	5,558	2,731	2,827	3,750	3,029	721	1,122	661	461
		Total 7	58,780	35,142	23,638	4,639	3,134	1,505	5,558	2,731	2,827	3,750	3,029	721	1,122	661	461
		Total III.—Feudatory State Service	**57,374**	**36,653**	**30,721**	**15,422**	**11,279**	**4,143**	**39,132**	**22,443**	**16,689**	**31,651**	**16,175**	**15,476**	**2,650**	**1,506**	**1,144**
		Total Class A	**75,775**	**42,089**	**33,686**	**24,008**	**14,057**	**9,946**	**62,520**	**34,799**	**27,721**	**35,560**	**18,216**	**17,344**	**3,348**	**1,929**	**1,419**
CLASS B.		**8.—Stock Breeding and Dealing.**															
		(a) *Horse and Horned Cattle.*															
	IV.—Live-Stock	Horse breeders and dealers	11	3	8	40	23	17	16	6	10	...	...	...	...	...	...
		Cattle breeders and dealers	290	138	152	316	223	93	4,183	2,491	1,689	6,723	3,662	3,061	1,522	907	615
		Cattle ground keepers and graziers	...	...	...	...	...	...	107	98	9	...	...	...	...	...	...
		Herdsmen	8,031	4,351	3,680	26,022	17,921	8,101	14	10	4	...	...	...	221	131	90
		Total 8 (a)	*8,332*	*4,492*	*3,840*	*26,378*	*18,167*	*8,211*	*4,320*	*2,608*	*1,712*	*6,723*	*3,662*	*3,061*	*1,743*	*1,038*	*705*
		(b) *Other Draught, etc., Animals.*															
		Elephant catchers	5	5	...	...	...	...	...	...	...	...	...	...	4	...	4
		Camel breeders and dealers	179	104	75	...	...	...	303	168	135	...	...	...	...	...	...
		Total 8 (b)	*184*	*109*	*75*	...	...	...	*303*	*168*	*135*	...	...	...	*4*	...	*4*

TABLE XVII.—Occupations.—Part B.—(Provincial Distribution)—*contd.*

OCCUPATION AND CLASS.			PROVINCIAL TOTAL.			DISTRIBUTION BY AGENCIES.								
						INDORE.			GWALIOR.			BHOPAL.		
Class.	Order.	Sub-order, Group and Occupation.	Total.	Males.	Females.	Total.	Males.	Females.	Total.	Males.	Females.	Total.	Males.	Females.
1	2	3	4	5	6	7	8	9	10	11	12	13	14	15
		(c) Small Stock.												
	IV.—Live-Stock—*contd.*	Sheep and goat breeders and dealers	31,535	17,269	14,266	262	110	152	12,367	6,679	5,688	825	450	375
		Pig breeders and dealers	48	32	16	23	16	7	...	...	...	...	...	...
		Total 8 (c)	31,583	17,301	14,282	285	126	159	12,367	6,679	5,688	825	450	375
		9.—Subsidiary Services to Stock.												
		(a) Training and Doctoring Live-Stock.												
		Veterinary surgeons	39	25	14	1	1	...	11	6	5	18	9	9
		Farriers	413	216	197	62	43	19	...	...	...	60	30	30
		Horse breakers and trainers	508	357	151	...	...	...	49	36	13	2	2	...
		Elephant „ „	1,182	646	536	...	...	...	92	87	5	3	2	1
		Total 9 (a)	2,142	1,244	898	63	44	19	152	129	23	83	43	40
		Total IV.—Live-Stock	97,177	58,225	38,952	1,815	1,235	580	17,997	9,868	8,134	9,428	5,809	3,619
		10.—Interest in Land.												
	V.—Agriculture	Land occupants, not cultivating	137,693	78,170	59,523	1,677	757	920	49,081	27,157	21,924	9,105	8,176	929
		Land occupants, cultivating	4,607,961	2,424,598	2,183,363	98,106	51,768	46,338	909,016	493,875	415,141	742,354	387,807	354,547
		Lessees of villages, etc.	9,698	5,103	4,595	...	...	...	...	...	...	7,085	3,668	3,417
		Total 10	4,755,352	2,507,871	2,247,481	99,783	52,525	47,258	958,097	521,032	437,065	758,544	399,651	358,893
		11.—Agricultural Labourers.												
		42. Farm servants	187,259	120,243	67,016	2	...	2	2	...	2	18,158	9,019	9,138
		43. Field labourers	3,048	1,971	1,077	2	2	...	8	8	...	665	372	293
		Total 11	190,307	122,214	68,093	4	2	2	10	8	2	18,823	9,391	9,431

Table XVII—B.—Occupations—(Provincial Distribution).

OCCUPATION AND CLASS.			DISTRIBUTION BY AGENCIES.														
			Bundelkhand.			Baghelkhand.			Western Malwa.			Bhopawar.			Guna.		
Class.	Order.	Sub-order, Group and Occupation.	Total.	Males.	Females.	Total.	Males.	Females.	Total.	Males.	Females.	Total.	Males.	Females.	Total.	Males.	Females.
			16	17	18	19	20	21	22	23	24	25	26	27	28	29	30
		(c) Small Stock.															
	IV.—Live-Stock—*contd.*	Sheep and goat breeders and dealers	14,524	7,637	6,887	801	431	370	1,90	1,446	463	...	...	...	847	516	331
		Pig breeders and dealers	...	...	...	25	16	9	...	...	...	...	...	...	...	...	...
		Total 8 (c)	14,524	7,637	6,887	826	447	379	1,909	1,446	463	...	...	...	847	516	331
		9.—Subsidiary Services to Stock.															
		(a) Training and Doctoring Live-Stock.															
		Veterinary surgeons	8	8	...	...	...	...	1	1	...	...	...	...	...	...	...
		Farriers	113	54	59	99	51	48	55	23	32	...	...	...	24	15	9
		Horse breakers and trainers	409	289	120	22	12	10	26	18	8	...	...	...	...	...	...
		Elephant " "	431	212	219	631	332	307	17	13	4	...	...	...	...	...	...
		Total 9 (a)	961	563	398	760	395	365	99	55	44	...	...	...	24	15	9
		Total IV—Live-Stock	**24,001**	**12,801**	**11,200**	**27,964**	**19,009**	**8,955**	**6,631**	**4,277**	**2,354**	**6,728**	**3,662**	**3,061**	**2,618**	**1,569**	**1,049**
		10.—Interest in Land.															
	V—Agriculture.	Land occupants, not cultivating	11,737	6,041	5,696	42,105	21,081	21,024	12,345	6,148	6,197	4,456	2,130	2,326	7,187	6,680	507
		Land occupants, cultivating	674,693	359,397	315,296	855,560	435,010	420,550	635,237	339,471	295,776	522,412	268,438	253,974	152,453	79,051	73,402
		Lessees of villages, etc.	201	139	62	1,630	763	597	497	267	230	...	...	...	555	266	289
		Total 10	686,631	365,577	321,054	899,025	456,854	442,171	666,209	355,667	310,542	526,868	2 70568	256,300	160,195	85,997	74,198
		11.—Agricultural Labourers.															
		Farm servants	...	...	...	168,887	111,091	57,796	...	...	...	...	...	...	210	133	77
		Field labourers	1,656	1,032	624	...	...	...	708	552	156	...	...	...	9	5	4
		Total 11	1,656	1,032	624	168,887	111,091	57,797	708	552	156	...	...	...	219	138	81

TABLE XVII.—Occupations.—Part B.—(Provincial Distribution)—*contd.*

OCCUPATION AND CLASS.			DISTRIBUTION BY AGENCIES.											
			PROVINCIAL TOTAL.			INDORE.			GWALIOR.			BHOPAL.		
Class.	Order.	SUB-ORDER, GROUP AND OCCUPATION.	TOTAL.	Males.	Females.	TOTAL.	Males.	Females.	TOTAL.	Males.	Females.	TOTAL.	Males.	Females.
1	2	3	4	5	6	7	8	9	10	11	12	13	14	15
CLASS B—*concld.*	V.—AGRICULTURE—*contd.*	**12.—Growers of Special Products and Trees.**												
		Betel vine, etc., growers	3,083	1,285	1,798	...	...	...	...	...	...	...	...	...
		Water nut growers	3,256	1,401	1,855	...	...	...	...	...	...	...	...	...
		Water melon growers	352	192	160	...	...	...	...	...	...	352	192	160
		Fruit growers	5	3	2	...	...	...	...	...	...	5	3	2
		Market gardeners	802	411	391	...	...	...	...	...	...	343	187	156
		Gardeners	3,951	2,207	1,744	467	366	101	715	375	340	174	81	93
		Forest officers	2	1	1	...	...	...	...	...	...	...	...	...
		Forest rangers, etc.	57	39	18	...	...	...	3	...	3	...	...	...
		Total 12	11,508	5,539	5,969	467	366	101	718	375	343	874	463	411
		13.—Agricultural Training and Supervision.												
		Agents and managers of landed estates	8,573	4,947	3,626	104	69	35	1,311	700	611	...	...	...
		Total 13	8,573	4,947	3,626	104	69	35	1,311	700	611	...	...	...
		Total V.—Agriculture	**4,965,740**	**2,640,571**	**2,325,169**	**100,358**	**52,962**	**47,396**	**960,136**	**522,115**	**468,021**	**778,241**	**409,505**	**368,736**
		Total Class B.	**5,062,917**	**2,698,796**	**2,364,121**	**102,173**	**54,197**	**47,976**	**978,133**	**531,178**	**446,155**	**787,669**	**415,314**	**372,355**
CLASS C.	VI.—PERSONAL AND HOUSEHOLD SERVICES.	**14.—Personal and Domestic Services.**												
		Barbers	112,368	60,086	52,282	3,912	2,231	1,681	21,421	11,332	10,089	28,860	15,256	13,604
		Ear pickers	53	1	52	...	...	...	...	...	...	...	...	...
		Washermen	54,187	28,568	25,619	1,628	955	673	15,733	8,226	7,507	16,293	8,389	7,904
		Water carriers	26,879	13,803	13,076	1,225	799	426	3,340	1,729	1,611	4,728	2,342	2,386
		Cooks	2,401	1,493	908	638	473	165	125	62	63	132	74	58
		Indoor servants	208,798	120,318	88,480	11,173	7,373	3,800	338	162	176	68,668	38,225	30,449
		Grooms, etc.	5,695	3,455	2,240	268	171	97	652	364	288	135	88	47
		Door keepers	2,000	1,227	773	6	6	...	233	166	67	...	...	...
		Domestic service, unspecified	78,488	41,588	36,900	20,542	10,255	10,287	32,673	16,847	15,826	73	1	72
		Total 14	490,869	270,539	220,330	39,392	22,263	17,129	74,515	38,888	35,627	118,889	65,375	54,514
		15.—Non-domestic Establishment.												
		Hotel and refreshment room-keepers, etc.	80	73	7	3	3	...	...	...	...	12	5	7
		Rest-house, serai keepers, etc.	45	26	19	...	...	...	...	...	...	...	...	...
		Total 15										12	5	[illegible]

Table XVII—B.—Occupations—(Provincial Distribution.)

Class.	Order.	Sub-order, Group and Occupation.	Bundelkhand. Total.	Bundelkhand. Males.	Bundelkhand. Females.	Baghelkhand. Total.	Baghelkhand. Males.	Baghelkhand. Females.	Western Malwa. Total.	Western Malwa. Males.	Western Malwa. Females.	Bhopawar. Total.	Bhopawar. Males.	Bhopawar. Females.	Guna. Total.	Guna. Males.	Guna. Females.
			16	17	18	19	20	21	22	23	24	25	26	27	28	29	30
CLASS B—concld.	V.—Agriculture—contd.	**12.—Growers of Special Products and Trees.**															
		Betel vine, etc., growers	3,083	1,285	1,798	...	...	...	...	...	...	...	...	...	...	...	...
		Water nut growers	2,791	1,401	1,390	465	...	465	...	...	...	...	...	...	...	...	...
		Water melon growers	...	...	...	...	...	...	...	...	...	...	...	...	...	...	...
		Fruit growers	...	...	...	...	...	...	...	...	...	...	...	...	...	...	...
		Market gardeners	444	215	229	...	...	...	...	...	...	...	...	...	15	9	6
		Gardeners	886	504	382	1,321	729	592	146	86	60	212	52	160	30	14	16
		Forest officers	...	...	...	...	...	...	...	...	...	2	1	1	...	...	...
		Forest rangers, etc.	52	37	15	2	2	...	...	...	...	...	...	...	...	...	...
		Total 12	7,256	3,442	3,814	1,788	731	1,057	146	86	60	214	53	161	45	23	22
		13.—Agricultural Training and Supervision.															
		Agents and managers of landed estates	636	307	329	6,522	3,871	2,651	...	...	...	...	...	...	...	...	...
		Total 13	636	307	329	6,522	3,871	2,651	...	...	...	...	...	...	...	...	...
		Total V.—Agriculture	696,179	370,358	325,821	1,076,222	572,547	503,675	667,063	356,305	310,758	527,082	270,621	256,461	16 0459	86,158	74,301
		Total Class B.	720,180	383,159	337,021	1,104,186	591,556	512,630	678,694	360,582	318,112	533,805	274,288	259,5 22	163,077	87,727	75,350
CLASS C.	VI.—Personal and Household Services.	**14.—Personal and Domestic Services.**															
		Barbers	22,881	11,982	10,899	12,700	7,066	5,634	14,077	7,693	6,384	48,26	2,557	2,269	3,691	1,969	1,722
		Ear pickers	53	1	52	...	...	...	...	...	...	...	...	...	...	...	...
		Washermen	12,564	6,611	5,953	1,483	725	758	2,656	1,720	936	1,574	779	795	2,256	1,163	1,093
		Water carriers	8,898	4,574	4,324	6,708	3,206	3,502	802	552	250	98	39	59	1,080	562	518
		Cooks	707	379	328	338	193	145	385	255	130	49	37	12	27	20	7
		Indoor servants	39,304	22,508	16,796	10,679	5,749	4,930	49,725	29,388	20,337	27,364	16,091	11,273	1,547	822	725
		Grooms, etc.	1,930	1,224	706	1,101	644	457	1,527	958	569	3	3	...	79	3	76
		Door-keepers	...	...	...	1,761	1,055	706	...	...	...	...	...	...	...	...	...
		Domestic service, unspecified	586	2	584	69	21	48	12,47	6,746	5,711	...	...	...	12,088	7,716	4,372
		Total 14	85,923	47,281	39,642	34,839	18,659	16,180	81,629	47,312	34,317	33,914	19,506	14,408	20,768	12,255	8,513
		15.—Non-domestic Establishment.															
		Hotel and refreshment room-keepers etc.	2	2	...	1	1	...	62	62	...	...	...	...	...	...	...
		Rest-house, serai keepers, etc.	37	25	12	8	1	7	...	...	...	...	...	...	...	...	...
		Total 15	39	27	12	9	2	7	62	62	...	...	...	...	...	...	...

TABLE XVII.—Occupations.—Part B.—(Provincial Distribution)—*contd.*

Class.	Order.	Sub-order, Group and Occupation.	Provincial Total. Total.	Provincial Total. Males.	Provincial Total. Females.	Indore. Total.	Indore. Males.	Indore. Females.	Gwalior. Total.	Gwalior. Males.	Gwalior. Females.	Bhopal. Total.	Bhopal. Males.	Bhopal. Females.
1	2	3	4	5	6	7	8	9	10	11	12	13	14	15
CLASS C—*concld.*		16.—Sanitation.												
	VI.—Personal and Household Services—*contd.*	Sanitary inspectors	21	7	14	...	...	...	...	...	...	...	...	...
		Sweepers and scavengers	35,185	18,612	16,573	2,191	1,362	829	10,516	5,659	4,857	7,370	4,055	3,315
		Total 16	35,206	18,619	16,587	2,191	1,362	829	10,516	5,659	4,857	7,370	4,055	3,315
		Total VI.—Personal and Household Services.	526,200	289,257	236,943	41,586	23,628	17,958	85,031	44,547	40,484	126,271	68,435	57,836
		Total Class C.	526,200	289,257	236,943	41,586	23,628	17,958	85,031	44,547	40,484	126,271	68,435	57,836
CLASS D.		17.—Animal Food.												
	VII.—Food and Drink	Milk and butter sellers	17,695	8,896	8,799	1,766	1,199	567	2,784	1,465	1,319	2,830	1,439	1,391
		Ghee preparers and sellers	2,044	1,122	922	5	5	...	1,154	659	495	42	34	8
		Cheese sellers	4	3	1	...	...	...	...	...	...	...	...	...
		Butchers	17,123	10,864	6,259	599	390	209	2,730	1,105	1,625	2,706	1,392	1,314
		Fowl and egg sellers	246	127	119	70	44	26	56	13	43	27	12	15
		Fish dealers	4,348	2,165	2,183	85	71	14	44	26	18	901	449	452
		Total 17	41,460	23,177	18,283	2,585	1,709	816	6,768	3,268	3,500	6,506	3,326	3,180
		18.—Vegetable Food.												
		Grain dealers	26,031	8,133	17,898	730	430	300	2,615	1,474	1,141	2,857	1,417	1,440
		Grain parchers	5,392	3,021	2,371	174	131	43	710	668	42	683	358	325
		Pulse and flour preparers and sellers	47,084	24,157	22,927	269	197	72	7,156	3,396	3,760	10,813	5,627	5,186
		Flour mill service	88	88	...	7	7	...	58	58	...	23	23	...
		Bakers	1,220	777	443	171	162	9	274	155	119	753	455	298
		Bread sellers	519	482	37	...	...	...	...	...	...	...	...	...
		Bran sellers	23	14	9	...	...	...	...	...	...	...	...	...
		Vegetable sellers	17,273	8,662	8,611	2,112	1,987	125	1,266	464	802	3,173	1,612	1,561
		Fruit sellers	796	373	423	52	44	8	294	126	168	92	53	39
		Cocoanut sellers	521	519	2	...	...	...	...	...	...	5	3	2
		Confectioners	6,634	3,705	2,869	508	335	173	1,964	1,145	819	2,243	1,238	1,005
		Sweetmeat sellers	2,813	1,726	1,087	...	...	...	239	145	94	820	691	137
		Total 18	108,304	[illegible]	[illegible]	4,023	3,293	730	14,576	7,631	6,945	21,470	11,477	9,993

Table XVI—B.—Occupations—(Provincial Distribution.)

Class.	Order.	Sub-order, Group and Occupation.	Bundelkhand. Total.	Bundelkhand. Males.	Bundelkhand. Females.	Baghelkhand. Total.	Baghelkhand. Males.	Baghelkhand. Females.	Western Malwa. Total.	Western Malwa. Males.	Western Malwa. Females.	Bhopawar. Total.	Bhopawar. Males.	Bhopawar. Females.	Guna. Total.	Guna. Males.	Guna. Females.
			16	17	18	19	20	21	22	23	24	25	26	27	28	29	30
CLASS C—concld.	VI.—Personal and Household Services—contd.	**16. Sanitation.**															
		Sanitary inspectors	21	7	14	...	...	...	...	...	...	...	...	...	...	...	...
		Sweepers and scavengers	3,857	1,794	2,063	1,683	860	823	5,831	3,003	2,828	1,579	772	807	2,18	1,107	1,051
		Total 16	3,878	1,801	2,077	1,683	860	823	5,831	3,003	2,828	1,579	772	807	2,158	1,107	1,051
		Total VI.—Personal and Household Services.	**90,840**	**49,109**	**41,781**	**36,531**	**19,521**	**17,010**	**87,522**	**50,377**	**87,145**	**35,493**	**20,278**	**15,215**	**22,926**	**13,362**	**9,564**
		Total Class C.	**90,840**	**49,109**	**41,781**	**36,531**	**19,521**	**17,010**	**87,522**	**50,377**	**87,145**	**35,493**	**20,278**	**15,215**	**22,926**	**13,362**	**9,564**
CLASS D.	VII.—Food and Drink.	**17.—Animal Food.**															
		Milk and butter sellers	1,472	719	753	3,415	1,124	2,291	2,249	1,206	1,043	2,365	1,282	1,083	814	462	352
		Ghee preparers and sellers	210	100	110	587	310	277	25	9	16	...	...	...	21	5	16
		Cheese sellers	...	...	...	4	3	1	...	...	...	...	...	...	...	...	...
		Butchers	2,493	1,254	1,239	804	416	388	7,052	5,909	1,143	426	226	200	313	172	141
		Fowl and egg sellers	36	21	15	49	29	20	8	8	...	...	..	...	...	...	...
		Fish dealers	1,189	611	578	61	42	19	341	165	176	1,719	793	926	8	8	...
		Total 17	5,400	2,705	2,695	4,920	1,924	2,996	9,675	7,297	2,378	4,510	2,301	2,209	1,156	647	509
		18.—Vegetable Food.															
		Grain dealers	3,343	1,182	1,461	10,985	...	10,985	1,163	811	352	3,553	1,693	1,860	785	426	359
		Grain parchers	1,480	730	750	1,204	595	609	651	317	334	405	172	233	85	50	35
		Pulse and flour preparers and sellers	24,632	12,764	11,868	3,468	1,706	1,762	718	439	279	28	28	...	...	...	...
		Flour mill service	...	...	...	...	...	...	...	...	...	...	...	...	...	...	...
		Bakers	2	...	2	10	4	6	9	...	9	1	1	...	...	...	...
		Bread sellers	455	437	18	...	...	...	60	41	19	4	4	...	...	...	...
		Bran sellers	11	11	...	12	3	9	...	...	...	...	...	...	...	...	...
		Vegetable sellers	1,129	559	570	7,234	2,712	4,522	1,454	712	742	485	367	118	420	249	171
		Fruit sellers	124	57	67	66	41	25	152	46	116	1	...	1	15	6	9
		Cocoanut sellers	...	...	...	516	516	...	...	...	...	...	...	...	...	...	...
		Confectioners	...	...	...	...	...	...	1,371	748	623	524	287	237	24	12	12
		Sweetmeat sellers	1,153	591	562	386	203	183	10	4	6	...	...	...	197	92	105
		Total 18	32,329	17,031	15,298	23,881	5,780	18,101	5,588	3,118	2,470	5,001	2,552	2,449	1,526	835	

TABLE XVII.—Occupations.—Part B.—(Provincial Distribution)—*contd.*

Class.	Order.	Sub-order, Group and Occupation.	Provincial Total. Total.	Provincial Total. Males.	Provincial Total. Females.	Indore. Total.	Indore. Males.	Indore. Females.	Gwalior. Total.	Gwalior. Males.	Gwalior. Females.	Bhopal. Total.	Bhopal. Males.	Bhopal. Females.
1	2	3	4	5	6	7	8	9	10	11	12	13	14	15
		19.—Drink, Condiments and Narcotics.												
	VII.—Food and Drink —*contd.*	Ice manufacturers and sellers	5	3	2	3	3	...	2	...	2	...	...	...
		Sodawater manufacturers	51	15	36	9	9	...	26	4	22	...	...	...
		Country spririt distillers and sellers	34,751	18,104	16,647	783	429	354	3,529	1,805	1,724	8,852	4,535	4,317
		Toddy drawers and sellers	45	9	36	...	...	...	...	...	...	45	9	36
		Tea sellers	21	19	2	1	1	...	...	...	...	...	...	...
		Sugar manufacturers and sellers	2	1	1	...	...	...	...	...	...	...	...	...
		Jaggery sellers	302	203	99	4	3	1	203	133	70	3	1	2
		Salt preparers and sellers	3,566	1,908	1,658	...	...	...	1,023	576	447	1,287	637	650
		Assafœtida, etc., sellers	1,500	799	701	...	...	...	...	...	...	318	162	156
		Pickle makers and sellers	35	10	25	...	...	...	2	...	2	30	7	23
		Grocers and general condiment dealers	26,463	14,168	12,295	1,399	900	499	3,438	1,801	1,637	18,134	9,607	8,527
		Betel-leaf sellers	14,431	8,221	6,210	515	297	218	2,152	1,139	1,013	2,673	1,517	1,156
		Tobacco manufacturers and sellers	6,687	3,371	3,316	632	625	7	734	405	329	614	340	274
		Snuff manufacturers and sellers	29	2	27	...	...	...	29	2	27	...	...	...
		Opium, etc., manufacturers and sellers	188	104	84	...	...	...	29	12	17	65	33	32
		Bhang and ganja preparers and sellers	297	215	82	...	...	...	64	39	25	128	128	...
		Total 19	88,373	7,152	41,221	3,346	2,267	1,079	11,231	5,916	5,315	32,149	16,976	15,173
		Total VII.—Food and Drink	**238,227**	**122,046**	**116,181**	**9,894**	**7,269**	**2,625**	**32,575**	**16,815**	**15,760**	**60,125**	**31,779**	**28,346**
		20.—Lighting.												
	VIII.—Light, Firing and Forage.	Oil pressers and sellers	87,307	47,967	39,340	2,184	1,145	1,039	18,165	9,428	8,737	16,464	11,570	4,894
		Candle makers and sellers	5	2	3	...	...	...	5	2	3	...	...	...
		Torch makers and sellers	92	56	36	6	...	6	17	12	5	...	...	...
		Match makers and sellers	2	2	...	1	1	...	1	1	...	...	...	...
		Total 20	87,406	48,027	39,379	2,191	1,146	1,045	18,188	9,443	8,745	16,464	1,570	4,894
		21.—Fuel and Forage.												
		Firewood and grass gatherers and sellers	19,601	15,994	3,607	434	359	75	2,949	1,348	1,601	1,348	642	706
		Coal dealers	611	318	293	41	40	1	80	31	49	149	75	74
		Charcoal burners	62	27	35	...	...	...	...	...	...	24	11	13
		Cow-dung fuel preparers and sellers	570	250	320	14	8	6	278	24	254	8	1	7
		Hay contractors, etc.	9	6	3	...	...	...	9	6	3	...	...	...
		Total 21	20,853	16,595	4,258	489	407	82	3,316	1,409	1,907	1,529	729	800
		Total VIII.—Light, Firing and Forage	**108,259**	**64,622**	**43,637**	**2,680**	**1,553**	**1,127**	**21,504**	**10,852**	**10,652**	**17,993**	**12,299**	**5,694**

Table XVII—B.—Occupations—(Provincial Distribution.)

CLASS D—*contd.*

Class.	Order.	Sub-order, Group and Occupation.	Bundelkhand. Total.	Bundelkhand. Males.	Bundelkhand. Females.	Baghelkhand. Total.	Baghelkhand. Males.	Baghelkhand. Females.	Western Malwa. Total.	Western Malwa. Males.	Western Malwa. Females.	Bhopawar. Total.	Bhopawar. Males.	Bhopawar. Females.	Guna. Total.	Guna. Males.	Guna. Females.
			16	17	18	19	20	21	22	23	24	25	26	27	28	29	30
		19.—Drink, Condiments and Narcotics.															
	VII.—Food and Drink —*contd.*	Ice manufacturers and sellers	...	...	...	...	...	...	...	...	...	...	...	...	...	...	...
		Sodawater manufacturers	14	...	14	...	...	...	2	2	...	...	...	...	...	...	...
		Country spirit distillers and sellers	5,805	2,861	2,944	5,129	2,595	2,534	4,244	1,791	2,453	5,034	2,730	2,304	1,375	1,358	17
		Toddy drawers and sellers	...	...	...	...	...	...	...	...	...	...	...	...	...	...	...
		Tea sellers	13	13	...	...	...	...	7	5	2	...	...	...	...	...	...
		Sugar manufacturers and sellers	2	1	1	...	...	...	...	...	...	...	...	...	...	...	...
		Jaggery sellers	...	...	...	...	...	...	92	66	26	...	...	...	...	...	...
		Salt preparers and sellers	522	353	169	691	316	375	...	...	...	...	...	...	43	26	17
		Assafœtida, etc., sellers	1	1	...	1	...	1	714	384	330	466	252	214	...	...	...
		Pickle makers and sellers	...	...	...	...	...	...	3	3	...	...	...	...	...	...	...
		Grocers and general condiment dealers	1,042	581	461	830	433	397	854	572	282	337	43	294	429	231	198
		Betel-leaf sellers	4,049	2,230	1,719	2,983	1,525	1,458	656	647	9	853	496	357	550	270	280
		Tobacco manufacturers and sellers	471	...	471	3,976	1,848	2,128	222	132	90	...	...	...	38	21	17
		Snuff manufacturers and sellers	...	...	...	...	...	...	...	...	...	...	...	...	...	...	...
		Opium, etc., manufacturers and sellers	5	1	4	...	...	...	89	58	31	...	...	...	...	...	...
		Bhang and ganja preparers and sellers	72	34	38	24	14	10	9	...	9	...	...	...	...	...	...
		Total 19	11,996	6,175	5,821	13,634	6,731	6,903	6,892	3,360	3,232	6,224	3,269	2,955	2,901	2,158	743
		Total VII.—Food and Drink	**49,725**	**25,911**	**23,814**	**42,485**	**14,485**	**28,000**	**22,155**	**14,075**	**8,080**	**15,785**	**8,122**	**7,6**	**5,588**	**3,640**	**1,948**
		20.—Lighting.															
	VIII.—Light, Firing, and Forage.	Oil pressers and sellers	18,301	9,380	8,921	13,239	6,472	67,67	9,162	4,929	4,233	6,568	3,43	3,133	3,224	1,608	1,616
		Candle makers and sellers	...	...	...	...	...	...	...	...	...	...	...	...	...	...	...
		Torch makers and sellers	63	38	25	6	6	...	...	...	...	...	...	...	...	...	...
		Match makers and sellers	...	...	...	...	...	...	...	...	...	...	...	...	...	...	...
		Total 20	18,364	9,418	8,946	13,245	6,478	6,767	9,162	4,929	4,233	6,568	3,435	3,133	3,224	1,608	1,616
		21.—Fuel and Forage.															
		Firewood and grass gatherers and sellers	522	245	277	12,862	12,862	...	836	287	549	556	207	349	94	44	50
		Coal dealers	311	150	161	22	14	8	...	...	...	8	8	...	...	...	...
		Charcoal burners	...	...	...	...	...	...	...	...	...	...	...	...	38	16	22
		Cow-dung fuel preparers and sellers	...	...	...	...	...	...	270	217	53	...	...	...	...	...	...
		Hay contractors, etc.	...	...	...	...	...	...	...	...	...	...	...	...	...	...	...
		Total 21	833	395	438	12,884	12,876	8	1,106	504	602	564	215	349	132	60	27
		Total VIII.—Light, Firing and Forage	**19,197**	**9,818**	**9,884**	**26,129**	**19,854**	**6,775**	**10,268**	**5,438**	**4,835**	**7,182**	**3,650**	**3,482**	**3,356**	**1,668**	**1,688**

TABLE XVII—Occupations.—Part B.—(Provincial Distribution)—*contd.*

Class.	Order.	Sub-order, Group and Occupation.	Provincial Total. Total.	Provincial Total. Males.	Provincial Total. Female.	Indore. Total.	Indore. Males.	Indore. Females.	Gwalior. Total.	Gwalior. Males.	Gwalior. Females.	Bhopal. Total.	Bhopal. Males.	Bhopal. Females.
1	2	3	4	5	6	7	8	9	10	11	12	13	14	15
		22.—Building Materials.												
	IX.—Buildings	Brick and tile makers and sellers	41,744	21,268	20,476	1,503	1	1,502	18,239	9,775	8,464	234	134	100
		Lime, chunam and shell burners and sellers.	3,577	1,929	1,648	15	6	9	198	107	91	103	53	50
		Stone quarry owners, contractors, etc.	2,564	1,245	1,319	...	...	...	455	455	...	452	217	235
		Total 22	47,885	24,442	23,443	1,518	7	1,511	18,892	10,337	8,555	789	404	385
		23.—Artificers in Building.												
		Building contractors	213	213	...	135	135	...	...	...	...	10	10	...
		Stone and marble workers	9,049	5,286	3,763	854	466	388	2,604	1,258	1,346	1,000	560	440
		Masons	16,216	8,929	7,287	875	639	236	9,506	5,338	4,168	1,835	1,020	815
		Mud wall builders	1,807	717	1,090	40	22	18	452	79	373	932	434	498
		Total 23	27,285	15,145	12,140	1,904	1,262	642	12,562	6,675	5,887	3,777	2,024	1,753
		Total IX.—Buildings	**75,170**	**39,587**	**35,583**	**3,422**	**1,269**	**2,153**	**31,454**	**17,012**	**14,442**	**4,566**	**2,428**	**2,138**
		24.—Railway Plant.												
	X.—Vehicles	Fitters	149	101	48	5	...	5	1	1	...	...	...	...
		Painters	17	17	...	...	...	...	...	...	...	...	...	...
		Platelayers	4	3	1	...	...	...	...	...	...	...	...	...
		Inspectors	83	51	32	61	45	16	4	3	1	7	2	5
		Lorrymen	162	93	69	...	...	...	...	...	...	...	...	...
		Trollymen	86	74	12	15	3	12	...	...	...	39	39	...
		Total 24	501	339	162	81	48	33	5	4	1	46	41	5
		25.—Carts, Carriages, etc.												
		Carriage makers and sellers	8	8	...	...	...	...	...	...	...	...	...	...
		Total 25	8	8	...	...	...	...	...	...	...	...	...	...
		Total X.—Vehicles	**509**	**347**	**162**	**81**	**48**	**33**	**5**	**4**	**1**	**46**	**41**	**5**

Class.	Order.	Sub order, Group and Occupation.	Bundelkhand. Total.	Males.	Females.	Baghelkhand. Total.	Males.	Females.	Western Malwa. Total.	Males.	Females.	Bhopawar. Total.	Males.	Females.	Guna. Total.	Males.	Females.
			16	17	18	19	20	21	22	23	24	25	26	27	28	29	30
		22.—Building Materials.															
	IX.—Buildings	Brick and tile makers and sellers	18,605	9,692	8,913	22	14	8	...	...	...	2	2	...	3,139	1,650	1,489
		Lime, chunam and shell burners and sellers.	2,841	1,574	1,267	207	92	115	153	64	89	...	...	...	60	33	27
		Stone quarry owners, contractors, etc.	93	...	93	776	178	598	...	...	...	425	200	225	363	195	168
		Total 22	21,539	11,266	10,273	1,005	284	721	153	64	89	427	202	225	3,562	1,878	1,684
		23.—Artificers in Building.															
		Building contractors	58	58	...	10	10	...	...	...	...	...	...	...	...	...	...
		Stone and marble workers	395	291	104	922	784	138	2,284	1,383	901	963	529	434	27	15	12
		Masons	1,573	865	708	419	215	204	1,943	824	1,119	12	1	11	53	27	26
		Mud wall builders	...	...	...	6	5	1	341	156	185	36	21	15	...	...	...
		Total 23	2,026	1,214	812	1,357	1,014	343	4,568	2,363	2,205	1,011	551	460	80	42	38
		Total IX.—Buildings	23,565	11,085	11,085	2,362	1,298	1,064	4,721	2,427	2,294	1,438	753	685	3,642	1,920	1,722
		24.—Railway Plant.															
	X.—Vehicles	Fitters	...	...	...	137	94	43	6	6	...	...	...	...	...	...	...
		Painters	...	...	...	17	17	...	...	...	...	...	...	...	...	...	...
		Platelayers	...	...	...	4	3	1	...	...	...	...	...	...	...	...	...
		Inspectors	...	...	...	4	1	3	...	...	...	...	...	...	...	...	...
		Lorrymen	...	...	...	162	93	69	7	...	7	...	...	...	...	...	...
		Trollymen	...	...	...	32	32	...	...	...	...	...	...	...	...	...	...
		Total 24	...	...	...	356	240	116	13	6	7	...	...	...	...	...	...
		25.—Carts, Carriages, etc.															
		Carriage makers and sellers	...	...	...	...	...	...	8	8	...	...	...	...	...	...	...
		Total 25	...	...	...	...	...	...	8	8	...	...	...	...	...	...	...
		Total X.—Vehicles	...	...	...	356	240	116	21	14	7	...	...	...	...	...	...

TABLE XVII.—Occupations.—Part B.—(Provincial Distribution)—*contd.*

Class.	Order.	Sub-order, Group and Occupation.	Provincial Total. Total.	Provincial Total. Males.	Provincial Total. Females.	Indore. Total.	Indore. Males.	Indore. Females.	Gwalior. Total.	Gwalior. Males.	Gwalior. Females.	Bhopal. Total.	Bhopal. Males.	Bhopal. Females.
1	2	3	4	5	6	7	8	9	10	11	12	13	14	15
		27.—Paper, etc.												
	XI.—Supplementary Requirements.	Paper makers and sellers	953	479	474	...	...	...	60	30	30	28	6	22
		Stationers	970	564	406	11	9	2	219	15	204	212	212	...
		Total 27	1,923	1,043	880	11	9	2	279	45	234	240	218	22
		28.—Books and Prints, etc.												
		Printers	30	20	10	11	7	4	...	...	...	1	1	...
		Book binders	71	43	28	19	19	...	21	9	12	4	4	...
		Book sellers	77	44	33	9	9	...	16	5	11	24	13	11
		Total 28	178	107	71	39	35	4	37	14	23	29	18	11
		29.—Watches, Clocks and Scientific Instruments.												
		Watch and clock repairers and sellers	187	124	63	27	23	4	22	10	12	108	75	33
		Total 29	187	124	63	27	23	4	22	10	12	108	75	33
		30.—Carving, Engraving, etc.												
		Turners	693	556	407	8	4	4	367	240	127	247	138	109
		Die sinkers	15	11	4	...	...	...	...	...	...	...	...	...
		Total 30	978	567	411	8	4	4	367	240	127	247	138	109
		31.—Toys, Curiosities, etc.												
		Toy makers and sellers	557	315	242	...	...	...	182	95	87	...	...	...
		Kite makers and sellers	19	9	10	...	...	...	19	9	10	...	...	...
		Hukka stem makers and sellers	494	299	195	...	...	...	35	22	13	293	192	101
		Tabut and tazia makers and sellers	23	9	14	...	...	...	23	9	14	...	...	...
		Curiosity dealers	60	27	33	...	...	...	60	27	33	...	...	...
		Total 31	1,153	659	494	...	...	...	319	162	157	293	192	101
		32.—Music and Musical Instruments.												
		Music and musical instrument dealers	66	39	27	...	...	...	...	...	...	...	...	...
		Drum makers	92	39	53	46	27	19	13	8	5	...	...	...
		Total 32	158	78	80	46	27	19	13	8	5	...	...	...

Table XVII-B.—Occupations—(Provincial Distribution).

Class.	Order.	Sub-order, Group and Occupation.	Bundelkhand. Total.	Bundelkhand. Males.	Bundelkhand. Females.	Baghelkhand. Total.	Baghelkhand. Males.	Baghelkhand. Females.	Western Malwa. Total.	Western Malwa. Males.	Western Malwa. Females.	Bhopawar. Total.	Bhopawar. Males.	Bhopawar. Females.	Guna. Total.	Guna. Males.	Guna. Females.
			16	17	18	19	20	21	22	23	24	25	26	27	28	29	30
		27.—Paper, etc.															
	XI.—Supplementary Requirements.	Paper makers and sellers	65	34	31	180	92	88	620	317	303	...	...	...	...	...	...
		Stationers	403	203	200	...	...	...	...	...	...	...	...	...	125	125	...
		Total 27	468	237	231	180	92	88	620	317	303	...	...	...	125	125	...
		28.—Books and Prints, etc.															
		Printers	7	6	1	...	...	...	11	6	5	...	...	...	...	...	...
		Book-binders	19	8	11	1	...	1	7	3	4	...	...	...	...	...	...
		Book-sellers	25	16	9	...	...	...	3	1	2	...	...	...	...	...	...
		Total 28	51	30	21	1	...	1	21	10	11	...	...	...	...	...	...
		29.—Watches, Clocks and Scientific Instruments.															
		Watch and clock repairers and sellers	6	2	4	15	9	6	9	5	4	...	...	...	...	...	...
		Total 29	6	2	4	15	9	6	9	5	4	...	...	...	...	...	...
		30.—Carving, Engraving, etc.															
		Turners	...	...	...	...	...	...	233	103	130	...	...	...	108	71	37
		Die sinkers	15	11	4	...	...	...	...	...	...	...	...	...	...	...	...
		Total 30	15	11	4	...	...	...	233	103	130	...	...	...	108	71	37
		31.—Toys, Curiosities, etc.															
		Toy-makers and sellers	122	75	47	239	136	103	12	9	3	2	...	2	...	...	...
		Kite-makers and sellers	...	...	...	...	...	...	...	...	...	...	...	...	...	...	...
		Hukka stem makers and sellers	5	2	3	155	79	76	6	4	2	...	...	...	...	...	...
		Tabut and Tazia makers and sellers	...	...	...	...	...	...	...	...	...	...	...	...	...	...	...
		Curiosity dealers	...	...	...	...	...	...	...	...	...	...	...	...	...	...	...
		Total 31	127	77	50	394	215	179	18	13	5	2	...	2	...		
		32.—Music and Musical Instruments.															
		Music and musical instrument dealers	66	39	27	...	...	...	...	...	...	...	...	...	...	...	...
		Drum makers	1	1	...	...	...	...	7	3	4	...	...	...	25	...	25
		Total 32	67	40	27	...	...	...	7	3	4	...	...	...	25	...	25

TABLE XVII.—Occupations.—Part B.—(Provincial Distribution)—*contd.*

Class.	Order.	Sub-order, Group and Occupation.	Provincial Total: Total.	Provincial Total: Males.	Provincial Total: Females.	Indore: Total.	Indore: Males.	Indore: Females.	Gwalior: Total.	Gwalior: Males.	Gwalior: Females.	Bhopal: Total.	Bhopal: Males.	Bhopal: Females.
1	2	3	4	5	6	7	8	9	10	11	12	13	14	15
		33.—Necklaces, Bracelets, Beads, Sacred Threads, etc.												
	XI.—Supplementary Requirements—*contd.*	Bangle makers and sellers	16,938	8,720	8,218	517	194	323	2,285	1,320	965	2,539	1,267	1,272
		Imitation jewellery makers and sellers	1,662	841	821	...	...	...	...	...	...	104	56	48
		Necklace makers and sellers	34	18	16	...	...	...	...	...	...	...	...	...
		Flower garland makers and sellers	1,313	793	520	23	23	...	407	245	162	293	126	167
		Sacred thread makers and sellers	12	7	5	...	...	...	7	2	5	...	...	...
		Total 33	19,959	10,379	9,580	540	217	323	2,699	1,567	1,132	2,936	1,149	1,487
		34.—Furniture.												
		Bedstead makers	18	12	6	...	...	...	...	...	...	...	...	...
		Furniture makers	13	7	6	...	...	...	...	...	...	13	7	6
		Looking-glass makers and sellers	19	14	5	...	...	...	3	1	2	...	...	...
		Total 34	50	33	17	...	...	...	3	1	2	13	7	6
		35.—Harness.												
		Saddlery makers and sellers	1,580	769	811	276	146	130	151	120	31	211	96	115
		Total 35	1,580	769	811	276	146	130	151	120	31	211	96	115
		36.—Tools and Machinery.												
		Knife grinders	3,189	1,777	1,412	89	52	37	636	342	294	823	471	352
		Tool grinders	128	75	53	...	...	...	...	...	...	...	...	...
		Mechanics	72	44	28	8	4	4	1	1	...	...	...	...
		Artisans, unspecified	2,167	1,126	1,041	102	59	43	9	5	4	4	2	2
		Total 36	5,556	3,022	2,534	199	115	84	646	348	298	827	473	354
		37.—Arms and Ammunition.												
		Gun menders and sellers	124	65	59	...	...	...	53	24	29	54	28	26
		Gunpowder makers and sellers	1,411	759	652	...	...	...	222	143	79	683	351	332
		Fire-work makers and sellers	1,164	628	536	...	...	...	721	390	331	108	53	55
		Sword makers and sellers	83	37	46	...	...	...	39	27	12	34	4	30
		Scabbard makers and sellers	263	147	116	...	...	...	42	21	21	...	...	...
		Bow and arrow makers and sellers	52	18	34	...	...	...	45	13	32	...	...	...
		Total 37	3,097	1,654	1,443	...	...	...	1,122	618	504	879	436	443
		Total XI.—Supplementary Requirements	34,819	18,485	16,384	1,146	576	570	5,658	3,133	2,525	5,783	3,102	2,681

Table XVII—B.—Occupations—(Provincial Distribution).

CLASS D—*contd.*

Class.	Order.	Sub-order, Group and Occupation.	Bundelkhand. Total.	Bundelkhand. Males.	Bundelkhand. Females.	Baghelkhand. Total.	Baghelkhand. Males.	Baghelkhand. Females.	Western Malwa. Total.	Western Malwa. Males.	Western Malwa. Females.	Bhopawar. Total.	Bhopawar. Males.	Bhopawar. Females.	Guna. Total.	Guna. Males.	Guna. Females.
			16	17	18	19	20	21	22	23	24	25	26	27	28	29	30
		33.—Necklaces, Bracelets, Beads, Sacred Threads, etc.															
	XI.—Supplementary Requirements—*contd*	Bangle makers and sellers	2,252	1,260	992	5,326	2,440	2,886	2,478	1,386	1,092	1,137	619	518	404	234	170
		Imitation jewellery makers and sellers	83	41	42	1,475	744	731	...	...	...	...	...	...	...	...	...
		Necklace makers and sellers	34	18	16	...	...	...	...	...	...	...	...	...	...	...	...
		Flower garland makers and sellers	289	126	163	206	206	...	26	25	1	...	...	...	69	42	27
		Sacred thread makers and sellers	...	...	...	5	5	...	...	...	...	...	...	...	...	...	...
		Total 33	2,658	1,445	1,213	7,012	3,395	3,617	2,504	1,411	1,093	1,137	619	518	473	276	197
		34.—Furniture.															
		Bedstead makers	...	...	...	12	6	6	6	6	...	...	...	...	...	...	...
		Furniture makers	...	...	...	...	...	...	...	...	...	...	...	...	...	...	...
		Looking-glass makers and sellers	...	...	...	12	12	...	...	...	...	...	...	...	4	1	3
		Total 34	...	...	...	24	18	6	6	6	...	...	...	...	4	1	3
		35.—Harness.															
		Saddlery makers and sellers	102	58	44	142	85	57	202	119	83	196	130	66	300	15	285
		Total 35	102	58	44	142	85	57	202	119	83	196	130	66	300	15	285
		36.—Tools and Machinery.															
		Knife grinders	252	142	110	...	...	...	875	470	405	393	232	161	121	68	53
		Tool grinders	...	...	...	128	75	53	...	...	...	...	...	...	...	...	...
		Mechanics	62	38	24	1	1	...	...	...	...	...	...	...	...	...	...
		Artisans, unspecified	15	11	4	...	...	...	2,037	1,049	988	...	...	...	...	...	...
		Total 36	329	191	138	129	76	53	2,912	1,519	1,393	393	232	161	121	68	53
		37.—Arms and Ammunition.															
		Gun menders and sellers	...	...	...	...	...	...	15	11	4	2	2	...	...	...	...
		Gunpowder makers and sellers	370	199	171	104	49	55	24	14	10	...	...	...	8	3	5
		Fire-work makers and sellers	90	53	37	139	77	62	60	29	31	...	...	...	46	26	20
		Sword makers and sellers	...	...	...	10	6	4	...	...	...	...	...	...	...	...	...
		Scabbard makers and sellers	221	126	95	...	...	...	...	...	...	...	...	...	...	...	...
		Bow and arrow makers and sellers	...	...	...	...	...	...	...	...	...	...	...	...	7	5	2
		Total 37	681	378	303	253	132	121	99	54	45	2	2	...	61	34	27
		Total XI.—Supplementary Requirements	4,438	2,430	2,008	8,216	4,061	4,155	6,631	3,560	3,071	1,730	988	747	1,217	519	627

TABLE XVII—Occupations.—Part B.—(Provincial Distribution)—*contd.*

OCCUPATION AND CLASS.			PROVINCIAL TOTAL.			DISTRIBUTION BY AGENCIES.								
						INDORE.			GWALIOR.			BHOPAL.		
Class.	Order.	Sub-order, Group and Occupation.	Total.	Males.	Females.	Total.	Males.	Females.	Total.	Males.	Females.	Total.	Males.	Females.
1	2	3	4	5	6	7	8	9	10	11	12	13	14	15
		38.—Wool and Fur.												
	XII.—Textile Fabrics and Dress.	Shawl weavers and sellers	46	31	15	...	...	...	...	...	...	...	...	...
		Felt workers and sellers	133	71	62	...	...	...	...	...	...	...	...	...
		Blanket weavers and sellers	10,435	5,843	4,592	180	101	79	533	316	217	3,750	2,057	1,693
		Woollen cloth manufacturers and sellers	124	51	73	...	...	...	...	...	...	...	...	...
		Fur dealers	21	9	12	...	...	...	...	...	...	...	...	...
		Total 38	10,659	6,005	4,754	180	101	79	533	316	217	3,750	2,057	1,693
		39.—Silk.												
		Silk weavers	3,513	1,962	1,551	2,324	1,232	1,092	258	223	35	63	176	187
		Braid makers and sellers	864	454	410	...	...	...	155	83	72	618	321	297
		Total 39	4,377	2,416	1,961	2,324	1,232	1,092	413	306	107	981	497	484
		40.—Cotton.												
		Cotton cleaners	46,947	24,482	22,425	1016	543	473	7,894	4,125	3,769	12,644	6,688	5,956
		" pressers	1,290	216	1,074	...	...	...	1,056	216	840	...	...	...
		" carpet makers and sellers	236	230	6	...	...	...	232	230	2	...	...	...
		" spinners	5,310	935	4,375	122	80	42	700	175	525	3,762	603	3,159
		Yarn beaters	17	5	12	5	5	...	...	...	...	2	...	2
		Cotton weavers	152,932	80,425	72,507	1,461	953	508	39,969	21,656	18,313	36,923	19,566	17,357
		Calenderers	2,627	1,384	1,243	...	...	...	...	...	...	774	379	395
		Cotton dyers	26,892	13,767	13,125	1,687	864	823	6,563	3,242	3,321	6,469	3,325	3,145
		Tape makers and sellers	9	3	6	...	...	...	...	...	...		3	6
		Total 40	236,260	121,447	114,813	4,291	2,445	1,846	56,414	29,644	26,770	60,583	30,564	30,019
		41.—Jute, Flax, Coir, etc.												
		Hemp rope makers and sellers	514	273	241	8	8	...	7	6	1	310	141	169
		Jute manufacturers	145	76	69	...	...	...	...	...	...	120	61	59
		Sacking and gunny makers and sellers	134	112	22	...	...	...	...	...	...	21	10	11
		Net makers and sellers	5	2	3	...	...	...	...	...	...	...	...	...
		Coir preparers and sellers	681	398	283	316	176	140	29	15	14	251	147	104
		Total 41	1,479	861	618	324	184	140	36	21	15	702	359	343

Table XVII—B.—Occupations—(Provincial Distribution).

Class.	Order.	Sub-order, Group and Occupation.	Bundelkhand. Total.	Bundelkhand. Males.	Bundelkhand. Females.	Baghelkhand. Total.	Baghelkhand. Males.	Baghelkhand. Females.	Western Malwa. Total.	Western Malwa. Males.	Western Malwa. Females.	Bhopawar. Total.	Bhopawar. Males.	Bhopawar. Females.	Guna. Total.	Guna. Males.	Guna. Females.
			16	17	18	19	20	21	22	23	24	25	26	27	28	29	30
		38.—Wool and Fur.															
	XII.—Textile Fabrics and Dress.	Shawl weavers and sellers	29	17	12	17	14	3	...	...	...	...	...	...	...	...	...
		Felt workers and sellers	133	71	62	...	...	...	...	...	...	...	...	...	...	...	...
		Blanket weavers and sellers	906	519	387	2,289	1,260	1,029	1,670	957	713	30	30	...	1,077	603	474
		Woollen cloth manufacturers and sellers	58	36	22	...	...	...	16	15	1	...	...	...	50	...	50
		Fur dealers	...	...	...	...	...	...	...	...	...	21	9	12	...	...	...
		Total 38	1,126	643	484	2,306	1,274	1,032	1,686	972	714	51	39	12	1,127	603	524
		39.—Silk.															
		Silk weavers	269	229	40	273	76	197	...	...	...	...	...	...	26	26	...
		Braid makers and sellers	...	...	...	...	...	...	9	7	2	55	27	28	27	16	11
		Total 39	269	229	40	273	76	197	9	7	2	55	27	28	53	42	11
		40.—Cotton.															
		Cotton cleaners	7,747	4,013	3,734	6,858	3,579	3,279	6,773	3,537	3,236	2,663	1,246	1,417	1,352	751	601
		" pressers	102	...	102	...	...	...	...	...	...	...	...	...	132	...	132
		" carpet makers and sellers	4	...	4	...	...	...	...	...	...	...	...	...	...	...	...
		" spinners	266	20	246	...	...	...	188	39	149	240	15	225	32	3	29
		Yarn beaters	...	...	...	...	...	...	...	...	...	...	...	...	10	...	10
		Cotton weavers	35,438	18,814	16,624	20,107	9,317	10,790	7,077	3,841	3,236	7,071	3,628	3,443	4,886	2,650	2,236
		Calenderers	173	173	...	...	...	...	1,468	721	747	...	...	...	212	111	101
		Cotton dyers	3,311	1,646	1,665	1,430	723	707	3,914	2,111	1,803	2,478	1,309	1,169	1,040	547	493
		Tape makers and sellers	...	...	...	...	...	...	...	...	...	...	...	...	...	...	...
		Total 40	47,041	24,666	22,375	28,395	13,619	14,776	19,420	10,249	9,171	12,452	6,198	6,254	7,664	4,062	3,602
		41.—Jute, Flax, Coir, etc.															
		Hemp rope makers and sellers	141	70	71	48	48	...	...	...	...	...	...	...	...	...	...
		Jute manufacturers	...	...	...	25	15	10	...	...	...	...	...	...	...	...	...
		Sacking and gunny makers and sellers	...	...	...	...	...	...	70	66	4	37	32	5	6	4	2
		Net makers and sellers	...	...	...	...	...	...	...	...	...	...	...	–	5	2	3
		Coir preparers and sellers	...	...	...	...	...	...	39	28	11	46	32	14	...	...	...
		Total 41	141	70	71	73	63	10	109	94	15	83	64	19	11	6	5

TABLE XVII.—Occupations.—Part B.—(Provincial Distribution)—*contd.*

Class.	Order.	Sub-order, Group and Occupation.	Provincial Total: Total.	Provincial Total: Males.	Provincial Total: Females.	Indore: Total.	Indore: Males.	Indore: Females.	Gwalior: Total.	Gwalior: Males.	Gwalior: Females.	Bhopal: Total.	Bhopal: Males.	Bhopal: Females.
1	2	3	4	5	6	7	8	9	10	11	12	13	14	15
CLASS D—*contd.*	XII.—Textile Fabrics and Dress—*contd.*	**42.—Dress.**												
		Tailors	57,187	30,429	26,758	3,735	2,161	1,574	6,658	3,484	3,174	14,905	7,881	7,024
		Darners	112	61	51	17	6	11	52	32	20	...	...	...
		Haberdashers	4,677	2,581	2,096	...	...	...	...	...	...	1,264	870	394
		Hat and cap makers and sellers	3	2	1	...	...	...	...	...	...	...	...	...
		Turban binders	50	30	20	21	12	9	...	...	...	3	3	...
		Umbrella makers and sellers	17	4	13	...	...	...	...	...	...	...	...	...
		Embroiderers	44	9	35	...	...	...	5	2	3	...	...	...
		Lace makers and sellers	3	2	1	...	...	...	...	...	...	1	1	...
		Fringe makers and sellers	1,591	488	1,103	...	...	...	410	275	135	6	6	...
		False plait makers and sellers	257	139	118	...	...	...	...	...	...	257	139	118
		Piece goods merchants	2,366	1,314	1,052	...	...	...	...	...	...	132	70	62
		Cloth merchants	11,675	6,240	5,435	567	411	156	3,12	1,692	1,500	4,883	2,494	2,389
		Total 42	77,982	41,299	36,683	4,340	2,590	1,750	10,317	5,485	4,832	21,451	11,464	9,987
		Total XII.—Textile Fabrics and Dress.	**330,857**	**172,028**	**158,829**	**11,459**	**6,552**	**4,907**	**67,718**	**35,772**	**31,941**	**87,467**	**44,941**	**42,526**
	XIII.—Metals and Precious Stones.	**43.—Gold, Silver and Precious Stones.**												
		Gold and silver dealers	551	541	10	...	...	...	...	...	...	...	...	...
		Assayers	9	7	2	5	5	...	...	...	...	...	...	...
		Mint servants	76	33	43	...	...	...	47	17	30	...	...	...
		Gold and silver workers	53,271	28,101	25,170	2,222	1,290	932	8,244	4,469	3,775	10,970	5,796	5,174
		Jewellery makers	469	250	219	...	...	...	66	27	39	52	25	27
		Gold beaters	37	37	...	...	...	...	...	...	...	...	...	...
		Goldsmiths' dust washers	1,017	361	656	5	4	1	273	128	145	102	39	63
		Enamellers	14	7	7	14	7	7	...	...	...	...	...	...
		Electroplaters	31	24	7	31	24	7	...	...	...	...	...	...
		Gilders	19	10	9	...	...	...	...	...	...	...	...	...
		Diamond dealers	46	15	31	...	...	...	...	...	...	...	...	...
		" diggers	272	139	133	...	...	...	...	...	...	...	...	...
		Pearl dealers	24	19	5	...	...	...	...	...	...	...	...	...
		Ring stone dealers	90	47	43	7	2	5	...	...	...	[illegible]	1	...
		Total 43	55,926	29,591	26,335	2,284	1,332	952	8,630	4,641	3,989	11,125	5,861	5,264
		44.—Brass, Copper and Bell-metal.												
		Brass pot makers and sellers	2,452	1,210	1,242	44	26	18	38	523	415	25	13	12
		Brass and copper wire drawers and sellers.	19	5	14	...	...	...	...	...	...	...	...	...
		Bell-metal workers and sellers	1,496	765	731	...	...	...	...	...	...	...	...	...
		General workers in brass	3,583	1,956	1,627	284	148	136	28	21	7	1,295	772	523
		Total 44	7,550	3,936	3,614	328	174	154	966	544	422	1,320	785	535

Table XVII—B.—Occupations—(Provincial Distribution).

Class.	Order.	Sub-order, Group and Occupation.	Bundelkhand. Total.	Bundelkhand. Males.	Bundelkhand. Females.	Baghelkhand. Total.	Baghelkhand. Males.	Baghelkhand. Females.	Western Malwa. Total.	Western Malwa. Males.	Western Malwa. Females.	Bhopawar. Total.	Bhopawar. Males.	Bhopawar. Females.	Guna. Total.	Guna. Males.	Guna. Females.
			16	17	18	19	20	21	22	23	24	25	26	27	28	29	30
		42.—Dress.															
	XII.—Textile Fabrics and Dress—*contd.*	Tailors	8,640	4,429	4,211	6,054	3,394	2,660	11,530	6,208	5,322	4,061	2,016	2,045	1,604	856	748
		Darners	43	23	20	...	...	...	...	...	...	...	...	...	...	...	...
		Haberdashers	3,146	1,639	1,507	...	...	...	223	63	160	...	...	...	44	9	35
		Hat and cap makers and sellers	3	2	1	...	...	...	...	...	...	...	...	...	...	...	...
		Turban binders	...	...	...	...	...	...	11	...	11	15	15	...	...	...	...
		Umbrella makers and sellers	...	...	...	17	4	13	...	...	...	...	...	...	...	...	...
		Embroiderers	...	...	...	...	...	...	30	3	27	...	...	...	9	4	5
		Lace makers and sellers	2	1	1	...	...	...	...	...	...	...	...	...	...	...	...
		Fringe makers and sellers	468	...	468	...	...	...	590	154	436	...	...	...	117	53	64
		False plait makers and sellers	...	...	...	...	...	...	...	...	...	...	...	...	...	...	...
		Piece goods merchants	...	...	...	...	...	...	2,135	1,189	946	...	...	...	99	55	44
		Cloth merchants	210	106	104	252	252	...	...	...	...	2,361	1,180	1,181	210	105	105
		Total 42	12,512	6,200	6,312	6,323	3,650	2,673	14,519	7,647	6,902	6,437	3,211	3,226	2,083	1,082	1,001
		Total XII.—Textile Fabrics and Dress.	**61,089**	**31,808**	**29,281**	**37,870**	**18,682**	**18,688**	**35,743**	**18,939**	**16,804**	**19,078**	**9,539**	**9,539**	**10,938**	**5,795**	**5,143**
		43.—Gold, Silver and Precious Stones.															
	XIII.—Metals and Precious Stones.	Gold and silver dealers	82	72	10	226	226	...	243	243	...	...	...	...	...	...	...
		Assayers	4	2	2	...	...	...	...	...	...	...	...	...	...	...	...
		Mint servants	...	...	...	...	...	...	29	16	13	...	...	...	...	...	...
		Gold and silver workers	9,671	5,015	4,656	7,839	3,972	3,867	8,504	4,510	3,994	4,318	2,255	2,063	1,503	794	709
		Jewellery makers	289	159	130	...	...	...	62	39	23	...	...	...	...	...	...
		Gold beaters	...	...	...	37	37	...	...	...	...	...	...	...	...	...	...
		Goldsmiths' dust washers	39	...	39	138	76	62	376	66	310	66	39	27	18	9	9
		Enamellers	...	...	...	...	...	...	...	...	...	...	...	...	...	...	...
		Electroplaters	...	...	...	...	...	...	...	...	...	...	...	...	...	...	...
		Gilders	19	10	9	...	...	...	...	...	...	...	...	...	...	...	...
		Diamond dealers	46	15	31	...	...	...	...	...	...	...	...	...	...	...	...
		" diggers	272	139	133	...	...	...	...	...	...	...	...	...	...	...	...
		Pearl dealers	24	19	5	...	...	...	...	...	...	...	...	...	...	...	...
		Ring stone dealers	82	44	38	...	...	...	...	...	...	...	...	...	...	...	...
		Total 43	10,528	5,475	5,053	8,240	4,311	3,929	9,214	4,874	4,340	4,384	2,294	2,090	1,521	803	718
		44.—Brass, Copper and Bell-metal.															
		Brass pot makers and sellers	436	291	145	722	169	553	...	...	...	111	111	...	176	77	99
		Brass and copper wire drawers and sellers	...	...	...	...	...	...	19	5	14	...	...	...	...	...	...
		Bell-metal workers and sellers	1,496	765	731	...	...	...	...	...	...	...	...	...	...	...	...
		General workers in brass	140	...	140	116	116	...	1,179	581	598	440	229	211	101	89	12
		Total 44	2,072	1,056	1,016	838	285	553	1,198	586	612	551	340	211	277	166	111

TABLE XVII.—Occupations.—Part B.—(Provincial Distribution)—*contd.*

OCCUPATION AND CLASS.			DISTRIBUTION BY AGENCIES.											
			PROVINCIAL TOTAL.			INDORE.			GWALIOR.			BHOPAL.		
Class.	Order.	Sub-order, Group and Occupation.	Total.	Males.	Females.	Total.	Males.	Females.	Total.	Males.	Females.	Total.	Males.	Females.
1	2	3	4	5	6	7	8	9	10	11	12	13	14	15
		45.—Tin, Zinc, Mercury and Lead.												
	XIII.—Metals and Precious Stones—*contd*.	Tin workers and sellers	705	374	331	72	68	4	4	2	2	424	214	210
		Lead workers and sellers	205	103	102	...	...	...	50	20	30	...	...	...
		General workers in tin, zinc and lead, etc.	602	307	295	10	5	5	...	...	...	91	54	37
		Total 45	1,512	784	728	82	73	9	54	22	32	515	268	247
		46.—Iron and Steel.												
		Blacksmiths	60,260	31,641	28,619	1,870	1,051	819	7,866	4,029	3,837	10,616	5,108	5,508
		Iron dealers	5,957	3,312	2,645	63	63	...	1,001	679	322	1	...	1
		Nail makers and sellers	136	69	67	...	...	...	136	69	67	...	...	...
		Total 46	66,353	35,022	31,331	1,933	1,114	819	9,003	4,777	4,226	10,617	5,108	5,509
		Total XIII.—Metals and Precious Stones	**131,341**	**69,333**	**62,808**	**4,627**	**2,693**	**1,934**	**18,658**	**9,984**	**8,669**	**23,577**	**12,022**	**11,555**
		47.—Glass and Chinaware.												
	XIV.—Glass, Pottery and Stoneware.	Bottle dealers	40	...	40	...	...	...	15	...	15	...	...	...
		Chinaware dealers	18	18	...	18	18	...	...	...	...	...	...	...
		Total 47	58	18	40	18	18	...	15	...	15	...	...	...
		48.—Earthen and Stoneware.												
		Potters	63,695	33,318	30,377	278	195	83	102	85	17	24,375	12,772	11,603
		Grindstone and millstone makers and sellers.	1,357	489	868	9	4	5	106	1	105	696	290	406
		Soapstone powder preparers and sellers	30	30	...	...	...	...	...	...	...	...	...	...
		Total 48	65,082	33,837	31,245	287	199	88	208	86	122	25,071	13,062	12,009
		Total XIV.—Glass, Pottery and Stoneware	**65,140**	**33,855**	**31,285**	**305**	**217**	**88**	**223**	**86**	**137**	**25,071**	**13,062**	**12,009**

Table XVII—B.—Occupations—(Provincial Distribution).

Class.	Order.	Sub-order, Group and Occupation.	Bundelkhand. Total.	Bundelkhand. Males.	Bundelkhand. Females.	Baghelkhand. Total.	Baghelkhand. Males.	Baghelkhand. Females.	Western Malwa. Total.	Western Malwa. Males.	Western Malwa. Females.	Bhopawar. Total.	Bhopawar. Males.	Bhopawar. Females.	Guna. Total.	Guna. Males.	Guna. Females.
			16	17	18	19	20	21	22	23	24	25	26	27	28	29	30
		45.—Tin, Zinc, Mercury and Lead.															
	XIII.—Metals and Precious Stones—contd.	Tin workers and sellers	94	35	59	...	...	...	102	52	50	2	2	...	7	1	6
		Lead workers and sellers	...	...	...	155	83	72	...	...	...	...	...	...	...	...	...
		General workers in tin, zinc and lead, etc.	...	...	...	501	248	253	...	...	...	...	...	...	...	...	...
		Total 45	94	35	59	656	331	325	102	52	50	2	2	...	7	1	6
		46.—Iron and Steel.															
		Blacksmith	11,586	6,160	5,426	14,129	7,709	6,420	9,220	4,932	4,288	3,770	1,992	1,778	1,803	660	543
		Iron dealers	...	...	...	4,654	2,466	2,188	...	...	...	...	...	...	238	104	134
		Nail makers and sellers	...	...	...	...	...	...	...	...	...	...	...	...	...	...	...
		Total 46	11,586	6,160	5,426	18,783	10,175	8,608	9,220	4,932	4,288	3,770	1,992	1,778	1,441	764	677
		Total XIII.—Metals and Precious Stones	**24,280**	**12,726**	**11,554**	**28,517**	**15,102**	**13,415**	**19,784**	**10,444**	**9,290**	**8,707**	**4,628**	**4,079**	**3,246**	**1,784**	**1,512**
		47.—Glass and Chinaware.															
	XIV.—Glass, Pottery and Stoneware.	Bottle dealers	23	...	23	2	...	2	...	...	...	...	...	...	...	...	...
		Chinaware dealers	...	...	...	...	...	...	...	...	...	...	...	...	...	...	...
		Total 47	23	...	23	2	...	2	...	...	...	...	...	...	...	...	...
		48.—Earthen and Stoneware.															
		Potters	39	...	39	15,976	8,261	7,715	16,734	8,754	7,980	5,627	2,919	2,708	564	332	232
		Grindstone and millstone makers and sellers	171	46	125	...	...	...	238	103	135	24	15	9	113	30	83
		Soapstone powder preparers and sellers	...	...	...	...	...	...	30	30	...	...	...	...	...	...	...
		Total 48	210	46	164	15,976	8,261	7,715	17,002	8,887	8,115	5,651	2,934	2,717	677	362	315
		Total XIV.—Glass, Pottery and Stoneware	**233**	**46**	**187**	**15,978**	**8,261**	**7,717**	**17,002**	**8,887**	**8,115**	**5,651**	**2,934**	**2,717**	**677**	**362**	**315**

TABLE XVII.—Occupations.—Part B.—(Provincial Distribution)—*contd.*

OCCUPATION AND CLASS.			PROVINCIAL TOTAL.			DISTRIBUTION BY AGENCIES.								
						INDORE.			GWALIOR.			BHOPAL.		
Class.	Order.	SUB-ORDER, GROUP AND OCCUPATION.	TOTAL.	Males.	Females.	TOTAL.	Males.	Females.	TOTAL.	Males.	Females.	TOTAL.	Males.	Females.
1	2	3	4	5	6	7	8	9	10	11	12	13	14	15
		49.—Timber and Wood.												
	XV.—WOOD, CANE AND LEAVES, ETC.	Timber dealers	595	319	276	5	...	5	...	...	...	113	6	107
		Bamboo „	2,650	1,602	1,048	173	164	9	185	141	44	456	201	255
		Wood-cutters	3,343	1,926	1,417	11	11	...	...	...	...	11	10	1
		Sawyers	73	46	27	34	23	11	...	...	...	20	15	11
		Carpenters	90,785	48,681	42,104	4,588	2,365	2,223	17,890	9,309	8,581	20,940	11,112	9,828
		Total 49	97,446	52,574	44,872	4,811	2,563	2,248	18,075	9,450	8,625	21,546	11,344	10,202
		50.—Canework, Matting and Leaves, etc.												
		Bamboo splitters, etc.	15,417	7,961	7,456	2	2	...	63	63	...	926	485	441
		Basket weavers	34,506	18,267	16,239	625	382	243	3,079	1,504	1,575	10,080	5,674	4,406
		Mat makers and sellers	2,898	1,225	1,673	120	52	68	30	30	...	1,765	941	824
		Screen makers and sellers	46	14	32	...	...	...	...	...	...	1	...	1
		Leaf-plate makers and sellers	2,698	1,242	1,456	20	13	7	691	310	381	48	17	31
		Comb makers and sellers	812	375	437	...	...	...	107	...	107	132	65	67
		Broom makers and sellers	229	139	90	...	...	...	119	72	47	17	7	10
		Pith and bark collectors	266	125	141	...	...	...	...	...	...	...	...	...
		Total 50	56,872	29,348	27,524	767	449	318	4,089	1,979	2,110	12,969	7,189	5,780
		Total XV.—Wood, Cane and Leaves, etc.	**154,318**	**81,922**	**72,396**	**5,578**	**3,012**	**2,566**	**22,164**	**11,429**	**10,735**	**34,515**	**18,533**	**15,982**
		51.—Gums, Wax and similar Forest Produce.												
	XVI.—DRUGS, GUMS, DYES, ETC.	Gum collectors	5,291	2,578	2,713	...	...	...	36	32	4	460	173	287
		Catechu preparers and sellers	2,903	1,613	1,290	...	...	...	...	...	...	127	80	47
		Lac collectors	200	200	...	...	...	...	...	...	...	...	...	...
		Sealing wax makers and sellers	1,632	649	983	...	...	...	...	...	...	45	22	23
		Honey collectors and sellers	22	15	7	...	...	...	21	14	7	...	...	...
		Total 51	10,048	5,055	4,993	...	...	...	57	46	11	632	275	357

OCCUPATION AND CLASS.			DISTRIBUTION BY AGENCIES.														
			BUNDELKHAND.			BAGHELKHAND.			WESTERN MALWA.			BHOPAWAR.			GUNA.		
Class.	Order.	Sub-order, Group and Occupation.	Total.	Males.	Females.	Total.	Males.	Females.	Total.	Males.	Females.	Total.	Males.	Females.	Total.	Males.	Females.
			16	17	18	19	20	21	22	23	24	25	26	27	28	29	30
		49.—Timber and Wood.															
	XV.—Wood, Cane and Leaves, etc.	Timber dealers	279	115	164	198	198	...	...	...	...	...	...	...	...	...	...
		Bamboo „	2	2	...	854	854	...	193	36	157	787	204	583	...	...	...
		Wood-cutters	...	...	...	1,353	...	1,353	59	...	59	20	16	4	1,889	1,889	...
		Sawyers	...	...	...	2	...	2	11	8	3	...	...	...	...	...	...
		Carpenters	15,304	8,271	7,033	8,261	4,409	3,852	15,861	9,066	6,795	6,554	3,357	3,197	1,387	792	595
		Total 49	15,585	8,388	7,197	10,668	5,461	5,207	16,124	9,110	7,014	7,361	3,577	3,784	3,276	2,681	595
		50.—Canework, Matting and Leaves, etc.															
		Bamboo splitters, etc.	1,036	530	506	12,394	6,202	6,192	336	19	317	660	660	...	...	...	..
		Basket weavers	19,137	9,919	9,218	...	...	...	710	339	371	8	8	...	867	441	426
		Mat makers and sellers	...	...	...	504	...	504	409	174	235	...	...	...	70	28	42
		Screen makers and sellers	18	11	7	19	...	19	8	3	5	...	...	...	...	...	...
		Leaf-plate makers and sellers	149	69	80	1,788	831	957	2	2	...	...	...	...	...	...	...
		Comb makers and sellers	225	101	124	330	197	133	18	12	6	...	...	...	...	...	...
		Broom makers and sellers	72	48	24	21	12	9	...	...	...	...	...	...	...	...	...
		Pith and bark collectors	...	...	...	266	125	141	...	...	...	...	...	...	...	...	...
		Total 50	20,637	10,678	9,959	15,328	7,637	7,955	1,483	549	934	668	668	...	937	469	468
		Total XV.—Wood, Cane and Leaves &c.,	**36,222**	**19,066**	**17,156**	**25,590**	**12,828**	**13,162**	**17,607**	**9,659**	**7,948**	**8,029**	**4,245**	**3,784**	**4,218**	**3,150**	**1,063**
		51.—Gums, Wax and similar Forest Produce.															
	XVI.—Drugs, Gums Dyes, etc.	Gum-collectors	4,795	2,373	2,422	...	...	...	...	...	...	...	...	...	...	...	...
		Catechu preparers and sellers	1,260	723	537	1,510	807	703	...	...	...	...	...	...	6	3	3
		Lac collectors	...	...	...	200	200	...	...	...	...	...	...	...	...	...	...
		Sealing wax makers and sellers	1,587	627	960	...	...	...	...	...	...	...	...	...	...	...	...
		Honey collectors and sellers	1	1	...	...	...	...	...	...	...	...	...	...	...	...	...
		Total 51	7,643	3,724	3,919	1,710	1,007	703	...	...	...	...	...	...	6	3	3

TABLE XVII.—Occupations.—Part B.—(Provincial Distribution)—*contd.*

Class.	Order.	Sub-order, Group and Occupation.	Provincial Total: Total.	Provincial Total: Males.	Provincial Total: Females.	Indore: Total.	Indore: Males.	Indore: Females.	Gwalior: Total.	Gwalior: Males.	Gwalior: Females.	Bhopal: Total.	Bhopal: Males.	Bhopal: Females.
1	2	3	4	5	6	7	8	9	10	11	12	13	14	15
CLASS D—concld.	XVI.—Drugs, Gums, Dyes, etc.—contd.	**52.—Drugs, Dyes, Pigments, etc.**												
		Chemists and druggists	4,260	2,265	1,995	9	7	2	...	...	...	2,858	1,521	1,337
		Soap makers and sellers	82	42	40	...	...	...	22	13	9	...	...	...
		Indigo workers, etc.	16	4	12	...	...	...	7	2	5	1	...	1
		Ink makers and sellers	34	25	9	...	...	...	18	12	6	...	...	...
		Antimony preparers and sellers	16	6	10	...	...	...	...	...	...	...	...	...
		Perfume preparers and sellers	1,273	779	494	58	39	19	203	118	85	403	265	138
		Total 52	5,681	3,121	2,560	67	46	21	250	145	105	3,262	1,786	1,476
		Total XVI.—Drugs, Gums, Dyes, etc.	**15,729**	**8,176**	**7,558**	**67**	**46**	**21**	**307**	**191**	**116**	**3,894**	**2,061**	**1,833**
	XVII.—Leather, Horns, Bones and Grease.	**53.—Leather, etc.**												
		Tanners, curriers, etc.	78,727	41,706	37,021	3,779	1,973	1,806	17,593	9,367	8,226	15,377	8,092	7,285
		Shoe makers and sellers	144,996	80,543	64,453	814	579	235	18,209	10,233	7,976	56,747	30,249	26,498
		Leather dyers	886	352	534	...	...	...	28	14	14	37	22	15
		Ghee pot makers and sellers	32	22	10	16	6	10	...	...	...	...	...	...
		Hide and bone dealers	3,482	1,882	1,600	3,060	1,621	1,439	...	...	...	...	...	...
		Total 53	228,123	124,505	103,618	7,669	4,179	3,490	35,830	19,614	16,216	72,161	38,363	33,798
		Total XVII.—Leather, Horns, Bones and Grease.	**228,123**	**124,505**	**103,618**	**7,669**	**4,179**	**3,490**	**35,830**	**19,614**	**16,216**	**72,161**	**38,363**	**33,798**
		Total Class D	**1,382,492**	**734,856**	**647,636**	**46,928**	**27,414**	**19,514**	**236,086**	**124,892**	**111,194**	**335,198**	**178,631**	**156,567**
CLASS E.	XVIII.—Commerce	**54.—Dealers in Money and Securities.**												
		Bankers	16,895	8,778	8,117	1,063	637	426	7,937	4,060	3,877	3,919	2,195	1,724
		Money lenders	18,090	9,131	8,959	355	193	162	191	66	125	3,637	1,855	1,782
		Money changers and testers	7,268	3,831	3,437	52	29	23	2,179	1,210	969	1,499	782	717
		Total 54	42,253	21,740	20,513	1,470	859	611	10,307	5,336	4,971	9,055	4,832	4,223

Table XVII B.—Occupations—(Provincial Distribution).

Class.	Order.	Sub-order, Group and Occupation.	Bundelkhand. Total.	Bundelkhand. Males.	Bundelkhand. Females.	Baghelkhand. Total.	Baghelkhand. Males.	Baghelkhand. Females.	Western Malwa. Total.	Western Malwa. Males.	Western Malwa. Females.	Bhopawar. Total.	Bhopawar. Males.	Bhopawar. Females.	Guna. Total.	Guna. Males.	Guna. Females.
			16	17	18	19	20	21	22	23	24	25	26	27	28	29	30
CLASS D—concld.		**52.—Drugs, Dyes, Pigments, etc.**															
	XVI.—Drugs, Gums, Dyes, etc.—contd.	Chemists and druggists	1,158	594	564	211	130	81	12	8	4	...	...	...	12	5	7
		Soap makers and sellers	...	...	...	60	29	31	...	...	...	...	...	...	...	...	...
		Indigo workers, etc.	...	...	...	...	...	...	6	2	4	...	...	...	2	...	2
		Ink makers and sellers	...	...	...	...	...	...	16	13	3	...	...	...	...	...	...
		Antimony preparers and sellers	...	...	...	...	...	...	16	6	10	...	...	...	...	...	...
		Perfume preparers and sellers	114	71	43	72	47	25	321	174	147	93	58	35	9	7	2
		Total 52	1,272	665	607	343	206	137	371	203	168	93	58	35	23	12	11
		Total XVI.—Drugs, Gums, Dyes, etc.	**8,915**	**4,389**	**4,526**	**2,058**	**1,218**	**840**	**371**	**208**	**168**	**93**	**58**	**35**	**29**	**15**	**14**
		53.—Leather, etc.															
	XVII.—Leather, Horns, Bones and Grease.	Tanners, curriers, etc.	456	189	267	2,081	1,158	923	21,832	12,105	9,727	9,351	4,956	4,395	8,258	3,866	4,392
		Shoe makers and sellers	46,337	25,150	21,187	17,231	10,576	6,655	441	273	168	231	123	108	4,986	3,360	2,626
		Leather dyers	41	9	32	...	...	...	587	217	370	...	...	...	193	90	103
		Ghee pot makers and sellers	...	...	...	...	...	...	...	...	...	16	16	...	...	...	...
		Hide and bone dealers	...	...	...	422	261	161	...	...	...	...	...	...	...	...	...
		Total 53	46,834	25,348	21,486	19,734	11,995	7,739	22,860	12,595	10,265	9,598	5,095	4,503	13,437	7,316	6,121
		Total XVII.—Leather, Horns, Bones and Grease.	**46,884**	**25,348**	**21,486**	**19,734**	**11,995**	**7,739**	**22,860**	**12,595**	**10,265**	**9,598**	**5,095**	**4,508**	**13,437**	**7,316**	**6,121**
		Total Class D	**274,498**	**144,017**	**130,481**	**209,140**	**107,469**	**101,671**	**157,113**	**86,286**	**70,877**	**77,191**	**40,007**	**37,184**	**46,838**	**26,190**	**20,148**
CLASS E.		**54.—Dealers in Money and Securities.**															
	XVIII.—Commerce	Bankers	137	80	57	...	...	...	3,010	1,344	1,666	...	...	...	829	462	367
		Money lenders	8,115	4,010	4,105	1,083	519	564	1,192	654	538	3,364	1,754	1,610	153	80	73
		Money changers and testers	912	445	467	...	...	...	1,714	932	782	404	201	203	508	232	276
		Total 54	9,164	4,535	4,629	1,083	519	564	5,916	2,930	2,986	3,768	1 955	1,813	1490	774	716

TABLE XVII.—Occupations.—Part B.—(Provincial Distribution)—*contd.*

OCCUPATION AND CLASS.			PROVINCIAL TOTAL.			DISTRIBUTION BY AGENCIES.								
						INDORE.			GWALIOR.			BHOPAL.		
Class.	Order.	Sub-order, Group and Occupation.	Total.	Males.	Females.	Total.	Males.	Females.	Total.	Males.	Females.	Total.	Males.	Females.
1	2	3	4	5	6	7	8	9	10	11	12	13	14	15
		55.—General Merchandise.												
	XVIII.—Commerce—*contd.*	General merchants	11,799	6,974	4,825	3,021	1,700	1,321	3,188	2,028	1,160	5,341	3,114	2,227
		Merchants, unspecified	54,482	27,844	26,638	198	161	37	5,156	260	4,896	...	...	...
		Merchants' clerks	1,397	796	601	...	...	...	5	...	5	90	88	2
		Total 55	67,678	35,614	32,06	3,219	1,861	1,358	8,349	2,288	6,061	5,431	3,202	2,229
		56.—Dealing, unspecified.												
		Shopkeepers, otherwise unspecified	136,101	70,703	65,398	14,479	8,071	6,408	34,682	18,894	15,788	1,247	669	578
		Pedlars	14,813	8,542	6,271	1,498	858	640	733	526	207	3,901	2,204	1,697
		Total 56	150,914	79,245	71,669	15,977	8,929	7,048	35,415	19,420	15,995	5,148	2,873	2,275
		57.—Middlemen, etc.												
		(a) Brokers, etc.												
		Brokers and Agents	8,425	4,031	4,395	1,655	926	729	3,397	1,236	2,161	290	112	178
		Auctioneers	2	1	1	2	1	1	...	...	...	...	...	...
		Total 57 (a)	*8,427*	*4,031*	*4,396*	*1,657*	*927*	*730*	*3,397*	*1,236*	*2,161*	*290*	*112*	*178*
		(b) Contractors and Farmers.												
		Farmers of ferries	1	1	...	...	...	...	...	...	...	...	...	...
		" " liquor and opium	14	10	4	14	10	4	...	...	...	...	...	...
		Contractors	4,146	2,316	1,830	428	248	180	1,405	807	598	688	350	338
		Total 57 (b)	*4,161*	*2,327*	*1,834*	*442*	*258*	*184*	*1,405*	*807*	*598*	*688*	*350*	*338*
		Total XVIII.—Commerce	**278,483**	**142,957**	**180,476**	**22,765**	**12,884**	**9,981**	**58,878**	**29,087**	**29,786**	**20,612**	**11,369**	**9,243**

Table XVII B.—Occupations—(Provincial Distribution).

Class.	Order.	Sub-order, Group and Occupation.	Bundelkhand. Total.	Males.	Females.	Baghelkhand. Total.	Males.	Females.	Western Malwa. Total.	Males.	Females.	Bhopawar. Total.	Males.	Females.	Guna. Total.	Males.	Females.
			16	17	18	19	20	21	22	23	24	25	26	27	28	29	30
		55.—General Merchandise.															
	XVIII.—Commerce—*contd.*	General merchants	9	8	1	28	28	...	125	26	99	...	...	...	87	70	17
		Merchants, unspecified	4,243	2,324	1,919	34	...	34	42,266	22,874	19,392	2,516	2,207	309	69	18	51
		Merchants' clerks	171	147	24	91	...	91	981	531	450	...	...	...	59	30	29
		Total 55	4,423	2,479	1,944	153	28	125	43,372	23,431	19,941	2,516	2,207	309	215	118	97
		56.—Dealing, unspecified.															
		Shopkeepers, otherwise unspecified	11,488	4,474	7,014	3,725	1,935	1,790	41,343	21,629	19,714	23,990	12,261	11,729	5,147	2,770	2,377
		Pedlars	25	15	10	676	676	...	5,457	2,907	2,550	...	...	...	2,523	1,356	1,167
		Total 56	11,513	4,489	7,024	4,401	2,611	1,790	46,800	24,536	22,264	23,990	12,261	11,729	7,670	4,126	3,544
		57.—Middlemen, etc.															
		(a) Brokers, etc.															
		Brokers and Agents	74	39	35	64	39	25	2,622	1,480	1,142	304	188	116	19	10	9
		Auctioneers	...	...	...	...	...	...	...	...	...	...	...	...	...	...	...
		Total 57 (a)	*74*	*39*	*35*	*64*	*39*	*25*	*2,622*	*1,480*	*1,142*	*304*	*188*	*116*	*19*	*10*	*9*
		(b) Contractors and Farmers.															
		Farmers of ferries	1	1	...	...	...	...	...	...	...	...	...	...	...	...	...
		" " liquor and opium	...	...	...	...	...	...	...	...	...	...	...	...	...	...	...
		Contractors	278	168	110	458	254	205	694	403	291	109	36	73	85	50	35
		Total 57 (b)	*279*	*169*	*110*	*459*	*254*	*205*	*694*	*403*	*291*	*109*	*36*	*73*	*85*	*50*	*35*
		Total XVIII.—Commerce	**25,458**	**11,711**	**13,472**	**6,160**	**3,451**	**2,709**	**99,404**	**52,780**	**46,624**	**30,687**	**16,647**	**14,040**	**9,479**	**5,078**	**4,401**

TABLE XVII.—Occupations.—PART B.—(Provincial Distribution)—*contd.*

Class.	Order.	Sub-order, Group and Occupation.	Provincial Total: Total.	Provincial Total: Males.	Provincial Total: Females.	Indore: Total.	Indore: Males.	Indore: Females.	Gwalior: Total.	Gwalior: Males.	Gwalior: Females.	Bhopal: Total.	Bhopal: Males.	Bhopal: Females.
1	2	3	4	5	6	7	8	9	10	11	12	13	14	15
		58.—Railway.												
		(a) Administration.												
	XIX.—Transport and Storage.	Officers	4	4	...	2	2	...	...	...	...	1	1	...
		Locomotive Superintendents	1	1	...	1	1	...	...	...	...	...	...	...
		Store-keepers	87	42	45	...	...	...	...	...	...	10	10	...
		Auditors	4	1	3	...	...	...	...	...	...	...	...	...
		Clerical staff, railway	548	332	216	19	3	16	32	7	25	94	91	3
		Total 58 (a)	*644*	*380*	*264*	*22*	*6*	*16*	*32*	*7*	*25*	*105*	*102*	*3*
		(b) Working Staff.												
		Station masters and assistants	289	146	143	40	...	40	31	16	15	82	49	33
		Guards, drivers, etc.	250	108	142	63	...	63	5	3	2	...	...	...
		Pointsmen, etc.	1,014	613	401	345	4	341	96	94	2	63	54	9
		Total 58 (b)	*1,553*	*867*	*686*	*448*	*4*	*444*	*132*	*113*	*19*	*145*	*103*	*42*
		59.—Road.												
		(a) Cart and Carriage Owners and Drivers.												
		Cart owners and drivers	5,818	3,785	2,033	1,225	1,019	206	768	435	333	361	169	192
		Drivers, stable servants, etc.	2,015	1,876	139	...	...	...	178	113	65	...	...	...
		Palki bearers	1,933	1,156	777	81	15	16	1,200	652	548	85	53	32
		Total 59 (a)	*9,766*	*6,817*	*2,949*	*1,256*	*1,034*	*222*	*2,146*	*1,200*	*946*	*446*	*222*	*224*
		(b) Carriers by Pack Animals.												
		Pack bullock owners and drivers	9,860	5,627	4,233	86	86	...	1,417	848	569	2,107	788	1,319
		Camel drivers	65	65	...	51	51	...	...	...	...	14	14	...
		Total 59 (b)	*9,925*	*5,692*	*4,233*	*137*	*137*	...	*1,417*	*848*	*569*	*2,121*	*802*	*1,319*
		60.—Water.												
		(b) Working Staff of Vessels.												
		Boatmen	874	485	389	29	29	...	232	67	165	54	53	1
		Total 60 (b)	*874*	*485*	*389*	*29*	*29*	...	*232*	*67*	*165*	*54*	*53*	*1*

OCCUPATION AND CLASS.			DISTRIBUTION BY AGENCIES.														
			Bundelkhand.			Baghelkhand.			Western Malwa.			Bhopawar.			Guna.		
Class.	Order.	Sub-order, Group and Occupation.	Total.	Males.	Females.	Total.	Males.	Females.	Total.	Males.	Females.	Total.	Males.	Females.	Total.	Males.	Females.
			16	17	18	19	20	21	22	23	24	25	26	27	28	29	30
		58.—Railway.															
		(a) Administration.															
	XIX.—Transport and Storage.	Officers	...	...	...	1	1	...	...	...	...	...	...	...	...	...	...
		Locomotive Superintendents	...	...	...	...	...	...	...	...	...	...	...	...	...	...	...
		Store-keepers	52	11	41	15	11	4	...	...	...	...	...	...	10	10	...
		Auditors	...	...	...	3	1	2	...	...	...	...	...	...	1	...	1
		Clerical staff, railway	57	57	...	24	...	24	322	174	148	...	...	...	...	...	...
		Total 58 (a)	*109*	*68*	*41*	*43*	*13*	*30*	*322*	*174*	*148*	...	...	...	*11*	*10*	*1*
		(b) Working Staff.															
		Station masters and assistants	32	20	12	104	61	43	...	...	...	...	...	...	...	...	...
		Guards, drivers, etc.	68	68	...	65	12	53	32	25	7	...	...	...	17	...	17
		Pointsmen, etc.	15	...	15	495	461	34	...	...	...	...	...	...	...	...	...
		Total 58 (b)	*115*	*88*	*27*	*664*	*534*	*130*	*32*	*25*	*7*	...	...	...	*17*	...	*17*
		59.—Road.															
		(a) Cart and Carriage Owners and Drivers.															
		Cart owners and drivers	1,111	841	270	462	285	177	1,277	592	685	540	410	130	74	34	30
		Drivers, stable servants, etc	1,567	1,567	...	16	16	...	1	1	...	...	...	...	253	179	74
		Palki bearers	256	138	118	98	57	41	26	13	13	216	216	...	21	12	9
		Total 59 (a)	*2,934*	*2,546*	*388*	*576*	*358*	*218*	*1,304*	*606*	*698*	*756*	*626*	*130*	*348*	*225*	*123*
		(b) Carriers by Pack Animals.															
		Pack bullock owners and drivers	1,251	640	611	496	322	174	1,593	674	919	1,995	1,769	226	915	500	415
		Camel drivers	...	...	...	...	...	...	...	...	...	...	...	...	...	...	...
		Total 59 (b)	*1,251*	*640*	*611*	*496*	*322*	*174*	*1,593*	*674*	*919*	*1,995*	*1,769*	*226*	*915*	*500*	*415*
		60.—Water.															
		(b) Working Staff of Vessels.															
		Boatmen	4	...	4	476	305	171	...	...	...	79	31	48	...	...	...
		Total 60 (b)	*4*	...	*4*	*476*	*305*	*171*	...	...	...	*79*	*31*	*48*	...	...	...

TABLE XVII.—Occupations.—Part B.—(Provincial Distribution)—*contd.*

Class.	Order.	Sub-order, Group and Occupation.	Provincial Total: Total.	Provincial Total: Males.	Provincial Total: Females.	Indore: Total.	Indore: Males.	Indore: Females.	Gwalior: Total.	Gwalior: Males.	Gwalior: Females.	Bhopal: Total.	Bhopal: Males.	Bhopal: Females.
1	2	3	4	5	6	7	8	9	10	11	12	13	14	15
CLASS E—*concld.*		**61.—Messages.**												
		(a) Post, etc.												
	XIX.—Transport and Storage—*contd.*	Postmasters and clerks	183	125	58	11	4	7	11	6	5	13	10	3
		Postal messengers and postmen	443	295	148	10	10	...	38	23	15	9	3	6
		Messengers (unspecified)	8	2	6	...	...	...	...	...	...	...	...	...
		Total 61 (a)	*634*	*422*	*212*	*21*	*14*	*7*	*49*	*29*	*20*	*22*	*13*	*9*
		(b) Telegraph.												
		Telegraph officers	2	2	...	...	...	...	...	...	...	...	...	...
		Signallers and messengers	166	90	76	38	21	17	22	20	2	21	10	11
		Total 61 (b)	*168*	*92*	*76*	*38*	*21*	*17*	*22*	*20*	*2*	*21*	*10*	*11*
		62.—Storage and Weighing.												
		Porters (general)	2,895	1,669	1,226	...	...	...	602	270	332	577	340	237
		Weighmen	4,220	2,966	1,254	54	32	22	1,771	1,526	245	631	450	181
		Watchmen (not village)	4,130	2,221	1,909	822	592	230	1,367	718	649	1,348	571	777
		Total 62	**11,245**	**6,856**	**4,389**	**876**	**624**	**252**	**3,740**	**2,514**	**1,226**	**2,556**	**1,361**	**1,195**
		Tot XIX.—Transport und Storage	**34,809**	**21,611**	**13,198**	**2,827**	**1,869**	**958**	**7,717**	**4,798**	**2,972**	**5,470**	**2,666**	**2,804**
		Total Class E	**308,242**	**164,568**	**143,674**	**25,592**	**14,703**	**10,889**	**66,643**	**33,885**	**32,758**	**26,082**	**14,035**	**12,047**
F.—PROFESSIONS.		**63.—Religion.**												
		(a) Priests, Ministers, etc.												
	XX.—Learned and Artistic Professions.	Priests, preachers, etc.	29,872	16,496	13,376	507	313	194	5,712	3,174	2,538	286	165	121
		Hail averters	140	94	46	...	...	...	140	94	46	...	...	...
		Amuletiers	61	41	20	...	...	...	...	...	...	...	...	...
		Total 63 (a)	*30,073*	*16,631*	*13,442*	*507*	*313*	*194*	*5,852*	*3,268*	*2,584*	*286*	*165*	*121*

Table XVII–B.—Occupations—(Provincial Distribution).

Class	Order	Sub-order, Group and Occupation	Bundelkhand Total	Bundelkhand Males	Bundelkhand Females	Baghelkhand Total	Baghelkhand Males	Baghelkhand Females	Western Malwa Total	Western Malwa Males	Western Malwa Females	Bhopawar Total	Bhopawar Males	Bhopawar Females	Guna Total	Guna Males	Guna Females
			16	17	18	19	20	21	22	23	24	25	26	27	28	29	30
CLASS E—*concld.*	XIX.—Transport and Storage—*contd.*	**61.—Messages.**															
		(a) *Post, etc.*															
		Postmasters and clerks	33	24	9	66	35	31	43	41	2	6	5	1	...	...	...
		Postal messengers and postmen	36	19	17	254	168	86	89	68	21	1	1	...	6	3	3
		Messengers (unspecified)	...	...	...	...	...	...	8	2	6	...	...	...	...	...	...
		Total 61 (a)	*69*	*43*	*26*	*320*	*203*	*117*	*140*	*111*	*29*	*7*	*6*	*1*	*6*	*3*	*3*
		(b) *Telegraph.*															
		Telegraph officers	...	...	...	2	2	...	...	...	...	...	...	...	...	...	...
		Signallers and messengers	13	9	4	61	23	38	4	2	2	4	2	2	3	3	...
		Total 61 (b)	*13*	*9*	*4*	*63*	*25*	*38*	*4*	*2*	*2*	*4*	*2*	*2*	*3*	*3*	...
		62.—Storage and Weighing.															
		Porters (general)	200	127	73	322	164	158	1,194	768	426	...	...	...	...	...	...
		Weighmen	566	325	241	511	262	249	636	327	309	11	11	...	40	33	7
		Watchmen (not village)	91	70	21	474	247	227	...	...	...	6	1	5	22	22	...
		Total 62	857	522	335	1,307	673	634	1,830	1,095	735	17	12	5	62	55	7
		Total XIX.—Transport and Storage	**5,352**	**3,916**	**1,436**	**3,945**	**2,433**	**1,512**	**5,225**	**2,687**	**2,538**	**2,858**	**2,446**	**412**	**1,362**	**796**	**566**
		Total Class E	**30,805**	**15,627**	**15,178**	**10,105**	**5,884**	**4,221**	**104,629**	**55,467**	**49,162**	**33,545**	**19,093**	**14,452**	**10,841**	**5,874**	**4,967**
F.—PROFESSIONS.	XX.—Learned and Artistic Professions.	**63.—Religion.**															
		(a) *Priests, Ministers, etc.*															
		Priests, preachers, etc.	7,995	4,258	3,737	3,148	1,690	1,458	11,935	6,751	5,184	...	...	...	289	145	144
		Hail averters	...	...	...	...	...	...	...	...	...	...	...	...	...	...	...
		Amuletiers	...	...	...	52	35	17	9	6	3	...	...	...	...	...	...
		Total 63 (a)	*7,995*	*4,258*	*3,737*	*3,200*	*1,725*	*1,475*	*11,944*	*6,757*	*5,187*	...	...	...	*289*	*145*	*144*

TABLE XVII.—Occupations.—Part B.—(Provincial Distribution)—contd.

OCCUPATION AND CLASS.			PROVINCIAL TOTAL.			DISTRIBUTION BY AGENCIES.								
						INDORE.			GAWLIOR.			BHOPAL.		
Class.	Order.	Sub-order, Group and Occupation.	Total.	Males.	Females.	Total.	Males.	Females.	Total.	Males.	Females.	Total.	Males.	Females.
1	2	3	4	5	6	7	8	9	10	11	12	13	14	15
		(b) Subsidiary Religious Services.												
	XX.—Learned and Artistic Professions—*contd.*	Religious mendicants	11,283	7,908	3,375	2,935	1,751	1,184	1,237	710	527	275	185	90
		Devotees	644	415	229	2	1	1	395	185	210	...	...	...
		Temple servants	26,865	15,638	11,227	2,170	1,272	898	7,361	4,404	2,957	4,093	2,259	1,834
		Burial ground servants	10	5	5	...	...	...	...	...	...	...	...	...
		Pilgrim conductors	184	167	17	...	...	...	159	143	16	...	...	...
		Total 63 (b)	*38,986*	*24,133*	*14,853*	*5,107*	*3,024*	*2,083*	*9,152*	*5,442*	*3,710*	*4,368*	*2,444*	*1,924*
		64.—Education.												
		Teachers, schoolmasters, etc.	2,026	1,241	785	249	179	70	301	218	83	218	129	89
		Total 64	2,026	1,241	785	249	179	70	301	218	83	218	129	89
		65.—Literature.												
		Authors and ballad-makers	12	7	5	1	...	1	...	...	...	...	...	...
		Private secretaries and clerks	837	460	377	...	...	...	...	...	...	...	...	...
		Public scribes	9,885	5,807	4,078	15	1	14	186	6	180	107	...	107
		Total 65	10,734	6,274	4,460	16	1	15	186	6	180	107	...	107
		66.—Law.												
		Pleaders and law agents	3,222	1,466	1,756	320	185	135	446	232	214	655	404	251
		Lawyers' clerks	33	27	6	33	27	6	...	...	...	...	...	...
		Stamp vendors	10	10	...	...	...	...	...	...	...	...	...	...
		Petition writers	206	120	86	26	...	26	46	46	...	26	10	16
		Total 66	3,471	1,623	1,848	379	212	167	492	278	214	681	414	267
		67.—Medicine.												
		(a) Practitioners.												
		Practitioners by diploma	644	287	357	42	37	5	2	2	...	7	5	2
		Practitioners without diploma	846	456	390	375	189	186	217	125	92	14	8	6
		Hakims, baids, etc.	2,976	1,487	1,489	65	52	13	680	361	319	868	264	604
		Dentists	1	1	...	1	1	...	...	...	...	...	...	...
		Vaccinators	38	26	12	8	5	3	...	...	...	2	2	...
		Midwifery	299	47	252	14	...	14	...	...	...	124	38	86
		Total 67 (a)	*4,804*	*2,304*	*2,500*	*505*	*284*	*221*	*899*	*488*	*411*	*1,015*	*317*	*698*

Table XVII B.—Occupations—(Provincial Distribution).

Class.	Order.	Sub-order, Group and Occupation.	Bundelkhand. Total.	Bundelkhand. Males.	Bundelkhand. Females.	Baghelkhand. Total.	Baghelkhand. Males.	Baghelkhand. Females.	Western Malwa. Total.	Western Malwa. Males.	Western Malwa. Females.	Bhopawar. Total.	Bhopawar. Males.	Bhopawar. Females.	Guna. Total.	Guna. Males.	Guna. Females.
			16	17	18	19	20	21	22	23	24	25	26	27	28	29	30
		(b) Subsidiary Religious Services.															
	XX.—Learned and Artistic Professions —*contd.*	Religious mendicants	330	157	173	121	87	34	3,332	2,132	1,200	2,648	2,637	11	405	249	156
		Devotees	207	201	6	...	–	...	39	27	12	1	1	...	...	...	...
		Temple servants	5,427	3,303	2,124	3,425	2,000	1,425	573	265	308	1,760	950	810	2,056	1,185	871
		Burial ground servants	10	5	5	...	...	...	...	...	...	...	...	...	...	...	...
		Pilgrim conductors	1	...	1	...	...	...	21	21	...	...	...	...	3	3	...
		Total 63 (b)	*5,975*	*3,666*	*2,309*	*3,546*	*2,087*	*1,459*	*3,965*	*2,445*	*1,520*	*4,409*	*3,588*	*821*	*2,464*	*1,437*	*1,027*
		64.—Education.															
		Teachers, schoolmasters, etc.	356	200	156	198	123	75	602	334	268	42	22	20	60	36	24
		Total 64	356	200	156	198	123	75	602	334	268	42	22	20	60	36	24
		65.—Literature.															
		Authors and ballad-makers	...	...	...	...	...	...	...	...	...	...	...	...	11	7	4
		Private secretaries and clerks	...	...	...	...	...	...	837	460	377	...	...	...	...	...	...
		Public scribes	9,565	5,791	3,774	...	...	...	...	...	...	9	9	...	3	...	3
		Total 65	9,565	5,791	3,774	...	...	...	837	460	377	9	9	...	14	7	7
		66.—Law.															
		Pleaders and law agents	60	60	...	982	109	873	372	216	156	343	227	116	44	33	11
		Lawyers' clerks	...	...	...	...	...	...	...	...	...	...	...	...	...	...	...
		Stamp vendors	6	6	...	...	...	...	4	4	...	...	...	...	...	...	...
		Petition writers	...	...	...	82	41	41	26	23	3	...	...	...	...	...	...
		Total 66	66	66	..	1,064	150	914	402	243	159	343	227	116	44	33	11
		67.—Medicine.															
		(a) Practitioners.															
		Practitioners by diploma	...	...	...	10	8	2	574	232	342	8	2	6	1	1	...
		Practitioners without diploma	17	7	10	48	29	19	168	98	70	...	...	...	7	...	7
		Hakims, baids, etc.	686	418	268	571	299	272	29	17	12	72	72	...	5	4	1
		Dentists	...	..	...	...	...	...	...	...	...	...	...	...	...	...	...
		Vaccinators	19	15	4	2	...	2	7	4	3	...	...	...	...	...	...
		Midwifery	...	...	...	50	3	47	97	6	91	10	...	10	4	...	4
		Total 67 (a)	*722*	*440*	*282*	*681*	*339*	*342*	*875*	*357*	*518*	*90*	*74*	*16*	*17*	*5*	*12*

TABLE XVII.—Occupations.—Part B.—(Provincial Distribution)—*contd.*

OCCUPATION AND CLASS.			PROVINCIAL TOTAL.			DISTRIBUTION BY AGENCIES.								
						INDORE.			GWALIOR.			BHOPAL.		
Class.	Order.	Sub-order, Group and Occupation.	Total.	Males.	Females.	Total.	Males.	Females.	Total.	Males.	Females.	Total.	Males.	Females.
1	2	3	4	5	6	7	8	9	10	11	12	13	14	15
		(b) Subsidiary Medical Services.												
	XX.—LEARNED AND ARTISTIC PROFESSIONS—*contd.*	Hospital assistants	40	20	20	7	...	7	...	...	...	11	7	4
		Asylum servants	5	1	4	...	...	...	...	...	...	...	...	...
		Apothecaries	59	51	8	36	36	...	...	...	...	...	...	...
		Compounders	99	51	48	15	13	2	...	...	...	16	6	10
		Dispensary servants	672	608	64	592	560	32	34	13	21	30	30	...
		Total 67 (b)	*875*	*731*	*144*	*650*	*609*	*41*	*34*	*13*	*21*	*57*	*43*	*14*
		68.—Engineering and Surveying.												
		(a) Engineers, Architects and Surveyors.												
		Administrative staff	42	31	11	...	...	...	7	1	6	...	...	...
		Civil Engineers	71	40	31	18	12	6	16	11	5	2	...	2
		Total 68 (a)	*113*	*71*	*42*	*18*	*12*	*6*	*23*	*12*	*11*	*2*	...	*2*
		(b) Subsidiary Staff.												
		Draughtsmen	124	67	57	40	14	26	2	2	...	2	2	...
		Total 68 (b)	*124*	*67*	*57*	*40*	*14*	*26*	*2*	*2*	...	*2*	*2*	...
		69.—Other sciences.												
		(b) Minor Sciences.												
		Astrologers and horoscope casters	1,394	634	760	85	50	35	1	...	1	9	3	6
		Total 69 (b)	*1,394*	*634*	*760*	*85*	*50*	*35*	*1*	...	*1*	*9*	*3*	*6*
		70.—Pictorial Art and Sculpture.												
		Painters	2,229	1,164	1,135	26	18	8	207	113	94	873	463	410
		Photographers	44	26	18	3	...	3	5	2	3	1	1	...
		Total 70	2,343	1,190	1,153	29	18	11	212	115	97	874	464	410

OCCUPATION AND CLASS.			DISTRIBUTION BY AGENCIES.														
			BUNDELKHAND.			BAGHELKHAND.			WESTERN MALWA.			BHOPAWAR.			GUNA.		
Class.	Order.	SUB-ORDER, GROUP AND OCCUPATION.	TOTAL.	Males.	Females.	TOTAL.	Males.	Females.	TOTAL.	Males.	Females.	TOTAL.	Males.	Females.	TOTAL.	Males.	Females.
			16	17	18	19	20	21	22	23	24	25	26	27	28	29	30
		(*b*) *Subsidiary Medical Services.*															
	XX.—LEARNED AND ARTISTIC PROFESSIONS.—*contd.*	Hospital assistants	...	...	...	13	8	5	...	...	...	9	5	4	...	...	...
		Asylum servants	5	1	4	...	...	...	...	...	...	...	...	...	...	...	...
		Apothecaries	23	15	8	...	...	...	...	...	...	...	...	...	...	...	...
		Compounders	...	...	...	68	32	36	...	...	...	...	...	...	...	...	...
		Dispensary servants	10	5	5	...	...	...	...	...	...	6	...	6	...	...	...
		Total 67 (b)	*38*	*21*	*17*	*81*	*40*	*41*	...	...	...	*15*	*5*	*10*	...	...	...
		68.—Engineering and Surveying.															
		(*a*) *Engineers, Architects and Surveyors.*															
		Administrative staff	...	...	...	...	...	...	35	30	5	...	...	...	...	...	...
		Civil Engineers	16	7	9	...	...	...	19	10	9	...	...	...	...	...	...
		Total 68 (a)	*16*	*7*	*9*	...	...	...	*54*	*40*	*14*	...	...	...	...	...	...
		(*b*) *Subsidiary Staff.*															
		Draughtsmen	23	13	10	57	36	21	...	...	...	...	...	...	...	...	...
		Total 68 (b)	*23*	*13*	*10*	*57*	*36*	*21*	...	...	...	...	...	...	...	...	...
		69.—Other Science.															
		(*b*) *Minor Sciences.*															
		Astrologers and horoscope casters	...	...	...	669	350	319	547	192	355	61	26	35	22	13	9
		Total 69 (b)	...	...	...	*669*	*350*	*319*	*547*	*192*	*355*	*61*	*26*	*35*	*22*	*13*	*9*
		70.—Pictorial Art and Sculpture.															
		Painters	129	88	41	57	14	43	994	463	531	13	5	8	...	...	...
		Photographers	23	17	6	...	...	...	12	6	6	...	...	...	...	...	...
		Total 70	152	105	47	57	14	43	1,006	469	537	13	5	8	...	...	...

TABLE XVII.—Occupations.—Part B.—(Provincial Distribution)—*contd.*

Class.	Order.	Sub-order, Group and Occupation.	Provincial Total. Total.	Provincial Total. Males.	Provincial Total. Females.	Indore. Total.	Indore. Males.	Indore. Females.	Gwalior. Total.	Gwalior. Males.	Gwalior. Females.	Bhopal. Total.	Bhopal. Males.	Bhopal. Females.
1	2	3	4	5	6	7	8	9	10	11	12	13	14	15
		71.—Music, Acting, Dancing.												
	XX.—Learned and Artistic Professions—*concld.*	Musicians (not military)	2,059	982	1,077	125	71	54	130	65	65	174	172	2
		Drummers	8,174	4,481	3,693	731	404	327	338	170	168	1,077	686	391
		Actors	1,570	795	775	...	...	...	...	...	...	175	80	95
		Singers and dancers	8,056	3,702	4,354	457	152	305	2,565	1,012	1,553	743	735	8
		Total 71	19,859	9,960	9,899	1,313	627	686	3,033	1,247	1,786	2,169	1,673	496
		Total XX.—Learned and Artistic Professions.	**114,802**	**64,859**	**49,943**	**8,898**	**5,343**	**3,555**	**20,187**	**11,089**	**9,098**	**9,788**	**5,654**	**4,134**
		72.—Sport.												
	XXI.—Sports and Amusements.	Shikaris and bird-catchers	1,028	607	421	93	52	41	323	177	146	123	85	38
		Total 72	1,028	607	421	93	52	41	323	177	146	123	85	38
		73.—Exhibitions and Games.												
		(a) Catching, Training and Exhibiting Animals.												
		Snake charmers	17	10	7	...	...	...	17	10	7	...	...	...
		Circus performers	13	7	6	...	...	...	...	...	...	13	7	6
		Total 73 (a)	*30*	*17*	*13*	...	...	...	*17*	*10*	*7*	*13*	*7*	*6*
		(b) Conjuring, Fortune-telling and other Exhibitions.												
		Buffoons	388	233	155	...	...	...	...	...	...	53	31	22
		Ballad reciters	870	384	486	28	17	11	570	247	323	...	...	...
		Exhibitors of puppets	55	...	55	...	...	...	...	...	...	...	...	...
		Conjurors	449	265	184	37	24	13	170	123	47	5	...	5
		Fortune-tellers	330	175	155	29	16	13	258	130	128	...	...	...
		Total 73 (b)	*2,092*	*1,057*	*1,035*	*94*	*57*	*37*	*998*	*500*	*498*	*58*	*31*	*27*

Table XVII B.—Occupations—(C Provincial Distribution)

CLASS F.—PROFESSIONS—*contd.*

OCCUPATION AND CLASS.			DISTRIBUTION BY AGENCIES.														
			BUNDELKHAND.			BAGHELKHAND.			WESTERN MALWA.			BHOPAWAR.			GUNA.		
Class.	Order.	Sub-order, Group and Occupation.	Total.	Males.	Females.	Total.	Males.	Females.	Total.	Males.	Females.	Total.	Males.	Females.	Total.	Males.	Females.
			16	17	18	19	20	21	22	23	24	25	26	27	28	29	30
		71.—Music, Acting, Dancing.															
	XX.—Learned and Artistic Professions—*concld.*	Musicians (not military)	125	46	79	31	31	...	919	317	602	527	280	247	28	...	28
		Drummers	118	69	49	18	...	18	5,887	3,149	2,738	...	...	...	5	3	2
		Actors	...	...	...	...	...	...	336	157	179	958	508	450	101	50	51
		Singers and dancers	1,292	422	870	1,366	650	716	1,551	673	878	...	...	...	82	58	24
		Total 71	1,535	537	998	1,415	681	734	8,693	4,296	4,397	1,485	788	697	216	111	105
		Total XX.—Learned and Artistic Professions.	**26,443**	**15,104**	**11,339**	**10,968**	**5,545**	**5,428**	**28,925**	**15,593**	**13,332**	**6,467**	**4,744**	**1,723**	**3,126**	**1,787**	**1,339**
		72.—Sport.															
	XXI.—Sports and Amusements.	Shikaris and Birdcatchers	43	24	19	81	37	44	165	133	32	150	77	73	50	22	28
		Total 72	43	24	19	81	37	4	165	133	32	150	77	73	50	22	28
		73.—Exhibitions and Games.															
		(a) Catching, Training and Exhibiting Animals.															
		Snake charmers	...	...	...	...	...	...	...	...	...	...	...	...	...	...	...
		Circus performers	...	...	...	...	...	...	...	...	...	...	...	...	...	...	...
		Total 73 (a)	...	...	...	...	...	...	...	...	...	...	...	...	...	...	...
		(b) Conjuring, Fortune-telling and other Exhibitions.															
		Buffoons	292	184	108	...	...	...	...	...	...	...	...	...	43	18	25
		Ballad reciters	93	66	127	22	18	4	57	36	21	...	...	...	...	...	...
		Exhibitors of puppets	...	...	...	...	...	...	...	...	...	...	...	...	55	...	55
		Conjurors	26	11	15	...	...	...	211	107	104	...	...	...	...	...	...
		Fortune-tellers	...	...	...	...	...	...	...	...	...	...	...	...	43	29	14
		Total 73 (b)	*511*	*261*	*250*	*22*	*18*	*4*	*268*	*143*	*125*	...	...	...	*141*	*47*	*94*

TABLE XVII.—Occupations.—Part B.—(Provincial Distribution)—*contd.*

OCCUPATION AND CLASS.			PROVINCIAL TOTAL.			DISTRIBUTION BY AGENCIES.								
						INDORE.			GWALIOR.			BHOPAL.		
Class.	Order.	Sub-order, Group and Occupation.	Total.	Males.	Females.	Total.	Males.	Females.	Total.	Males.	Females.	Total.	Males.	Females.
1	2	3	4	5	6	7	8	9	10	11	12	13	14	15
CLASS F.—PROFESSIONS—*concld.*	XXI.—Sports and Amusements—*contd.*	(c) *Acrobatics and Athletics.*												
		Tumblers, acrobats and wrestlers	3,745	3,337	408	61	61	...	160	96	64	2,783	2,757	26
		Total 73 (c)	*3,745*	*3,337*	*408*	*61*	*61*	...	*160*	*96*	*64*	*2,783*	*2,757*	*26*
		(d) *Service of places of Entertainment.*												
		Billiard-room managers	35	15	20	7	1	6	...	...	...	...	...	...
		Total 73 (d)	*35*	*15*	*20*	*7*	*1*	*6*	...	...	...	...	...	...
		Total XXI.—Sports and Amusements.	**6,980**	**5,083**	**1,897**	**255**	**171**	**84**	**1,498**	**783**	**715**	**2,977**	**2,880**	**97**
		Total Class F	**121,782**	**69,892**	**51,840**	**9,153**	**5,514**	**3,639**	**21,685**	**11,872**	**9,813**	**12,765**	**8,534**	**4,231**
G.—INDEFINITE AND INDEPENDENT.	XXIII.—Indefinite.	**74.—Unskilled Labour.**												
		(a) *Special Branches.*												
		Well sinkers	19	17	2	...	...	...	...	...	...	...	...	...
		Road labourers	492	365	127	...	...	...	46	28	18	...	...	...
		Railway labourers	785	477	308	...	...	...	205	134	71	5	...	5
		Gangmen	562	540	22	468	468	...	...	...	...	86	68	18
		Miners (unspecified)	1,128	742	386	...	...	...	...	...	...	...	...	...
		Total 74 (a)	*2,986*	*2,141*	*846*	*468*	*468*	...	*251*	*162*	*89*	*91*	*68*	*23*
		(b) *General Branches.*												
		General labour	2,190,999	1,032,907	1,158,092	91,765	47,885	43,880	214,924	107,923	107,001	550,662	278,330	272,332
		Total 74 (b)	*2,190,999*	*1,032,907*	*1,158,092*	*91,765*	*47,885*	*43,880*	*214,924*	*107,923*	*107,001*	*550,662*	*278,330*	*272,332*
		75.—Undefined, etc.												
		Undefined and disreputable means of livelihood.	4,004	1,444	2,560	239	130	109	1,315	495	820	263	85	178
		Total 75	**4,004**	**1,444**	**2,560**	**239**	**130**	**109**	**1,315**	**495**	**820**	**263**	**85**	**178**
		Total XXIII.—Indefinite	**2,197,989**	**1,036,492**	**1,161,497**	**92,472**	**48,483**	**43,989**	**216,490**	**108,580**	**107,910**	**551,016**	**278,483**	**272,533**

Table XVII B.—Occupations—(Provincial Distribution).

Class.	Order.	Sub-order, Group and Occupation.	Bundelkhand. Total.	Bundelkhand. Males.	Bundelkhand. Females.	Baghelkhand. Total.	Baghelkhand. Males.	Baghelkhand. Females.	Western Malwa. Total.	Western Malwa. Males.	Western Malwa. Females.	Bhopawar. Total.	Bhopawar. Males.	Bhopawar. Females.	Guna. Total.	Guna. Males.	Guna. Females.
			16	17	18	19	20	21	22	23	24	25	26	27	28	29	30
CLASS F.—PROFESSIONS—concld.	XXI.—Sports and Amusements—contd.	*(c) Acrobatics and Athletics.*															
		Tumblers, acrobats and wrestlers	349	218	131	193	115	78	111	51	60	88	39	49	...	...	...
		Total 73 (c)	*349*	*218*	*131*	*193*	*115*	*78*	*111*	*51*	*60*	*88*	*39*	*49*	...	...	...
		(d) Service of places of Entertainment.															
		Billiard-room managers	...	...	...	...	...	...	28	14	14	...	...	...	...	...	...
		Total 73 (d)	...	...	...	...	...	...	*28*	*14*	*14*	...	...	...	...	...	...
		Total XXI.—Sports and Amusements.	**908**	**508**	**400**	**296**	**170**	**126**	**572**	**341**	**231**	**238**	**116**	**122**	**191**	**69**	**122**
		Total Class F	**27,346**	**15,607**	**11,739**	**11,264**	**5,715**	**5,549**	**29,497**	**15,934**	**13,563**	**6,705**	**4,860**	**1,845**	**3,317**	**1,856**	**1,461**
CLASS G.—INDEFINITE AND INDEPENDENT.	XXIII.—Indefinite.	**74.—Unskilled Labour.**															
		(a) Special Branches.															
		Well sinkers	...	...	...	...	...	...									
		Road labourers	...	...	...	446	337	109	19	17	2	...	...	...	...	...	...
		Railway labourers	15	...	15	560	343	217	...	...	...	...	...	...	...	...	...
		Gangmen	...	...	..	8	4	4	...	...	...	...	...	...	...	...	...
		Miners (unspecified)	...	...	...	1,128	742	386	...	...	...	...	...	...	...	...	...
		Total 74 (a)	*15*	...	*15*	*2,142*	*1,426*	*716*	*19*	*17*	*2*	...	...	...	...	...	...
		(b) General Branches.															
		General labour	270,298	129,158	141,140	321,642	110,364	211,278	436,018	209,438	226,580	231,092	111,986	119,106	74,598	37,823	36,775
		Total 74 (b)	*270,298*	*129,158*	*141,140*	*321,642*	*110,364*	*211,278*	*436,018*	*209,438*	*226,580*	*231,092*	*111,986*	*119,106*	*74,598*	*37,823*	*36,775*
		75.—Undefined, etc.															
		Undefined and disreputable means of livelihood.	1,036	404	632	381	72	309	384	150	234	80	56	24	306	52	254
		Total 75	1,036	404	632	381	72	309	384	150	234	80	56	24	306	52	254
		Total XXIII.—Indefinite	**271,349**	**129,562**	**141,787**	**324,165**	**111,862**	**212,308**	**436,421**	**209,605**	**226,816**	**231,172**	**112,042**	**119,130**	**74,904**	**37,875**	**37,029**

TABLE XVII.—Occupations.—Part B.—Provincial Distribution.—*contd.*

OCCUPATION AND CLASS.			PROVINCIAL TOTAL.			DISTRIBUTION BY AGENCIES.								
						INDORE.			GWALIOR.			BHOPAL.		
Class.	Order.	Sub-order, Group and Occupation.	Total.	Males.	Females.	Total.	Males.	Females.	Total.	Males.	Females.	Total.	Males.	Females.
1	2	3	4	5	6	7	8	9	10	11	12	13	14	15
		76.—Property and Alms.												
		(a) Property and Allowances.												
	XXIV.—INDEPENDENT OF WORK.	House-rent, shares, etc.	628	327	301	21	18	3	23	11	12	415	263	152
		Allowances from patrons	1,205	388	817	45	21	24	...	...	...	96	50	46
		Total 76 (a)	*1,833*	*715*	*1,118*	*66*	*39*	*27*	*23*	*11*	*12*	*511*	*313*	*198*
		(b) Charity and Endowment.												
		Scholarship	234	207	27	20	20	...	32	23	9	...	...	...
		Mendicancy (not religious)	269,187	145,904	123,283	13,805	3,131	10,674	37,663	26,157	11,506	80,290	38,407	41,883
		Total 76 (b)	*269,421*	*146,111*	*123,310*	*13,825*	*3,151*	*10,674*	*37,695*	*26,180*	*11,515*	*80,290*	*38,407*	*41,883*
		77.—Supported at the public charge.												
		(a) Pension.												
		Pensioners, Civil	1,371	710	661	610	383	227	...	...	...	26	11	15
		„ Military	1,276	683	593	...	...	...	...	...	...	125	105	20
		„ (Unspecified)	1,260	583	677	...	...	...	314	162	152	106	106	...
		Total 77 (a)	*3,907*	*1,976*	*1,931*	*610*	*383*	*227*	*314*	*162*	*152*	*257*	*222*	*35*
		(b) Prisoners.												
		Prisoners	1,548	1,270	278	288	285	3	745	735	10	238	...	238
		Total 77 (b)	*1,548*	*1,270*	*278*	*288*	*285*	*3*	*745*	*735*	*10*	*238*	...	*238*
		Total XXIV.—Independent of Work	**276,709**	**150,072**	**126,637**	**14,789**	**3,858**	**10,931**	**38,777**	**27,088**	**11,689**	**81,296**	**38,942**	**42,354**
		Total Class G	**2,474,698**	**1,186,564**	**1,288,134**	**107,261**	**52,341**	**54,920**	**255,267**	**135,668**	**119,599**	**632,312**	**317,425**	**314,887**
		Total of all Classes	**10,318,812**	**5,395,536**	**4,923,276**	**372,792**	**201,944**	**170,848**	**1,757,509**	**948,805**	**808,704**	**2,006,859**	**1,052,777**	**954,082**

OCCUPATION AND CLASS.			DISTRIBUTION BY AGENCIES.														
			BUNDELKHAND.			BAGHELKHAND.			WESTERN MALWA.			BHOPAWAR.			GUNA.		
Class.	Order.	Sub-Order, Group and Occupation.	TOTAL.	Males.	Females.	TOTAL.	Males.	Females.	TOTAL.	Males.	Females.	TOTAL.	Males.	Females.	TOTAL.	Males.	Females.
			16	17	18	19	20	21	22	23	24	25	26	27	28	29	30
		76.—Property and Alms.															
		(a) Property and Allowances.															
	XXIV.—INDEPENDENT OF WORK.	House-rent, shares, etc.	18	10	8	19	2	17	120	23	97	12	...	12	...	...	...
		Allowances from patrons	390	...	390	638	283	355	34	32	2	...	...	...	2	2	...
		Total 76 (a)	*408*	*10*	*398*	*657*	*285*	*372*	*154*	*55*	*99*	*12*	...	*12*	*2*	*2*	...
		(b) Charity and Endowment.															
		Scholarship	...	...	...	19	10	9	163	154	9	...	...	...	...	...	...
		Mendicancy (not religious)	15,709	5,201	10,508	16,966	15,639	1,327	67,067	38,396	28,671	24,540	13,726	10,814	13,147	5,247	7,900
		Total 76 (b)	*15,709*	*5,201*	*10,508*	*16,985*	*15,649*	*1,336*	*67,230*	*38,550*	*28,680*	*24,540*	*13,726*	*10,814*	*13,147*	*5,247*	*7,900*
		77.—Supported at the public charge.															
		(a) Pension.															
		Pensioners, Civil	377	219	158	88	...	88	252	97	155	...	...	...	18	...	18
		" Military	766	306	460	300	187	113	85	85	...	...	...	...	...	...	...
		" (Unspecified)	...	...	...	126	...	126	101	...	101	561	263	298	52	52	...
		Total 77 (a)	*1,143*	*525*	*618*	*514*	*187*	*327*	*438*	*182*	*256*	*561*	*263*	*298*	*70*	*52*	*18*
		(b) Prisoners.															
		Prisoners	...	...	...	56	37	19	150	146	4	68	64	4	3	3	...
		Total 77 (b)	...	...	...	*56*	*37*	*19*	*150*	*146*	*4*	*68*	*64*	*4*	*3*	*3*	...
		Total XXIV.—Independent of Work	**17,260**	**5,736**	**11,524**	**18,212**	**16,158**	**2,054**	**67,972**	**38,933**	**29,039**	**25,181**	**14,053**	**11,128**	**13,222**	**5,304**	**7,918**
		Total Class G	**288,609**	**135,298**	**153,311**	**342,877**	**128,020**	**214,357**	**504,393**	**248,538**	**255,855**	**256,353**	**126,095**	**130,258**	**88,126**	**43,179**	**44,947**
		Total of all Classes	**1,508,053**	**784,906**	**723,147**	**1,737,606**	**872,222**	**865,384**	**1,619,368**	**851,933**	**767,435**	**978,652**	**502,832**	**475,820**	**337,873**	**180,117**	**157,856**

TABLE A.

Christians by Sect and Race.

Part I.

NOTE.—This table applies only to persons enumerated on the British India Schedule

Table A.—Christians by Sect and Race.—Part I.

AGENCIES.	TOTAL CHRISTIAN.			DISTRIBUTION BY SECT.																														
				CHURCH OF ENGLAND.								ROMAN CATHOLIC.								PRESBYTERIAN.								PROTESTANT.							
				TOTAL.		Foreign.		Eurasian.		Native.		TOTAL.		Foreign.		Eurasian.		Native.		TOTAL.		Foreign.		Eurasian.		Native.		TOTAL.		Foreign.		Eurasian.		Native.	
	TOTAL.	Males.	Females.	Males.	Females.	Males.	Females.	Males.	Females.	Males.	Females.	Males.	Females.	Males.	Females.	Males.	Females.	Males.	Females.	Males.	Females.	Males.	Females.	Males.	Females.	Males.	Females.	Males.	Females.	Males.	Females.	Males.	Females.	Males.	Females.
1	2	3	4	5	6	7	8	9	10	11	12	13	14	15	16	17	18	19	20	21	22	23	24	25	26	27	28	29	30	31	32	33	34	35	36
INDORE . . .	3,452	2,662	790	1,730	326	1,685	271	18	35	27	20	711	397	291	118	54	36	366	243	97	43	66	21	...	...	31	22	...	...	...	...	...	...	...	...
GWALIOR . . .	199	157	42	126	24	125	23	1	1	...	...	10	14	6	12	4	2	...	...	7	4	7	4	...	...	...	...	4	...	4	...	...	...	...	...
BHOPAL . . .	98	54	44	17	23	13	11	2	9	2	3	31	16	6	3	16	9	9	4	1	3	1	3	...	...	...	...	...	...	...	...	...	...	...	...
BUNDELKHAND . .	652	560	92	463	48	461	46	1	1	1	1	63	37	59	28	1	...	3	9	4	2	4	2	...	...	...	...	...	...	...	...	...	...	...	...
BAGHELKHAND . .	213	118	95	67	45	49	24	16	21	2	...	29	33	12	14	9	4	8	15	7	8	2	6	5	2	...	...	8	5	7	5	1	...	...	...
WESTERN MALWA .	751	559	192	329	93	301	69	20	19	8	5	171	51	74	12	35	24	62	15	24	25	23	14	...	...	1	11	2	3	...	...	...	...	2	3
BHOPAWAR . .	20	14	6	8	2	8	2	...	...	...	...	5	1	3	...	1	...	1	1	1	3	...	...	...	...	1	3	...	...	...	...	...	...	...	...
GUNA . . .	18	15	3	9	1	8	...	1	1	...	...	3	2	...	...	3	2	...	...	...	...	...	...	...	...	...	...	2	...	...	...	2	...	...	...
Total .	5,408	4,139	1,264	2,749	562	2,650	446	59	87	40	29	1,028	551	451	187	128	77	449	287	141	88	108	50	5	2	33	36	16	8	11	5	3	...	2	3

AGENCIES.	DISTRIBUTION BY SECT.																															
	WESLEYAN.								METHODIST.								UNSECTARIAN.								CONGREGATIONALIST.							
	TOTAL.		Foreign.		Eurasian.		Native.		TOTAL.		Foreign.		Eurasian.		Native.		TOTAL.		Foreign.		Eurasion.		Native.		TOTAL.		Foreign.		Eurasian.		Native.	
	Males.	Females.	Males.	Females.	Males.	Females.	Males.	Females.	Males.	Females.	Males.	Females.	Males.	Females.	Males.	Females.	Males.	Females.	Males.	Females.	Males.	Females.	Males.	Females.	Males.	Females.	Males.	Females.	Males.	Females.	Males.	Females.
	37	38	39	40	41	42	43	44	45	46	47	48	49	50	51	52	53	54	55	56	57	58	59	60	61	62	63	64	65	66	67	68
INDORE . . .	102	...	102	...	...	...	...	...	15	22	14	21	...	1	1	...	4	1	4	1	...	...	...	...	...	1	...	1	...	...	...	...
GWALIOR . . .	7	...	7	...	...	...	...	...	2	...	1	...	1	...	...	...	...	...	...	...	...	...	...	...	...	...	...	...	...	...	...	...
BHOPAL . . .	2	...	2	...	...	...	...	...	1	...	...	...	...	...	1	...	...	1	...	...	...	1	...	...	...	...	...	...	...	...	...	...
BUNDELKHAND . .	25	3	25	3	...	...	...	...	2	1	2	1	...	...	...	...	1	...	1	...	...	...	...	...	...	...	...	...	...	...	...	...
BAGHELKHAND . .	5	4	2	1	3	3	...	...	1	...	...	...	1	...	...	...	...	...	...	...	...	...	...	...	...	...	...	...	...	...	...	...
WESTERN MALWA .	11	1	11	1	...	...	...	...	8	7	5	7	3	...	...	...	2	3	1	...	1	3	...	...	...	...	...	...	...	...	...	...
BHOPAWAR . .	...	...	...	...	...	...	...	...	...	...	...	...	...	...	...	...	...	...	...	...	...	...	...	...	...	...	...	...	...	...	...	...
GUNA . . .	...	...	...	...	...	...	...	...	...	...	...	...	...	...	...	...	1	...	1	...	...	...	...	...	...	...	...	...	...	...	...	...
Total .	152	8	149	5	3	3	...	...	29	30	22	29	5	1	2	...	8	5	7	1	1	4	...	...	...	1	...	1	...	...	...	...

Table A.—Christians by Sect and Race.—Central India.

AGENCIES.	DISTRIBUTION BY SECT.																															
	Evangelical.								Episcopalian.								Baptist.								Lutheran.							
	Total.		Foreign.		Eurasian.		Native.		Total.		Foreign.		Eurasian.		Native.		Total.		Foreign.		Eurasian.		Native.		Total.		Foreign.		Eurasian.		Native.	
	Males.	Females.	Males.	Females.	Males.	Females.	Males.	Females.	Males.	Females.	Males.	Females.	Males.	Females.	Males.	Females.	Males.	Females.	Males.	Females.	Males.	Females.	Males.	Females.	Males.	Females.	Males.	Females.	Males.	Females.	Males.	Females.
	69	70	71	72	73	74	75	76	77	78	79	80	81	82	83	84	85	86	87	88	89	90	91	92	93	94	95	96	97	98	99	100
Indore	1	...	1	...	...	...	...	...	1	...	1	...	...	...	...	...	1	...	1	...	...	...	...	...	...	...	...	...	...	...	...	...
Gwalior	...	...	...	...	...	...	...	...	...	...	...	...	...	...	...	...	...	...	...	...	...	...	...	...	1	...	1	...	...	...	...	...
Bhopal	...	...	...	...	...	...	...	...	...	...	...	...	...	...	...	...	...	...	...	...	...	...	...	...	...	...	...	...	...	...	...	...
Bundelkhand	...	...	...	...	...	...	...	...	...	...	...	...	...	...	...	...	...	...	...	...	...	...	...	...	...	...	...	...	...	...	...	...
Baghelkhand	...	...	...	...	...	...	...	...	1	...	1	...	...	...	...	...	...	...	...	...	...	...	...	...	...	...	...	...	...	...	...	...
Western Malwa	...	...	...	...	...	...	...	...	...	...	...	...	...	...	...	...	9	3	7	2	...	...	2	1	...	...	...	...	...	...	...	...
Bhopawar	...	...	...	...	...	...	...	...	...	...	...	...	...	...	...	...	...	...	...	...	...	...	...	...	...	...	...	...	...	...	...	...
Guna	...	...	...	...	...	...	...	...	...	...	...	...	...	...	...	...	...	...	...	...	...	...	...	...	...	...	...	...	...	...	...	...
Total	1	...	1	...	...	...	...	...	2	...	2	...	...	...	...	...	10	3	8	2	...	...	2	1	1	...	1	...	...	...	...	...

AGENCIES.	DISTRIBUTION BY SECT.																							
	Agnostic.								Society of Friends.								Not Returned.							
	Total.		Foreign.		Eurasian.		Native.		Total.		Foreign.		Eurasian.		Native.		Total.		Foreign.		Eurasian.		Native.	
	Males.	Females.	Males.	Females.	Males.	Females.	Males.	Females.	Males.	Females.	Males.	Females.	Males.	Females.	Males.	Females.	Males.	Females.	Males.	Females.	Males.	Females.	Males.	Females.
	101	102	103	104	105	106	107	108	109	110	111	112	113	114	115	116	117	118	119	120	121	122	123	124
Indore	...	...	...	...	...	...	...	...	...	...	...	...	...	...	...	...	...	...	...	...	...	...	...	...
Gwalior	...	...	...	...	...	...	...	...	...	...	...	...	...	...	...	...	...	...	...	...	...	...	...	...
Bhopal	...	...	...	...	...	...	...	...	2	1	2	1	...	...	...	...	...	...	...	...	...	...	...	...
Bundelkhand	1	...	1	...	...	...	...	...	...	...	...	...	...	...	...	...	1	1	...	...	...	...	1	1
Baghelkhand	...	...	...	...	...	...	...	...	...	...	...	...	...	...	...	...	...	...	...	...	...	...	...	...
Western Malwa	1	...	1	...	...	...	...	...	...	...	...	...	...	...	...	...	2	6	...	...	...	...	2	6
Bhopawar	...	...	...	...	...	...	...	...	...	...	...	...	...	...	...	...	...	...	...	...	...	...	...	...
Guna	...	...	...	...	...	...	...	...	...	...	...	...	...	...	...	...	...	...	...	...	...	...	...	...
Total	2	...	2	...	...	...	...	...	2	1	2	1	...	...	...	...	8	7	...	...	...	...	8	7

TABLE A—*continued.*

Races.

Part II.

NOTE.—This Table applies only to persons enumerated on the British India Schedule.

TABLE A.—Part II.—Races—*continued.*

DISTRIBUTION BY RACE.

AGENCIES.	Total Christian.			A—Foreign.																				
				Total.			Church of England.		Roman Catholic.		Presbyterian.		Protestant.		Wesleyan.		Methodist.		Unsectarian.		Congregationalist.		Evangelical.	
	Total.	Males.	Females.	Total.	Males.	Females.	Males.	Females.	Males.	Females.	Males.	Females.	Males.	Females.	Males.	Females.	Males.	Females.	Males.	Females.	Males.	Females.	Males.	Females.
1	2	3	4	5	6	7	8	9	10	11	12	13	14	15	16	17	18	19	20	21	22	23	24	25
Indore	3,452	2,662	790	2,598	2,165	433	1,685	271	291	118	66	21	...	...	102	...	14	21	4	1	...	1	1	...
Gwalior	199	157	42	190	151	39	125	23	6	12	7	4	4	...	7	...	1	...	...	...	...	...	...	...
Bhopal	98	54	44	42	24	18	13	11	6	3	1	3	...	...	2	...	...	...	...	...	...	...	...	...
Bundelkhand	652	560	92	633	553	80	461	46	59	28	4	2	...	...	25	3	2	1	1	...	...	...	...	...
Baghelkhand	213	118	95	123	73	50	49	24	12	14	2	6	7	5	2	1	...	...	...	...	...	...	...	...
Western Malwa	751	559	192	528	423	105	301	69	74	12	23	14	...	...	11	1	5	7	1	...	...	...	...	...
Bhopawar	20	14	6	13	11	2	8	2	3	...	...	...	...	...	...	...	...	...	...	...	...	...	...	...
Guna	18	15	3	9	9	...	8	...	...	...	...	...	...	...	...	...	...	...	1	...	...	...	...	...
Total	5,408	4,189	1,264	4,136	3,409	727	2,650	446	451	187	108	50	11	5	149	5	22	29	7	1	...	1	1	...

DISTRIBUTION BY RACE.

AGENCIES.	A.—Foreign—*contd.*										B.—Eurasian.																
	Episcopalian.		Baptist.		Lutheran.		Agnostic.		Society of Friends.		Total.			Church of England.		Roman Catholic.		Presbyterian.		Protestant.		Wesleyan.		Methodist.		Unsectarian.	
	Males.	Females.	Males.	Females.	Males.	Females.	Males.	Females.	Males.	Females.	Total.	Males.	Females.	Males.	Females.	Males.	Females.	Males.	Females.	Males.	Females.	Males.	Females.	Males.	Females.	Males.	Females.
	26	27	28	29	30	31	32	33	34	35	36	37	38	39	40	41	42	43	44	45	46	47	48	49	50	51	52
Indore	1	...	1	...	...	...	...	...	...	...	144	72	72	18	35	54	36	...	...	...	...	...	...	...	1	...	...
Gwalior	...	...	...	...	1	...	...	...	...	...	9	6	3	1	1	4	2	...	...	...	...	...	...	1	...	...	...
Bhopal	...	...	...	...	...	...	...	...	2	1	37	18	19	2	9	16	9	...	...	...	...	...	...	...	...	...	1
Bundelkhand	...	...	...	...	...	...	1	...	...	...	3	2	1	1	1	1	...	...	...	...	...	...	...	...	...	...	...
Baghelkhand	1	...	...	...	...	...	...	...	...	...	65	35	30	16	21	9	4	5	2	1	...	3	3	1	...	...	...
Western Malwa	...	...	7	2	...	...	1	...	...	...	105	59	46	20	19	35	24	...	...	...	...	...	...	3	...	1	3
Bhopawa	...	...	...	...	...	...	...	...	...	...	1	1	...	...	...	1	...	...	...	...	...	...	...	...	...	...	...
Guna	...	...	...	...	...	...	...	...	...	...	9	6	3	1	1	3	2	...	...	2	...	...	...	...	...	...	...
Total	2	...	8	2	1	...	2	...	2	1	878	199	174	59	87	128	77	5	2	8	...	8	8	5	1	1	4

Table A.—Part II.—Races.—Central India.

DISTRIBUTION BY RACE.

AGENCIES.	C.—NATIVE.																
	TOTAL.			Church of England.		Roman Catholic.		Presbyterian.		Protestant.		Methodist.		Baptist.		Not returned.	
	TOTAL.	Males.	Females.	Males.	Females.	Males.	Females.	Males.	Females.	Males.	Females.	Males.	Females.	Males.	Females.	Males.	Females.
	53	54	55	56	57	58	59	60	61	62	63	64	65	66	67	68	69
INDORE	710	425	285	27	20	366	243	31	22	...	...	1	...	...	...	...	...
GWALIOR	...	...	...	...	...	...	...	...	...	...	...	...	...	...	...	...	...
BHOPAL	19	12	7	2	3	9	4	...	...	...	...	1	...	...	...	...	...
BUNDELKHAND	16	5	11	1	1	3	9	...	...	...	...	...	...	...	...	1	1
BAGHELKHAND	25	10	15	2	...	8	15	...	...	...	...	...	...	...	...	...	...
WESTERN MALWA	118	77	41	8	5	62	15	1	11	2	3	...	...	2	1	2	6
BHOPAWAR	6	2	4	...	...	1	1	1	3	...	...	...	...	...	...	...	...
GUNA	...	...	...	...	...	...	...	...	...	...	...	...	...	...	...	...	...
Total	894	531	363	40	29	449	287	33	36	2	3	2	...	2	1	3	7

TABLE B.

Christians by Race and Age.

NOTE.—This Table applies only to persons enumerated on the British India Schedule.

TABLE B.—Christians by Race and Age.

AGENCIES.	TOTAL.			A.—NON-ASIATICS.											B.—EURASIANS.											C.—NATIVES.										
				All ages.			0—14		15—34		35—49		50 and over.		All ages.			0—14		15—34		35—49		50 and over.		All ages.			0—14		15—34		35—49		50 and over.	
	Total.	Males.	Females.	Total.	Males.	Females.	Males.	Females.	Males.	Females.	Males.	Females.	Males.	Females.	Total.	Males.	Females.	Males.	Females.	Males.	Females.	Males.	Females.	Males.	Females.	Total.	Males.	Females.	Males.	Females.	Males.	Females.	Males.	Females.	Males.	Females.
1	2	3	4	5	6	7	8	9	10	11	12	13	14	15	16	17	18	19	20	21	22	23	24	25	26	27	28	29	30	31	32	33	34	35	36	37
Indore	3,452	2,662	790	2,598	2,165	433	177	174	1,834	205	126	48	28	6	144	72	72	22	31	20	22	21	15	9	4	710	425	285	137	94	153	124	87	32	48	35
Gwalior	199	157	42	190	151	39	9	16	124	15	13	4	5	4	9	6	3	...	...	4	1	2	2	...	...	...	...	...	...	...	...	...	...	...	...	...
Bhopal	98	54	44	42	24	18	5	3	9	10	8	4	2	1	37	18	19	9	8	6	9	2	1	1	1	19	12	7	...	2	9	5	3	...	...	...
Bundelkhand	652	560	92	633	553	80	34	31	483	39	34	10	2	...	3	2	1	...	...	2	...	...	1	...	...	16	5	11	3	5	2	4	...	1	...	1
Baghelkhand	213	118	95	123	73	50	15	18	31	24	16	6	11	2	65	35	30	15	14	14	9	4	6	2	1	25	10	15	1	8	6	5	2	1	1	1
Western Malwa	751	559	192	528	423	105	50	42	328	43	39	16	6	4	105	59	46	16	18	22	19	18	6	3	3	118	77	41	19	20	34	12	19	5	5	4
Bhopawar	20	14	6	13	11	2	1	...	5	1	4	...	1	1	1	1	...	...	...	...	...	...	...	1	...	6	2	4	...	2	1	2	1	...	...	...
Guna	18	15	3	9	9	...	1	...	5	...	2	...	1	...	9	6	3	...	1	5	1	1	...	...	1	...	...	...	...	...	...	...	...	...	...	...
Total	5,408	4,139	1,264	4,136	3,409	727	292	284	2,819	337	242	88	56	18	378	199	174	62	72	78	61	48	31	16	10	894	531	363	160	131	205	152	112	39	54	41

TABLE C.

Literate by Language known (Provincial Summary).

NOTE.—This Table applies only to persons enumerated on the British India Schedule.

TABLE C.—Literate by Language known (Provincial Summary).

Class.	Group.	Caste, Tribe or Race.	Religion.	Total Literate.			Total knowing English.		
				Total.	Males.	Females.	Total.	Males.	Females.
A.—Agricultural.	1.—Military and Dominant.	Rajput	Hindu	580	567	13	27	27	...
		Chauhan	Do.	60	57	3	5	5	...
		Thakur	Do.	8	8	...	...	...	...
		Bhadauria	Do.	1	1	...	...	...	...
		Rathor	Do.	12	12	...	1	1	...
		Rawat	Do.	6	6	...	1	1	...
		Kachwa	Do.	5	5	...	...	...	...
		Raghubansi	Do.	1	1	...	...	...	...
		Pawar	Do.	44	43	1	...	...	...
		Sikarwari	Do.	2	2	...	...	...	...
		Surajbansi	Do.	2	1	1	...	...	...
		Bhatti	Do.	2	2	...	...	...	...
		Salunki	Do.	2	2	...	...	...	...
		Jat	Do.	134	133	1	6	6	...
		Maratha	Do.	407	396	11	38	38	...
		Gujar	Do.	38	36	2	3	3	...
		Chhatri	Do.	32	32	...	5	5	...
		Sikh	Do.	505	499	6	9	9	...
			Total 1	1,841	1,803	38	95	95	...
	2.—Minor Agricultural	Kotwar	Hindu	2	2	...	...	...	...
		Kumawat	Do.	2	2	...	...	...	...
		Koli	Do.	185	183	2	31	31	...
		Mali	Do.	48	48	...	8	8	...
		Balai	Do.	5	5	...	1	1	...
		Ahir	Do.	181	177	4	12	12	...
		Tamboli	Do.	35	35	...	2	2	...
		Kunbi	Do.	65	61	4	11	11	...
		Lodha	Do.	66	66	...	6	6	...
		Patel	Do.	1	1	...	...	...	...
		Kachhi	Do.	17	17	...	1	1	...
		Nayak	Do.	64	62	2	...	...	...
		Murai	Do.	25	24	1	3	3	...
		Kurmi	Do.	43	42	1	9	9	...
		Ghosi	Do.	4	4	...	...	...	...
		Dhanuk	Do.	5	5	...	4	4	...
		Barai	Do.	1	1	...	...	...	...
		Nayata	Do.	1	1	...	1	1	...
			Total 2	750	736	14	89	89	...
	4.—Forest and Hill Tribes.	Kol	Hindu	3	3	...	2	2	...
		Kirar	Do.	1	...	1	...	...	...
		Bhil	Do.	1	1	...	...	...	...
		Mina	Do.	4	4	...	...	...	...
		Pahri	Do.	1	1	...	1	1	...
		Aboriginals unspecified	Aboriginal	81	81	...	...	...	...
			Total 4	91	90	1	3	3	...
			Total Class A	2,682	2,629	58	187	187	...
B.—Professional.	5.—Priests	Brahman	Hindu	2,376	2,280	96	357	355	2
		Dakshni	Do.	2	2	...	...	...	...
		Telangi	Do.	20	18	2	7	7	...
			Total 5	2,398	2,300	98	364	362	2
	6.—Devotees	Sadhu	Hindu	5	5	...	...	...	...
		Bairagi	Do.	8	8	...	...	...	...
		Gosain	Do.	16	15	1	...	...	...
		Jati	Do.	6	6	...	...	...	...
		Jati	Jain	2	2	...	...	...	...
			Total 6	37	36	1	...	...	...
	9.—Writers	Kayasth	Hindu	315	295	20	15	15	...
		Bengali	Do.	2	2	...	2	2	...
		Khatri	Do.	56	53	3	13	13	...
			Total 9	373	350	23	30	30	...
	10.—Astrologers	Dakot	Hindu	2	2	...	...	...	...
	11.—Musicians and Ballad reciters.	Bhat	Do.	27	27	...	3	3	
			Total Class B	2,887	2,715	122	397	395	2

TABLE C.—Literate by Language known (Provincial Summary)—*contd.*

Class.	Group.	Caste, Tribe or Race.	Religion.	Total Literate. Total.	Total Literate. Males.	Total Literate. Females.	Total knowing English. Total.	Total knowing English. Males.	Total knowing English. Females.
C.—Commercial.	14.—Traders	Mehesri	Hindu	303	303	...	7	7	...
		Bijawargi	Do.	46	45	1	2	2	...
		Gujrati	Do.	13	13	...	1	1	...
		Bania	Do.	98	98	...	...	...	...
		Dhusar	Do.	7	7	...	...	...	...
		Jeswar	Do.	14	14	...	...	...	...
		Nima	Do.	1	1	...	1	1	...
		Parwal	Do.	5	5	...	2	2	...
			Jain	3	3	...	...	...	...
		Mahajan	Hindu	284	281	3	17	17	...
			Jain	39	39	...	...	...	...
		Agarwal	Hindu	1,400	1,394	6	28	28	...
			Jain	21	21	...	1	1	...
		Saraogi	Do.	183	183	...	6	6	...
		Oswal	Do.	143	142	1	5	5	...
		Digambari	Do.	3	3	...	...	...	...
			Total 14	**2,563**	**2,552**	**11**	**70**	**70**	...
	16.—Carriers	Banjara	Hindu	4	4	...	...	...	...
			Total Class C.	**2,567**	**2,556**	**11**	**70**	**70**	...
D.—Artisans and Village Menials.	17.—Goldsmiths	Sonar	Hindu	110	108	2	5	5	...
	18.—Barbers	Nai	Do.	84	84	...	8	8	...
		Bari	Do.	3	3	...	...	...	...
			Total 18	**87**	**87**	...	**8**	**8**	...
	19.—Blacksmiths	Lohar	Hindu	41	40	1	2	2	...
	20.—Carpenters and Turners.	Sutar	Do.	55	52	3	7	7	...
		Lakhera	Do.	3	3	...	1	1	...
		Sailawat	Do.	3	3	...	1	1	...
			Total 20	**61**	**58**	**3**	**9**	**9**	...
	21.—Brass and Copper-smiths.	Kasera	Hindu	1	1	...	...	...	...
	22.—Tailors	Darzi	Do.	66	64	2	8	7	1
	23.—Weavers, Calenderers and Dyers.	Kori	Do.	6	6	...	...	...	...
		Kandera	Do.	1	1	...	...	...	...
		Momin	Do.	1	1	...	...	...	...
		Chhipa	Do.	6	6	...	...	...	...
			Total 23	**14**	**14**	...	...	...	...
	24.—Washermen	Dhobi	Hindu	25	25	...	1	1	...
	25.—Cotton cleaner	Pinjara	Do.	1	1	...	...	...	...
	26.—Shepherds and Wool weavers.	Gadaria	Do.	41	39	2	5	5	...
		Rebari	Do.	3	3	...	...	...	...
			Total 26	**44**	**42**	**2**	**5**	**5**	...
	27.—Oil-pressers	Teli	Hindu	84	82	2	1	1	...
	28.—Potters	Kumhars	Do.	11	11	...	2	2	...
	30.—Salt, etc., Workers	Lunia	Do.	24	22	2	...	...	...
	35.—Fishermen, Boatmen, Palki Bearers, Cooks, etc.	Bhujwa	Do.	29	29	...	...	...	...
		Bhoi	Do.	12	12	...	1	1	...
		Kahar	Do.	84	83	1	4	4	...
		Madrasi	Do.	6	6	...	2	2	...
		Mallaha	Do.	1	1	...	...	...	...
		Dhimar	Do.	1	1	...	...	...	...
		Halwai	Do.	1	1	...	...	...	...
			Total 35	**134**	**133**	**1**	**7**	**7**	...
	36.—Distillers and Toddy-drawers.	Kalal	Hindu	53	50	3	5	5	...
	37.—Butchers	Khatik	Do.	9	9	...	...	...	...
	38.—Leather Workers	Mochi	Do.	62	62	...	9	9	...
		Jatha	Do.	1	1	...	1	1	...
		Chamar	Do.	89	87	2	9	9	...
			Total 38	**152**	**150**	**2**	**19**	**19**	...
	38.—A	Mahar	Hindu	150	146	4	9	9	...
		Parwari	Do.	102	98	4	9	9	...
		Mang	Do.	5	5	...	...	...	...
			Total 38 A	**257**	**249**	**8**	**18**	**18**	...

TABLE C.—Literate by Language known (Provincial Summary)—*contd.*

Class.	Group.	Caste, Tribe or Race.	Religion.	Total Literate. Total.	Total Literate. Males.	Total Literate. Females.	Total knowing English. Total.	Total knowing English. Males.	Total knowing English. Females.
D.—Artisans and Village Menials—*contd.*	39.—Scavengers	Chandal	Hindu	2	2	...	...	...	...
		Mehtar	Do.	56	54	2	...	...	...
			Total 39	58	56	2	...	...	...
			Total Class D	**1,232**	**1,202**	**30**	**90**	**89**	**1**
E.—Vagrant—Minor Artisans and Performers, etc.	41.—Earth-workers and Stone dressers.	Beldars	Hindu	12	12	...	...	...	...
	44.—Hunters and Fowlers, etc.	Baheliya	Do.	4	4	...	...	...	...
		Pasi	Do.	19	19	...	...	...	...
			Total 44	23	23	...	...	...	...
	45.—Miscellaneous and disreputable livers.	Sethbax	Hindu	2	2	...	2	2	...
		Hindu	Do.	338	335	3	40	39	1
		Kheria	Do.	1	1	...	...	...	...
		Karad	Do.	1	1	...	...	...	...
		Bhagor	Do.	2	2	...	...	...	...
		Babjabu	Do.	1	1	...	...	...	...
		Shudra	Do.	1	...	1	...	...	...
		Musalman	Musalman	373	343	30	9	9	...
			Total 45	719	685	34	51	50	1
	46.—Tumblers and Acrobats.	Nat	Hindu	8	8	...	...	...	...
			Total Class E.	**762**	**728**	**34**	**51**	**50**	**1**
F.—Races and Nationalities.	48.—Tribal Communities of Foreign Asiatic origin or reputed descent.	Pathan	Musalman	764	734	30	52	50	2
		Shekh	Do.	1,137	1,071	66	137	132	5
		Saiyad	Do.	378	363	15	29	29	...
		Moghal	Do.	42	41	1	3	3	...
		Parsi	Parsi	348	183	165	145	137	8
		Jew	Jew	33	24	9	6	6	...
			Total 48	2,702	2,416	286	272	257	15
	50.—Non-Asiatic Races	Europeans	Christians	3,461	2,982	479	3,296	2,821	475
	51.—Europeans	Eurasians	Eurasians	153	85	68	146	82	64
	52.—Christians, Converts	Christians, Converts, Native	Christians	284	219	65	121	94	27
			Total Class F.	**6,600**	**5,702**	**898**	**3,985**	**3,854**	**581**
		TOTAL OF ALL CLASSES		**16,680**	**15,532**	**1,148**	**4,780**	**4,145**	**585**

Supplementary Statement of Area and Population.

Supplementary Statement of Area and Population.

Native States, and Cantonments, etc., under British Occupation.	Area in square miles.	Number of: Towns.	Number of: Villages.	Number of: Occupied houses.	Population. Males. In towns.	Males. In villages.	Males. Total.	Females. In towns.	Females. In villages.	Females. Total.	Both Sexes. In towns.	Both Sexes. In villages.	Both Sexes. Total.	Number of persons per square mile.	Number of towns per square mile.	Number of villages per square mile.	Number of houses per square mile.	Number of persons per occupied house.
1	2	3	4	5	6	7	8	9	10	11	12	13	14	15	16	17	18	19
Gwalior	25,846'3	22	9,551½	600,894	172,543	1,631,641	1,804,184	151,690	1,422,900	1,574,590	324,233	3,054,541	3,378,774	135'94	'0009	'38	24'42	5'56
Gwalior Residency		...	1	279	...	672	672	...	573	573	...	1,245	1,245					
Sipri Cantonment		...	1	567	...	1,743	1,743	...	1,214	1,214	...	2,957	2,957					
Agar Cantonment		...	1	571	...	2,532	2,532	...	1,499	1,499	...	4,031	4,031					
Guna Cantonment		...	1	1,343	...	2,729	2,729	...	1,964	1,964	...	4,693	4,693					
Nimuch Cantonment		1	...	6,503	8,763	...	8,763	6,528	...	6,528	15,291	...	15,291					
Sirdarpur Cantonment		...	1	591	...	1,744	1,744	...	1,391	1,391	...	3,135	3,135					
Bagli		...	55	3,337	...	7,579	7,579	...	7,096	7,096	...	14,675	14,675					
Raghogarh		...	104	3,191	...	9,569	9,569	...	8,563	8,563	...	18,132	18,132					
Gurrah		...	57	1,669	...	5,775	5,775	...	5,079	5,079	...	10,854	10,854					
Parone		...	39	1,670	...	4,268	4,268	...	3,716	3,716	...	7,984	7,984					
Dharnaoda		...	30	851	...	2,608	2,608	...	2,279	2,279	...	4,887	4,887					
Sirsi		...	35	978	...	2,473	2,473	...	2,205	2,205	...	4,678	4,678					
Umri		...	27	582	...	1,669	1,669	...	1,388	1,388	...	3,057	3,057					
Bhadaura		...	12	505	...	1,631	1,631	...	1,499	1,499	...	3,130	3,130					
Khiaoda		...	6	223	...	542	542	...	465	465	...	1,007	1,007					
Agra Barkhera		...	34	1,374	...	3,922	3,922	...	3,518	3,518	...	7,440	7,440					
Guaranteed Estates		1	96	6,237	3,380	11,012	14,392	3,400	9,941	13,341	6,780	20,953	27,733					
Indore	9,715'9	10	3,511½	224,204	79,501	498,541	578,042	69,799	452,149	521,948	149,300	950,690	1,099,990	117'45	'001	'36	24'84	4'93
Indore Residency		1	...	1,681	6,099	...	6,099	3,246	...	3,246	9,345	...	9,345					
Mhow Cantonment		1	...	5,494	18,300	...	18,300	13,473	...	13,473	31,773	...	31,773					
Mehidpur Cantonment		...	1	26	...	47	47	...	29	29	...	76	76					
Bhopal	6,996'9	5	3,167	189,693	48,154	443,731	491,885	44,027	416,574	460,601	92,181	860,305	952,486	137'71	'0008	'45	27'45	5'01
Sehore Cantonment		1	...	2,438	6,084	...	6,084	5,040	...	5,040	11,124	...	11,124					
Khaniadhana	111'0	...	47	1,967	...	7,923	7,923	...	6,948	6,948	...	14,871	14,871	133'97	...	'42	17'72	7'56
Dewas (Senior Branch)	882'5																	
Dewas (Junior Branch)		1	474	28,778	8,051	72,636	80,687	7,017	64,369	71,386	15,068	137,005	152,073	172'32	'001	'53	32'59	5'28
Jaora	691'5	2	327	23,866	13,762	47,328	61,090	13,202	43,358	56,560	26,964	90,686	117,650	188'78	'002	'50	38'5	4'90
Piplauda		...	24	2,753	...	6,487	6,487	...	6,305	6,305	...	12,792	12,792					
Panth Piplauda	...	...	10	855	...	2,154	2,154	...	1,939	1,939	...	4,093	4,093	...	...	...	...	...
Ratlam	729'5	1	218	20,670	15,322	30,633	45,955	14,500	28,705	43,205	29,822	59,338	89,160	122'22	'001	'29	28'33	4'31
Sitamau	198'5	1	91	5,930	3,017	14,588	17,605	2,844	12,858	15,702	5,861	27,446	33,307	107'51	'005	'45	29'87	5'61
Sailana	309'8	1	76	7,158	2,626	13,519	16,145	2,487	12,880	15,367	5,113	26,399	31,512	108'17	'003	'24	23'13	4'40
Rajgarh	957'2	1	631	23,055	3,339	61,280	64,619	3,137	51,733	54,870	6,476	113,013	119,489	130'13	'001	'67	25'08	5'18
Suthalia		...	20	954	...	2,689	2,689	...	2,392	2,392	...	5,081	5,081					
Narsinghgarh	669'6	1	419	20,602	4,548	57,788	62,336	4,013	49,931	53,944	8,561	107,719	116,280	173'65	'001	'62	30'76	5'64
Khilchipur	272'9	...	223	7,757	...	19,574	19,574	...	16,728	16,728	...	36,302	36,302	133'02	...	'81	28'42	4'67
Kurwai	144'6	...	92	4,098	...	11,319	11,319	...	10,468	10,468	...	21,787	21,787	150'67	...	'63	28'34	5'31

Native States, and Cantonments, etc., under British Occupation.	Area in square miles.	Number of: Towns.	Number of: Villages.	Number of: Occupied houses.	Males: In towns.	Males: In villages.	Males: Total.	Females: In towns.	Females: In villages.	Females: Total.	Both Sexes: In towns.	Both Sexes: In villages.	Both Sexes: Total.	Number of persons per square mile.	Number of towns per square mile.	Number of villages per square mile.	Number of houses per square mile.	Number of persons per occupied house.
1	2	3	4	5	6	7	8	9	10	11	12	13	14	15	16	17	18	19
Maksudangarh	...	...	77	2,642	...	7,751	7,751	...	6,671	6,671	...	14,422	14,422	...	...	...	...	...
Basoda	49·5	...	22	1,488	...	3,481	3,481	...	3,229	3,229	...	6,710	6,710	165·67	...	·54	36·74	4·50
Mahomedgarh	29·1	...	17	895	...	2,513	2,513	...	2,207	2,207	...	4,720	4,720	161·51	...	·58	30·75	5·27
Pathari	29·6	...	19	926	...	2,428	2,428	...	2,388	2,388	...	4,816	4,816	162·70	...	·64	31·28	5·20
Pindara Jagir	13·9	...	5	504	...	1,279	1,279	...	1,214	1,214	...	2,493	2,493	179·35	...	·36	36·25	4·92
Dhar	1,775·0	2	530	33,573	12,889	73,686	86,575	11,887	71,012	82,899	24,776	144,698	169,474	95·81	·001	·29	18·91	5·04
Jhabua } Ratanmal }	12,57·8	...	736	25,082	...	60,401	60,401	...	59,386	59,386	...	119,787	119,787	96·19	...	·59	20·09	4·78
Ratanmal		...	13	190	...	642	642	...	570	570	...	1,212	1,212					
Burwani	1,178·8	1	343	16,922	2,930	38,773	41,703	3,124	35,439	38,563	6,054	74,212	80,266	68·09	·0008	·29	14·35	4·74
Ali Rajpur	860·1	...	326	12,462	...	36,548	36,548	...	33,543	33,543	...	70,091	70,091	81·39	...	·37	14·48	5·62
Guaranteed Thakurats (Bhopawar Agency.)	...	...	88	6,056	...	14,993	14,993	...	14,486	14,486	...	29,479	29,479	...	...	...	...	...
Guaranteed Bhumiats (Bhopawar Agency.)	121·5	...	190	4,365	...	12,322	12,322	...	11,555	11,555	...	23,877	23,877	196·51	...	1·56	35·92	5·47
Jobat	121·6	...	61	2,669	...	7,745	7,745	...	7,302	7,302	...	15,047	15,047	123·74	...	·50	21·94	5·63
Kathiwara	70·8	...	46	696	...	1,759	1,759	...	1,812	1,812	...	3,571	3,571	50·43	...	·66	9·54	5·13
Mathwar	129·0	...	35	627	...	1,570	1,570	...	1,421	1,421	...	2,991	2,991	23·18	...	·27	4·86	4·77
Rewa } Sutna }	12,676·6	2	5,430	278,153	15,957	742,681	758,638	14,440	735,865	750,305	30,397	1,478,546	1,508,943	119·07	·0001	·42	21·95	5·42
Sutna		...	1	159	...	367	367	...	144	144	...	511	511					
Nagode	501·4	1	334	17,742	2,714	39,031	41,745	2,728	39,624	42,352	5,442	78,655	84,097	167·73	·001	·66	35·38	4·74
Maihar	406·0	1	183	15,836	3,179	35,348	38,527	3,278	35,741	39,019	6,457	71,089	77,546	191·00	·002	·45	39·00	4·89
Sohawal	212·9	...	173	8,775	...	21,768	21,768	...	22,085	22,085	...	43,853	43,853	205·98	...	·81	41·24	4·99
Kothi	168·8	...	67	4,511	...	11,177	11,177	...	11,479	11,479	...	22,656	22,656	134·21	...	·39	26·72	5·02
Urchha	2,079·8	1	658	62,726	9,200	163,789	172,989	8,410	151,621	160,031	17,610	315,410	333,020	160·12	·0004	·31	30·15	5·26
Panna	2,492·0	1	858	49,044	7,766	115,703	123,469	6,939	108,925	115,864	14,705	224,628	239,333	96·03	·0004	·34	19·68	4·88
Datia	912·5	3	454	31,057	20,027	78,158	98,185	19,026	69,229	88,255	39,053	147,387	186,440	204·31	·003	·49	34·03	6·00
Chhatarpur } Nowgong Cantonment } Belhari }	1,157·9	1	315	30,546	6,604	83,800	90,404	6,353	77,391	83,744	12,957	161,191	174,148	162·67	·0008	·27	28·63	5·68
Nowgong Cantonment		1	...	1,826	6,946	...	6,946	3,956	...	3,956	10,902	...	10,902					
Belhari		...	2	780	...	1,662	1,662	...	1,653	1,653	...	3,315	3,315					
Charkhari	702·9	1	270	25,236	6,668	67,619	74,287	6,400	62,421	68,821	13,068	130,040	143,108	203·59	·001	·38	35·90	5·67
Bijawar	965·0	1	299	27,778	4,114	60,995	65,109	3,429	54,876	58,305	7,543	115,871	123,414	127·99	·001	·30	28·78	4·44
Ajaigarh	771·4	...	361	18,426	...	47,915	47,915	...	45,133	45,133	...	93,048	93,048	120·62	...	·47	23·88	5·04
Samthar	178·1	1	90	7,600	4,192	17,126	21,318	3,673	15,550	19,223	7,865	32,676	40,541	227·62	·005	·50	42·67	5·33
Baoni	122·5	...	53	5,376	...	9,556	9,556	...	8,885	8,885	...	18,441	18,441	150·54	...	·43	43·88	3·43
Baraundha	217·4	...	59	3,802	...	9,500	9,500	...	9,096	9,096	...	18,596	18,596	85·99	...	·27	17·48	4·88
Alipura	72·8	...	28	3,423	...	8,021	8,021	...	7,259	7,259	...	15,280	15,280	209·89	...	·38	47·01	4·46
Gaurihar	73·1	...	15	1,848	...	5,199	5,199	...	4,949	4,949	...	10,148	10,148	138·82	...	·20	25·28	5·49
Paldeo	28·0	...	19	1,979	...	4,845	4,845	...	4,538	4,538	...	9,383	9,383	335·10	...	·67	70·67	4·74
Jaso	72·1	...	56	1,770	...	4,397	4,397	...	4,433	4,433	...	8,830	8,830	122·46	...	·77	24·54	4·98

Supplementary Statement of Area and Population—*concld.*

Native States, and Cantonments, etc., under British Occupation.	Area in square miles.	Number of: Towns.	Number of: Villages.	Number of: Occupied houses.	Population. Males. In towns.	Males. In villages.	Males. Total.	Females. In towns.	Females. In villages.	Females. Total.	Both Sexes. In towns.	Both Sexes. In villages.	Both Sexes. Total.	Number of persons per square mile.	Number of towns per square mile.	Number of villages per square mile.	Number of houses per square mile.	Number of persons per occupied house.
1	2	3	4	5	6	7	8	9	10	11	12	13	14	15	16	17	18	19
Lugasi	46·6	...	12	1,047	...	3,672	3,672	...	3,276	3,276	...	6,948	6,948	149·09	...	·25	22·43	6·63
Sarila	32·5	...	10	1,243	...	2,837	2,837	...	2,785	2,785	...	5,622	5,622	172·67	...	·30	38·24	4·52
Garauli	36·7	...	16	1,091	...	2,829	2,829	...	2,700	2,700	...	5,529	5,529	150·65	...	·43	29·72	5·06
Bhaisaunda	12·0	...	7	929	...	2,468	2,468	...	2,287	2,287	...	4,755	4,755	396·25	...	·58	77·41	5·11
Beri	32·0	...	6	904	...	2,369	2,369	...	2,156	2,156	...	4,525	4,525	141·04	...	·19	28·25	5·005
Bihut	16·0	...	8	760	...	2,301	2,301	...	2,138	2,138	...	4,439	4,439	277·43	...	·05	47·5	5·84
Pahra	10·1	...	10	825	...	2,147	2,147	...	2,003	2,003	...	4,150	4,150	410·89	...	·99	81·68	5·03
Jigni	22·3	...	6	791	...	2,020	2,020	...	1,882	1,882	...	3,902	3,902	174·97	...	·26	35·47	4·93
Taraon	14·5	...	10	717	...	1,727	1,727	...	1,700	1,700	...	3,427	3,427	236·34	...	·62	49·44	4·77
Rebai	7·6	...	4	786	...	1,684	1,684	...	1,689	1,689	...	3,373	3,373	443·81	...	·52	103·42	4·44
Tori Fatehpur	} 85·0	...	8	2,363	...	4,827	4,827	...	4,770	4,770	...	9,597	9,597	} 171·83	...	...	...	...
Bijna		...	4	561	...	1,196	1,196	...	1,130	1,130	...	2,326	2,326		...	...	...	...
Kampta Rajaula		...	3	358	...	934	934	...	651	651	...	1,585	1,585		...	·18	40·8	4·21
Banka Pahari		...	1	237	...	547	547	...	551	551	...	1,098	1,098		...	...	...	...
Dhurwai	...	...	8	353	...	895	895	...	879	879	...	1,774	1,774	...	...	...	...	...
Tonk	878·1	3	698	40,218	13,225	83,120	96,345	11,565	73,225	84,790	24,790	156,345	181,135	206·12	·003	·79	45·80	4·50
Manpur (British)	6·7	...	32	1,075	...	2,880	2,880	...	2,462	2,462	...	5,342	5,342	797·31	...	4·77	160·44	4·96
Grand Total	78,165·2	70	32,458	1,965,092	509,900	4,895,347	5,405,247	449,611	4,482,072	4,931,683	959,511	9,377,419	10,336,930	132·24	·00008	·41	25·14	5·26

SUPPLEMENTARY TABLE,

Shewing the population of Central India (Native States and British occupations) by religions.

NOTE.—In column 3 one town has been entered against Dewas (S. B.) and one against Dewas (J. B.), but those towns are really one, hence the total for States 6, 7 and 8 in Indore Agency is 1.

The grand total at the end of this table exceeds the grand total of those tables which are prepared by Agencies, inasmuch as the Gwalior and Indore Districts in Meywar are not included in the latter.

Supplementary Table, shewing the population of Central

STATE.	NUMBER OF TOWNS AND VILLAGES.			Number of occupied houses.	ALL RELIGIONS.			HINDU.	
	Total.	Towns.	Villages.		Total.	Males.	Females.	Males.	Females.
1	2	3	4	5	6	7	8	9	10
1. GWALIOR—									
Indore Agency	103	...	103	6,274	33,747	17,829	15,918	12,713	11,389
Gwalior "	3,941	10	3,931	272,087	1,710,703	924,075	786,628	817,744	693,780
Bhopal "	1,558½	3	1,555½	85,351	426,195	225,238	200,957	188,153	168,162
Western Malwa "	2,461	8	2,453	160,928	830,868	438,156	392,712	318,791	285,899
Bhopawar "	458	...	458	33,511	131,905	67,734	64,171	29,607	28,495
Guna "	1,039	...	1,039	41,231	233,078	124,563	108,515	101,890	88,926
Meywar "	13	1	12	1,512	12,278	6,589	5,689	5,238	4,507
TOTAL	9,573½	22	9,551½	600,894	3,378,774	1,804,184	1,574,590	1,474,136	1,281,158
2. INDORE—									
Indore Agency	389	2	387	44,326	211,039	113,922	97,117	89,995	76,461
Bhopal "	568½	...	568½	29,398	151,913	80,213	71,700	52,713	46,768
Bundelkhand "	25	...	25	3,791	17,056	8,651	8,405	7,864	7,703
Western Malwa "	1,236	6	1,230	81,409	395,598	207,886	187,712	150,016	136,432
Bhopawar "	1,271	2	1,269	63,471	318,544	164,248	154,296	98,521	93,217
Meywar "	31	...	31	1,809	5,840	3,122	2,718	1,758	1,491
TOTAL	3,521½	10	3,510½	224,204	1,099,990	578,042	521,948	400,867	362,072
3. BHOPAL	3,172	5	3,167	189,693	952,486	491,885	460,601	349,289	325,460
4. KHANIADHANA	47	...	47	1,967	14,871	7,923	6,948	6,519	5,662
5. GUARANTEED ESTATES	97	1	96	6,237	27,733	14,392	13,341	10,793	10,082
TOTAL FOR STATES 4 AND 5 IN GWALIOR AGENCY	144	1	143	8,204	42,604	22,315	20,289	17,312	15,744
6. DEWAS (Senior Branch)—									
Indore Agency	113	1	112	6,468	38,708	20,377	18,331	15,695	14,111
Western Malwa Agency	75	...	75	4,337	24,822	13,301	11,521	8,844	7,774
Bhopal "	39	...	39	2,787	15,909	8,612	7,297	6,163	4,989
Bhopawar "	15½	...	15½	600	2,950	1,532	1,418	940	876
TOTAL	242½	1	241½	14,192	82,389	43,822	38,567	31,642	27,750
7. DEWAS (Junior Branch)—									
Indore Agency	123	1	122	7,206	33,505	17,838	15,667	14,084	12,231
Western Malwa Agency	61	...	61	3,680	19,338	10,229	9,109	7,962	7,081
Bhopal "	34	...	34	3,099	13,891	7,266	6,625	5,359	4,859
Bhopawar "	15½	...	15½	601	2,950	1,532	1,418	941	877
TOTAL	233½	1	232½	14,586	69,684	36,865	32,819	28,346	25,048
8. BAGLI	55	...	55	3,337	14,675	7,579	7,096	5,188	4,923
TOTAL FOR STATES 6, 7, 8 IN INDORE AGENCY	530	1	529	32,115	166,748	88,266	78,482	65,176	57,721
9. JAORA	329	2	327	23,866	117,650	61,090	56,560	42,408	39,089
10. RATLAM	219	1	218	20,670	89,160	45,955	43,205	25,213	23,931
11. SITAMAU	92	1	91	5,930	33,307	17,605	15,702	15,042	13,410
12. SAILANA	77	1	76	7,158	31,512	16,145	15,367	9,504	9,151
13. PIPLAUDA	24	...	24	2,753	12,792	6,487	6,305	4,689	4,578
14. PANTH PIPLAUDA	10	...	10	855	4,093	2,154	11,939	1,464	1,294
TOTAL FOR STATES 9 TO 14 IN WESTERN MALWA AGENCY	751	5	746	61,232	288,514	149,436	139,078	98,320	91,453
15. RAJGARH	632	1	631	23,055	119,489	64,619	54,870	49,179	41,902
16. NARSINGHGARH	420	1	419	20,602	116,280	62,336	53,944	50,428	43,612
17. KHILCHIPUR	223	...	223	7,757	36,302	19,574	16,728	15,547	13,392
18. KURWAI	92	...	92	4,098	21,787	11,319	10,468	9,153	8,410
19. MAKSUDANGARH	77	...	77	2,642	14,422	7,751	6,671	5,438	4,681
20. AGRA BARKHERA	34	...	34	1,374	7,440	3,922	3,518	3,265	2,960
21. BASODA	22	...	22	1,488	6,710	3,481	3,229	2,579	2,368
22. SUTHALIA	20	...	20	954	5,081	2,689	2,392	1,952	1,803
23. PATHARI	19	...	19	926	4,816	2,428	2,388	2,097	2,023
24. MUHAMADGARH	17	...	17	895	4,720	2,513	2,207	1,863	1,606
25. PINDARA JAGIR	5	...	5	504	2,493	1,279	1,214	760	724
TOTAL FOR STATES 15 TO 25 IN BHOPAL AGENCY	1,561	2	1,559	64,295	339,540	181,911	157,629	142,261	123,484

India (Native States and British occupations) by religions.

MUSALMAN.		JAIN.		ABORIGINAL.		CHRISTIAN.		PARSI.		SIKH.		JEW.	
Males.	Females.	Males.	Females.	Males.	Females.	Males.	Females.	Males.	Females.	Males.	Females.	Males.	Females.
11	12	13	14	15	16	17	18	19	20	21	22	23	24
1,028	835	136	121	3,952	3,572	...	...	...	...	...	...	...	...
41,258	34,595	4,992	4,389	59,977	53,765	99	99	2	...	3	...	...	...
14,369	12,521	1,291	1,273	21,418	18,996	7	5	...	...	...	...	...	...
34,805	31,287	8,609	7,650	75,813	67,782	109	74	23	13	5	6	1	1
2,810	2,415	1,018	987	34,298	32,274	...	...	1	...	...	...	...	...
4,054	3,317	1,907	1,686	16,700	14,582	...	...	...	...	12	4	...	...
293	257	454	369	604	556	...	...	...	...	...	...	...	...
98,617	**85,227**	**18,407**	**16,475**	**212,762**	**191,527**	**215**	**178**	**26**	**13**	**20**	**11**	**1**	**1**
14,110	11,881	2,177	1,769	7,351	6,796	130	102	4	6	155	102	...	...
5,905	5,325	653	595	20,940	19,010	2	2	...	...	...	...	...	...
227	203	278	238	282	261	...	...	...	...	...	...	...	...
10,929	10,356	2,440	2,155	44,488	38,766	6	...	2	...	5	3	...	...
9,266	8,798	1,611	1,547	54,851	50,734	2	...	2	...	...	...	...	...
43	31	5	4	1,316	1,192	...	...	...	...	...	...	...	...
40,775	**36,594**	**7,164**	**6,308**	**129,228**	**116,759**	**140**	**104**	**8**	**6**	**160**	**105**	...	...
47,078	42,230	2,770	2,643	92,531	90,054	106	106	11	14	100	94	...	...
118	84	253	246	1,032	956	1	...	...	...	...	...	...	...
438	419	17	10	3,141	2,828	2	2	...	...	1	...	...	...
556	**503**	**270**	**256**	**4,173**	**3,784**	**3**	**2**	...	...	**1**	...	...	...
2,334	2,018	185	186	2,163	2,013	...	...	...	...	...	3	...	...
668	664	131	114	3,658	2,969	...	...	...	...	...	...	...	...
1,099	1,084	31	22	1,319	1,202	...	...	...	...	...	...	...	...
113	87	18	16	460	439	1	...	...	...	...	...	...	...
4,214	**3,853**	**365**	**338**	**7,600**	**6,623**	**1**	...	...	...	...	**3**	...	...
1,521	1,328	113	88	2,120	2,019	...	...	...	...	...	1	...	...
409	342	65	57	1,793	1,629	...	...	...	...	...	...	...	...
855	813	86	82	966	871	...	...	...	...	...	...	...	...
112	87	17	15	461	439	1	...	...	...	...	...	...	...
2,897	**2,570**	**281**	**242**	**5,340**	**4,958**	**1**	...	...	...	...	**1**	...	...
354	311	286	258	1,751	1,604	...	...	...	...	...	...	...	...
7,465	**6,734**	**932**	**838**	**14,691**	**13,185**	**2**	...	...	...	...	**4**	...	...
7,790	7,270	1,677	1,433	9,188	8,755	14	4	12	9	1	...	...	...
5,232	4,808	3,017	2,624	12,445	11,803	41	33	4	5	3	1	...	...
937	797	74	75	1,552	1,420	...	...	...	...	...	...	...	...
853	731	587	565	5,198	4,918	2	2	1	...	...	...	...	...
370	290	254	288	1,174	1,149	...	...	...	...	...	...	...	...
52	36	10	7	628	602	...	...	...	...	...	...	...	...
15,234	**13,932**	**5,619**	**4,992**	**30,185**	**28,647**	**57**	**39**	**17**	**14**	**4**	**1**	...	...
3,266	2,823	121	104	12,052	10,037	...	...	...	...	1	4	...	...
2,275	1,987	23	30	9,607	8,311	...	...	...	...	3	4	...	...
668	607	...	2	3,359	2,727	...	...	...	...	...	...	...	...
1,381	1,301	32	34	753	723	...	...	...	...	...	...	...	...
241	167	...	...	2,072	1,823	...	...	...	...	...	...	...	...
232	170	2	2	423	386	...	...	...	...	...	...	...	...
466	456	29	25	407	380	...	...	...	...	...	...	...	...
49	44	...	...	688	545	...	...	...	...	...	...	...	...
207	227	74	82	50	56	...	...	...	...	...	...	...	...
359	345	46	28	245	228	...	...	...	...	...	...	...	...
251	257	...	...	268	230	...	...	...	...	...	...	...	...
9,395	**8,384**	**327**	**307**	**29,924**	**25,446**	...	...	...	...	**4**	**8**	...	...

Supplementary Table, shewing the population of Central

STATE.	NUMBER OF TOWNS AND VILLAGES.			Number of occupied houses.	ALL RELIGIONS.			HINDU.	
	Total.	Towns.	Villages.		Total.	Males.	Females.	Males.	Females.
1	2	3	4	5	6	7	8	9	10
26. RAGHOGARH	104	...	104	3,191	18,132	9,569	8,563	7,364	6,615
27. GURRAH	57	...	57	1,669	10,854	5,775	5,079	3,845	3,362
28. PARONE	39	...	39	1,670	7,984	4,268	3,716	3,526	3,069
29. DHARNAODA	30	...	30	851	4,887	2,608	2,279	2,164	1,909
30. SIRSI	35	...	35	978	4,678	2,473	2,205	1,751	1,504
31. BHADAURA	12	...	12	505	3,130	1,631	1,499	1,346	1,243
32. UMRI	27	...	27	582	3,057	1,669	1,388	1,403	1,161
33. KHIAODA	6	...	6	223	1,007	542	465	453	367
TOTAL FOR STATES 26 TO 33 IN GUNA AGENCY	310	...	310	9,669	53,729	28,535	25,194	21,852	19,230
34. DHAR—									
Bhopawar Agency	528	2	526	33,156	167,505	85,479	82,026	49,854	47,796
Bhopal "	4½	...	4½	408	1,945	1,080	865	930	746
Western Malwa "	...	...	...	9	24	16	8	16	8
TOTAL	532½	2	530½	33,573	169,474	86,575	82,899	50,800	48,550
35. JHABUA	736	...	736	25,082	119,787	60,401	59,386	10,932	10,809
36. BARWANI	344	1	343	16,922	80,266	41,703	38,563	14,923	13,912
37. ALI RAJPUR	326	...	326	12,462	70,091	36,548	33,543	2,857	2,521
38. GUARANTEED THAKURAETS	88	...	88	6,056	29,479	14,993	8,430	8,430	8,152
39. GUARANTEED BHUMIATS	190	...	190	4,365	23,877	12,322	11,555	3,449	3,075
40. JOBAT	61	...	61	2,669	15,047	7,745	7,302	461	372
41. KATHIWADA	46	...	46	696	3,571	1,759	1,812	52	63
42. MATHWAR	35	...	35	627	2,991	1,570	1,421	102	71
43. RATANMAL	13	...	13	190	1,212	642	570	285	250
TOTAL FOR STATES 34 TO 43 IN BHOPAWAR AGENCY	2,371½	3	2,368½	102,642	515,795	264,258	251,537	92,291	87,775
44. REWA—									
Baghelkhand Agency	5,430	2	5,428	277,912	1,507,719	758,019	749,700	496,942	486,809
N.-W. Provinces	2	...	2	241	1,224	619	605	517	490
TOTAL	5,432	2	5,430	278,153	1,508,943	758,638	750,305	497,459	487,299
45. NAGODE—									
Baghelkhand Agency	324	1	323	16,727	78,798	39,118	39,680	32,327	32,895
Central Provinces	11	...	11	1,015	5,299	2,627	2,672	1,996	2,023
TOTAL	335	1	334	17,742	84,097	41,745	42,352	34,323	34,918
46. MAIHAR	184	1	183	15,836	77,546	38,527	39,019	30,365	30,584
47. SOHAWAL	173	...	173	8,775	43,853	21,768	22,085	18,806	19,045
48. KOTHI	67	...	67	4,511	22,656	11,177	11,479	8,934	9,112
TOTAL FOR STATES 44 TO 48 IN BAGHELKHAND AGENCY	6,191	4	6,187	325,017	1,737,095	871,855	865,240	589,887	580,958
49. URCHHA	659	1	658	62,726	333,020	172,989	160,031	156,221	143,914
50. PANNA	859	1	858	49,044	239,333	123,469	115,864	103,822	96,580
51. DATIA	457	3	454	31,057	186,440	98,185	88,255	91,084	81,675
52. CHHATARPUR	316	1	315	30,546	174,148	90,404	83,744	83,965	77,459
53. CHARKHARI	271	1	270	25,236	143,108	74,287	68,821	67,794	62,333
54. BIJAWAR	300	1	299	27,778	123,414	65,109	58,305	58,904	52,456
55. AJAIGARH	361	...	361	18,426	93,048	47,915	45,133	4 ,637	38,001
56. SAMTHAR	91	1	90	7,600	40,541	21,318	19,223	19,414	17,572
57. BAONI	53	...	53	5,376	18,441	9,556	8,885	7,964	7,288
58. BARAUNDHA	59	...	59	3,802	18,596	9,500	9,096	7,564	7,224
59. ALIPURA	28	...	28	3,423	15,280	8,021	7,259	7,385	6,663
60. GAURIHAR	15	...	15	1,848	10,148	5,199	4,949	4,811	4,555
61. TORI FATEHPUR	8	...	8	2,363	9,597	4,827	4,770	4,473	4,368
62. PALDEV	19	...	19	1,979	9,383	4,845	4,538	4,395	4,137
63. JASSO	56	...	56	1,770	8,830	4,397	4,433	3,772	3,842
64. LUGASI	12	...	12	1,047	6,948	3,672	3,276	3,559	3,156
65. SARILA	10	...	10	1,243	5,622	2,837	2,785	2,611	2,559
66. GARAULI	16	...	16	1,091	5,529	2,829	2,700	2,676	2,550
67. BHAISONDA	7	...	7	929	4,755	2,468	2,287	2,093	1,960
68. BERI	6	...	6	904	4,525	2,369	2,156	2,092	1,834
69. BIHAT	8	...	8	760	4,439	2,301	2,138	2,187	2,033
70. PAHRA	10	...	10	825	4,150	2,147	2,003	1,958	1,841
71. JIGNI	6	...	6	791	3,902	2,020	1,882	1,852	1,738
72. TARAON	10	...	10	717	3,427	1,727	1,700	1,612	1,603

India (Native States and British occupations) by religions—*contd.*

MUSALMAN.		JAIN.		ABORIGINAL.		CHRISTIAN.		PARSI.		SIKH.		JEW.	
Males.	Females.	Males.	Females.	Males.	Females.	Males.	Females.	Males.	Females.	Males.	Females.	Males.	Females.
11	12	13	14	15	16	17	18	19	20	21	22	23	24
449	408	315	189	1,441	1,351	...	...	...	...	...	...	...	...
149	111	84	79	1,697	1,527	...	...	...	...	...	...	...	...
105	67	1	...	636	580	...	...	...	...	...	...	...	...
113	86	66	63	265	221	...	...	...	...	...	...	...	...
12	5	...	...	710	696	...	...	...	...	...	...	...	...
37	20	20	16	228	220	...	...	...	...	...	...	...	...
48	42	31	24	186	161	...	...	...	...	1	...	...	...
1	...	2	1	86	97	...	...	...	...	...	...	...	...
914	**739**	**519**	**872**	**5,249**	**4,853**	...	...	...	...	**1**	...	...	...
6,684	6,295	1,913	1,687	27,022	26,240	1	...	4	5	1	3	...	...
98	82	...	...	52	37	...	...	...	...	...	...	...	...
..	...	...	...	...	...	...	...	...	...	...	...	...	...
6,782	**6,377**	**1,913**	**1,687**	**27,074**	**26,277**	**1**	...	**4**	**5**	**1**	**3**	...	...
1,219	994	1,118	1,067	47,128	46,513	...	...	4	3	...	...	...	...
1,704	1,546	153	152	24,916	22,951	2	1	2	...	3	1	...	...
822	761	71	75	32,797	30,186	1	...	...	...	...	...	...	...
596	540	368	315	5,598	5,479	...	...	1	...	...	...	...	...
393	288	32	18	8,448	8,174	...	...	...	...	...	...	...	...
117	99	8	7	7,159	6,824	...	...	...	...	...	...	...	...
25	16	...	...	1,682	1,733	...	...	...	...	...	...	...	...
10	10	...	...	1,458	1,340	...	...	...	...	...	...	...	...
3	...	...	...	354	320	...	...	...	...	...	...	...	...
11,671	**10,631**	**3,663**	**3,321**	**156,614**	**149,797**	**4**	**1**	**11**	**8**	**4**	**4**	...	...
18,693	17,865	157	148	242,058	244,763	125	98	...	...	44	17	...	...
13	20	...	...	89	95	...	...	...	...	...	...	...	...
18,706	**17,885**	**157**	**148**	**242,147**	**244,858**	**125**	**98**	...	...	**44**	**17**	...	...
1,446	1,384	42	39	5,303	5,362	...	...	...	...	...	...	...	...
58	64	4	7	569	578	...	...	...	...	...	...	...	...
1,504	**1,448**	**46**	**46**	**5,872**	**5,940**	...	...	...	...	...	...	...	...
1,141	1,093	44	26	6,976	7,316	1	...	...	...	...	...	...	...
675	645	3	4	2,284	2,391	...	...	...	...	...	...	...	...
167	194	...	...	2,076	2,173	...	...	...	...	...	...	...	...
22,193	**21,265**	**250**	**224**	**259,355**	**262,678**	**126**	**98**	...	...	**44**	**17**	...	...
4,858	4,649	3,279	3,154	8,625	8,311	5	3	...	...	1	...	...	...
3,278	2,917	844	836	15,484	15,518	8	4	...	...	33	9	...	...
4,116	3,927	13	7	2,971	2,646	1	...	...	...	...	...	...	...
3,079	2,863	331	380	3,029	3,042	...	...	...	...	...	...	...	...
3,249	3,182	175	163	3,068	3,143	1	...	...	...	...	...	...	...
1,317	1,176	1,104	1,089	3,784	3,584	...	...	...	...	...	...	...	...
1,554	1,415	187	169	5,533	5,546	3	2	...	...	1	...	...	...
1,332	1,139	40	24	532	488	...	...	...	...	...	...	...	...
1,195	1,217	21	11	376	369	...	...	...	...	...	...	...	...
120	107	...	...	1,816	1,765	...	...	...	...	...	...	...	...
518	467	20	19	98	110	...	...	...	...	...	...	...	...
151	149	...	...	237	245	...	...	...	...	...	...	...	...
223	240	29	33	101	128	1	1	...	...	...	...	...	...
94	79	...	...	356	322	...	...	...	...	...	...	...	...
74	53	...	...	551	538	...	...	...	...	...	...	...	...
83	84	...	...	30	36	...	...	...	...	...	...	...	...
184	190	...	...	42	36	...	...	...	...	...	...	...	...
90	79	...	...	63	71	...	...	...	...	...	...	...	...
54	47	...	...	321	280	...	...	...	...	...	...	...	...
101	114	5	3	171	205	...	...	...	...	...	...	...	...
73	76	...	...	41	29	...	...	...	...	...	...	...	...
35	38	...	...	154	124	...	...	...	...	...	...	...	...
131	108	...	...	37	36	...	...	...	...	...	...	...	...
34	25	...	...	81	72	...	...	...	...	...	...	...	...

Supplementary Table, shewing the population of Central

STATE.	NUMBER OF TOWNS AND VILLAGES.			Number of occupied houses.	ALL RELIGIONS.			HINDU.	
	Total.	Towns.	Villages.		Total.	Males.	Females.	Males.	Females.
1	2	3	4	5	6	7	8	9	10
73. REBAI	4	...	4	786	3,373	1,684	1,689	1,565	1,569
74. BELHARI	2	...	2	780	3,315	1,662	1,653	1,459	1,435
75. BIJNA	4	...	4	561	2,326	1,196	1,130	1,097	1,037
76. DHURWAI	8	...	8	353	1,774	895	879	872	855
77. KAMTA RAJAULA	3	...	3	358	1,585	934	651	907	629
78. BANKA PAHARI	1	...	1	237	1,098	547	551	496	496
TOTAL FOR STATES 49 TO 78 IN BUNDELKHAND AGENCY	3,659	9	3,650	284,356	1,480,095	769,309	710,786	689,241	633,362
79. TONK (Rajputana)—									
BHOPAL AGENCY	391	1	390	20,432	93,856	50,488	43,368	44,579	38,839
GUNA	188	1	187	10,657	46,473	24,290	22,183	22,835	20,721
WESTERN MALWA	122	1	121	9,129	40,806	21,567	19,239	19,593	17,342
TOTAL	701	3	698	40,218	181,135	96,345	84,790	87,007	76,902
Total Feudatories	32,484	65	32,419	1,942,539	10,236,505	5,346,341	4,890,164	4,027,639	3,655,319
MHOW CANTONMENT	1	1	...	5,494	31,773	18,300	13,473	11,131	8,779
NIMUCH „	1	1	...	6,503	15,291	8,763	6,528	5,935	4,402
SEHORE CANTONMENT AND AGENCY	1	1	...	2,438	11,124	6,084	5,040	4,495	3,867
NOWGONG CANTONMENT AND AGENCY	1	1	...	1,826	10,902	6,946	3,956	4,097	2,556
INDORE RESIDENCY	1	1	...	1,681	9,345	6,099	3,246	4,460	2,333
MANPUR (BRITISH PARGANA)	32	...	32	1,075	5,342	2,880	2,462	1,292	1,051
GUNA CANTONMENT AND AGENCY	1	...	1	1,343	4,693	2,729	1,964	1,835	1,486
AGAR CANTONMENT AND AGENCY	1	...	1	571	4,031	2,532	1,499	1,613	1,017
SARDARPUR CANTONMENT AND AGENCY	1	...	1	591	3,135	1,744	1,391	862	660
SIPRI CANTONMENT	1	...	1	567	2,957	1,743	1,214	1,189	860
GWALIOR RESIDENCY	1	...	1	279	1,245	672	573	560	494
SUTNA AGENCY AND CANTONMENT	1	...	1	159	511	367	144	181	62
MEHIDPUR CANTONMENT	1	...	1	26	76	47	29	38	27
Total for Cantonments, etc., under British Occupation	44	5	39	2,553	100,425	58,906	41,519	37,688	27,594
Grand Total	32,528	70	32,458	1,965,092	10,336,930	5,405,247	4,931,683	4,065,827	3,682,918

India (Native States and British occupations) by religions—*concld.*

MUSALMAN.		JAIN.		ABORIGINAL.		CHRISTIAN.		PARSI.		SIKH.		JEW.	
Males.	Females.	Males.	Females.	Males.	Females.	Males.	Females.	Males.	Females.	Males.	Females.	Males.	Females.
11	12	13	14	15	16	17	18	19	20	21	22	23	24
96	98	...	...	23	22	...	...	...	...	...	...	...	...
174	188	4	2	25	28	...	...	...	...	...	...	...	...
49	41	1	...	49	52	...	...	...	...	...	...	...	...
10	12	2	4	11	8	...	...	...	...	...	...	...	...
9	9	...	...	18	13	...	...	...	...	...	...	...	...
26	27	8	8	17	20	...	...	...	...	...	...	...	...
26,307	24,716	6,063	5,902	47,644	46,787	19	10	...	...	35	9	...	...
5,575	4,247	329	280	...	...	5	2	...	...	...	...	...	...
1,313	1,357	142	105	...	...	...	...	...	...	...	...	...	...
1,283	1,255	691	642	...	...	...	...	...	...	...	...	...	...
8,171	6,859	1,162	1,027	...	...	5	2	...	...	...	...	...	...
288,076	257,814	47,146	42,665	982,356	933,517	677	540	73	55	373	253	1	1
4,481	3,752	97	95	...	...	2,300	615	214	205	45	6	32	21
2,258	1,868	81	76	...	...	418	116	59	60	2	...	10	6
1,261	1,033	83	56	...	...	36	33	5	6	204	45	...	...
1,999	1,270	28	21	...	...	557	91	2	...	263	18	...	...
1,191	684	96	52	...	...	266	100	80	74	5	3	1	...
215	169	6	3	1,366	1,239	...	...	1	...	...	...	...	...
593	354	35	41	...	...	15	3	...	...	251	80	...	...
631	379	49	37	...	...	21	4	3	...	215	62	...	...
115	84	...	...	757	642	10	5	...	...	...	...	...	...
356	274	78	71	...	...	120	9	...	...	...	...	...	...
82	49	...	...	...	...	30	30	...	...	...	...	...	...
184	81	...	...	...	...	2	1	...	...	...	...	...	...
9	2	...	...	...	...	...	...	...	...	...	...	...	...
13,375	9,999	553	452	2,123	1,881	3,775	1,007	364	345	985	214	43	27
301,451	**267,818**	**47,699**	**43,117**	**984,479**	**935,398**	**4,452**	**1,547**	**437**	**400**	**1,358**	**467**	**44**	**28**

Table showing the percentage of the total population belonging to the Principal Religions.

Table showing the percentage of the total population belonging to the principal religions.

NAMES OF STATES, ETC.	HINDU.	MAHOMEDAN.	JAIN.	ABORIGINAL.	CHRISTIAN.	OTHERS.
GWALIOR	81·54	5·44	1·03	11·96	·01	...
INDORE	69·35	7·03	1·22	22·36	·02	·02
BHOPAL	70·84	9·37	·56	19·16	·02	·02
KHANIADHANA	81·91	1·29	3·35	13·37	...	...
GUARANTEED ESTATES (GWALIOR)	75·27	3·09	·09	21·53	...	...
DEWAS (SENIOR BRANCH)	72·08	9·79	·85	17·26	...	...
DEWAS (JUNIOR BRANCH)	76·62	7·84	·75	14·77	...	...
BAGLI	68·89	4·53	3·69	22·86	...	...
JAORA	69·27	12·80	2·64	15·25	·01	·01
RATLAM	55·11	11·26	6·32	27·19	·07	·01
SITAMAU	85·42	5·20	·44	8·92	...	...
SAILANA	59·19	5·02	3·65	32·10	·01	...
PIPLAUDA	72·44	5·18	4·23	18·16	...	...
PANTH PIPLAUDA	67·37	2·15	·41	30·05	...	...
RAJGARH	76·22	5·09	·18	18·48	...	...
NARSINGHGARH	80·87	3·66	·04	15·40	...	...
KHILCHIPUR	79·71	3·51	...	16·76	...	...
KURWAI	80·61	12·31	·30	6·77	...	...
MAKSUDANGARH	70·16	2·82	...	27·00	...	...
AGRA BARKHERA	83·67	5·40	·05	10·87	...	...
BASODA	73·72	13·74	·80	11·73	...	...
PUTHALIA	73·90	1·83	...	24·26	...	...
PATHARI	85·54	9·01	3·23	2·20	...	...
MAHOMADGARH	73·49	14·91	1·56	10·02	...	...
PINDARA JAGIR	59·52	20·37	...	19·97	...	...
RAGHOGARH	77·09	4·72	2·77	15·39	...	...
GURRAH	66·39	2·39	1·50	29·70	...	...
PARONE	82·60	2·15	·01	15·23	...	...
DHARNAODA	83·34	4·07	2·62	9·94	...	...
SIRSI	69·58	·36	...	30·05	...	...
BHADAURA	82·71	1·82	1·15	14·31	...	...
UMRI	83·87	2·94	1·79	11·35	...	·03
KHIAODA	81·42	·09	·29	18·17	...	...
DHAR	58·62	7·70	2·12	31·48	...	...
JHABUA	18·14	1·84	1·82	78·17	...	...
BARWANI	35·92	4·04	·37	59·63	...	...
ALI RAJPUR	7·67	2·25	·20	89·85	...	...
GUARANTEED THAKURATS (BHOPAWAR AGENCY)	56·25	3·85	2·31	37·56	...	...
GUARANTEED BHUMIATS (ditto)	27·32	2·85	·20	69·61	...	...
JOBAT	5·53	1·43	·09	92·92	...	...
KATHIWADA	3·22	1·14	...	95·63	...	...
MATHWAR	5·78	·66	...	93·54	...	...
RATANMAL	44·14	·24	...	55·61	...	...
REWA	65·26	2·42	·02	32·27	·01	...
NAGODE	82·33	3·51	·10	14·04	...	...
MAIHAR	78·59	2·88	·09	18·43	...	...
SOHAWAL	86·31	3·01	·01	10·66	...	...
KOTHI	79·64	1·50	...	18·75	...	...
URCHHA	90·12	2·85	1·93	5·08	...	...
PANNA	83·73	2·58	·70	12·95	...	·01
DATIA	92·66	4·31	...	3·01	...	...
CHHATARPUR	92·69	3·41	·40	3·48	...	...
CHARKHARI	90·92	4·49	·23	4·34	...	...
BIJAWAR	90·23	2·02	1·77	5·97	...	...
AJAIGARH	84·51	3·19	·38	11·90	...	...
SAMTHAR	91·23	6·09	·15	2·51	...	...
BAONI	82·70	13·07	·17	4·03	...	...
BARAUNDHA	79·52	1·21	...	19·25	...	...
ALIPURA	91·93	6·44	·25	1·36	...	...
GAURIHAR	92·29	2·95	...	4·74	...	...
TORI FATEHPUR	92·12	4·82	·64	2·38	·02	...
PALDEC	90·93	1·84	...	7·22	...	...
JASU	86·22	1·43	...	12·33	...	...
LUGASI	96·64	2·40	...	·95	...	...
SARILA	91·96	6·65	...	1·38	...	...
GEROLI	94·51	3·05	...	2·42	...	...
BHAISAUNDA	85·23	2·12	...	12·63	...	...
BERI	86·76	4·75	·17	8·30	...	...
BEHUT	95·06	3·35	...	1·57	...	...
PAHRA	91·54	1·75	...	6·69	...	...
JIGNI	92·00	6·12	...	1·87	...	...
TARAON	93·81	1·72	...	4·46	...	...
REBAI	92·91	5·75	...	1·33	...	...
BELHARI	87·30	10·92	·18	1·59	...	...
BIJNA	91·74	3·86	·04	4·34	...	...
DHURWAI	97·35	1·24	·33	1·07	...	...
KAMTA RAJAULA	96·90	1·13	...	1·95	...	...
BANKA PAHARI	90·34	4·82	1·45	3·37	...	...

Table showing the percentage of the total population belonging to the principal religions—*contd.*

NAMES OF STATES, ETC.	HINDU.	MAHOMEDAN.	JAIN.	ABORIGINAL.	CHRISTIAN.	OTHERS.
TONK	90·49	8·29	1·20	...	...	...
MHOW	62·68	25·91	·60	...	9·17	1·63
NIMACH	67·60	26·98	1·02	...	3·49	·88
SEHORE	75·53	20·21	1·24	...	·62	2·33
NOWGONG	61·02	29·98	·44	...	5·94	2·59
INDORE RESIDENCY	72·69	20·06	1·58	...	3·91	1·74
MANPUR (BRITISH)	43·86	7·18	·16	48·76	...	·01
GUNA	70·76	20·17	1·61	...	68	7·05
AGAR	65·24	25·05	2·13	...	·62	6·95
SARDARPUR	48·54	6·34	...	44·62	·47	...
SIPRI	69·29	21·30	5·03	...	4·36	...
GWALIOR RESIDENCY	84·65	10·52	...	...	4·81	...
SUTNA	47·55	51·85	...	...	·58	...
MEHIDPUR	85·52	14·47	...	...	...	...